AF248747

Butter
Unsalted Butter

A is for ARCHIVE
WARHOL'S WORLD FROM A TO Z

Matt Wrbican

Edited by Abigail Franzen-Sheehan
Contributions by Blake Gopnik and Neil Printz

The Andy Warhol Museum, Pittsburgh
in association with
Yale University Press, New Haven and London

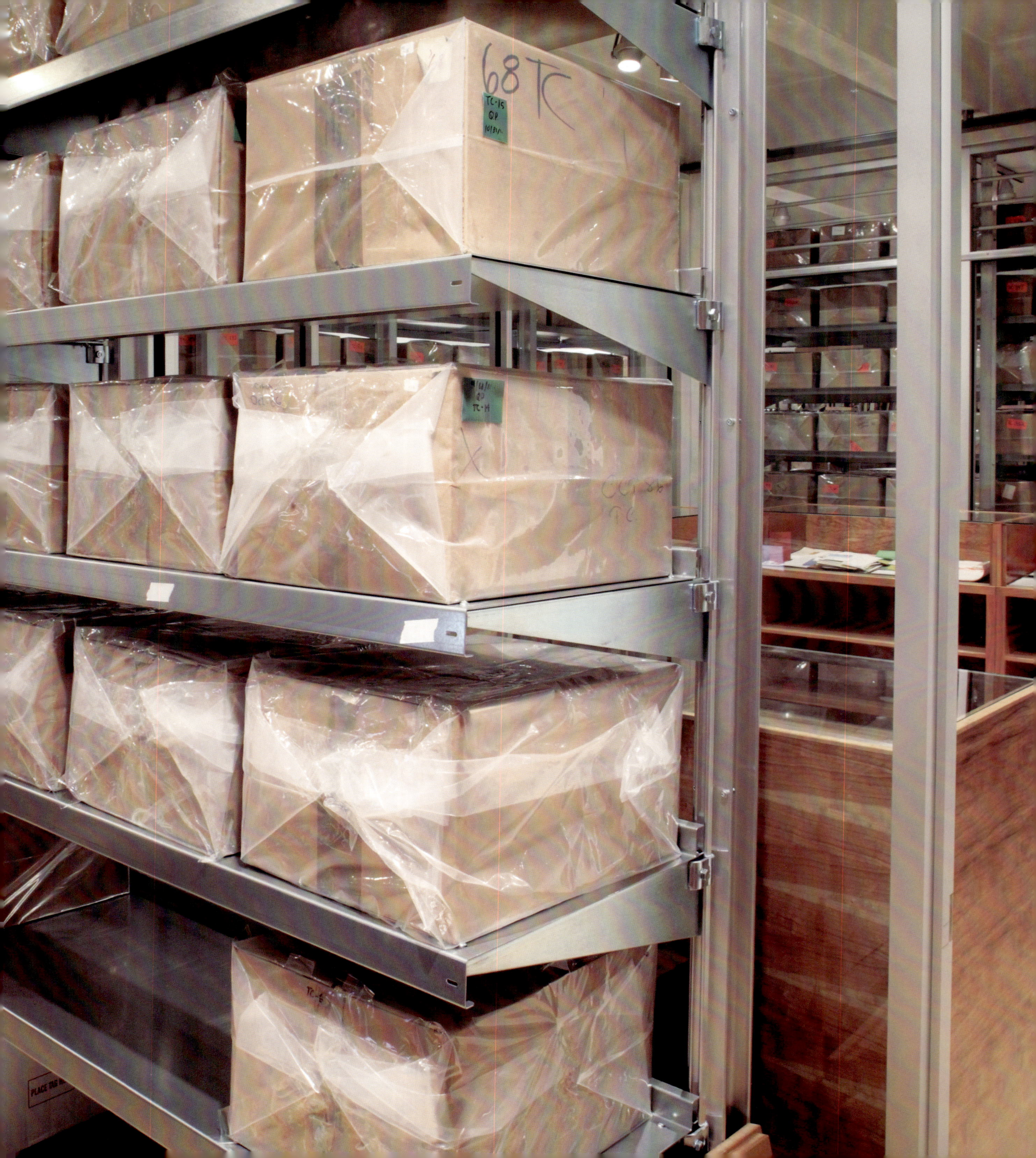

Contents

A to Z

Matt Wrbican

Foreword

Work long enough in the archives of The Andy Warhol Museum, and you start getting the curious sense that *Andy is watching*. Uncover a batch of his wig receipts, and he whispers about how the toupees made him itch. Track down the performances he went to—thanks to piles of his ticket stubs—and he chuckles when you finally realize that he cared more about grand opera and ballet than Broadway shows. On the many nights when I stayed late to talk Warhol with Matt Wrbican, the museum's legendary archivist, I always felt that I had to carefully consider every Warholian thought that I uttered, lest The Master (Andy, not Matt) hear foolishness come out of my mouth.

I imagine that every artist's archive produces feelings like that, just from the sheer presence of its hero in every object. But there may be something more particular going on with Warhol. The archives he left behind don't simply bear witness to his life as an artist. In some sense, they themselves exemplify what this life was about and what drove it. That's because they produce as much confusion and chaos as clarity, and, if you work with them long enough, you start to realize that this carefully cultivated *uncertainty*—not blotted ink or silkscreens or Polaroid film—was Warhol's most cherished art supply.

At first you imagine that the archives' hundreds of thousands of objects (no one has ever come close to counting them) will shine light into even the darkest corners of Warhol Land. And this book does indeed present more than a few such corners, better illuminated than ever before.

With "I is for Illusions," Wrbican gives long overdue attention to Warhol's fascination with 3-D effects. Those go along with his lifelong taste for the very latest technology, as witnessed in the archives' piles of receipts for the latest in stereos, cameras, and cassette decks. This technophilia reveals a surprising bro side to a man who always reveled in being deliciously light in his loafers, and in the effect this studied levitation had on others.

Warhol's compulsive collecting (read, *hoarding*) has often been written up, but you can't really understand it until you've taken in the dozens and dozens (and dozens) of dental models that Wrbican discusses in "T is for Tooth Fairy." As far as we can tell, Warhol bought most of his heap of fake teeth on a single shopping trip in 1982. Multiply such trips by 365, over something like 30 years, and you get a sense of Warhol's manic acquisitional drive. But dig still deeper into his archive and life, and you realize that his collecting was more about a true fascination with the peculiar than it was about the joy of simply *having*. When he could use fine art to spot the peculiar in the everyday— to recognize the puzzling paintings that soup cans want to become—he was at his happiest.

And those paintings are truly more puzzling than almost ever gets recognized. The hundreds, maybe thousands, of art-critical clippings that survive in Warhol's archives reveal interpretations that must range more widely than for anyone else in the history of Western art. From the moment they were first shown, the thirty-two *Campbell's Soup Can* paintings that launched Warhol's career were greeted with diametrically opposite readings: They were (take your pick) either coruscating condemnations of American consumer culture or glorious celebrations of its democratic freedoms.

The one observer who refused to cut this Gordian knot was Warhol himself, who, after all, famously said, "just look at the surface: of my paintings and films and me, and there I am. There's nothing behind it." Or, rather, who never said any such thing, as we learn in the chapter of this book titled "G is for Gretchen." What's especially important about that tale of the reporter who put words in Warhol's mouth is not that Gretchen Berg did it; writers have been playing fast and loose with quotes since at least the New Testament. What matters is that, in this case and in so many others, Warhol was perfectly happy to have himself portrayed, and often to portray himself, as an empty-headed naïf who made great art by accident—when the truth was that he was as sophisticated as they come, with a deep knowledge of cutting-edge modern art and culture. (The college textbooks in his archives, with their extensive underlinings, go some way toward proving this, as do the serious books that he left behind when he died. There's plenty to show that he read them.)

Unlike almost any other artist in history (or—scarier thought—maybe just like most of them), Warhol turns out to be the very least reliable witness to his own art and life and ideas, as eager to steer you wrong as to set you straight. Always in search of the odd and the striking, he knew that fibs and misdirection were generally more compelling than truth, and that there was no law to stop him from serving them up.

And here's where we come back to that notion of uncertainty as Warhol's main art supply. Because the sheer quantity of raw information that Warhol left behind in his archives does as much to muddy the Warholian waters as to make things clear in his art and life. The archives' 610 *Time Capsules*, carefully stuffed by Warhol with all the documents and detritus of his career as an artist, give the impression of a trove of data meant to help ease the task of future Warholians. But the vast quantity and weirdness of this unedited hoard actually does as much to forestall any final conclusions about who and what Warhol was, as a person and an artist, as to make such conclusions pop out. After a few dozen hours in the Warhol archives, you start to get the very definite feeling that he's messing with you, daring you to find order and meaning in the chaos that he's left behind, just as he dared his first viewers to sum up the sense of some paintings of soup cans.

Was Warhol a sweetheart or a cold calculator?
A dedicated artist or a committed social climber?
A genius or a lucky fool?
As he himself would always have answered:
Yes.

Blake Gopnik

Editor's Preface

The Andy Warhol Museum is an undeniably cool place to work—not only to be surrounded by the art that fills seven floors of this historic building but also to be part of the mindset of Warhol, which still infuses the place. Warholian traits of openness, obsessive inquiry, humor, and collaboration are all channeled into the day-to-day labors of the gallery attendants, educators, and curators on the front lines and into the dedicated work of the registrars, archivists, and researchers behind the scenes. Each in unique ways sustains Warhol's art, physically and conceptually. As the museum marks its twenty-fifth anniversary, it is my immense privilege to work on this publication, which preserves and celebrates a rich history of fascinating stories told in museum exhibitions through our Archive collection.

Matt Wrbican began his work with the Archive of Andy Warhol shortly after the artist's death in 1987. Together with Fred Hughes, Tim Hunt, and Neil Printz, he began documenting the artist's *Time Capsules* and vast collection. Wrbican is above all else an intense researcher and intellectual. His writing about and curating from within Warhol's Archive have been nothing less than extraordinary. When I started at the museum in 1996 as an artist educator, there was nothing more intimidating than giving a tour through or near the Archive only to have Wrbican visit my desk later in the day and tell me which detail I had relayed that was not quite right. Over the years, we worked together to create copious label copy and educational curriculum materials. As I took on new roles at The Warhol, he trusted more but was no less exacting. His exhibitions, whether small in scale or filling floors with content, always made an exhaustive investigation into the archival evidence of a theme. In the museum's early decades, funds were not available to create publications for most exhibitions. Years of research were buried in paper records and computer files.

A is for Archive is our conservancy of some of this rich legacy. Titled after Warhol's own alphabet books of the 1950s, *A is an alphabet*, *A was a lady...*, the book is an anthology of essays that are adaptations from material exhibited from the Archive. It is not chronological but can be read through from A to Z. Alternatively, each chapter is meant to stand on its own, and we invite readers to jump in wherever their interests lie. Many of the images in this publication are previously unpublished and represent the endless future research opportunities that remain within Warhol's Archive. Part picture book, part storybook, part historical research, *A is for Archive* strives to present various dichotomies—the simultaneous embrace of high and low, the compulsive collecting in large quantities and the singular focus on details, the familiar and the unknowable—that were all part of Warhol's art and life.

Abigail Franzen-Sheehan
Editor
Director of Publications
The Andy Warhol Museum

Matt Wrbican and the Early Days of the Archive

On May 15, 1994, when The Andy Warhol Museum opened its doors in Pittsburgh, the fledgling staff of the newly minted institution had already been at work for several years. They were installed in Warhol's last studio, a T-shaped former Con Edison substation in Midtown Manhattan, around the corner from the Empire State Building, that now served as the headquarters of the Andy Warhol Foundation for the Visual Arts. This was where I first encountered a former art student with long hair and a soul patch on his chin; he had an MFA in intermedia and electronic art from Carnegie Mellon and hailed from Pittsburgh—Matt Wrbican, then the assistant archivist of The Andy Warhol Museum.

It was the summer of 1993, and I had just begun working on the catalogue raisonné of Warhol's paintings, sculptures, and drawings under the aegis of the Warhol Foundation. I was assigned a desk at the blunt end of a small corridor on the third floor of the 33rd Street studio, sandwiched between the office of the foundation's curator, Tim Hunt, and a large open area where Warhol's films and video collections were stored. I spent most of my time, however, in a small room on the floor above, where the "Study Collection," as it was then called, was housed: an accumulation of photographs, photostats, documents, and other loose ephemera that had been brought over from Warhol's town house at 57 East 66th Street and meticulously assembled by Matt in fifty-odd acid-free solander boxes. Matt became my guide not only to the Study Collection but also to the other troves of archival materials: nearly two hundred "Miscellaneous Boxes" stacked in metal shelves in the basement of 33rd Street, as well as "A," "B," and "M" boxes and trunks stored in the foundation's capacious Chelsea warehouse. And, of course, there were the storied *Time Capsules*.

I quickly realized that there could be no more matchless fit of artist, archivist, and hometown boy than Matt Wrbican at The Andy Warhol Museum. Every Friday morning for eight months before the museum opened, from August 1993 to April 1994, Matt, Vincent Fremont—Warhol's longtime studio manager and friend—and I would meet up in another small, windowless room in the warehouse to open one of the six hundred–plus *Time Capsules*, or two, if we had the time. Matt would unseal and photograph the numbered cardboard box; Vincent and I would don white cotton gloves; then Vincent would proceed to remove the contents one piece at a time, identifying each image, opening each magazine, reading letters and postcards, gallery announcements, catalogues, invoices, and bills, plucking souvenirs from the unknown lode. Matt typed with speed and precision, inventorying the box's contents on his laptop, while Vincent spoke on tape, providing a nonstop oral history. Narrative and typing might cease from time to time, just long enough for Matt to photograph or me to photocopy an especially memorable or significant fragment of that history. Once we had "finished the box," we would reassemble its contents as best we could in their "original" order.

One day, I remember confiding to Matt that I had discovered the source image of one of Warhol's paintings in a Study Collection box. He gently reminded me that I hadn't "discovered" anything. He was right, of course; it had been there all along. What Matt didn't say was that he had put the image there in the first place for researchers like me to find, and what he was too modest to say, but as every Warhol researcher soon learns, is that Matt just about knew the entire contents of the Archive by heart.

Neil Printz
Editor of the Andy Warhol Catalogue Raisonné
March 5, 2018

Andy Warhol began collecting autographs during his child-hood. He would write a letter to a movie star whom he admired and ask for a signed photo—a request that film studios of the period expected their actors to fulfill. Warhol carefully pasted those he received into a photo album, which grew to contain over thirty photos of stars of the 1930s and 1940s, including Glenn Ford, Jane Russell, and Mae West; Warhol's most prized possession was his hand-colored photo of film star Shirley Temple, autographed to Warhol in 1941. When he became a celebrity in his own right, he would rarely turn down a request for an autograph, as he knew just how important they can be to those who seek stardom. He signed numerous copies of his magazine, *Interview*; promoted his publications with signing events in bookstores; and was known to sign his name to soup cans, clothing, and even body parts.

As for his artwork, he signed it all until his mother joined him in New York in 1952. Her unique, florid, old-world cursive style proved popular with art directors and other clients; soon, she was signing Andy's name to his drawings. Branching out from his commercial work into Pop Art in the early 1960s, Warhol explored ways to be

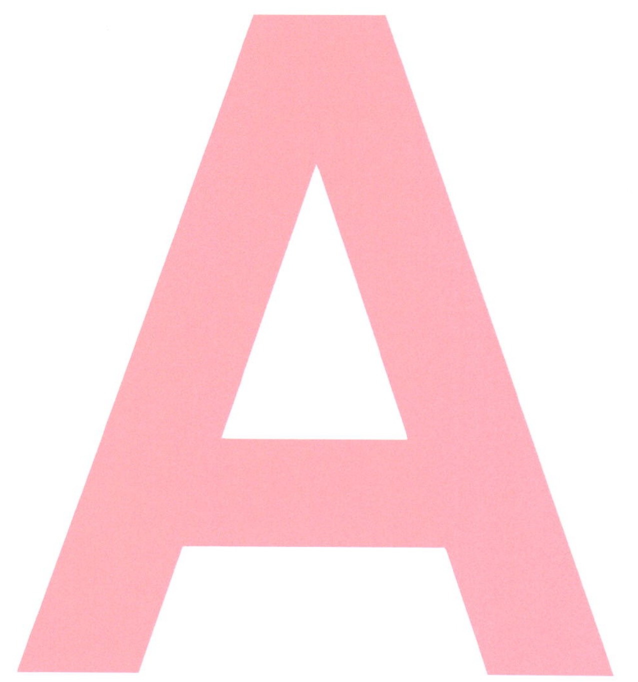

A
is for AUTOGRAPH

This chapter is based on the exhibition *Celebrity Signings: Autographed Memorabilia from Warhol's Archives*, which displayed about thirty objects in the Archives Study Center, March 3–July 7, 2002.

more avant-garde with his signature and arrived at a satis-factory method. He signed many paintings on their stretcher bars, which were hidden from view, using an electric hot iron, and affixed adhesive seals to the boxes holding his Pop print portfolios. The seals and iron bore his signature in an easily imitated script font. His occasional preference for the unconventional stance of not signing a finished painting created problems with collectors. His close friend Brigid Berlin (Brigid Polk) was once quoted in a national magazine as saying that she signed all of his art; some of his studio assistants signed his works as well.[1]

Warhol often gave art as presents to family and friends. He gave a small *Marilyn Monroe* painting to a young niece; as she was showing it off, her friend noticed that it wasn't signed and said it should be returned for the signature that would make it "real art." Sadly, it was the last time the little girl saw her *Marilyn*; she mailed it to her famous uncle, but it was never returned. The Archive contains the mailing-package material from the niece, confirming that Warhol received the artwork.

Warhol was also the recipient of signed or personalized gifts from famous friends, including *The Beatles Christmas Album*, autographed to Warhol by John Lennon and his wife, the artist Yoko Ono. After Lennon's murder in 1980, Warhol took an interest in the well-being of their son, Sean, attend-ing the boy's birthday parties and proposing that he make an annual portrait of Sean. As an expression of appreciation for the gifts bestowed by Warhol, Sean gave him an "Imagine" postcard with a personalized inscription. Sometimes these "gifts" were also "requests" for assistance, as with the auto-graphed recording of David Bowie's 1971 album, *Hunky Dory*. It was sent to Warhol by Bowie's agent, asking the artist for a blurb to help promote the album. The package included the typed lyrics to Bowie's song "Andy Warhol" and a hand-written list of the record's song titles. It is not known whether Warhol ever submitted the blurb, but Bowie's admiration for Warhol remained constant. Twenty-five years later, in 1996, Bowie played the role of Warhol in the film *Basquiat*, borrow-ing archival objects from the museum to help look the part. When the items were returned, a little gift was found hidden inside the coat: a winning $5 lottery ticket, signed and dated by Bowie—a gift that surely would have pleased Warhol.

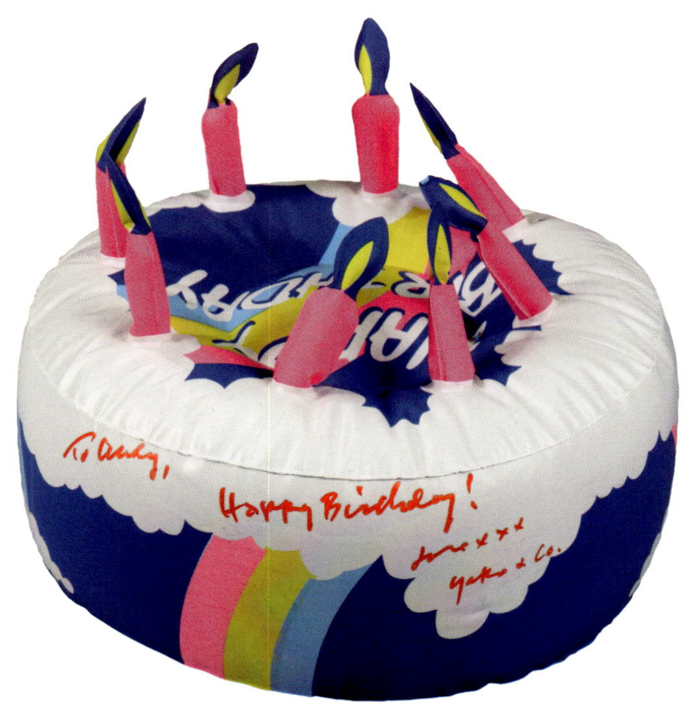

Sports

A wide array of competitors is represented in Warhol's auto-graph collection, many of whom are the subjects of his *Athletes* series. In 1977 Warhol was commissioned to create a cycle of portraits featuring some of the most iconic athletes of the day, from tennis legend Chris Evert to basketball star Kareem Abdul-Jabbar, both of whom signed Warhol's Studio guest book. Warhol considered star athletes to be the equal of movie stars and enjoyed their portrait sessions.

Entertainment

Warhol's scrapbook from 1972 to 1978 is a treasure trove of entertainment signatures. The book documents life at his weekend home in Montauk, Long Island, and contains auto-graphs and photos of Truman Capote, Dick Cavett, Catherine Deneuve, Jackie Kennedy Onassis, Elizabeth Taylor, and many other celebrities of the time. It also includes a note from rock star Mick Jagger, whose band the Rolling Stones rented the Montauk home as a base of operations during a US tour in the 1970s (see "L is for Loose Lips and LPs").

Inflatable birthday cake inscribed by Yoko Ono to Warhol, n.d.

Art

Late in his career, after visiting the Hollywood Walk of Fame, Warhol embarked on a small number of unusual sculptures mimicking what he saw, but in a portable mode: cardboard boxes filled with concrete into which he signed his name. Warhol also created *Sidewalk* (1983), based on famous signatures. He photographed the illustrious sidewalk known as the Forecourt of the Stars at Grauman's Chinese Theatre in Hollywood (now TCL Chinese Theatre). Warhol chose the handprints of actors Judy Garland, Cary Grant, Jack Nicholson, and Shirley Temple.

NOTE

1. In his memoir *POPism*, Warhol confesses to the mistake he made in flippantly telling a West Coast magazine that Brigid Berlin executed his paintings for him (Andy Warhol and Pat Hackett, *POPism: The Warhol Sixties* [Orlando, FL: Harcourt Brace Jovanovich, 1980], 313–14). This was not true. Nationally syndicated columnist Joyce Haber picked up the story, and it created a panic among collectors. Warhol promptly issued a retraction.

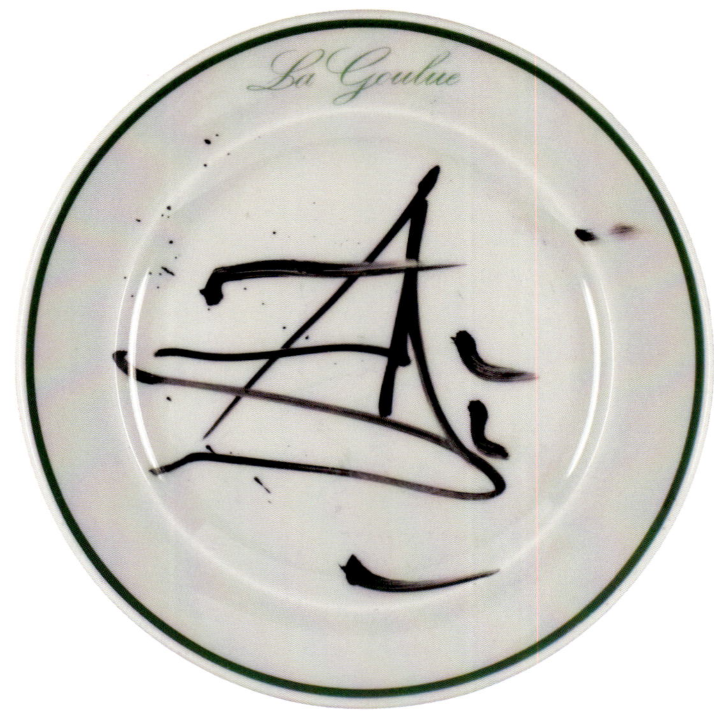

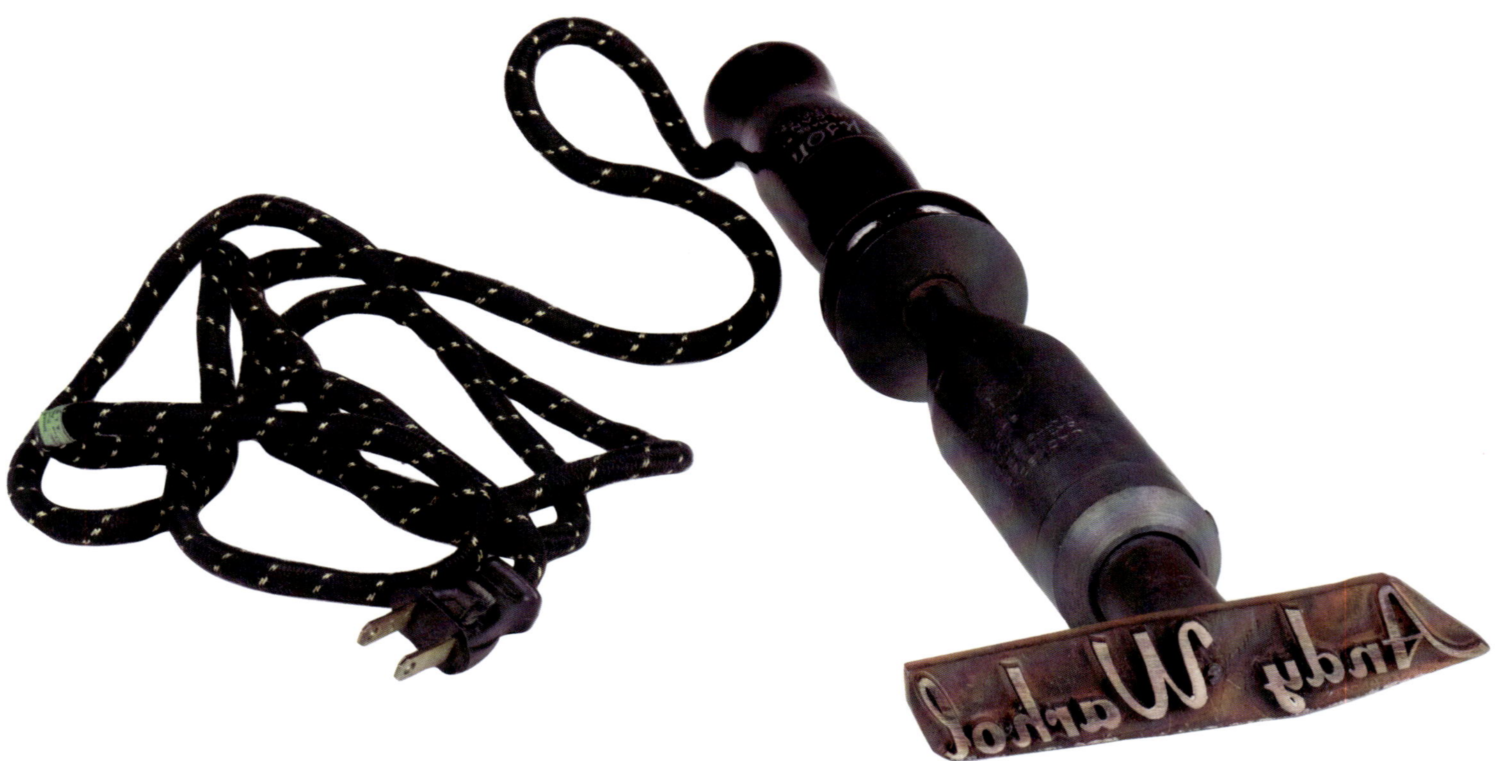

La Goulue plate signed by Salvador Dalí, n.d.

Electric Andy Warhol signature branding iron, n.d.

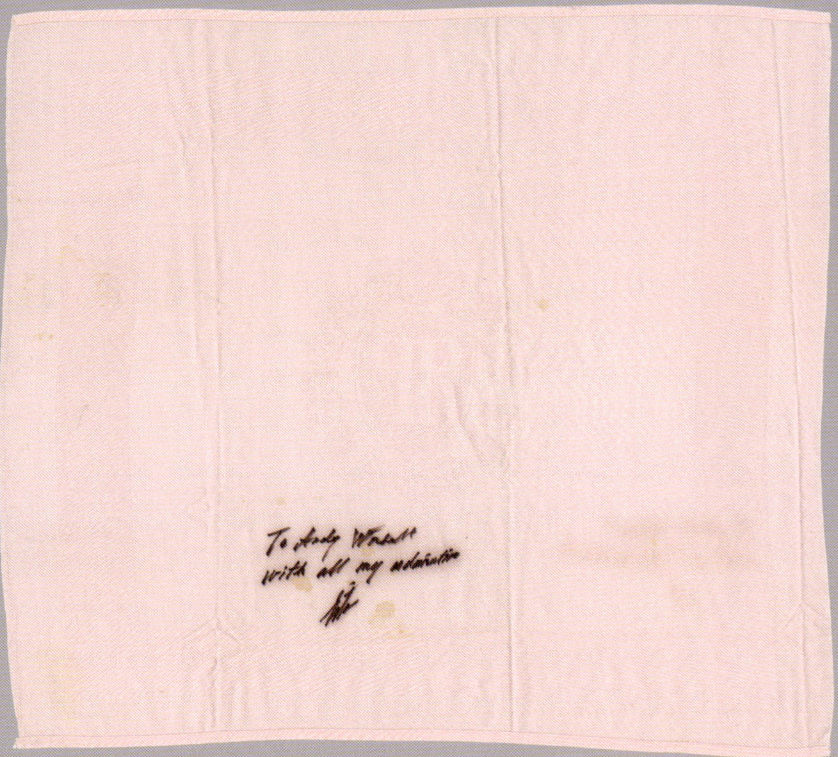

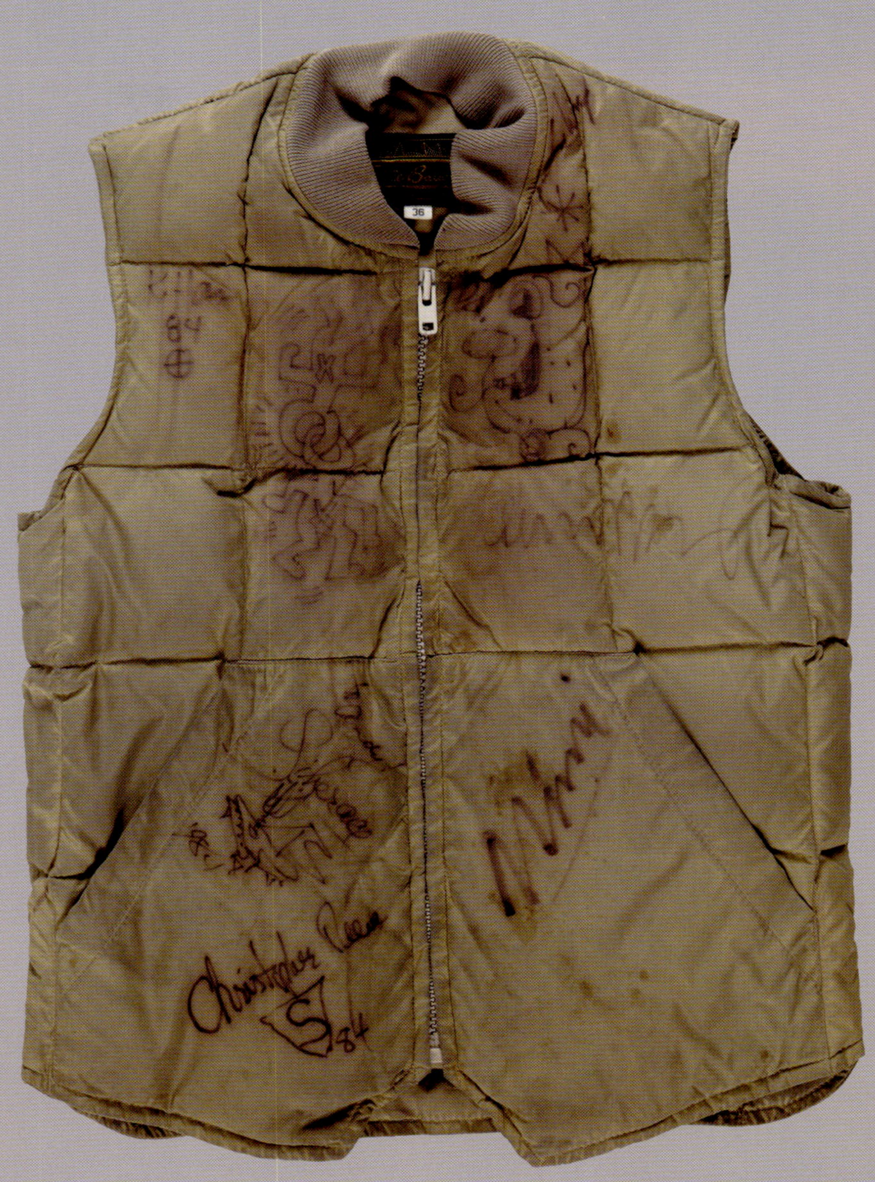

Signed note from Robert Rauschenberg on Warhol's personal stationery, ca. 1984

Plaza Hotel napkin inscribed by artist and designer Erté to Warhol, n.d.

Eddie Bauer ski vest signed and dated with graffiti art and doodles by Jean-Michel Basquiat, Keith Haring, L.A. II, Liberace, Mimi, Christopher Reeve, and Kenny Scharf, 1984

13

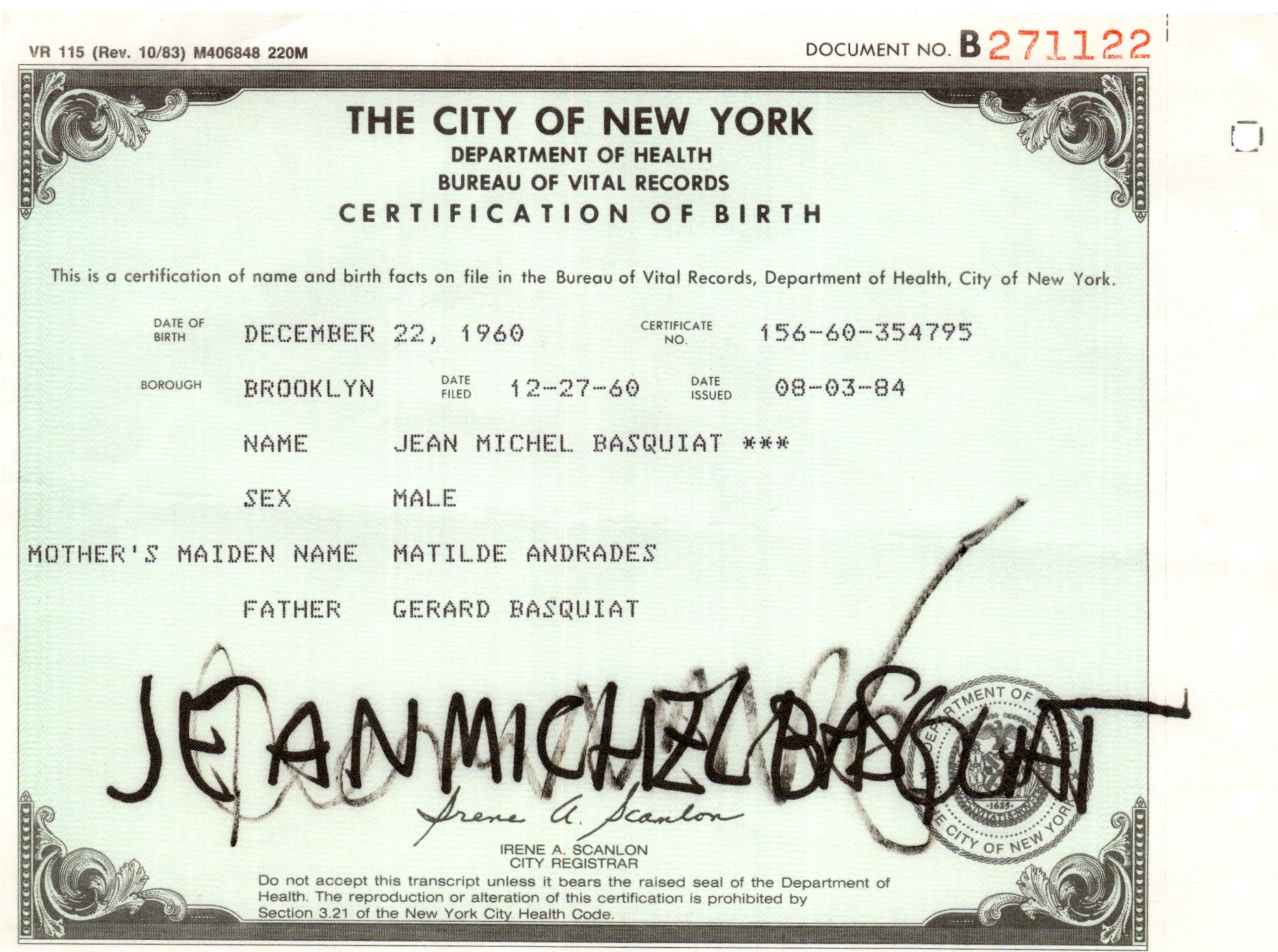

Jean-Michel Basquiat's birth certificate with his signature, issued 1984

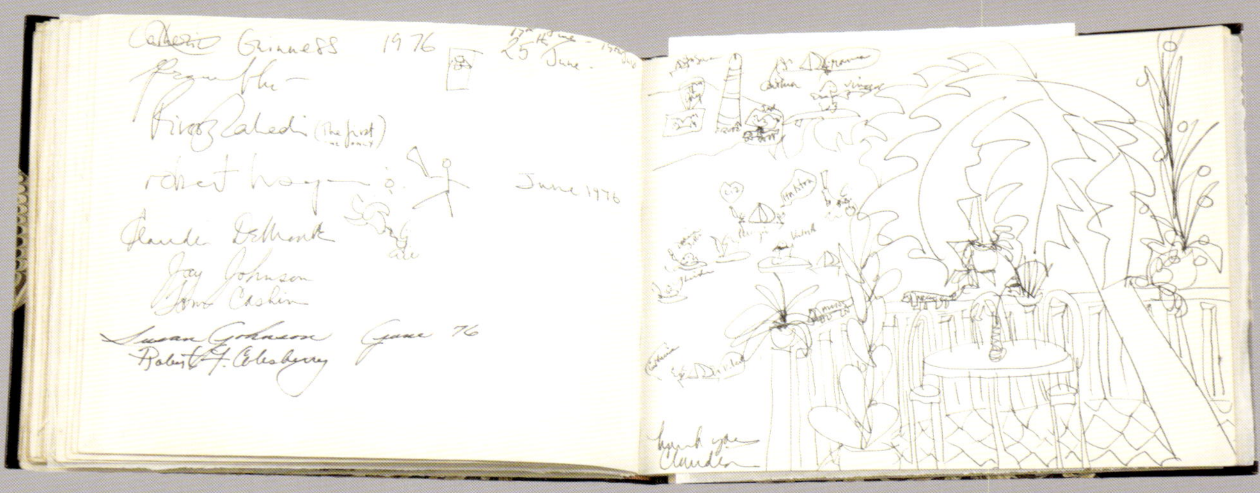

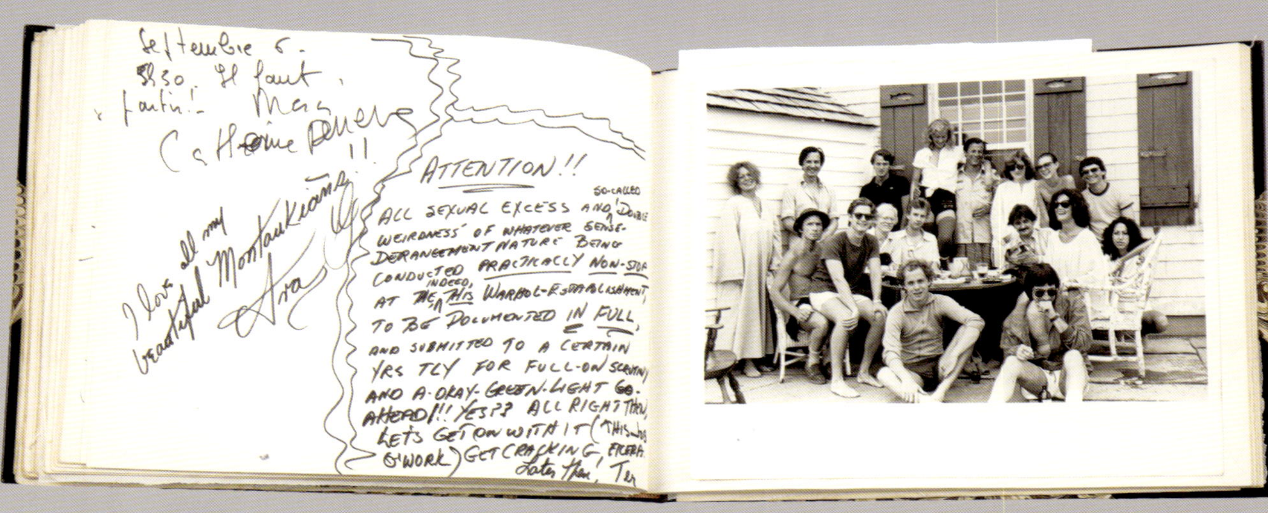

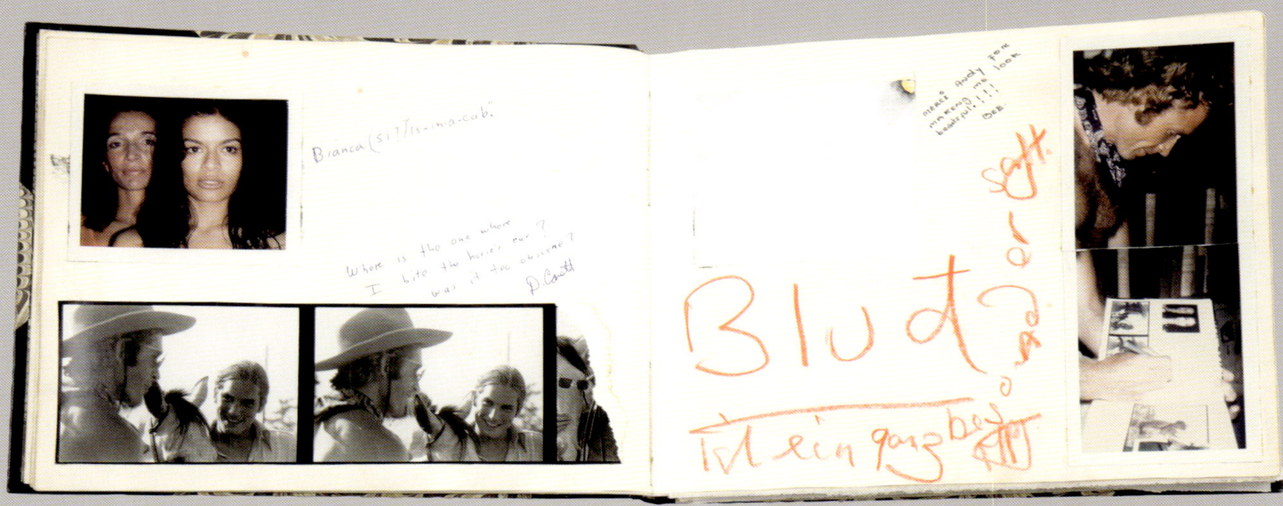

Three spreads from Warhol's scrapbook, which he kept at his Montauk vacation home, inscribed by guests including Dick Cavett, Catherine Deneuve, Catherine Guinness, and Jay Johnson, 1972–78

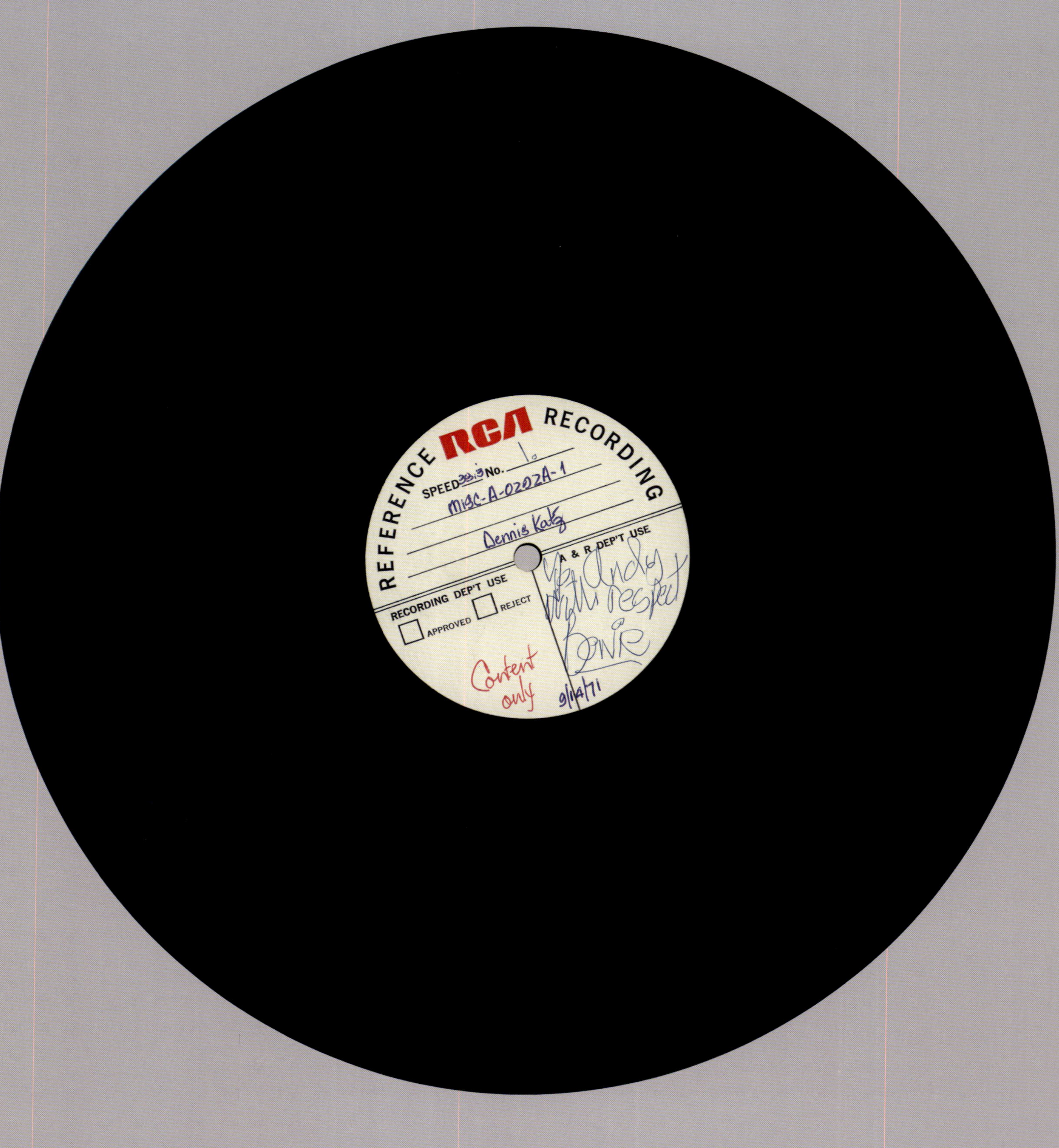

Pre-release copy of *Hunky Dory* by David Bowie inscribed to Warhol, 1971

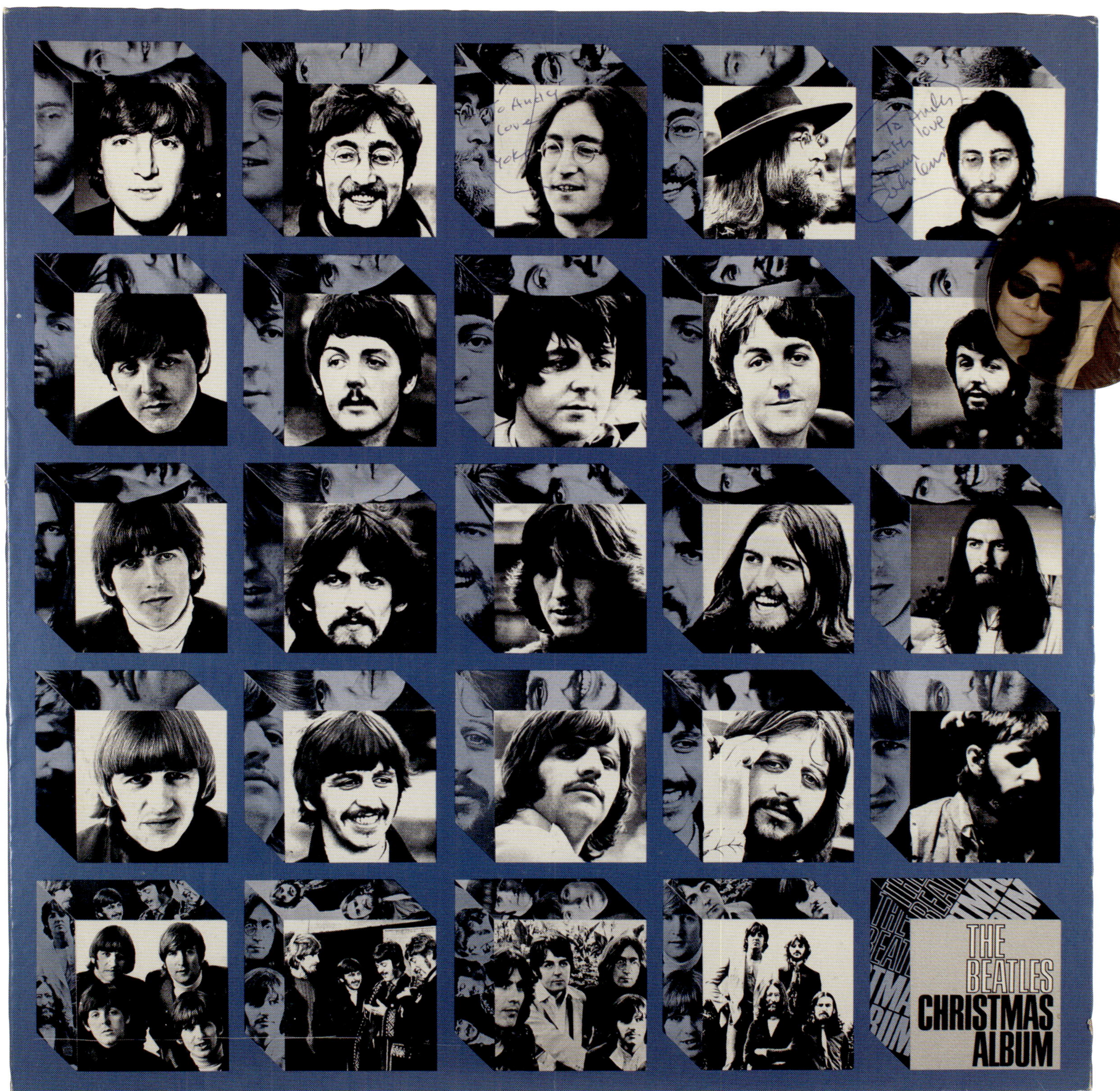

The Beatles Christmas Album inscribed by John Lennon and Yoko Ono
to Warhol, 1970

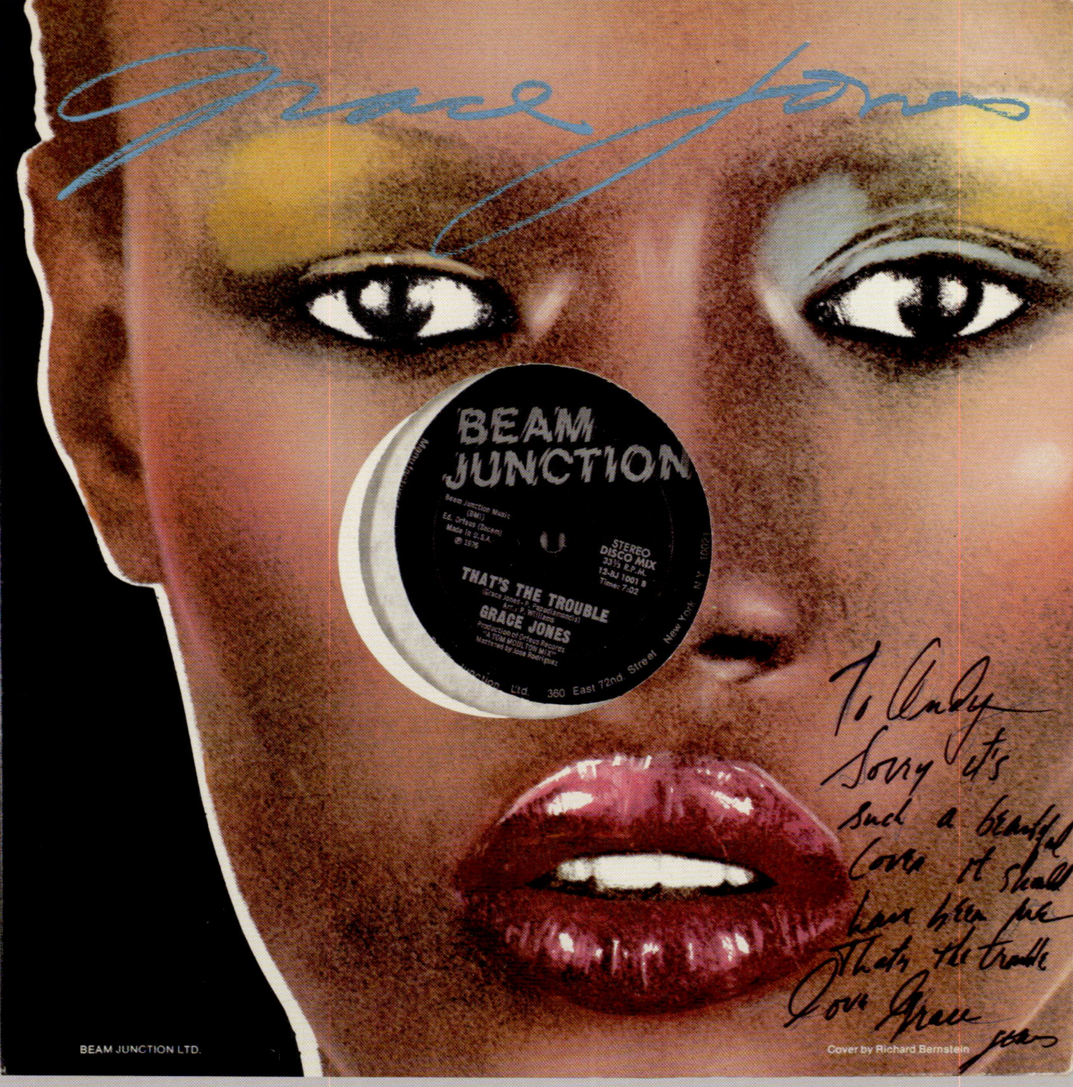

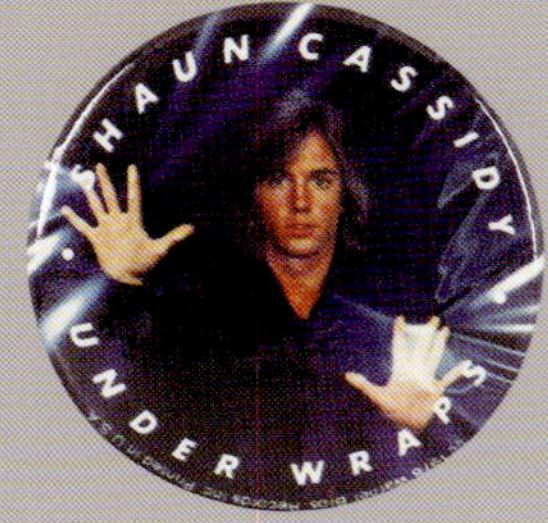

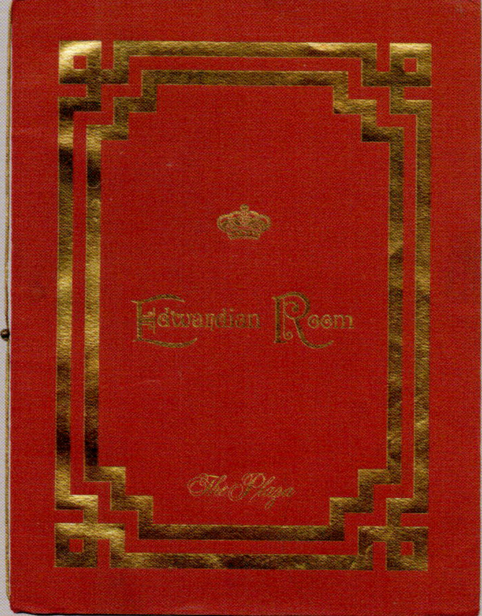

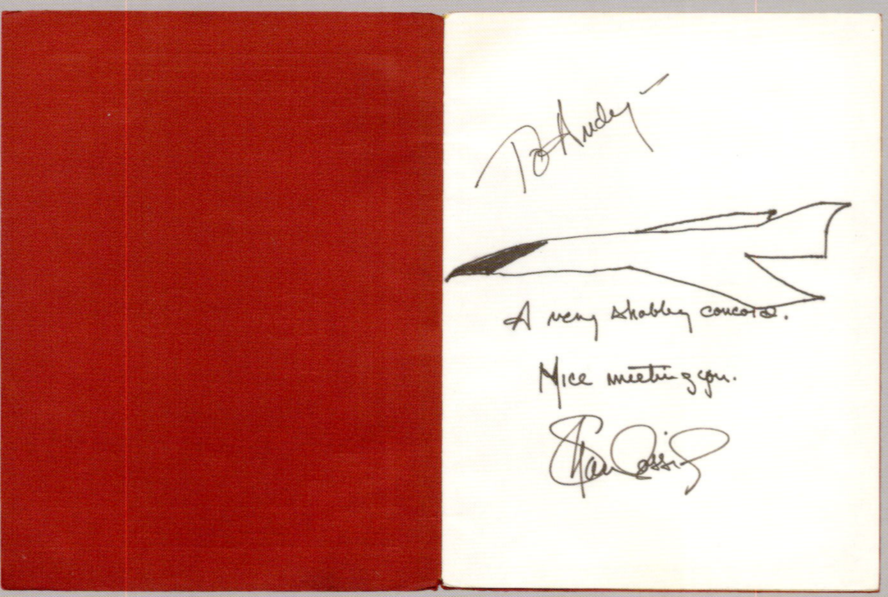

That's the Trouble by Grace Jones inscribed to Warhol, 1976

Promotional button for *Under Wraps* by Shaun Cassidy and menu from the Edwardian Room at the Plaza Hotel inscribed by Cassidy to Warhol, ca. 1978

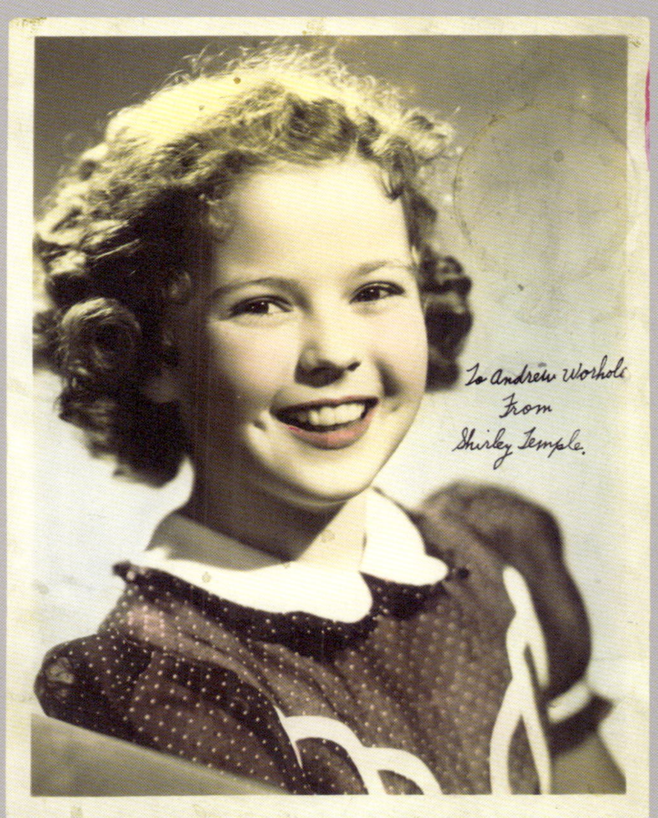

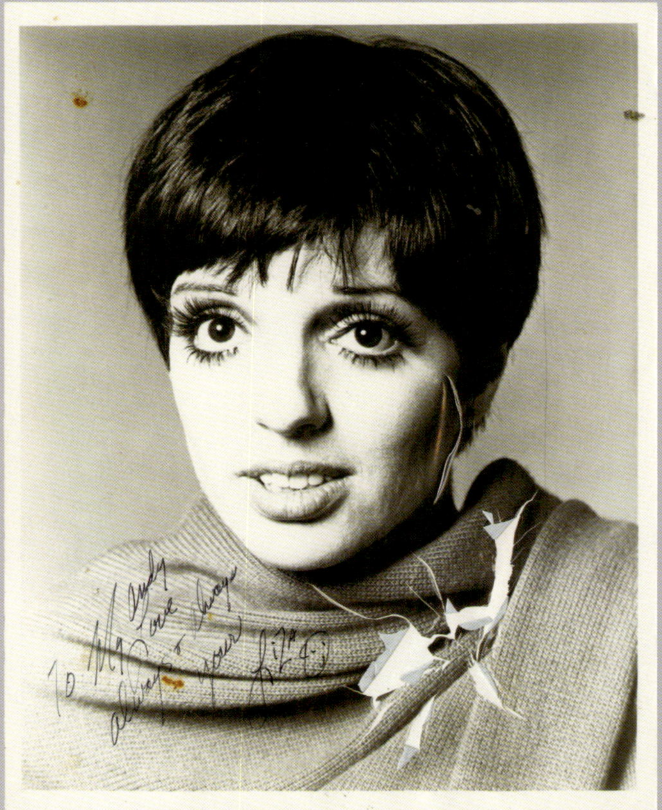

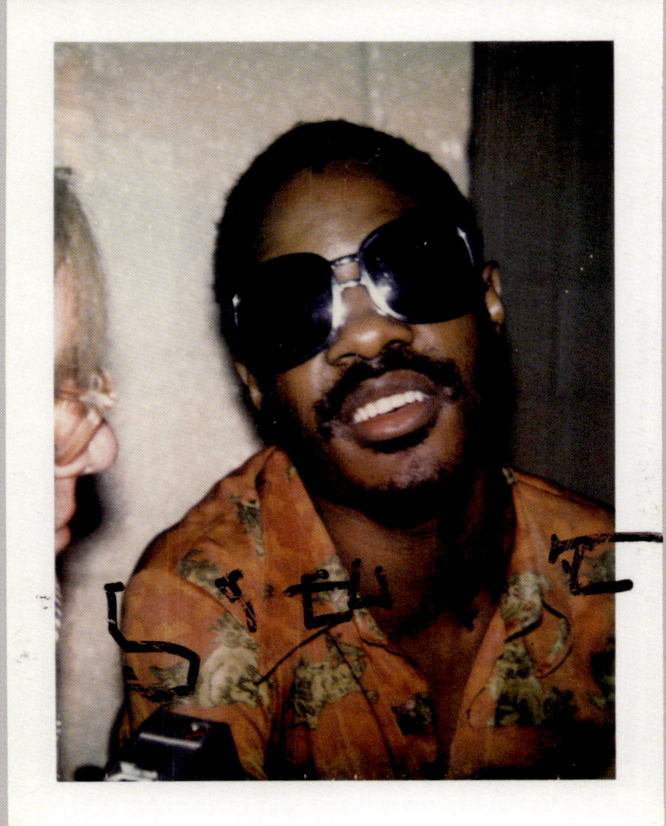

Hand-colored photograph of Shirley Temple inscribed to "Andrew Warhola," 1941

Andy Warhol, *Stevie Wonder*, 1972, signed by Wonder

Photograph of Liza Minnelli inscribed to Warhol, 1970s

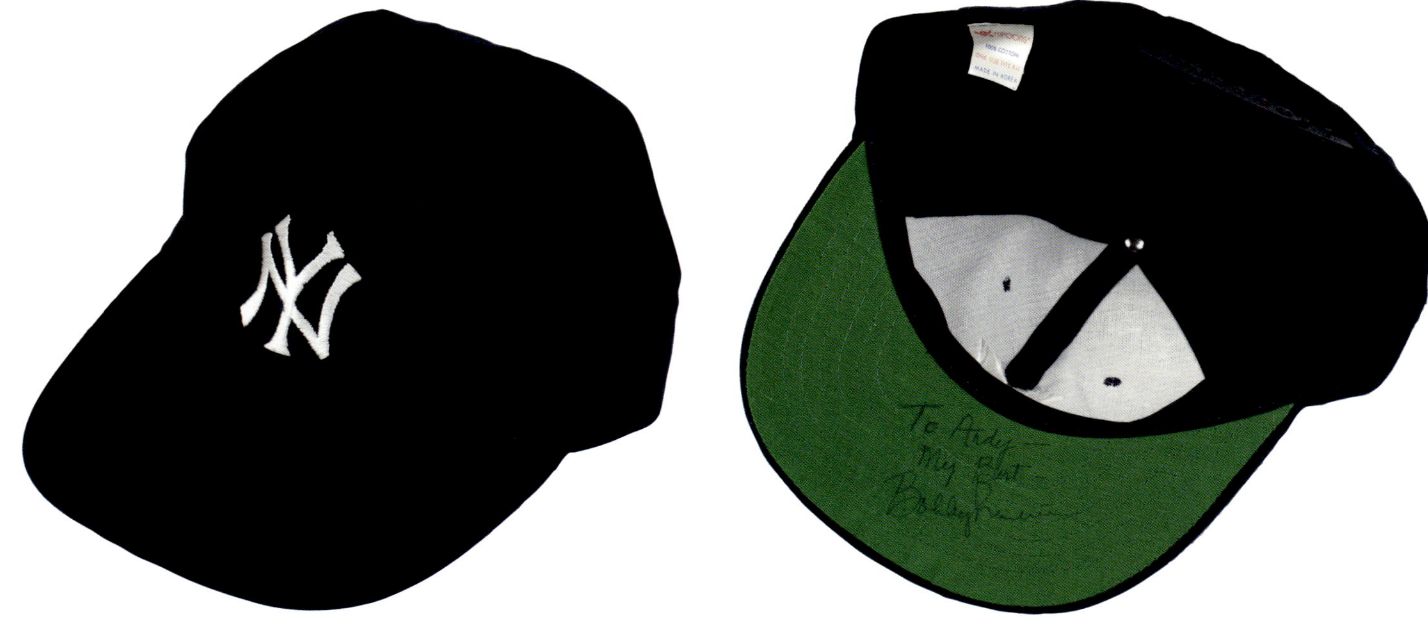

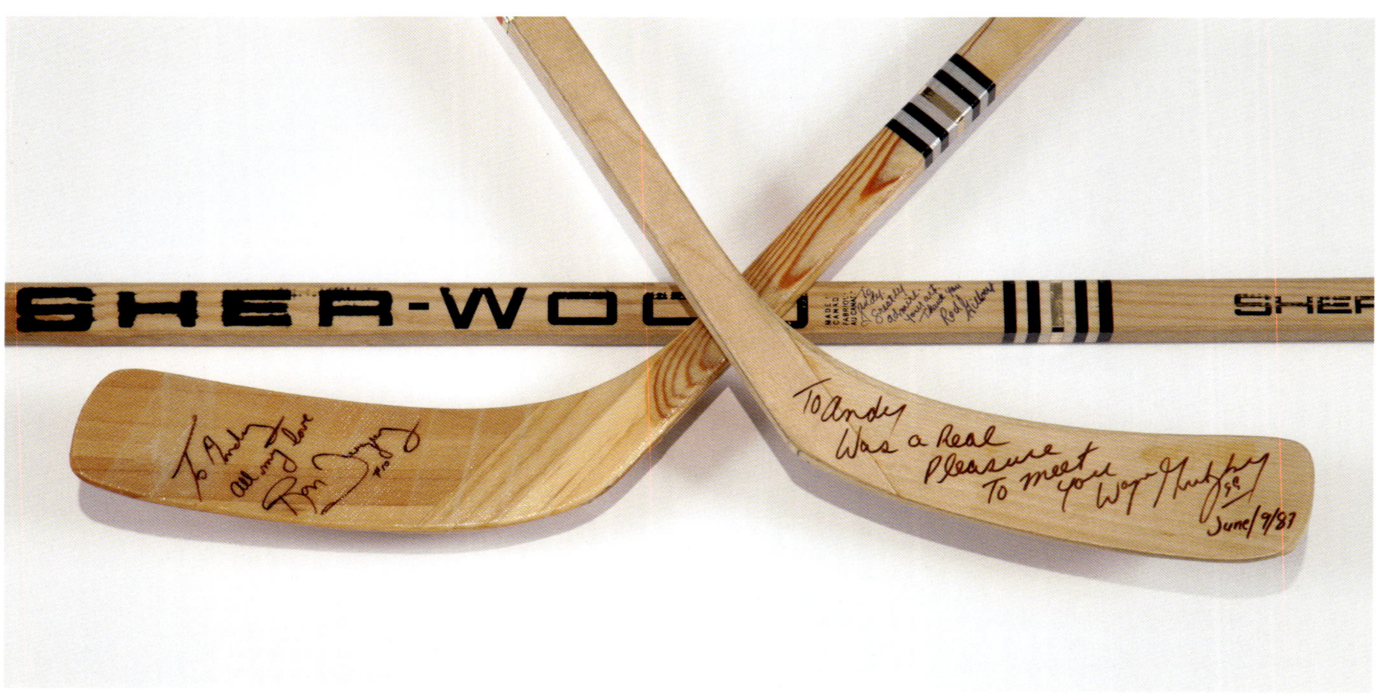

New York Yankees hat inscribed by Bobby Murcer to Warhol, ca. 1979–83

Hockey sticks inscribed by Rod Gilbert, Ron Duguay, and Wayne Gretzky to Warhol, 1978, 1982, 1983

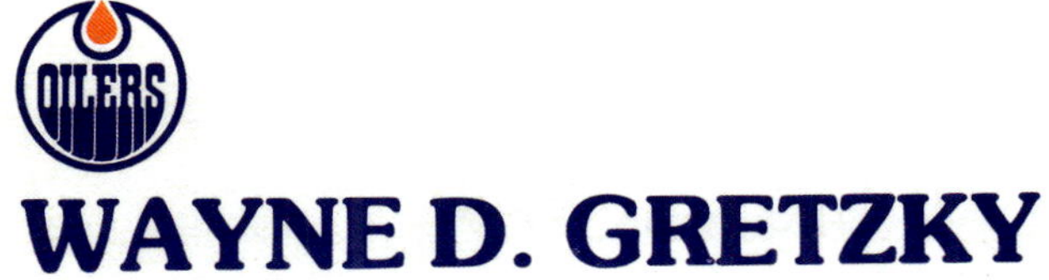

July 7, 1983

Mr. Andy Warhol
860 Broadway
New York, New York

Dear Mr. Warhol:

Just a short note to thank you for the enjoyable afternoon I spent at
your studio. As I mentioned to you, I have several works of your art
presently hanging in my residence and certainly consider it an honor
to be considered as a subject of your work.

I'm looking forward to seeing the finished prints and would be happy to
provide you with any further assistance you my require. Once again
Andy, thank you.

Sincerely yours,

Wayne Gretzky

/jk

7424 - 118th AVENUE, EDMONTON, ALBERTA T5B 4M9
(MERAK INVESTMENTS LTD.)

Letter from Wayne Gretzky to Warhol, July 7, 1983

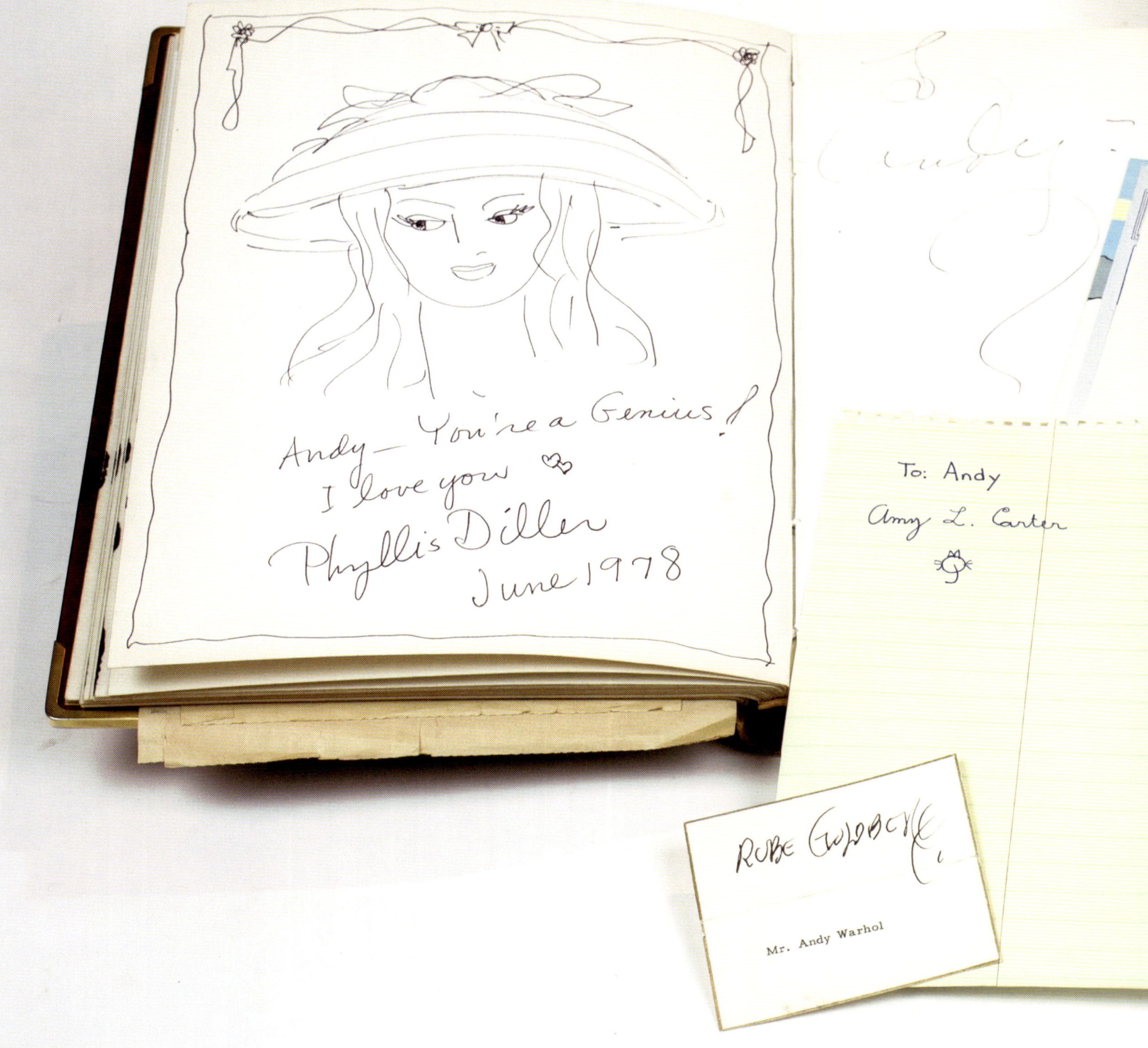

(clockwise from top) Note from comedian Milton Berle to Warhol, n.d.; Drinking glass signed by Nick Rhodes, ca. 1984; Cassette case signed by Richard James Burgess, ca. 1984; *Tintin in Tibet* inscribed by Hergé to Warhol, April 27, 1972 (Hergé/Moulinsart); Note from Amy Carter to Warhol, late 1970s; Place card for Warhol signed by Rube Goldberg, ca. 1970–75; Page from the Factory guestbook inscribed by comedienne Phyllis Diller to Warhol, June 1978

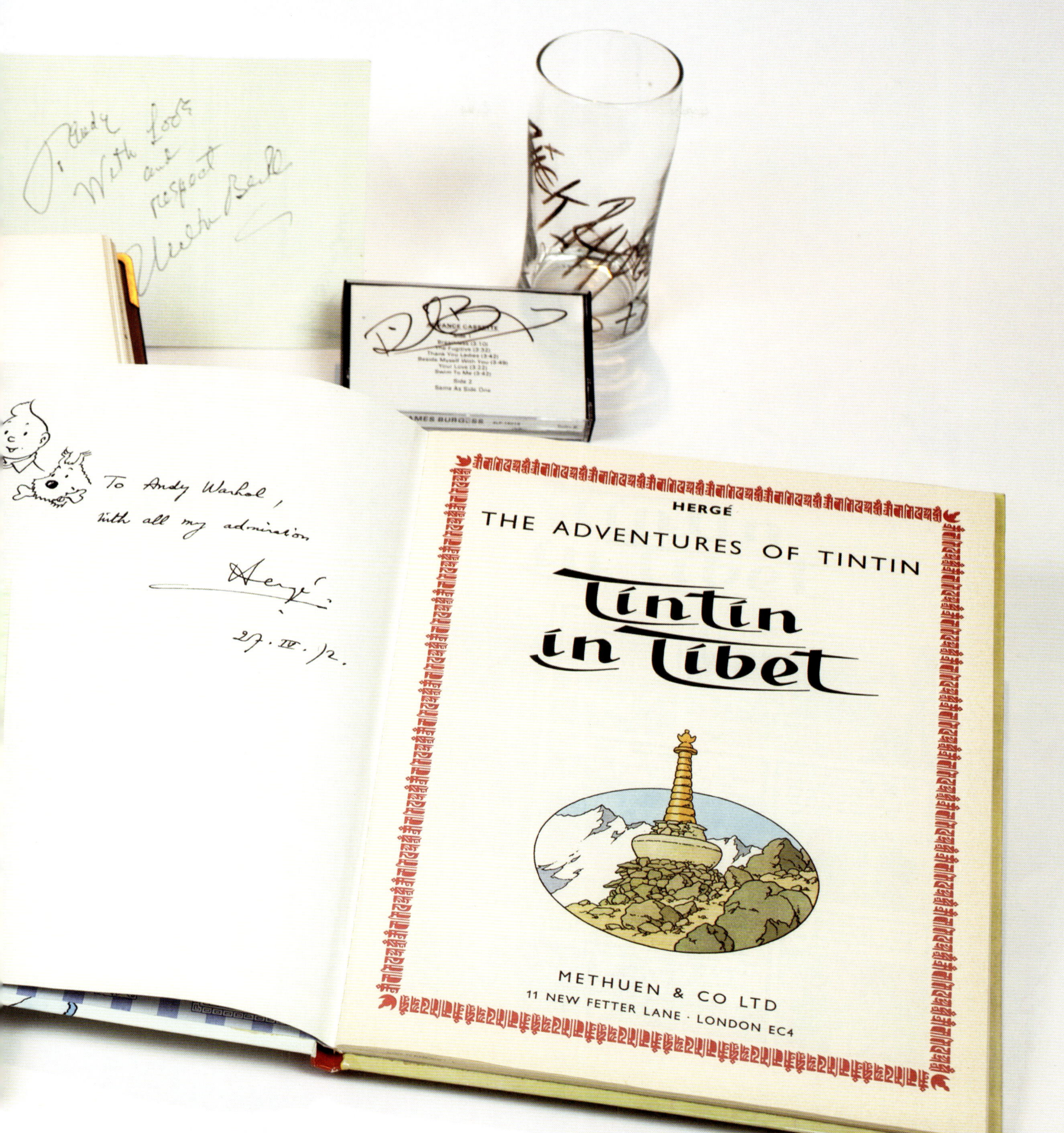
HERGÉ
THE ADVENTURES OF TINTIN
Tintin in Tibet
METHUEN & CO LTD
11 NEW FETTER LANE · LONDON EC4
To Andy Warhol,
with all my admiration
Hergé
27·IV·72

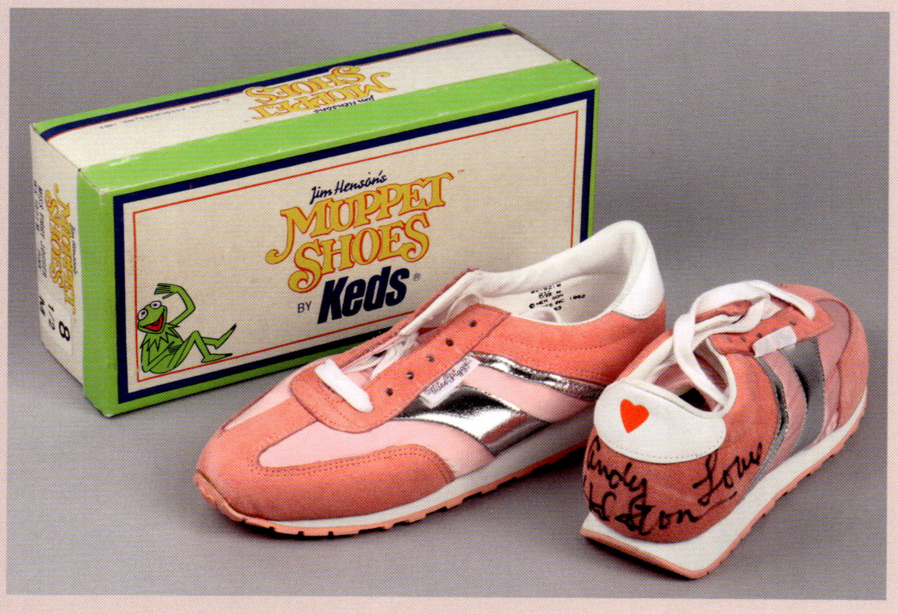

The best.... and more!!
More is better....
The most is the best!!!

Love Van Furstenberg

Live your
fantasies.

March 2nd.
1978

GianniVersace

ANDY,   I LOVE TO SEE YOU
SOON

Love Gi

G.V. FASHION IMPORTS Inc. • 600 Madison Avenue • New York, N.Y. 10022 • (212) 223-0575/6 • Telex: 238491

Miss Piggy Joggers inscribed by Halston to Warhol, 1980–83

Page from the Factory guestbook inscribed by Diane von Furstenberg to Warhol, March 2, 1978
Note from Gianni Versace to Warhol, n.d.

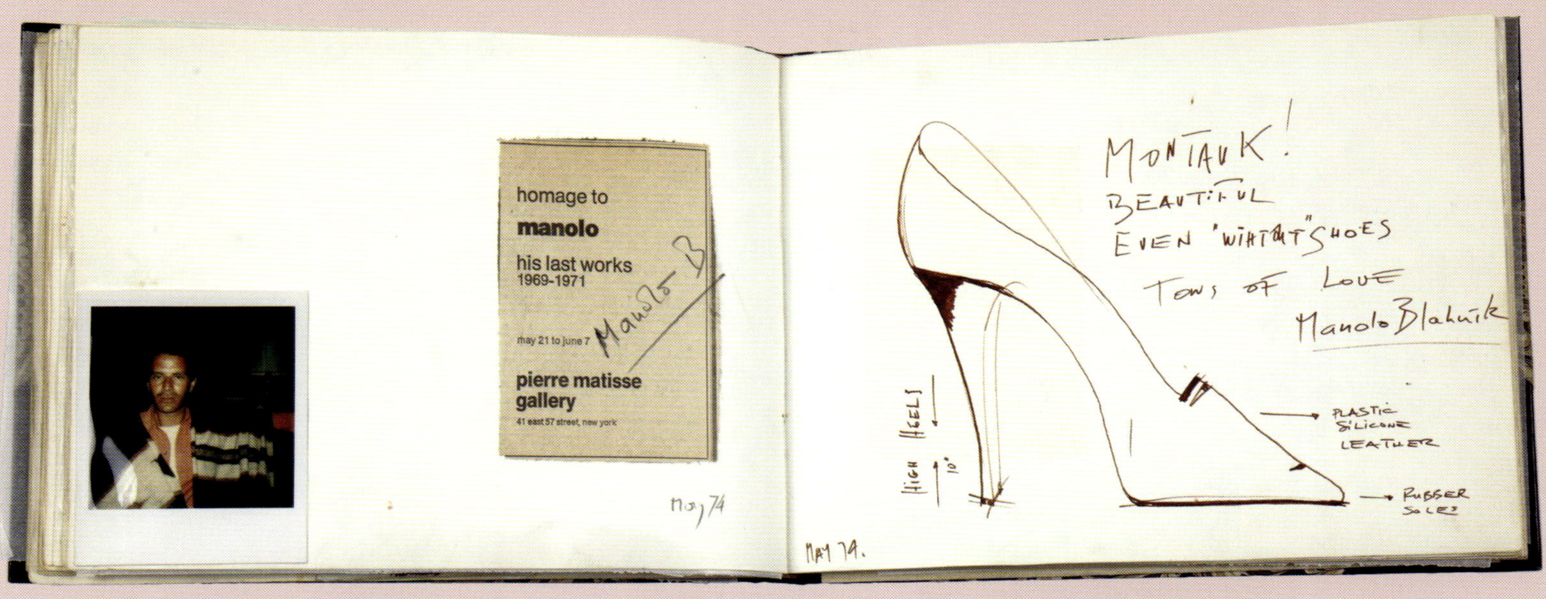

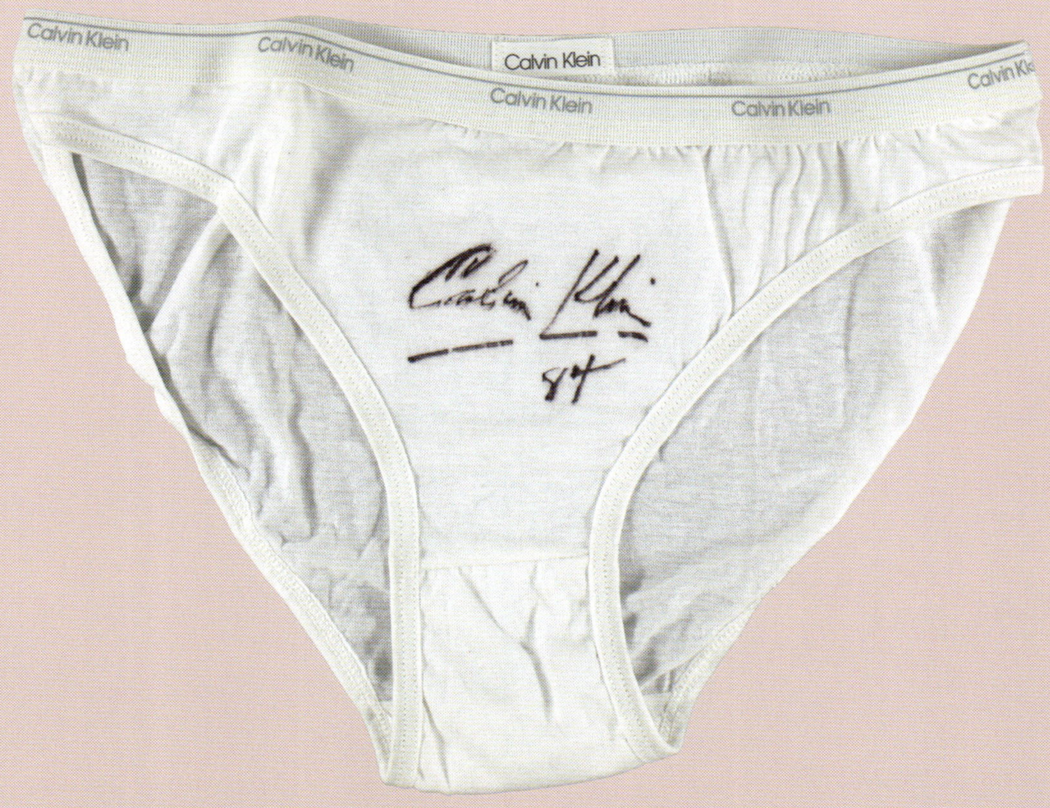

Inscription from Manolo Blahnik to Warhol in the Montauk scrapbook,
May 1974

Calvin Klein men's underwear signed by the designer, 1984

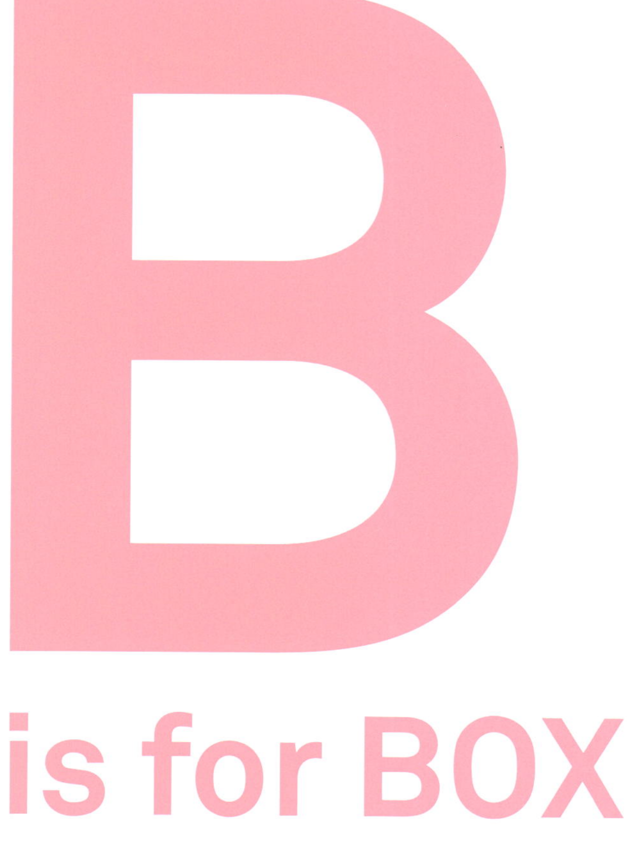

B
is for BOX

Perhaps most renowned for his *Brillo Boxes* (1964), Warhol based another sculpture on utilitarian cardboard boxes— a work that would span two decades and later fill his archive and is so large it has never been displayed all at once. While preparing to move his studio in Manhattan in 1974, Warhol began assembling a strange, modular sculpture, which he called *Time Capsules*. This work consists of 610 containers with an average of 800 objects in each. Most of the containers are standard cardboard boxes each measuring about 10 by 18 by 14 inches. There are also 40 filing cabinet drawers and one large trunk. The collection is considered an artwork because that is how Fred Hughes, Warhol's longtime friend, business associate, and executor, described the artist's thinking on the boxes when he was asked to discuss Warhol's art and collection with a small group of representatives of the three founding partners of The Andy Warhol Museum.[1] In Hughes's words, "[Warhol] thought of them as sculpture."[2]

The former vice president of Warhol Enterprises and longtime colleague and friend, Vincent Fremont, claims credit for the concept and the title. He felt that by having Warhol fill a box at a time and call each one a *Time Capsule*

This chapter features highlights from *Time Capsule 79*, whose contents date from 1941 to 1972 and were on display in the Archives Study Center, January 27–November 7, 2004.

it would be a way to motivate him to clean up the mess in their old studio. Then they could continue the process at their new studio. Warhol liked the idea so much that he also began making *Time Capsules* in his home. He wanted to exhibit them all on a large shelving unit in an art gallery. Each box would be for sale but could not be opened for inspection prior to purchase; the price of every *Time Capsule* would be identical, a price that was often changing in his mind. "Took a few time capsule boxes to the office.…Some day I'll sell them for $4,000–$5,000 apiece. I used to think $100, but now I think that's my new price."[3] The show never came to pass, however, and none of the boxes was sold. After the artist's death in 1987, the *Time Capsules* were each assigned a unique number, to document how many existed and to help with record keeping, and then transferred to The Andy Warhol Museum in their entirety.[4]

The *Time Capsules* contain a vast amount of personal ephemera, correspondence, and telephone messages, ideas and notes for Warhol's creations, and even artworks. Everything from Polaroids and phonograph records to perfumes and tiny bottles of liquor has been catalogued as part of the work. One box is filled with hundreds of black-and-white photographs taken by Warhol in the 1980s; another holds three original Warhol portraits of Bella Abzug buried amid correspondence, kazoos, and bags of cookies. Some boxes are filled entirely with his mother's belongings (see "J is for Julia"), while dozens of others are filled with newspapers (see "H is for Headlines").

Each *Time Capsule* provides information on Warhol's interests and activities, as well as current events. This chapter features highlights from *Time Capsule 79*, the contents of which date from 1941 to 1972, with the majority from 1964 to 1966. The mid-1960s were an especially prolific and dynamic period in Warhol's career as an emerging Pop artist and filmmaker.

Commercial Art and Financial Records

Throughout the 1950s and into the early 1960s, Warhol's art was largely made for commercial clients. *Time Capsule 79* contains documentation of this period. The large drawing in his blotted-line style is an example of this work, shown in its final form in a recording of Ravel's *Daphnis and Chloe*, made for RCA Victor in 1955. Invoices Warhol sent to his clients in 1960 and work orders that he received from them are telling records of his success. A *New York Times* envelope contains Warhol's 1099 tax form for their commissions in 1961, totaling $2,925, or more than $24,000 in 2018 values.[5]

At times, Warhol's mother, Julia Warhola, collaborated with him on his art projects, adding her charming handwriting to illustrations. An example of her script is seen on Warhol's green-and-blue stationery, and several *Time Capsules* contain her drawings and personal ephemera. Julia moved to New York in 1952, living with her son from then until 1971, a year before her death in 1972. She cooked and cared for him, and even when Warhol was involved in a frenetic social life with New York's cultural avant-garde and celebrities, she insisted that he attend Mass.

Another important early collaborator, and one of Warhol's first boyfriends, was photographer Edward Wallowitch. Two Wallowitch photos from 1961 were found in *Time Capsule 79*. Warhol used Wallowitch's photos as sources for many of his works, selectively tracing over them and then making blotted-line drawings.

Clipping from unidentified newspaper with excerpt from "A Psychodelic [*sic*] Sparkle," Tuesday, February 28, 1967

Art Source Materials

Warhol placed his ideas for artworks, reference materials, and even original works in the *Time Capsules*. Like hidden gems, these items were stashed away for decades but are now being catalogued and added to the pantheon of his oeuvre and related scholarship. *Time Capsule 79* contains source material for multiple bodies of work and contemporaneously published examples of completed works. *Miriam Davidson (20 Times)* (1965), featured on the cover of *Canadian Art* magazine in January 1966, shows Warhol's use of repetition and photography.[6] He first used photobooth photos for the self-portrait he provided to the catalogue for the 1963 *Popular Image* show at the Washington Gallery of Modern Art, Washington, DC, and used them again to illustrate an article for *Harper's Bazaar* in June 1963; a fragment of the illustration remains in *Time Capsule 79*. Art dealer John Weber's photobooth self-portraits adorn his letter to Warhol from November 1963. Warhol also used Polaroid photos; two self-portraits and five of actor Denis Deegan dating from about 1963 are in the box.

The image of Warhol on the exhibition announcement "Personality of the Artist" is from a photobooth photo. The flyer publicized his *Boxes* show at the Stable Gallery in 1964 and suggests that his work is deeper than the surface: "It takes us to a place which we have not seen and possibly have not sensed before."[7] This was the second time the gallery promoted Warhol's work using unconventional material. In 1962, the gallery used college student Suzy Stanton's essay as a handout for Warhol's first Pop Art show in New York. The paper was written for a class with Lawrence Alloway, champion of British Pop artists in the 1950s, and parodied both the class and the art.

Several items in this *Time Capsule* figured in the conception of other famous works by Warhol. Warhol made the stencils "Cream of" and "Onion" for his *Campbell's Soup* images of 1962. The small cow-head stencil and a postcard recall his *Cow* wallpaper. Mug shots of two criminals depicted in Warhol's *Thirteen Most Wanted Men* mural, created for the New York World's Fair of 1964, accompany the stencils. The *Mona Lisa* tear sheets are the sources for Warhol's versions of the Leonardo da Vinci work. They come from the catalogue for the only US exhibition of the painting, held at the National Gallery of Art, Washington, DC, and the Metropolitan Museum of Art, New York, respectively, in 1963.[8]

A lesser-known creative project is referenced in a letter to Warhol from United Scenic Artists. This document has helped to confirm that Warhol designed costumes for a Broadway play, James Thurber's *The Beast in Me*, in 1963. He wasn't a union member, so he received barely visible credit for this work.

Celebrities in the Media

The popular press was very important to Warhol, keeping him abreast of cultural trends and of his portrayal in the public eye. *Time Capsule 79* contains many periodicals from the 1960s, capturing the politics and entertainment of the era. Amid the movie magazines are alternative publications such as the *East Village Other*, which protested the war in Vietnam, and *Kiss*, which promoted sexual openness (see "U is for Underground").

Highlights include Fabian, teen idol of the 1950s and 1960s and lifelong performer, donning the cover of *Stardom* in 1959. TV's late-night star Johnny Carson appeared in *Look* magazine in 1966; he had hosted *The Tonight Show* for four years, with twenty-six more to go.[9] In the *Status & Diplomat* magazine article "The Restless Ones," model Donyale Luna describes her upcoming role in Warhol's film of *Snow White*, which was never finished.[10] In a *Life* magazine article from September 1960, actor Fredric March transforms into his role in Stanley Kramer's *Inherit the Wind*, based on the infamous Scopes "Monkey Trial" of 1925, on the teaching of evolution.[11] The film starred Spencer Tracy and Gene Kelly as well.

Also included is a book of print ads and puff reviews publicizing the 1941 film *Penny Serenade*, a story about infertility and adoption. Cary Grant was nominated for an Oscar for his performance in the film. Warhol received an autographed photo of its beautiful female star, Irene Dunne, that same year, as well as photos of Fredric March and many others.

Among other celebrity materials, the *Time Capsule* contains a grouping of ephemera related to Marilyn Monroe. A clipping sent to Warhol from "Max" promotes the book *Violations of the Child Marilyn Monroe*, which purports to tell the story of her childhood abuses. There is an announcement card for a show of paintings by Warhol's friend Harold Stevenson at Feigen-Herbert Gallery in New York City. The gallery also screened *Some Like It Hot*, a comedy in which Jack Lemmon and Tony Curtis impersonate women, and which was Monroe's most successful film.

Film Materials

Warhol's insatiable interest in famous lives—both the glamorous and the seamy sides—became inspiration for his art. In the early 1960s, he created drawings based on ads for beauty products endorsed by Joan Crawford and Hedy Lamarr. He also fashioned an unusual portrait combining the faces of four stars—Crawford, Marlene Dietrich, Greta Garbo, and Sophia Loren—and later produced portraits of Marlon Brando, Monroe, Elvis Presley, and others.[12] In 1966, when Lamarr was arrested for shoplifting, Warhol made his film *Hedy*. He also interpreted the life of Lana Turner in his movie *More Milk, Yvette* (1965) and that of Lupe Velez in *Lupe* (1965).

Time Capsule 79 contains many references to Warhol's films. This box includes the May 1968 issue of *Avant-Garde* magazine, featuring Warhol's female Superstars. The Superstars were Warhol's favored roster of performers—charismatic personalities drawn from within his circle of friends, lovers, and colleagues, instead of professional actors. The Superstars were tasked with roles that were loosely scripted or in unscripted scenarios. In this setup, there was often little distinction between the performed and the real. Warhol frequently provoked his Superstars to act out on film but also captured their captivating beauty while doing no more than lounging around. Most of the Superstars were given stage names: Susan Bottomly, for example, became International Velvet; Ingrid von Scheven became Ingrid Superstar; and Isabelle Collin Dufresne, Ultra Violet.

Between 1964 and 1966, Warhol shot more than six hundred *Screen Tests* of friends, artists, actors, and lesser-known visitors to the Factory. They included Roderick Clayton, who spent a brief period in the Factory and afterward wrote a letter to Warhol (found in *Time Capsule 79*) describing his job measuring the ears of Air Force pilots in 1966; he added that it is a "far cry from when you painted my nails and I vowed not to get up tight whirling in silver vinylcrucifying [*sic*] skeletons and so." Clayton sat for four Warhol *Screen Tests* in 1966.

Billy Linich (Billy Name) also sat for a *Screen Test*, but he was usually found behind the camera, lighting Warhol's films or documenting the goings-on at the Factory. Warhol first met Linich when he was a waiter at Serendipity 3, a restaurant that Warhol frequented in the 1950s and early 1960s. At that time, Linich was also a lighting designer for dance and theater performances; he appears as such in the program for "A Concert of Dance." After meeting Warhol, Linich assumed the same role for Warhol's films and productions. They were briefly lovers in 1964. Linich, like all the Superstars, changed his identity—to Billy Name—when he began working on Warhol's *Exploding Plastic Inevitable* shows in 1966. *Time Capsule 79* contains one of Linich's photos of Warhol with a Liz Taylor portrait. Linich decorated the photo with a word balloon filled with the names of the cast of Warhol's film *Vinyl* (1965), based on Anthony Burgess's *A Clockwork Orange*. Dialogue from *Vinyl* was also published in the December 1965 issue of *Clyde* magazine.

The artist Ray Johnson was a friend of both Warhol and Linich. In May 1963, Johnson arranged for the three of them to attend a bodybuilders' competition. The program for the event is in this box, along with Johnson's "correspondance" collages, which were sent to a third party with instructions to resend them to Warhol (see "S is for Stamp").

The Velvet Underground

Time Capsule 79 also contains material pertaining to one of the most influential bands in the history of rock and roll, a band that Warhol managed in 1966: the Velvet Underground. Its principal members included John Cale, Sterling Morrison, Lou Reed, and Maureen Tucker. They formed in 1965, performing live music for poetry/film shows at the

Film-Makers' Cinematheque in New York. The Velvet Underground's influences included the poet Delmore Schwartz, doo-wop music, and the composers John Cage and La Monte Young. In turn, their songs have influenced an array of musicians from David Bowie to Galaxie 500. The Velvet Underground was inducted into the Rock and Roll Hall of Fame on January 17, 1996. Warhol began to work with the Velvets after seeing them perform at the Cafe Bizarre in Greenwich Village in December 1965. He soon introduced the former model Nico (Christa Paeffgen) as the group's chanteuse. Together they performed in New York and on tour in Warhol's performances *Up-Tight* and *The Exploding Plastic Inevitable*, and at the New York club the Gymnasium. Warhol created the well-known banana cover for the group's first album. The band was a significant presence in the artist's films, books, and performances. After leaving Warhol's orbit in the summer of 1967, the Velvets endured personnel changes and recorded three studio albums until their final performance in the summer of 1970.

Warhol kept ephemera relating to the time he spent with the band, including red tickets to the Velvet Underground's performance at Rutgers University in March 1966, which reveal various names for the performance, among them "Andy Warhol's Underground New York" and "Rutgers Up-Tight." Stored with the tickets is a schedule listing Warhol's shows at the Cinematheque in February 1966; these were intended as a retrospective of his films starring Edie Sedgwick, who was then also listed as a dancer with the Velvet Underground. Additional ephemera include a photo of Sedgwick and Warhol; a page of singer/songwriter Lou Reed's essay "Life among the Poobahs," which was published in *Aspen* magazine in December 1966; a 1965 interview with Bob Dylan; and a torn handwritten guest list for the Rutgers show that includes journalist Al Aronowitz, pop star Donovan (whose son portrayed Gerard Malanga in the 1996 film *I Shot Andy Warhol*), and actor Peter Fonda, whom Warhol included in his commissioned artwork for a cover of *Time* magazine in 1970, titled *The Flying Fondas*.[13]

Receipts and invoices for electrical equipment, most from late March and early April 1966, bear the name of filmmaker Danny Williams, whom Warhol was romancing at the time. Williams was responsible for the technical

aspects of Warhol's performances featuring the Velvets, eventually known as *The Exploding Plastic Inevitable*. Among the receipts is an Ohio Turnpike toll card from the Velvets' trip to Michigan in March 1966. Other invoices are from Warhol's lawyers, Barovick, Konecky, and Litvinoff; these documents detail fees for many projects related to the Velvet Underground and indicate that Warhol was paying a portion of his legal fees with his art in 1966. Lastly, the box holds invoices for a banana image, dated August 1966, which Warhol used as the cover of the Velvet Underground's first album, released in March 1967.

Ultimately, for the Museum and for Warhol scholarship, it is very fortunate that Warhol never realized his vision of a gallery installation of the *Time Capsules* or sold them to unknown collectors. The *Time Capsules* are now all in one place and stand together in their inexplicable completeness. Each is a wealth of information, and collectively they provide an assortment of exceptional primary documents for research not only into the world and work of Warhol but also into American culture in the twentieth century.

NOTES

1. The tripartite committee that met to form The Andy Warhol Museum was represented by executive staff of the Warhol Foundation, the Dia Center for the Arts, and the Carnegie Museums of Pittsburgh. The formal agreement was signed on October 8, 1992.

2. Fred Hughes's statement was in reply to a question posed by the first director/curator of the Warhol Museum, Mark Francis, who wished to know Warhol's thoughts on the *Time Capsules*. At that time, the *Time Capsules* had never been exhibited and were barely known outside of the artist's inner circle.

3. Andy Warhol and Pat Hackett, eds., *The Andy Warhol Diaries* (New York: Hachette Book Group, 1989), 762.

4. An attempt was made to number the *Time Capsules* chronologically; however, after a portion were given sequential numbers, additional boxes were located in storage that predated the next available numbers. These boxes were given negative numbers. Examples in this book include *Time Capsule -10* (see "X is for X-Rated") and *Time Capsule -27* (see "J is for Julia").

5. "1961 dollars in 2018 | Inflation Calculator," FinanceRef Inflation Calculator, Alioth Finance, http://www.in2013dollars.com/1961-dollars-in-2018.

6. *Canadian Art*, no. 100 (January 1966), cover image of Andy Warhol's *Miriam Davidson (20 Times)* (1965), with article by Ellen H. Johnson, "The Image Duplicators—Lichtenstein, Rauschenberg and Warhol," p. 12, with inscription "To Andy With Love, Ellen H. Johnson." In 1967 *Canadian Art* changed its name to *Artscanada*.

7. Gene Swenson, "The Personality of the Artist," exhibition announcement poster, *Andy Warhol at Stable Gallery*, April 21–May 9, 1964. The Andy

Warhol Museum, Pittsburgh; Founding Collection, Contribution The Andy Warhol Foundation for the Visual Arts, Inc. TC79.201.2.1.

8. This exhibition was the only time the *Mona Lisa* has been on view in the United States. Then–First Lady Jackie Kennedy arranged with André Malraux, French minister for cultural affairs, to have Leonardo's master-piece exhibited in Washington, DC, and New York. It was on view at the National Gallery, January 9–February 3, and at the Metropolitan Museum of Art, February 7–March 4.

9. Betty Rollin, "Johnny Carson, the Prince of Chitchat, Is a Loner," *Look* 30, no. 2 (January 25, 1966): 98–102.

10. Jerome Agel, "The Restless Ones," *Status & Diplomat* 18, no. 205 (June/July 1967): 64–65, 79.

11. "A New Image of Bryan: March Plays in Scopes Trial Film," *Life* 49, no. 13 (September 26, 1960): 77–78.

12. The portrait, *Female Movie Star Composite* (ca. 1962), lists the initials of each actress beside the feature Warhol used to create the faces, from hairline to chin: "GG," Greta Garbo's hairline; "J.C," Joan Crawford's eyes; "M.D," Marlene Dietrich's nose and cheekbones; and "SL," Sophia Loren's lips and chin.

13. Peter, his sister Jane, and their father, Henry Fonda, were all included in Warhol's artwork for *Time* magazine.

Additional research for this chapter was provided by Erin Byrne, Matt Gray, and Brianna Treleven. Photographic layouts designed by Becky Shock and Brianna Treleven.

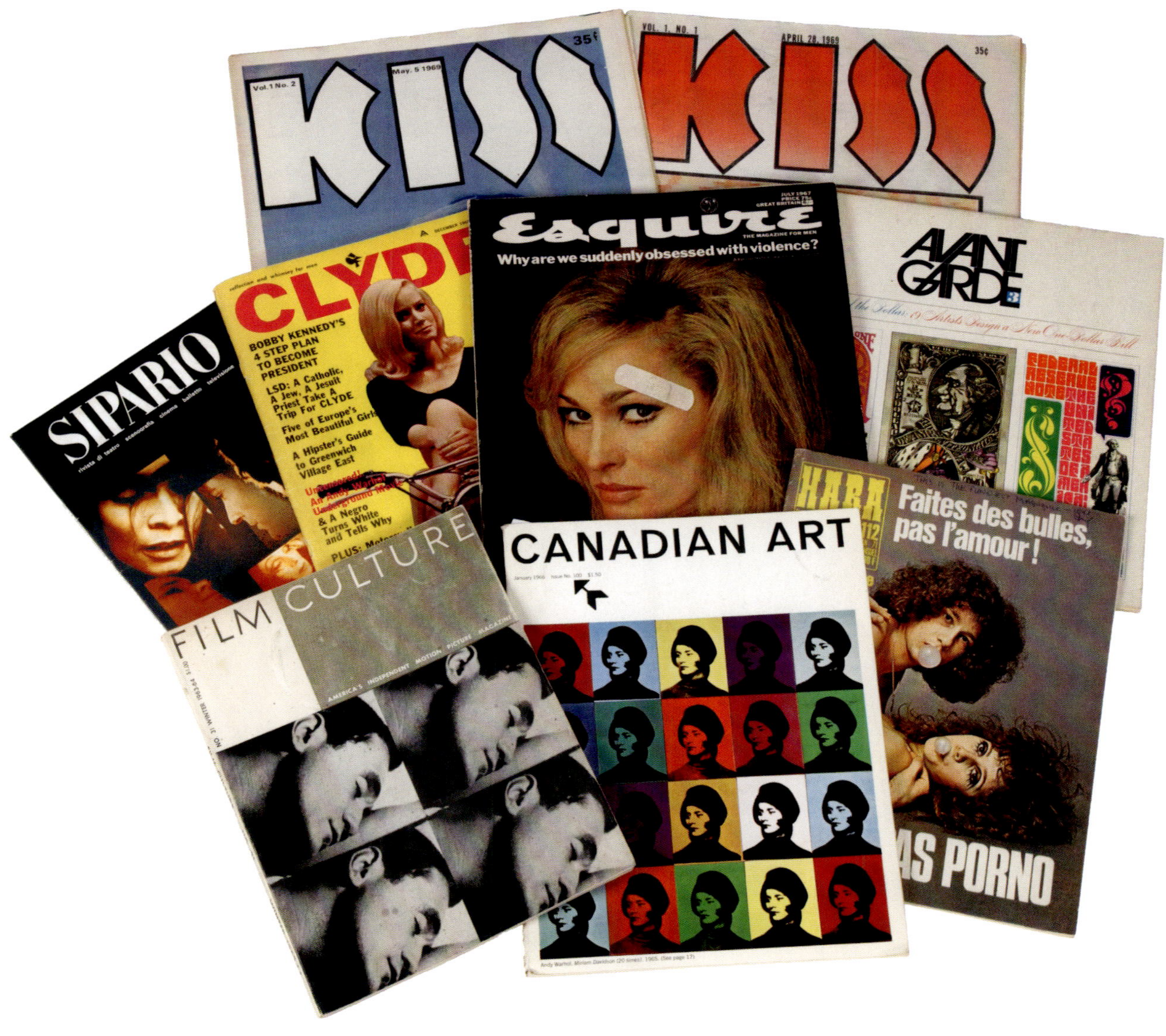

Group of magazines from *Time Capsule 79*

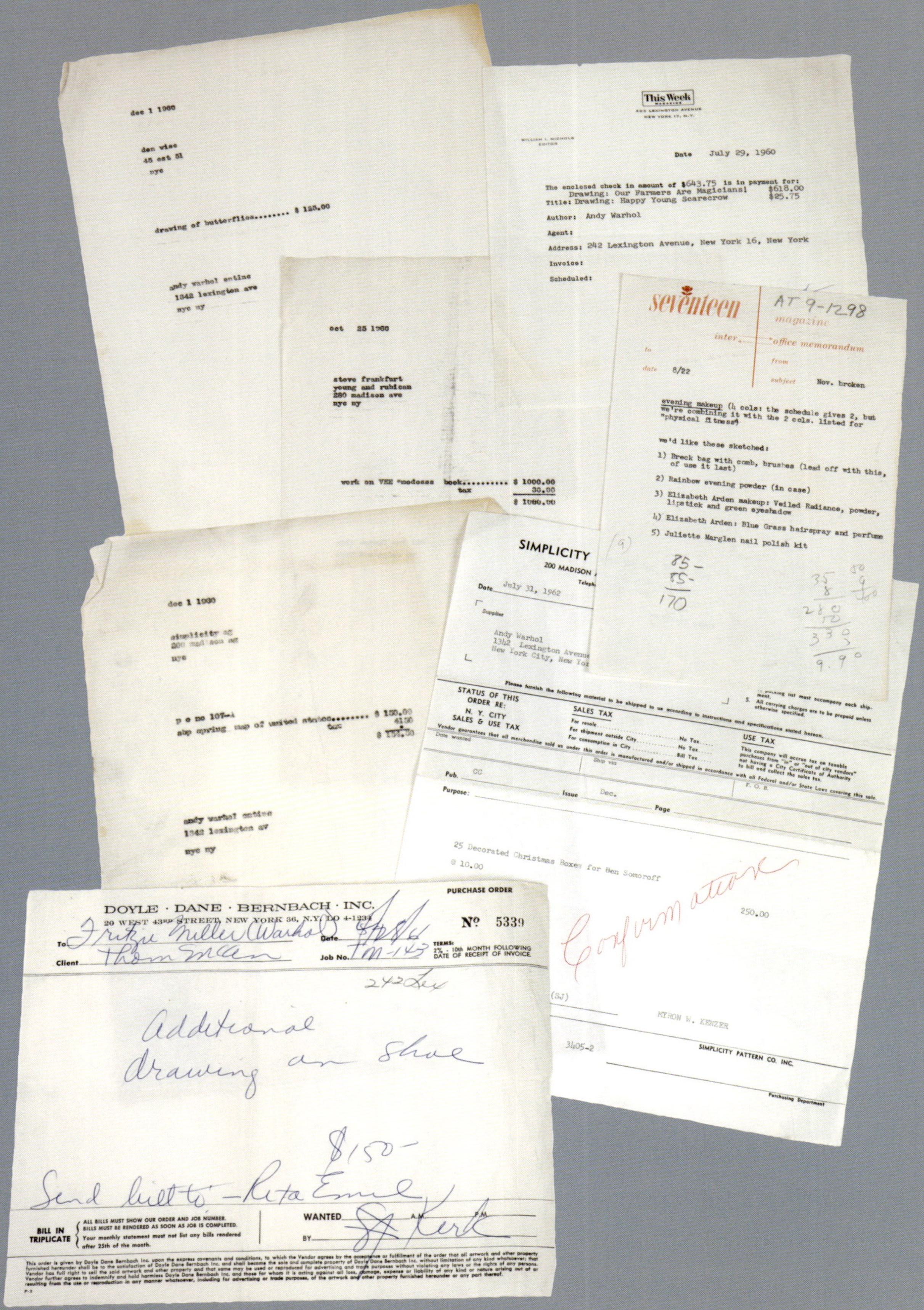

Financial records for various commercial assignments completed by Warhol from *Time Capsule 79*

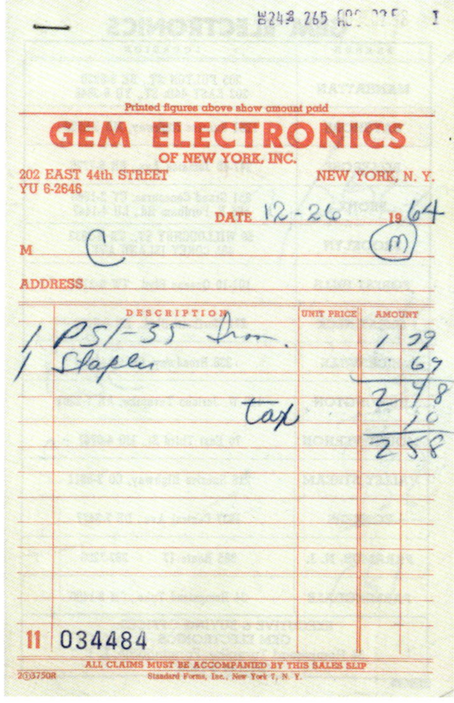

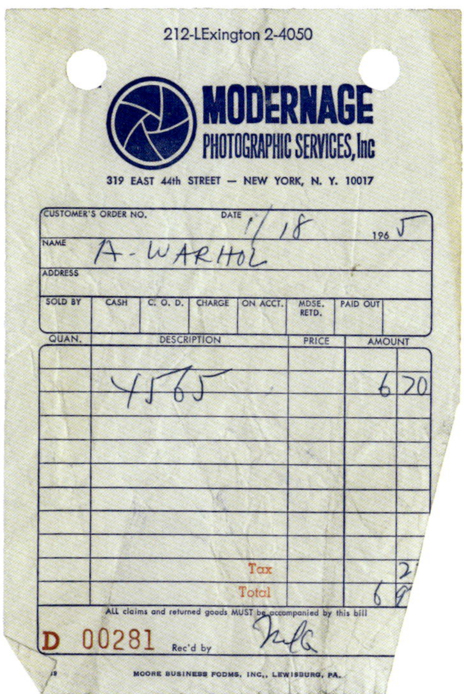

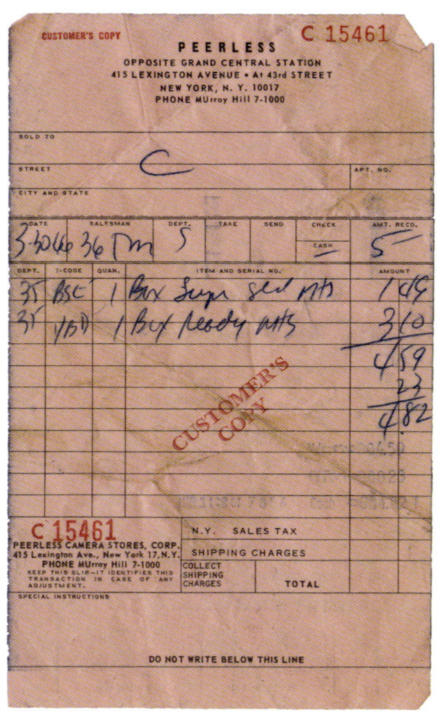

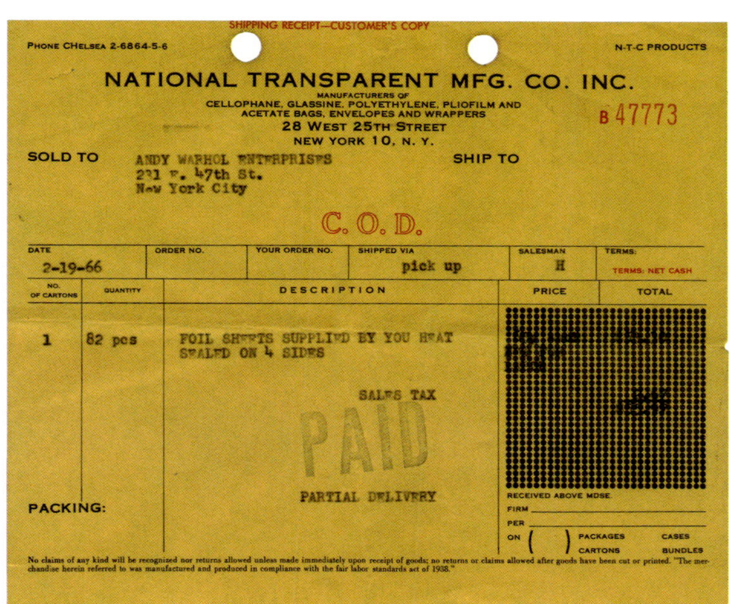

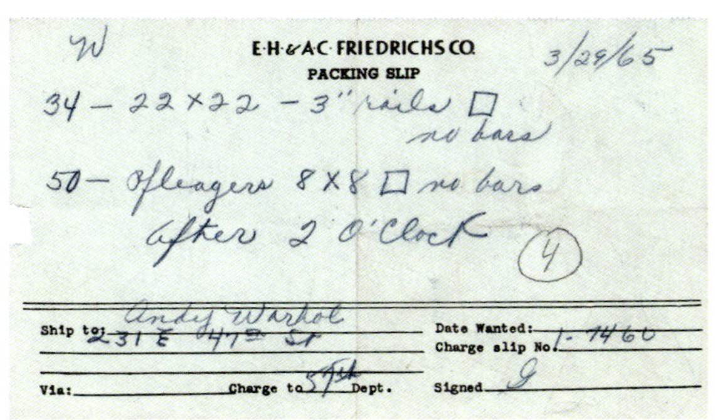

Receipts, 1964–66, for Warhol's supplies for paintings, films, and the sculpture *Silver Clouds*, 1966

(middle row, right) Andy Warhol business stationery envelope with lettering in Julia Warhola's handwriting, ca. 1959

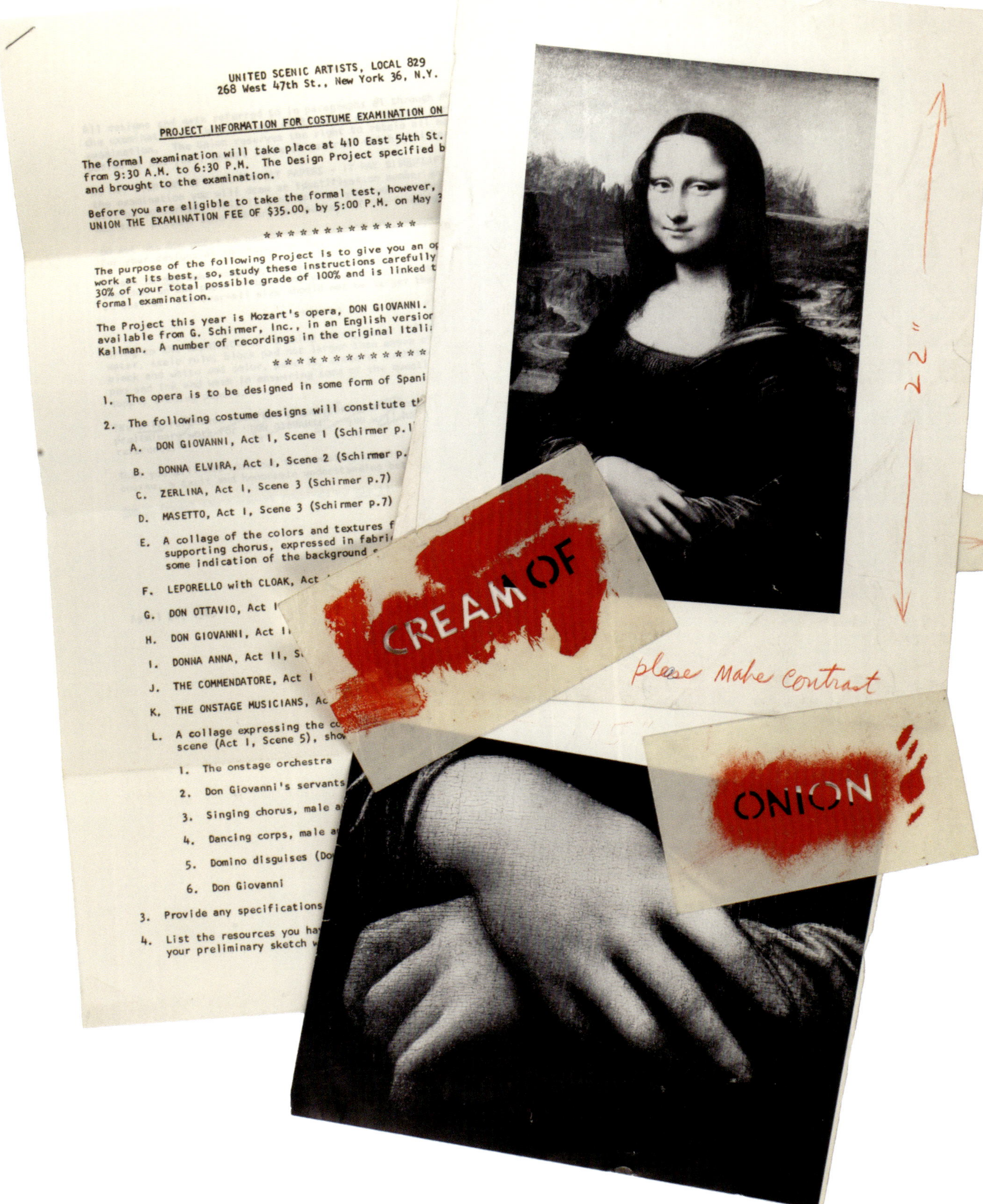

Warhol's source materials for *Mona Lisa* paintings, soup can stencils,
and United Scenic Artists' examination instructions for theater costume
design work from *Time Capsule 79*, ca. 1962–63

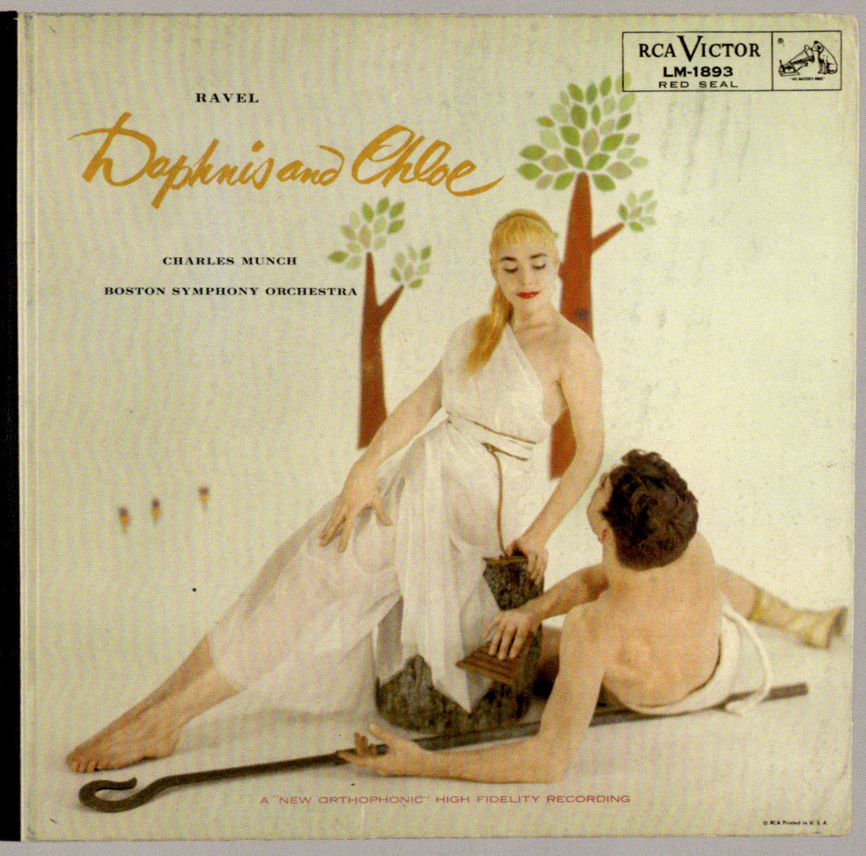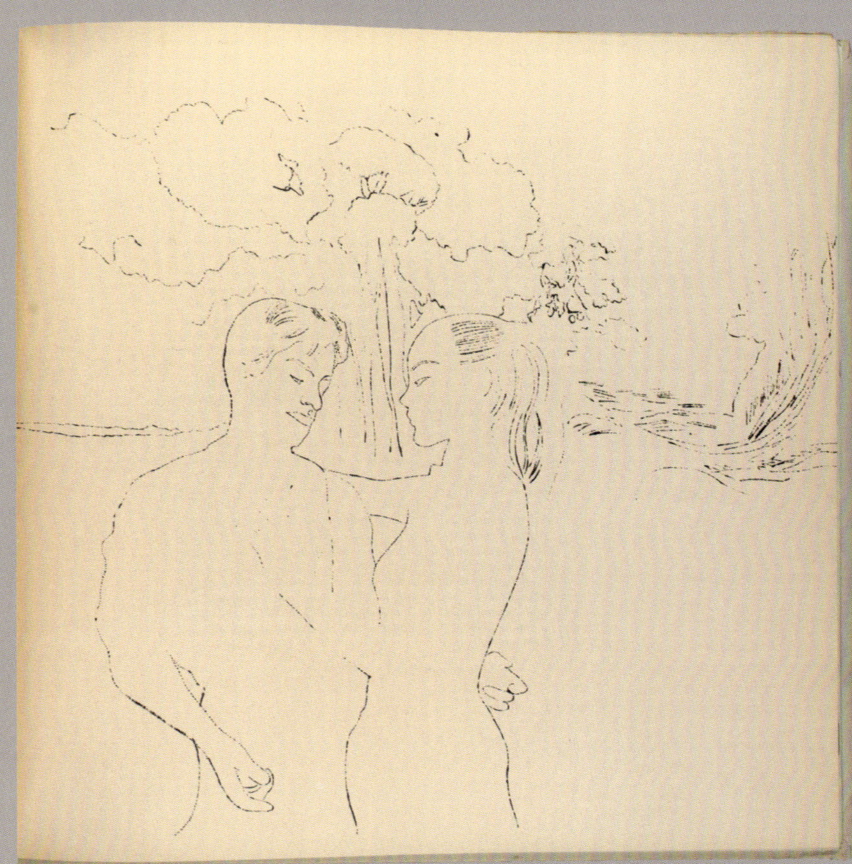

Vinyl record jacket for Ravel's *Daphnis and Chloe*, RCA Victor, with
original illustrations by Warhol on interior pages, 1955

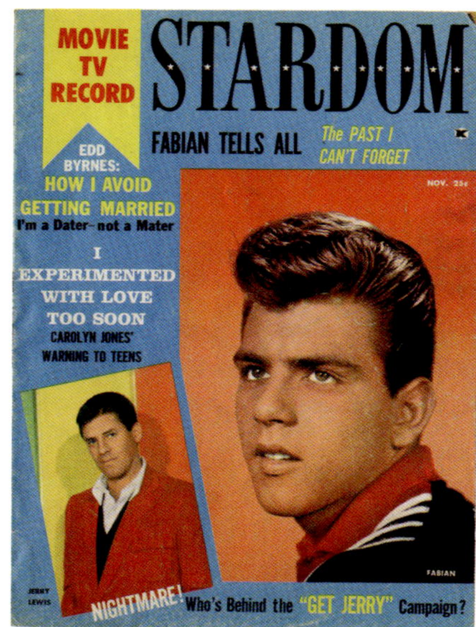

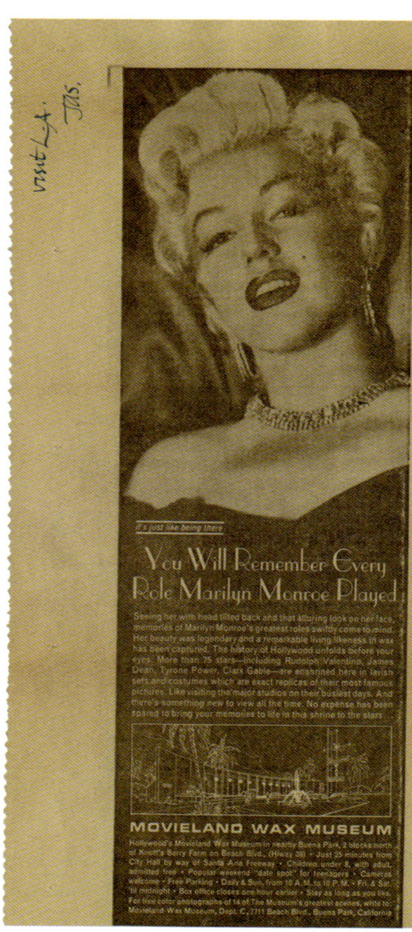

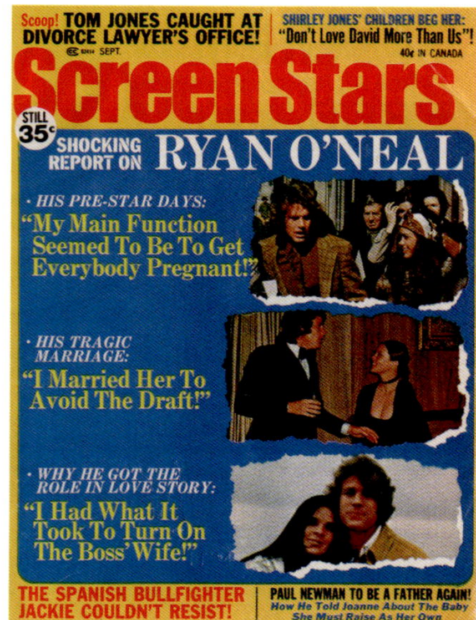

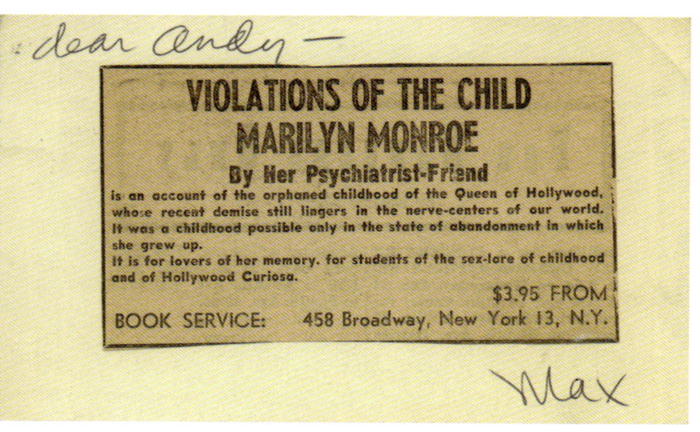

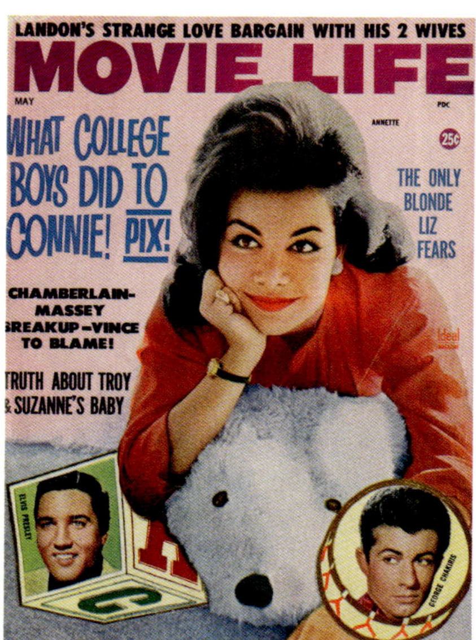

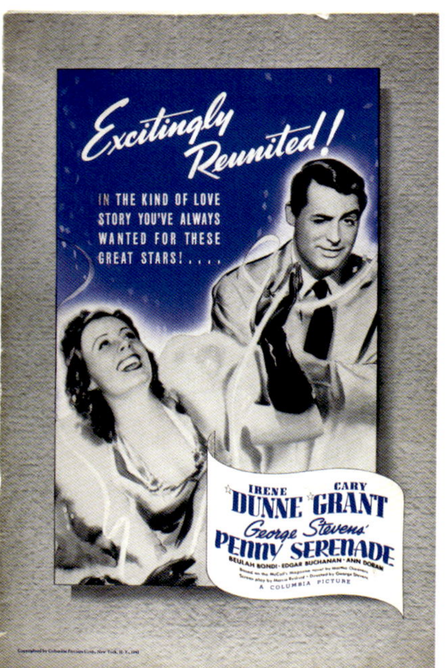

Movie star materials from *Time Capsule 79* (clockwise from top left) *Stardom* with Fabian and Jerry Lewis on the cover, November 1959; Advertisement for the Movieland Wax Museum with photo of Marilyn Monroe, 1963; *Screen Stars* with Ryan O'Neal on the cover, September 1971; Promotional book for *Penny Serenade*, starring Irene Dunne and Cary Grant, 1941; *Movie Life* with Annette Funicello on the cover, May 1963; Postcard to Warhol with newspaper clipping promoting a book about Marilyn Monroe, 1963

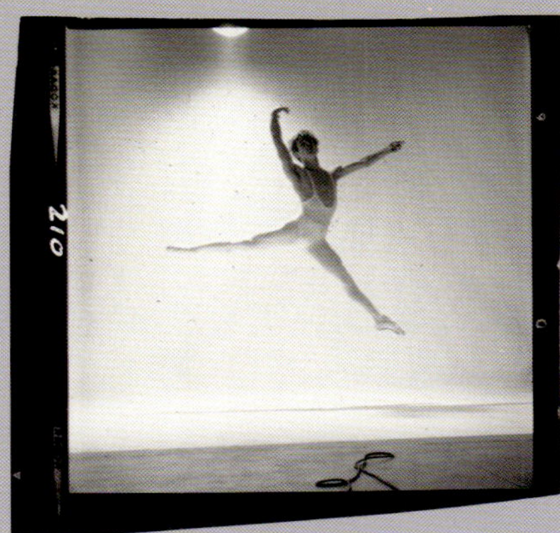

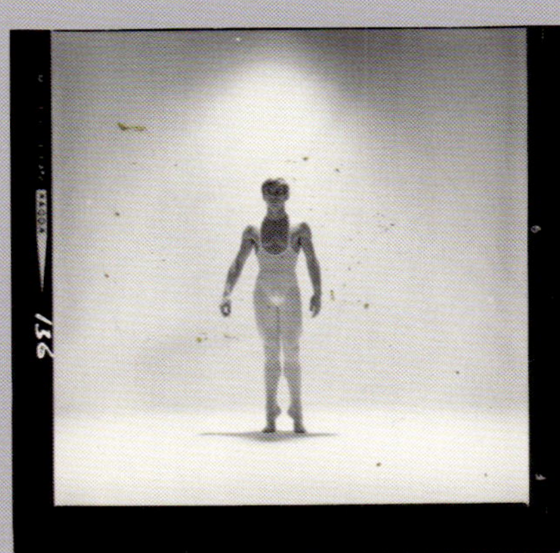

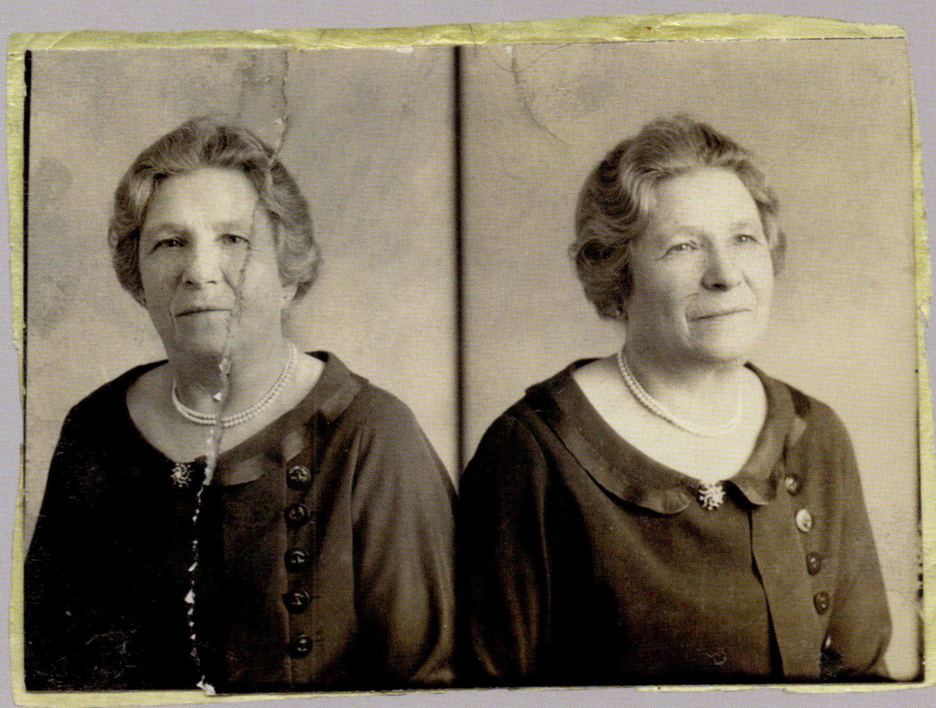

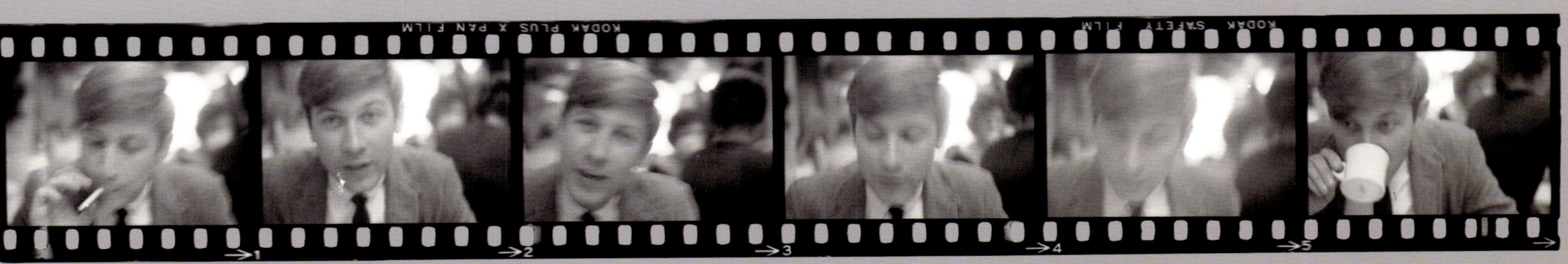

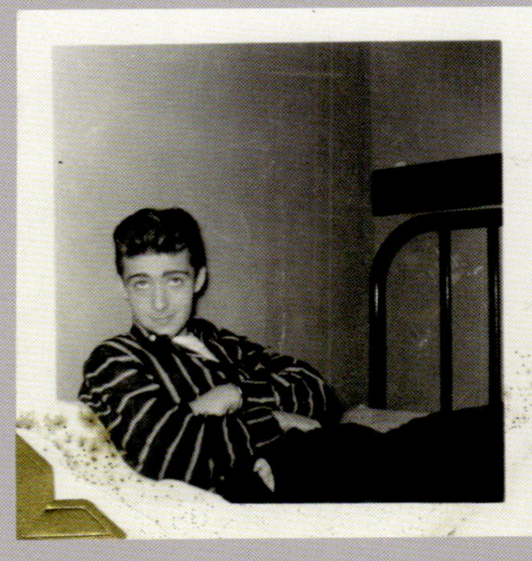

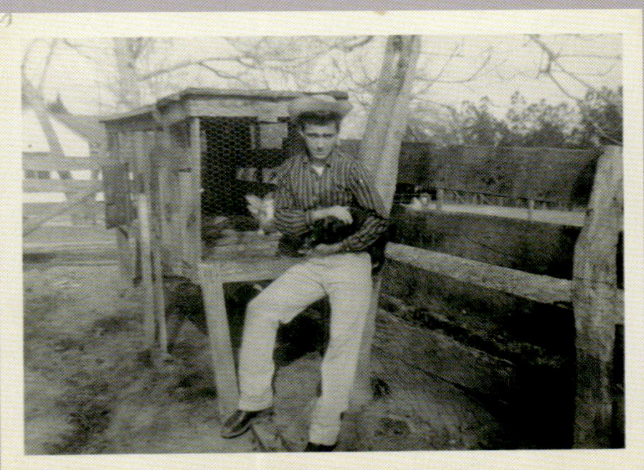

Two contact prints of Rudolf Nureyev dancing, n.d.

Double portrait photograph of a woman, possibly the artist May Wilson, 1962

Photographer unknown, Unidentified man drinking coffee and smoking, n.d.

Two photographs of an unknown man in bed and holding a rabbit, ca. 1966

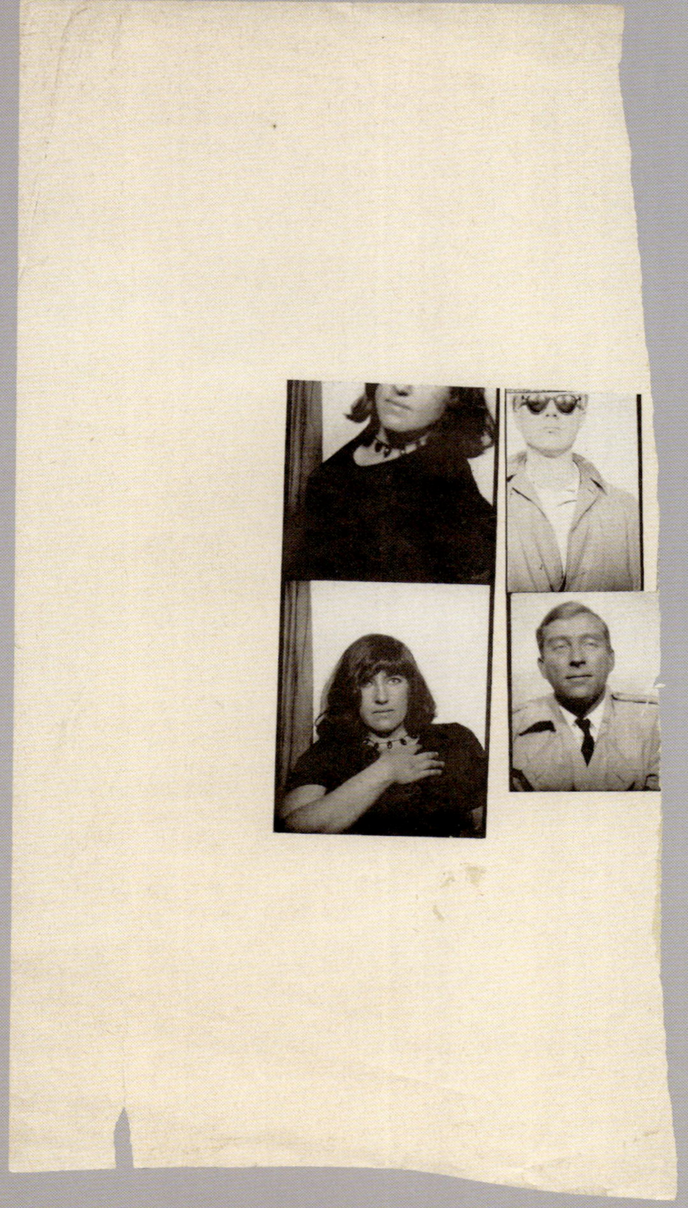

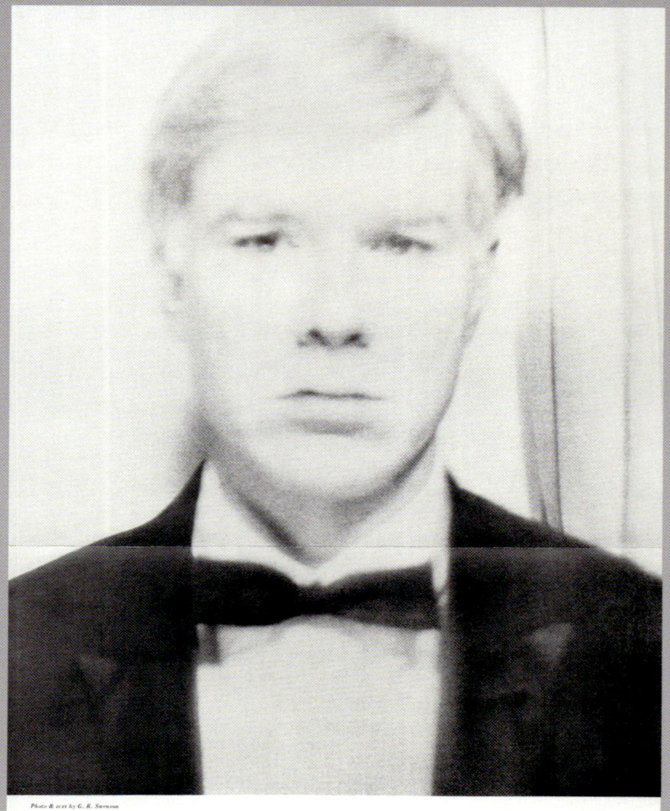

Photo & text by G. R. Swenson

THE PERSONALITY OF THE ARTIST

An understanding of the works of Angus Sinclair, the late Scottish philosopher, might be helpful in understanding the paintings and boxes of Andy Warhol, although the artist might deny it. As for Warhol's images, we ought to be wary of reading any articulated philosophy into them. If anything, these objects on canvas and store boxes speak the "language in which inanimate things speak" (the language Hofmannsthal's Lord Chandos wanted to learn). "I want to be a machine," the painter has said, misleading many; his work does suppress those symptoms of modern art — personality and creativity — which have been sanctified to the point of blasphemy.

Art criticism has been as resistant to allowing the object to make feelings as most psychiatrists have been to allowing, for example, the head of government as a source for personal neurosis (except psychoanalytically through identification, a childhood fear of sexual authority, etc.). The paintings and boxes of Warhol *are* feelings, as much as paint in Abstract-Expressionist painting is paint; the artist's works have almost nothing to do with his white streaked hair or his pale skin.

Sinclair, in the "Sensations, Perceptions, Feelings, Emotions and Things" chapter of *Conditions of Knowing*, states that "experiencing things and objects as things and objects is the outcome of holding certain attitudes, and to hold and apply these requires a constant effort." That suggests an attitude to which few of us have come. Sinclair, in a footnote, suggests that we could probably develop a sensitivity to radar if it became necessary. To try to understand works of art which are not the result of personality may make us aware of an analogous need.

With a touch of prescience, Warhol's specific art has provided us with a means of seeing and feeling a place (things) which we have not seen and possibly have not sensed before.

APRIL 21 – MAY 9   OPENING 5-7, APRIL 21   STABLE GALLERY   33 EAST 74TH STREET, NEW YORK

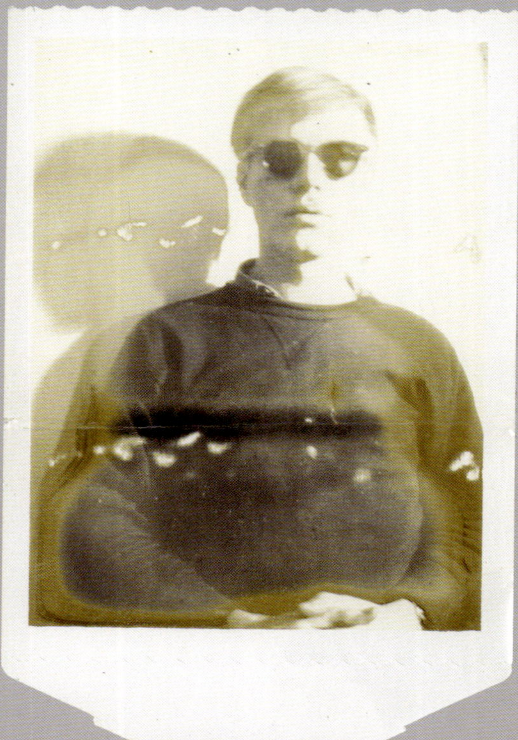

Clipping from "New Faces, New Forces, New Names in the Arts," *Harper's Bazaar*, designed by Warhol with photobooth photos, featuring Rosalyn Drexler, Warhol, and John Bedenkapp, 1963

Announcement for exhibition *Andy Warhol: The Personality of the Artist* at the Stable Gallery, New York, 1964

Photographer unknown, *Andy Warhol*, early 1960s

Group of items related to the Velvet Underground from
Time Capsule 79, 1966

Pets were a constant in Warhol's life as daily, trusted companions. Reframing the maxim of actor Will Rogers, Warhol wrote, "I never met an animal I didn't like."[1] Some he elevated to the status of subjects for his art in many media; others left their footprints—literally—on his art. Warhol always enjoyed domestic animals, from the Warhola family's lovable mutt, Lucy, in the 1940s, to his dozen or so Siamese cats named Sam (and one Hester) in the 1950s. In the 1960s, the Silver Factory's resident cats were named Black Lace and White Pussy, and his dachshunds in the 1970s were Amos and Archie.[2] The dogs and cats owned by his friends, including Brigid Berlin's (Brigid Polk's) pugs, Fame and Fortune, found their way into his photographs and social life. Although pets can sometimes be troublesome or break our hearts, most of us would agree with Warhol's statement in his book *America* (1985):

But some people have found a way to satisfy their TV dreams. They have pets, and having pets is just like having a television family. TV parents never have any real problems with their children, and owners don't have too much trouble with pets. Pets make a family that's always loyal, will do just

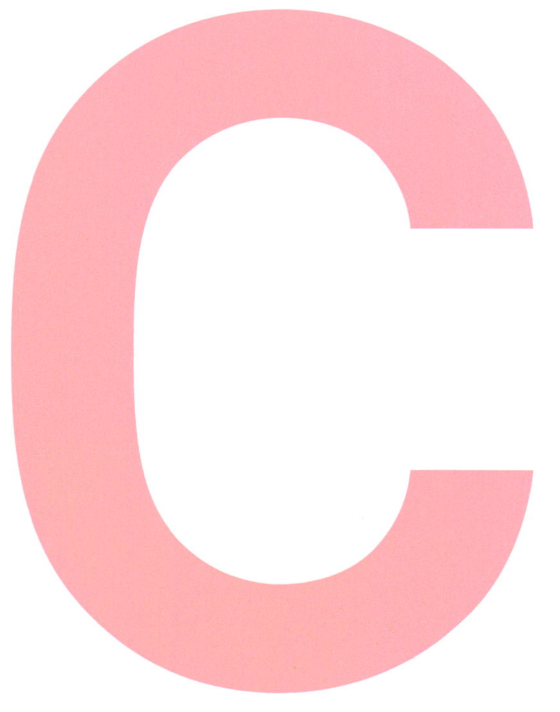

is for CANIS MAJOR

This chapter features highlights from works and materials shown in the exhibition *Canis Major: Andy Warhol's Dogs and Cats (And Other Party Animals)*, January 12–May 4, 2008.

about anything to make you happy, never criticize, love you till the end of the earth, and never expect much in return.

You can get a cat that calls to you every morning when you go out the door, just like a TV mother; a dog that always has that sad, cute face when you scold it, just like TV children; a pet that comes running to the door all excited just because you're coming home, like a TV wife; and one that sulks in the corner when it doesn't get its way, just like a TV husband or father.

Most of the time one pet can even do all these things. So even if you're sort of poor, but you have all these television hopes and dreams, pets are really the answer.[3]

Dogs

In the early 1970s, Jed Johnson, Warhol's boyfriend at the time, convinced him to get a dog. They decided on a small black-and-tan short-haired dachshund whom they named Archie, and a few years later they purchased a second dachshund, Amos. Warhol and Johnson were very fond of their two dogs. Warhol treated Archie as his alter ego, bringing him to parties and posing with him in photographs. In 1975 Archie received a gift from another dog, Finnegan Richardson.[4] Finnegan was owned by Brenda Richardson, a curator at the Baltimore Museum of Art, where Warhol had an exhibition at the time. The card is inscribed, "Try not to fret—Andy will be home soon! In the meantime, here's a treat to help your loneliness—from your friend in Baltimore—Finnegan Richardson." The Archive contains a large quantity of ephemera relating to Amos and Archie, including dog sweaters, vaccination records, licenses, veterinary bills, and photographs.

A much larger dog stood guard at the Factory from about 1970 to 1987. Warhol was an avid collector of almost everything, including taxidermy: a lion, a peacock, a penguin, and a moose head. The best known of these was a harlequin Great Dane—the big dog, known as Cecil, the name given to it by Warhol and his associates. Recent scholarship by canine photographer and genealogist Kerrin Winter-Churchill has solved many of the mysteries surrounding this magnificent creature, including his true identity (Ador Tipp Topp), his pedigree as a Westminster

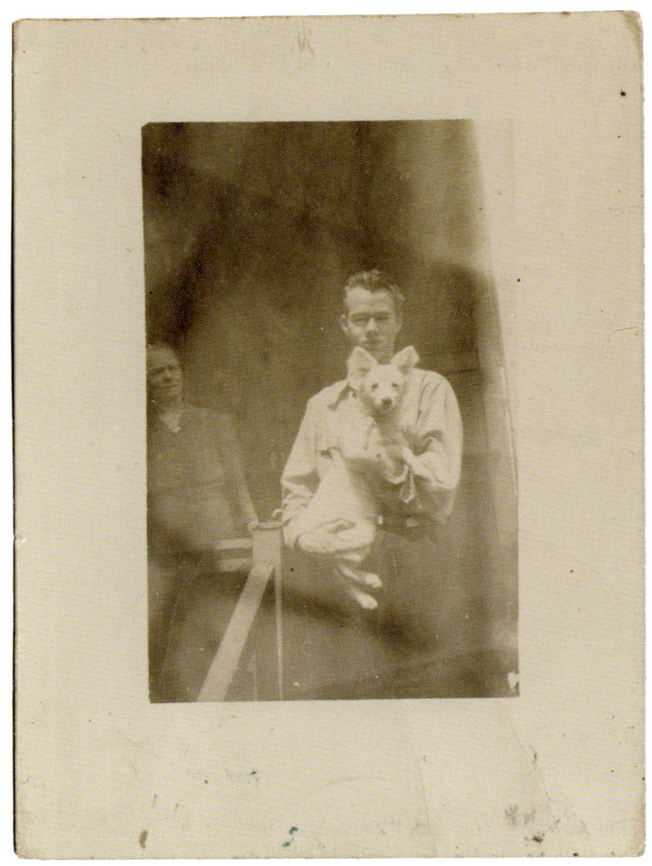

champion, and the strange tale of how he arrived at Warhol's door by way of Yale University.

The animal was a champion show dog born in Germany in 1921 and purchased with his half sister, Addy, in 1922 by Charles Ludwig, a founding member of the parent club for the breed in the United States. He first showed Ador and Addy at the Bronx Kennel Club in October 1922, where they both won blue ribbons. Soon after, Ador was sold to Gerdus H. Wynkoop of Long Island, who entered him in ten more shows, in which he gained enough merit points to earn the title of champion by 1924, when he won Best of Breed at the Westminster Kennel Club show, the most illustrious dog competition in America.

After Ador's death in 1930, his remains were sent to the Yale Peabody Museum of Natural History at Yale University, New Haven, Connecticut, where they were mounted and

Warhol with the family's dog, Lucy, and Julia Warhola at Dawson Street, ca. 1946

displayed with eleven other breeds in what was known colloquially at the time as the "Dog Hall of Fame."[5] However, by 1945 the canine display was removed to storage and forgotten. In 1964 Scott Elliot, a Yale drama student, was sent to the Peabody to borrow some birds for a play titled *The Grebe*. He found the birds and also bought all twelve dog mounts for $10 each, intending to use them as models in an art school he wished to open. When Elliot had to move a few months later, many of the mounts were left with a friend, who put them in rented storage, which went unpaid. Several years later, Elliot owned an antiques store in Manhattan's East Village and heard about a harlequin Great Dane in another shop on 3rd Avenue. On Elliot's arrival, Ador's new owner told Elliot that the dog had belonged to film director Cecil B. DeMille, so he was asking $300—too steep for it to return to Elliot's care. However, the price was less of an issue for Warhol, who soon after bought the story and the Great Dane.

Ador's current appearance differs from his championship form. His coat was actually black and white; exposure to sunlight has faded it to brown. Also, at some point his ears had broken off and were repaired, but their new vertical form is truer to late twentieth-century ideals for the breed than the original rounded shape.

Cats

The first of Warhol's books to be properly bound, *25 Cats Name Sam and One Blue Pussy* (1956), has a text consisting of just four words—"Sam" and "one blue pussy," all attributed to the designer Charles Lisanby. One of the words is repeated on fifteen of its sixteen pages: "Sam." At the time, Warhol and his mother, Julia, lived with many Siamese cats, which he hoped to develop into a breeding business on the side. The felines proved difficult to sell or even give away, though, as they were said to be inbred. This is the first of Warhol's artists' books to include his mother's fanciful handwriting, which was a much-desired aspect of his advertising work.

Many of Warhol's drawings for his books were inspired by other printed materials. Two sources for the *25 Cats* drawings were Walter Chandoha's book *All Kinds of Cats*

(1952) and an earlier book titled *Sam* (1937), by Edward Quigley and John Crawford. Although those titles were not found in Warhol's Archive, another, *The Personality of the Cat* (1958), bears the dedication, "From 9 cats and one blue curator all named Sam," in the unmistakable handwriting of Warhol's friend Sam Wagstaff, former curator at the Wadsworth Atheneum and the Detroit Institute of Arts.

The last of Warhol's realized artists' books from that time pays tribute to his mother, who was also honored by professional societies for graphic arts. *Holy Cats by Andy Warhol's Mother* (1960) presents Julia Warhola's strangely hilarious drawings of cats matched with folksy captions in her unique handwriting. Its pages are a cheerfully random spectrum of colors. The text is uncredited, but its voice suggests Julia's words. A brief manuscript (possibly written by Dick Heard) held in one of Warhol's *Time Capsules* is titled "Holy Cats Pussy Heaven," but its style differs greatly from that of the book. *Holy Cats* has only recently been correctly dated; an invoice from Warhol's printer, Seymour Berlin of Record Offset Printing, gives December 1960.

NOTES

1. Will Rogers was known for, among other things, his statement "I never met a man I didn't like." Rogers was a Native American of the Cherokee Nation, who with his rope tricks and original humor became a star of vaudeville, and then was a journalist, the host of a weekly radio show, and finally a movie star. Warhol likely would've heard his radio program in the 1930s and seen his movies.

2. Warhol's studio space was called the "Silver Factory" from 1964 to 1968. Black Lace and White Pussy were the cats' names as told to the author by Billy Linich (Billy Name) around 1997. The name White Pussy also appears on posters announcing Warhol's film *Harlot* (1965). More recently, Name recalled their names as Ruby and Lacy; see Billy Name, interview by Eric Shiner, in *13 Most Wanted Men: Andy Warhol and the 1964 World's Fair*, ed. Larissa Harris and Media Farzin (Queens, NY: Queens Museum of Art/The Andy Warhol Museum, 2014), 82.

3. Andy Warhol, *America* (New York: Harper & Row, 1985), 192.

4. The gift was a dog treat, based on the correspondence.

5. The collection at the Yale Peabody Museum was formally known as the Leon F. Whitney Dog Collection and was part of the Division of Vertebrate Zoology.

Additional research for this chapter was provided by Erin Byrne, Matt Gray, and Brianna Treleven. Photographic layouts designed by Becky Shock, Brianna Treleven, and Kristin Britanik.

Andy Warhol, *"Do You See My Little Pussy,"* 1958

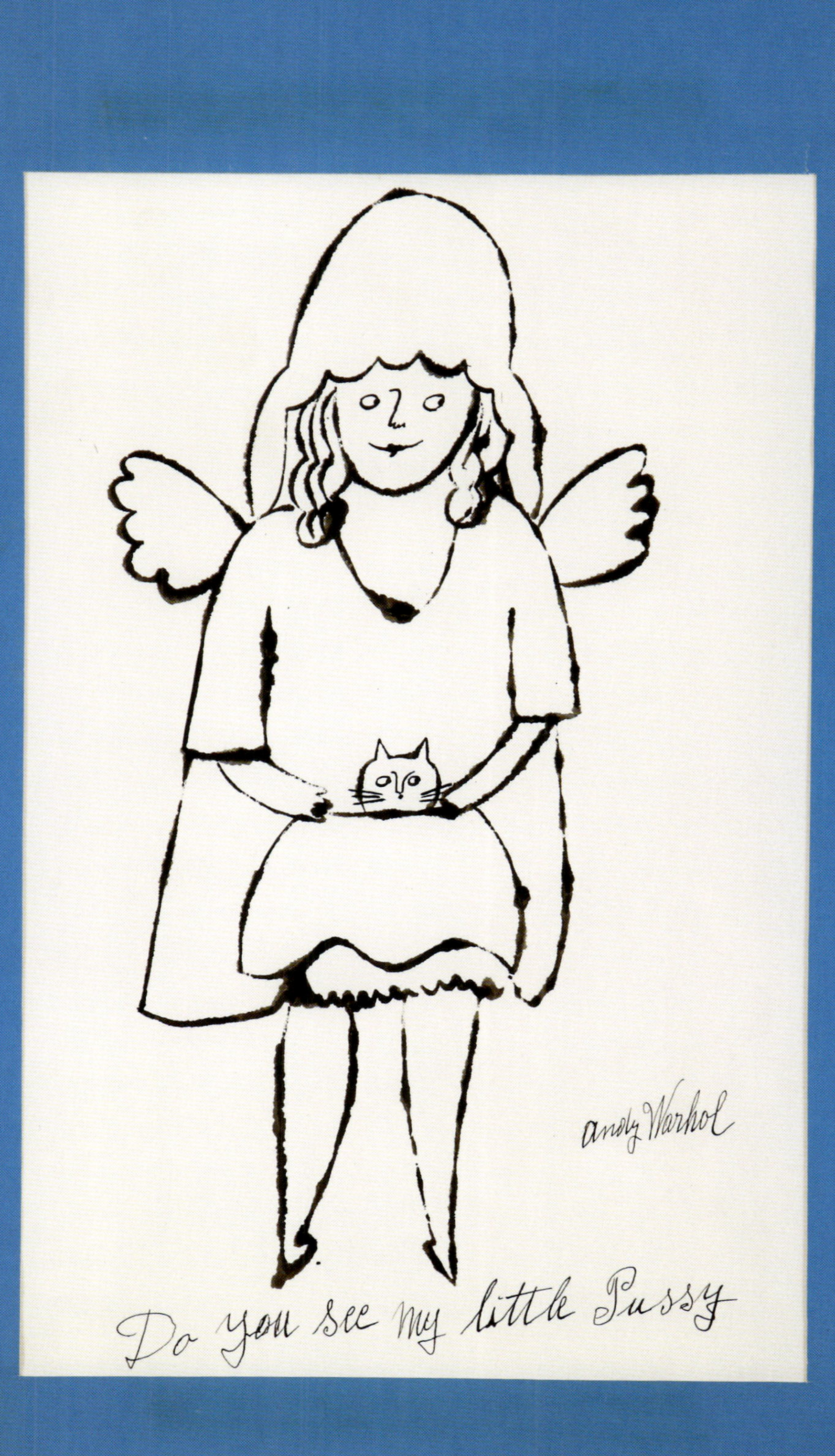

andy Warhol
Do you see my little Pussy

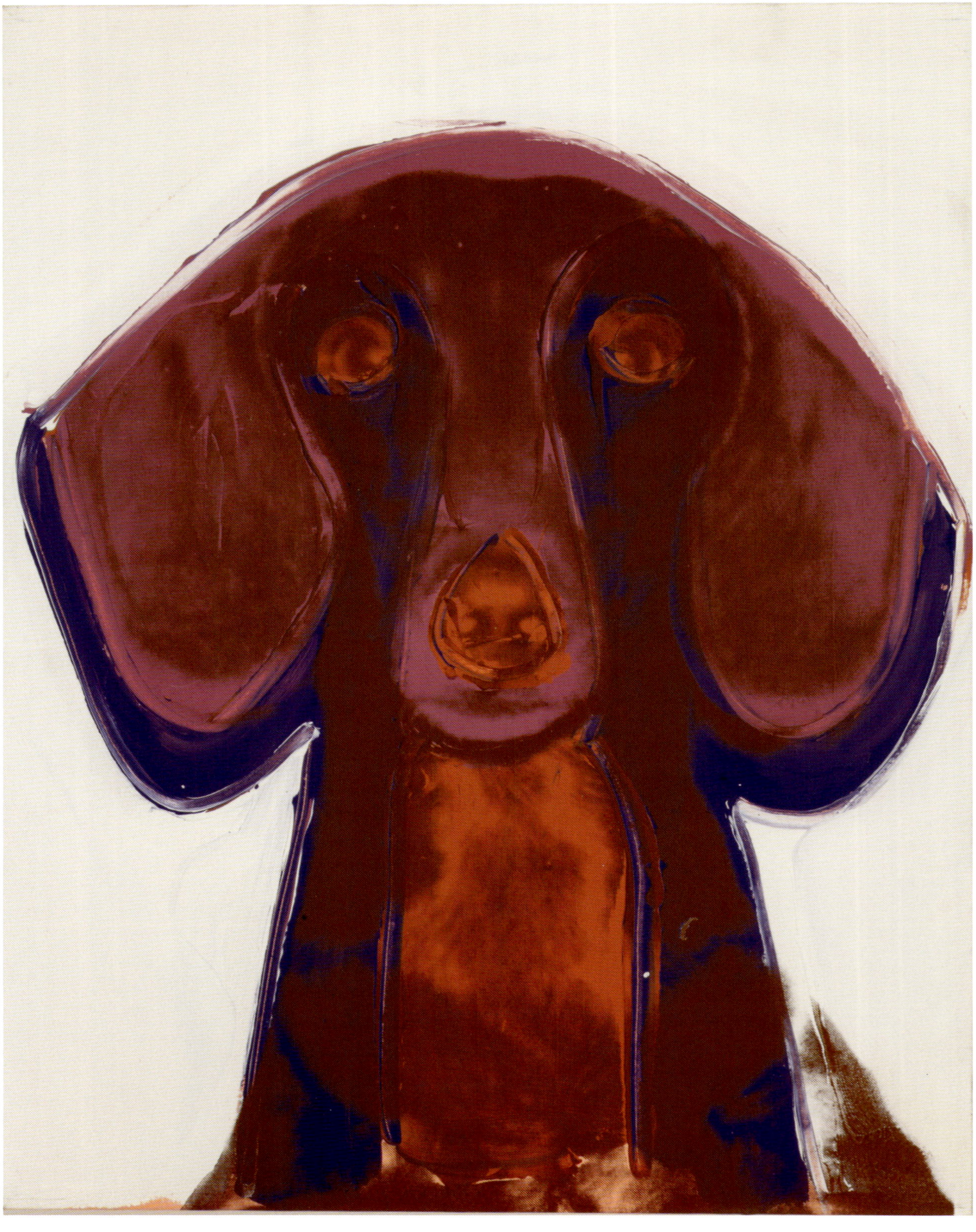

Andy Warhol, *Cats and Dogs (Maurice)*, 1976

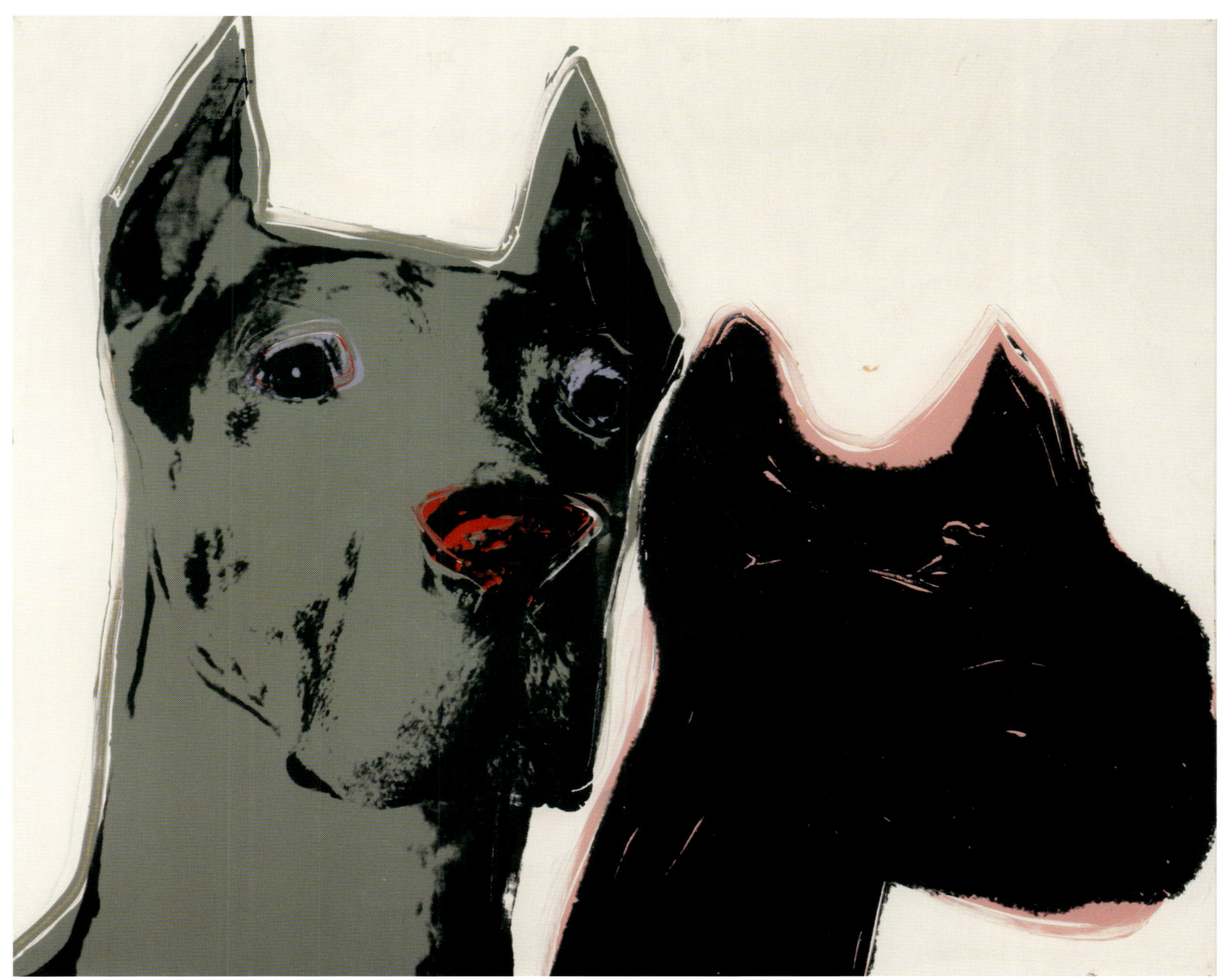

Andy Warhol, *Cats and Dogs (Cecil)*, 1976

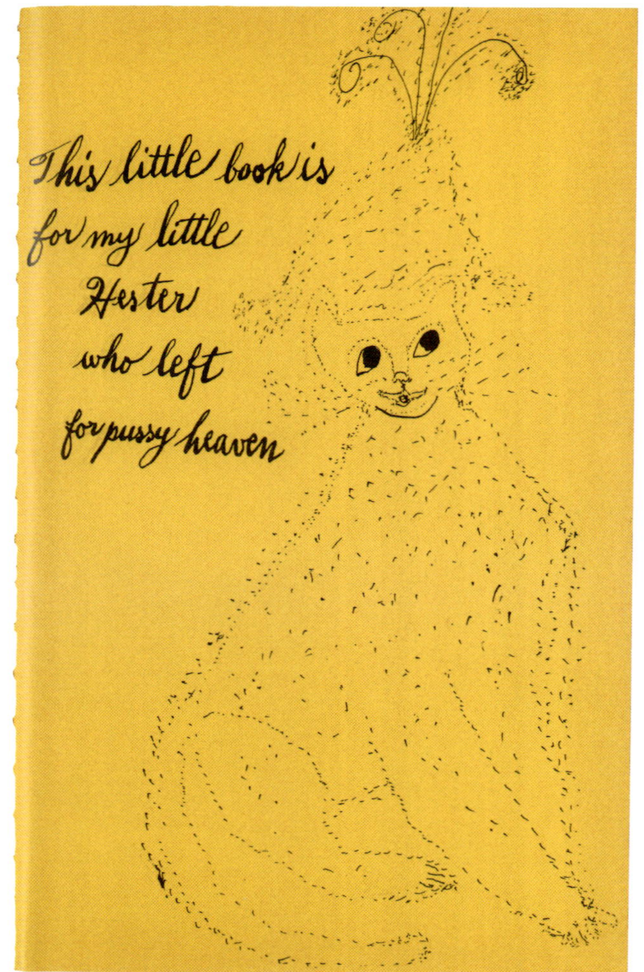

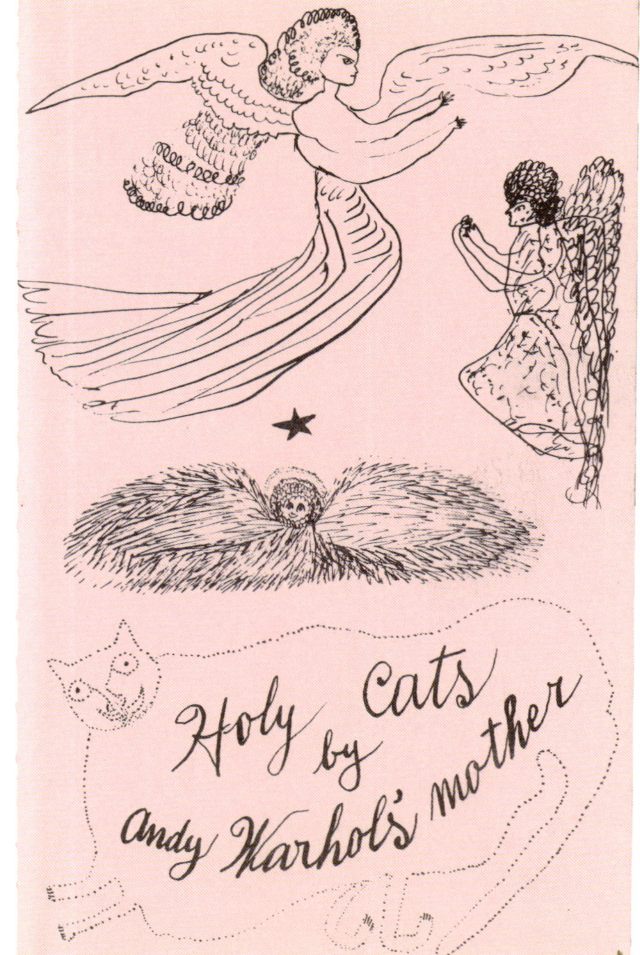

Julia Warhola, *Holy Cats by Andy Warhol's Mother*, 1960

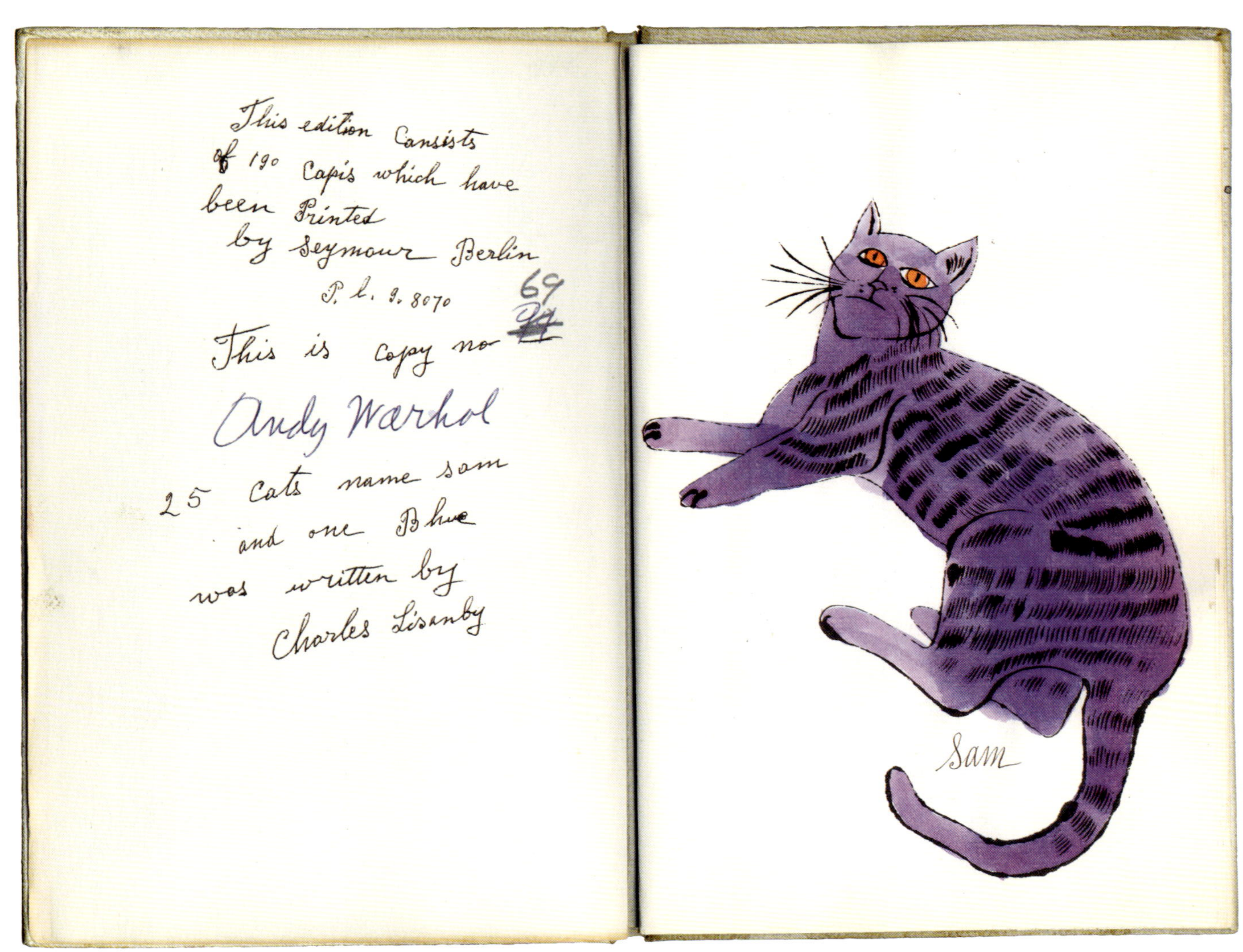

Andy Warhol, *25 Cats Name Sam and One Blue Pussy*, 1956

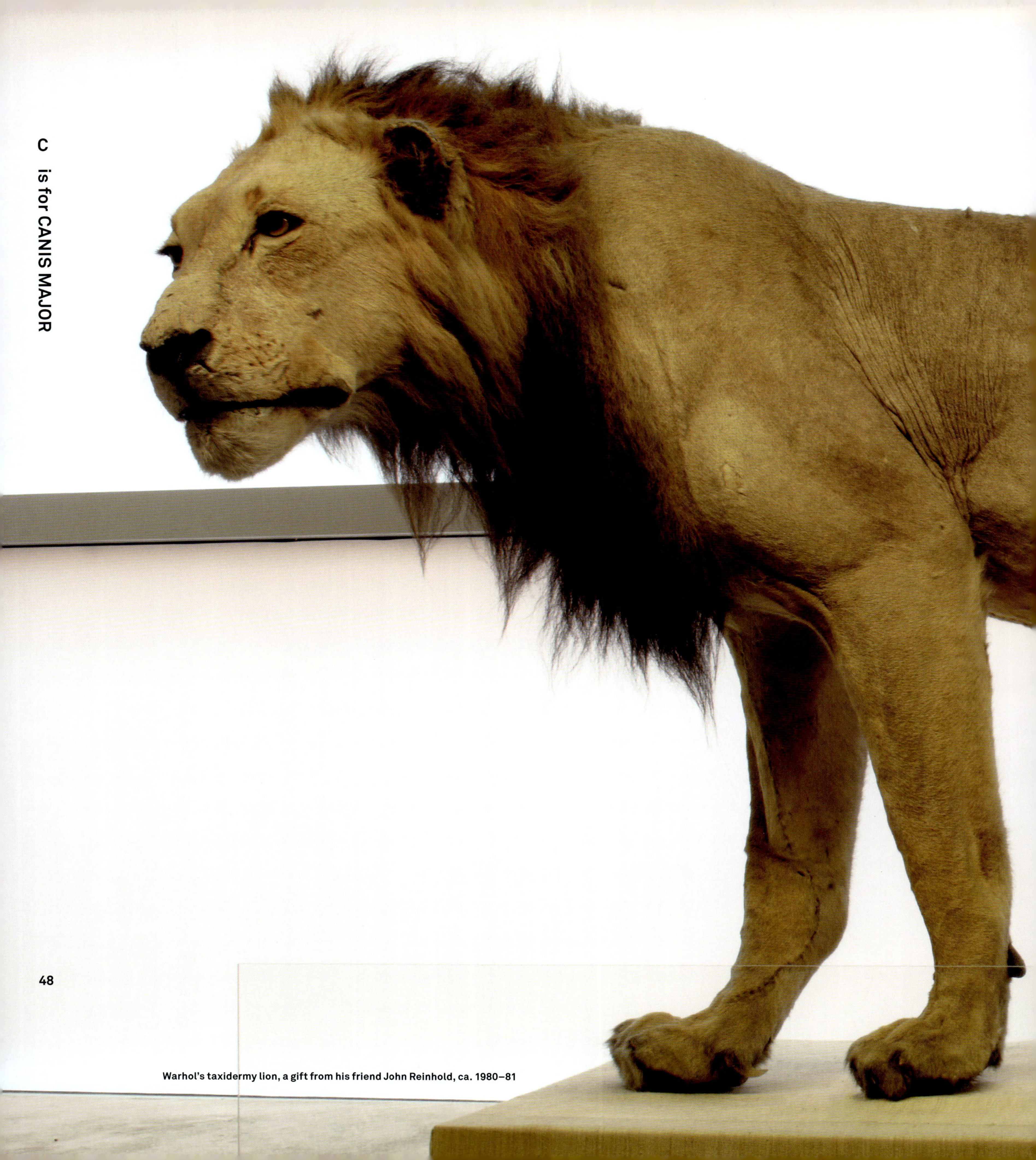

Warhol's taxidermy lion, a gift from his friend John Reinhold, ca. 1980–81

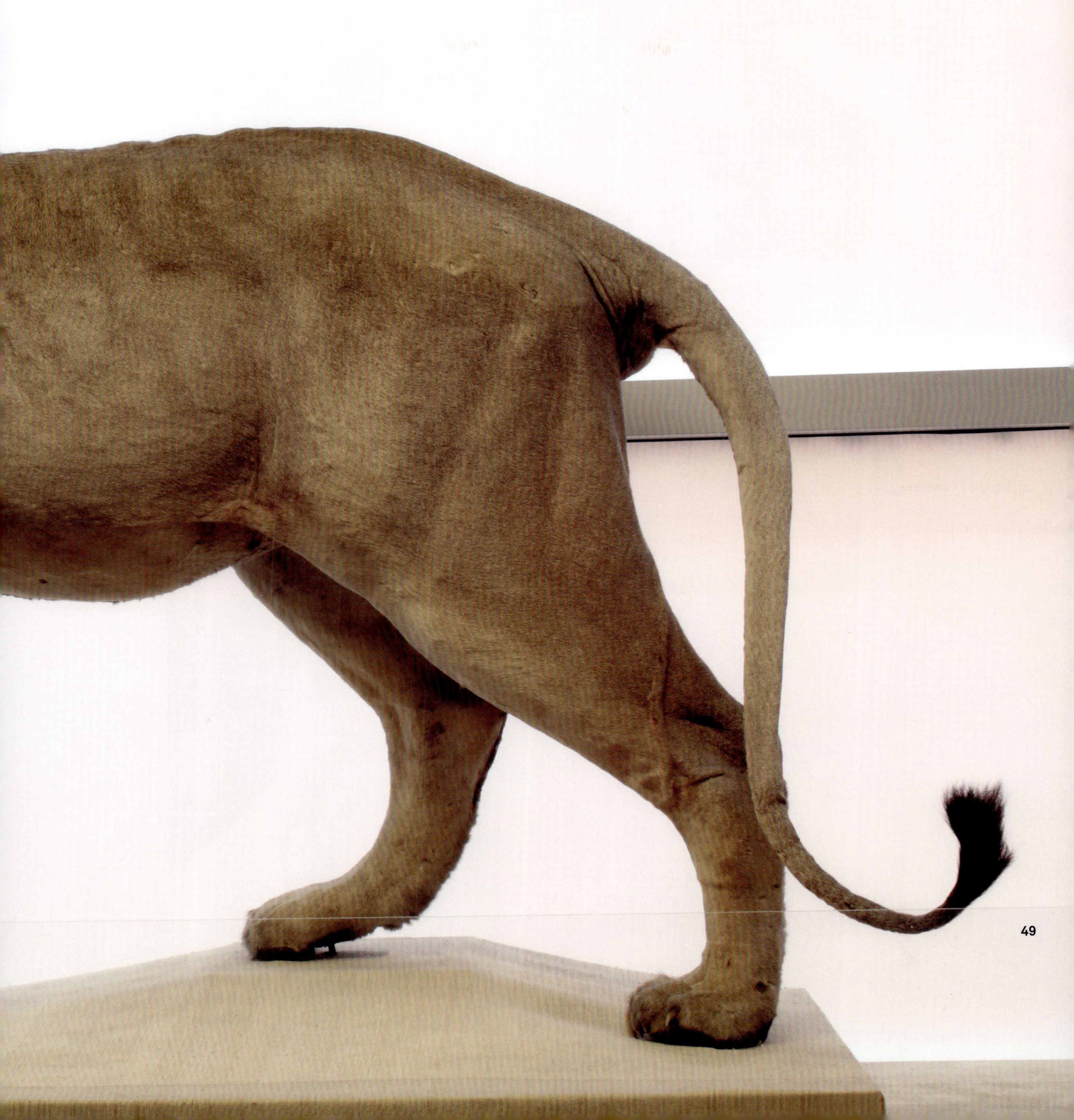

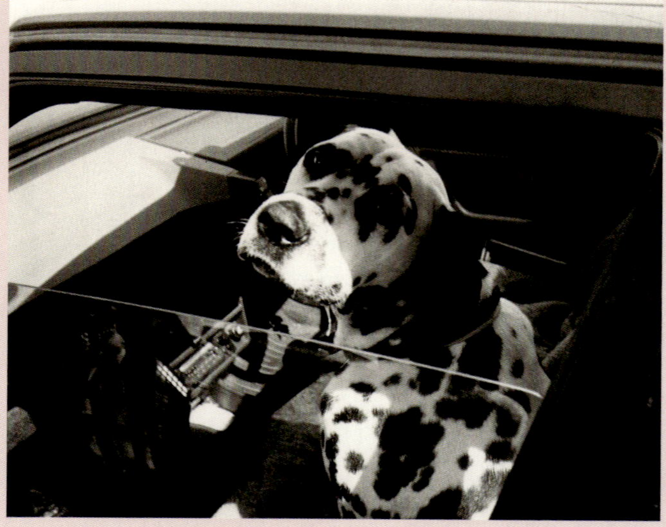

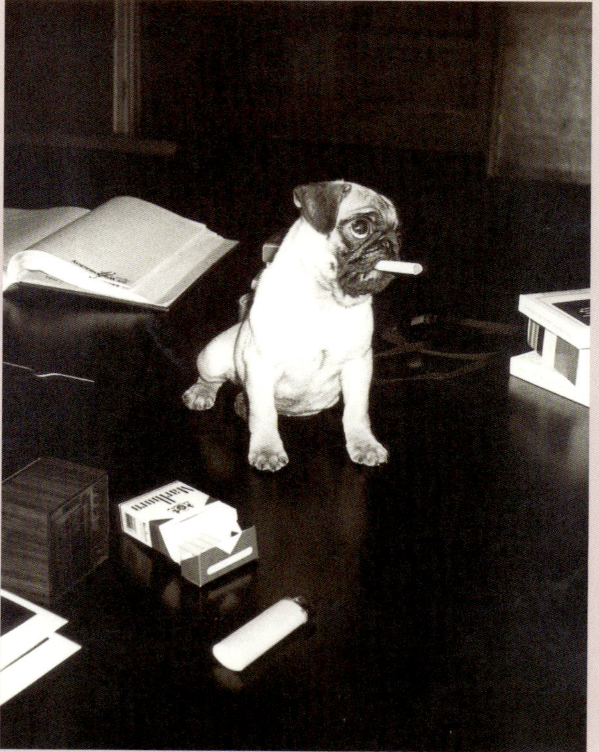

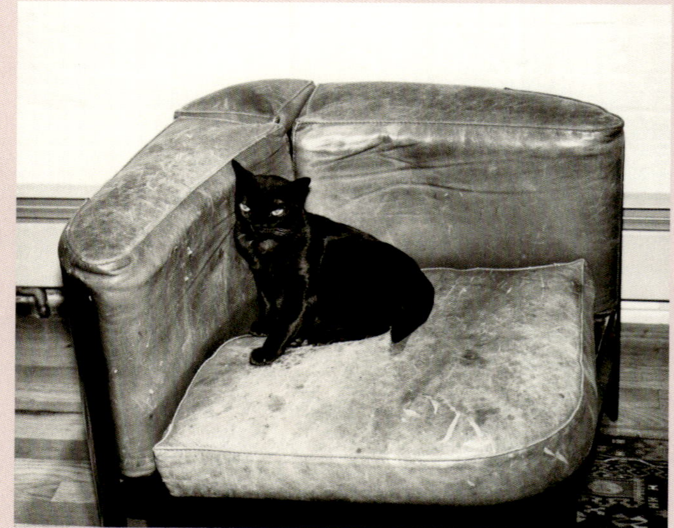

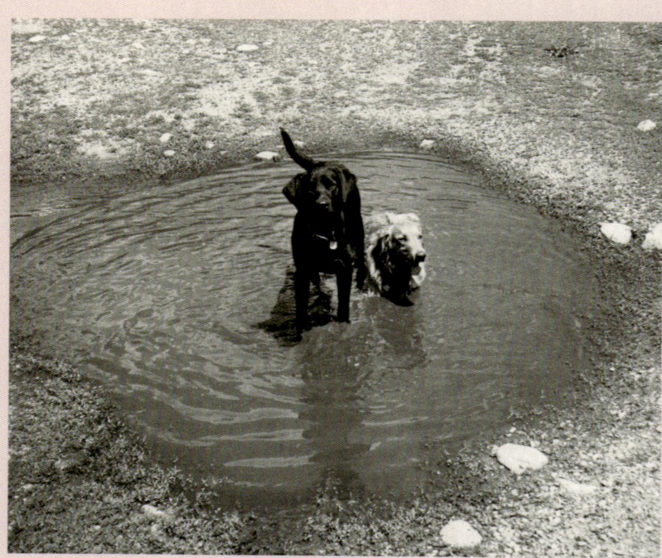

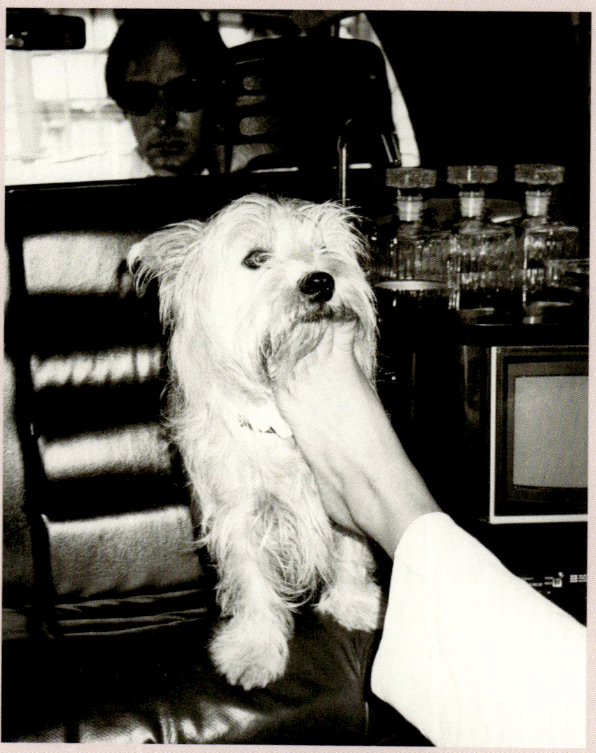

(clockwise from top left) Andy Warhol, *Dalmatian*, ca. 1976–86; *Pug*, ca. 1984; *West Highland White Terrier ("Westie")*, ca. 1976–86; *Black Labrador and Golden Retriever*, ca. 1976–86; *Cat*, ca. 1976–86

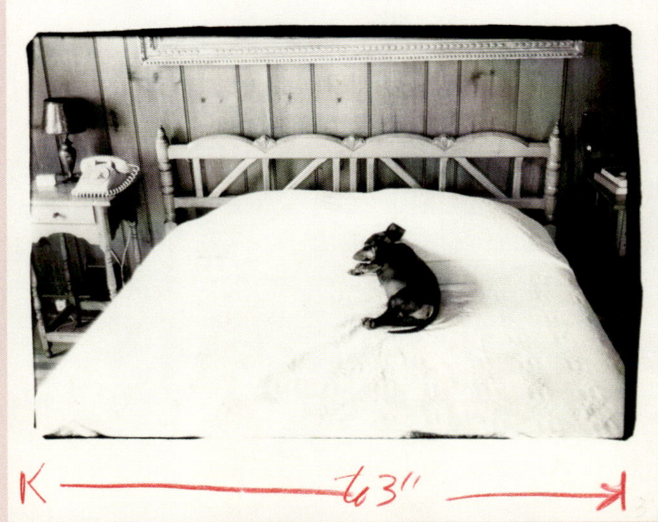
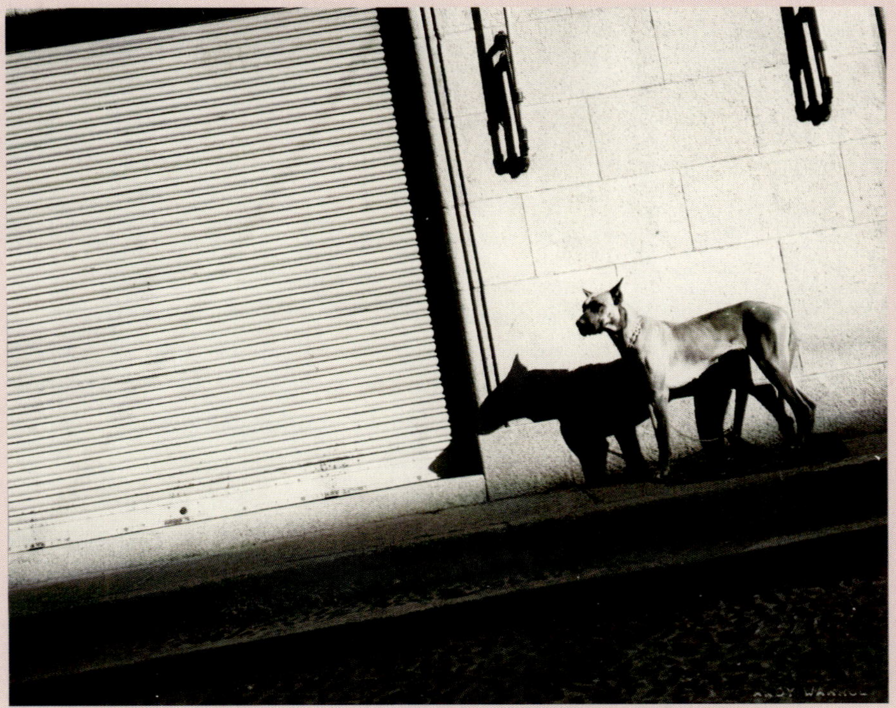
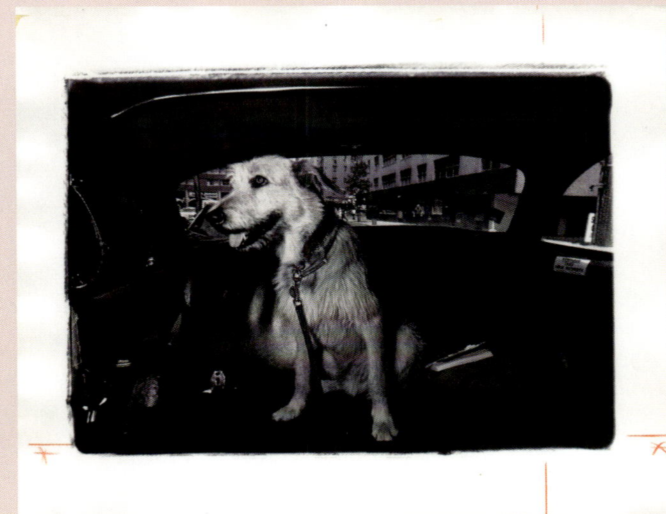
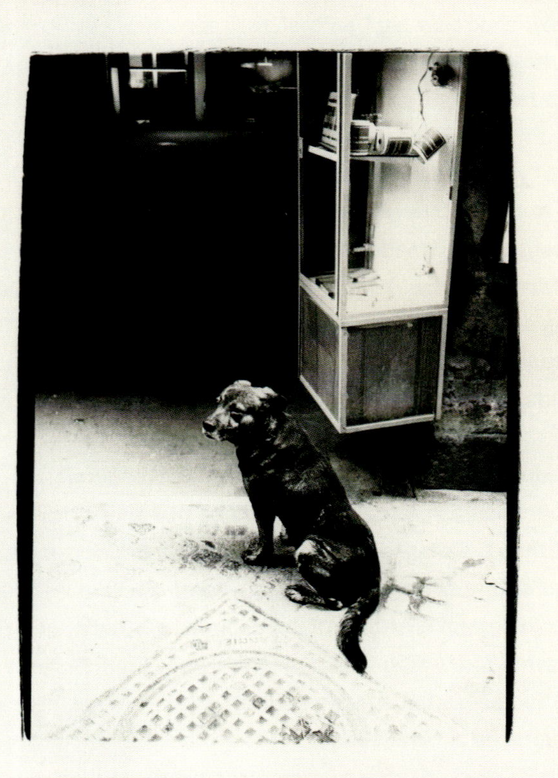
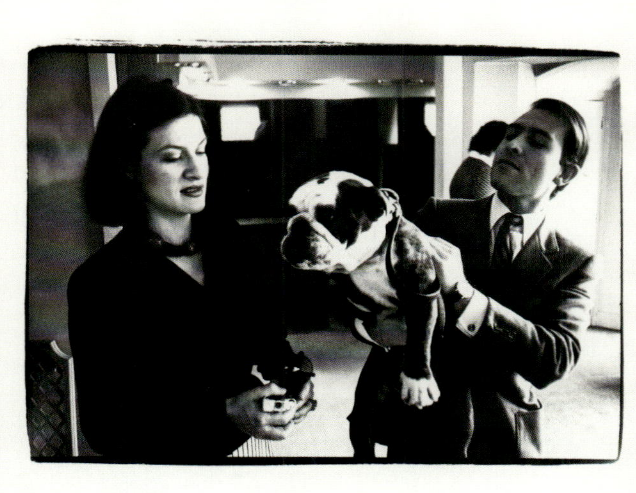

(clockwise from top left) Andy Warhol, *Dog*, ca. 1976–86; *Great Dane*, 1983; *Great American Mutt*, ca. 1976–86; *Paloma Picasso and Raphael Lopez Sanchez*, 1980; John Bean Studios, New York, *Sandy (Dog from the Broadway Musical "Annie")*, 1977

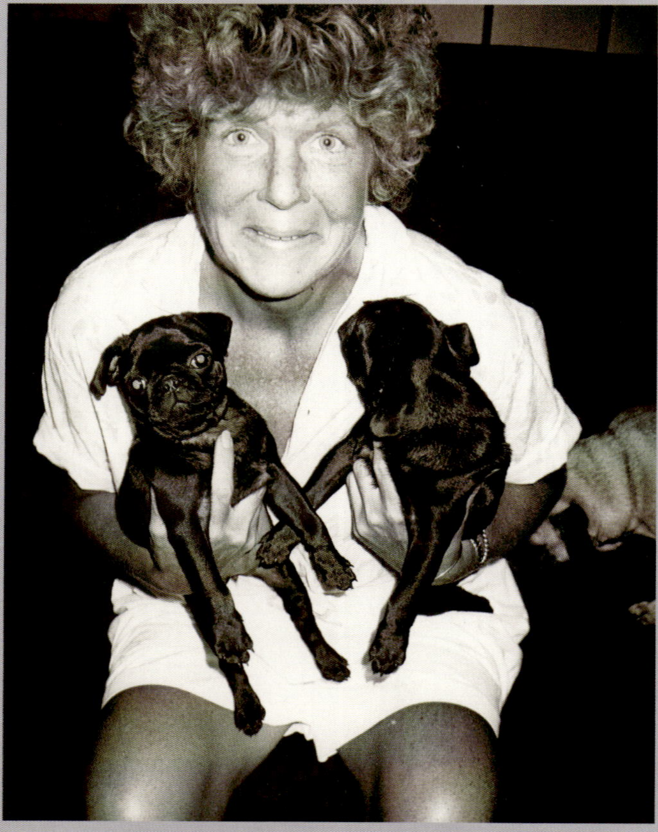

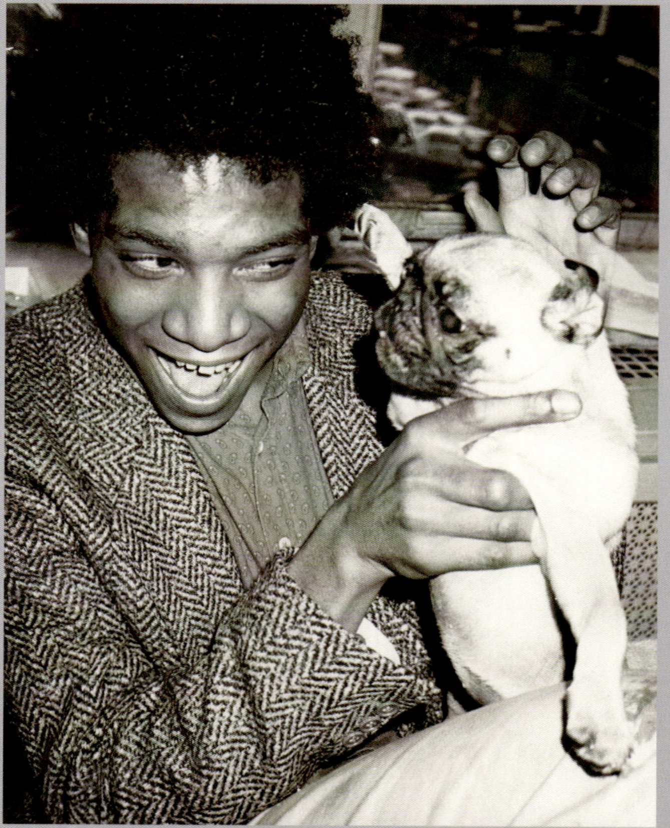

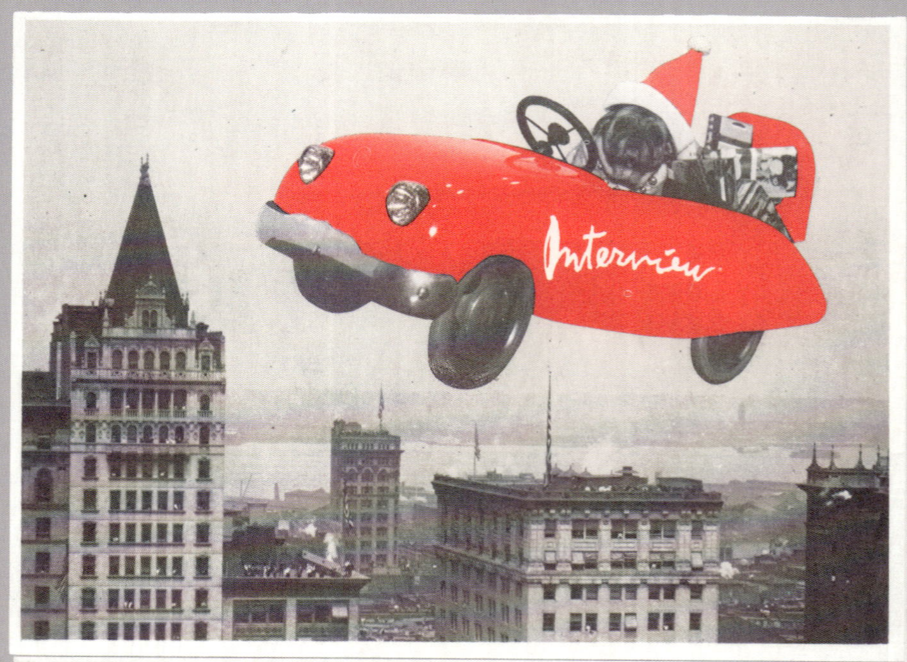

52

Andy Warhol, *Brigid Berlin*, ca. 1981; *Jean-Michel Basquiat and Dog*, 1984   *Interview* magazine "Santa Paws" Christmas card, n.d.

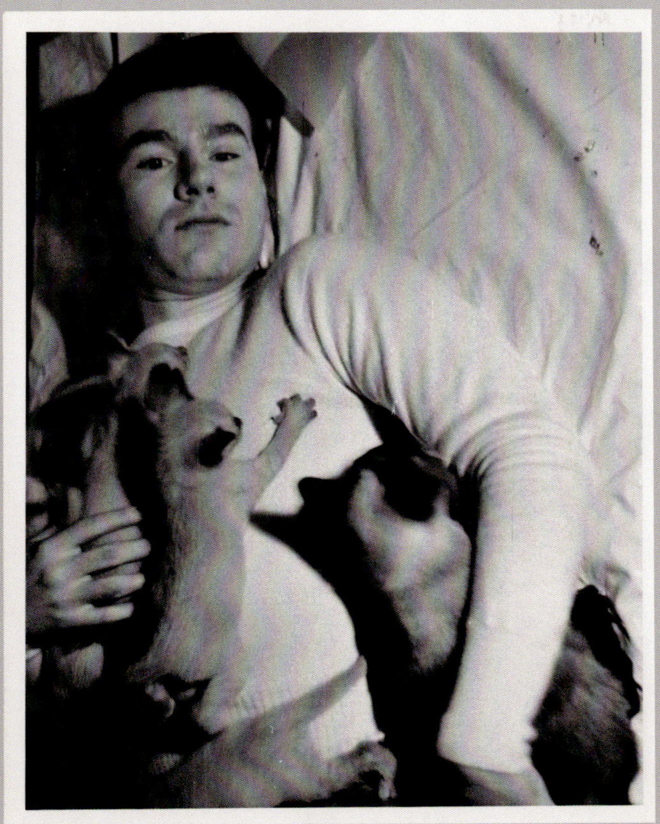

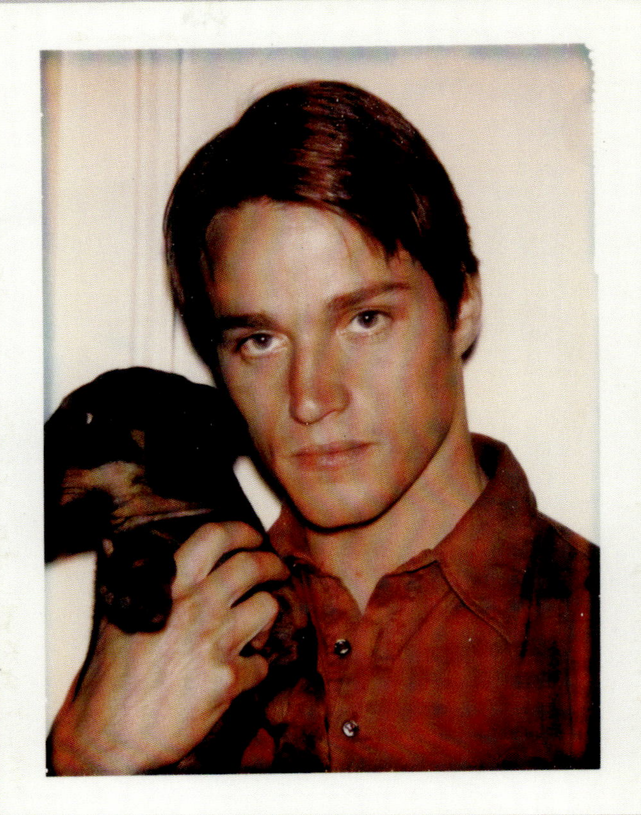

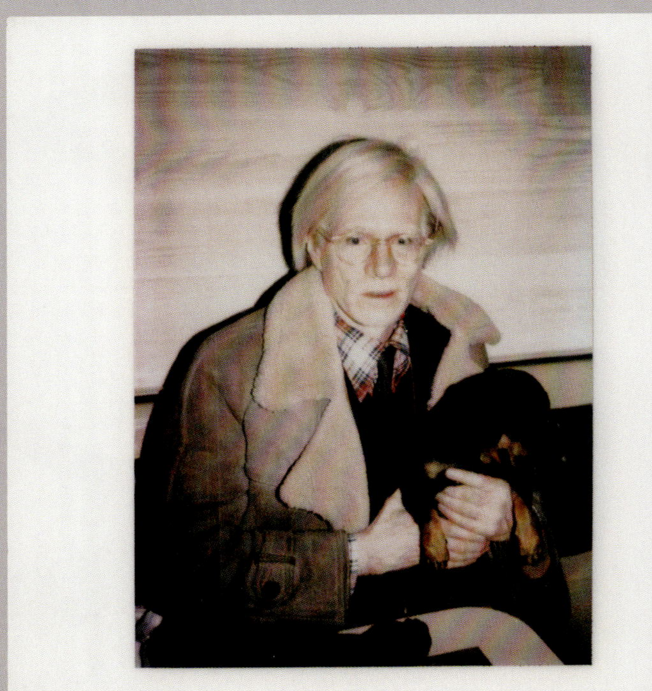

Edward Wallowitch, *Andy Warhol in Bed with Cats*, ca. 1957

Photographer unknown, *Andy Warhol Holding Archie*, ca. 1977

Andy Warhol, *Jed Johnson*, 1973

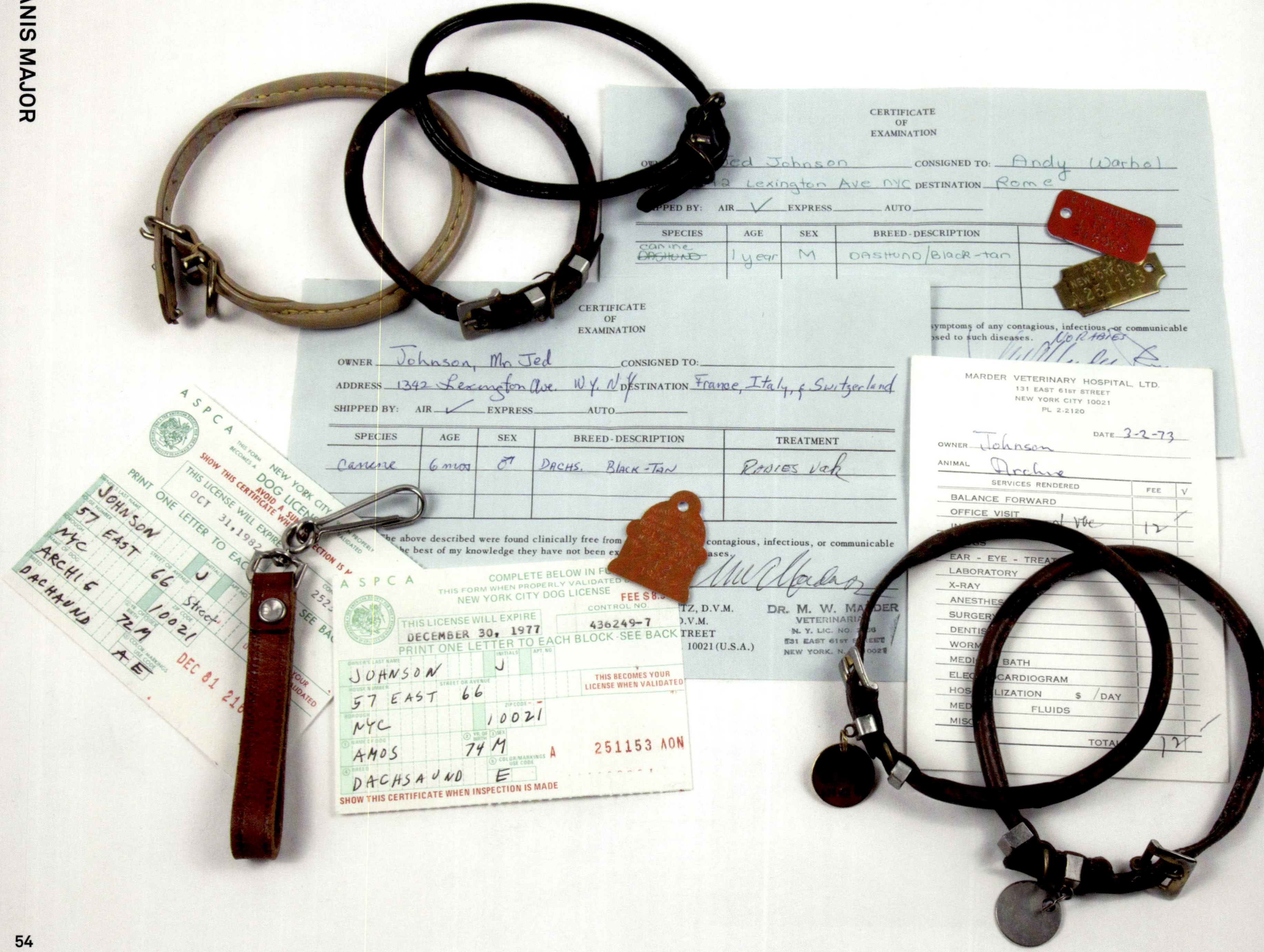

Dog collars, tags, and papers for Amos and Archie, dachshunds owned by
Jed Johnson and Warhol

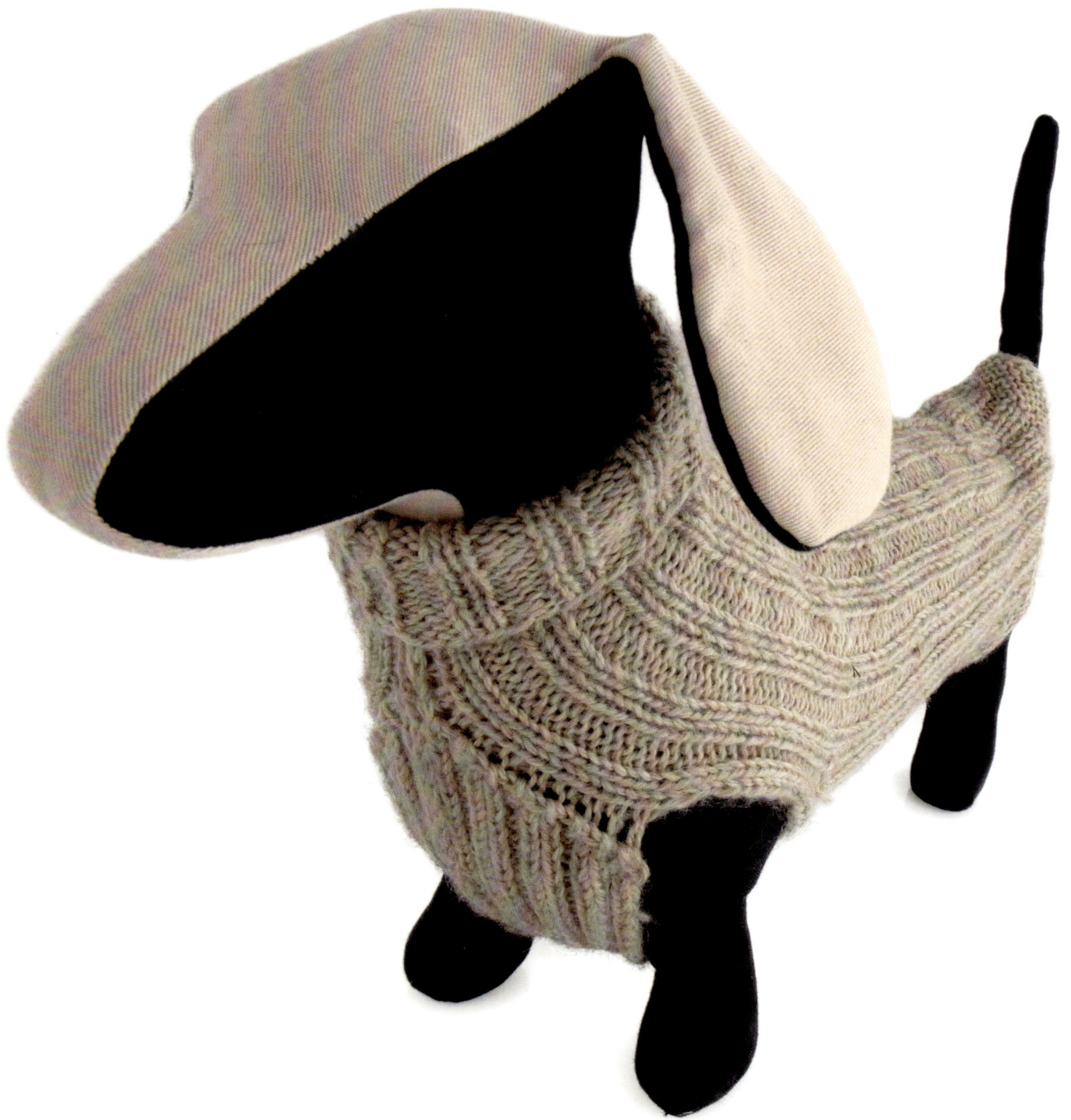

Beige dog sweater possibly worn by Amos or Archie

In 1947 Marcel Duchamp created one of his many now-legendary art environments at the *Exposition Internationale du Surréalisme* in Paris. In one gallery, known as *Rain Room*, water rained down onto a billiard table, a marble sculpture, and the floor from a long pipe attached to the ceiling. Twenty-three years later, at the Osaka World's Fair of 1970, Andy Warhol exhibited *Rain Machine (Daisy Waterfall)* (1970)—a sculptural environment consisting in part of water showering from dozens of brass nozzles into long troughs, from which it was continuously pumped back up to the pipe overhead (see "I is for Illusions").

In 1921 Duchamp and his close friend and fellow artist Man Ray collaborated on the film *The Baroness Shaves Her Pubic Hair*, in which the outrageously original Baroness Elsa von Freytag-Loringhoven does just that (nearly all of the film, however, was destroyed during processing). Forty-six years later, in 1967, Warhol shot a half-hour reel, "Gerard" (also known as "Gerard Has His Hair Removed with Nair"), for his epic twenty-five-hour film ***** (Four Stars)*, in which his assistant's woolly body is smoothed by four women, using a commercial depilatory.

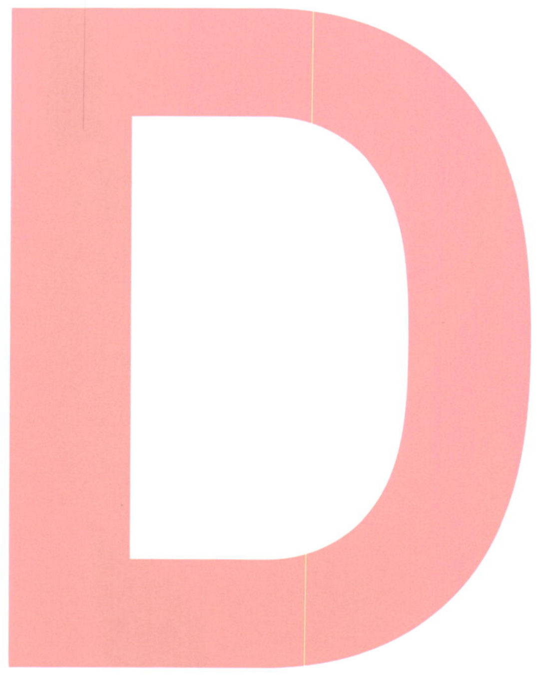

D
is for DUCHAMP

The paired works in this chapter comprise an edited selection from the expansive museum exhibition *Twisted Pair: Marcel Duchamp / Andy Warhol*, May 23–September 12, 2010.

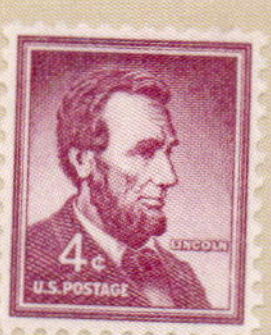

These are just a few strikingly similar works by the two artists, and there are many more. The paired works in this chapter echo each other across decades in a variety of media, including film, painting, sculpture, installation, published works, and ephemera and written statements. The artists even posed for similar photographs. Both artists' early works were notorious and iconoclastic in their own time but are now recognized as important touchstones of modern art history. These include Duchamp's Dada *Fountain* (1917) and Warhol's Pop Art *Campbell's Soup Cans* (1962). Among their shared interests and themes are optical-effect experiments, language and puns, pseudonyms, sexuality and identity, fame, and death. To generate new art, both Duchamp and Warhol mined their personal archives and recycled their previous works. In other, equally interesting ways, the artists are in complete opposition.

Duchamp may have had more influence on Warhol than any other artist. Although the creative kinship between the two was noted as early as 1962, recent Duchamp scholarship and access to Warhol's personal papers, many held in The Andy Warhol Museum Archive, have underscored Warhol's enduring interest in and indebtedness to Duchamp. As an art collector, Warhol owned *Fountain*, *Prière de toucher* (1947), *Female Fig Leaf* (1950), and about thirty other Duchamp works and related objects—a significant number, considering Duchamp's limited output.

In electricity, the simple twisted pair of copper wires is perhaps the most fundamental construct; one positive and one negative insulated wire that, through technological convenience, make modern life possible. In contemporary art, the work of Marcel Duchamp and Andy Warhol has played a comparable role. The phrase "twisted pair" also acknowledges that the general public still regards both figures as bizarre, and, considered together, they do make quite a pair.

RSVP card from Marcel Duchamp to Warhol, April 14, 1965

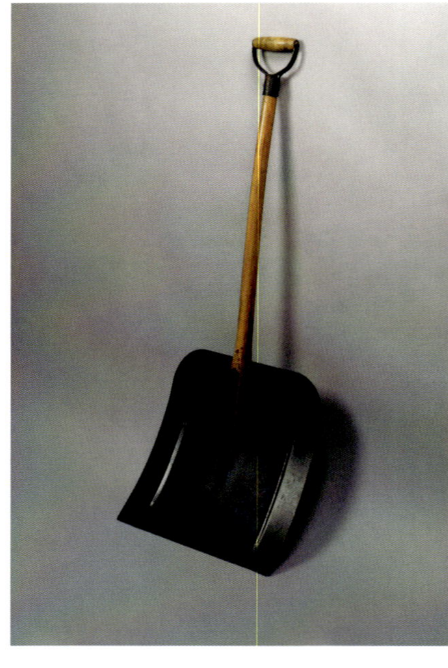

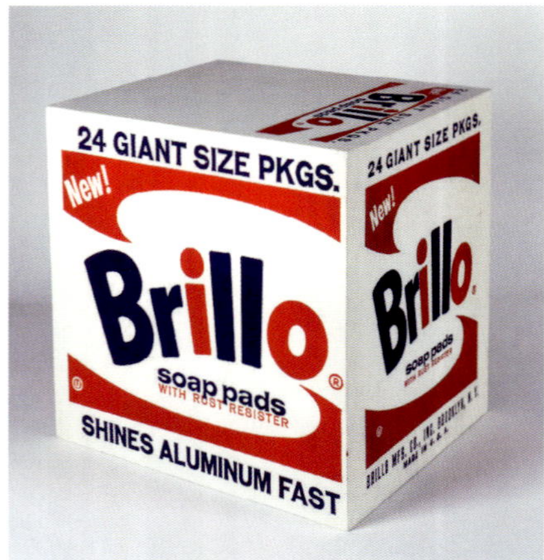

The Readymade / The Everyday

At first, the works of both Duchamp and Warhol were considered shocking, largely because they used materials and depicted subjects that were "outside" the realm of art. However, the two artists were eventually revered for their avant-garde approach.

As a student in the 1940s, Warhol encountered the work of Duchamp, for whom ideas were the crux of art. Many of Duchamp's statements, works, and ideas have direct parallels with Warhol's oeuvre and life. Duchamp aspired to put painting "at the service of the mind" and invented the readymade—declaring that a small number of manufactured objects (a snow shovel, a urinal, and so on), chosen because of his *indifference* to them, were works of art. Although Duchamp preferred not to align himself with any particular movement, this radical notion assured him a preeminent place among the artists of Dada, who questioned not only the prevailing art standards of their time but also (being in the midst of the horrors of World War I) the legitimacy of Western civilization. The initial version of Duchamp's work *In Advance of the Broken Arm* (1915) was a snow shovel that he bought at a hardware store in New York City. Like many of his readymades, the original was lost, possibly having been discarded. A Duchamp shovel was in Warhol's art collection, copy number 5 of the 1964 edition of eight examples.

Warhol depicted everyday objects in paintings and sculptures using the industrial technique of silkscreen printing. Starting in 1964, he created a series of painted plywood sculptures that almost perfectly mimicked common shipping cartons for grocery items such as Del Monte canned peaches, Mott's apple juice, Heinz tomato ketchup, Campbell's tomato juice, Kellogg's Corn Flakes cereal, and Brillo soap pads. He asked his assistants to go to the supermarket near his home and retrieve the empty cardboard boxes (otherwise destined for the trash), which he then sent off to be made into silkscreens for his art.

Signature Pieces

Duchamp's readymade *Fountain*—a common porcelain urinal resting on its back—was regarded as so offensive at the time of its creation that it was the only piece excluded from an art exhibition by the Society of Independent Artists that had announced that all submitted works would be accepted.

Warhol's *Campbell's Soup Cans* series was equally shocking for the simple banality of its subject matter; Duchamp himself commented on the paintings, "If you take a Campbell's Soup can and repeat it fifty times, you are not interested in the retinal image. What interests you is the concept that wants to put fifty Campbell's Soup cans on

Marcel Duchamp, *In Advance of the Broken Arm*, 1915/63

Andy Warhol, *Brillo Soap Pads Box*, 1964

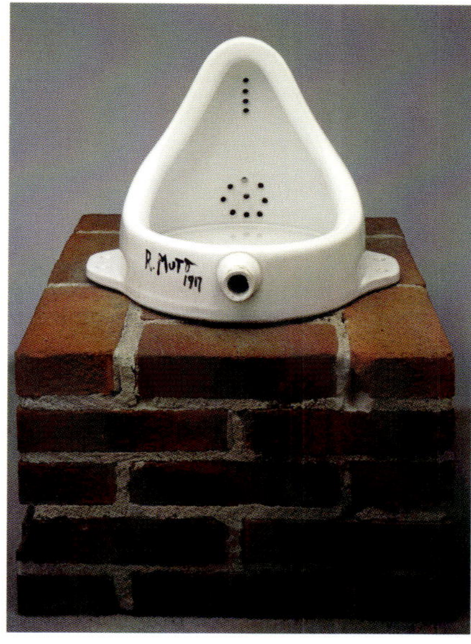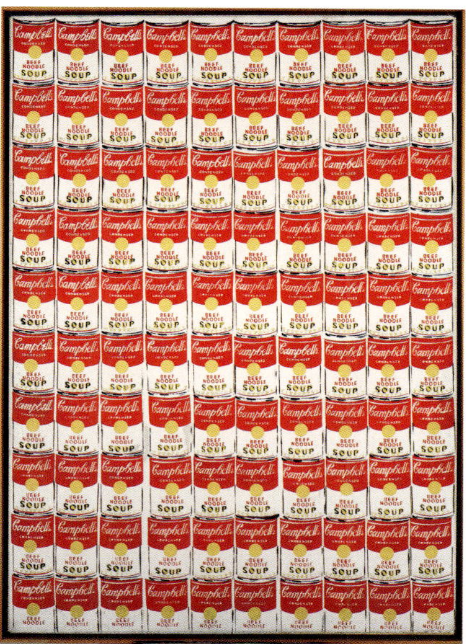

a canvas."[1] When first exhibited as a group in 1962, the thirty-two nearly identical soup-can images were ridiculed in a nearby gallery, which displayed a pyramid of actual cans of soup for sale at 33¢ for two cans, with the notice "Don't Be Misled. Get the Original." This mocking tone echoed the scorn directed at Duchamp's painting *Nude Descending a Staircase, No. 2* (1912) when it was displayed in the famous Armory Show of 1913 in New York, Chicago, and Boston.

For some of his best-known images, such as *Marilyn Monroe*, *Electric Chair*, and *Flowers*, Warhol, much like Duchamp, created several series over many decades. His first *Campbell's Soup Can* is a hand-painted work that predates the stenciled paintings and is in the museum's collection. Warhol created two similar stenciled paintings and a sculpture, *Campbell's Soup Cans Box* (1962), as well as the cycle of thirty-two hand-painted single cans first shown in Los Angeles in 1962, plus several more similar to that series, measuring approximately 20 by 16 inches each; several are slightly larger.

At the same time, Warhol made a series of monumental hand-painted single cans, measuring about 6 by 4 feet; the museum's collection includes three of these. After featuring the packaging design of Campbell's tomato juice in his *Box* sculptures of 1964, Warhol returned to the iconic can in 1965 in a cycle of paintings with radically altered colors; these were followed by two series of printed shopping bags in 1965 and 1966, two suites of editioned prints in 1968 and 1969, the series *Retrospectives and Reversals* in 1979/80, hand-painted images in the early 1980s, and, finally, a series of paintings of the packaging for Campbell's new dry soup mixes in 1986. In addition to these, other objects on this theme with which Warhol has been associated also exist, such as aluminum sculptures, a necktie, a paper dress, and prints on plastic. In many ways, the soup can is his signature work.

Often lampooned for them, Warhol created these everyday depictions of soup cans in mockery of Abstract Expressionism. At Carnegie Mellon University in the late 1970s, art professor Bruce Breland was fond of telling a story about his days as a young art professor around 1960 in New York City, in New York State's SUNY system. He had developed a friendship with a young abstract painter, Roy Lichtenstein, and they spent many hours together in galleries and museums, at openings, and in Lichtenstein's Lower Manhattan studio.[2] Breland recalled that the Abstract Expressionist painters openly referred to their compositions as "soup," which they were constantly trying to perfect, as if they were recipes for paintings. Obviously, with this information, Warhol's soup cans take on a whole new meaning, especially since the abstract

Marcel Duchamp, *Fountain*, 1917/63

Andy Warhol, *100 Cans*, 1962

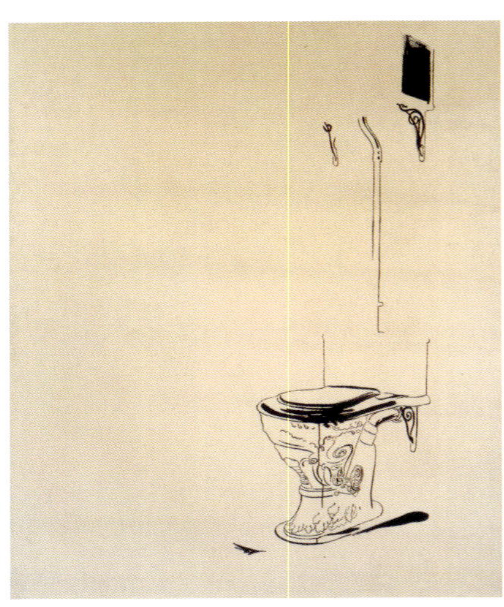

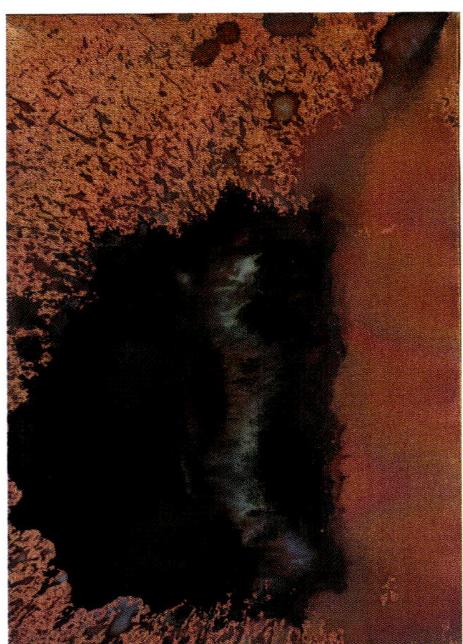

painters didn't care for Warhol's art. He tried several times to be admitted into the Tanager Gallery's co-op of mostly abstract artists, some of whom had been Warhol's classmates at Carnegie Tech. He might have thought, "If you want soup, I'll give you soup." His works were a provocation, for those who were in the know.

Scandal

Much of the shock value of *Fountain* derives from the fact that it is not only an everyday object but also a utilitarian one—a urinal—that is not held in high esteem and, moreover, is often considered vulgar and shameful. Much as *Immersion (Piss Christ)* (1987), Andres Serrano's beautiful photograph of a crucifix in a golden light (which was, in fact, urine), offended government, religion, and the wider public alike when it was shown in 1989, *Fountain* continues to shock.

The original readymade *Fountain* was lost or destroyed shortly after the controversy of 1917. The first recorded copy of *Fountain* was acquired in Paris and exhibited in New York City in 1950, and another (current whereabouts unknown) was sold at auction in Paris three years later. In 1963 Ulf Linde made a copy of *Fountain* in Sweden that was signed by Duchamp in Milan the following year.

Duchamp included a drawing of *Fountain* in his print *Four Readymades* (1964). Warhol owned a signed copy of *Fountain* from a 1964 edition of eight along with four copies, his being *hor série* (outside of the edition), each created from blueprint drawings and cast from a handmade clay model that was based on Alfred Stieglitz's 1917 photograph of the original. Warhol is said to have doggedly pursued and finally acquired his copy by trading three of his portraits to one of his art dealers in 1973.

Warhol chose the lowly toilet as the subject of one of his early hand-painted Pop paintings, *Toilet* (1961). Yet, in contrast to Duchamp, he selected an extremely ornate late nineteenth-century model, which he found in an illustrated catalogue of plumbing supplies. At about the same time, he unsuccessfully experimented with urine as a medium, applying it directly to primed canvas.[3] In the mid-1970s, Warhol returned to the concept, but this time he infused his seemingly vulgar art with a scientific component. Before his assistants urinated on the canvas, it was first covered with metallic paints containing copper or bronze, which, when combined with the salts and other minerals in urine, naturally oxidized and turned darker hues (usually a range of lush greens) in complex forms reminiscent of Abstract Expressionist paintings of the 1950s. Warhol could not find a gallery in the United States

Andy Warhol, *Toilet*, 1961

Andy Warhol, *Oxidation Painting*, 1978

(See also Marcel Duchamp, *Fountain*, 1917/63, on page 59)

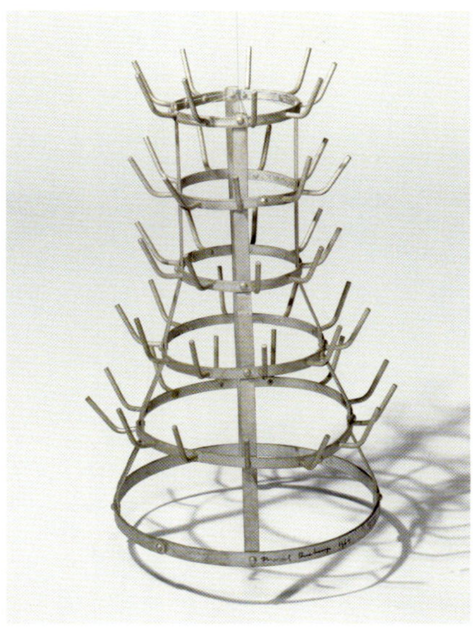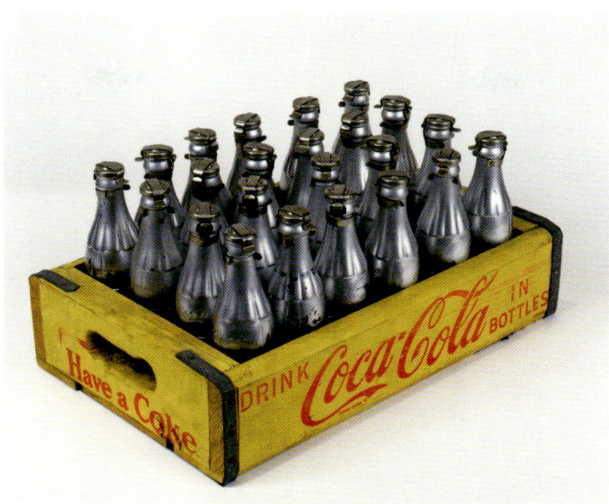

that was willing to exhibit the *Oxidations* (1978) until 1985, when the paintings were finally displayed at the Gagosian Gallery in New York.

Puns

In 1914 Duchamp purchased a bottle rack from a department store in Paris. While in New York City two years later, he wrote to his sister, Suzanne, asking her to rescue the object from his abandoned studio and inscribe upon it a deliberately nonsensical phrase he had devised. However, she had already cleaned out his studio and in the process had unwittingly discarded not only *Bottle-Rack* (1914) but also another readymade, *Bicycle Wheel* (1913). In 1921 Duchamp re-created the original, lost *Bottle-Rack* for his sister. Man Ray realized another version in 1959; Robert Rauschenberg produced one in 1960; and Duchamp, another one in 1961. Art dealer Irving Blum (who gave Warhol his first gallery show of Pop Art— of the *Campbell's Soup Cans*) produced yet one more in 1963, while an edition of eight plus four was published in 1964. Duchamp also included a drawing of *Bottle-Rack* in *Four Readymades*.

Warhol's *You're In* (1967) can be interpreted as a reference to Duchamp's *Bottle-Rack*. Racks for drying precious glass bottles were a common item in Duchamp's day; by Warhol's time, commercial culture had moved on, and empty glass bottles for products were returned in exchange for a nominal deposit, usually in the wood crates in which the product was shipped. Warhol's title is a pun on social status and bodily waste, suggesting the arbitrariness of social standing. Warhol intended to fill his silver bottles with cologne and sell them as art in the Philadelphia exhibition *The Museum of Merchandise* (1967). Coca-Cola objected to the use of its trademarked bottles, and Warhol skirted the issue by offering the scent for sale in its original packaging, with a free silver bottle.

Marcel Duchamp, *Bottle-Rack*, 1914/64

Andy Warhol, *You're In*, 1967

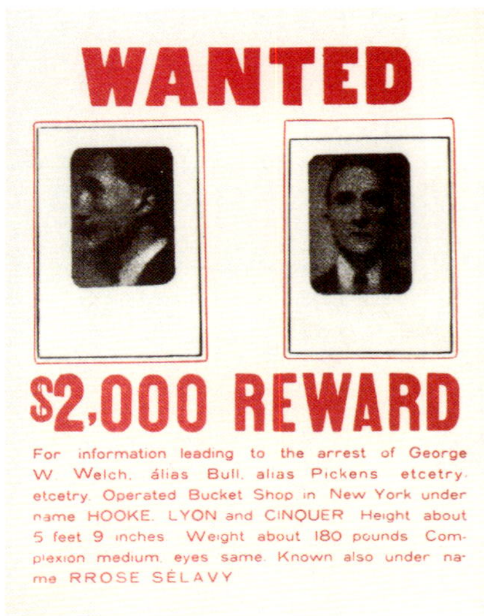

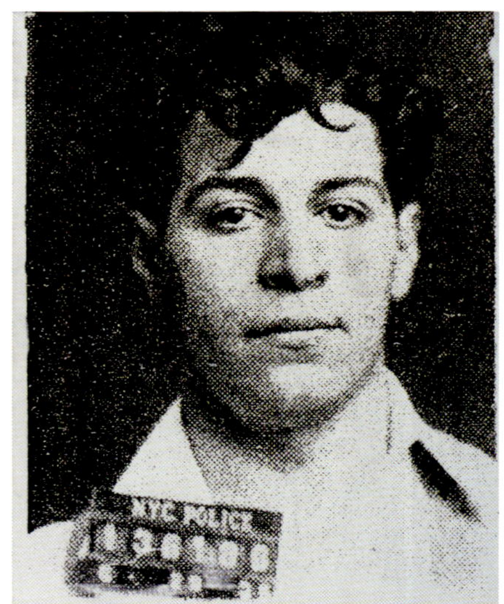

Most Wanted

Duchamp's design for the poster for his retrospective exhi-bition at the Pasadena Art Museum in 1963 reproduces a lost work, *Wanted: $2,000 Reward / Marcel Duchamp* (1923), in which the artist posed as a criminal in imitation of typical police mug shots, by pasting photos of himself on a fake "wanted poster" such as might be found in amusement parks and post offices. Warhol made a special point of attending the opening of that show, scheduling his own exhibition of *Elvis* and *Liz* paintings to open at the Ferus Gallery in Los Angeles within days of the Duchamp show. Several photos document Warhol's attendance at Duchamp's opening celebration; he also shot a short film of the Duchamp exhibition.

Warhol owned a copy of Duchamp's Pasadena poster. The show—Duchamp's first retrospective—was held when the artist was seventy-six years old. The curator was Walter Hopps, who was already very familiar with Warhol's work and had been a partner with Irving Blum at the Ferus Gallery. Hopps had received Duchamp's permission to make copies of three of Duchamp's works for the show; David Hayes, a curator at the Guggenheim Museum in New York, was engaged to produce them.[4] Hayes and Warhol were friends; the 1962 datebook that Warhol filled with tickets and receipts confirms eight meetings between them that year, including what was probably a holiday dinner on December 23 with dealer Ileana Sonnabend and artist Robert Rauschenberg.[5]

One year after Duchamp's Pasadena exhibition, Warhol used the wanted-poster template to produce a large mural depicting a series of thirteen criminals for the New York State Pavilion of the World's Fair in New York City. Warhol's images and title were taken directly from a New York City Police Department booklet called *The Thirteen Most Wanted Men*, published in 1961. Officials of the fair objected to the mural and ordered that it be covered with a large tarpaulin. Following much publicity, Warhol permitted the work to be obscured with silver paint, after first cheekily suggesting that it be replaced with a portrait of the fair's director, Robert Moses. Though the mural was destroyed, Warhol also made canvas portraits of the criminals.

In 1965 the New York poetry journal *Kulchur* published a photographic portrait of Warhol next to a photo of a modified version of *Wanted: $2,000 Reward* (probably the version on the Pasadena poster) in which the images of Duchamp were replaced with slightly smaller photos of poet Ted Berrigan and artist Joe Brainard (see "U is for Underground"). The magazine's layout makes it appear that Warhol is glancing directly at the two substitute pho-tos. Berrigan and Brainard each sat for a Warhol *Screen Test* on March 3, 1965.

Marcel Duchamp, *A Poster Within a Poster (Pasadena exhibition poster)* (detail), 1963

Andy Warhol, *Most Wanted Men No. 2, John Victor G.*, 1964

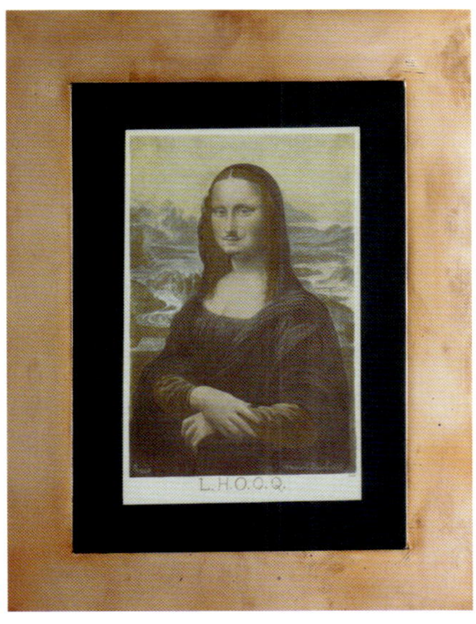 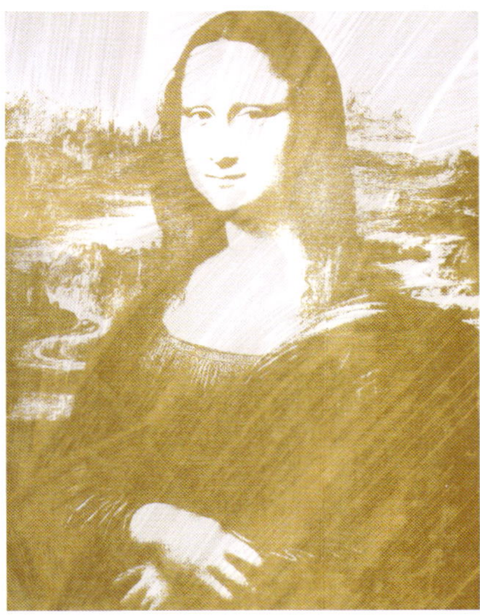

Art History

Duchamp and Warhol both referenced masterpieces of Western art in their work. Of the two artists, Warhol did so with far greater frequency and reverence.

Duchamp made his first *L.H.O.O.Q.* in 1919, and all of his versions of Leonardo da Vinci's *Mona Lisa* (*La Gioconda*, 1503–6) seem to have been created with mischief in mind. Aside from the naughty-schoolboy aspect of the added facial hair, by simply enunciating the letters in French the title of his work reads, "Elle a chaud au cul," or "She has a hot ass" (an oblique reference to Leonardo's alleged homosexuality, a topic that fascinated Warhol). Another, more recent reading of the work is that the initial version was printed by Duchamp with slightly modified facial features so that Leonardo's lady bears a resemblance to Duchamp; the beard and mustache that he applied were meant to test the observation skills of his audience and prevent them from seeing his subtler alleged modification.

Warhol's homages to Leonardo's well-known portrait began in 1963, when the painting was on a highly publicized brief visit to the United States, arranged jointly by the US and French governments. Warhol found his reproduction of the painting in his copy of the catalogue that was published for the tour. One of his numerous silk-screened renditions consists of thirty repetitions of Leonardo's image, titled *Thirty Are Better than One* (1963).

The illustrated copy of *L.H.O.O.Q.* is probably an extra example of the three hundred from 1941 using the pochoir (stencil) technique featured in Duchamp's *Boîte-en-valise* (1935–41); it is based on the original of 1919. The numerous versions of *L.H.O.O.Q.* make it perhaps closest in that regard to Warhol's *Soup Cans*: after the initial work appeared in 1919, Duchamp's friend Francis Picabia created a variant in 1920 for the magazine *391*, followed by a large-scale version in 1930, one signed to Max Ernst in 1960, an edition of thirty-eight in 1964, two printed dish towels in 1965, and a "shaved" version in an edition of about one hundred from 1965.[6]

Marcel Duchamp, *L.H.O.O.Q.*, 1919/41

Andy Warhol, *Mona Lisa*, ca. 1979

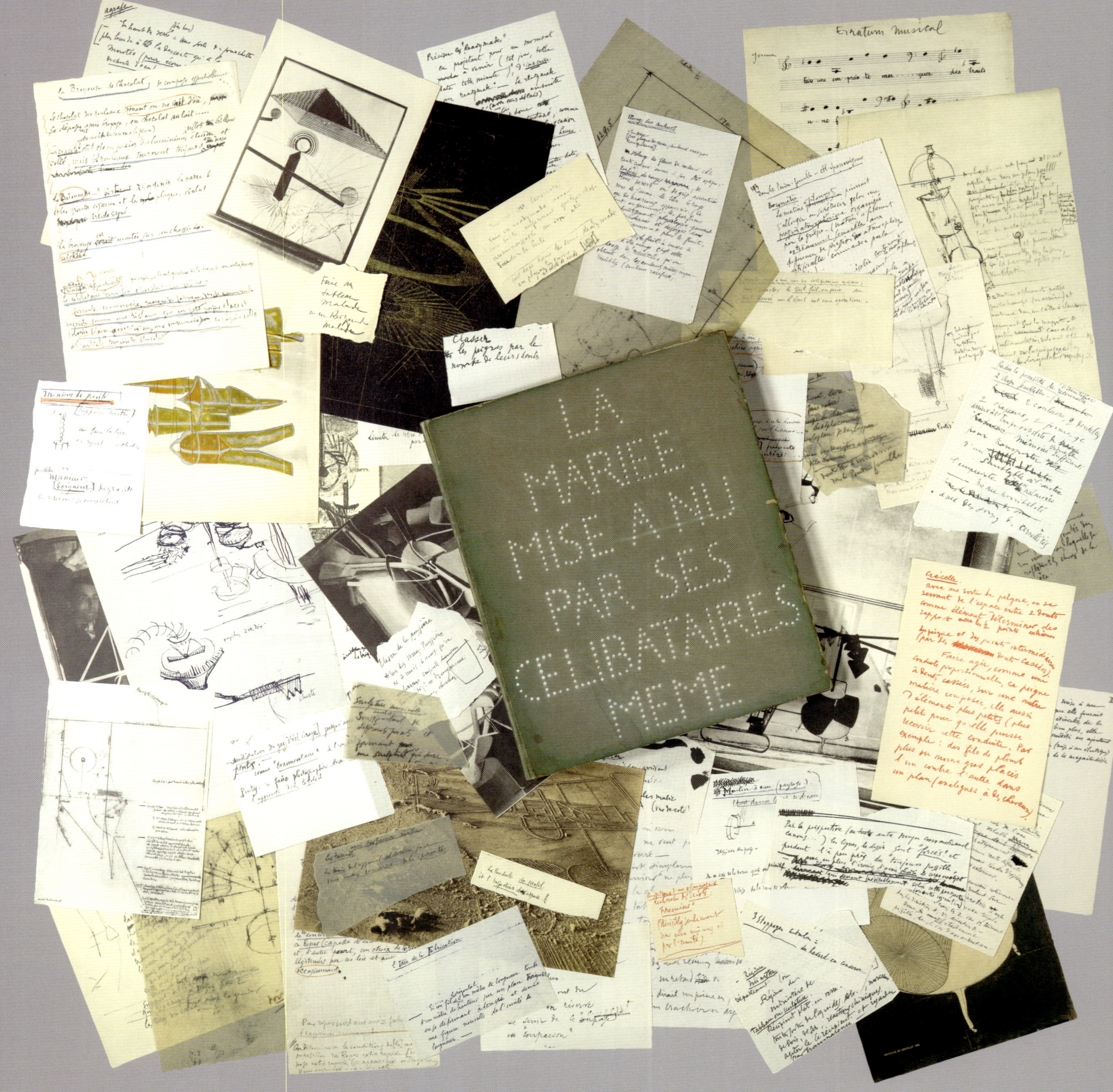

64

Marcel Duchamp, *The Bride Stripped Bare by Her Bachelors, Even (The Green Box)*, September 1934

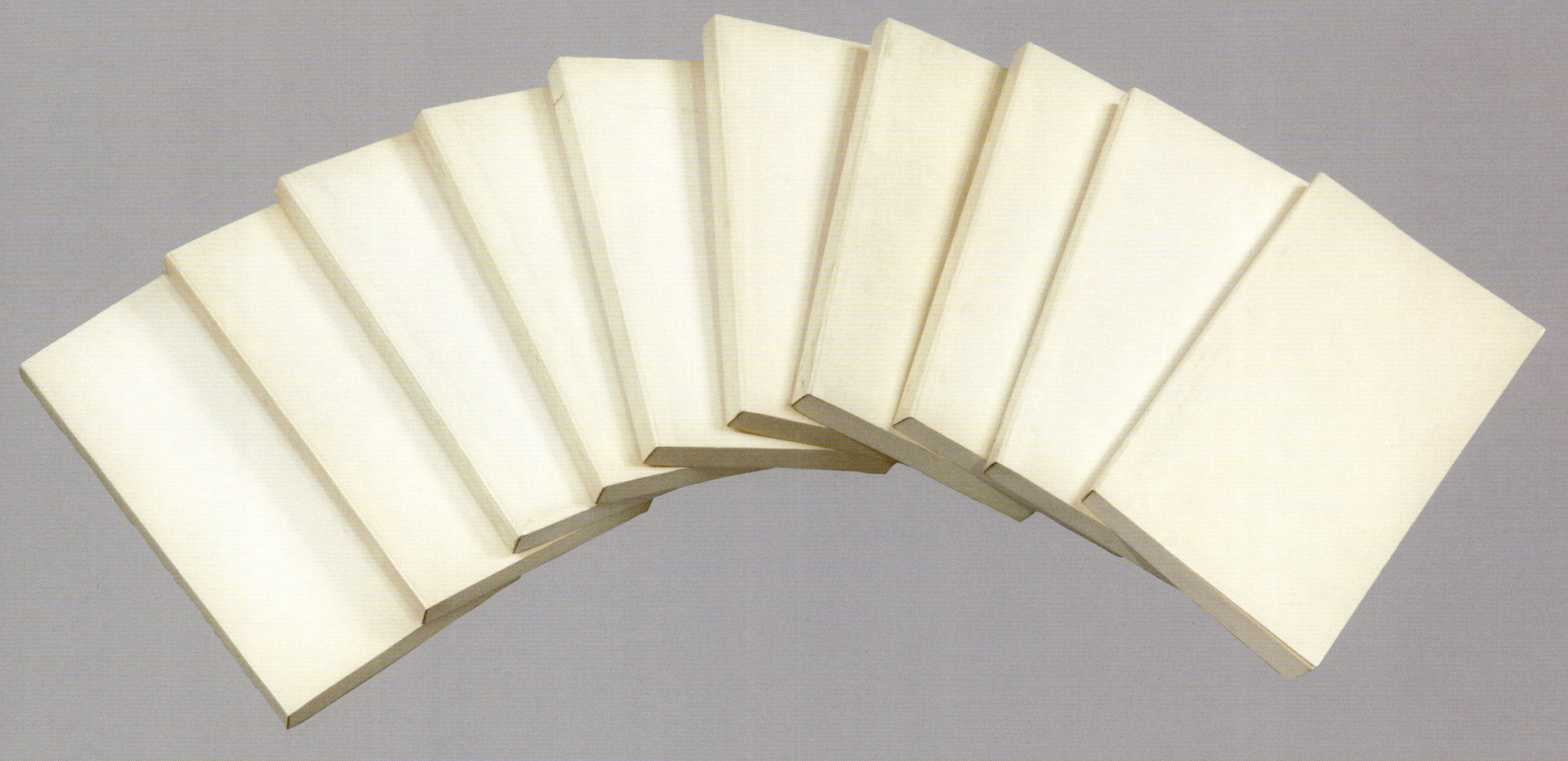

Andy Warhol, blank books, known as "trip books," ca. 1968

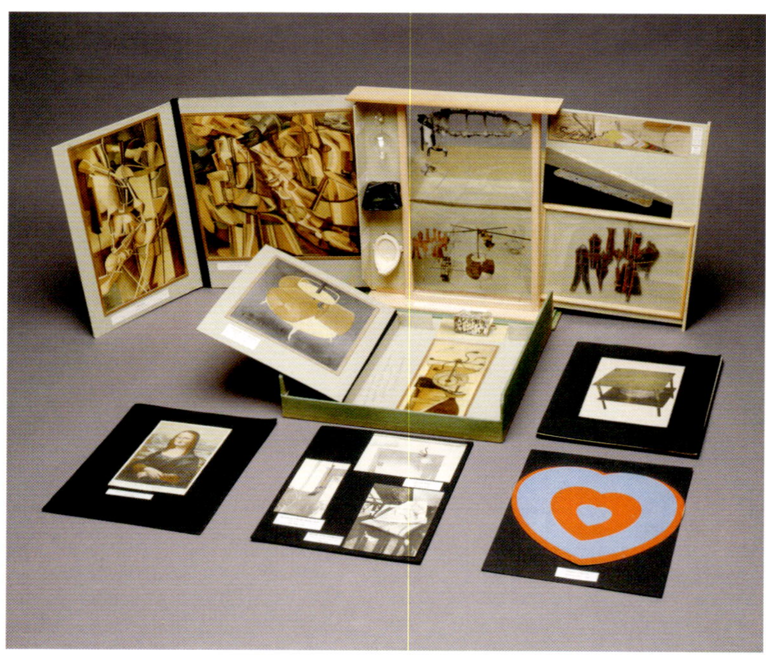

Archive as Art

A l'infinitif (*In the Infinitive*) consists of precise facsimile reproductions of seventy-nine of Duchamp's handwritten notes made over many decades, dating to the years of his discovery of the readymade. It was the last of three such "notes in a box" projects that he created; the previous ones were *The Box of 1914* (in 3 copies) and *The Bride Stripped Bare by Her Bachelors, Even* (better known as *The Green Box* of 1934, in 320 numbered copies). Some art historians have compared his efforts to Leonardo's notebooks. A fourth box of notes was published posthumously by Duchamp's heirs in 1980. Warhol owned copy 31 of *In the Infinitive*.

Outside of phone numbers and a few jottings of ideas, Warhol was not much of a note maker, though he attempted a project of keeping his ideas in a series of small white notebooks, known at the time as "trip books." He seems to have filled only one, while thirteen more exist that were never used. The project dates from about 1968. Warhol shared Duchamp's obsession with packing his papers with the intent of selling them, as evidenced by his massive *Time Capsules* project. *Time Capsule 2* contains a letter sent to Warhol in 1968 by a college student, requesting an answer to the question, "Do you think there is any relation between your work in art and the readymades of Duchamp?"

Marcel Duchamp, *Boîte-en-valise* (*Box in a Valise*), 1961

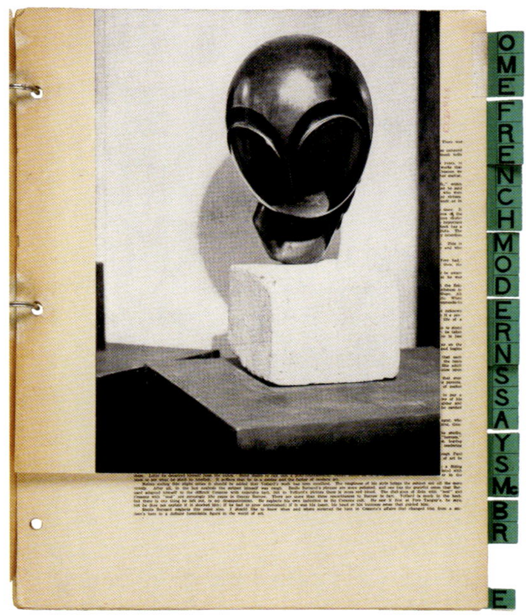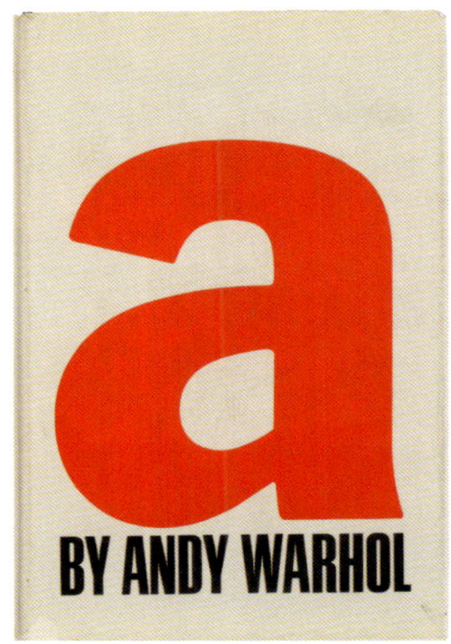

Books

Duchamp's radically designed book *Some French Moderns Says McBride* (1922) contains excerpts from the art criticism published by Henry McBride between 1915 and 1922. Each successive text is printed in a progressively larger type, except for the last, which wouldn't fit on the remaining three pages. The final page thus returns to the very small type of the first text. By printing the book's title and publisher on tabbed dividers, which typically are used to alphabetize material or place it into other categories, the design subverts the organizational practices and values of the modern business office. Similarly, the design of Warhol's *a* (1968) makes innovative use of the top margin of every page. It reprints a short phrase from the text below rather than simply indicating the current chapter. Billy Linich (Billy Name), as Warhol's editor, takes credit for this idea and the choice of each phrase. Warhol's title, of course, is also quite radical; it's a reference to amphetamine, the drug of choice for many characters in the book.

Warhol's book is usually referred to as *a: a novel* for clarity. The text of *a* was transcribed from his tape recordings, most of which are in the Warhol Museum's collection. Each of the twenty-four chapters is divided in half and was transcribed from a one-hour tape, making the book a record of events over a twenty-four-hour period, although in fact those hours were scattered between 1965 and 1967.

While almost every character in *a* is based on a real person (Warhol, or one of his numerous associates and friends), nearly all are given pseudonyms in the book; Warhol is Drella, a nickname he went by at the time, and a contraction of "Dracula" and "Cinderella." The transcriptions were done by several young women, and their inconsistencies, frequent use of onomatopoeia, and typographical errors were all retained in the final product.[7]

Marcel Duchamp, *Some French Moderns Says McBride*, 1922

Andy Warhol, *a: a novel*, 1968

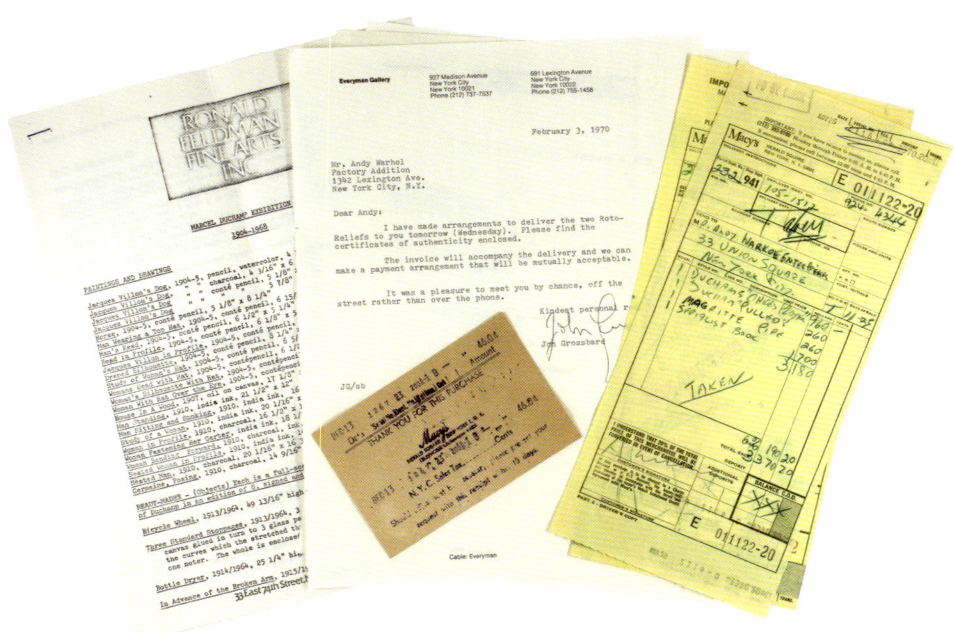

Warhol Collects Duchamp

As noted above, Warhol owned some thirty works and related objects by Duchamp; some of these are included in the auction catalogues for the 1988 sale of Warhol's estate. (See "I is for Illusions" for one of several copies of Duchamp *Rotoreliefs* owned by Warhol.) Warhol also owned several books about Duchamp; at that time, there were very few monographs published on the artist. Warhol's datebook for 1962 includes a receipt for the purchase of an unidentified volume on Duchamp, probably the American edition of Robert Lebel's *Sur Marcel Duchamp* (1959). Warhol also owned the published catalogue raisonné of Duchamp's work by Arturo Schwarz, *The Complete Works of Marcel Duchamp* (1969).

Critical Comparisons

Art critics and other writers have noted connections between the work of Duchamp and Warhol, but few art exhibitions have explored them. One of the first seems to have been *The Arena of Love* at the Dwan Gallery in Los Angeles in January 1965. In this group show, Warhol's massive diptych *Marilyn's Lips* (1962) was shown along with, although not beside, Duchamp's *Female Fig Leaf*, their friend Bill Copley's paintings, and others. The following year, at the Institute of Contemporary Art in Philadelphia, critic/curator Gene Swenson presented *The Other Tradition*, which aimed to correct the then-prevalent misperception that only art concerned with formal properties (mainly abstraction) could be of legitimate interest. Again, Duchamp and Warhol were included in this large and important group show.

Six more years would pass before *Realität, Realismus, Realität* was presented at several museums in West Germany in 1972. This was a much more focused exhibition of works by Duchamp, Warhol, and the brilliant German conceptual/performance artist Joseph Beuys. The catalogue ends with a photo of a hand-painted sign from Beuys's 1964 performance declaring, "Das Schweigen von Marcel Duchamp wird Überbewertet" ("The Silence of Marcel Duchamp is Overrated"). Beuys and Warhol would later collaborate on a few occasions in the 1980s.

Correspondence about and receipts for Marcel Duchamp artworks purchased by Warhol, 1969

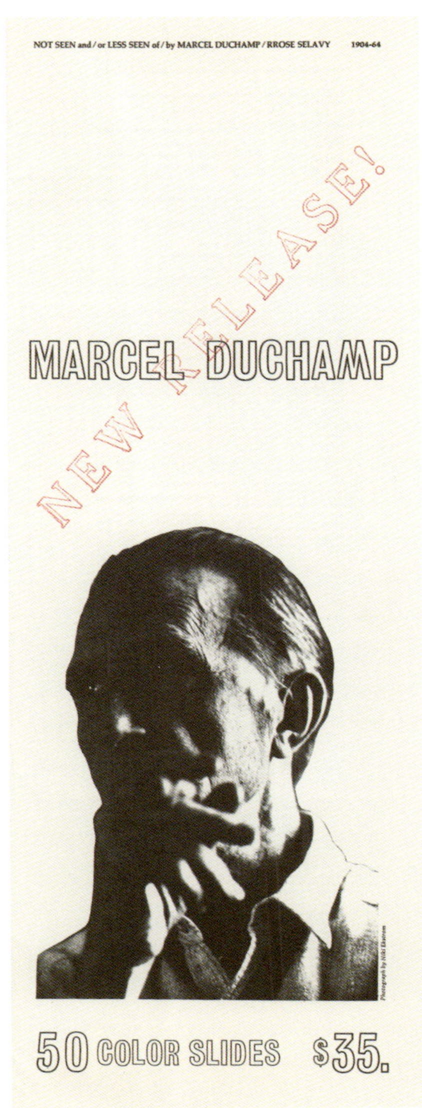

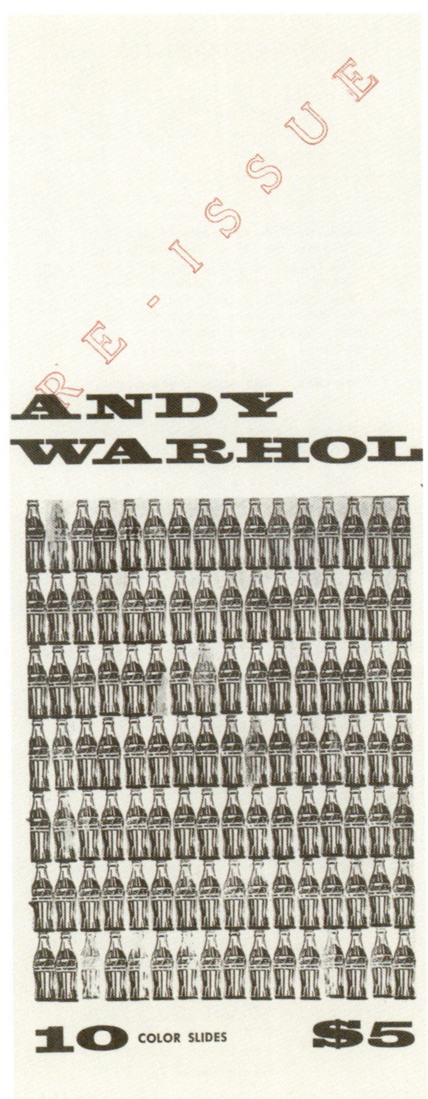

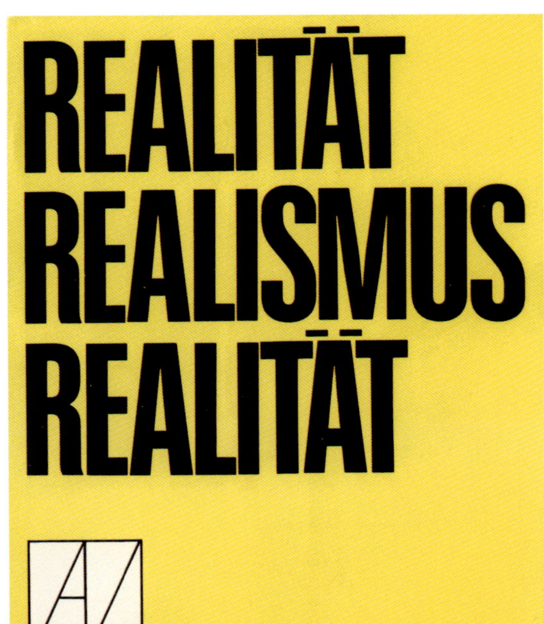

Pamphlets from Portable Gallery Press sent to Warhol in 1965

Exhibition catalogue for *Realität, Realismus, Realität*, Von der Heydt-Museum, Wuppertal, Germany, from *Time Capsule 90*

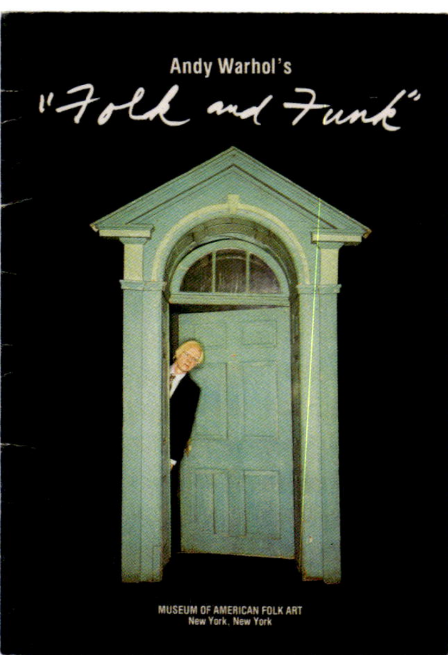

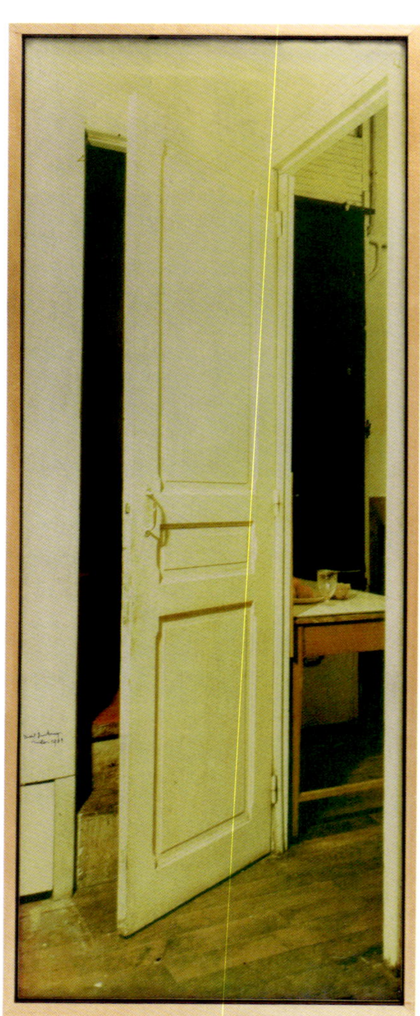

Doors

Images of doors were chosen for the covers of publications related to Duchamp and Warhol. In 1965, for an exhibition of Mary Sisler's important collection of Duchamp's work at Cordier & Ekstrom Gallery, a color photograph of his *Door: 11, rue Larrey, Paris* was printed on the catalogue cover. "A door which is always opened and always closed" is Duchamp's riddle-like description of the unusual door, which he designed for his Paris studio in 1927. It consists of a single door pivoted on hinges mounted between two doorways, so that only one doorway can be blocked or opened at any given moment. Beyond serving this function, it defied the old French adage "Il faut qu'une porte soit ouverte ou fermée" ("A door must be either open or closed"). Duchamp's door, therefore, openly contradicts the assumed notion of mutual exclusivity.[8] Warhol's collection of folk art was publicly displayed at the Museum of American Folk Art in New York City in 1977. His antique door was chosen for the exhibition catalogue cover, with Warhol himself peeking through it, as if to welcome visitors to the show (by this time, he rarely entertained guests at his home). The door was free-standing, much like a sculpture in the middle of a room. "I like the door best; you can go in and out of it and still go nowhere," he told a journalist reporting on the exhibition.[9]

Exhibition catalogue for *Andy Warhol's Folk and Funk* at the Museum of American Folk Art, New York, 1977

Marcel Duchamp, *Door: 11, rue Larrey, Paris* (*Porte: 11, rue Larrey, Paris*), 1927

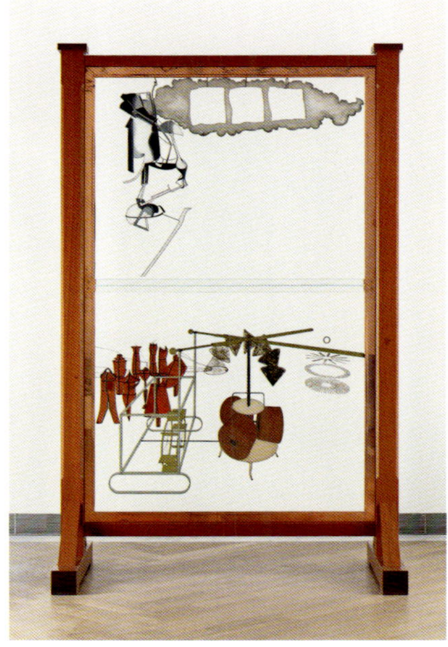

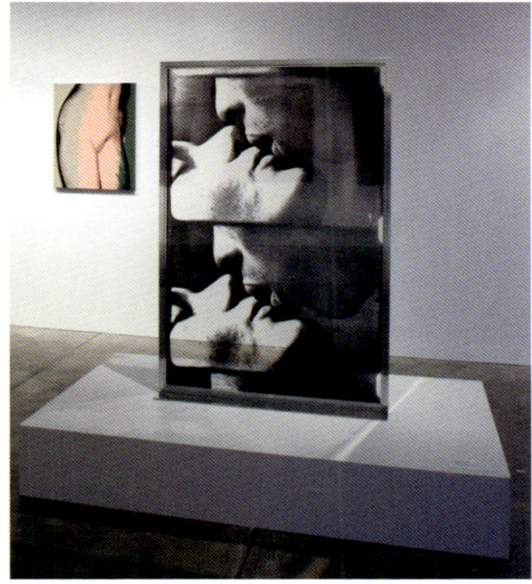

Sexuality

The Bride Stripped Bare by Her Bachelors, Even (1915–23)—also known as *The Large Glass*—is Duchamp's deliberately unfinished magnum opus, his intricate and mysterious representation of mechanized sexuality, with the female bride in the top half and the male bachelors below, unable to reach their object of desire. The ideas he imbued in the piece—such as modern technology, love, and postpone-ment—evolved from his earlier oil paintings and have been the subject of intense study using the multitude of related notes and drawings that the artist saved and painstakingly reproduced in a numbered edition of the same title, also known as *The Green Box* (1934). All of the images in *The Large Glass* have specific names and func-tions attributed to them; for example, in the upper half are the Bride, three Draft Pistons, and the Milky Way, and in the lower half are the Sieves, the Glider, the Malic Moulds, and the Oculist Witnesses.

In New York, Duchamp periodically but carefully toiled on the artwork for nearly a decade before losing interest in the laborious process and deciding to move on to newer ideas. After *The Large Glass* was first exhibited in Brooklyn in 1926, it shattered into hundreds of shards, and in the early 1930s, Duchamp spent weeks methodically reassem-bling it. The delicate pattern of repaired cracks in the origi-nal is almost identical in the upper and lower halves of *The*

Large Glass. The original—which is in the collection of the Philadelphia Museum of Art—is too fragile to travel. There are a small number of nearly exact reproductions approved by the artist. Warhol owned an example of Duchamp's etching of *The Large Glass*.

In a format similar to that of Duchamp's *Large Glass*, Warhol's erotic sculpture *Large Kiss* (1965) presents two enlarged frames, bisecting the work into upper and lower halves, from his 1964 film *Kiss*. He used the format again in *Large Sleep* (1965), another sculpture based on two frames from a film, in this case his first one, *Sleep* (1963). The imperceptible differences between the film frames (each representing 1/24th of a second) in both sculptures evoke the similarities of the pattern of cracks in the origi-nal *Large Glass*. As with *The Large Glass*, these works by Warhol are neither paintings nor traditional sculptures, although at times they have been classified as prints as well as sculpture.

Marcel Duchamp, *La mariée mise à nu par ses célibataires, même* (*The Bride Stripped Bare by Her Bachelors, Even*), also known as *The Large Glass*, 1915–23, replica by Ulf Linde, Henrik Samuelson, and John Stenborg, 1991–92, after the 1961 version

Andy Warhol, *Large Kiss* (installation view), 1965

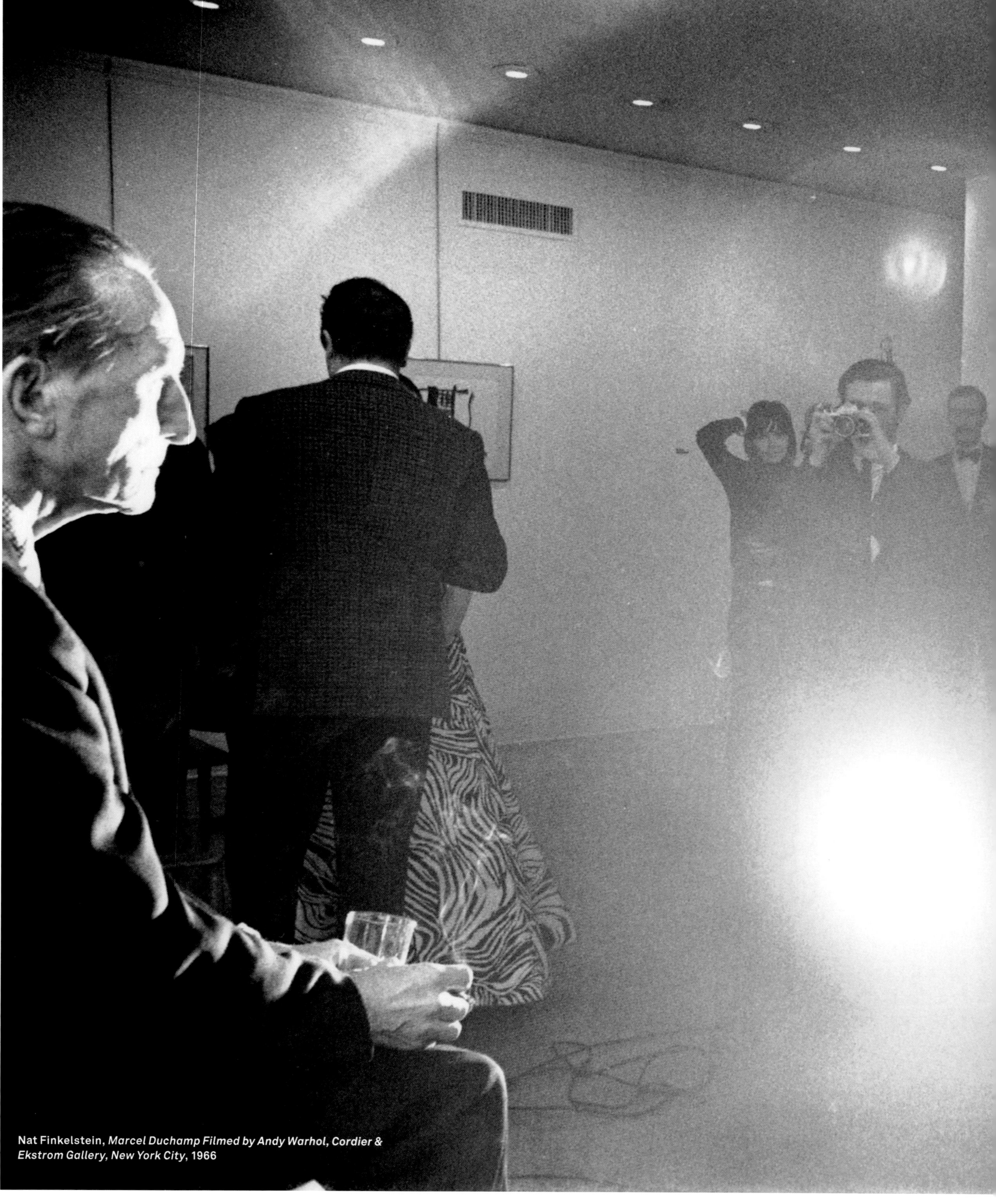

Nat Finkelstein, *Marcel Duchamp Filmed by Andy Warhol, Cordier & Ekstrom Gallery, New York City*, 1966

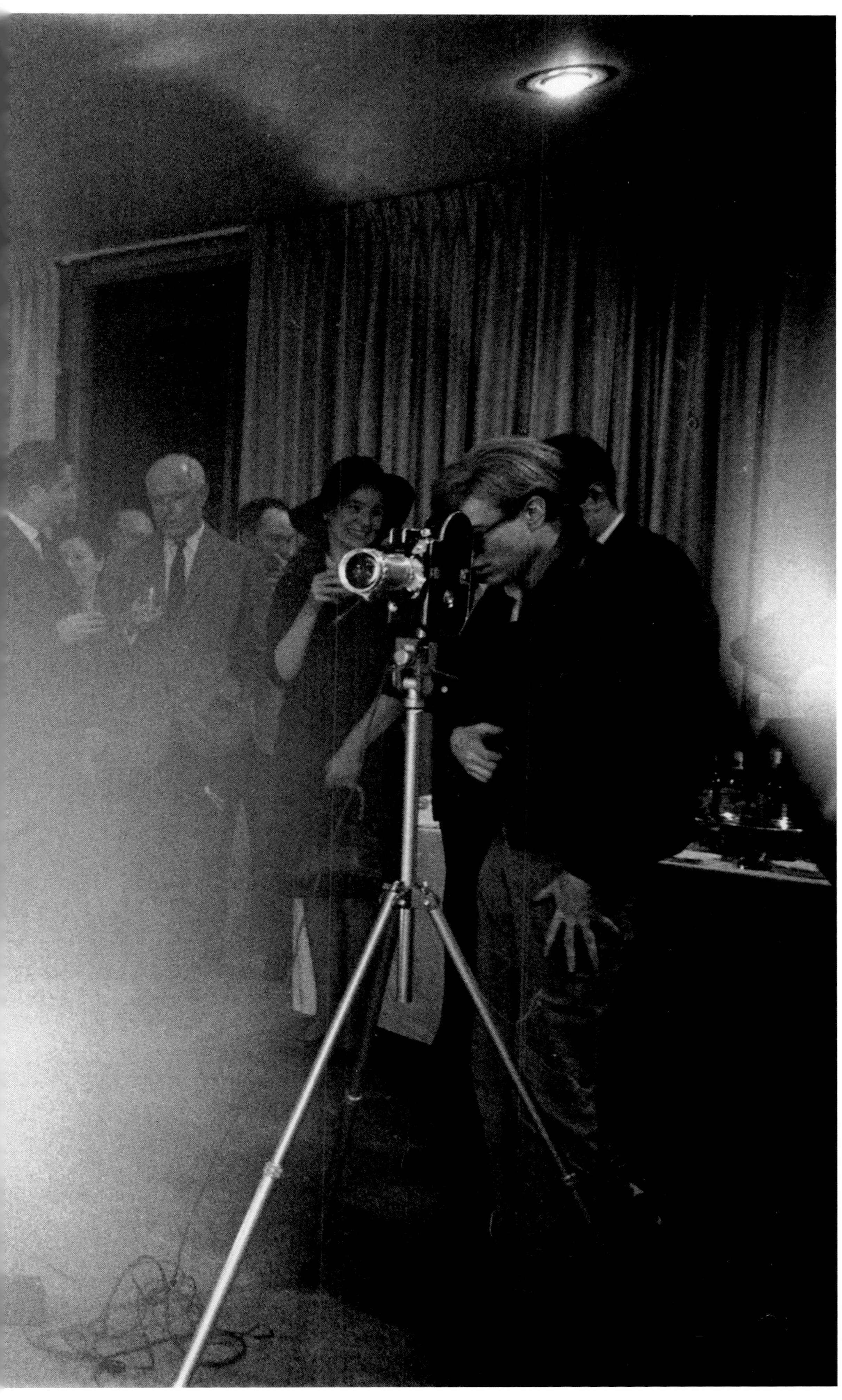

cordier & ekstrom, inc.

10 November, 1965

Dear Warhol:

I wrote to you in April to ask you if you would like to take part in a show for the benefit of the American Chess Foundation which will take place at the Cordier & Ekstrom Gallery from February 8 until February 26, 1966. A copy of my letter is enclosed herewith.

Not having had a reply, I am writing to you again, not to urge you to participate if you have decided that you do not wish to, but merely to make sure that my letter came to your attention.

The deadline for delivery of works was originally set for November 1st., but we find that we can extend it to December 1st. and if absolutely necessary, even to December 15th.

If I do not hear from you before December 1st., I shall take that to mean that you will not be among the participants.

With kindest regards,

Sincerely yours,

MARCEL DUCHAMP

Mr. Andy Warhol
1342 Lexington Avenue
New York City

978 MADISON AVENUE · NEW YORK 21, NEW YORK · TELEPHONE YUKON 8-8857 · CABLE CORDIEKS

Correspondence from Marcel Duchamp to Warhol, on Cordier & Ekstrom
Gallery letterhead, November 10, 1965

Interactions between the Artists

Duchamp's devotion to the game of chess led to the exhibition *Hommage à Caissa* in New York City in February 1966, with the proceeds from art sales to benefit the Marcel Duchamp Fund of the American Chess Foundation. Duchamp invited about two dozen artists to participate in the exhibition at Cordier & Ekstrom Gallery, including Warhol.

As each artist returned the RSVP card, Duchamp created a collage from the cards that would serve as the poster design; however, Warhol's card is missing from the poster. While it was known that Warhol participated in the exhibition by making his film portrait *Screen Test: Marcel Duchamp* during the opening, it was unclear whether he had brazenly crashed the party (as some have suggested) or had indeed been invited until Duchamp's two letters of invitation and the blank RSVP card were discovered in Warhol's *Time Capsules*. Describing the experience of sitting for Warhol, Duchamp referred to him as a cameraman: "I like Warhol's spirit. He's not just some painter or movie-maker. He's a *filmeur* and I like that very much."[10]

In making his portrait of Duchamp, Warhol shot three separate three-minute rolls of film, only one of which is currently available for screening. At one point during the film, Duchamp's gaze drifts downward, and he smiles; this might be in reaction to a beautiful young Italian woman (Benedetta Barzini) touching his thigh, a gesture apparently encouraged by Warhol. In later interviews, Warhol said that he had the financial support to film a twenty-four-hour-long project. Warhol was near-fatally shot in June 1968 and Duchamp died in October of that year, so it was never realized. This film project might be the reason that Duchamp noted Warhol's name in his datebook on January 8, 1968.

In an interview filmed by David Bailey in about 1972, Teeny Duchamp and John Cage speculated as to whether Warhol played chess. Cage stated, "He doesn't look like a chess player," to which Teeny replied, "I think he has a kind of chess player's mind though, which is very curious."[11]

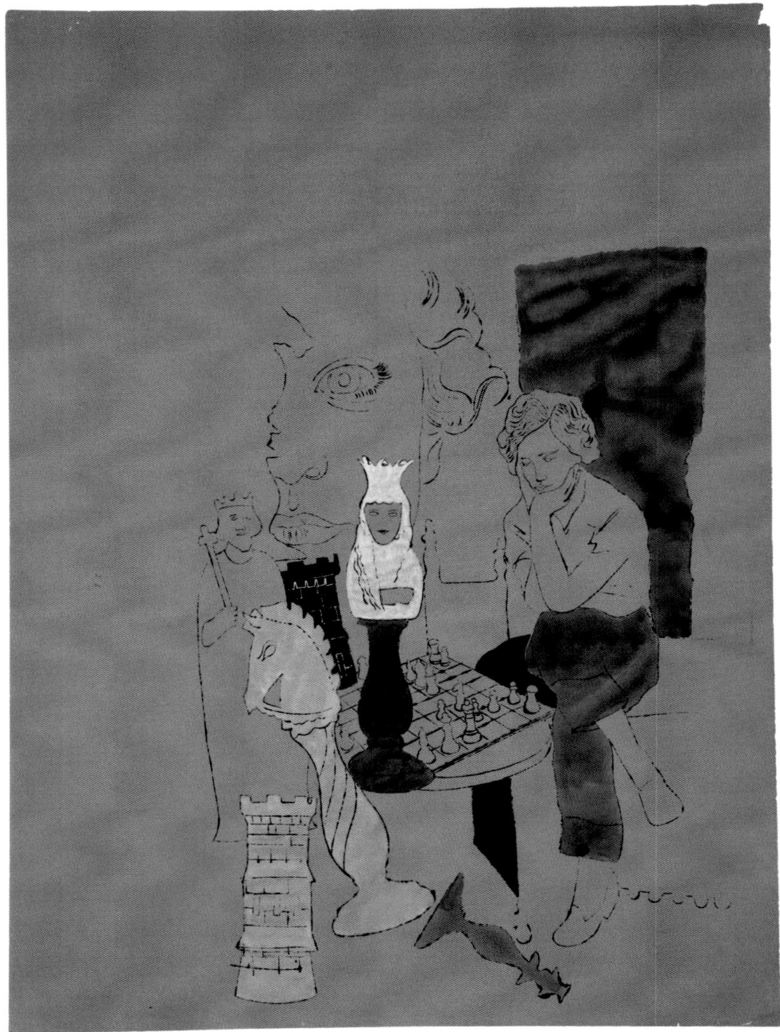

Andy Warhol, *Chess Player*, 1950s

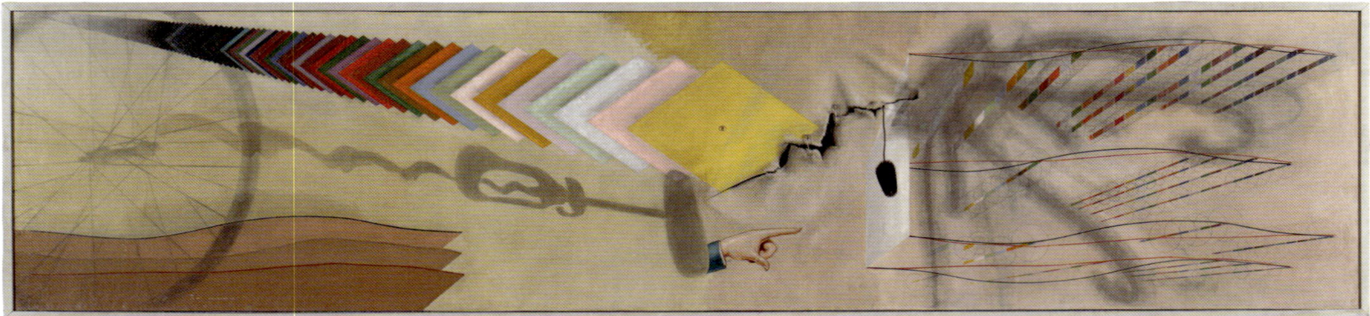

Secrets / Shadows

Near the end of his life, Duchamp focused on the theme of shadows with *Suite of Transparent Shadows* (1967), silk-screened silhouettes of his readymades *Bicycle Wheel* and *Bottle-Rack*. This work was printed on transparent sheets of plastic, much like the graphic-arts "acetates" that Warhol relied upon to make all of his photo-silkscreened works—almost his entire oeuvre from 1962 to 1987.

The Corkscrew's Shadow (1918) is probably the most ephemeral of Duchamp's works: it vanishes depending on the light. In an interview with Gene Swenson in 1963, Warhol discussed a new series of paintings made with fluorescent paint and featuring a similar use of light effects: "My next series will be pornographic pictures. They will look blank; when you turn on the black lights, then you see them—big breasts and . . . if a cop came in, you could just flick out the lights or turn on the regular lights—how could you say that was pornography?"[12] The first of these works featured the curvy torso of an anonymous nude woman, published in *Playboy* magazine in 1966. Late in life, he used the same painting medium in his enormous series of works based on Leonardo's *Last Supper* (1498).

Warhol's monumental abstract *Shadows* series (1979) was based on photographs that for many years were left mysteriously unidentified. They are now believed to be images of shadows found in Warhol's office/studio known as the Factory. Duchamp's *With Hidden Noise* (1916/63) contains a mysterious object that rattles around inside the ball of twine when the object is shaken (the object has never been ascertained). Duchamp asked his friend and patron Walter Arensberg to select the item and not tell him what it was.

Both artists recognized the potency of maintaining an air of mystery, encouraging their audience to never stop speculating about their lives and their work. Duchamp, the more reticent of the two, became more widely known after he "stopped" making art, whereas Warhol encouraged the media to spread news about him, including the simplifications and lies that he planted himself.

Marcel Duchamp, *Tu m'*, 1918, depicting shadows of readymades including the corkscrew

NOTES

1. David Bourdon, *Warhol* (New York: Abrams, 1989), 88.

2. At the author's recommendation, Bruce Breland was interviewed for the Oral History project of the Roy Lichtenstein Foundation.

3. Unlike Warhol's later *Oxidation* paintings, which were made of urine on metallic paint (which chemically reacted to one another, causing interesting coloration), the *Piss* paintings of the early 1960s were urine on primed canvas that appeared as a yellow stain. Warhol did not like the effect. In an interview in 1976, the artist recollected that he had thought of them as "diseased" and he put them away. "Appendix 4: Piss Paintings," *The Andy Warhol Catalogue Raisonné: Paintings and Sculpture, 1961–1963*, ed. George Frei and Neil Printz (New York: Phaidon, 2002), 469.

4. Hayes was the son of Mary Sisler, heir to the Firestone tire and rubber fortune. He encouraged his mother to collect Duchamp's work, and her collection was exhibited widely before it was sold. Like Warhol, Hayes owned a copy of Duchamp's *Boîte-en-valise*.

5. In 1963, upon the request of Billy Klüver, Warhol designed the cover of a vinyl LP recording of interviews with Pop artists, for a group exhibition at the Washington Gallery of Modern Art. The work, *Giant Size $1.57*, was based on one of five small collages made by Hayes (the sheet of artist's paper with four collages and a large cut-out rectangle is in Warhol's *Time Capsule 70*).

6. Another variant of *L.H.O.O.Q.* is a stenciled drawing of only the beard and mustache that was published in an edition of about two hundred in 1941.

7. Some of this information is based on the PhD research of Lucy Mulroney, in the Grove Press archive at Syracuse University, and corrects several notions that were previously and mistakenly understood about the book.

8. The information on *Door: 11, rue Larrey, Paris* draws heavily upon Francis Naumann's essay, "Marcel Duchamp: A Reconciliation of Opposites," in *Marcel Duchamp: Artist of the Century*, ed. Rudolf Kuenzli and Francis M. Naumann (Cambridge, MA: MIT Press, 1989), 20–40.

9. Judy Klemesrud, "A Party for Warhol's Folk and Funk," *New York Times*, September 20, 1977, as quoted in Bourdon, *Warhol*, 365.

10. Jennifer Gough-Cooper, Jacques Caumont, and Pontus Hultén, *Marcel Duchamp: Work and Life / Ephemerides on and about Marcel Duchamp and Rrose Sélavy, 1887–1968* (Cambridge, MA: MIT Press, 1993).

11. David Bailey, *Andy Warhol* (London: Associated Television Corporation; television film, duration unknown). Includes interview with Cage, filmed before or during 1972.

12. G. R. Swenson, "What Is Pop Art? Answers from 8 Painters, Part I," *Artnews* 62, no. 7 (November 1963), reprinted in *I'll Be Your Mirror: The Selected Andy Warhol Interviews*, ed. Kenneth Goldsmith (New York: Carroll & Graf, 2004), 19.

Andy Warhol, *Shadows*, ca. 1978

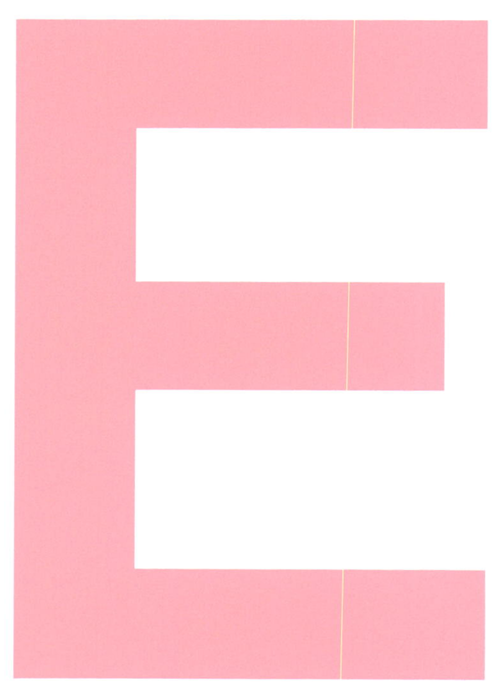

E
is for EDIE

This chapter highlights lesser-known archival material that was displayed in the large exhibition *Edie Sedgwick: From Silver Hill to the Silver Factory*, June 10–September 2, 2001.

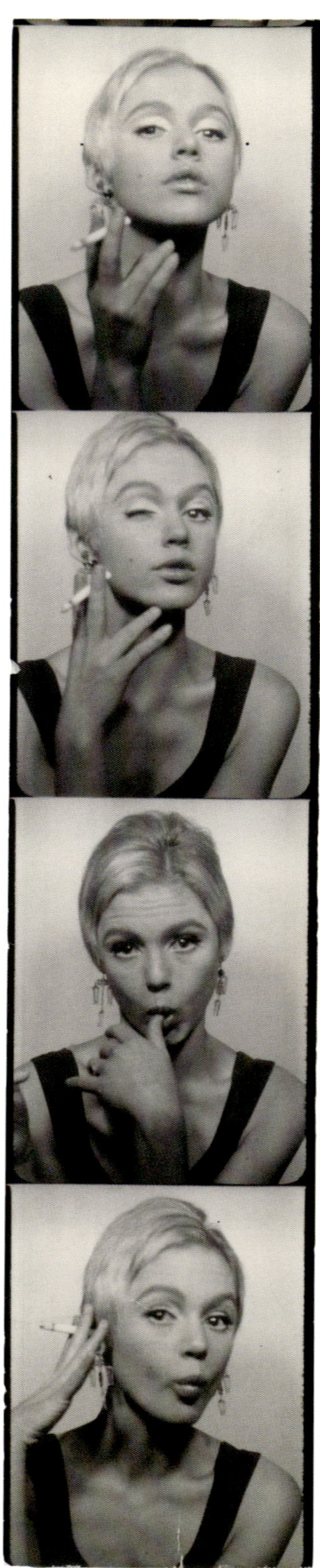

The most glamorous and tragic of Andy Warhol's Super-stars, Edith Sedgwick made headlines as his radiant "Girl of the Year" for 1965.[1] She starred in nearly every film—more than twenty-five—that Warhol made that year. They often attended parties together, and gossip columnists noted that the two were difficult to tell apart, dressed alike in striped shirts, Sedgwick's short hair colored silver to match Warhol's. When *Esquire* magazine asked Warhol who should portray him in a film, he answered, "I'd want Edie Sedgewick [*sic*] to play me. She does everything better than I do."[2]

Her unique style and extraordinary beauty were featured in both *Vogue* and *Life* magazines. Magazine editors, includ-ing the famed Diana Vreeland, who labeled the twenty-two-year-old a "youthquaker" in a 1965 issue of *Vogue*, embraced her natural incandescence and personal style.[3] Sedgwick instinctively paired black tights that she had worn since her teen years with oversized tops and loose dangling ear-rings that dusted her shoulder blades—an inexpensive, easy-to-wear look that was totally her own. However, she conceded the praise for her appearance was slightly absurd: "I was Girl of the Year and superstar and all that crap.... Everything I did was really underneath, I guess, motivated by psychological disturbances. I'd make a mask out of my face because I didn't realize I was quite beauti-ful, God blessed me so. I practically destroyed it. I had to wear heavy black eyelashes like bat wings, and dark lines under my eyes, and cut all my hair off, my long, dark, hair. Cut it off and strip it silver and blond and all those little maneuvers I did out of things that were happening to my life that upset me. I'd freak out in a very physical way. And it was all taken as a fashion trend."[4]

Edith Minturn Sedgwick was born into a life of privilege, one of eight siblings in a prominent family, and grew up riding horses on their six-thousand-acre California ranch. For her, 1965 began by dodging death in a New Year's Eve car accident near home, the same night that her brother Bobby fatally slammed his motorcycle into a New York bus. Only months before, their brother Minty had committed suicide at Silver Hill, a private psychiatric hospital in New Canaan, Connecticut, where he had been placed by their father to be "cured" of his homosexuality.

In the fall of 1962, after Sedgwick's discovery of her father's extramarital affairs and her objection to his sexual advances on his daughters, she was institutionalized at Silver Hill, in part to treat her bulimia. Sedgwick briefly tells the story of her committal to Silver Hill in a tape recording made by Warhol. Despite treatment, her eating disorder continued unabated, and she was subsequently moved to Bloomingdale, the Westchester County division of New York Hospital. Once her bulimia was under relative control (it plagued her throughout her adult life), Sedgwick was released, and she moved to Cambridge, Massachusetts, in the fall of 1963. She began to study art with her cousin Lily Saarinen, a sculptor, artist, and educator who taught at Pratt Institute in Brooklyn, the School of the Museum of Fine Arts, Boston, and MIT in Cambridge.[5] Of her private student and cousin, Saarinen disclosed, "She was the most talented young person I've taught art to. She'd come in late and very tired. She'd have her friends come in, and pretty soon more came. She was very insecure about men, though all the men loved her. She was chic and adorable. Pretty soon my life was Edie because I couldn't do anything else."[6]

In sketchbooks, on loose paper, and even on her apart-ment walls, Sedgwick drew all kinds of animals and figura-tive compositions. Her wildlife subjects included horses, deer, squirrels, mice, and camels, among others. Although most of her representations were naturalistic and unsenti-mental, her delicately drawn mice were dressed in cos-tumes and arranged in anthropomorphic and somewhat humorous poses, as if from children's storybooks. Sedgwick also worked with clay. During the year she studied with Saarinen in Cambridge, she continually returned to sculpt-ing a horse. Her teacher and friends commented on Sedgwick's intense focus on perfecting its equine form.

While living in Cambridge, Sedgwick discovered a vibrant, bohemian hub of intelligent and endlessly fasci-nating people, many of whom were students at Harvard. She began hanging around the famed Harvard Square bar, Casablanca, and quickly became a magnetic center for a close group of friends including Danny Fields, Tommy Godwin, Ed Hennessey, Ed Hood, Donald Lyons, Chuck Wein, and others. Even though she lived in Cambridge for only a short time, her friends quickly recognized her

Andy Warhol, *Edie Sedgwick*, ca. 1965

vulnerability and allure. Lyons remarked, "I knew Edie in Cambridge....She seemed to blossom in this setting, seemed to be happy for the first time. One got the impression of this wounded creature who was just opening up to life."[7] Within a year, Sedgwick wanted more, professing that she needed "to see what was really going on in the world."[8] Immediately following her twenty-first birthday, when she reached legal age to receive the benefits of her trust fund, she drove her Mercedes-Benz to New York City. Many of her friends had already trod the same path from Cambridge to New York, and more would follow. In January of 1965, Sedgwick met Andy Warhol at a party held in the New York penthouse apartment of advertising mogul and Hollywood producer Lester Persky. Warhol was captivated.

Persky, their host, described the meeting, "Although [Edie] was always surrounded by these somewhat manqué people, she herself always had a fantastic poise. And it was at my house, at this marble table, that I brought the two—Andy and Edie—together. Andy, as I recall, sucked in his breath and did the usual popeye thing and said, 'Oh, she's bee-you-ti-ful.'...He was *very* impressed."[9] Warhol quickly issued Sedgwick an invitation to visit the Factory. Chuck Wein, who was acting as Sedgwick's de facto manager when she first arrived in New York, described her beguiling presence at Persky's. "[Edie] was doing her dance there—a sort of balletlike rock 'n' roll. We'd had an idea of opening up an underwater discotheque where Edie'd dance her ballet to Bach played at rock 'n' roll tempo. So Andy invited us down to the Factory the next day."[10]

At the time, Sedgwick was studying jazz ballet, and her movements reflected an enchanting combination of freeform style and athleticism. Friends often described her deft incorporation of cartwheels and acrobatic spins into the self-choreographed dances she spontaneously performed at clubs and private parties. Warhol began filming her almost immediately. He would later place her onstage, incorporating her dancing into his multimedia performance artwork, *The Exploding Plastic Inevitable*, but it was in front of the camera that she shone most brightly. Warhol explained, "Edie was incredible on camera—just the way she moved. And she never stopped moving for a second—even when she was sleeping, her hands were wide awake....

The great stars are the ones who are doing something you can watch every second, even if it's just a movement inside their eye."[11]

Even though Sedgwick's presence at the Factory seemed pervasive, she was actually present for only about a year. But during that time, she graced some of Warhol's most memorable films and became an immortal icon of the Silver Factory years. In March 1965, within two months of their first meeting, she made her first appearance in a Warhol film. *Vinyl* was Warhol's and playwright Ronald Tavel's loose adaptation of Anthony Burgess's novel *A Clockwork Orange*. Filled with boys playacting S&M poses, the film stars Gerard Malanga as the tortured juvenile delinquent. Sedgwick drops into this milieu and steals the show. As Tavel himself put it, "When [Edie] showed up...[Warhol] asked her to sit right on the set. She said, 'What do I do?' [Warhol] said, 'Well, there's no part for you. So just sit there.' And she ended up stealing the film and becoming a star overnight."[12]

Poor Little Rich Girl, which came after other bit parts in *Bitch* and *Horse* (all 1965), is considered Sedgwick's first starring vehicle. It is also the first film in what was to be called *The Poor Little Rich Girl Saga*, Warhol's ultimately unrealized idea for a twenty-four-hour film of a day in Sedgwick's life. She starred in several other films that were made for this project, including *Restaurant*, *Face*, and *Afternoon*, all from 1965. Filmmaker and critic Jonas Mekas wrote about *Poor Little Rich Girl* at the time, claiming it surpassed everything cinema verité had done up until that point. "It is a piece that is beautiful, sad, unrehearsed, and says about the life of the rich girl today more than ten volumes of books can say. It was an old dream of Cesare Zavattini to make a film 2 hours long which would show 2 hours in the life of a woman, minute by minute....Miss Sedgwick happened to be the most suitable person for such a film, with the proper personality; with a rich, complex, and very open personality, able to relax in front of the camera and be free and not hide anything and reflect everything. It is not an easy part to play, it is not an easy film to make."[13]

In the spring of that year, Warhol teamed up with Tavel again to film *Kitchen*. The loose plot centers on an unhappy

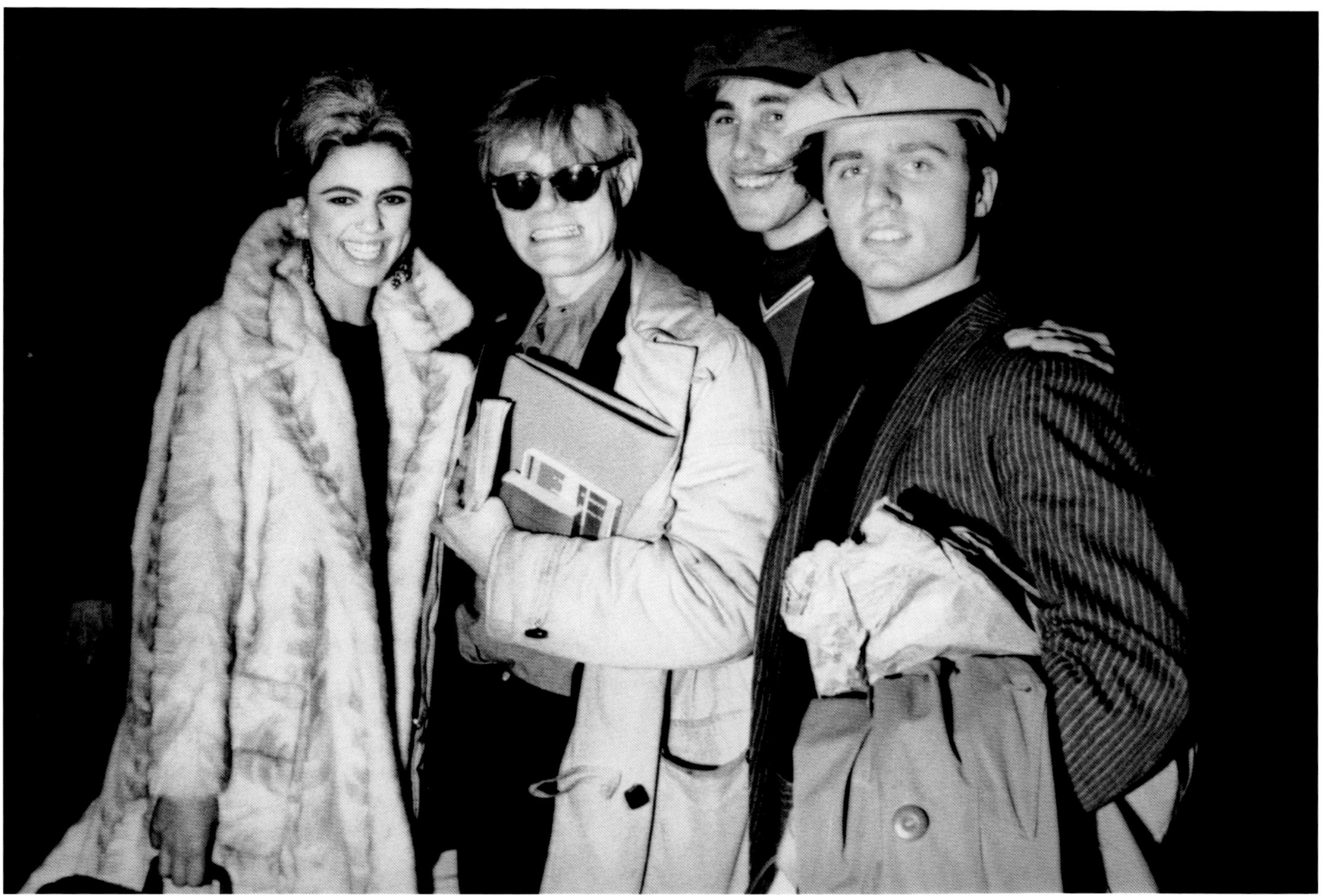

heterosexual couple (Roger Trudeau and Sedgwick) who keep getting interrupted by other characters, including the "houseboy," René Ricard. Sedgwick continually forgets her lines and sneezes throughout the film, her cue for receiving help with the script. In August, Sedgwick was involved with another memorable milestone in Warhol's multimedia career: starring in one of his first video productions. The Norelco Company had loaned the artist an early model of a portable consumer video system for him to try out and ultimately endorse. Sedgwick was one of his first subjects; he later screened the video portrait for her on a television monitor and filmed her watching it. In the resulting film, *Outer and Inner Space* (1965), we see Sedgwick seated in front of a television screen that features her own face; as the videotape plays, she interacts with the likeness. When the film is projected in double screen, often as many as four images of Sedgwick are on-screen at the same time.

As noted above, Sedgwick appeared in almost every film Warhol made in 1965—over twenty-five—including nine of his short, silent portrait films called *Screen Tests*; *Beauty #2*; and *Lupe*, in which she portrayed the death of Hollywood actress Lupe Velez. Outside of the Factory, Sedgwick accompanied Warhol to openings, exhibitions, clubs, private parties, discotheques, and media interviews. Weather permitting, she frequently topped her signature look with a fur coat. Sedgwick owned several, including one made of genuine leopard skin and another of snow-white mink. Recognizable everywhere, the casually worn fur coats signaled her idiosyncratic synthesis of old establishment money and new underground fame.

In May of 1965, Edie traveled with Warhol and a small entourage to Paris, London, Madrid, and Tangier. The trip began in Paris, where they attended the opening of Warhol's *Flowers* show at Galerie Ileana Sonnabend and roamed among the City of Lights' famed nightclubs and cafés. Warhol observed Sedgwick's captivating joie de vivre: "Edie had arrived in France wearing a white mink coat over her t-Shirt and tights and carrying one

David McCabe, *Edie Sedgwick, Andy Warhol, Chuck Wein, and Gerard Malanga*, 1965, reprinted 1996 little suitcase. When she 'unpacked' at the hotel, I saw that the only thing she'd brought with her was another white mink coat! She wore one of them to Castel's that night and when someone offered to check her coat, she clutched it around her and said, 'No! it's all I've got on!'…The French adored her—and she adored Paris; she'd lived there for a while when she was nineteen, studying art."[14]

Sedgwick projected a magnetism on camera and in person that few have articulated as perfectly as her friend Danny Fields. "You just fell in love with her. No matter what—if you were straight or gay or what. No matter, you just fell in love with her. She was so beautiful and so helpless and so rich and so 'bananas.'"[15] John Cale, the classically trained musician and cofounder of the experimental rock group the Velvet Underground, met Sedgwick at the Factory and fell for her, becoming one of her many brief romantic entanglements. "The affair lasted about six weeks, me living with her. Although desperate and on her last legs with Andy, she still possessed all the elemental magic, frayed beauty and presence of Marilyn Monroe…. She was really a beautiful creature to be around."[16]

Sedgwick left the Factory in 1966, convinced that Warhol was mistreating her. Already taking massive doses of drugs—amphetamines to get up each day and barbiturates to sleep—she now increased the volume and variety. The last five years of Sedgwick's life were largely spent in and out of hospitals in New York and California for psychiatric care and treatment for drug addiction, including extensive shock therapy, with only sporadic film work. The production of her last film, *Ciao! Manhattan*, began in 1967 but was not completed until 1972. Written and directed by John Palmer and David Weisman, it was by all accounts a nightmare. In 1967, while shooting *Ciao!*, her residence accidentally caught on fire a second time due to her carelessness with a cigarette. According to her roommate, she eventually burned her mattress five more times. That same year, she made one final film with Warhol, titled *Ondine and Edie*. Her costar, himself deeply addicted, spoke about her tragedy: "It's absolutely the most excruciating piece of footage you'll ever see in your life. It's a whole reel of the total collapse of a person…. Edie trying to be charming and delightful, smoking cigarette after cigarette, talking to me about things she thinks I'll enjoy, playing actors and actresses weirdly…and it just didn't work. It begins to get really painful because she is so obviously coming apart at the seams."[17]

In August 1967, she made a series of short films with British filmmaker Richard Leacock, commissioned for a Boston Opera production of Alban Berg's tragic *Lulu*. A few months later, Sedgwick's father died while she was confined to Gracie Square Hospital in New York. According to Sedgwick, she experienced a mad sequence of destructive drug-induced events, including falling into a coma. She spent the year in five different hospitals. Her mother had her released in late 1968 and took her home to California. Although Sedgwick and Warhol were now estranged, she contacted him in June of 1968 while he was in the hospital recovering from his gunshot wound (see "Q is for Quick"). Her handwritten note filled a greeting card with expressions of love, alarm, and tremendous care for Warhol.

Soon after returning to California, she was arrested for narcotics and sentenced to five years' probation. In August 1969, her psychiatrist recommended that she enter Cottage Hospital in Santa Barbara, where she continued to abuse drugs, and where she showed off a scrapbook of her old press clippings while complaining bitterly about Warhol to her doctors. She became involved with an outlaw motorcycle gang, the Vikings. She was back in Cottage Hospital from January 17 to June 4, 1971, for shock treatments, which appeared to help her, according to Michael Post, a twenty-year-old fellow patient. Sedgwick and Post fell in love and married on July 24, 1971, at her family's ranch.

Before the wedding, Sedgwick's participation in the filming of *Ciao! Manhattan* resumed with her doctor's permission in 1970. Sedgwick decided to have breast-augmentation surgery, which caused a dramatic discontinuity in her appearance. The film screenwriters attributed this to diet and exercise. French director Roger Vadim, who had an acting part in *Ciao!*, felt that she was being mistreated and promised her a role in his upcoming film, *Pretty Maids All in a Row*. The promised role never materialized. After the wedding, Sedgwick's life seems to have been somewhat happy, although she was still dependent on pills. Her last night, November 15, 1971, was spent attending a fashion show at the Santa Barbara Museum of Art, which was filmed for the PBS program *An American Family*. The next morning, her husband found her body in their bed; she had died of a barbiturate overdose.

Sedgwick's life and family are chronicled in *Edie: American Girl* (1982). The book, a mosaic-like assemblage of oral histories, narrates Sedgwick's story in first-person voices. Authored by Jean Stein and edited by George Plimpton, the book was an immediate success and drew attention from all parts of the globe for both its content and construction. Warhol responded to his depiction in the book by writing in his diary:

Tuesday, March 16, 1982
Paul Morrissey came down and he said that Jean Stein called him and read him something that René Ricard had said about him in her Edie *book, and he told her that if she printed it he'd sue her, and she said she was going to print it anyway.... I called her and said, "You know, Jean,... I hear that you put me down in your book." And she said, "Oh, well-well-well-I-I-it's tape recorded, it's taped interviews." And I said, "Oh, so then other people put me down." And she goes, "Well-I-I didn't-didn't really say that."*[18]

Tuesday, June 15, 1982
In the book [Edie] *is this photograph of this totally wrong birth certificate for me. I just don't understand it. For Andrew Warhola, and it's from a different city and it says October 29, 1930, I think. Where could they have gotten a thing like that? What is it?*[19]

Tuesday, September 21, 1982
I saw George Plimpton and his wife Freddy, and when she saw me she began running around me and acting just nuts. She felt guilty because George helped Jean Stein with the Edie *book.... And I told her, "Look, I don't know what you're carrying on about. I don't care about the stupid book."... And I could see Jon [Gould, Warhol's boyfriend at the time] talking to George and later he told me he told George how could he put those things in the book about me when he knew me personally and he knew they weren't true and that Edie was away from the Factory for years before she died.*[20]

NOTES

1. The phrase "Girl of the Year" was likely a moniker Warhol adopted from fan magazines.

2. "ME? A movie about *me*? Manny, it's a natural," *Esquire*, January 1966, 48.

3. In the August 1, 1965, issue of *Vogue* magazine, then edited by Diana Vreeland, "Youth Quakers, people are talking about…" (p. 112) christened Sedgwick one of the stars in the works and a "youthquaker." Others featured in the article included Bill Cosby, Zubin Mehta, Liza Minnelli, Larry Poons, Joan Rivers, and Frank Stella.

4. Jean Stein and George Plimpton, *Edie: American Girl* (New York: Grove Press, 1982), 302.

5. Lily Saarinen received her training at the Art Students League in New York City and the Cranbrook Academy of Art in Michigan, where she met her husband, architect and industrial designer Eero Saarinen.

6. Stein and Plimpton, *Edie*, 119.

7. Stephen Shore and Lynne Tillman, *The Velvet Years: Warhol's Factory, 1965–67* (New York: Thunder's Mouth Press, 1995), 126.

8. Melissa Painter and David Weisman, *Edie: Girl on Fire* (San Francisco: Chronicle Books, 2006), 35.

9. Stein and Plimpton, *Edie*, 180.

10. Ibid., 179.

11. Andy Warhol and Pat Hackett, *POPism: The Warhol Sixties* (Orlando, FL: Harcourt Brace Jovanovich, 1980), 137.

12. Ronald Tavel, interviewed by Patrick Smith, in *Warhol: Conversations about the Artist* (Ann Arbor, MI: UMI Research Press, 1988), 312.

13. Jonas Mekas, "Movie Journal," *Village Voice* (New York), April 29, 1965, 13.

14. Warhol and Hackett, *POPism*, 141–42.

15. Smith, *Warhol: Conversations about the Artist*, 286.

16. John Cale and Victor Bockris, *What's Welsh for Zen: The Autobiography of John Cale* (New York: Bloomsbury, 2000), 85.

17. Stein and Plimpton, *Edie*, 347.

18. Andy Warhol and Pat Hackett, eds., *The Andy Warhol Diaries* (New York: Hachette Book Group, 1989), 442.

19. Ibid., 456.

20. Ibid., 471.

Additional research for this chapter was provided by Signe Warner Watson.

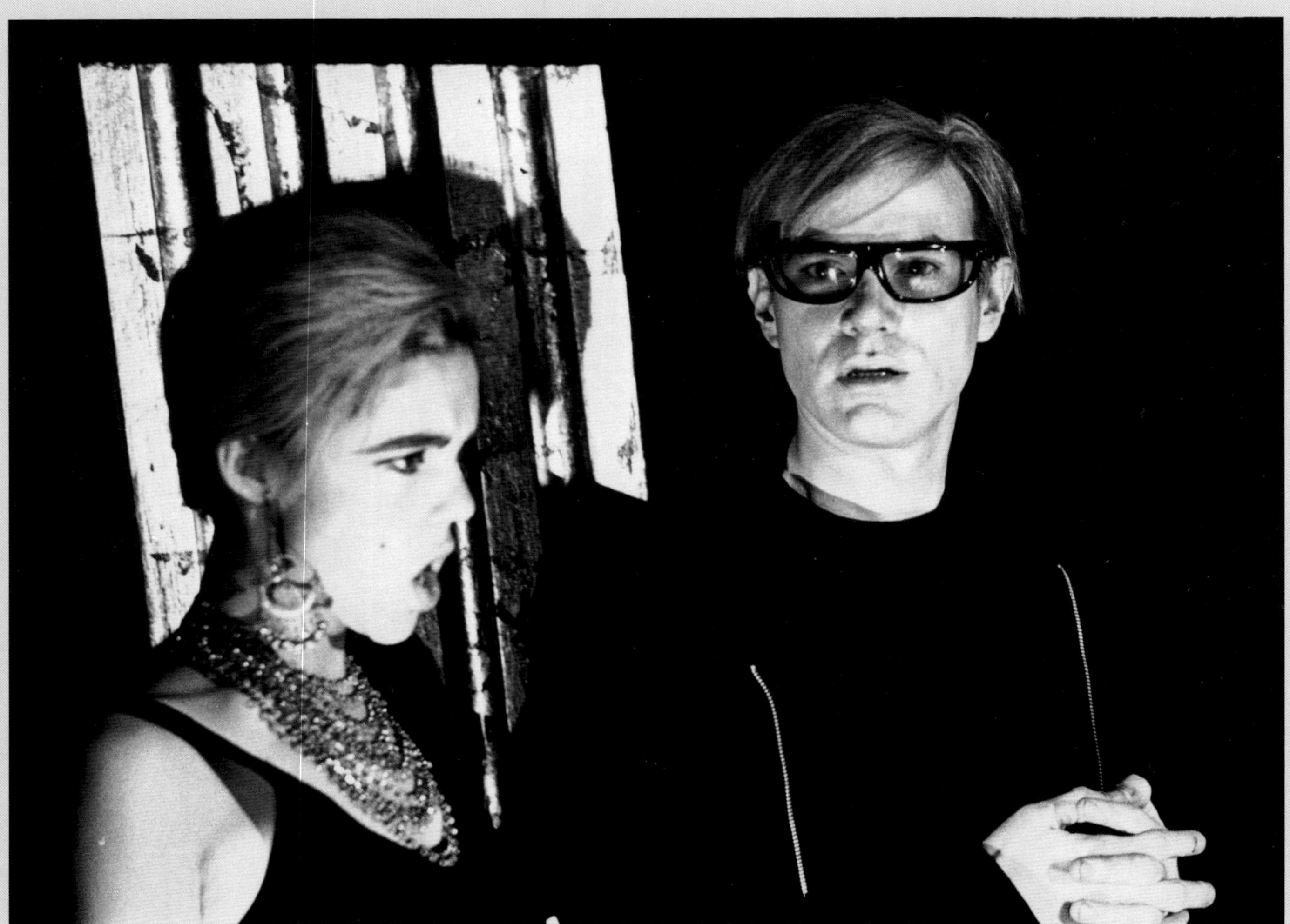

Stephen Shore, *Edie Sedgwick and Andy Warhol*, ca. 1965

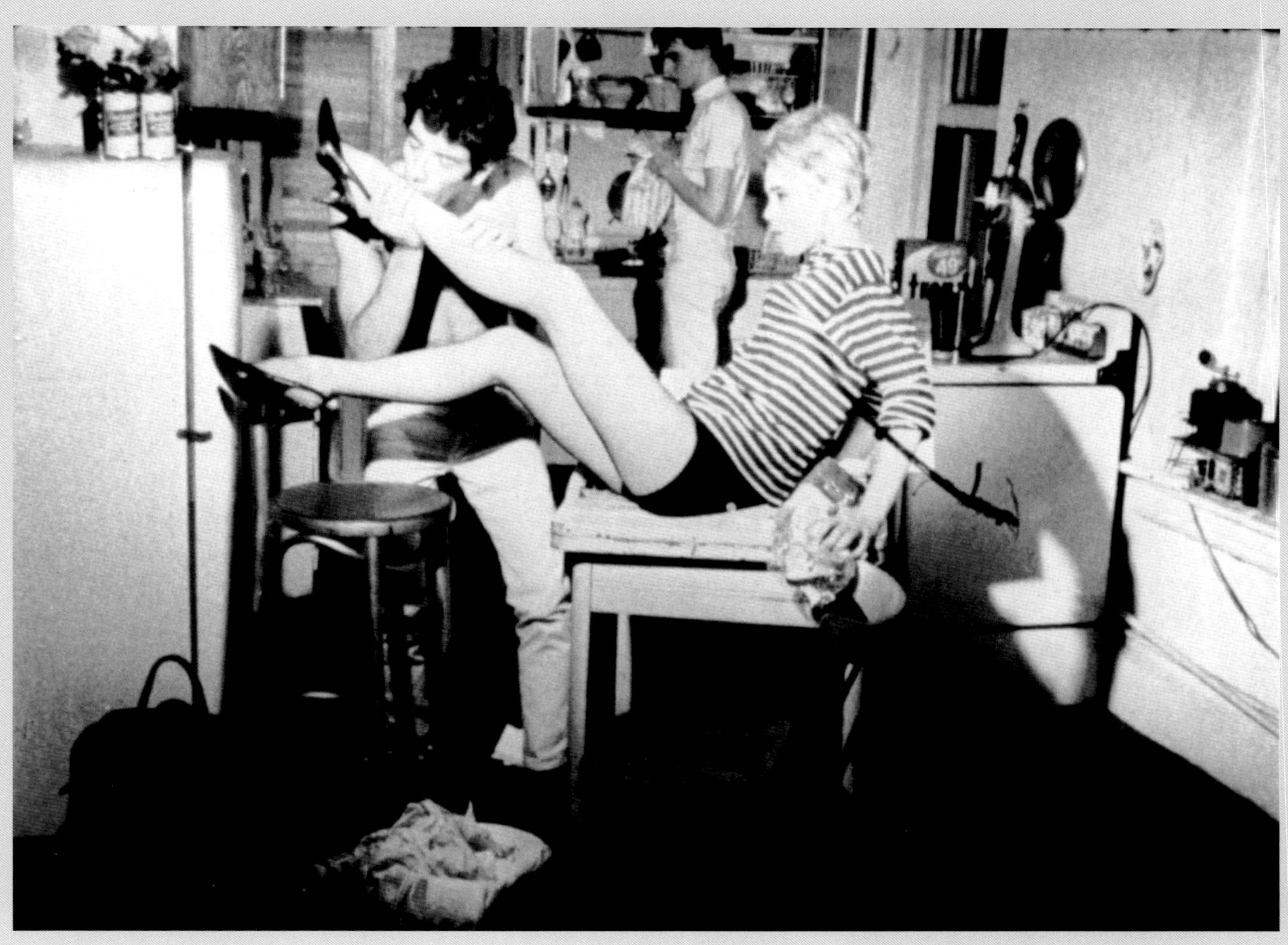

Andy Warhol, film still from *Kitchen*, with Edie Sedgwick, Roger Trudeau,
and René Ricard, 1965

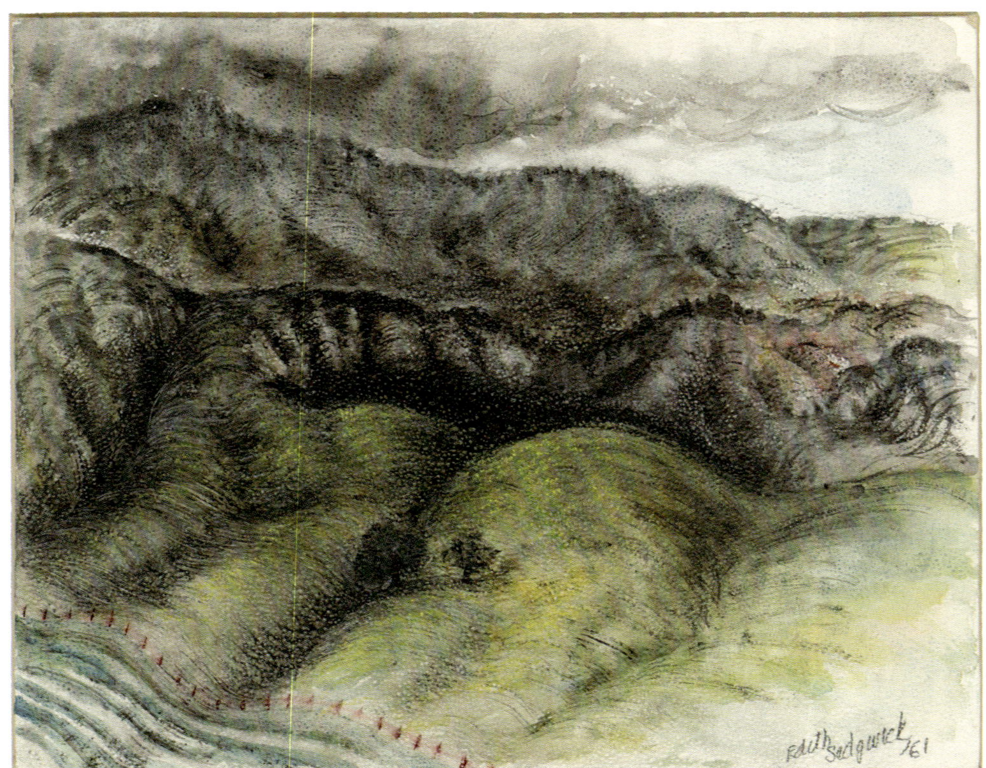

Edie Sedgwick, *Mice*, 1963

Edie Sedgwick, *Landscape*, 1961

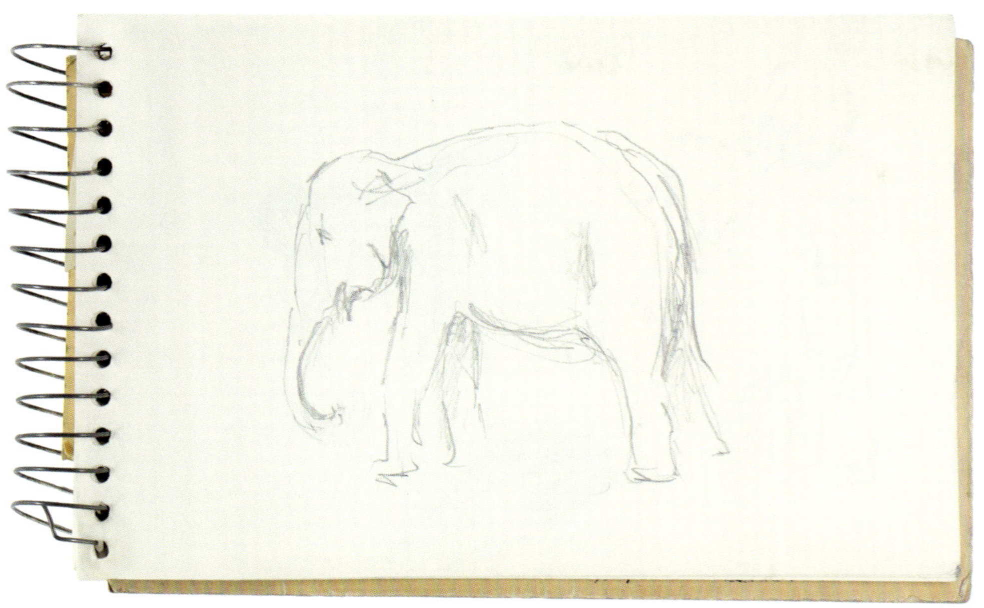

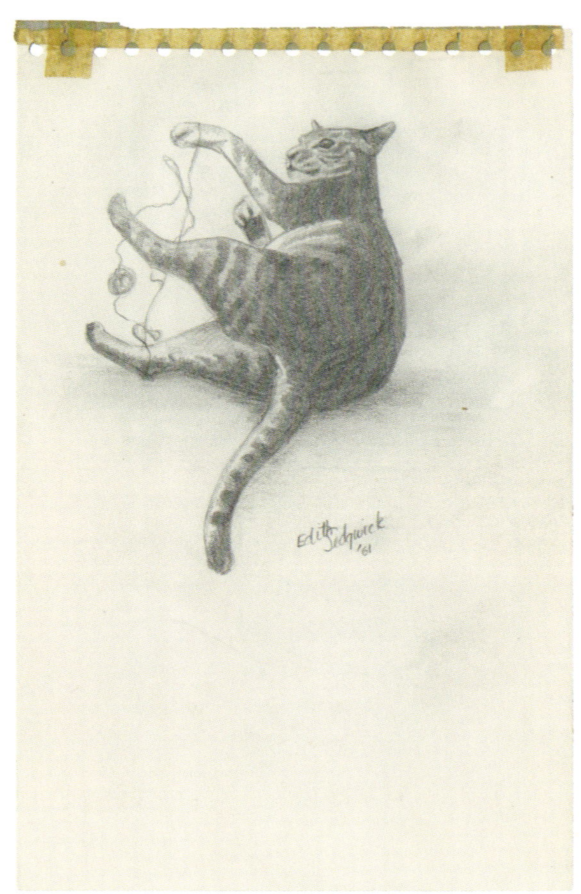

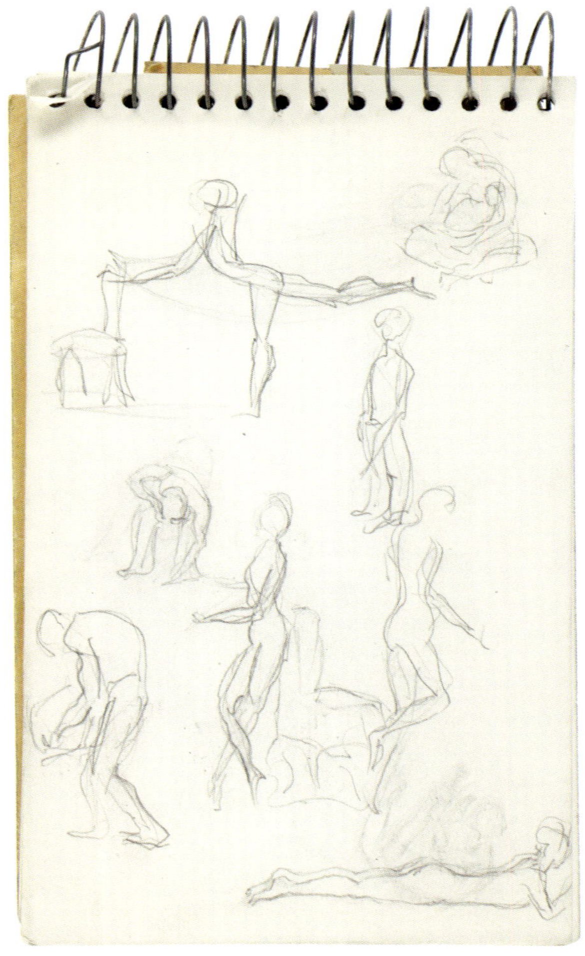

Two pages from Edie Sedgwick's sketchbook containing graphite
drawings of animals, people, still lives, and interiors, 1963

Edie Sedgwick, *Cat with Yarn*, 1961

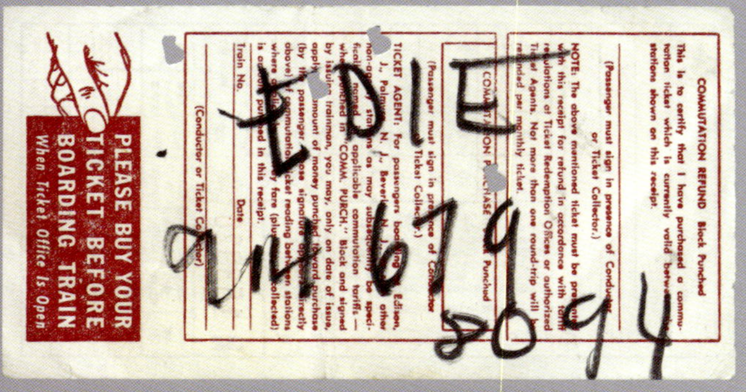

June 4th, 1968

Darling Andy,
I was horribly upset to hear how you were severely injured. I am *With All Good Wishes* saying prayers for you --- don't know how much good they do, but at least you will know I care, and care tremendously.

You are one of the few people who really matter to me, and I can't bear the thought of anything bad happening to you. I hope this letter finds you well on the way to recovery and with it I send you *all* my love.

Bundles of hugs and kisses,
♡
Edie ☺

EDITH M. SEDGWICK
722 WEST 168TH St.
NEW YORK
NEW YORK 10032

John Beatrix Potter's original illustration for
The Tale of Two Bad Mice
© FREDERICK WARNE & CO LTD, LONDON & NEW YORK

Pennsylvania Railroad ticket with "Edie 914 679 8094" written by Warhol, ca. 1965

Mental Hygiene Reeducation: Talks to Patients, ca. 1962. Sedgwick designed the leather cover as a therapeutic project for patients while at Silver Hill. The book contains pamphlets bound together.

Get-well card from Edie Sedgwick to Warhol, posted June 4, 1968

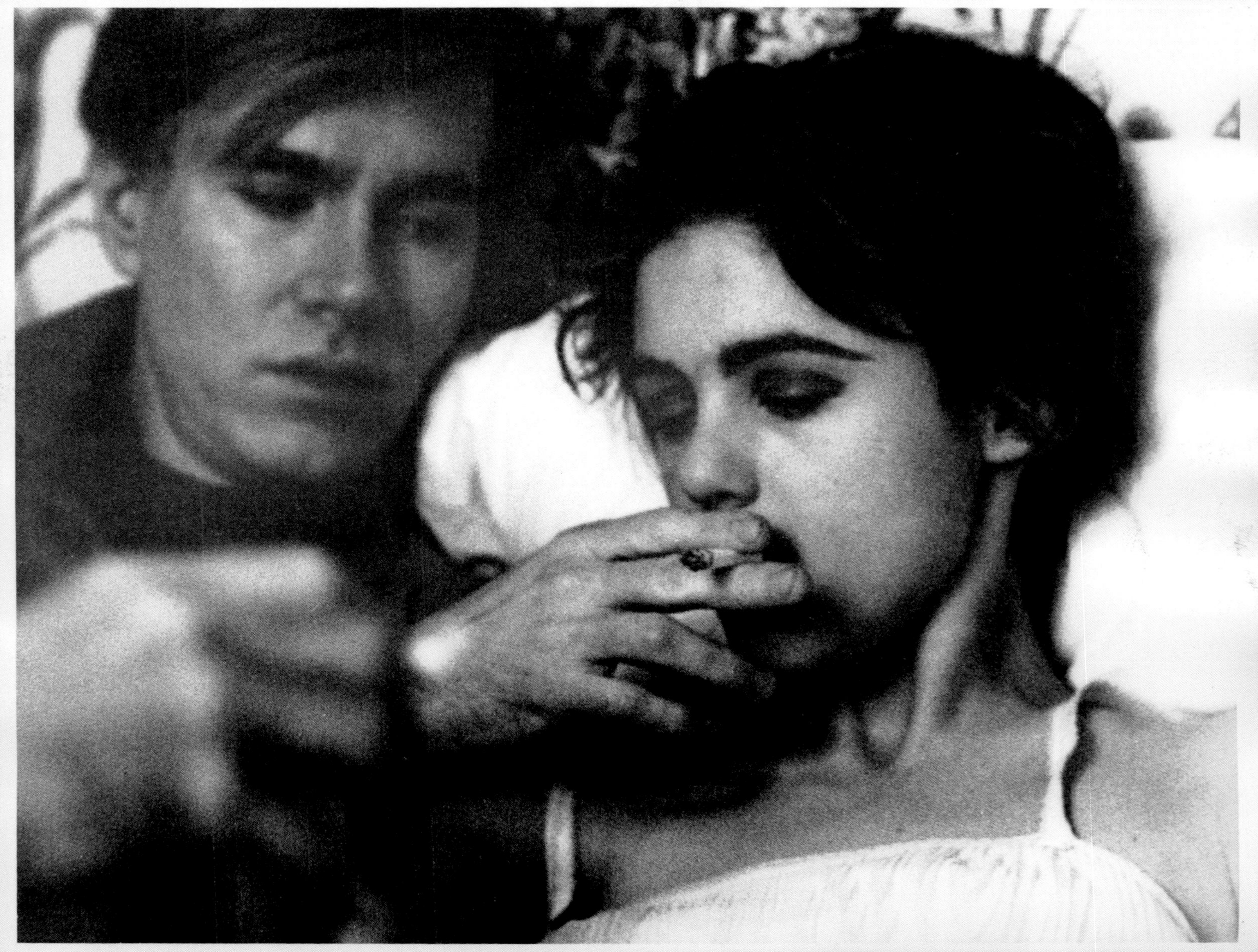

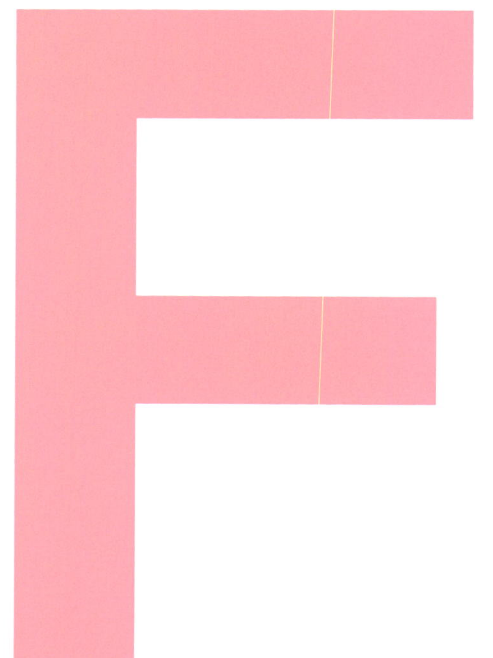

is for FASHION

Jordan Crandall: What is your favorite thing to wear?
AW: I just wear the same thing every day.
JC: Are you an impulsive shopper?
AW: Yes.
JC: Clothing?
AW: I buy anything. But I can't wear anything. I just put it in the closet. I wear Stephen Sprouse black pants, black T-shirt, black turtleneck, black shirt, black leather jacket and Adidas shoes.[1]

In one of his last interviews, with the young journalist Jordan Crandall, Andy Warhol alludes to the bulk and boundaries of his wardrobe. The artist was friends with many fashion designers, including Diane von Furstenberg, Halston, Betsey Johnson, Calvin Klein, Karl Lagerfeld, Tiger Morse, Yves Saint Laurent (see "Y is for Yves"), and Stephen Sprouse. He admired and collected exceptional designer clothing and jewelry. His personal fashion proclivities, however, favored a uniform. His typical daily garb was tweaked in order to follow trends, with more dramatic changes decade by decade.

For much of the 1950s, Warhol presented a relatively conservative look by today's standards, in button-down

This chapter was created from permanent collection displays of Warhol's personal clothing over the past twenty years as part of the Archival Collection.

shirts and khaki trousers. Yet, he was noticed by art directors for the paradox he presented. To some he appeared as "Raggedy Andy," a sorry young man in scruffy khakis and badly worn shoes. Others who knew him just as well saw a young man flaunting his commercial success in Brooks Brothers shirts and the latest three-button suits. He was accessible in garb, yet quirky—he pulled beautiful drawings out for review not from a briefcase or portfolio but from a paper bag, implying some lack of grandeur and sophistication, but revealing the sublime. His growing success allowed him to supplement his more pedestrian white shirts, narrow neckties, and penny loafers with hand-tailored suits. In 1956, during his trip around the world, Warhol was fitted for a cashmere suit in Hong Kong. As with much of his clothing, he later gave it to his family members in Pittsburgh for their use.[2]

In the early 1960s, Warhol pushed himself and shifted his focus to create ambitious fine art in the new style known as Pop Art. His work of the time is arguably the most creative and inventive of his career. He combined his past experience with new professional and social connections and new media. His audacious work was based on modern life, from bland soup cans to images of ghastly tragedies, to close-up depictions of intimate daily events such as eating, kissing, and sleeping, to the full sensory assault that was his music/film/light show called *The Exploding Plastic Inevitable*. Warhol transformed his costume accordingly with this shift from commercial art to fine art and underground film.

In 1965 Warhol attended the opening of his show of *Flowers* paintings at Galerie Ileana Sonnabend in Paris, where he announced to the press that he was retiring from painting to devote himself to making movies. He bought a Breton striped shirt, probably while in France; the design is a common French sailor's shirt that dates to 1858. It's similar to the shirt Picasso wears in photos that were widely seen in the early 1950s. Usurping Picasso's brand, the shirt briefly became the Factory's virtual uniform in 1965–66, with Sedgwick, John Cale, and others photographed wearing the deep navy-blue stripes. Warhol paired this look with finely crafted Cuban-heeled Beatle boots, made in Italy, and either black cotton or colorful suede jeans. He also

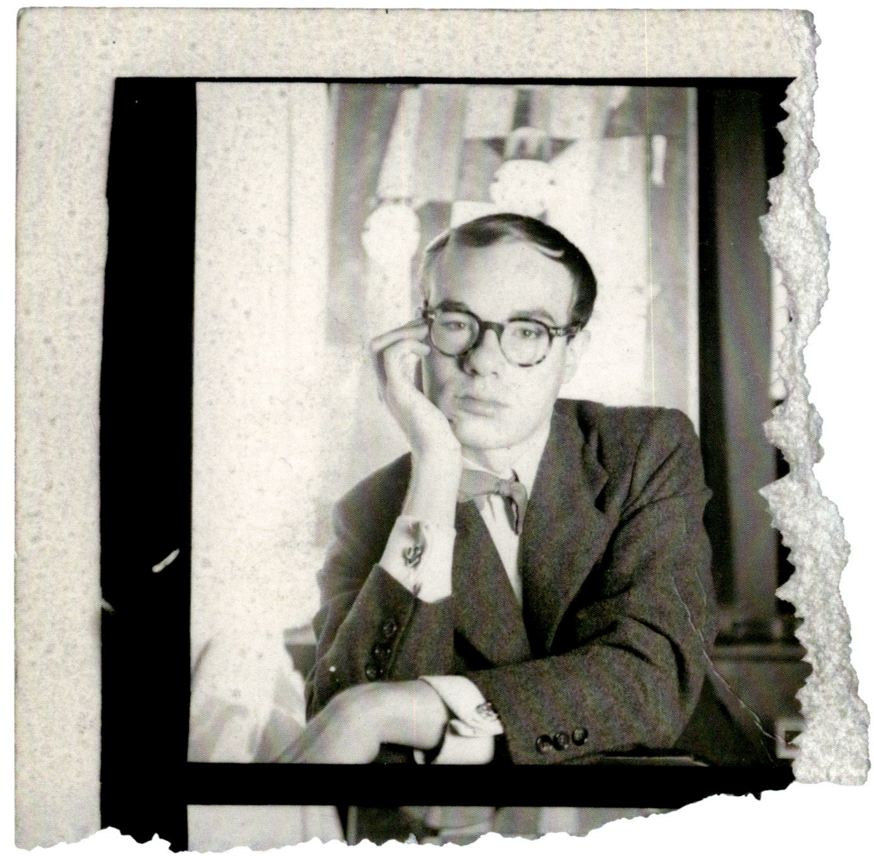

wore lightweight dancer's tights and a leather motorcycle jacket in cold weather. When his daily schedule was particularly busy, Warhol layered formal and informal clothes, such as black tuxedo trousers over jeans. He also mixed fashions, attending formal events in a tuxedo jacket, white shirt, and tie paired with comfortable denim jeans and cowboy boots.

Warhol returned to wearing coats and ties in the 1970s, deftly mixing quietly patterned sport coats and loud plaid neckties with the decorative stitching of cowboy boots and plain blue-denim jeans. Yves Saint Laurent's safari jackets were fashionable, and Warhol owned many of them. After he was shot in the abdomen in 1968, he began to wear corsets to help support his internal organs; they were dyed in a variety of pastel colors. In the 1980s, basic black was the rage. Warhol's look included a black turtleneck paired with

Melton-Pippin, *Andy Warhol*, ca. 1953

jeans and white sneakers, with a small backpack. In winter, he added insulated trousers, a cashmere scarf, leather boots, and a hooded leather jacket—all in black.

Cowboy Boots

Warhol was a foot fetishist who had a special fondness for cowboy boots. He owned more than fifteen pairs, some of which were gifts—but most he seems to have purchased for himself. The boots are in a wide range of materials, and some look unused, whereas others are well worn or bear paint drippings. One of his favorite brands was Lucchese, but Warhol seemed happy to wear the work of many other makers as well.

His boot buying started around the time when he was in Arizona shooting *Lonesome Cowboys* (1968). This film was his take on the Hollywood Western, which Warhol knew well from obsessive movie watching in his youth; the scrapbook of movie-star photos he assembled as a child includes a full-page image of Gene Autry, known as "The Singing Cowboy." Fred Hughes, a native Texan who joined Warhol's staff in 1967, also influenced the artist's love of boots. (Hughes, who was well versed in the legends and imagery of America's Old West, eventually rose to a high position within Andy Warhol Enterprises and was named the executor of Warhol's estate.)

On the advice of his friends John and Kimiko Powers, Warhol bought ranch land in Colorado in about 1976 and registered a cattle brand based on his initials, "A\W" (the W was set sideways). He never used the land as a working ranch (preferring to keep it naturally beautiful), but he created a large series of artworks based on themes of the Old West, titled *Cowboys and Indians*, in 1986.

Wigs

Warhol began wearing a wig in the mid-1950s. Initially a subtle hairpiece, it later became an essential aspect of his look: reportedly painted silver in the 1960s, more natural in the 1970s, and less so in the 1980s. Perhaps more than any other accessory, his wig was a protective shield covering up a vulnerability. This is supported by Warhol's own

acknowledgment in his *Diaries* on October 30, 1985, when he recalls, "Okay, let's get it over with. Wednesday. The day my biggest nightmare came true."[3] Warhol was at a book signing for *America* (1985) at Rizzoli Bookstore in SoHo when midway through the afternoon a woman pulled off his wig and threw it over the balcony to a man below, who then ran out of the store with it. Aghast, shaken, and mortified, Warhol pulled his coat hood over his head and kept signing. His account goes on to describe how it hurt, physically and mentally, and was "like getting shot again" (see "Q is for Quick"). After relaying the information to Pat Hackett, Warhol never wanted to revisit the episode.

Warhol didn't wear a cap under his wigs, just wig tape to keep them in place. From the quantity and condition of the seventy-nine wigs catalogued in the Archive, it is safe to conclude that he wore a wig extensively and then, instead of having it cleaned, replaced it with a new one. Some were stored in actual wig boxes, others were stuffed into manila envelopes. The latter are often matted together, and the mashed hairs now stay at very odd angles. Some wigs are in good condition, but most are not, given the poor storage they received when put into retirement. Nearly all the wigs were manufactured by Paul Bochicchio Inc. in New York. The labels sewn on the underside are inscribed, "An Original Hairpiece by Paul—147 W. 42 St., NY." They are made up of natural and synthetic hair, dyed either blond or silvery gray with a dark-brown patch at the back.

The wig contributed immensely to Warhol's distinctive look, making him instantly recognizable. In the mid-1980s, he considered creating an edition of about forty framed wigs as a work of art but abandoned the idea after completing only two of them. Around the same time, a few of Warhol's wigs were given a punk-style trim by artist Jean-Michel Basquiat.

Corsets

Following Warhol's shooting in 1968, the surgical reconstruction of his internal organs necessitated the artist's wearing a corset to hold his midsection in proper alignment. The Archive contains fifty of these corsets in white and twenty-six in various Easter-egg colors, hand-dyed

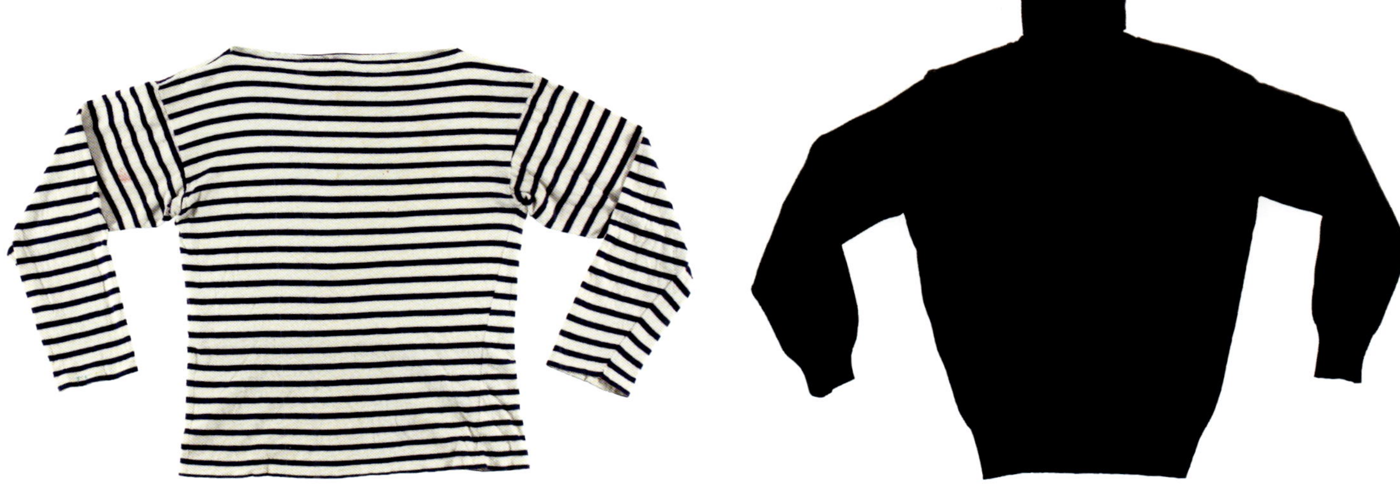

by Warhol's close friend Brigid Berlin (Brigid Polk). Warhol wore an extra small; when cinched around his waist, the circumference was less than twenty-six inches.

Leather Jackets

In 1966 Warhol started to wear a black leather motorcycle jacket, with many zippers and metal snaps. It gave him the look of a street tough, corresponding to the image of the Velvet Underground, the rock and roll band he had recently taken under his wing as "producer" (in the movie-studio sense of the term: provider of financial support and promotion).

Two years later, Warhol changed to a far more genteel jacket: cut like a sport coat lacking lapels, primarily light brown with red details at the collar and breast pocket. Warhol wore cloth jackets throughout the 1970s and returned to leather in the 1980s. He acquired several jackets that were hand-painted by Stefano Castronovo. One of these is silver leather and bears a portrait of Warhol on the back and 1960s-style Pop imagery on the sleeves. Another is white leather with a portrait of Basquiat on the back and a depiction of his work on the front; Warhol wore this jacket to the opening of the exhibition of Basquiat/Warhol collaboration paintings in 1985. Other jackets in this series that were owned by Warhol include several bearing images of saints and major events in Catholicism.

Also at this time, Warhol acquired a black leather hooded jacket designed by Calvin Klein. He wore it with

great frequency, including to the exhibition for his *Last Supper* paintings (1986), shown in Milan in February 1987. At the party, Warhol informally layered the jacket over a blue hoodie for the softball team of the Ford Modeling Agency, which was then representing the artist. Photographs taken during Warhol's final public appearance feature the artist again wearing the jacket, performing as a runway model in a fashion show at the nightclub the Tunnel. Years afterward, when the jacket entered the collection of The Andy Warhol Museum, staff discovered a taxi receipt in the breast pocket. Dated February 19, 1987, at 4:48 in the afternoon, it records one of Warhol's last cab rides.

NOTES

1. Jordan Crandall, "Andy Warhol," *Splash*, no. 6 (1986), reprinted in *I'll Be Your Mirror: The Selected Andy Warhol Interviews*, ed. Kenneth Goldsmith (New York: Carroll & Graf, 2004), 352.

2. Warhol gave a dark cloth coat to his older brother, John (now in the collection of John's son Donald Warhola), that is unremarkable at first glance, but inside it is lined with a bright-magenta fabric. This distinctive color matches both the exhibition announcements for the *Wild Raspberries* exhibition in 1959 and the self-published book of the same name. The coat has a tailor's label with Warhol's name and a date of 1958, which might suggest that this coat was meant to be worn by Warhol at the opening of *Wild Raspberries*. If so, it would be an early example of his take on the life-as-art idea, a prelude to his wearing a jacket painted with Jean-Michel Basquiat's portrait to the opening of the exhibition of their collaboration paintings in 1985.

3. Andy Warhol and Pat Hackett, eds., *The Andy Warhol Diaries* (New York: Hachette Book Group, 1989), 700.

Additional research for this chapter was provided by Erin Byrne, Matt Gray, and Brianna Treleven. Photographic layouts designed by Becky Shock, Brianna Treleven, and Kristin Britanik.

Warhol's striped, sailor-style shirt, 1965

Halston cashmere and silk turtleneck worn by Warhol, 1985

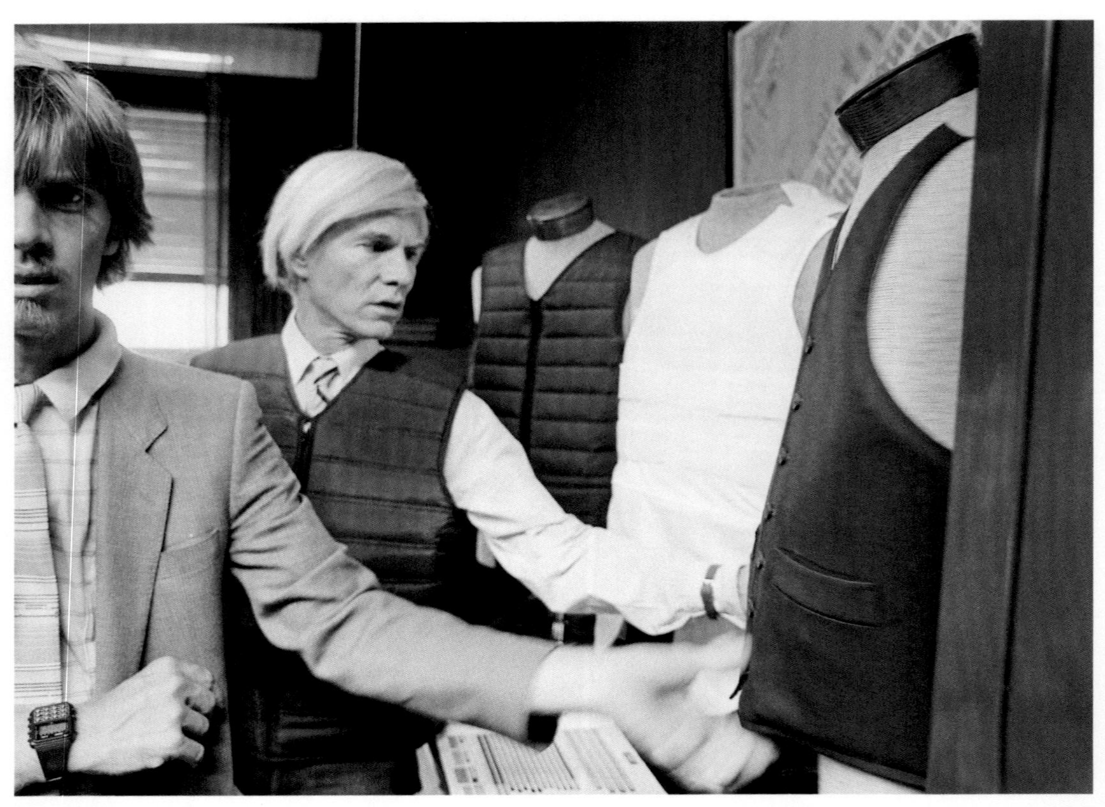

Robert J. Levin, *Andy Warhol Choosing a Bulletproof Vest, New York City*, 1981

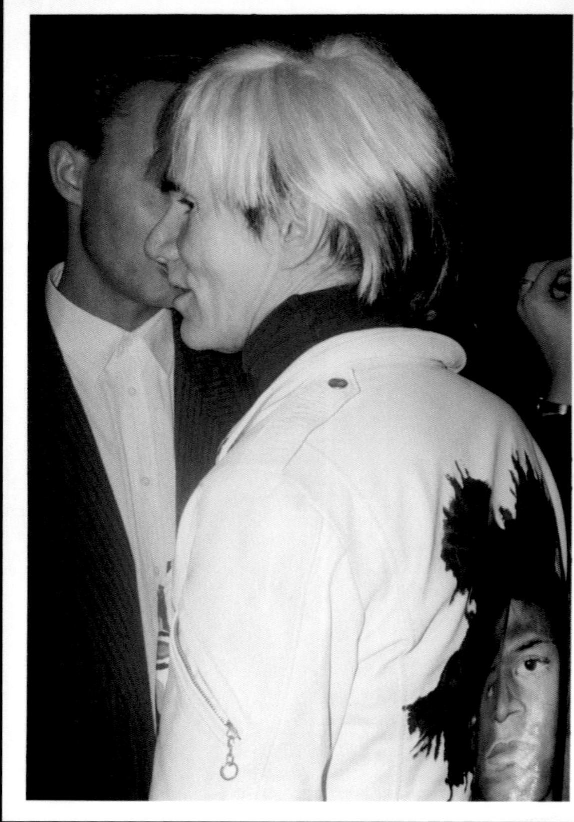

Patrick McMullan, *Andy Warhol at the Palladium Saturday, September 14, 1985*, 1985 (Patrick McMullan/Getty Images)

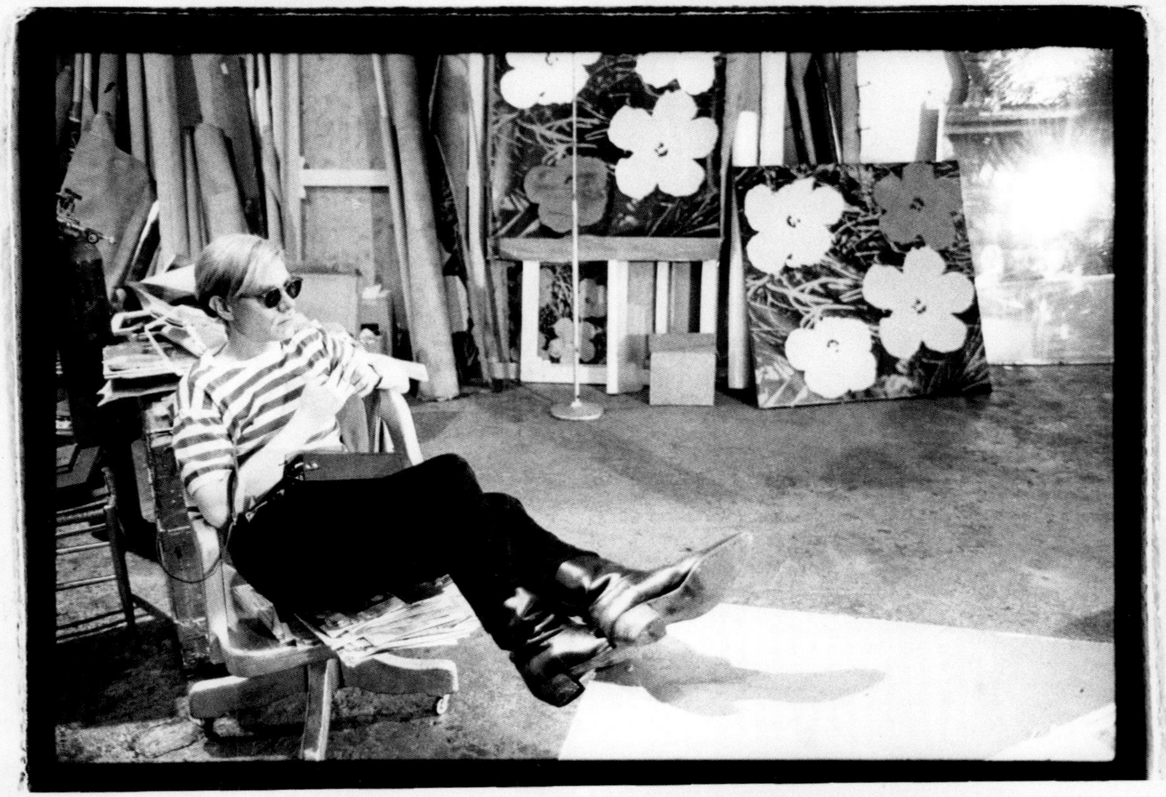

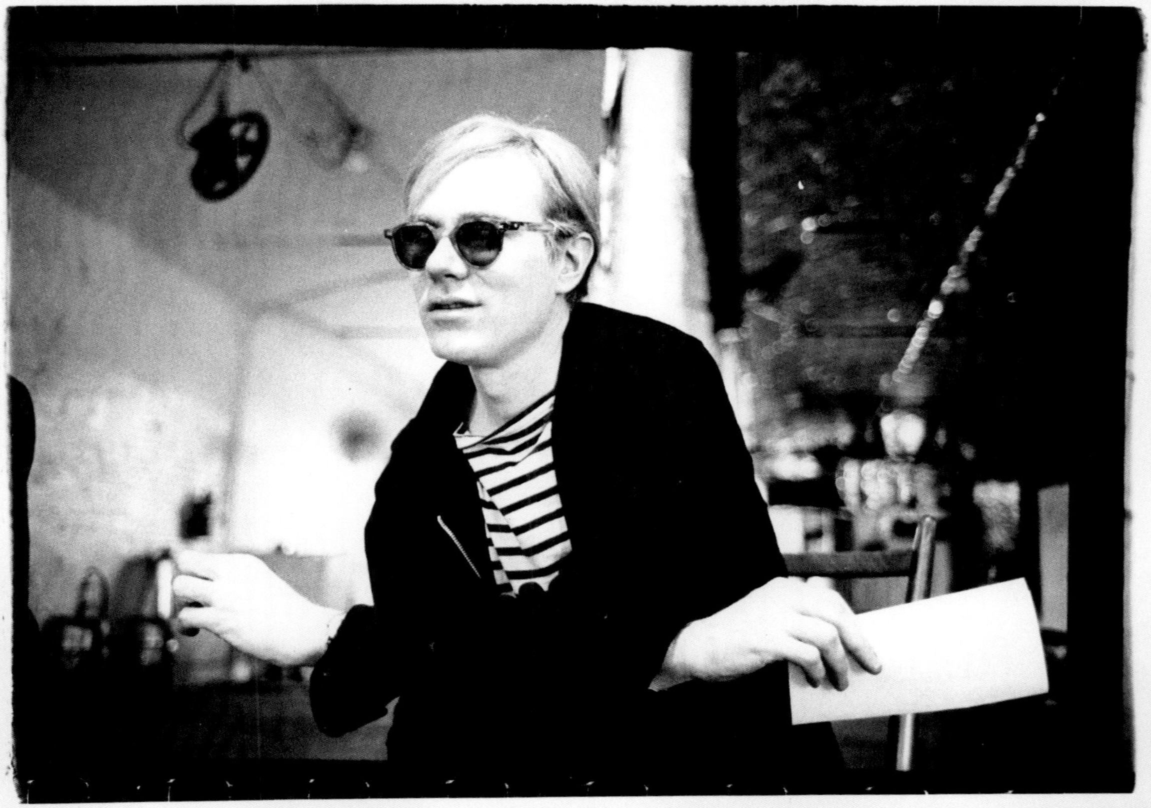

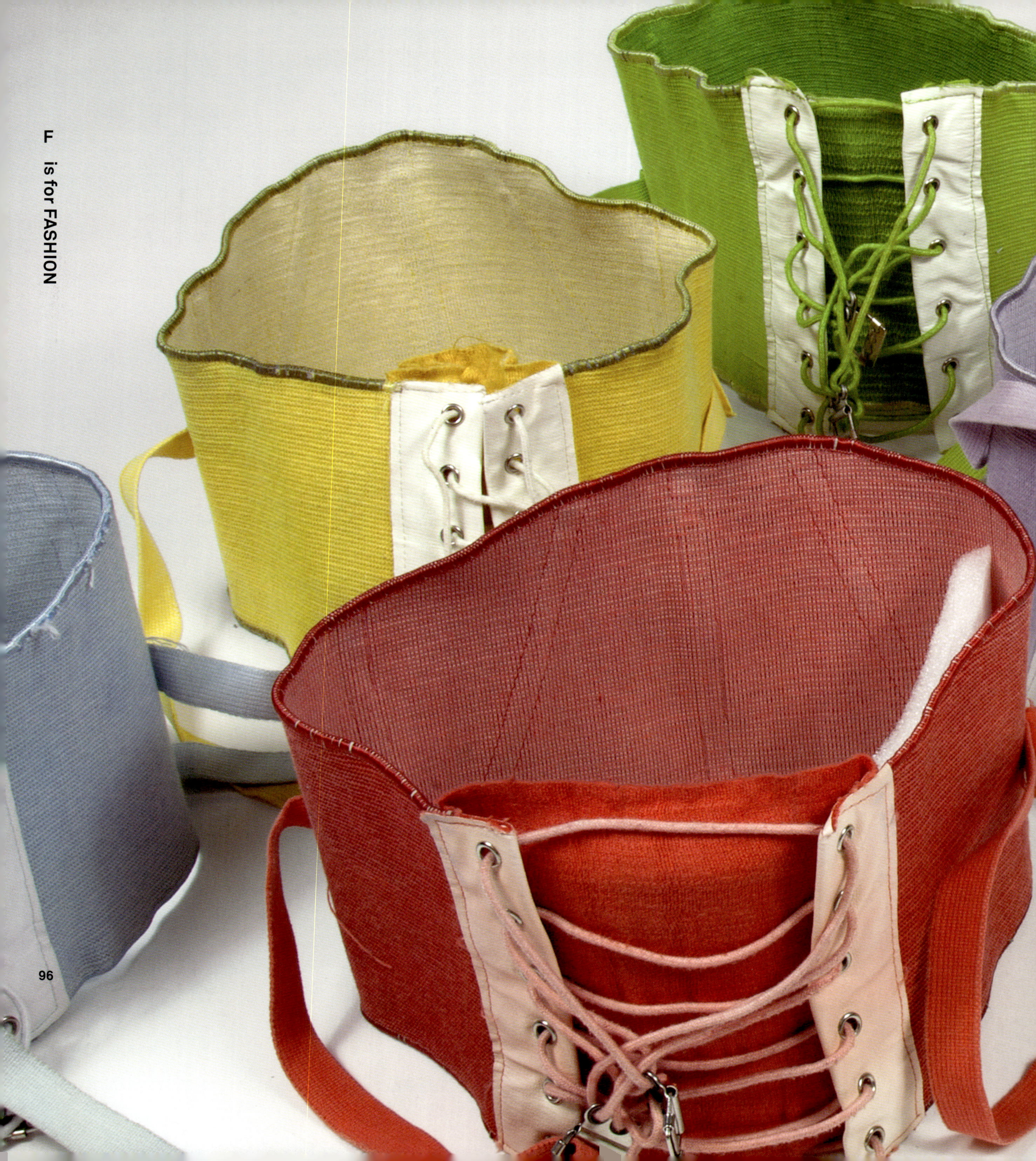
F   is for FASHION

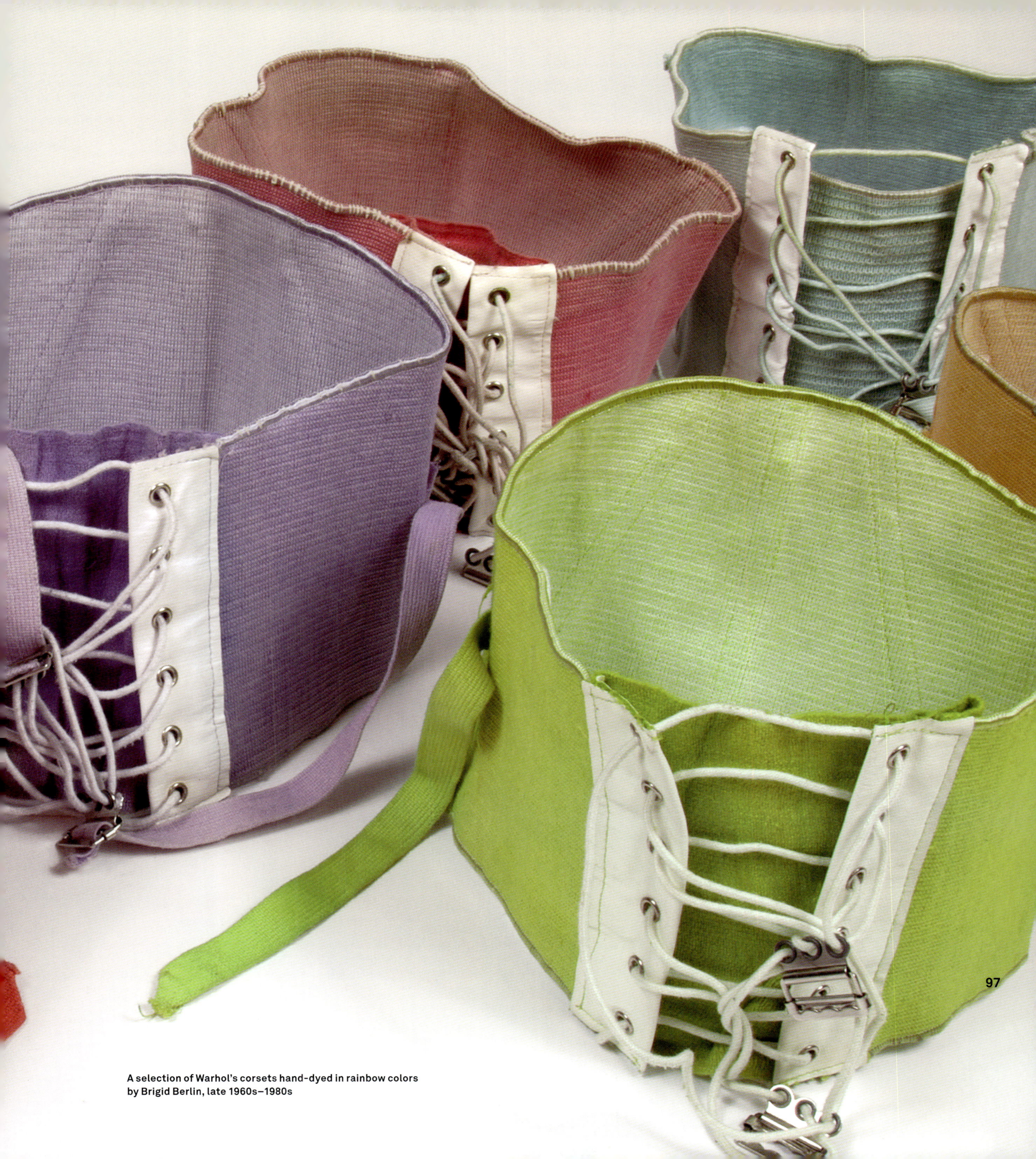

A selection of Warhol's corsets hand-dyed in rainbow colors
by Brigid Berlin, late 1960s–1980s

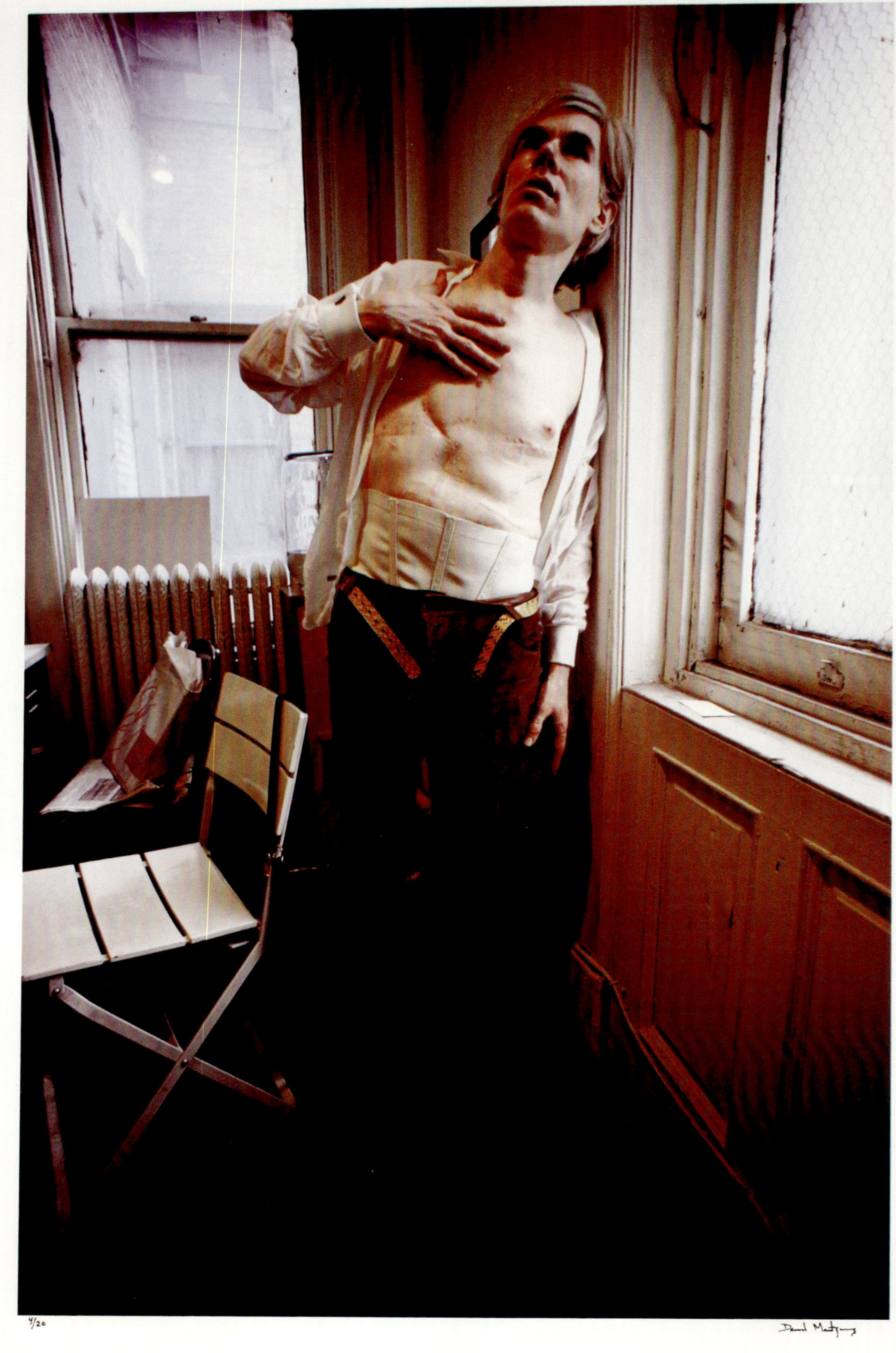

David Montgomery, *Andy in Repose*, June 1969, reprinted 2005

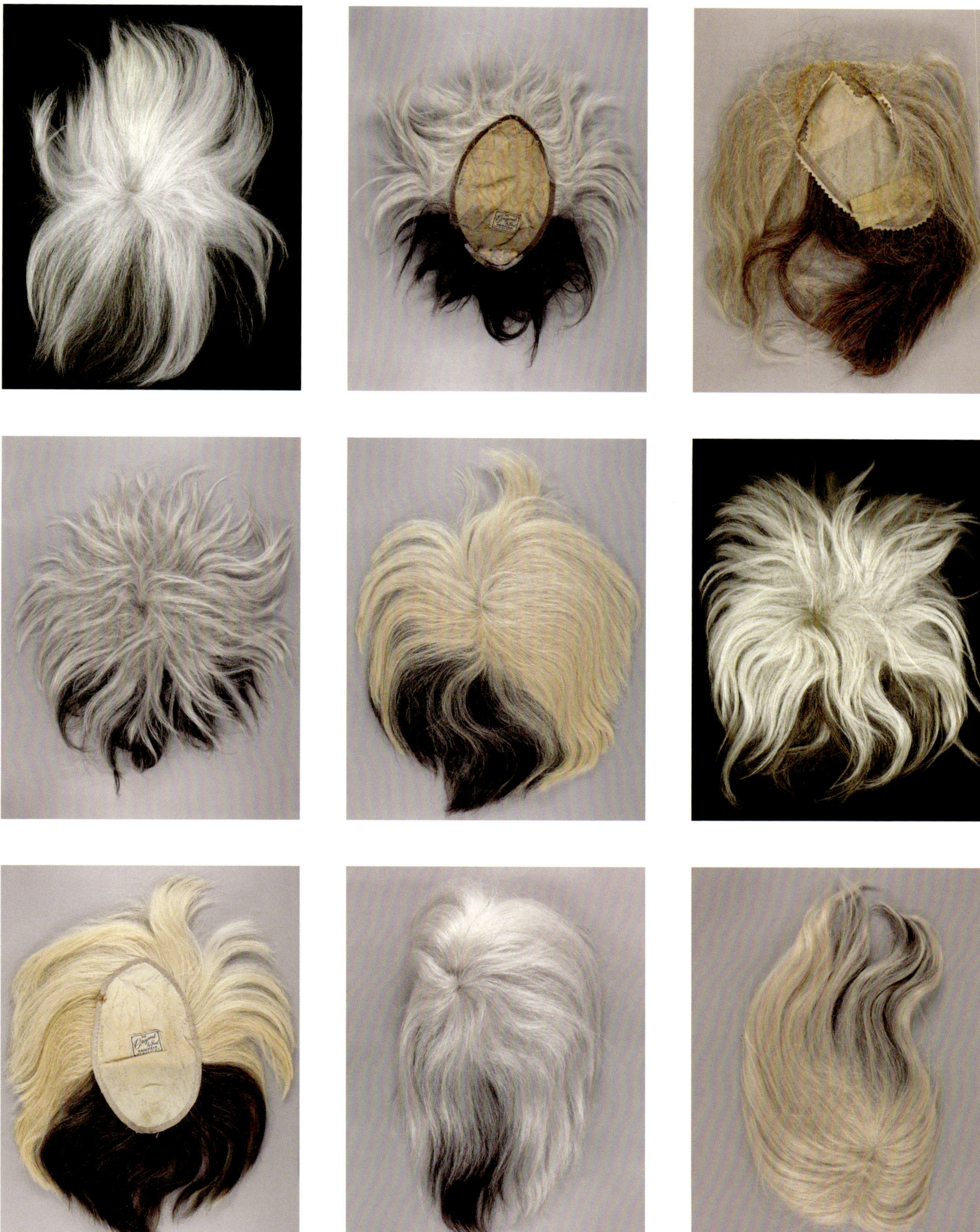

Wigs worn by Warhol manufactured by Paul Bochicchio Inc., 1980s

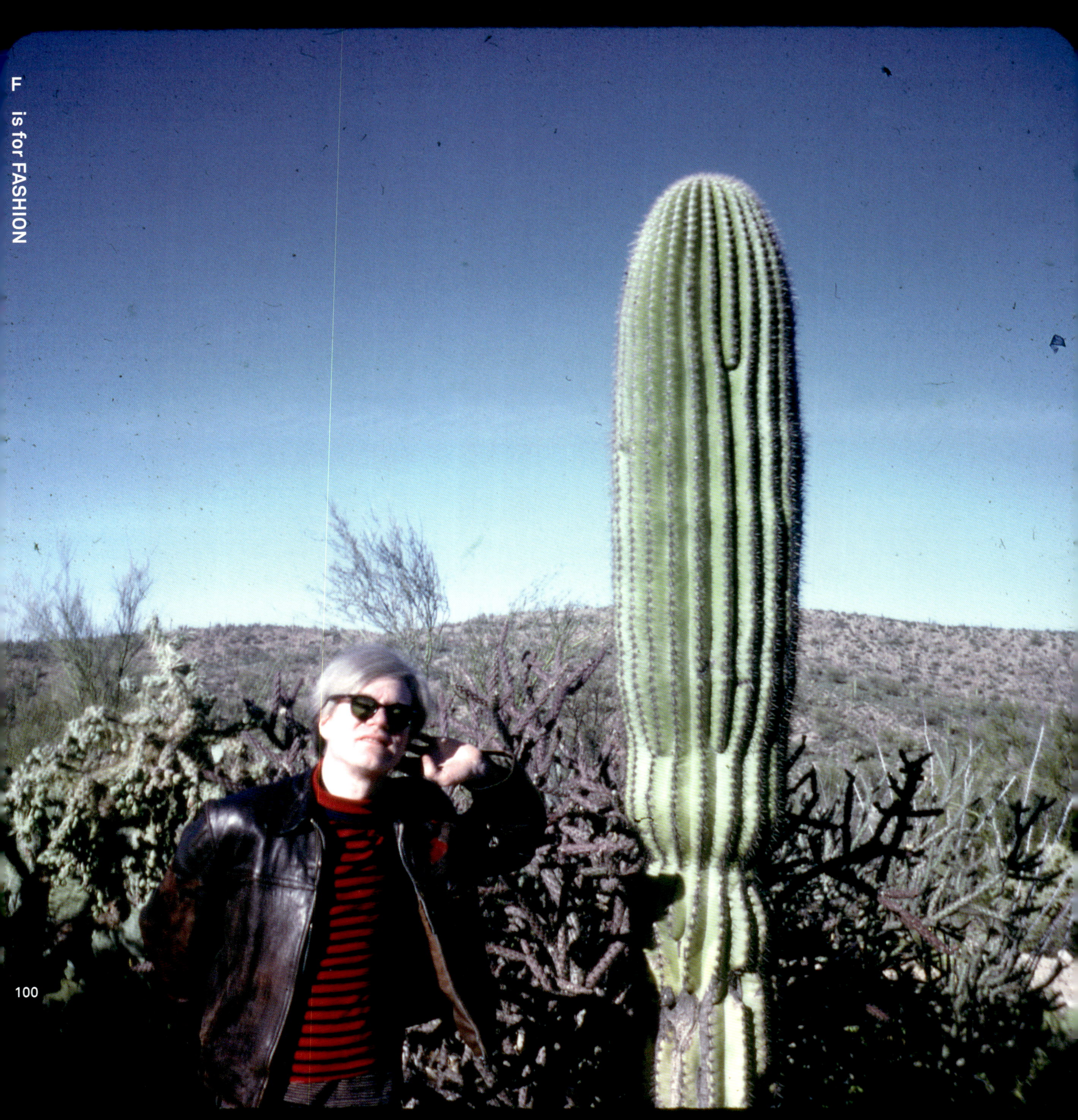
F
is for FASHION
100

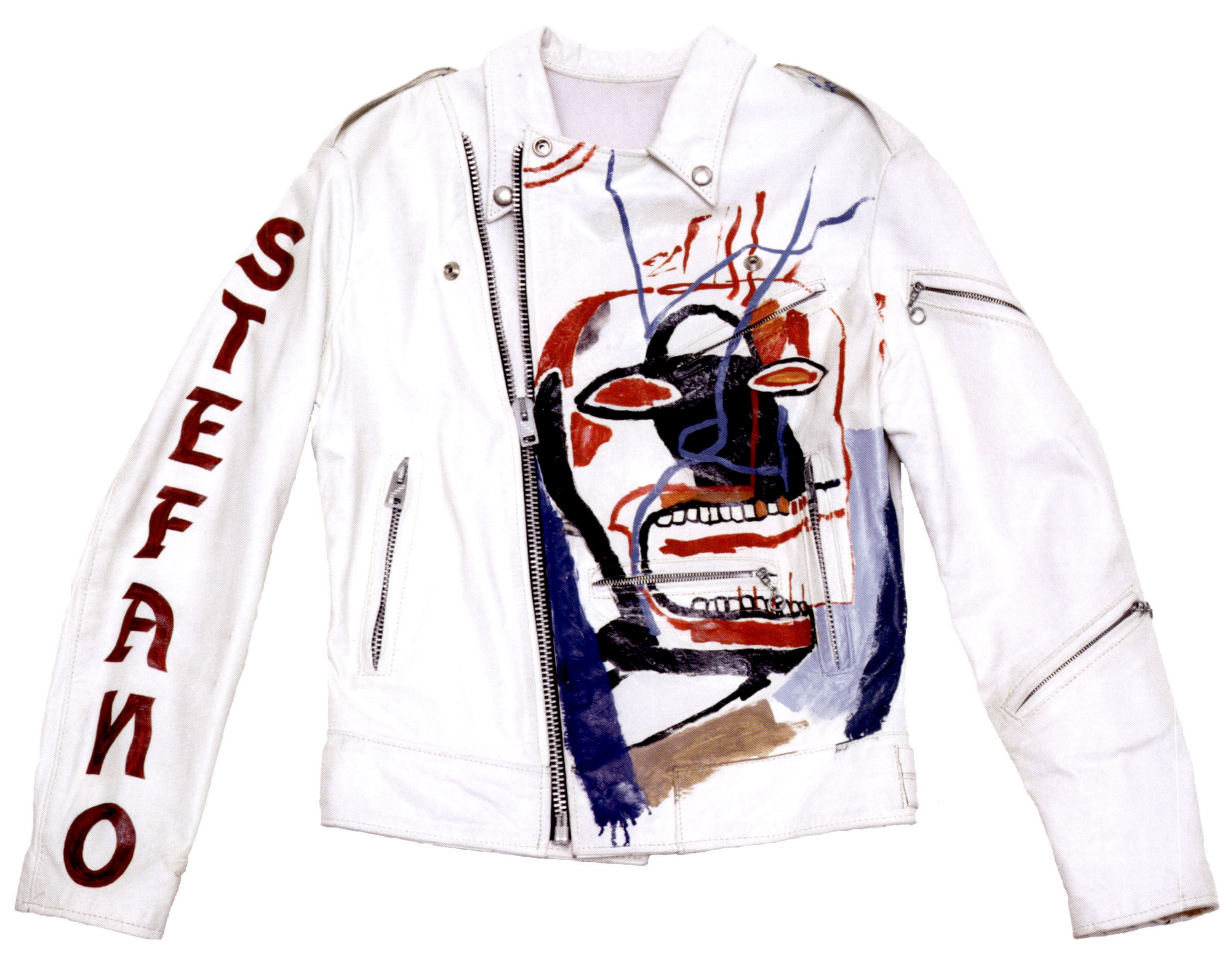

Warhol wearing leather jacket near Tucson, Arizona, 1968

Stefano Castronovo, *Jean-Michel Basquiat Leather Jacket*, 1985

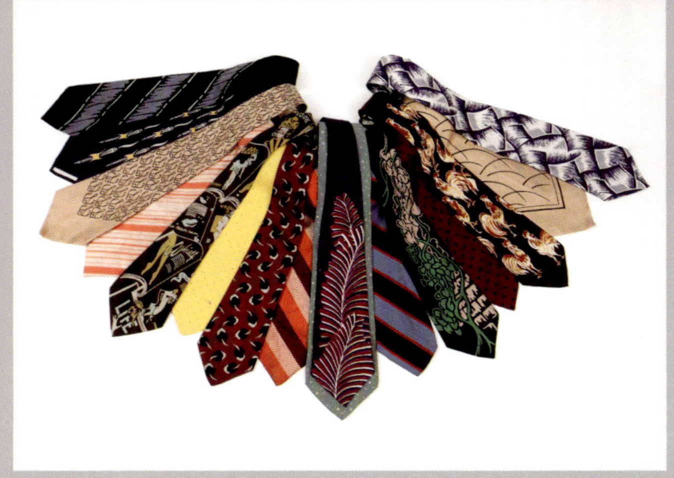

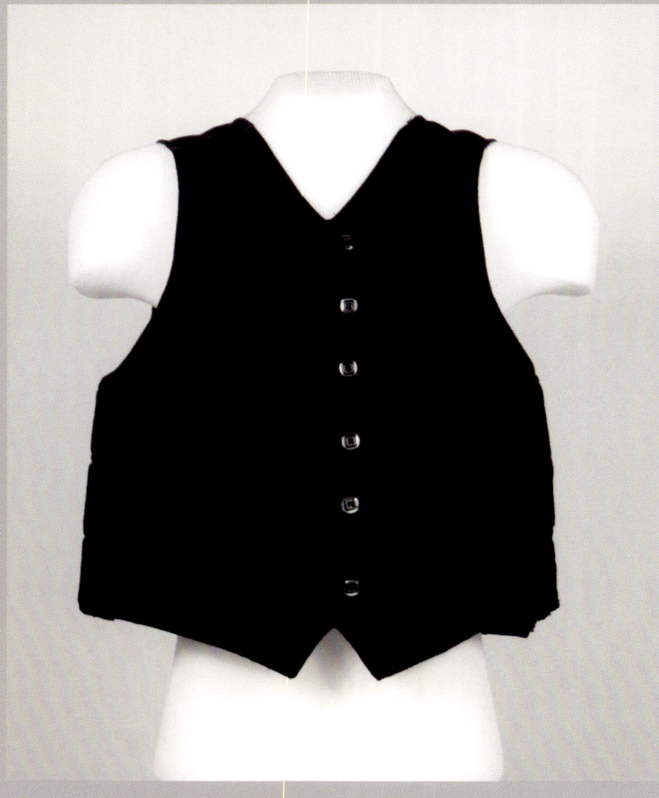

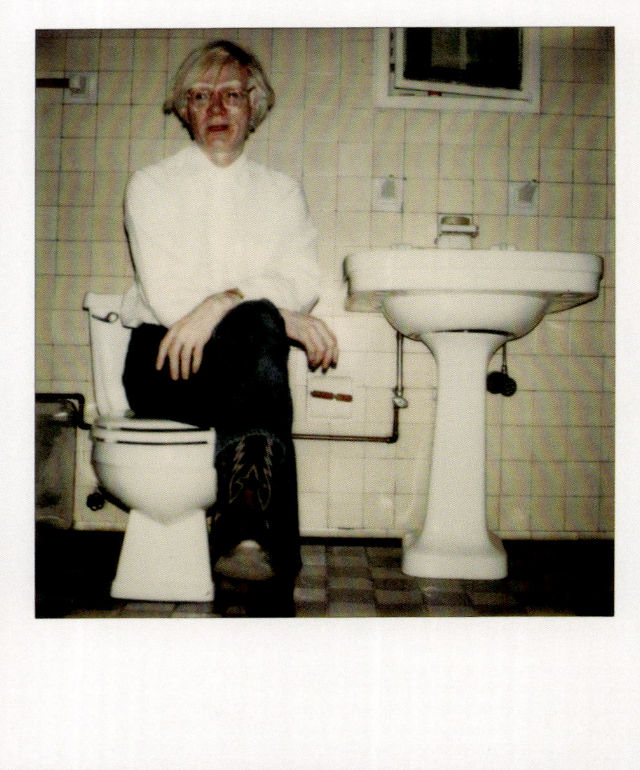

Photographer unknown, *Andy Warhol*, 1950s

Warhol's bulletproof vest, 1981

A selection of Warhol's neckties

Photographer unknown, *Andy Warhol*, ca. 1978

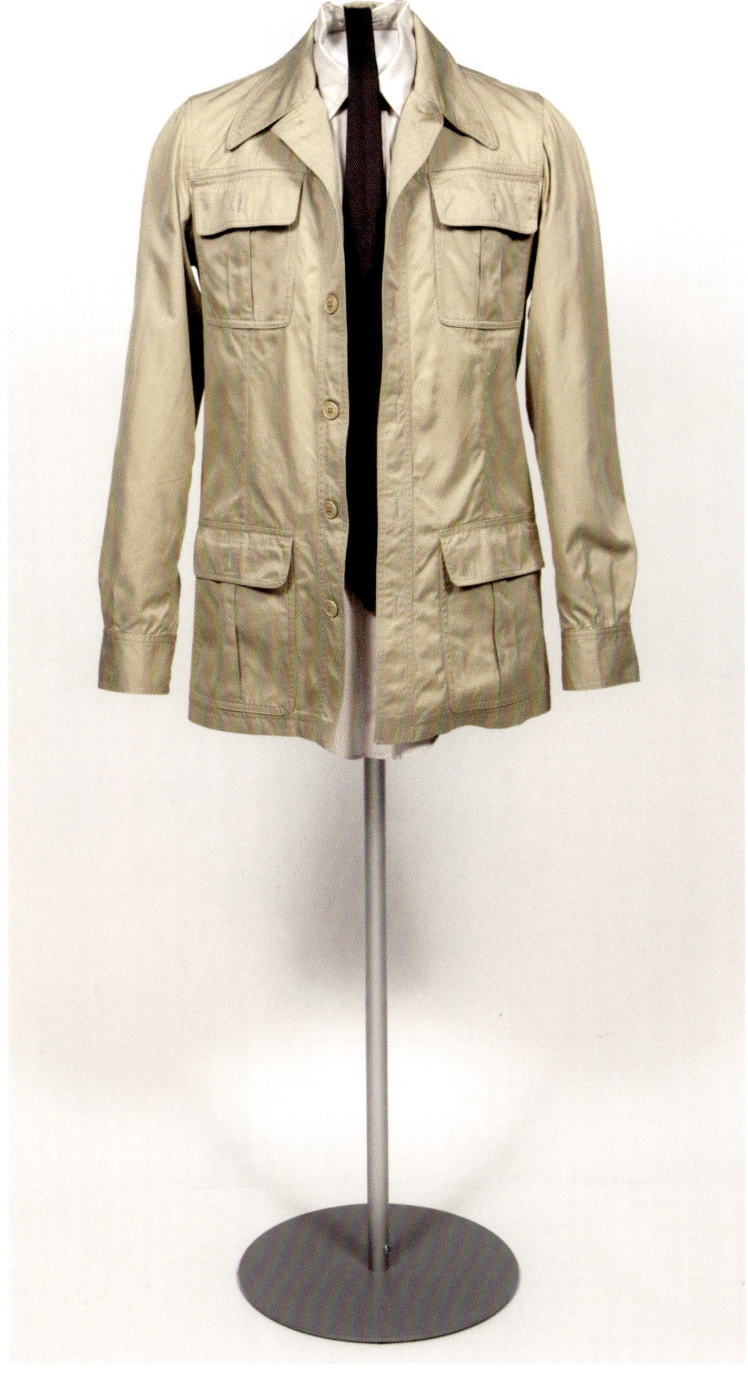

Warhol's Yves Saint Laurent "safari jacket" layered over white shirt and skinny tie, an outfit regularly worn in the 1970s

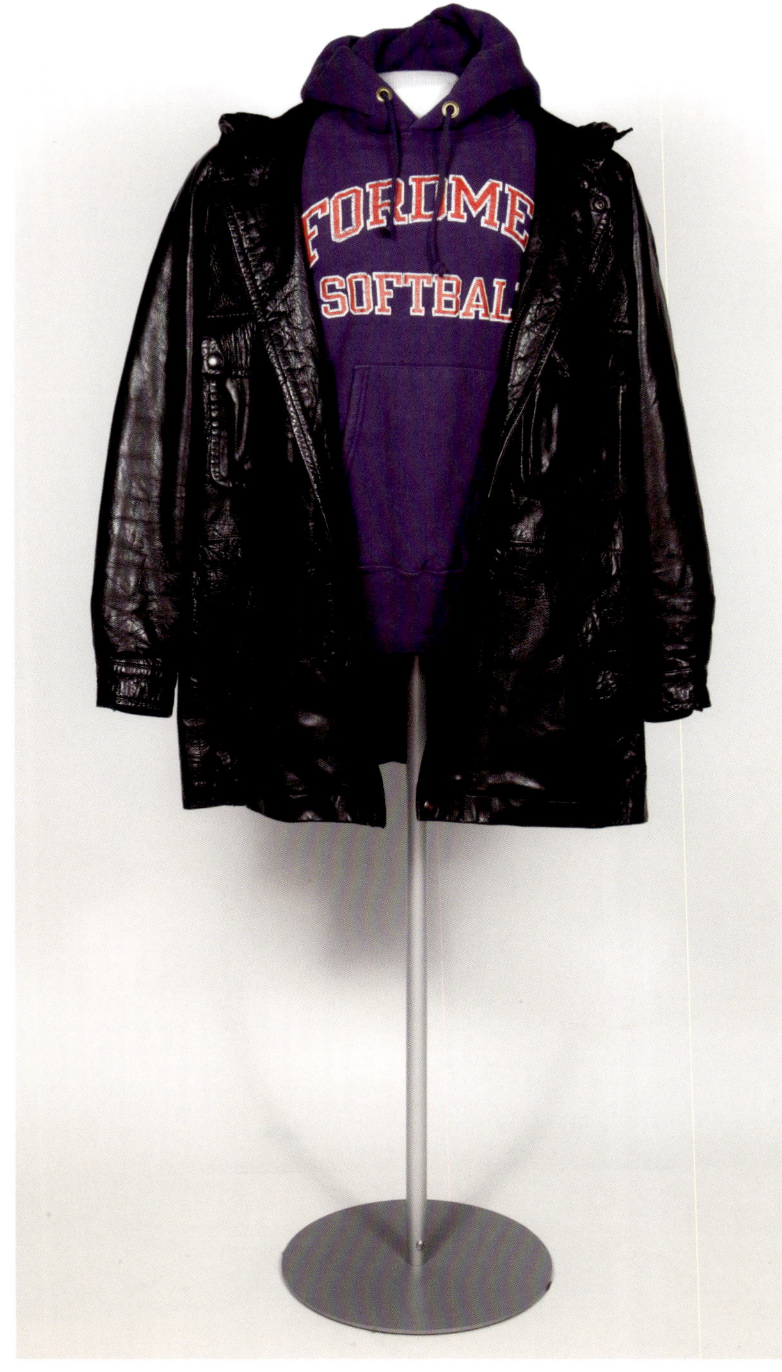

Black leather Calvin Klein jacket and blue hoodie for the Ford Modeling Agency softball team, worn by Warhol to the opening exhibition for his *Last Supper* paintings in Milan in February 1987

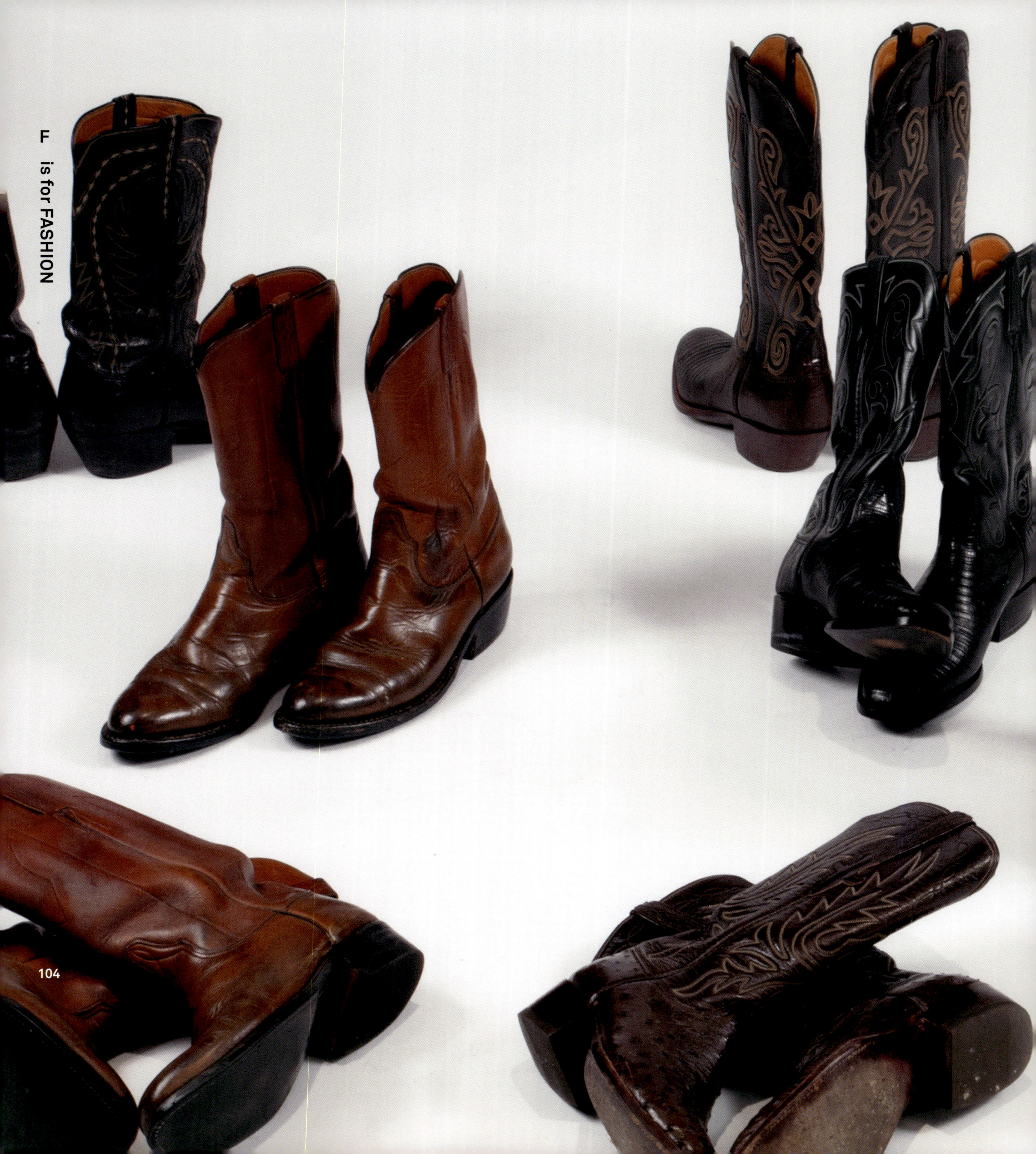
F   is for FASHION

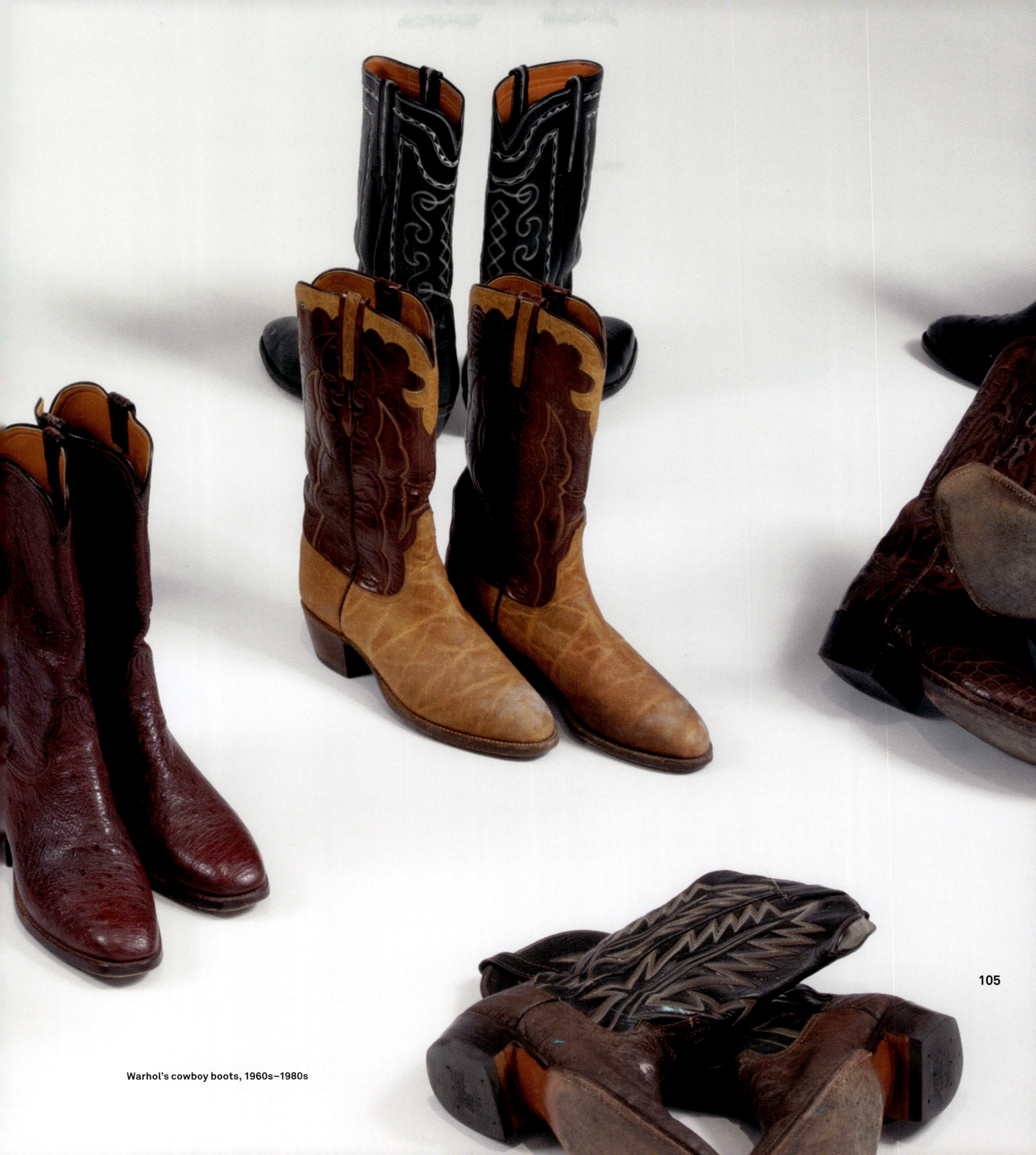

Warhol's cowboy boots, 1960s–1980s

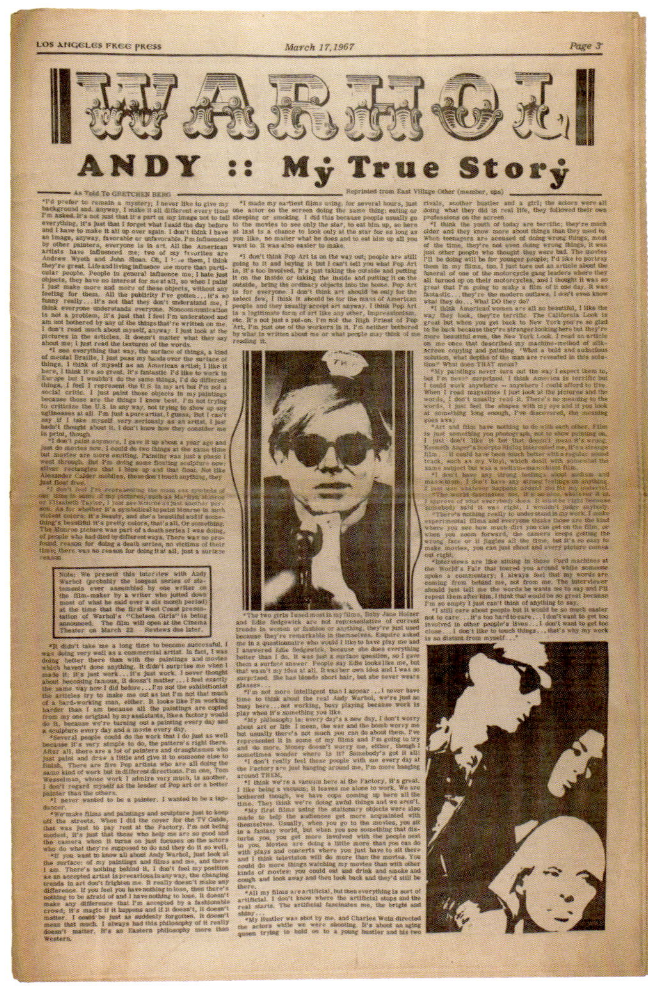

WARHOL

ANDY :: My True Story

As Told To GRETCHEN BERG

Reprinted from East Village Other (number, six)

"I'd prefer to remain a mystery; I never like to give my background and, anyway, I make it all different every time I'm asked. It's not just that it's part of my image not to tell everything, it's just that I forget what I said the day before and I have to make it all up over again. I don't think I have an image, anyway, favorable or unfavorable. I'm influenced by other painters, everyone is in art. All the American artists have influenced me; two of my favorites are Andrew Wyeth and John Sloan. Oh, I love them, I think they're great. Life and living influence me more than particular people. People in general influence me; I hate just objects, they have no interest for me at all, so when I paint I just make more and more of these objects, without any feeling for them. All the publicity I've gotten...it's so funny really...It's not that they don't understand me, I think everyone understands everyone. Noncommunication is not a problem, it's just that I feel I'm understood and am not bothered by any of the things that're written on me. I don't read much about myself, anyway; I just look at the pictures in the articles. It doesn't matter what they say about me; I just read the textures of the words.

"I see everything that way, the surface of things, a kind of mental Braille. I just pass my hands over the surface of things. I think of myself as an American artist; I like it here, I think it's so great. It's fantastic. I'd like to work in Europe but I wouldn't do the same things, I'd do different things. I feel I represent the U.S. in my art but I'm not a social critic. I just paint those objects in my paintings because those are the things I know best. I'm not trying to criticize the U.S. in any way, not trying to show up any uglinesses at all. I'm just a pure artist, I guess. But I can't say if I take myself very seriously as an artist. I just hadn't thought about it. I don't know how they consider me in print, though.

"I don't paint anymore. I gave it up about a year ago and just do movies now. I could do two things at the same time but movies are more exciting. Painting was just a phase I went through. But I'm doing some floating sculpture now; silver rectangles that I blow up and that float. Not like Alexander Calder mobiles, these don't touch anything, they just float free.

"I don't feel I'm representing the main sex symbols of our time in some of my pictures, such as Marilyn Monroe or Elizabeth Taylor. I just see Monroe as just another person. As for whether it's symbolical to paint Monroe in such violent colors: it's beauty, and she's beautiful and if something's beautiful it's pretty colors, that's all. Or something. The Monroe picture was part of a death series I was doing, of people who had died by different ways. There was no profound reason for doing a death series, no victims of their time; there was no reason for doing it at all, just a surface reason."

> Note: We present this interview with Andy Warhol (probably the longest series of statements ever assembled by one writer on the film-maker by a writer who jotted down most of what he said over a six month period) at the time that the first West Coast presentation of Warhol's "Chelsea Girls" is being announced. The film will open at the Cinema Theater on March 22. Reviews due later.

"It didn't take me a long time to become successful. I was doing very well as a commercial artist. In fact, I was doing better there than with the paintings and movies which haven't done anything. It didn't surprise me when I made it. It's just work...it's just work. I never thought about becoming famous, it doesn't matter...I feel exactly the same way now I did before...I'm not the exhibitionist the articles try to make me out as but I'm not that much of a hard-working man, either. It looks like I'm working harder than I am because all the paintings are copied from my one original by my assistants, like a factory would do it, because we're turning out a painting every day and a sculpture every day and a movie every day.

"Several people could do the work that I do just as well because it's very simple to do, the pattern's right there. After all, there are a lot of painters and draughtsmen who just paint and draw a little and give it to someone else to finish. There are five Pop artists who are all doing the same kind of work but in different directions. I'm one, Tom Wesselman, whose work I admire very much, is another. I don't regard myself as the leader of Pop art or a better painter than the others.

"I never wanted to be a painter. I wanted to be a tap-dancer.

"We make films and paintings and sculpture just to keep off the streets. When I did the cover for the TV Guide, that was just to pay rent at the Factory. I'm not being modest, it's just that those who help me are so good and the camera when it turns on just focuses on the actors who do what they're supposed to do and they do it so well.

"If you want to know all about Andy Warhol, just look at the surface of my paintings and films and me, and there I am. There's nothing behind it. I don't feel my position as an accepted artist is precarious in any way, the changing trends in art don't frighten me. It really doesn't make any difference. If you feel you have nothing to lose, then there's nothing to be afraid of and I have nothing to lose. It doesn't make any difference that I'm accepted by a fashionable crowd. It's magic if it happens and if it doesn't, it doesn't matter. I could be just as suddenly forgotten. It doesn't matter that much. I always had this philosophy of it really doesn't matter. It's an Eastern philosophy more than Western.

"I made my earliest films using, for several hours, just one actor on the screen doing the same thing: eating or sleeping or smoking. I did this because people usually go to the movies to see only the star, to eat him up, so here at last is a chance to look only at the star for as long as you like, no matter what he does and to eat him up all you want to. It was also easier to make.

"I don't think Pop Art is on the way out; people are still going to it and buying it but I can't tell you what Pop Art is, it's too involved. It's just taking the outside and putting it on the inside or taking the inside and putting it on the outside, bring the ordinary objects into the home. Pop Art is for everyone. I don't think art should be only for the select few, I think it should be for the mass of American people and they usually accept art anyway. I think Pop Art is a legitimate form of art like any other, Impressionism, etc. It's not just a put-on. I'm not the High Priest of Pop Art, I'm just one of the workers in it. I'm neither bothered by what is written about me or what people may think of me reading it."

"The two girls I used most in my films, Baby Jane Holzer and Edie Sedgwick are not representations of current trends in women or fashion or anything, they're just used because they're remarkable in themselves."

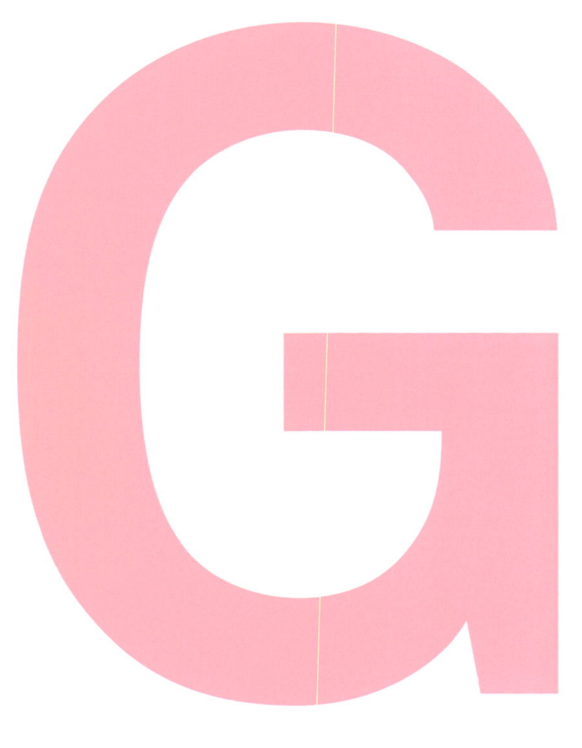

is for GRETCHEN

This chapter is based on the exhibition *Gift of Gretchen Berg: The True Story of "My True Story,"* April 20–August 5, 2007.

With the Factory's stereo playing Stravinsky's *Petrushka*, photojournalist and writer Gretchen Berg began her interview of Warhol in early 1966; after several more sessions, and much editing, it was published with the teen-idol title "Andy Warhol: My True Story." This interview is now widely regarded as the best that Warhol ever gave, filled with many of his most famous and most perceptive quotes. However, many of these quotes aren't his but instead are Berg's, who carefully condensed the conversation to make it appear that she was eliminating her voice, although in fact the interview is composed largely of her words— queries to which Warhol either agreed or disagreed. Confronted with his reticence, Berg felt the need to liven things up for the reader. There are moments, however, when Warhol is more expressive: in discussing his films and in describing the script that Valerie Solanas (who is not named) asked him to produce.

Commenting on the experience, Berg stated, "I had a good collaborator."[1] Warhol may well have taken a cue from her, as he went on to use this collaborative method for most of his later published writings. Listening to the audio version of Berg's interview with Warhol offers a different experience than that of reading the typescript. Whereas the typescript portrays Warhol as garrulous and unmasked, the audio reveals a much more elusive figure.

The following are selections from the unedited transcription of the interview. The transcription of the original recording was done by Robert Taylor. The quotation selections are by the author. Berg's selections in bold are those she choreographed into a now-famous Warhol "quote" that follows below the transcription.

GB: Do you often find these unknown people like Miss Holzer and Miss Sedgwick to use in your films?
AW: Well it just sort of happened. I use people like Jack Smith, and Taylor Mead, Beverly Grant, and Mario Montez.
GB: Why do you like to use them, these particular people?
AW: Oh, well, they're so good.
GB: Do they fit into any particular pattern that you have in mind?
AW: Well, when we used them they were mostly all sort of period costume kind of things. The Jane thing is more

up-to-date "real" kind of things than the things with Edie.
GB: So are they artificial?
AW: But then **everything is sort of artificial**/real. So, **I don't know where**—
GB: One stops and the other—
AW: Yeah.
GB: Is that the world then in general?
AW: Yeah, I guess so; it's all illusion, I think.
GB: You don't really believe too much in sight value?
AW: Uhh, no. Well, usually it's so different. So, you have to accept the people by their sight value, or things—
GB: Do you do that?
AW: Yeah.
GB: But you know that it's all artificial underneath?
AW: Oh, yeah.
GB: And **that's what fascinates you, the artificial**?
AW: Yeah, I guess so. Oh, yeah! Oh, I guess it is.
GB: Bright shiny kinds of things?
AW: Yeah.
GB: I'm simplifying.
AW: Yeah.

"All my films are artificial but then everything is sort of artificial. I don't know where the artificial stops and the real starts. The artificial fascinates me, the bright and shiny."[2]

GB: Now, Mr. Warhol, could **I** have some of your background in art, please, or would you **prefer** that **to remain a mystery**?
AW: Uhhhhh, a mystery.
GB: A mystery?
AW: Yeah.
GB: You **never like to give** your **background**?
AW: Uhhh, no.
GB: No?
AW: No.
GB: And no one knows about it then, it has not been recorded before, then?
AW: No, **I make it all up every time**.
GB: I see, everyone gets a **different**—
AW: Yes.
GB: Of course; is this **part of your image**?

"Warhol, Andy :: My True Story" by Gretchen Berg, *Los Angeles Free Press*, March 17, 1967, originally printed in the *East Village Other*, November 1, 1966

AW: Uhhhhhhhhhhhh, no, **it's just that I forget** everything. Every day's a new day, and I'm just forgetful.
GB: What it was originally?
AW: Yeah.

"I'd prefer to remain a mystery, I never like to give my background, and, anyway, I make it all up different every time I'm asked. It's not just that it's part of my image not to tell everything, it's just that I forget what I said the day before and I have to make it all up over again."[3]

GB: Did you always **want to be a painter**?
AW: Uhhhh, no. I don't know. **No.**
GB: Did you want to be anything in particular?
AW: I wanted to be able to tap dance, which I never really learned how.
GB: Is that your only disappointment?
AW: Well, I wasn't really disappointed.

"I never wanted to be a painter, I wanted to be a tap dancer."[4]

GB: It's all there on the surface then; it's what we can see.
AW: Well, I like—I guess, yeah.
GB: What do you like?
AW: The surface.
GB: Then that's all that we can see; **if we want to know about Andy Warhol, we just look at your paintings and your films and that's—**
AW: Yeah.
GB: There's nothing profound **underneath—**
AW: No.

"If you want to know all about Andy Warhol, just look at the surface: of my paintings and films and me, and there I am. There's nothing behind it."[5]

Berg's own story is one filled with creative influences. Her family introduced her to the magical worlds of the word and the image—primarily as related to cinema—when she was very young. Many of her family members worked in film, radio, and television; their combined résumés represent a Who's Who of twentieth-century Western culture.

Her father, Herman G. Weinberg, was involved in the early days of the film industry as a filmmaker and subtitler of about four hundred films, including many classics, and was a friend of Louise Brooks, Charlie Chaplin, Marlene Dietrich, Fritz Lang, Ernst Lubitsch, Jean Renoir, Josef von Sternberg, Erich von Stroheim, Orson Welles, and other actors, writers, and directors. He later taught filmmaking for many years at City College of New York, published several books on film, and wrote a frequent column in the journal *Film Culture* called "Coffee, Brandy, and Cigars." Berg's uncle Eric Arthur wrote for the radio serial *The Shadow* and worked with Orson Welles and journalist Edward R. Murrow. Another uncle, Max Weinberg, helped to found the Publicists Guild in Los Angeles. Berg's godmother was Mary Ellen Bute, an important figure in early avant-garde animated abstract film. Berg's godfather was the director Erich von Stroheim. Naturally, these connections opened many doors for her.

Berg's mother, Etta Pollano, was born in Odessa, Ukraine, in 1912 and immigrated with her parents to the United States when she was nine or ten. Her parents were Peter and Sophia Simon Pollano (Poliakoff or Poliakov in Russian; presumably, as recent Jewish immigrants, they had changed their name to assimilate to American culture). They settled in Pittsburgh, but Pollano left for New York City shortly after graduation, gravitating toward the intellectual and artistic life she dreamed of, fueled by books and movies. There, she met Herman G. Weinberg through a mutual friend, the film historian Lewis Jacobs, in about 1936, and they married soon after. At the time, Herman was a subtitler of foreign-language films and operated a cinema that screened them, the 55th Street Playhouse. (One of his colleagues in this theater was Ed Sullivan, who many years later became the host of one of the best-known television variety shows.)

Born in 1943, Gretchen was the couple's only child; sometime in 1945–46, her parents separated. A few years later, Etta became ill with liver cancer; she died in 1950. Gretchen's father began taking his young daughter to the cinema and to meet his close friends in that world, granting her a firsthand education in the great masters of the silver—and often silent—screen. Berg describes her childhood as somewhat like that of the character Scout in *To Kill a Mockingbird*. With her father, she occasionally visited the Connecticut country home of Dada filmmaker Hans Richter and explored the woods nearby. Her first drawings came about when she stole charcoal from Richter's studio and then waited until she was alone at home to secretly make her art. More formally, she attended children's art classes at the Museum of Modern Art and later at the School of Visual Arts, Cooper Union, and the Art Students League, where her mother modeled and was friendly with the painters John Groth and Norman Rabin. Etta also had friends who were professional dancers, and as a child Gretchen took ballet classes at Carnegie Hall.

In 1948 the family moved to a quiet, furnished apartment hotel at Broadway and 71st Street, the Hotel Robert Fulton. Berg remembers it having "an atmosphere of the past, similar to O. Henry stories." The building's name was later changed to Coliseum House. She spent her childhood there with friends—neighbors from the building, who were all marginal figures from the edge of society, not middle class—in the upstairs "television room" (at a time when TVs were uncommon), surrounded by old, unused furniture. She has fond memories of them running around the hotel, hanging out of windows, and immersing themselves in other unsupervised pleasures. Inspired by TV programs, Berg and her friends acted out stories with small home-made toy figures of metal, rubber, and wood, and some early plastic toys from Cracker Jack and cereal boxes. Among the television films that fascinated her were *The Lodger*, *The Mystery of Edwin Drood*, *Hangover Square*, and *Gunga Din*. Life in the hotel had a profound effect on her, giving her a love of history and of interiors that evoked film sets on which dramas were played out. Henry Hathaway's espionage film *The House on 92nd Street* (1945) was shot near her home and visually captures the streets of her youth, a place and time for which she still yearns. Berg left her father's home in 1966, moving first to the Midtown Wellington Hotel for a year, then to the East Village with her boyfriend on St. Mark's Place, across the street from the poet W. H. Auden, whom they didn't know personally but referred to as "The Professor."

Through her father's long-standing position as a columnist for *Film Culture*, the New York journal of cinema, Berg published several short pieces in its pages early on, under the name Gretchen Weinberg: an appreciation of the Canadian animator Norman McLaren, a brief note on the 1962 New York Film Festival, and a few of her drawings. Her first interview was with the New Zealand filmmaker and kinetic sculptor Len Lye, published in *Film Culture* in the summer of 1963. This was followed by interviews with director Roman Polanski and her godmother, filmmaker Mary Ellen Bute.[6] In her interviews, which she considers "meditations," she strived to project a feeling of intimacy between the reader and the subject, revealing aspects of the subject that would not otherwise be known.

Her first writing under the shortened name Gretchen Berg was a hybrid of private correspondence and observations of film director Fritz Lang (of *Metropolis* and *M* fame, among many others) and his friends in the St. Moritz hotel on Central Park South; this was published in *Cahiers du Cinema* in two parts. Through her father's friendship with Lang, Gretchen had extraordinary access to the great director. Working with her father, Berg then interviewed Baron Nicholas de Gunzberg (also known as Julian West, the producer of Carl Th. Dreyer's *Vampyr* in 1932); the interview appeared in *Film Culture* in 1964.

In 1965 Berg attended a screening of one of Warhol's films with her friend Sheldon Renan, who also wrote for *Film Culture*. Berg approached Warhol to ask for an interview. He agreed to her request but warned that he usually had little to say. She began her work with Warhol early in 1966 (possibly February) and continued into the summer; after months of editing, the interview was published in the *East Village Other* in November; it was subsequently reprinted in *Cahiers du Cinema* in 1967 and picked up by the Underground Press Syndicate and published widely. On meeting Warhol, Berg felt that he was a kindred spirit.

Berg went on to write additional pieces for *Film Culture* and other publications. Other famous interviewees include Ernest Pintoff, animator, director of television shows, and film producer; Richard Roud, director of the New York Film Festival; and Paul Morrissey, director and Warhol associate. She also completed interviews with photographers Barbara

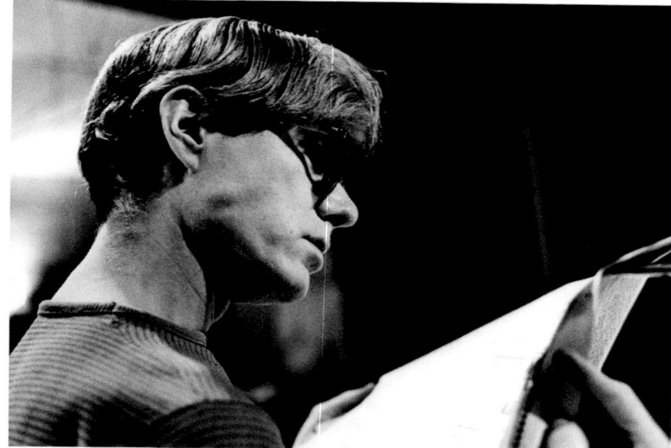

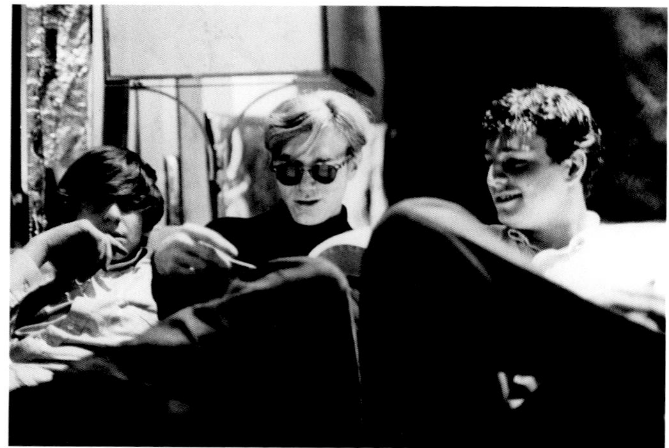

Morgan, Jill Freedman, and Peter Beard, the playboy/adventurer/photographer who was Warhol's good friend and collaborator.

More than her many lengthy personal encounters with important creative figures, the work of which Berg is most proud is her cycle of photos of teenage demonstrators, a series she calls *Troublemakers*. She started the series in about 1965 with images of youths protesting the United States' engagement in the Vietnam War and, later, conditions in the public schools. She continued the series into the mid-1970s and then broadened it with photographs of anti-nuclear demonstrators in the early 1980s.

In addition to the archival materials related to the "True Story," the museum collection holds a number of photographs by Berg of Warhol and his associates. She documented the Factory during her time there in the summer of 1966 and again in 1972. Many of Berg's images of the Warhol studios in 1972 were commissioned for a magazine story on Paul Morrissey, but the project was canceled. A year later, Berg saw Warhol for the last time. As she remembers, he was coming out of a film at the Paris Theatre, near the Plaza Hotel on 58th Street, and she called out his name and said hello, but Warhol didn't recognize her, and kept walking past.

NOTES

1. Gretchen Berg in conversation with the author, March 2007.

2. Gretchen Berg, "Andy Warhol: My True Story," *East Village Other*, November 1, 1966, 9–10, in *I'll Be Your Mirror: The Selected Andy Warhol Interviews*, ed. Kenneth Goldsmith (New York: Carroll & Graf, 2004), 93.

3. Ibid., 87.

4. Ibid., 89.

5. Ibid., 90.

6. The Roman Polanski interview is in *Sight & Sound* (Winter 1963–64), 32–33, and the Mary Ellen Bute interview is in *Film Culture* 35 (1964–65), 25–28.

Gretchen Berg, *Andy Warhol, Summer 1966*, reprinted 2006

Gretchen Berg, *Joey Freeman, Andy Warhol and Unidentified Man, Summer 1966*, reprinted 2006

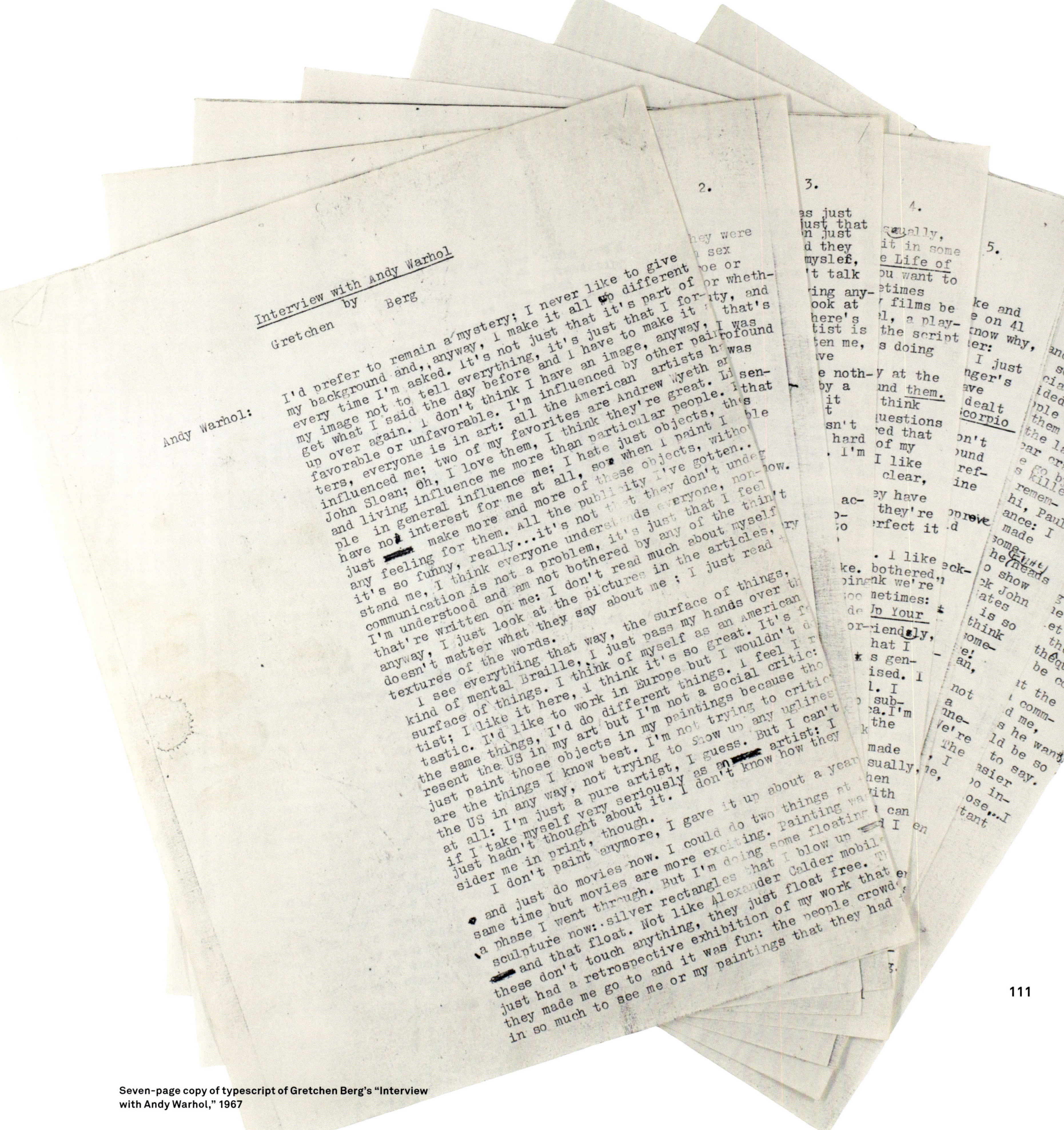

Seven-page copy of typescript of Gretchen Berg's "Interview with Andy Warhol," 1967

Andy Warhol's collection of newspaper headlines began with one in the *Pittsburgh Press* in 1946, which announced that he had been awarded a prize in college. From this, Warhol's interest in the immediate public record of the news of the day eventually grew to epic proportions. The entire contents of dozens of his *Time Capsules* are devoted to headlines, often the tabloid sensationalism of the *New York Post*, from 1967 to 1987.

Many of Warhol's newspaper works are related to his *Disaster* series (1963), including *"Pirates Sieze Ship…"* [*sic*] (1961) and *129 Die in Jet* (1962), very likely because newspapers—especially the tabloids that he favored—emphasize tragedy. In a subtle way, Warhol's painting *A Boy for Meg* (1962), although celebrating the birth of a royal, Princess Margaret's son the Viscount Linley, may also represent a *Disaster*. As Warhol wrote, "Being born is like being kidnapped. And then sold into slavery."[1] His painting *Hospital*, one of the major works in the *Disaster* series, shows a doctor holding a newborn in a delivery room.

Warhol's artworks based on newspaper headlines appeared as early as 1956, with his drawing *The Princton Leader* [*sic*], among the very first Pop Art works by Warhol,

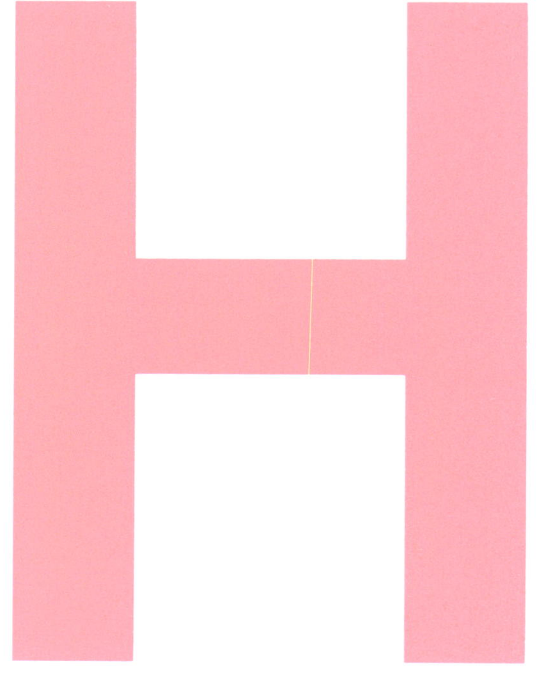

H
is for HEADLINES

This chapter is based on an exhibition of newspaper materials in the Archives Study Center, August 17, 2001–January 13, 2002.

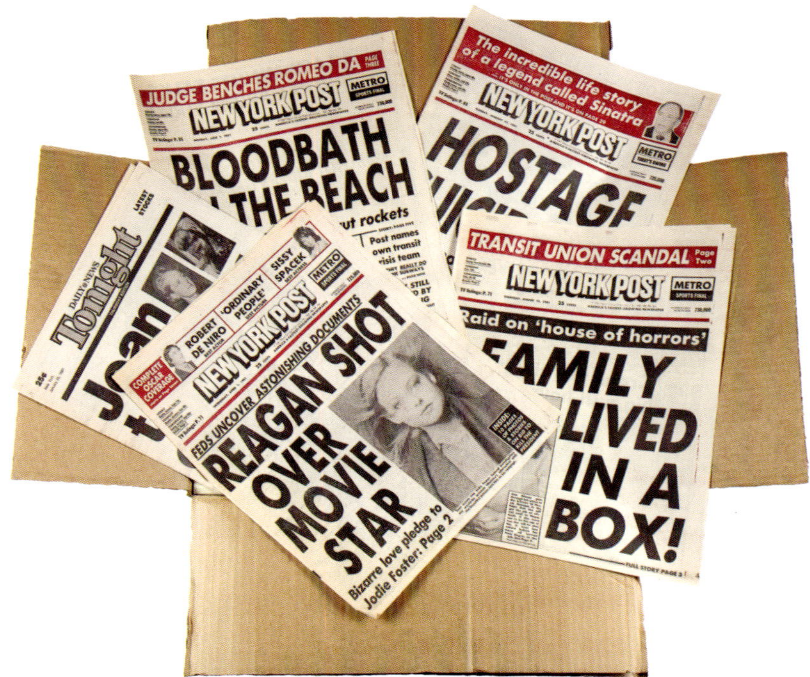

if the date on the newspaper, August 23, 1956, is an accurate date for the work. The drawing includes a fabricated story about his friend Charles Lisanby, stating that Lisanby had completed an apprenticeship as a plumber and steamfitter in Kentucky, when in fact he was a designer for the New York theater. Warhol and Lisanby had concluded an eight-week round-the-world trip only ten days before the date on the paper. But *The Princton Leader* may also belong in the *Disaster* series, because Warhol's hoped-for relationship ended in disaster when his advances were rebuffed by Lisanby.

Two of the New York papers that he collected and based works on (the *Mirror* and the *Journal American*) were owned by the Hearst Corporation, long known for its sensationalist packaging of the news. The president of Hearst from 1943 to 1973, Richard E. Berlin, had a daughter, Brigid, who was one of Warhol's best and oldest friends. Taking the name Brigid Polk, she notoriously starred in Warhol's film *The Chelsea Girls* (1966), demonstrating her technique of poking an amphetamine-loaded hypodermic needle through her jeans and earning her similar-sounding nom de plume.

Warhol was obsessed with celebrity culture, and his publication *Interview* was devoted to it. He began a series of portraits of Marilyn Monroe soon after her death in August 1962. The headline announcing the tragedy appeared on Warhol's thirty-fourth birthday (also the seventeenth anniversary of the nuclear bombing of Hiroshima, whose mass destruction Warhol included in the *Disaster* series), and he saved several more in the days that followed. He collected many other celebrity headlines that he found in supermarket tabloids like the *National Enquirer*. This paper and its cousins *National Star Chronicle*, *Midnight*, and *Inside News* published extremely exploitative headlines complete with gruesome photographs. Many of them were undeniably brutal. The papers also consistently played to readers' fears of unconventional sexuality and ran a large number of stories about freak occurrences of blindness. Their journalistic descendants currently found in checkout lines are a pale shadow of the editions that Warhol saved.

The suggestion of dread and tragedy is obscured in several Warhol works. In the large, brightly colored print *Daily News* (1967), the headline "LBJ to Kremlin: Y'All Come" is obliterated with a page of flower silhouettes intended for

Andy Warhol, *Time Capsule 322* (closed and open), 1981–82

use by graphic designers. His print portfolio *Flash* (1967), on the theme of the assassination of President John F. Kennedy, repeats the flower silhouettes overlaid on a headline, in this case the *New York World-Telegram* of November 22, 1963, with the headline "PRESIDENT SHOT DEAD."

Warhol's own celebrity tragedy made the tabloid headlines on June 4, 1968, when he was shot and very nearly killed by Valerie Solanas, a frustrated and mentally ill writer who wanted Warhol to produce her play. She made an appearance in one of Warhol's films, *I, a Man* (1967), but Warhol was unwilling to give her writing a chance. "Andy Warhol Fights for Life," screamed the *New York Post*, and his life was saved after a five-hour operation. However, Warhol's name was quickly dropped from the front page when Sirhan Sirhan killed Senator Robert F. Kennedy on June 5, while Kennedy was campaigning in Los Angeles for the presidency.

The assassination attempt on Warhol profoundly changed his ability to work for many months. Many in the art world assumed that he had given up painting. However, Warhol created some of his most ambitious works during the following decade. In 1972, when President Richard Nixon's visit to China was making headlines, Warhol created monumental paintings, prints, and drawings of Chairman Mao Tse-tung. Warhol picked up a darker subject in 1976 with his *Skull* paintings, presenting the traditional vanitas image in small and large canvases. The paintings of this symbol of mortality marked the beginning of Warhol's return to critical attention after his near-death experience.

At the same time, Warhol continued collecting headlines. The contents of *Time Capsule 232* consist almost entirely of front pages from New York's two remaining tabloid newspapers, the *New York Post* and the slightly less sensational *Daily News*. Many of the headlines date from the first three months of 1980 and focus on the Iran hostage crisis, during which fifty-two Americans were held hostage in Iran after the US embassy in Tehran was violently seized by Iranian revolutionaries on November 4, 1979. The captives were finally released on January 20, 1981, after 444 days of imprisonment. This traumatic event was the subject of nearly every US newspaper's front-page headline for its entire duration.

Shortly thereafter, Warhol returned to the headline as a source for his art. A series of three paintings titled *Fate Presto* (1981) is based on the front page of *Il Mattino* of November 26, 1980, reporting on the aftermath of an earthquake in Naples that killed two thousand people. These paintings repeat the eight-foot height of *129 Die in Jet* but differ in that they're silkscreened in three versions: near-replica black on white, reversal white on black, and ghostlike white on white. In the museum's collection are large fragments of these images, which Warhol used as tests in deciding on the final works. They are silkscreened on clear Mylar and coated with "diamond dust," a very finely ground glass that glitters like precious gems.

In 1983 he created works based on a headline proclaiming, "Race Slay Teenager Gets 5 to 15 Years / Judge Blasts Lynch," which were intended as gifts to his friends. The headline referred to the beating death of a thirty-four-year-old African American transit worker, William Turks, by a group of white teenagers in Brooklyn, including Gino Bova, who was the first of four defendants to stand trial for manslaughter. Judge Sybil Hart Kooper stated, "There was a lynch mob on Avenue X that night. The only thing missing was a rope and a tree." Bova received the maximum sentence and a further rebuke from the judge: "You said you're sorry a man is dead. You didn't say you're sorry you killed him." Warhol based several other works that same year on headlines reporting the suicide bombing of the US Marine base in Beirut. Other news banners can be found in his collaborations with Jean-Michel Basquiat, including the grim phrase "Plug Pulled on Coma Mom."

In 1984 Warhol and Basquiat worked on a series of large collaborative paintings in Warhol's expansive studio at 860 Broadway, at the northwest corner of Union Square. During this time an unusual collaborative sculpture was also created. According to Warhol's assistants, the untitled work was made in direct response to the death of Basquiat's friend, the graffiti artist Michael Stewart, who was choked by the police in Union Square, fell into a coma, and died thirteen days later.[2]

Basquiat, Warhol, and two assistants, Agusto Bugarin and Jay Shriver, all had a hand in creating the work. It was Warhol's idea to smash a large stretched canvas, which

Bugarin and Shriver performed, no doubt reflecting both the violence of the police (the medical examiner noted that Stewart died of "physical injury to the spinal cord in the upper neck") and the artists' anger. Basquiat was responsible for pouring the pink paint all over the canvas-turned-sculpture, and Shriver attached smaller paintings (*Beware of Dog*, *Artist Could Have Been Choked*) to the larger pink wreckage. While the sculpture was in progress, art dealer Bruno Bischofberger visited and suggested that Italian artist Francesco Clemente become involved as well. Clemente contributed a drawing of a face, which he placed on the sculpture as if it were an easel. The final sculpture gives the impression of a destroyed painting, or even the aftermath of an earthquake.

Three years later, news of Warhol's unexpected death shook the art world and made front-page news around the globe. Warhol's photo appeared with the headline "Is God Dead?" on the cover of the *Village Voice*.[3] It seemed to many that cultural life in New York had changed dramatically and irrevocably. Warhol's longtime friend Brigid Berlin supposedly remarked, "I guess the 60s are finally over."

NOTES

1. Andy Warhol, *The Philosophy of Andy Warhol (From A to B and Back Again)* (New York: Harcourt Brace Jovanovich, 1975), 96.

2. Songwriters Lou Reed and Michelle Shocked, filmmaker Spike Lee, and artist Keith Haring also created works to commemorate the tragedy of Michael Stewart's death at the hands of police.

3. *Village Voice* (New York), May 5, 1987, 1.

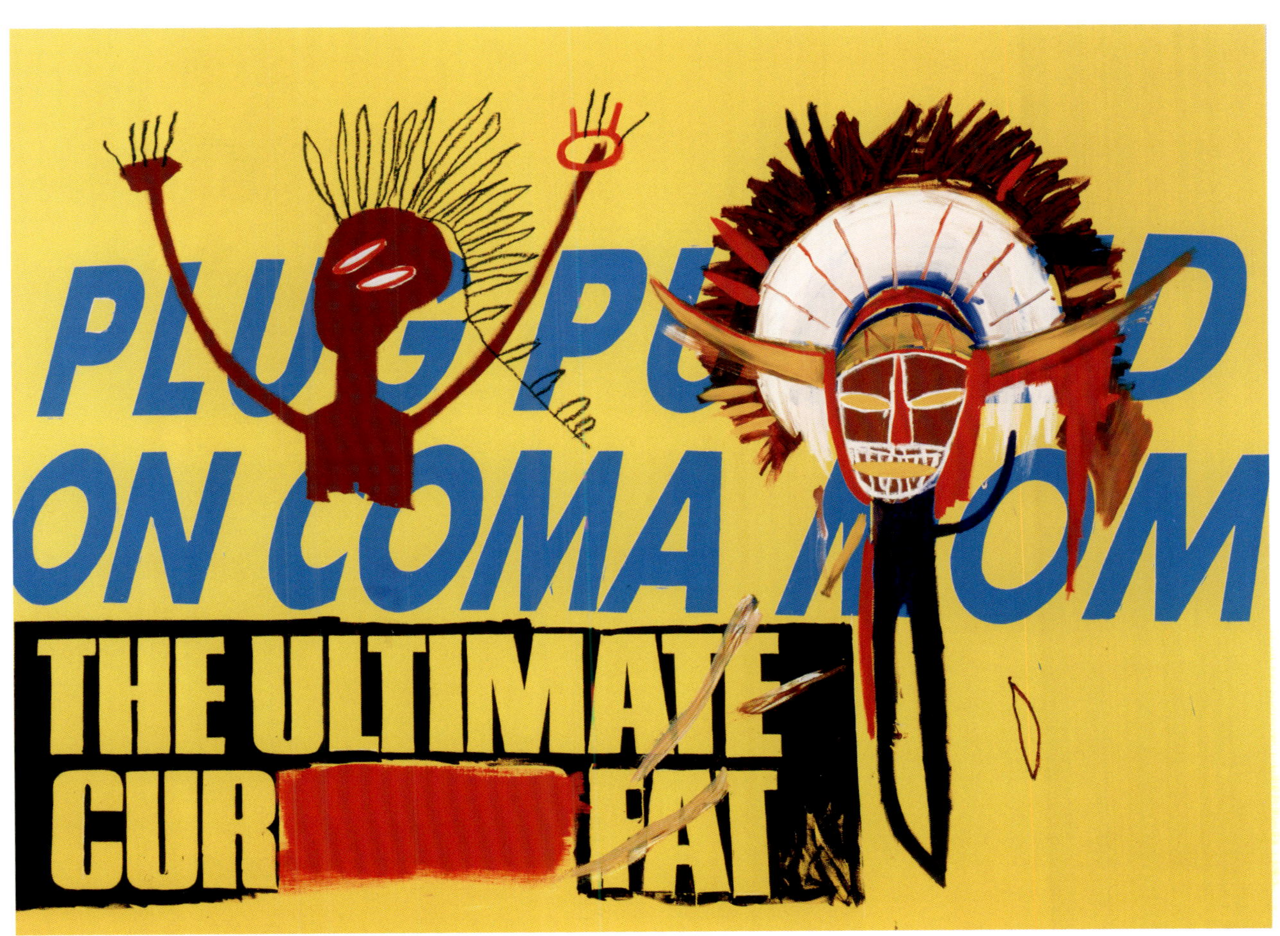

Jean-Michel Basquiat and Andy Warhol, *Collaboration*, 1984–85

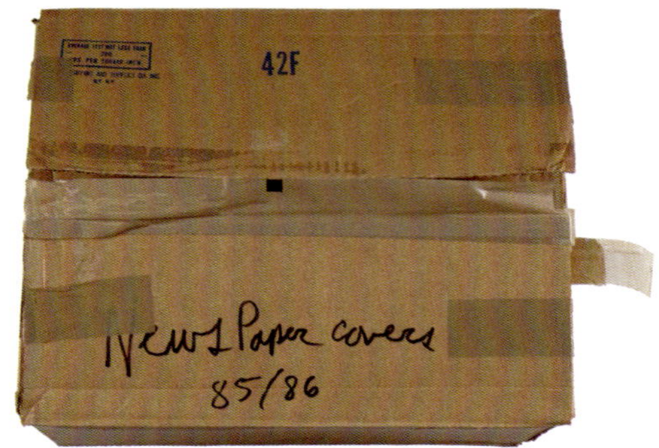

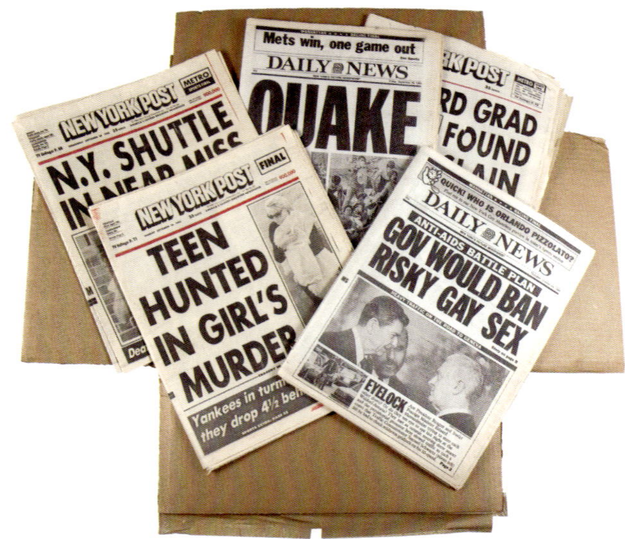

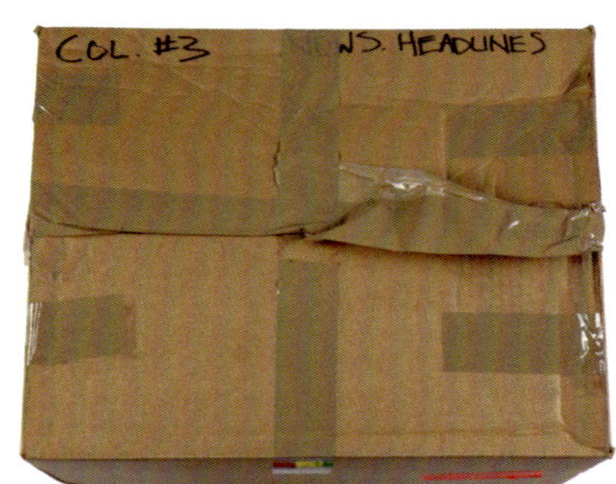

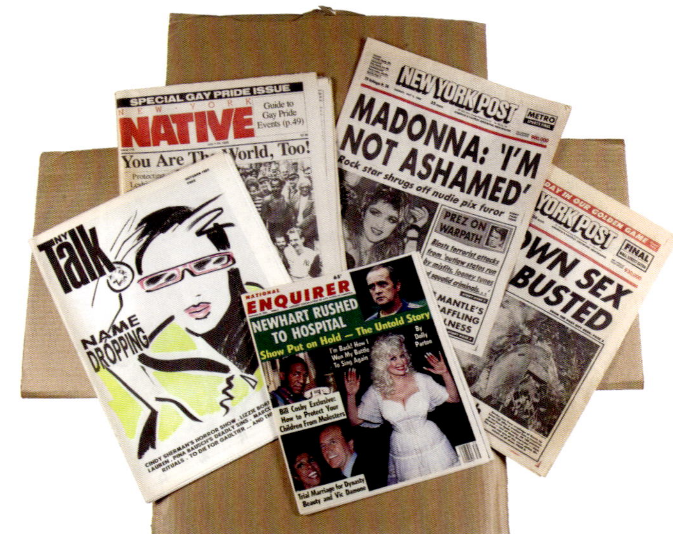

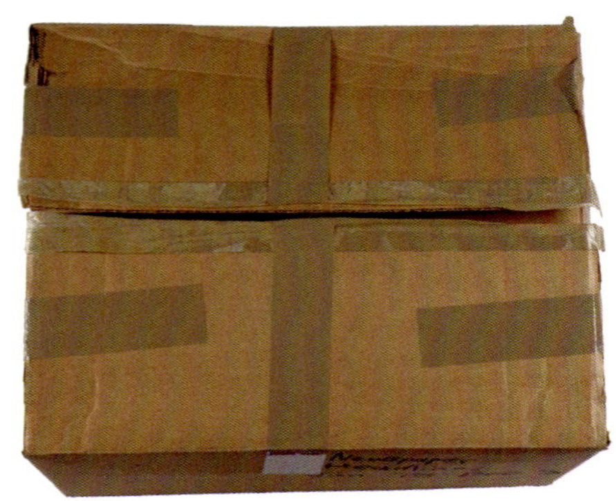

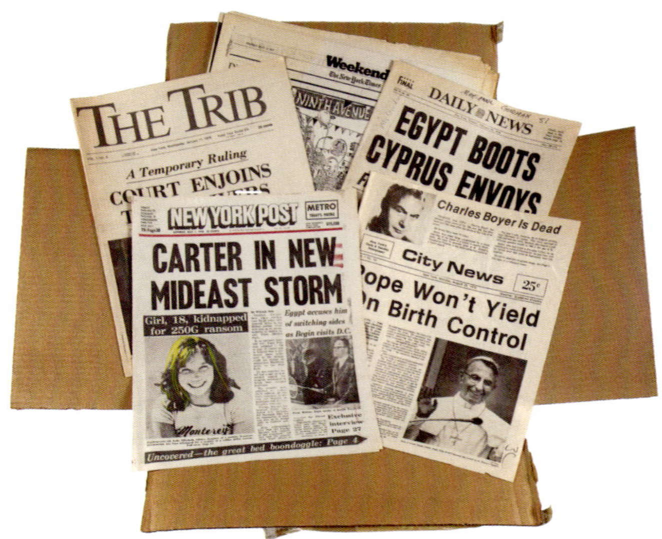

Andy Warhol, (top) *Time Capsule 433* (closed and open), 1985; (middle)
Time Capsule 465 (closed and open), 1983–87; (bottom) *Time Capsule 189*
(closed and open), 1976–78

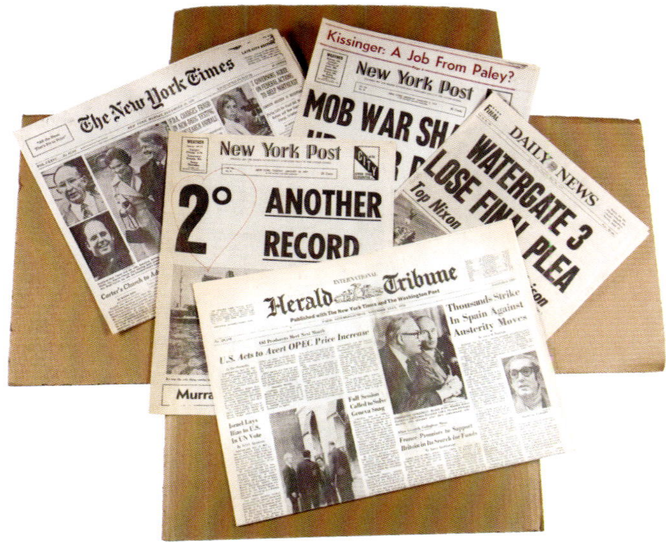
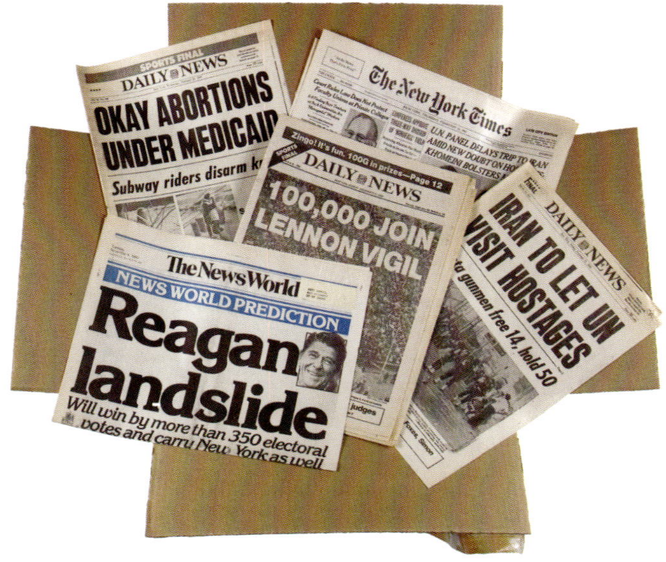
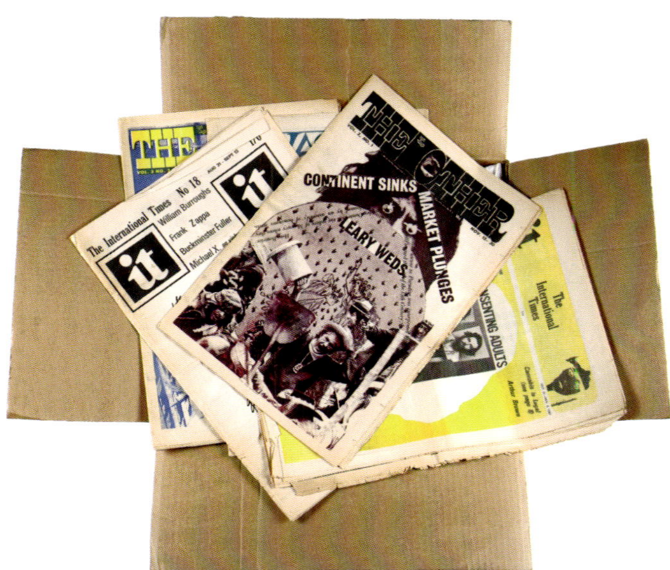
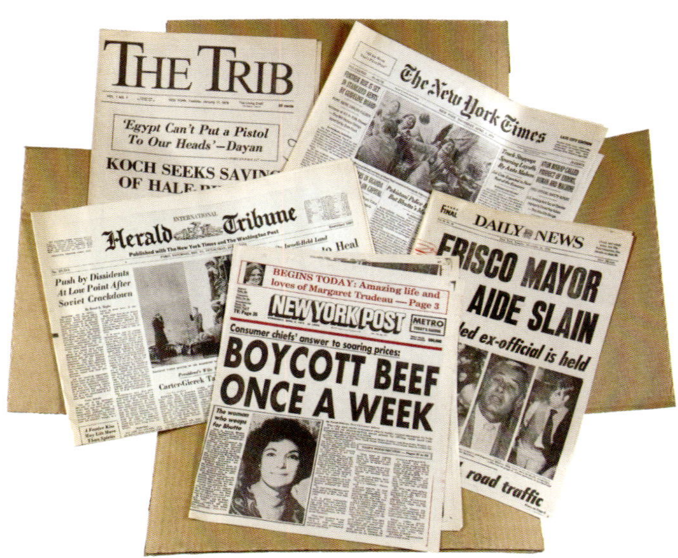
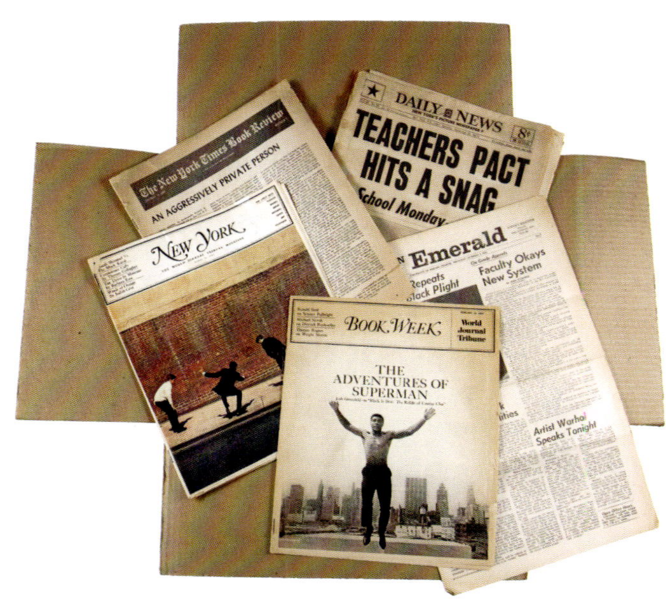
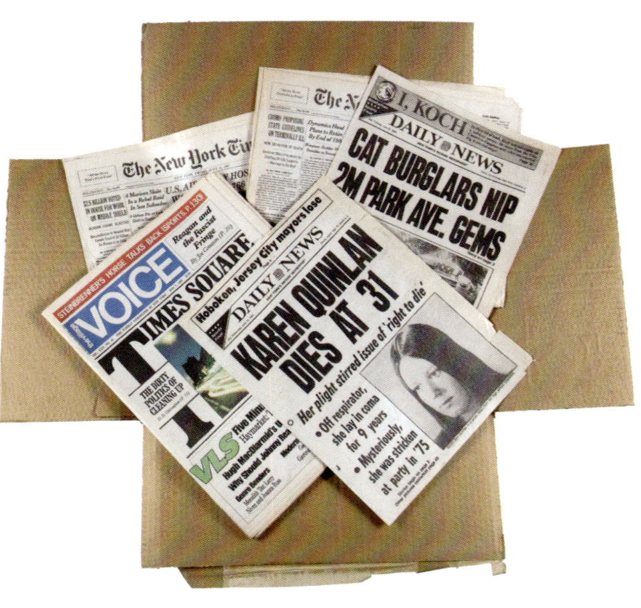

Andy Warhol, (top) *Time Capsule 170*, 1975–77; *Time Capsule 316*, 1979–81; (middle) *Time Capsule -5*, 1967; *Time Capsule 529*, 1977–79; (bottom) *Time Capsule -6*, 1967–68; *Time Capsule 428*, 1984–86

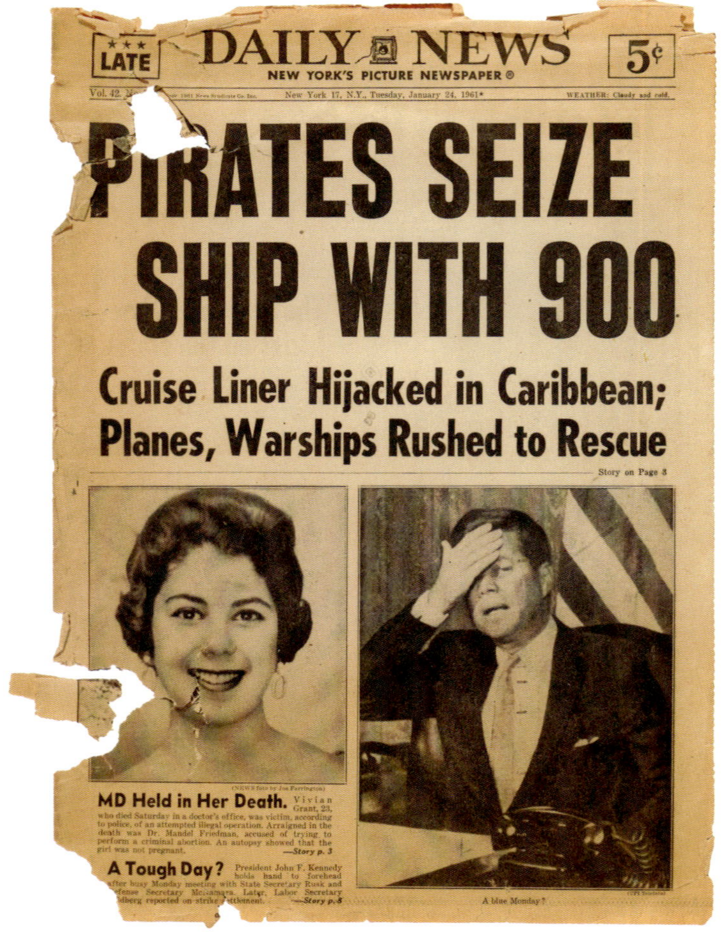

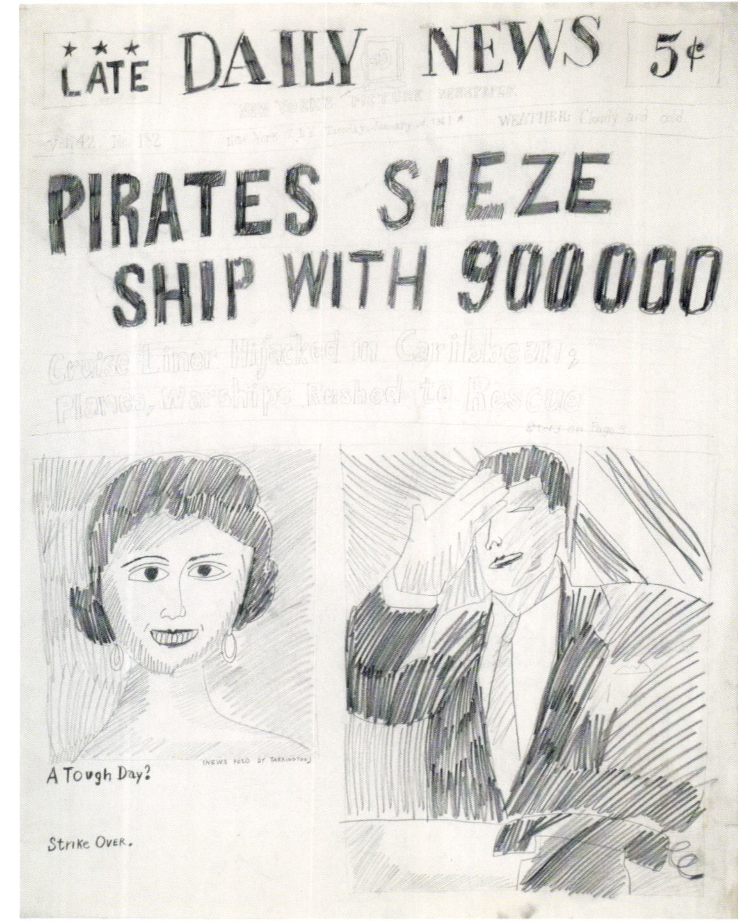

Newspaper headline "Pirates Seize Ship with 900," *Daily News*, January 24, 1961, source material for drawing

Andy Warhol, *"Pirates Sieze Ship . . . ,"* 1961

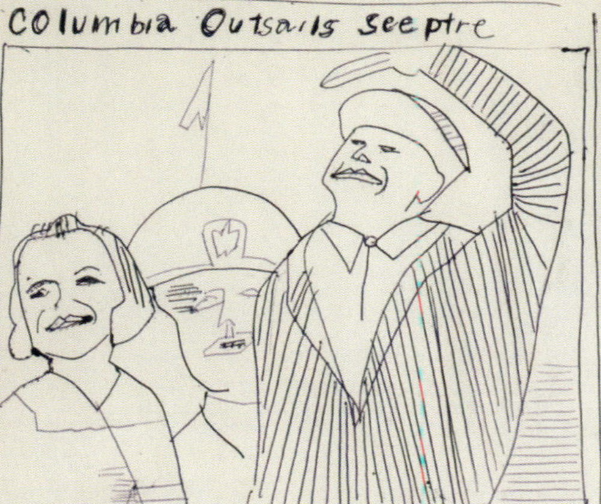

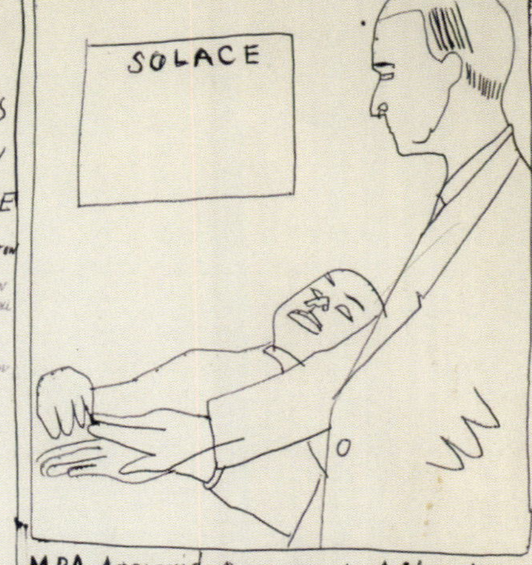

Andy Warhol, *Journal American*, ca. 1959

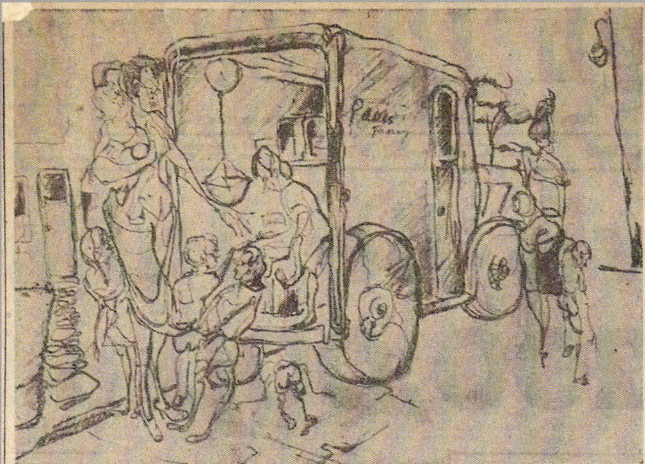

"THEY HAD SO MANY CHILDREN," according to artist-huckster Andy Warhola, "they didn't know what to do." So the mothers brought them to his vegetable truck while they chatted. His prize-winning drawings satirize customers of a huckster route in Oakland and Homestead last Summer.

Bilbo War Graft Charges To Be Aired

Meade Announces Start of Hearings

WASHINGTON, Nov. 23 (UP)—Chairman James M. Mead announced today that his Senate War Investigating Subcommittee will start open hearings Dec. 12 on charges Senator Theodore G. Bilbo received gifts from Mississippi war contractors.

The hearings will be held here, the New York Democrat said.

Another Senate group—the Campaign Investigating Committee—will hold hearings in Jackson, Miss., beginning Dec. 2 on anti-Negro charges against the Mississippi Democrat.

Mr. Mead said the charges before his group concern "certain transactions alleged to have been entered into by Senator Bilbo and certain war contractors."

Senator Bilbo has asked the War Investigating Committee for a bill of particulars on charges against him.

Assistant Committee Counsel Francis D. Flanagan has outlined the charges as follows:

1—That Senator Bilbo received a $25,000 contribution from a Mississippi war contractor in September, 1942.

2—That he received from $6000 to $8000 from other war contractors in 1941 and 1942. Senator Bilbo allegedly turned the money over for the unsuccessful 1942 Senatorial campaign of Senate Sergeant-at-Arms Wall Doxey, who was questioned today at a highly secret meeting of Mead's Subcommittee.

3—That war contractors built an artificial lake—with an island in the middle—on Senator Bilbo's Poplarville, Miss., estate; built his "Dream House No. 2" on the island, later furnished it for him, and that a war contractor gave him a new Cadillac.

4—That Senator Bilbo solicited funds to construct a parsonage for the Juniper Grove Baptist Church in Poplarville and later built the parsonage, but still holds title to the dwelling and has not let the minister move in.

Doxey Questioned

Mead made the announcement after Doxey was questioned for an hour and a half.

Mead ordered a committee in-

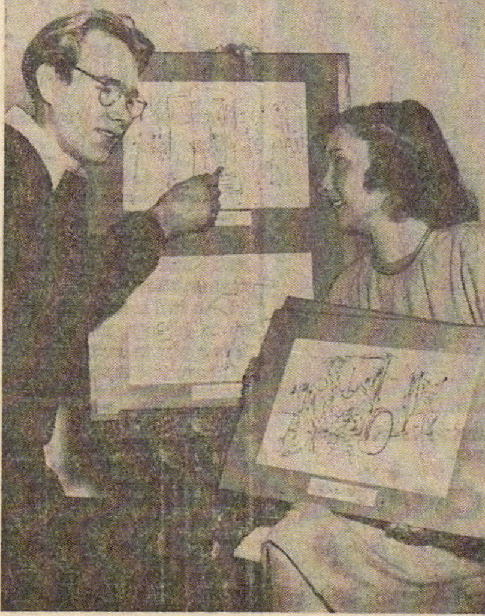

SATIRE OF TOMATO-SQUEEZERS is explained by Andy Warhola to Jane Bicht, fellow art student at Carnegie Tech. His sketches won one of the Leisser Art awards. He's 18, a graduate of Schenley High.

Artist-Huckster Sketches Customers and Wins Prize

Series of Drawings Shows Everything From Idle Rich to Scrambling Poor

Never squeeze the tomato, lady. You may find yourself in Carnegie Institute.

For two months this Summer the good housewives of Pittsburgh squeezed the tomatoes, bananas and assorted produce of Andy Warhols, 18-year-old artist-huckster.

Now the pinch is on the other foot. Andy, a Carnegie Tech art student, has satirized them with a prize-winning set of drawings.

Penned Sketches

As the huckster's wagon went its lazy way through Oakland and Homestead, Andy did something besides dish out vegetables and try

Prosecutor Floors Fascist Leader

Georgian Angered by Remark in Court

ATLANTA, Ga., Nov. 23 (UP)—The smashing right fist of Georgia's

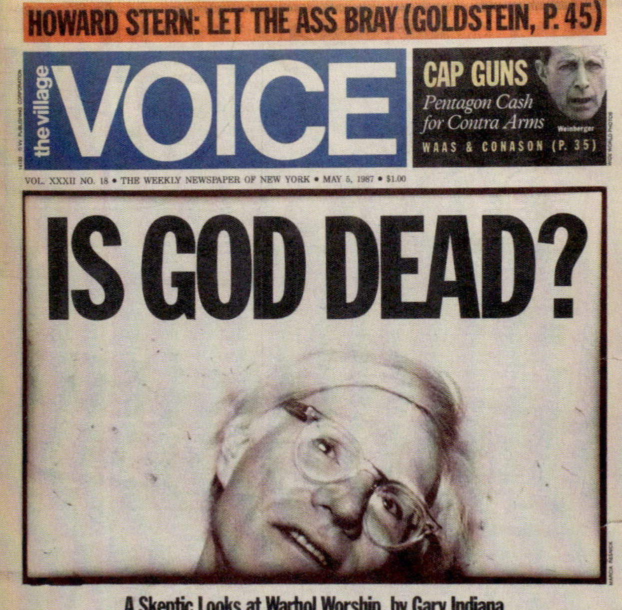

Warhol's first mention in a newspaper, "Artist-Huckster Sketches Customers and Wins Prize," *Pittsburgh Press*, Sunday, November 24, 1946

Village Voice, May 5, 1987

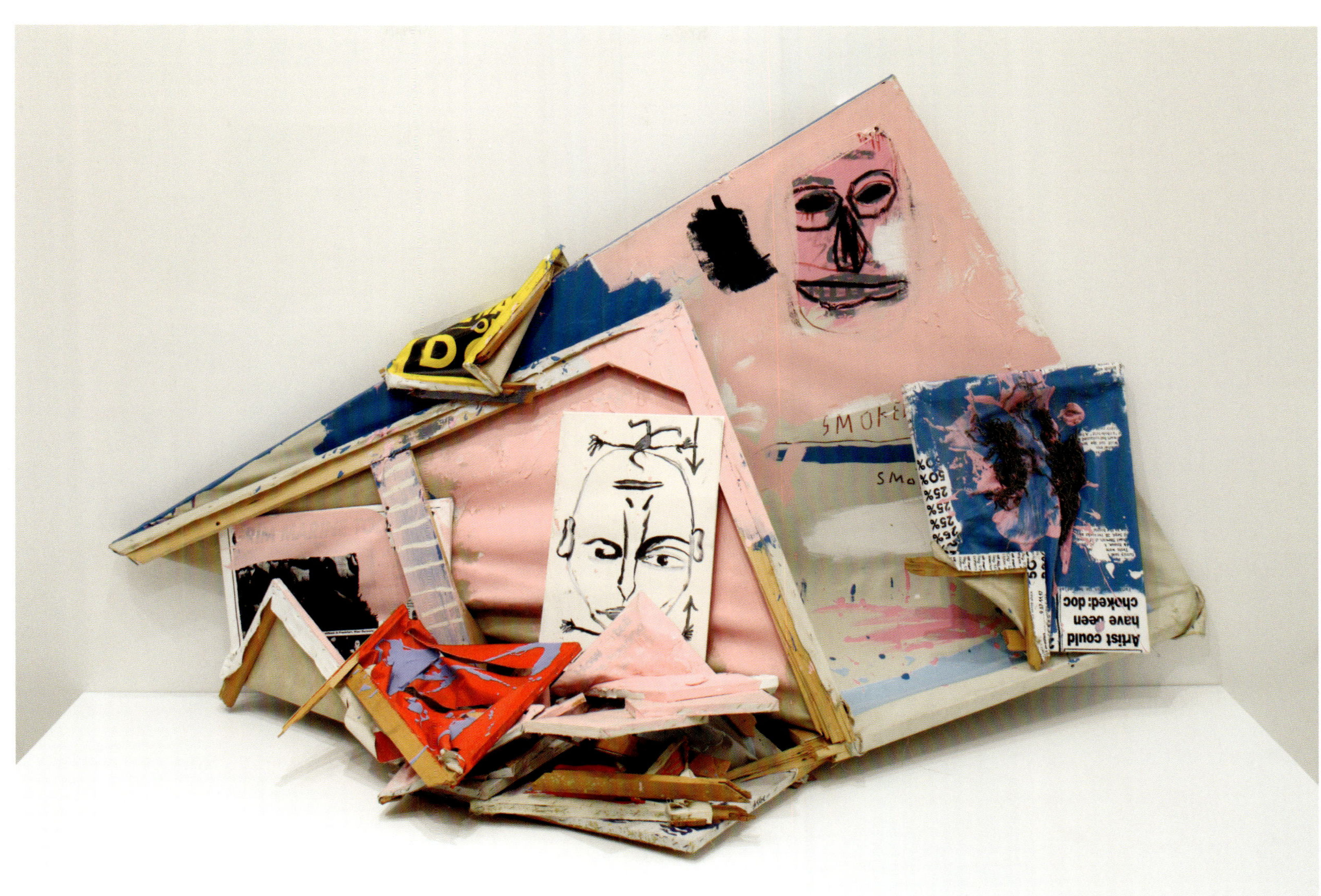

Jean-Michel Basquiat, Francesco Clemente, and Andy Warhol,
Collaboration, ca. 1984

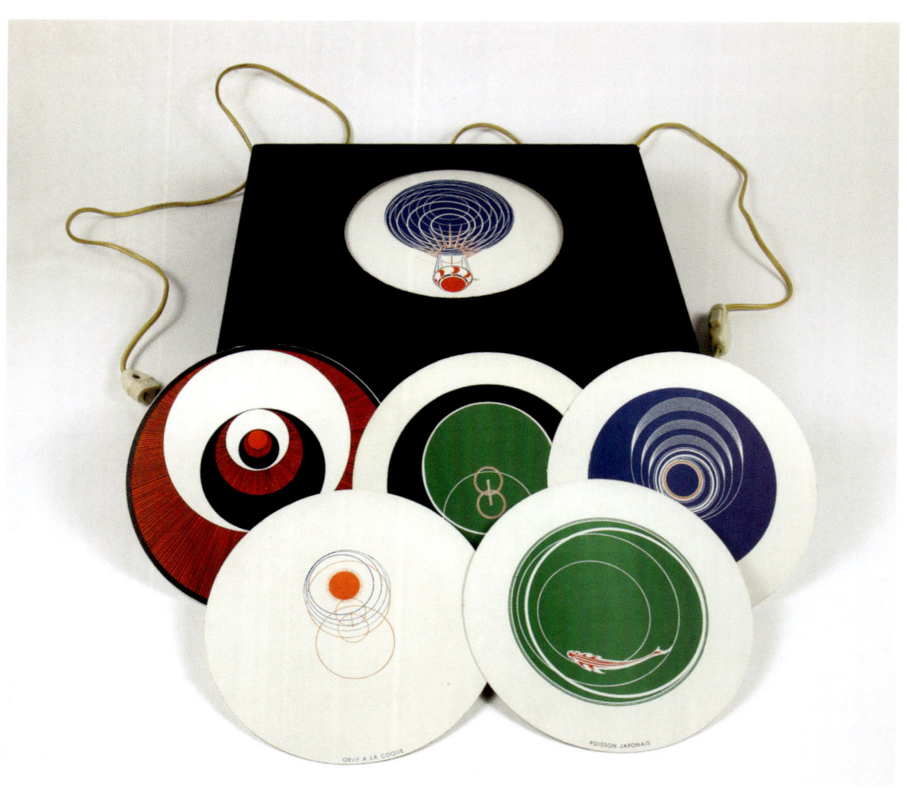

is for ILLUSIONS

This chapter is based on the exhibition *IN 3-D! Illusions of Depth*, in the Archives Study Center, December 11, 2004–September 11, 2005.

Throughout his career, Andy Warhol was interested in the three-dimensional illusions, broadly known as "3-D," that are created by stereo cards, anaglyphs, lenticular images, polarized images, and holograms. Due to their appearance and subject matter, these objects are often considered kitsch—which for Warhol was not a negative but an appealing quality. From images of prosaic landscapes and landmarks to unusual taxidermic animals and female impersonators, the antique stereo cards in Warhol's collection run the gamut. The cards and viewers in the Archive date from the nineteenth and early twentieth centuries. In 1957 Warhol created a work for a commercial client based on the appearance and style of these antique objects, which were among the most popular and common amusements of their time.

The technology for viewing two dimensions in three advanced exponentially during Warhol's lifetime. In 1953 Leonard Maurer produced the first 3-D comic (starring Mighty Mouse) using his patented anaglyphic "illustereo" process. Maurer also made the special glasses needed to view the images. The monochrome image seen through the glasses has a depth that can be startling. The craze of 3-D imagery quickly appeared in magazines and in movies such as *It Came from Outer Space* (1953) and *Creature from the Black Lagoon* (1954).

Warhol painted a small series of works in the early 1960s that attempted to mimic the anaglyphic 3-D illusion of depth that was discovered in the previous decade and created by images rendered in color opposites. Anaglyphs are properly viewed through a pair of red-and-green or orange-and-blue glasses. *Album of a Mat Queen* (1962) is an early Warholian experiment printed in orange and blue. Other works by Warhol in this category include *Statue of Liberty* (1962), *Optical Car Crash* (1963), and the portrait *Patty Oldenburg* (1962). His illusions were unsuccessful but are fascinating regardless.

Along with Warhol, many photographers and inventors became interested in three-dimensional illusions at this time. Their research led to the emergence of lenticular printed images. This technique splices and interlaces two different images under a layer of plastic rounded ridges (lenticular lenses). When the printed card is tilted back and forth, the eye sees a 3-D image or a movement between the two pictures. Arthur Rothstein's *Untitled (Bust of Edison with Five Inventions)* (1964) was the first mass-produced lenticular print, appearing in *Look* magazine that year. From June 1965 through March 1971, the covers of *Venture* magazine were lenticular images. The lenticular prints in the Warhol Archive include postcards and promotional materials and suggest his continued interest in 3-D imagery.

Forever incorporating new processes in his art, Warhol produced at least two works that use lenticular technology. The cover of *Andy Warhol's Index (Book)* (1967) is printed on lenticular plastic, and *Rain Machine (Daisy Waterfall)* (1970), a sculpture, incorporates multiple lenticular prints. *Index (Book)* was the first of several Warhol projects that challenge the usual definition of a book, all dating to the period of 1967–68. The *Index* was initiated by the photographer Nat Finkelstein through his agency, Black Star; he pitched it for publication by Random House with a design realized by David Paul, overseen by editor Christopher Cerf. On Warhol's behalf, the production and design were directed by Billy Linich (Billy Name). A note in the publisher's archives indicates that Jerome Agel was consulted on the project. Agel is known for his bold design work on several books from the period, including significant titles by Marshall McLuhan and R. Buckminster Fuller.

Cerf encouraged Warhol to be as "revolutionary" as possible in his thinking on the *Index (Book)* and sent him many objects for inspiration, though a number of his suggestions proved to be too expensive to include (such as "blinking" lenticular eyes). On the other hand, permission was granted from the owners of the commercial brands that appear in the book: Baby Ruth candy bars, Hunt's tomato paste, Campbell's juice, and Brillo soap pads.

The finished *Index (Book)* includes several pop-ups—two dimensions turned into three: a small red accordion that emits a groaning "Bronx cheer," a triple-gatefold multilayered and rainbow-hued graphic of the profile of Bob Dylan's nose, a spring-mounted circle printed with quotes by critics of Warhol's films, and a pop-out polyhedron that literally bursts from the book with the help of a sturdy rubber band. The final special feature of the *Index (Book)* is an inflatable rubber balloon. In virtually every copy of the book, the

Warhol owned this Marcel Duchamp *Rotorelief*, 1965, consisting of six cardboard discs that create various optical effects when spun on a turntable balloon has fused the pages together so that only its unmistakable shape is apparent, however, in early mockups the balloon is quite visible and is printed with the book's title.[1]

Warhol also held a keen interest in holograms. The earliest-known holograms by an established artist were self-portraits made by Bruce Nauman, shown in 1969 in New York and California.[2] Inspired by Nauman's work with 3-D imagery, Warhol originally intended to use a hologram in the *Rain Machine*, for its ghostly quality. However, it couldn't be achieved at the large scale that he desired. Instead, opting for the less glamorous or less new and exciting medium, Warhol created lenticular prints of a group of four daisies, which were the backdrop for his *Rain Machine* sculpture. The following year he made a second version of this piece, using a different lenticular print of a single daisy.

The first version of Warhol's sculpture *Rain Machine* was exhibited at Expo '70 in Osaka, Japan. Three variants of this unusual piece were executed; each consists of a grid of seventy *Daisy* lenticular prints mounted on a wall, behind a wall-like shower of water, falling into troughs from which it is pumped back into the overhead sprinklers. The second version is in the museum's collection and replaces the image of four flowers with a single bold daisy. It is rarely exhibited because of the humidity that it releases into the building. This version was first shown in the *Art and Technology* exhibition at the Los Angeles County Museum of Art in 1971.

Keeping pace with the times and working in Warhol's film studio, Paul Morrissey shot *Flesh for Frankenstein* (also known as *Andy Warhol's Frankenstein*) in a 3-D process known as Spacevision in 1973.[3] Spacevision used a split prism to expose two images, one above the other.[4] The 3-D effect was visible only on a silver or aluminized screen. Though *Flesh for Frankenstein* was ostensibly a horror film, Morrissey wanted to use 3-D more for humorous effect than for shock value. Combining sex and gore, the film allowed viewers to experience such effects as human guts being thrust out of the screen. Like all 3-D films, it had to be viewed through special glasses.

Warhol collected 3-D works by other artists, including Marcel Duchamp's *Rotoreliefs* (1965). Duchamp was interested in these optical tricks, having himself created not only the *Rotoreliefs* (which the artist referred to as "playtoys" and patented) but also anaglyphs, stereo images, and kinetic sculptures that produced 3-D illusions. Warhol owned six sets of the *Rotoreliefs*, which are intended to be viewed on a wall, mounted in a black velvet–covered turntable designed by the artist. When each card rotates correctly, Duchamp's skillful use of skewed circles, thick and thin lines, and other simple means results in an illusion of depth.

Warhol is one of several well-known public figures to have sat for a hologram portrait by Jason Sapan: *Andy Warhol* (1977). Sapan recalled the process: "I shot it in 35 mm black and white negative stock on a Mitchell Mark II (R 35) motion picture camera on Kodak film stock back in 1976. Paul Morrissey was there taking stereo realist slides of the shoot. But later when I asked him how they came out he said they were lost at the developing and never seen again. What a loss!…Andy was the easiest model to work with. The entire shoot took 24 minutes and was the easiest I can remember. Andy was very cooperative and quiet. With his shock of white hair and gaunt facial features he was easy to capture in three dimensions."[5] Sapan considers his holographic portrait of Warhol to be one of his best, regarding Warhol's gracefulness and high level of cooperation as contributing to the quality of the work. This hologram, also known as a "multiplex holographic stereogram," was exhibited on several occasions in New York's Museum of Holography. The work shows Warhol pausing to glance up at the viewer before turning a page of *Interview* magazine. Despite Warhol's fascination with holograms, he never created one.

NOTES

1. Three mock-ups of *Index (Book)* are in the collection of the Williams College Museum of Art.

2. The exhibition announcement for *Making Faces* has red-and-green images. Held in 1969, this was Nauman's first solo show at the Leo Castelli Gallery.

3. Paul Morrissey was one of Warhol's most important and trusted collaborators in filmmaking from 1965 to 1974. Warhol was the producer of *Flesh for Frankenstein*, which Morrissey wrote and directed.

4. Spacevision borrowed from the same principles as Mauer's "illustereo" process.

5. Jason Sapan, telephone interview with the author, November 2004.

Research assistance for this chapter was provided by Archives interns Bill Zollinger and Jacob Jenson. Additional object research provided by Brianna Treleven. Photographic layouts designed by Becky Shock.

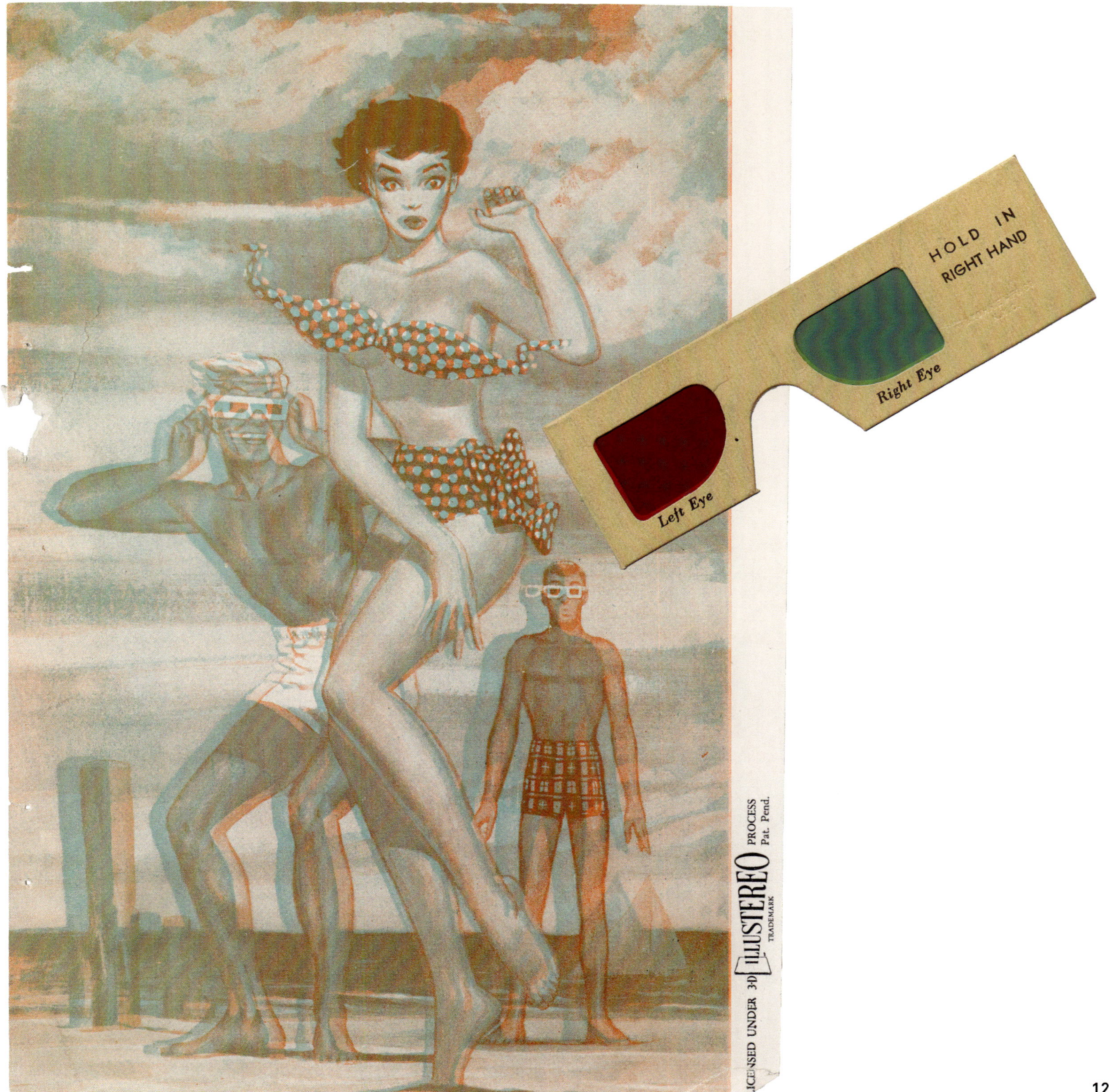

Anaglyphic illustration of beach scene, 1950s

3-D glasses with red and green filters, made by Brownie Manufacturing Co., 1950s

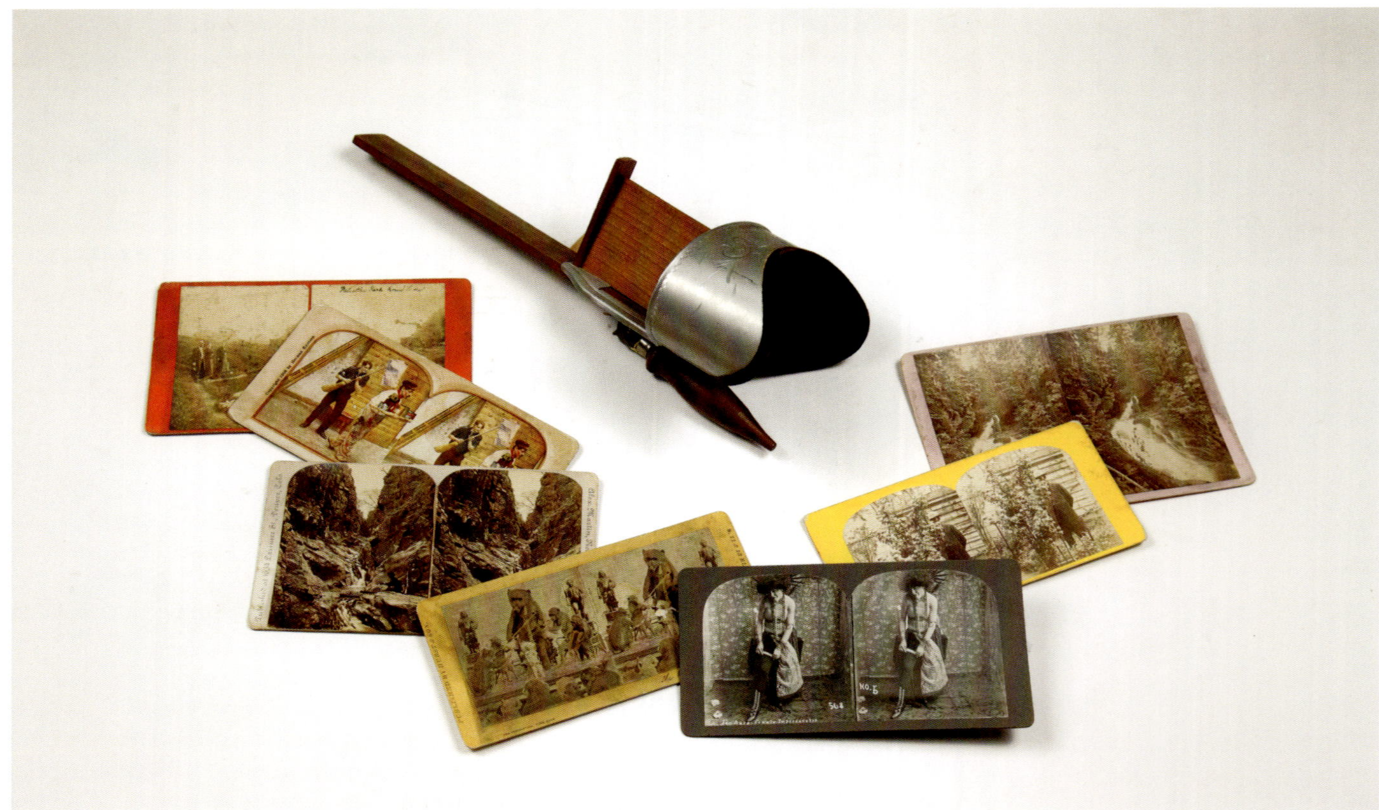

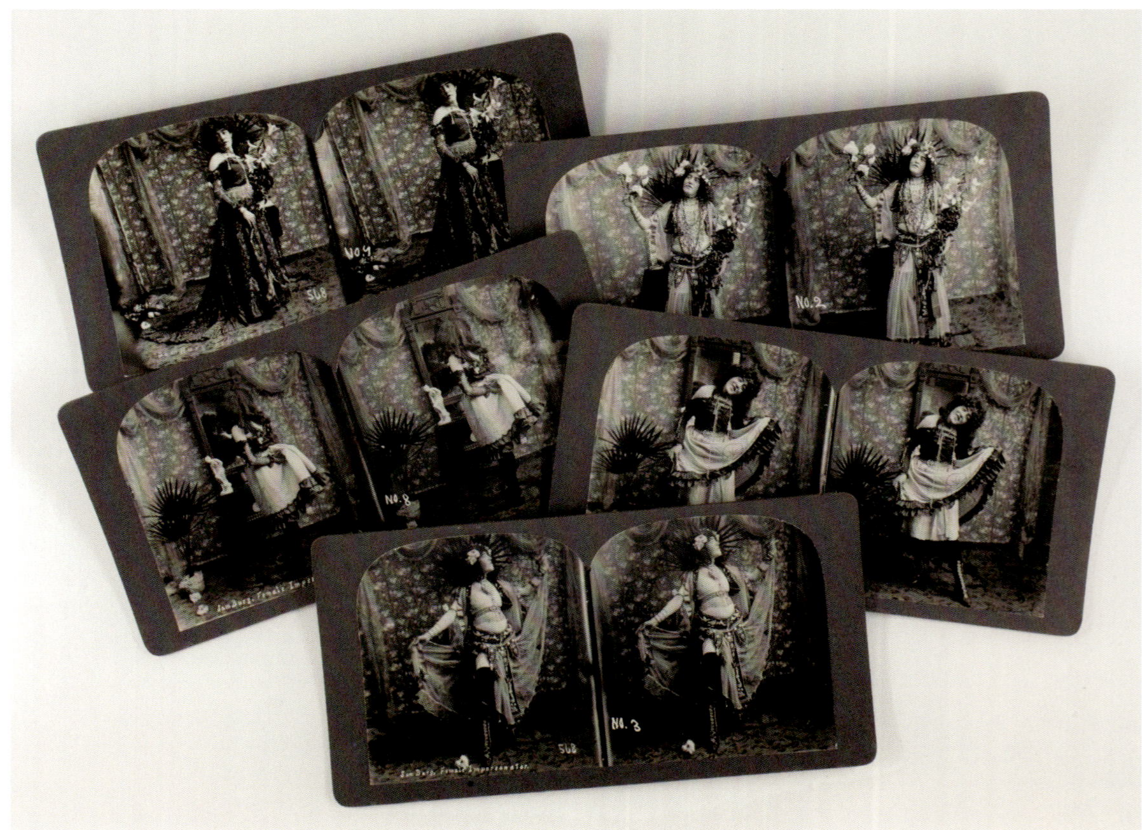

Holmes-type wood and aluminum stereoscope with seven different stereo cards

Five stereo cards depicting female impersonator Sam Burg, n.d.

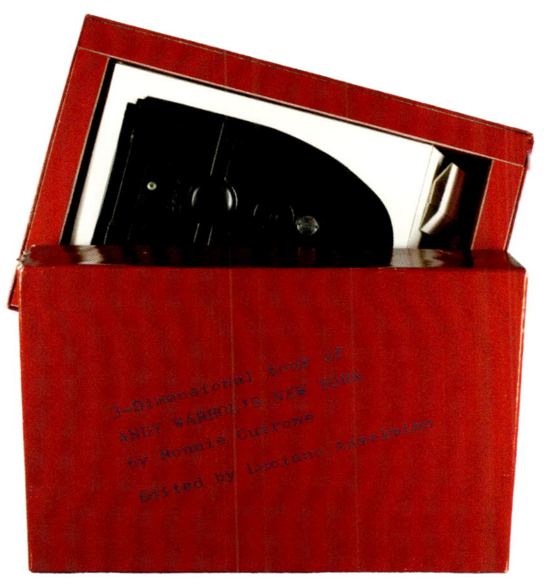
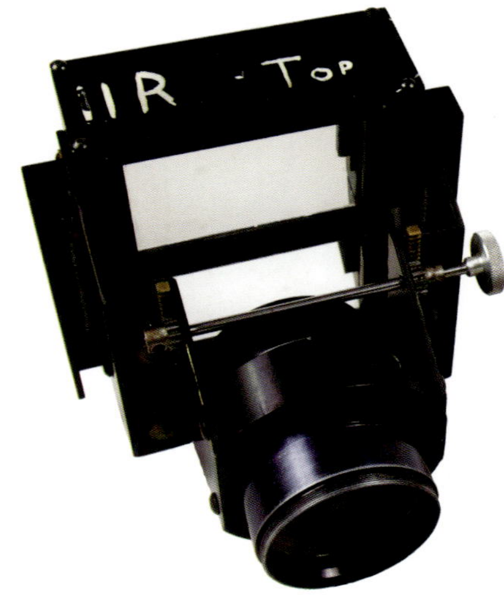
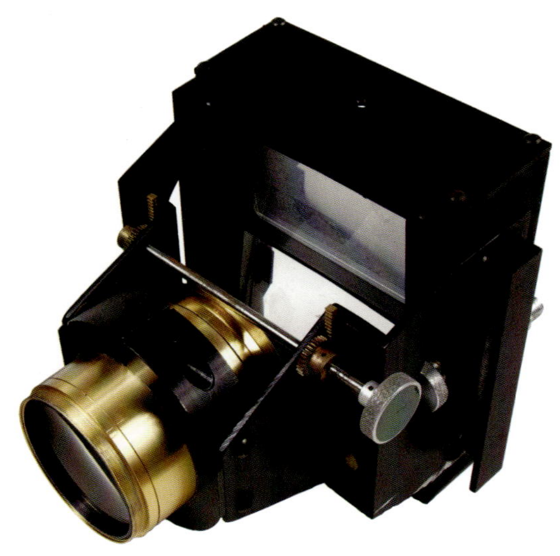

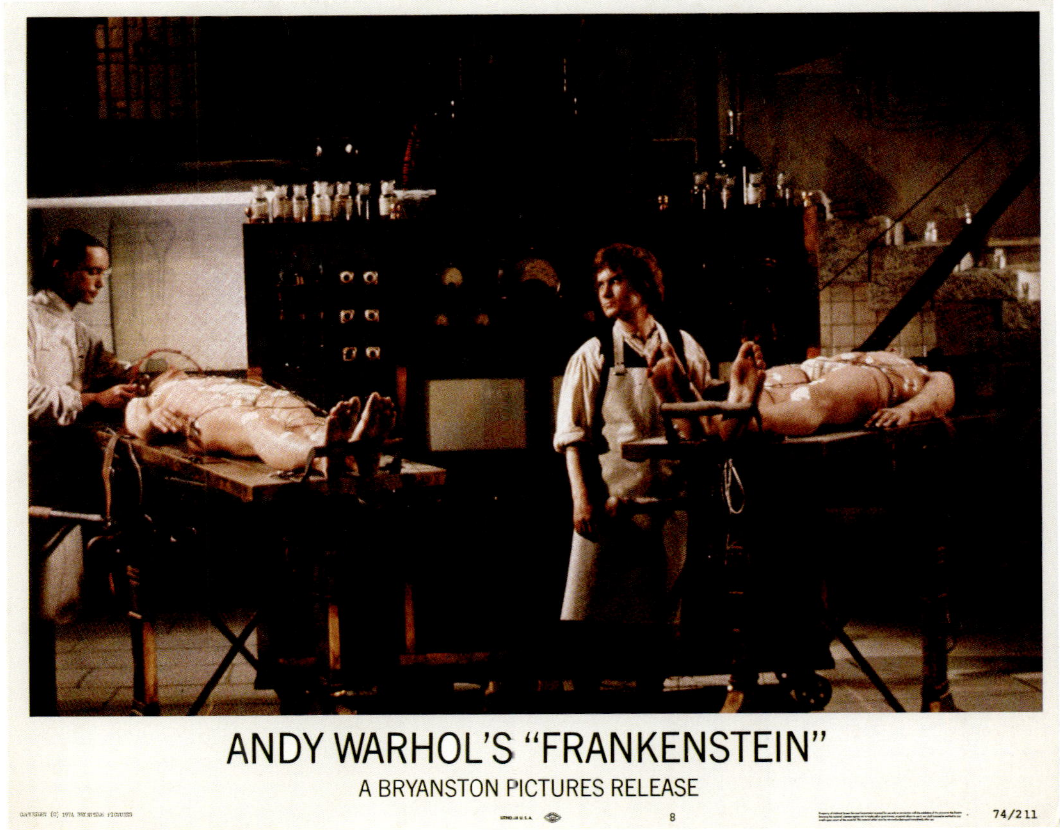

**Ronnie Cutrone, *3-Dimensional Tour of Andy Warhol's New York*, 1975.
The box contains a stereoscope and a typewritten description of
stereoscopic slides.**

Lobby card for *Andy Warhol's Frankenstein*, 1974

**Two Polarator lenses used by Warhol and Paul Morrissey to film *Andy
Warhol's Frankenstein*, 1974**

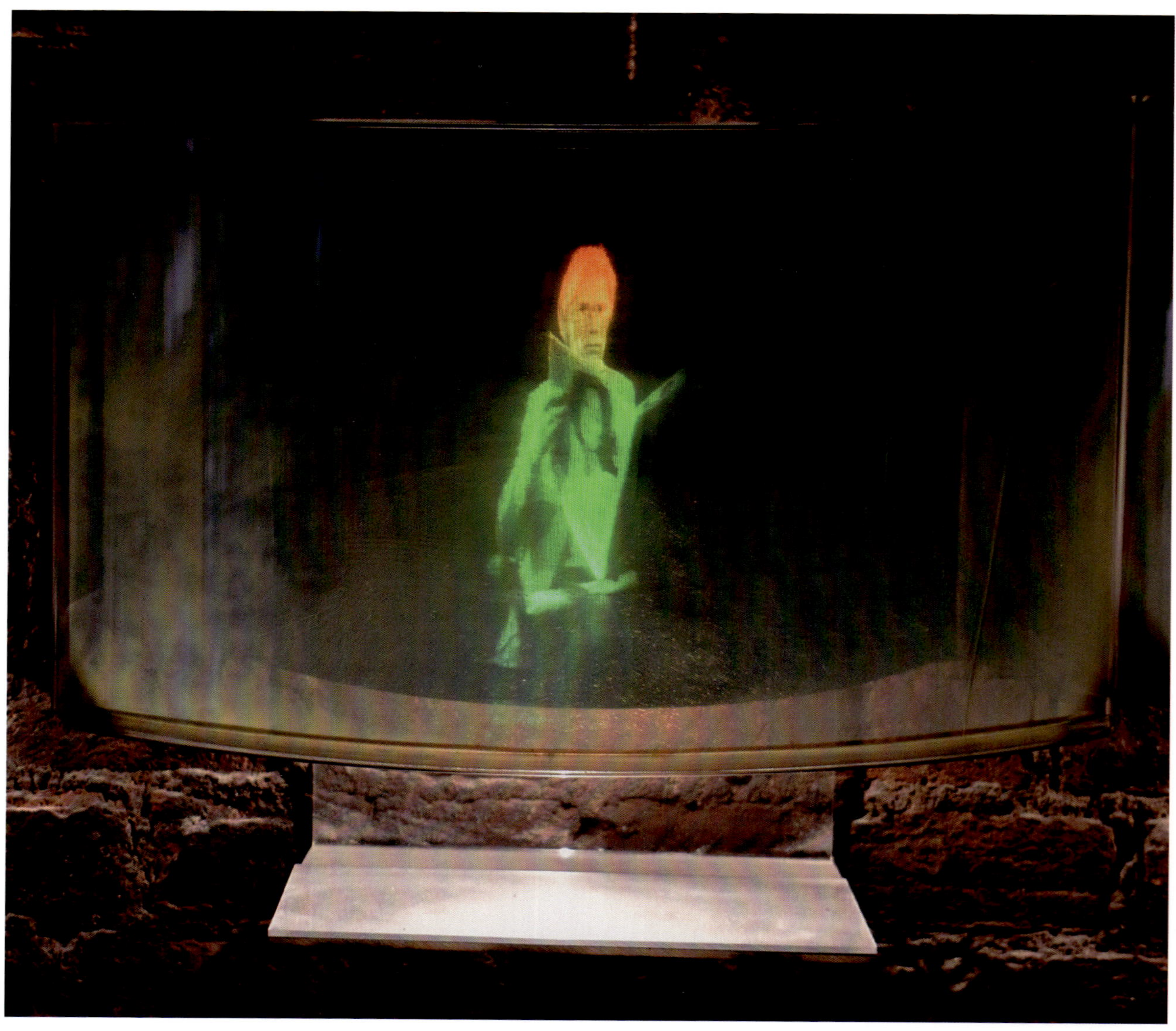

Jason Arthur Sapan, *Andy Warhol*, 1977, hologram of Warhol wearing a
seersucker suit and reading *Interview* magazine (© Jason Arthur Sapan)

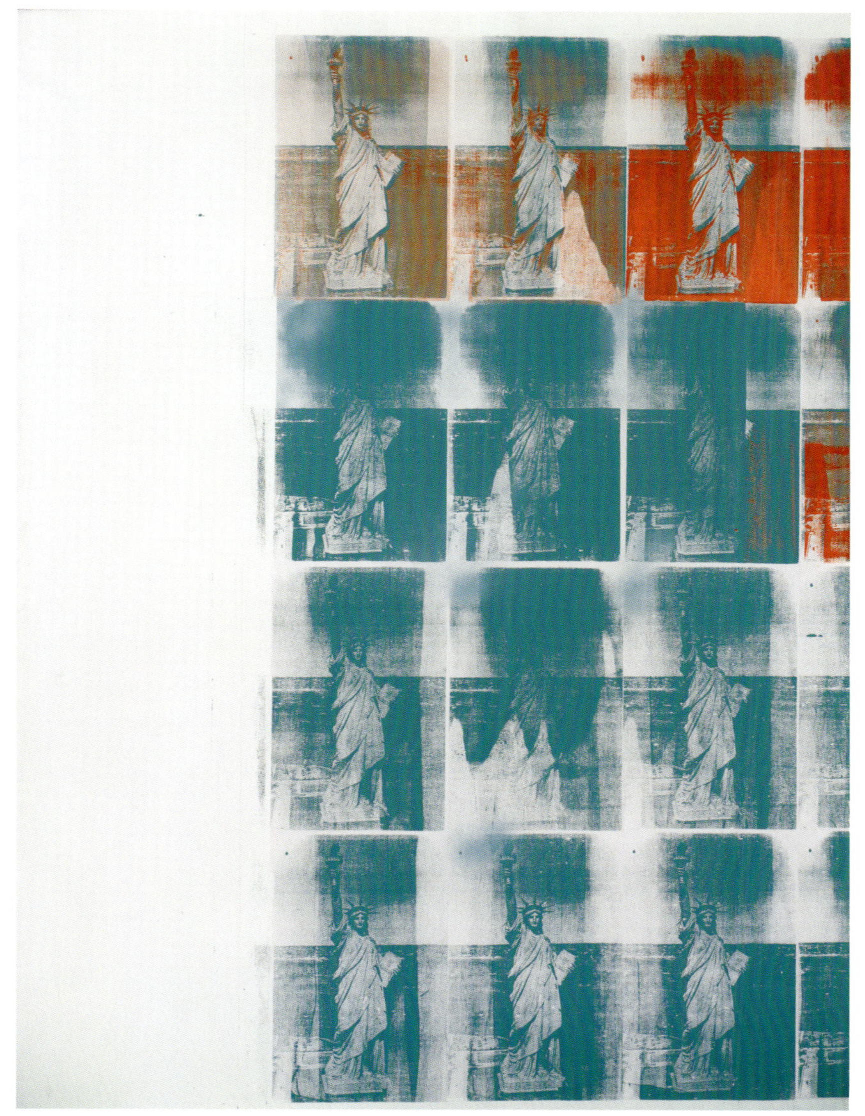

Andy Warhol, *Statue of Liberty*, 1962

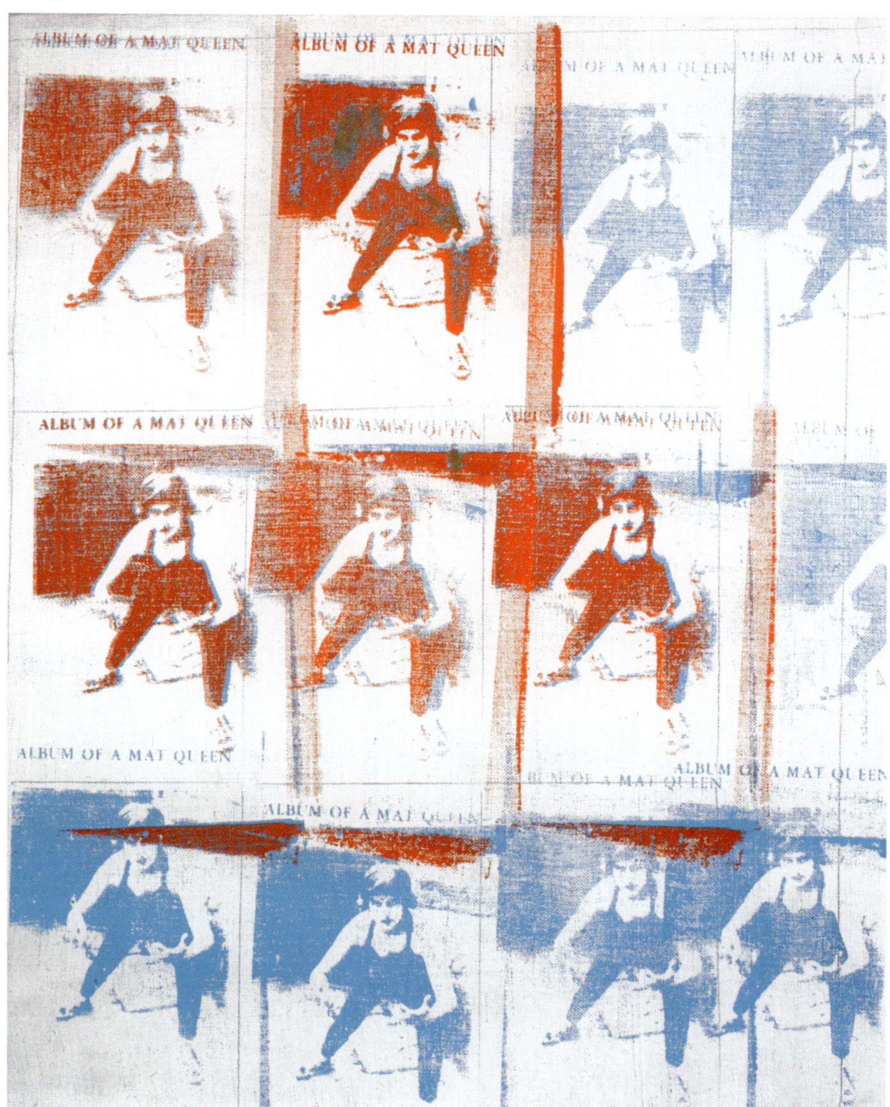

Andy Warhol, *Album of a Mat Queen*, 1962

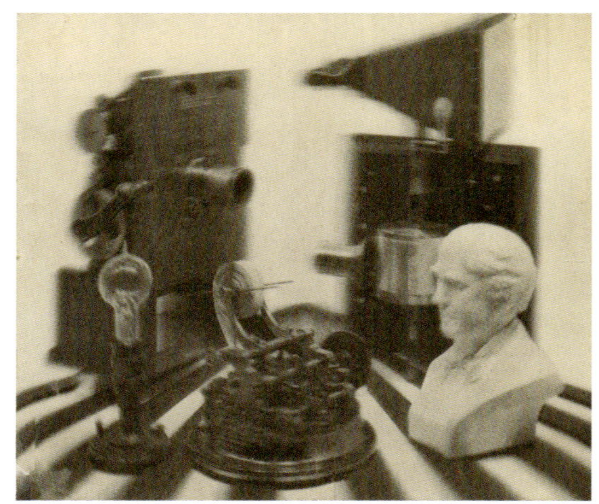

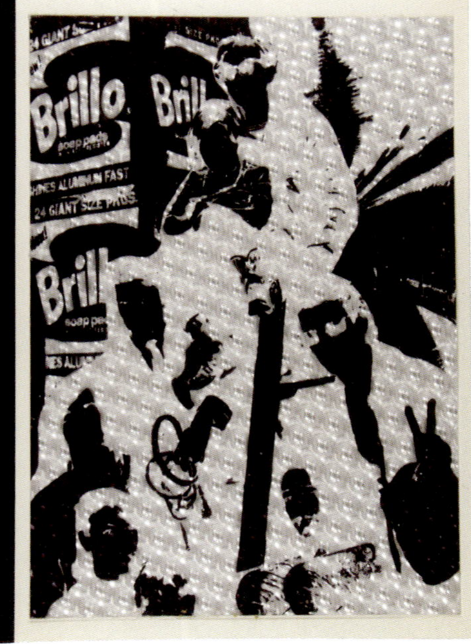

Arthur Rothstein, *Untitled (Bust of Edison with Five Inventions)*, 1964, the first mass-produced lenticular print

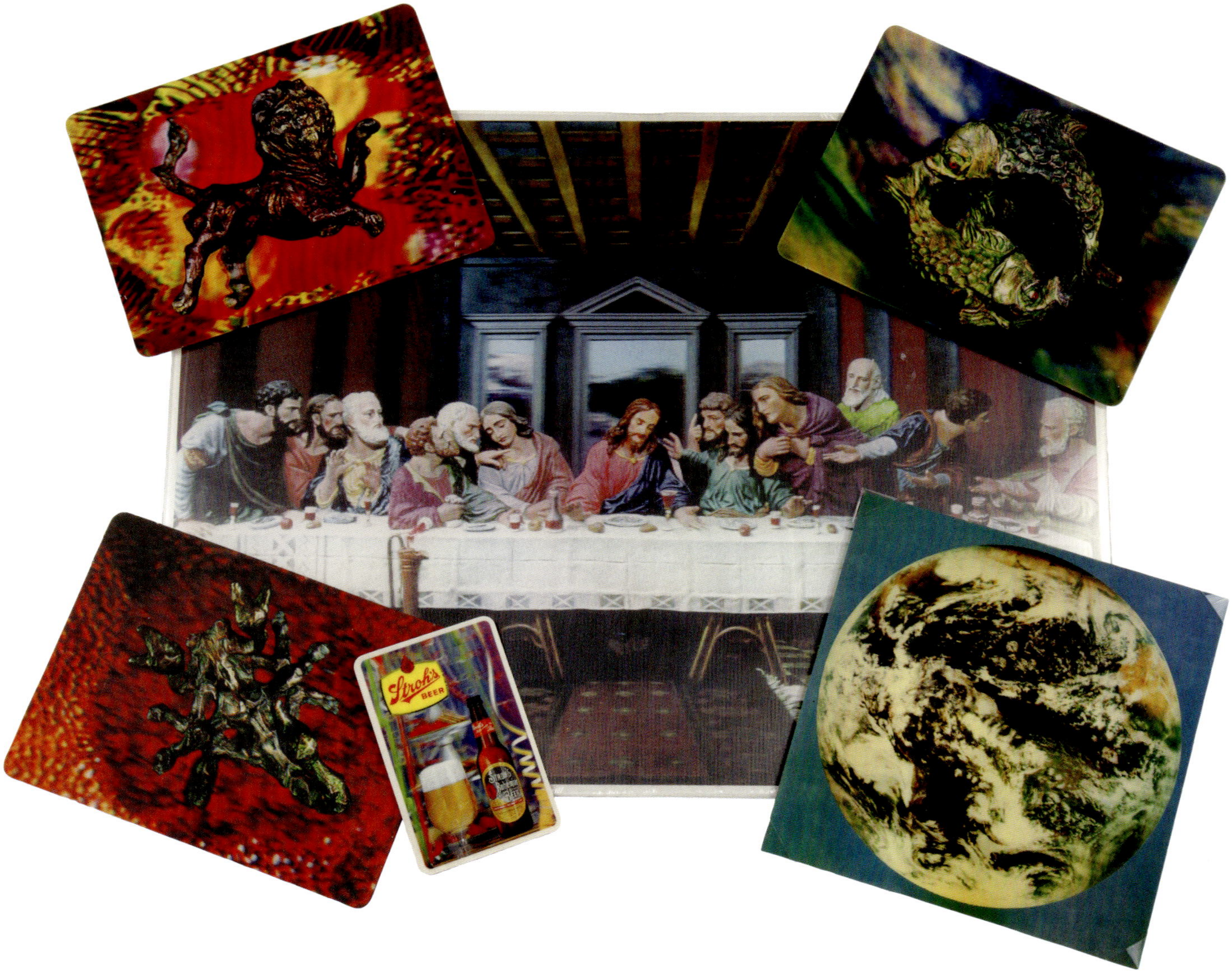

Lenticular prints from Warhol's collection, including the *Last Supper*, various zodiac symbols, Stroh's Beer, and Earth

Andy Warhol, *Andy Warhol's Index (Book)*, 1967, with lenticular photograph on front cover and pop-up interior pages

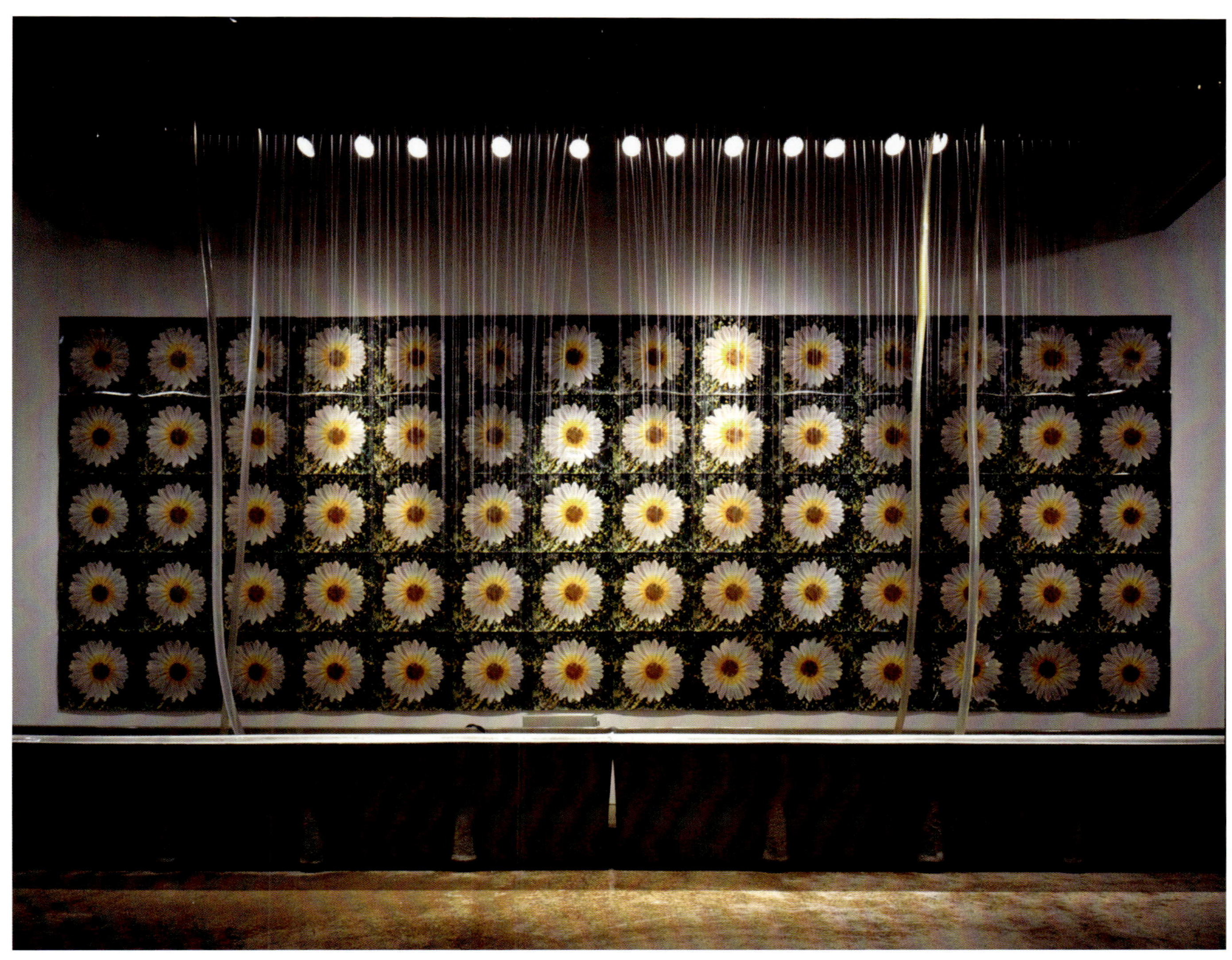

Andy Warhol, *Rain Machine (Reconstruction of Los Angeles Version 1/2)*, reconstruction by Maurice Tuchman and Martin Beck, 1988

Julia Zavacky Warhola immigrated to the United States in 1921. Each leg of her long journey is recorded on her passport, a single well-worn piece of paper marred by deep creases from being carefully folded and unfolded by anxious hands. The passport and other vital documents were found in a *Time Capsule*, miraculously preserved considering their age and mileage. Julia's husband, Andrej (Andrei), had immigrated on November 12, 1912, aboard the SS *George Washington*, sailing from Bremen, Germany, to New York, and settling in Pittsburgh.[1] The couple had been "married for only three years before Andrei departed for America, and tragically just weeks later Julia would bury their first child, a girl named Maria, who was born on November 2, 1912, and died on December 4. Nine long years later, Julia was ultimately able to join Andrei. The documents reveal that on October 12, 1920, Julia traveled from her Carpatho-Rusyn village of Mikova to the city of Prague, where she was granted permission by the American Consulate to travel to the United States.[2] She then acquired visas to travel through Germany and Belgium, crossing the English Channel and arriving in Dover, England, before departing for the United States

J
is for JULIA

This chapter features highlights from *Time Capsule 20*, in the Archives Study Center, March 5–October 12, 2008, and *Time Capsule -27*, part of the exhibition *Andy Warhol's Time Capsules*, October 3, 2004–January 2, 2005, as well as recently discovered archival materials.

from Liverpool in steerage class aboard the SS *Celtic* on June 11, 1921. The transatlantic voyage would take ten days before she finally arrived at Ellis Island on June 21. From there she most likely traveled by train to Pittsburgh.

Julia's much-delayed immigration to the United States and reunion with her husband may have been affected by the outbreak of World War I, which raged across Europe and prevented most Atlantic crossings between 1914 and 1918. This turmoil was coupled with the widespread fear of immigrants that led to the United States' Immigration Act of 1921. The new law would mark the first time that the United States decided to limit immigration from a specific region; the number of immigrants from Southern and Eastern European countries was reduced by about 500,000 people annually. Finally reunited, Andrei and Julia settled into new lives together in Pittsburgh, moving among several rented apartments until they eventually bought a home at 3252 Dawson Street in 1922. The couple had three sons, Paul, John, and their youngest, Andrew, born in 1928.

The family's life was arduous, as it was for many Americans in the 1920s and 1930s. Andrei worked as a building mover for the Eichleay Engineering company. This job consisted of lifting a building up from its foundation onto huge, greased timbers and then moving it to a new, predetermined location. During the Great Depression, Julia supplemented the family's income by making and selling fanciful floral bouquets that she created from empty tin cans and crepe paper.

As a child, Warhol was frail and spent much time alone. His mother nursed him through critical illnesses and shielded him from the taunts of peers intolerant of the boy who did not take part in their sports.[3] Having creative leanings of her own, Julia recognized her son's talent while he was very young. She encouraged his interest in the arts. The young Warhol projected cartoons on his bedroom walls and grew interested in photography. He took pictures with the family's camera, and they eventually bought him his own Kodak Brownie. An area of the basement in the family's new home was cleared for use as a darkroom. From about 1937 to 1941, Andy attended the Tam O' Shanter free art classes at the Carnegie Institute.

The Warholas derived much comfort and strength from their faith in God. Devout Byzantine Catholics, they regularly walked to St. John Chrysostom Church in Greenfield from their home in the Soho area of the Hill District and, later, South Oakland.[4] Julia displayed a color reproduction of Leonardo da Vinci's *Last Supper* in their Pittsburgh home along with holy cards of the saints and encouraged her children's religious practice. Many of Warhol's friends remarked that he kept his prayer book close at hand as an adult.

In 1945 Andy was admitted to the Carnegie Institute of Technology (now Carnegie Mellon University), enrolling in

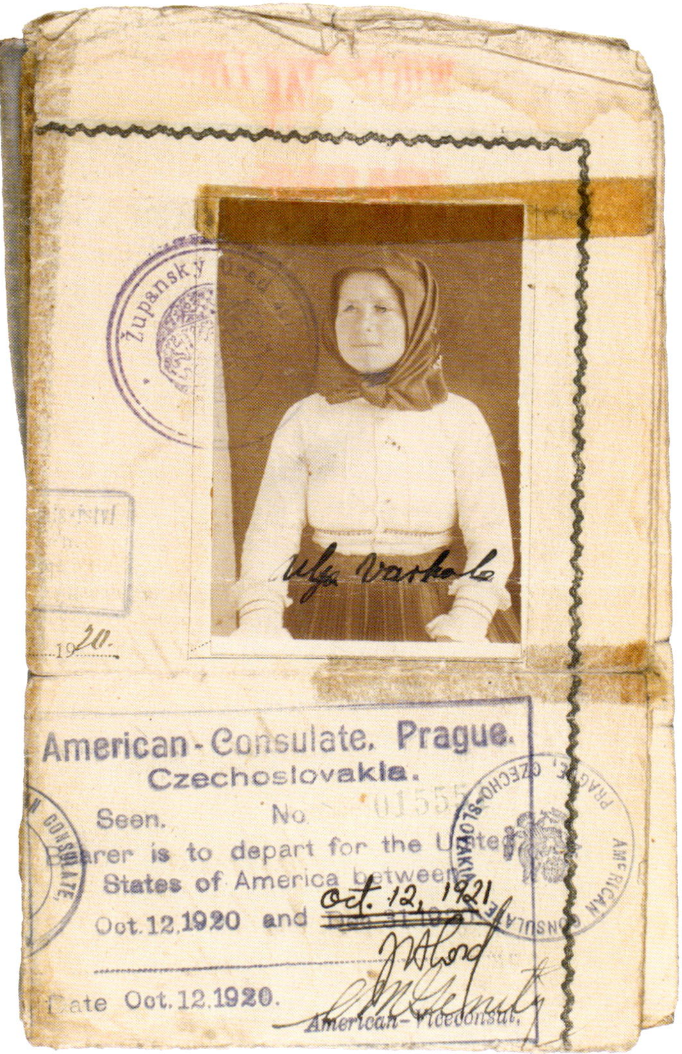

Julia Warhola's passport, 1920

the Department of Painting and Design.[5] After graduating in 1949 with a degree in pictorial design, Warhol moved to New York City, where he was joined by his mother three years later. Mother and son lived together, and she continued to cook and care for him.

During Warhol's early commercial years, Julia was his first assistant and collaborator. Warhol incorporated her beautiful handwriting, learned in her homeland, into his design work, even having Julia sign her son's name to his art. Warhol also turned her handwriting into several custom-made Letrasets, allowing him and his assistants to rapidly add flourishes of her script to the many advertisements in progress. Julia's whimsical curlicue script earned her two professional awards, both credited to "Andy Warhol's Mother." The first was from the American Institute of Graphic Arts in 1957 for her artwork on the LP *The Story of Moondog*, which consisted entirely of her handwriting, and the second was from the Art Director's Club in 1959, for the business stationery she designed for her son, bearing his studio address of 242 Lexington Avenue (see "B is for Box"). Julia Warhola was a highly original, though untrained, artist in her own right. Her favorite subjects were angels and cats, of which she drew hundreds. Warhol had many of these drawings published as a book, titled *Holy Cats by Andy Warhol's Mother* (1960; see "C is for Canis Major").

It is not surprising that many *Time Capsules* contain personal material of Julia's, given that she lived with Warhol for nearly two decades. *Time Capsule -27* is perhaps the most intimate, inscribed on the cardboard box, "Andy Warhol's Mother's Clothes." This *Time Capsule* holds personal clothing, including scarves, blouses, aprons, hats, and silk flowers; an illustrated nursery-rhyme book; and documentation relating to Julia's close association with Saint Mary's Catholic Church in New York City. It also features correspondence with members of her family, some of it written in her native Carpatho-Rusyn. She maintained a frequent correspondence with her family in Pittsburgh and in Europe, often sending them small cash gifts to be donated to their local church. Julia also supported the Holy Trinity Monastery in Butler, Pennsylvania; their solicitations and Christmas cards appear throughout the Archive.

Pittsburgh and New York are mixed together in the jumble of material from *Time Capsule 20*. The blue-and-white edition of the Greek Catholic Union Almanac Kalendar for 1968, published in Munhall, Pennsylvania, contains an inserted newspaper article related to Senator Robert F. Kennedy's assassination by Sirhan Sirhan on June 5 of that year, two days after Warhol was shot and nearly killed by Valerie Solanas (see "Q is for Quick"). These combined events were extremely traumatic for Julia. Another clipping inserted in the Kalendar is a memorial for President John F. Kennedy, outlined in black. Also found in this *Time Capsule* was Julia's plastic patient's card from New York Hospital, where her son Andy would pass away in 1987.

In Julia's later years, Warhol made films and videos of her, eventually painting a series of posthumous portraits of his beloved mother. Even when he partook in a frenetic social life with New York's cultural avant-garde and celebrities, Julia insisted that he attend Mass. She lived with him until 1971, a year before her death in 1972. She is commonly viewed as one of the most influential forces in Warhol's artistic development.

NOTES

1. There are multiple spellings of Warhol's father's name on immigration documents.

2. The Carpatho-Rusyns are a stateless Eastern European people from a region including the Carpathian Mountains, now encompassing parts of Slovakia, Poland, and Ukraine.

3. Warhol did not participate in organized sports in school, but in a conversation with the author during a rare visit to the museum (2005), Warhol's childhood friend, the late Nick Kish, remembered riding sleds in the winter and playing outside with the artist.

4. The Byzantine Rite Catholic Church originated in the Orthodox Christian faith, first introduced to the Eastern Slavs by the Greek Saints Cyril and Methodius in the ninth century and subsequently reinforced by missionaries. Two hundred years later, the Great Schism divided Christianity between Western Rome and Eastern Constantinople. Between 1596 and 1700, the Carpatho-Rusyns gradually separated from the Eastern Orthodox Church, which cleaved to Constantinople. They established a communion with the Roman Catholic Church, professing its dogmas and acknowledging the primacy of papal authority, while also trying to preserve their rich Eastern liturgical and spiritual heritage.

5. Andrei Warhola saved several thousand dollars for Andy to attend college before he died from an illness in 1942.

Additional research for this chapter was provided by Erin Byrne. Photographic layouts designed by Becky Shock.

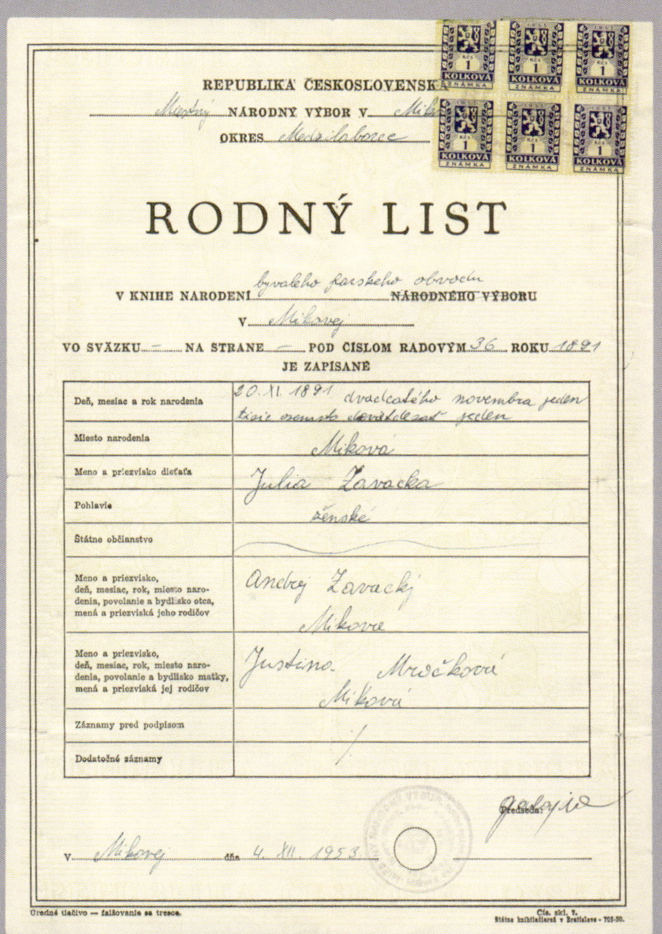

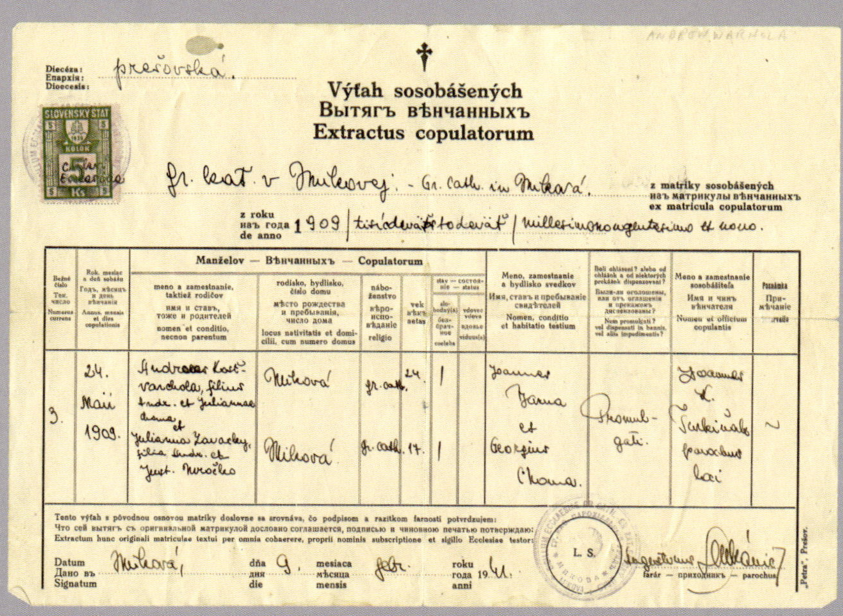

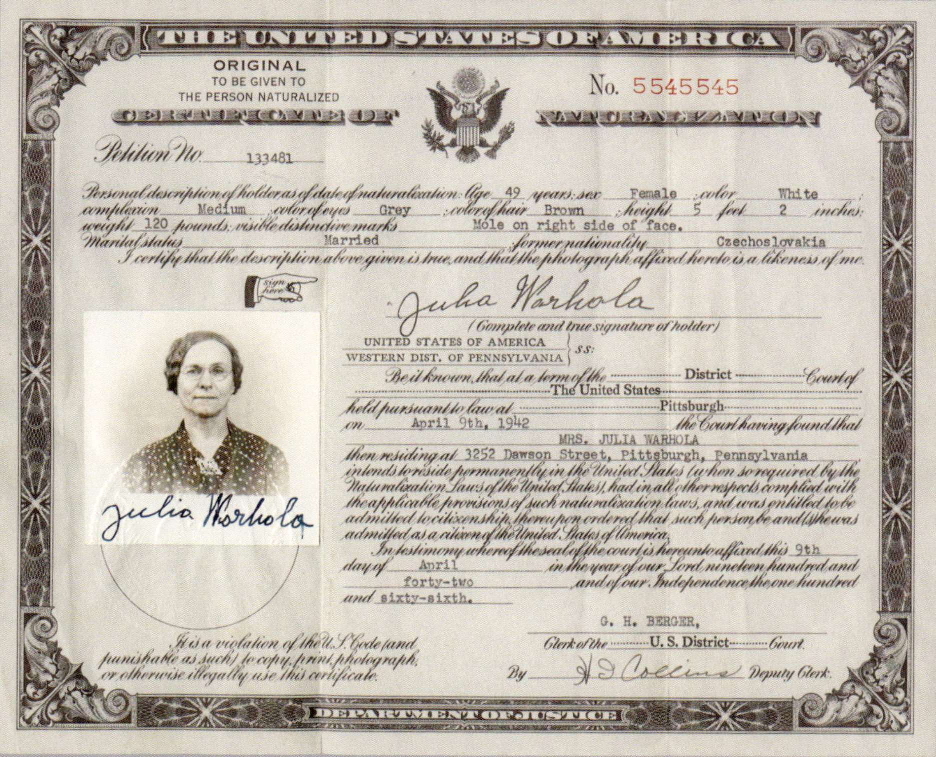

Julia Warhola's birth certificate, issued 1953

Julia Warhola's certificate of naturalization, 1942

Marriage certificate for Julia and Andrei Warhola, May 24, 1909

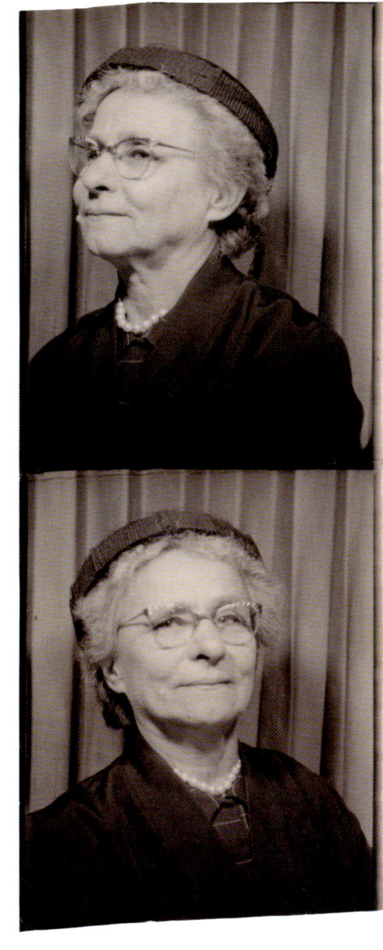

Photobooth strip of Julia Warhola, ca. 1960s

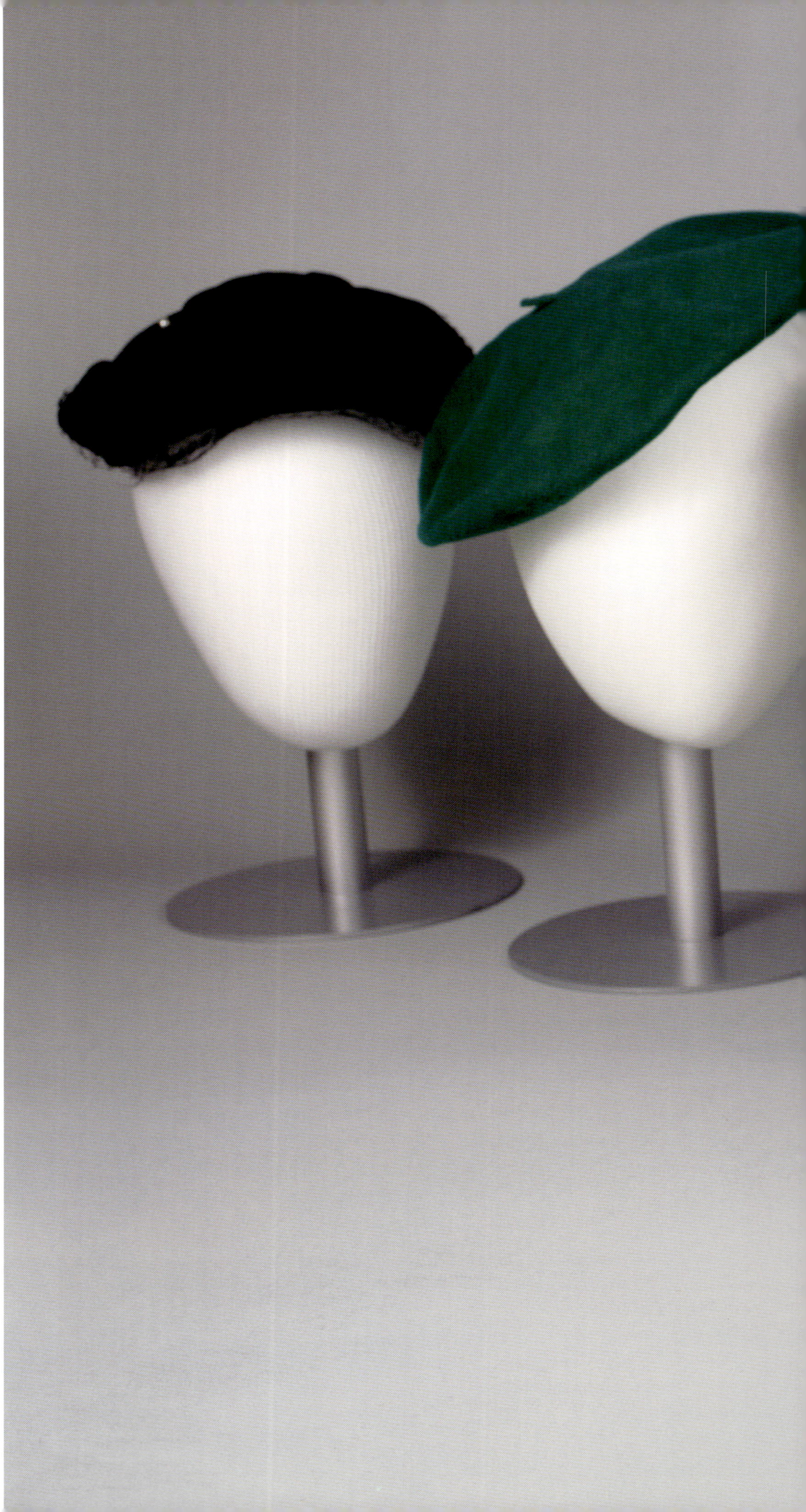

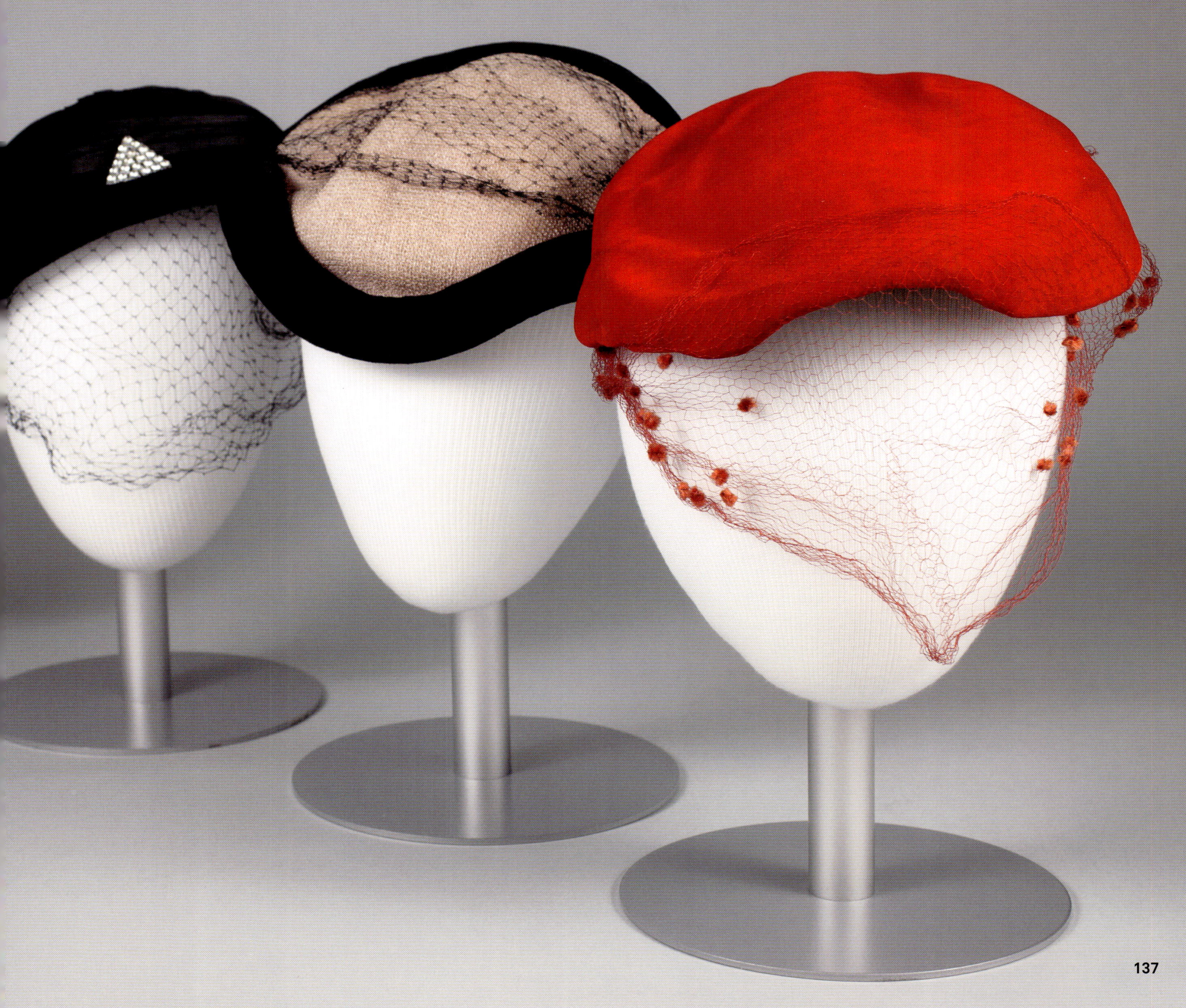

Selection of Julia Warhola's hats

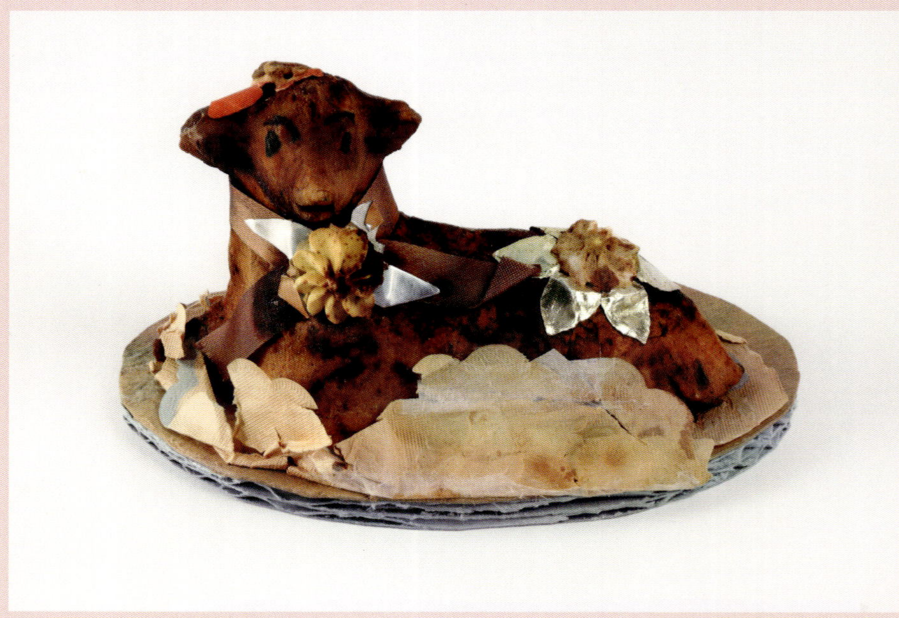

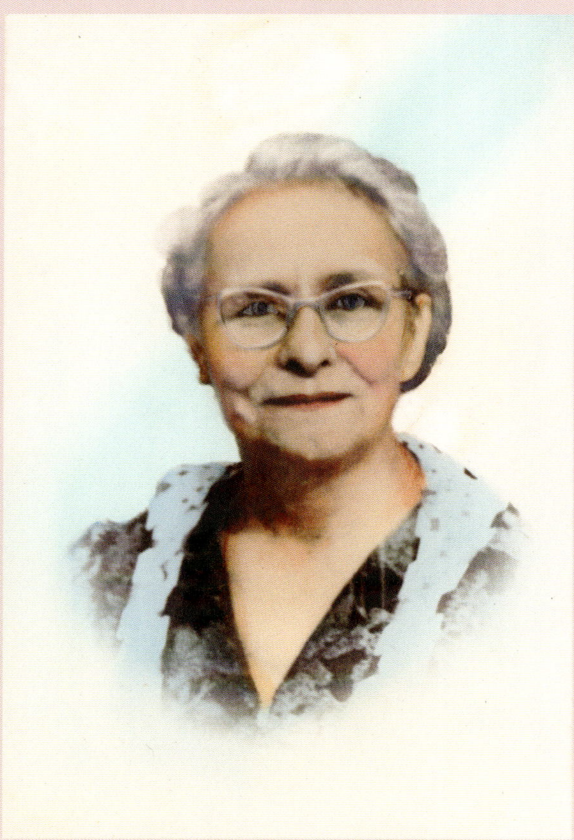

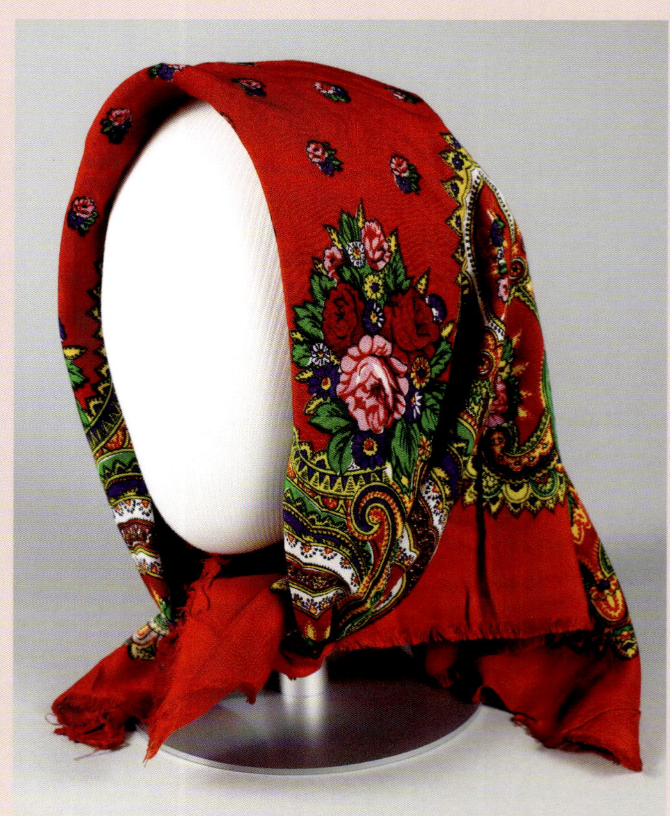

Selection of items that belonged to Julia Warhola from *Time Capsule -27* and the Archive: molded candy marzipan lamb, hand-colored photograph of Julia, n.d., and Czechoslovakian-style floral pattern scarf

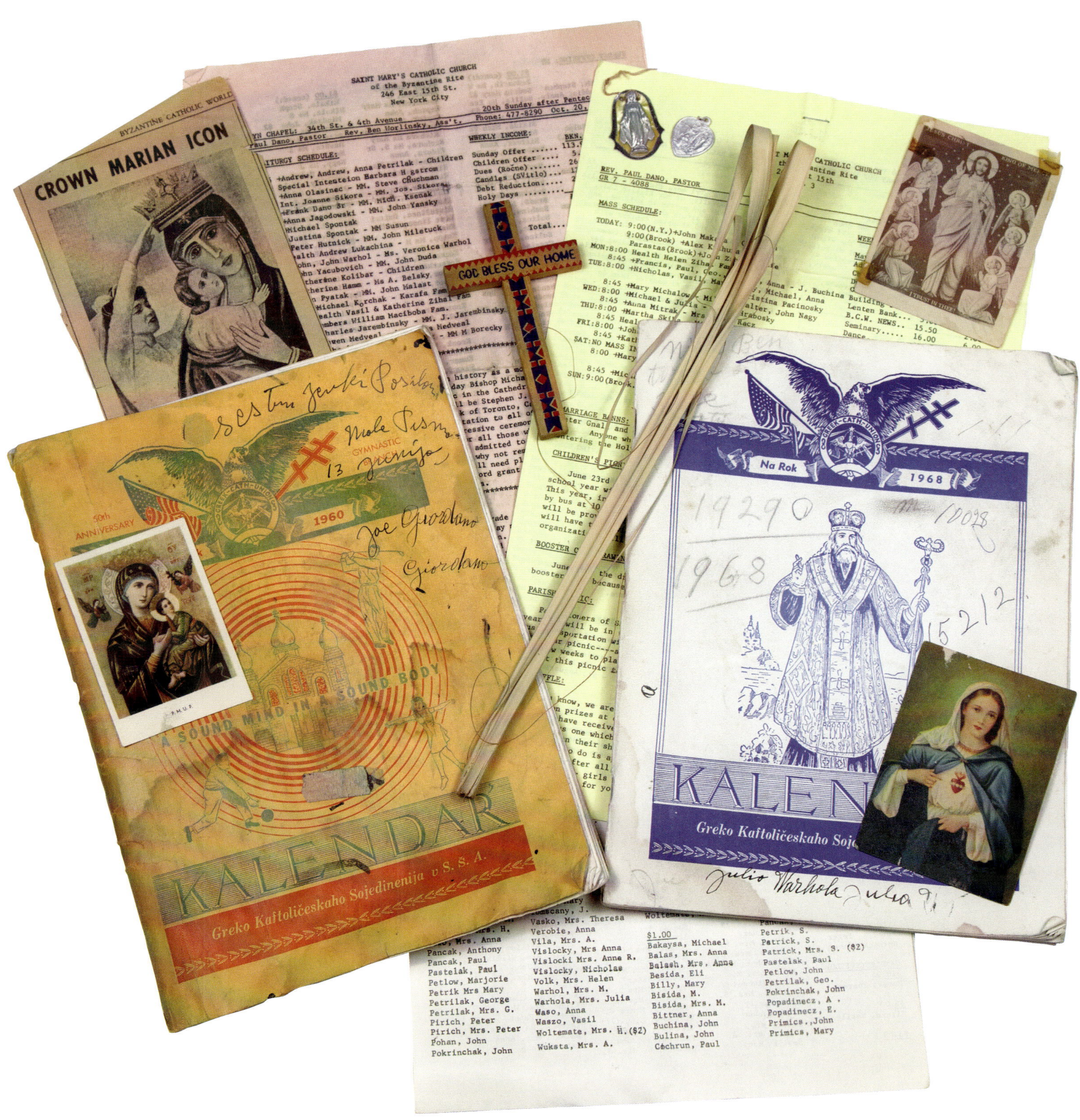

Group of religious objects owned by Julia Warhola, 1960s

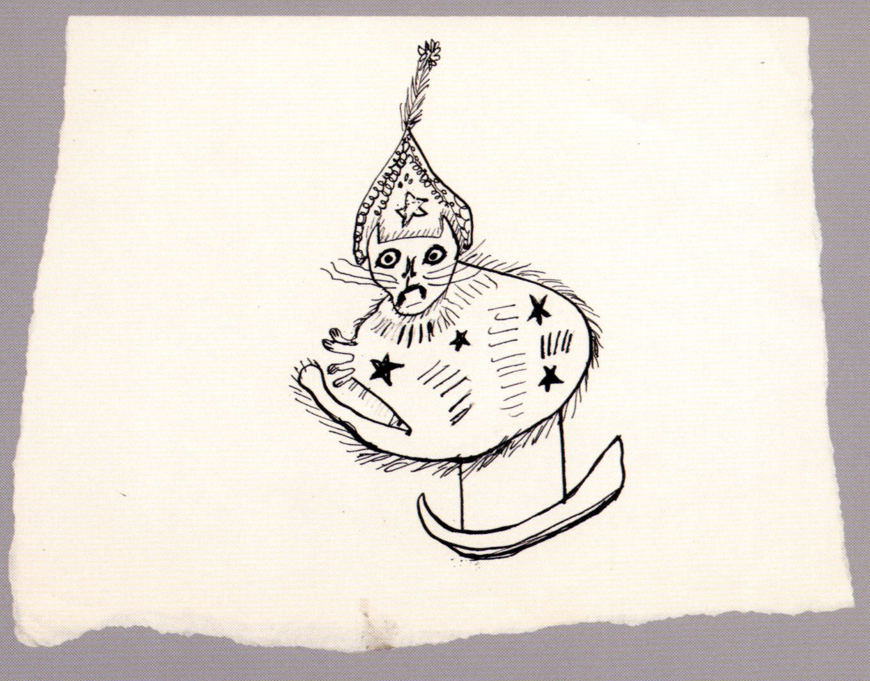

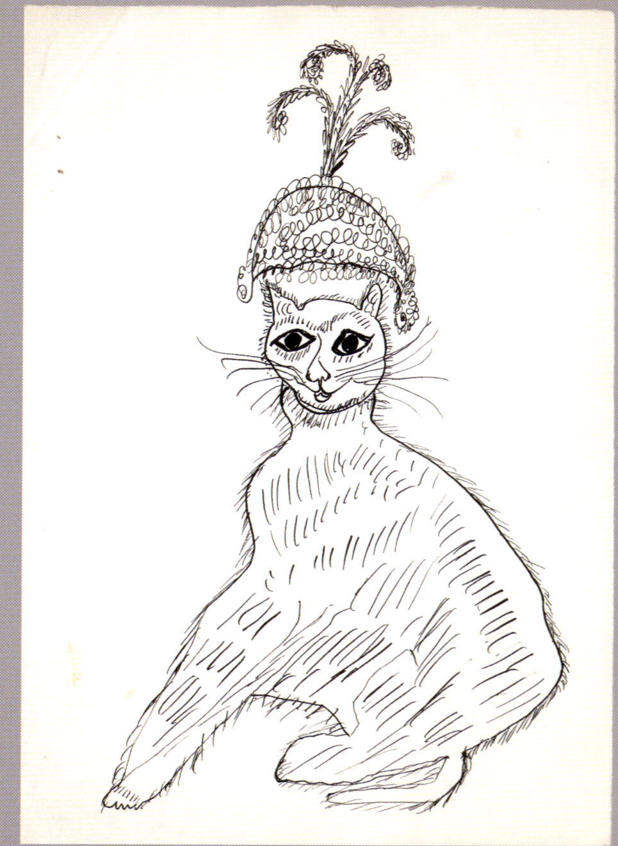

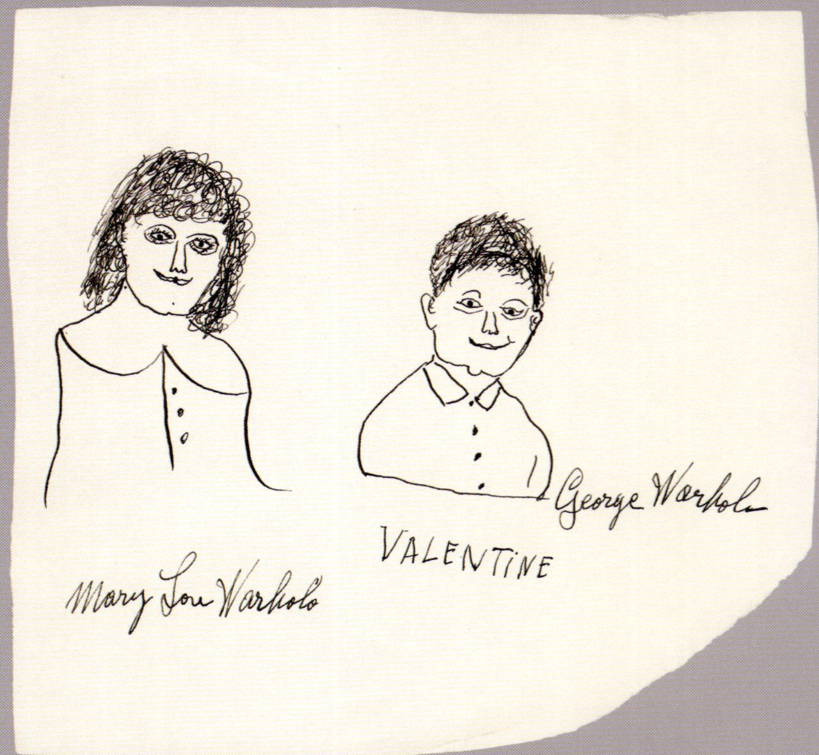

140

Julia Warhola, *Cat with a Hat Reclining on a Hat*, n.d.; *Cat with a Hat*, n.d.;
Mary Lou Warhola and George Warhola (Julia's grandchildren), n.d.

the story of moondog Prestige 7099

moondog is a poet who versifies in sound, a diarist overcome by love, curiosity and amusement by everything that reaches his ears, all of which he transposes into a symphony of himself. it may be the roar from the streets; it may be the casual chatter in a room or, best of all it will be that secret music that seeps through imagination and memory. These experiences, so dull to the dull but so alive to him, he orchestrates into a record of those enchanting conversations everyone can hold with himself would he only listen for a bemused moment. They make up the script of that unique tragi-comedy, the story of anyone's life. Picking up our ears would be so easy, yet it is seldom done.

But when moondog compels us to do it, we are entranced and delivered willingly into new worlds of meaning.

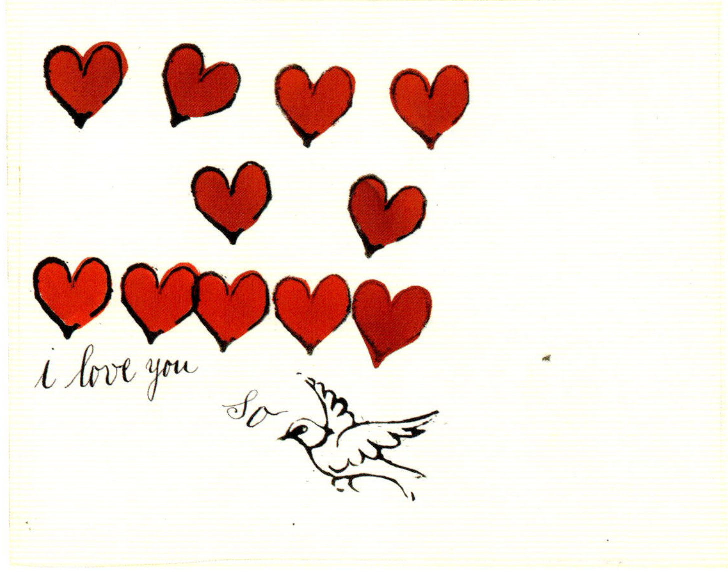

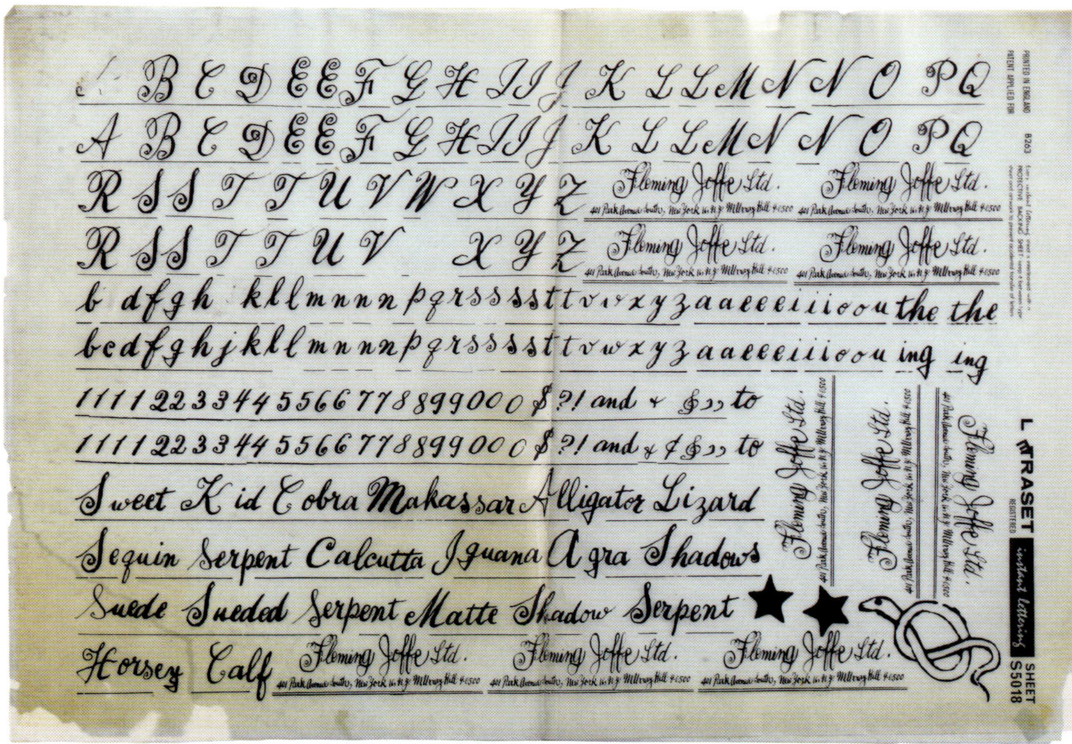

Vinyl record jacket for *The Story of Moondog*, Prestige Records, with calligraphy by Julia Warhola, ca. 1957

Andy Warhol, *"I Love You So,"* 1950s

Letraset of Julia Warhola's handwriting, ca. 1963

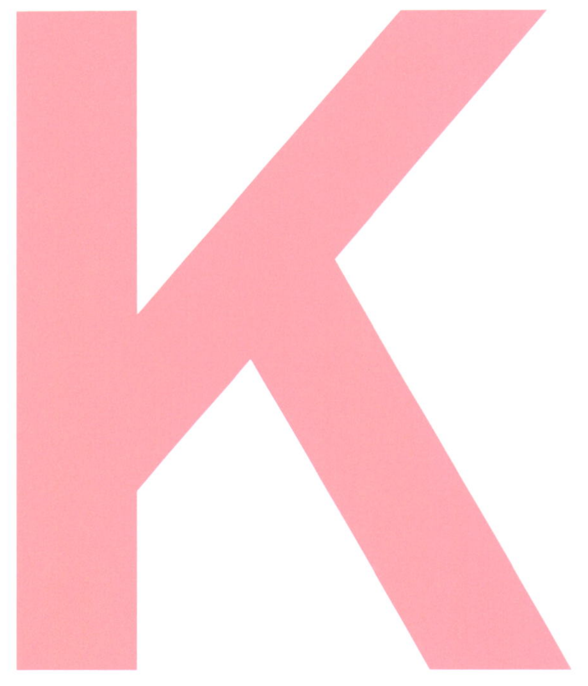

"Kronk" was one of Billy Name's favorite words from his Aerial Canon of concrete poetry.[1] Best known for his iconic photographs that captured the aesthetic of the Silver Factory in the 1960s and for his creative lighting displays in Warhol films, Name was a good friend to Warhol and to The Andy Warhol Museum. The Archive contains unusual documentation of this relationship.

The artist Billy Name was born William Linich on February 22, 1940, in Poughkeepsie, New York. As a teenager, he idolized film stars such as Marlon Brando in *The Wild One* (1953), and James Dean in *Rebel Without a Cause* (1955). After graduating from high school in 1958 as president of his class, he gravitated to the arts although he had no formal training in them. He moved to Greenwich Village with a friend and discovered the scene at the San Remo restaurant on the corner of Bleecker and MacDougal Streets. The San Remo attracted a diverse, creative crowd, including Leonard Bernstein, Judith Malina, Ned Rorem, Simone Signoret, and Tennessee Williams. It was also a hangout for the Beat poets Allen Ginsberg, Jack Kerouac, and others. Linich befriended many dynamic people there, such as Nick Cernovich, a lighting designer for avant-garde

is for KRONK

This chapter is compiled from two exhibitions: *Kronk!*, in the Archives Study Center, March 19–August 31, 1997, and *Billy Name: Factory Fotos 1963–68*, July 25–September 28, 1997.

dance and theater in New York; writer Robert Heide; Robert Olivo, better known as the actor Ondine; and composer La Monte Young. Cernovich and Linich shared an interest in Zen philosophy. Cernovich taught stage lighting and set design to Linich and introduced him to the intensely creative community of experimental artists from Black Mountain College in North Carolina. Through this link, Linich met other artists and writers, including the collage/correspondence artist Ray Johnson. He attended numerous avant-garde film screenings (including works by Stan Brakhage and Stan VanDerBeek) and performances. Following these initiations into aesthetic awareness, Linich was hooked. He traveled to Spoleto for the 1960 Festival of Two Worlds as Cernovich's assistant, lighting the operas, plays, and other stage productions. Around that time, he also journeyed to San Francisco, visiting the poet Diane di Prima and dancer Freddy Herko. Eventually, he took over Cernovich's lighting-design position at the Judson Dance Theater in New York. Linich also became involved in the downtown New York poetry avant-garde, working on publications such as *The Floating Bear* and *The Sinking Bear*, with Johnson, di Prima, and others.

Billy Linich first met Andy Warhol in 1959 while working at the New York café Serendipity 3, and again in about 1962 when Johnson invited them both to attend a bodybuilding competition at the Brooklyn Academy of Music (see "B is for Box"). The third time they met was in late 1963 at a haircutting party in Linich's Lower East Side apartment, which he had covered entirely with mirrors and aluminum foil, or "silver." Linich learned the skill of haircutting from his great-uncle Andy Gusmano, a barber, and he often held salons for members of the downtown art world, usually on Friday nights at his apartment. The party inspired Warhol to feature him in his new film, *Haircut* (1963). Shortly after, when Warhol rented a new studio on 47th Street in January 1964, he asked Linich to decorate it like his silver apartment. This process took several months and prompted Linich to live in the studio, now christened the Factory, after the hat factory that was formerly on the premises. The Silver Factory (1964–68) made its debut with a huge invitation-only celebration on the opening night of Warhol's *Boxes* exhibition, which Linich installed at the artist's

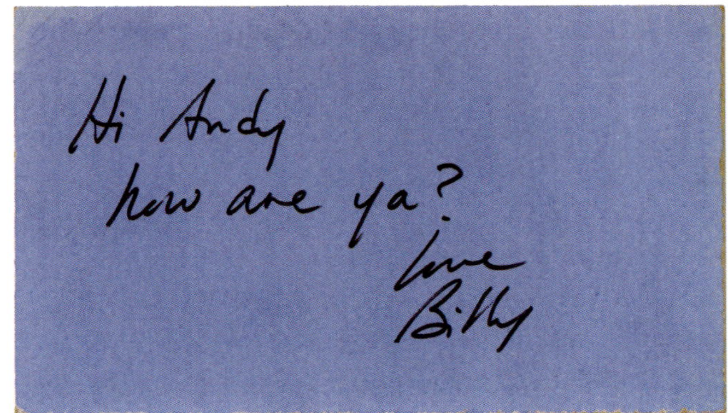

request, at the Stable Gallery in April 1964. The cream of New York's cultural worlds attended, and the unattributed decor made the gossip columns the next day.

Around that same time, Warhol gave Linich his 35-millimeter single-lens reflex camera and asked him to record the Factory's daily events and shoot production stills of the films to which Warhol was beginning to devote more and more of his energy. Linich taught himself the art and craft of photography through how-to books, popular magazines, experimentation, and daily practice. His knowledge of theatrical lighting played a significant role in the look of his photos, many of which captured the film sets he had illuminated. His intimate understanding of the Factory demimonde, along with a moderate-length telephoto lens, permitted him to capture emotions and expressions that may have been suppressed for another photographer.

Linich appeared in a number of Warhol's films: three versions of *Haircut* (1963), *Couch* (1964), *13 Most Beautiful Boys* (1964–65), *Lupe* (1965), and an unreleased all-male version of *Nude Restaurant* (1967). He was also one of four participants in the off-screen dialogue soundtrack of *Harlot* (1965), starring Mario Montez.

Billy Linich became Billy Name in 1966, when he needed a stage identity for his role in *The Exploding Plastic Inevitable*, Warhol's multimedia performance show. A mail-in reply form in a magazine, which requested the sender's name, triggered the idea. Warhol thought it was "cute," and Billy Name was born. An essential member of Warhol's Factory,

143

Note from Billy Name to Warhol, 1960s

Billy Name became known as the unofficial Factory foreman, famous for his dramatic lighting of Warhol's films and particularly for his photos of the Factory scene. Warhol said that Name's photos were "the only thing that ever came close" to depicting the ambience of the Silver Factory. The photographs were originally used for publicity and were published as Factory Fotos in almost every magazine or newspaper story about Warhol. Name's photo of Warhol with International Velvet, Nico, and Mary Woronov was seen nationwide in ads and posters for the epic film *The Chelsea Girls* (1966). Many of the photos appeared in *Andy Warhol's Index (Book)* (1967), Warhol's first book of his Pop period and his first to be mass-produced (see "I is for Illusions").

About two hundred of Name's Factory Fotos were featured in the central section of the catalogue for Warhol's 1968 Stockholm retrospective, the artist's first solo show in a major museum. Two of the Velvet Underground's studio albums utilized Name's photos: a small detail from a photo showing a tattoo of a skull subtly printed in black on black for the cover of the band's second album, titled *White Light / White Heat*; and informal photos of the band lounging on the Factory couch for the cover of their eponymous third record. Name's portraits also adorned the cover of Nico's 1967 solo album, *Chelsea Girl*. In 1980 Warhol again used many of Name's photos to illustrate his memoir of the 1960s, *POPism*.[2] This accumulated exposure burned the images into the era's consciousness as darkly glamorous icons of the 1960s avant-garde. Name's images from the 1960s are usually high-contrast and grainy, due to the lighting and his use of high-speed film. Their subjects include all of Warhol's Superstars of the period, caught by turns at their most flamboyant, ethereal, gritty, luminous, or sensual. The Archive contains several rare hand-colored black-and-white images of stunning beauty.

Name was working in his photography darkroom late in the afternoon of June 3, 1968, when he heard yelling, then gunfire and more voices. He opened the door and saw Warhol lying in a pool of blood, shot in the chest by the writer Valerie Solanas (see "Q is for Quick"). Rushing over to him, Name cradled Warhol's head in his arms and sobbed. Name remembers that Warhol told him, "Don't make me laugh, Billy. Please. It hurts too much."[3] Soon after this violent assault, from which Warhol nearly died, Name began to slowly withdraw from most of the Warhol crowd, although he continued to live at the Factory. He gradually became more deeply involved in the study of astrology and Eastern and occult mysticism. He spent most of his time studying in the darkroom and permitted only Lou Reed and Ondine access to his room, because they shared his interests. Eventually, Name realized that he needed to leave the Factory, and sometime in the winter of 1969–70 he departed, leaving a note to Warhol saying that he was "not here anymore but I am fine. Love, Billy." He gave no clues of his plans or whereabouts, and his New York friends assumed he had simply disappeared.

Name left New York City, visited his family in Poughkeepsie for a short time, and then traveled to Washington, DC, where he witnessed the demonstrations against the Vietnam War. He made his way further south to New Orleans and then hitchhiked through Boulder, Colorado, to San Francisco, where he again visited Diane di Prima. The Bay area was the locus of the era's counterculture, and Name immersed himself in metaphysical philosophy, one of many prevailing cultural interests of the period. He lived a hermit's existence in California and spent long periods in intense self-examination, through which he discovered concrete poetry and conceptual sculpture. In 1977 Name went home once more to Poughkeepsie. He reestablished his New York connections, contacting Andy Warhol and Henry Geldzahler, a former curator at the Metropolitan Museum of Art and fellow Warhol associate. In 1986 he started the Mid-Hudson Arts & Science Center. He also exhibited locally and developed a co-op with artists from the area.

Andy Warhol died on February 22, 1987, Name's forty-seventh birthday. Name attended Warhol's memorial service, held at St. Patrick's Cathedral on April 1, and was reunited with dozens of old friends after two decades. As Warhol's estate was slowly sorted out, discovered among his enormous collection of furniture was a beat-up old steamer trunk, painted silver. Name had originally found it in the basement of the Factory in 1964, and it had become part of the Factory scene: used as a seat by Edie Sedgwick in Warhol's 1965 film *Vinyl*; as a table surface for movie projectors; and, finally, as storage for Name's possessions, including a large cache of photographic negatives and vintage prints. The contents were returned to the artist on the order of the executor of Warhol's estate, Fred Hughes, who knew Name well from their brief time together with Warhol in the late 1960s.

In subsequent decades, Name's classic photos of the 1960s gained new life, inspiring artists, photographers, and the fashion world with their aesthetic qualities and status as documents of an incredible moment in American art. He also produced new works of conceptual photography and sculpture and continued to develop his Aerial Canon of concrete poetry, which is based on the vowel system and was, for Name, a way of transforming energy into the form of vocalized sounds. One of his major concerns was ensuring that he passed on to others the insights of the gracious, inspiring artists he had known.

The Andy Warhol Museum and its staff, researchers, and visitors are recipients of Name's generosity. Name attended the museum's grand-opening weekend in 1994 and returned to Pittsburgh several times afterward to deliver a public talk, sign copies of the latest book of his photos, attend the 1997 opening of *Billy Name: Factory Fotos 1963–68*, and, finally, attend the museum's twentieth-anniversary star-studded party in 2014. Name appeared on-screen in the museum's introductory film (produced for the twentieth anniversary), along with Brigid Berlin (Brigid Polk), Bob Colacello, Vincent Fremont, Paul Warhola, and other significant figures in Warhol's life. He passed away two years later, on July 18, 2016.

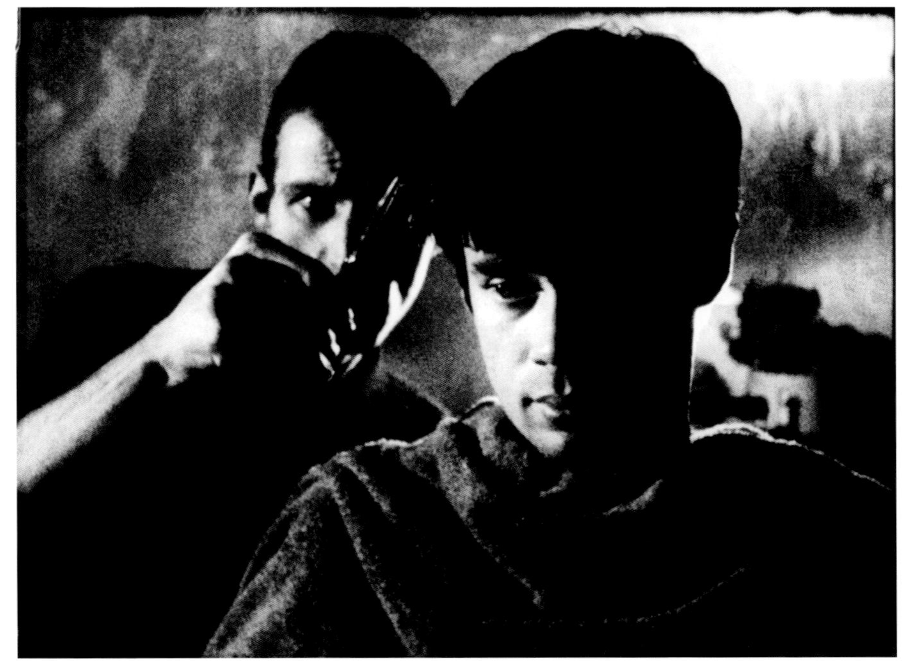

Andy Warhol, *Haircut (No. 1)*, 1963, Billy Name pictured

NOTES

1. The author visited Name at his home in Poughkeepsie, New York, a couple of times. One of these visits led to Name's lending the museum a group of archival materials for the small exhibition *Kronk!*

2. Andy Warhol and Pat Hackett, *POPism: The Warhol Sixties* (Orlando, FL: Harcourt Brace Jovanovich, 1980).

3. Steven Watson, *Factory Made: Warhol and the Sixties* (New York: Pantheon, 2003), 331.

Research assistance for this chapter was provided by Geralyn Huxley and Greg Pierce of the museum's Department of Film and Video. Photographic layouts designed by Becky Shock.

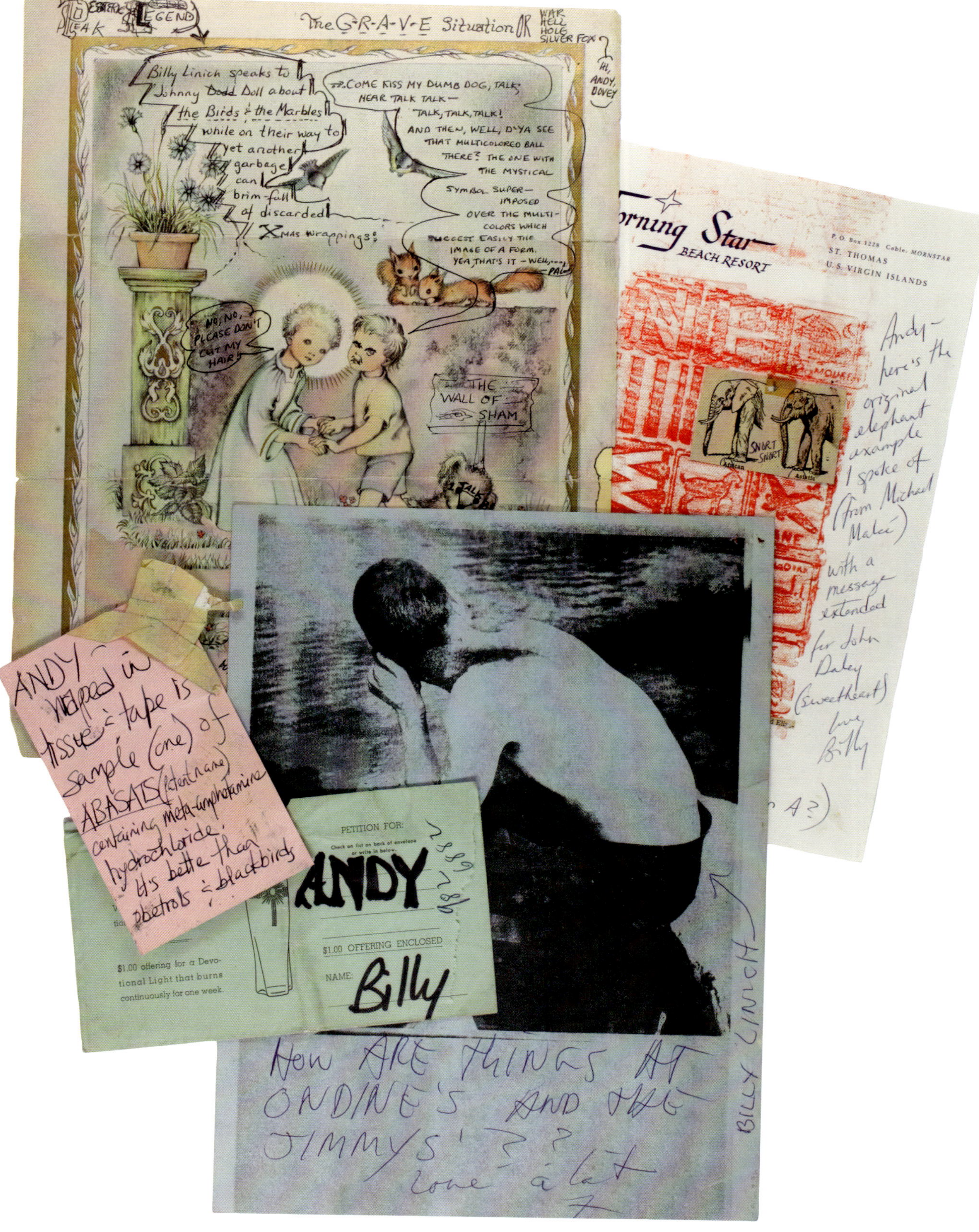

Grouping of correspondence, with drawings and poems given
to Warhol by Billy Name, 1960s

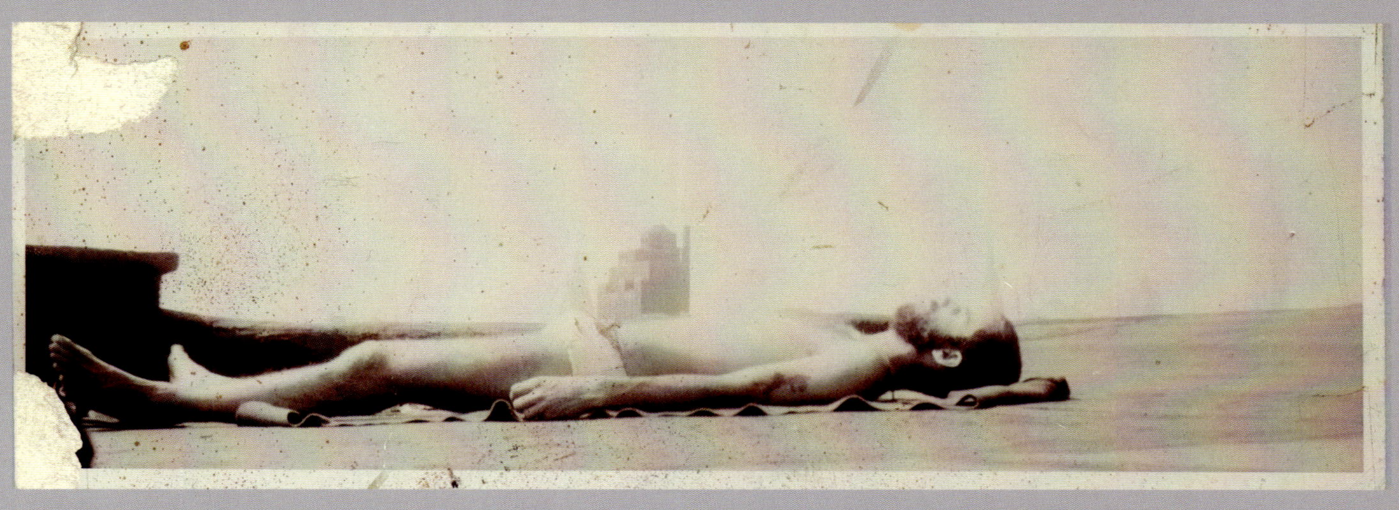

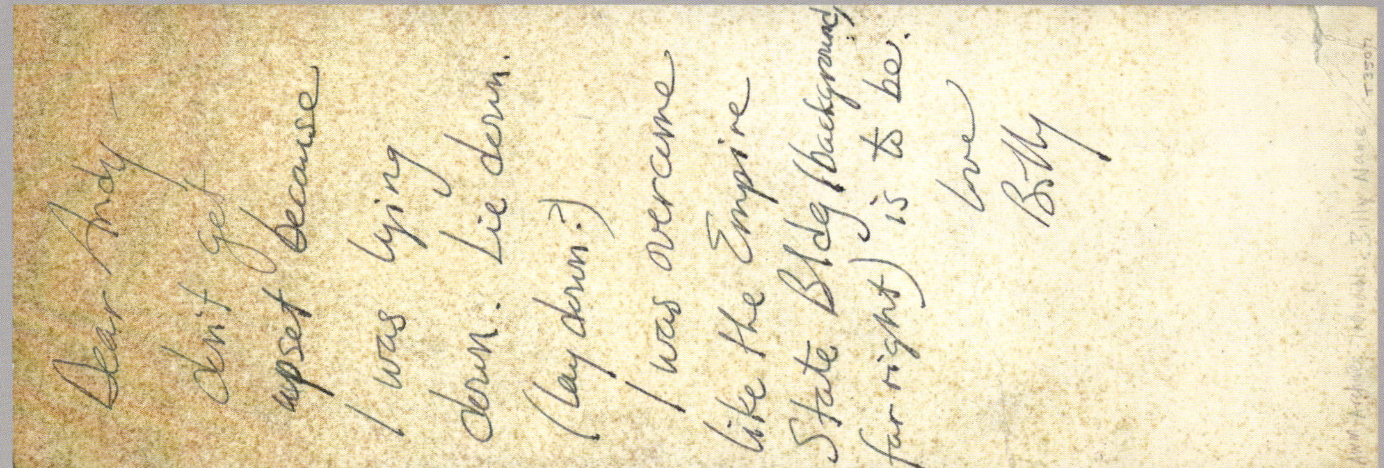

Michael (Felix) Katz, *Billy (Name) Linich on a Rooftop in New York*,
ca. 1964, with a note on the back to Warhol

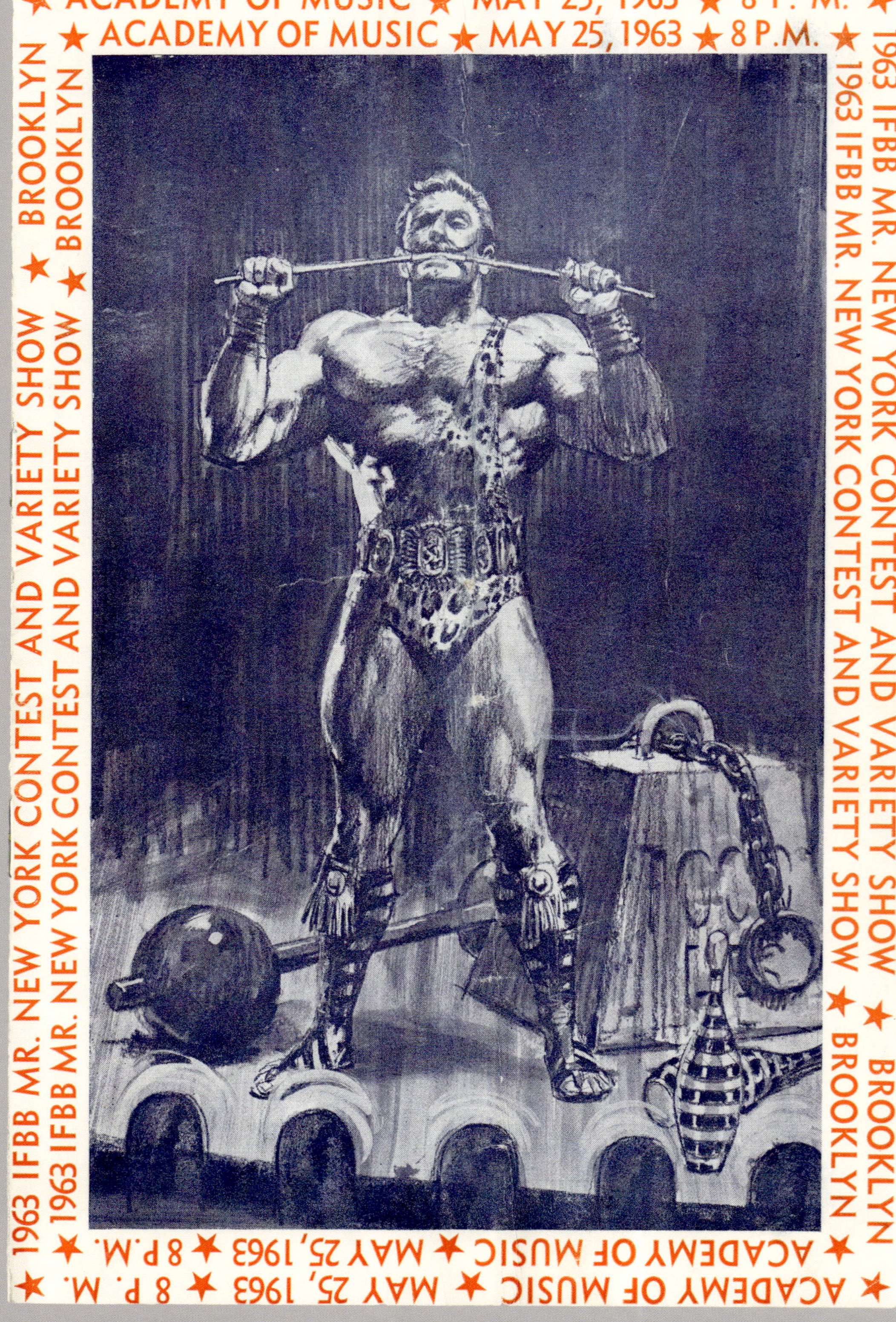

Program for the I.F.B.B. Mr. New York Contest and Variety Show,
May 25, 1963, where Warhol met Billy Name for the second time

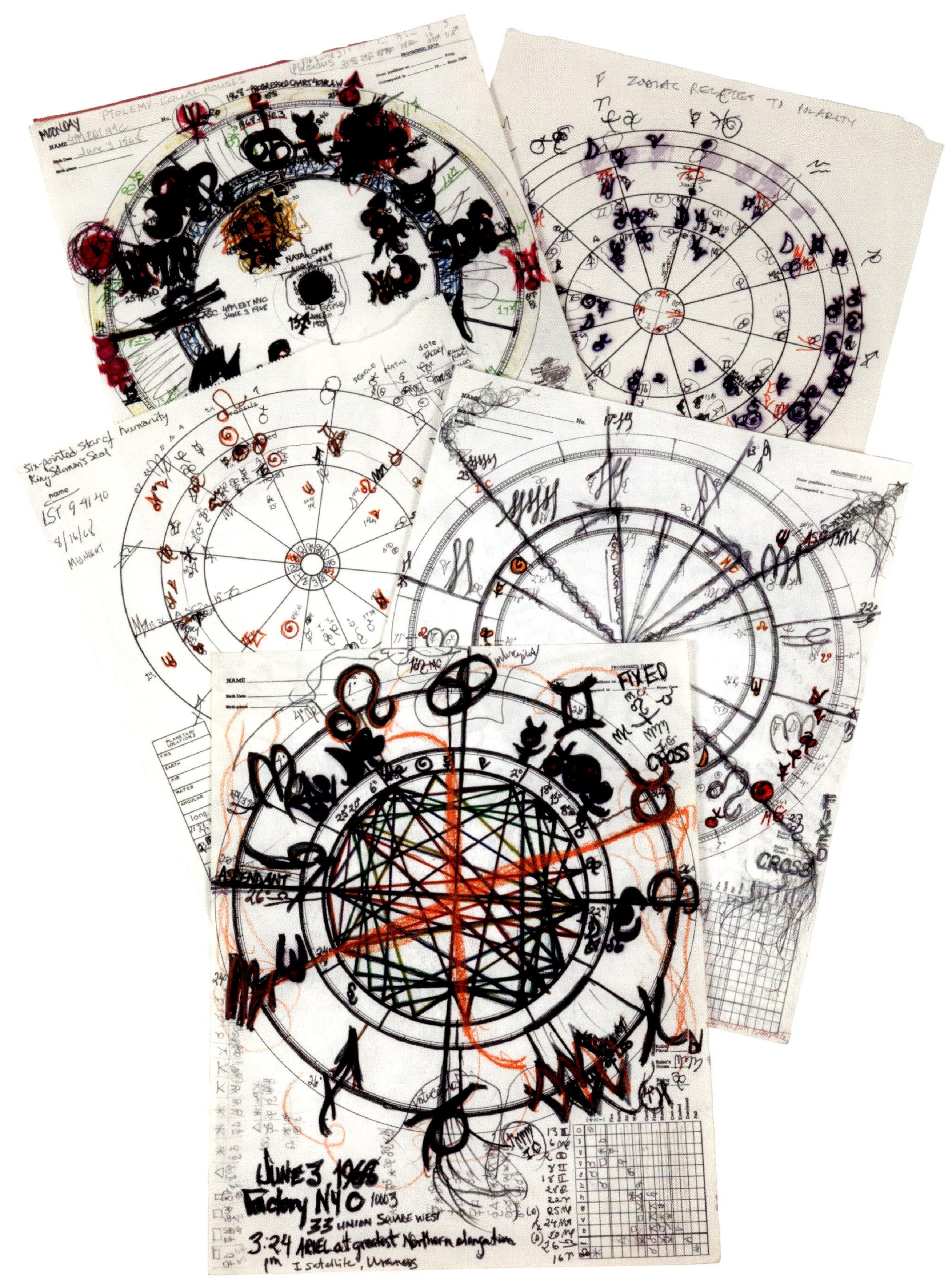

Five of nineteen astrology charts drawn by Billy Name at the Factory
in 1968, including one (at bottom) drawn for the day and very minute that
Warhol was shot

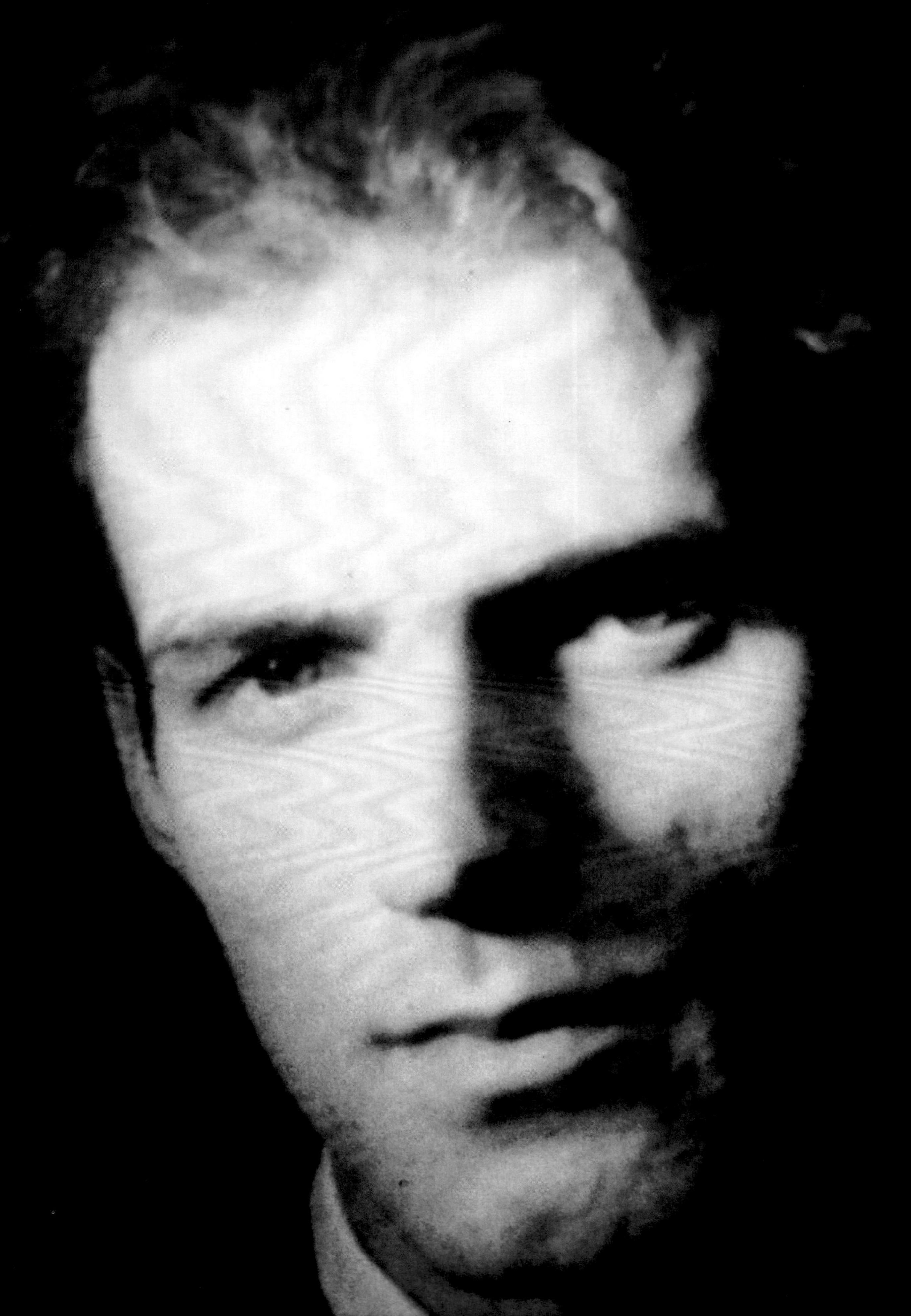

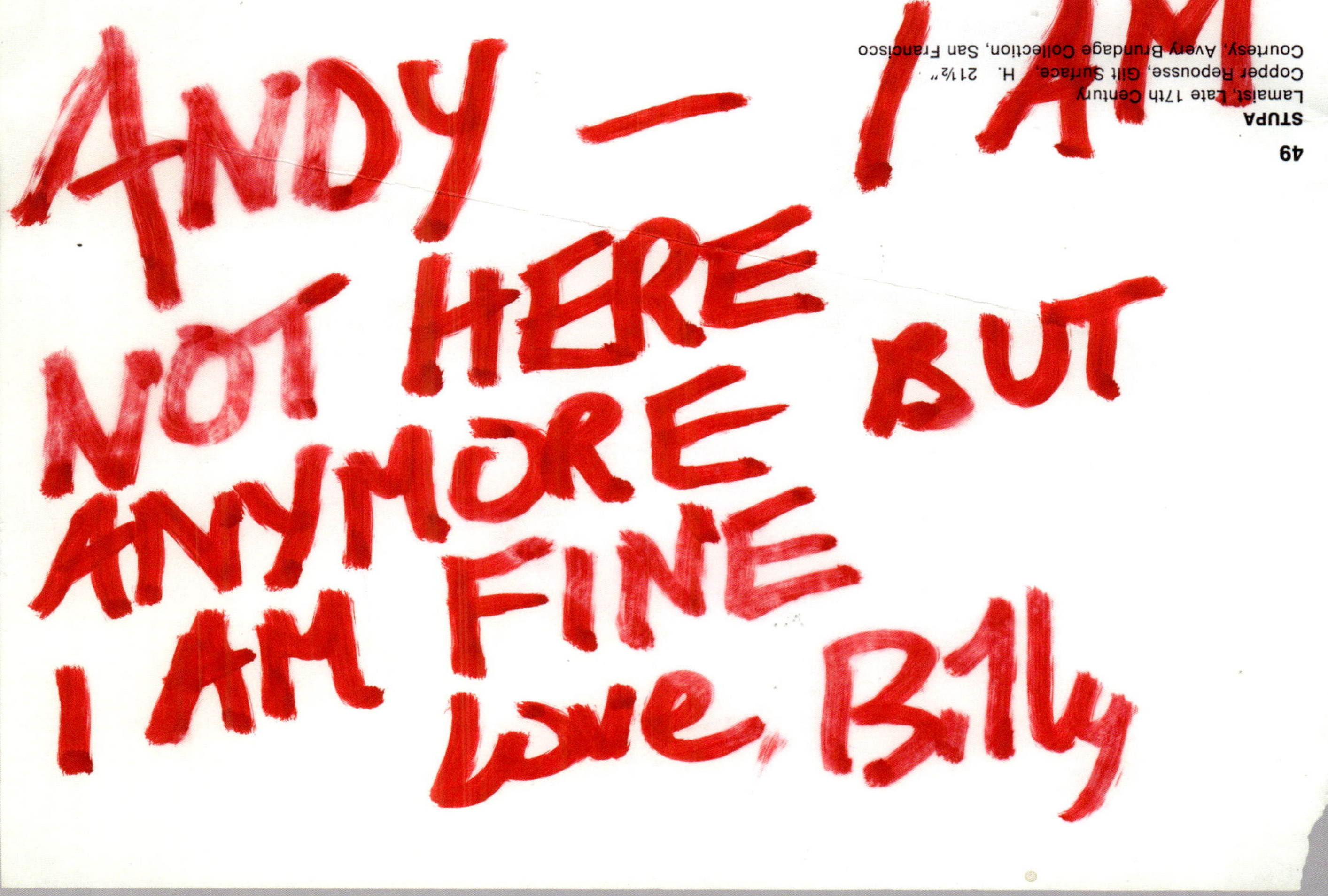

Andy Warhol, *Screen Test: Billy Linich [ST193]* (detail), 1964

Farewell note from Billy Name to Warhol, ca. 1969

Warhol first met rock-and-roll superstar Mick Jagger in 1964, at a party given by Warhol Superstar Baby Jane Holzer. Warhol admired Jagger for his looks, his supremely confident stage presence, his celebrity as lead singer of the Rolling Stones, and his business savvy. Warhol shot dozens of Polaroids for the two album covers that he designed for the band, *Sticky Fingers* (1971) and *Love You Live* (1977), and for his portraits of Jagger (1975). Warhol was also approached to design an earlier cover, *Through the Past, Darkly* (1969), but the project was never completed. One of Warhol's biographers claims that the artist wanted to cast Jagger in a film in 1964. Many objects from Warhol's Archive illuminate their subsequent friendship.

A decade later, the band rented Warhol's secluded property at the eastern tip of Long Island as a rehearsal space for its North American tour in 1975. That year, Warhol created portrait paintings and a print portfolio of portraits of Jagger. They remained friends until Warhol's passing in 1987. For years after, potted poinsettias were delivered to the Warhol Foundation offices in New York City at Christmastime, a posthumous gift to Warhol from Jagger.

L is for LOOSE LIPS & LPs

This chapter is based on content from two exhibitions: *Loose Lips*, in the Archives Study Center, September 15–November 13, 2005, and *Starf*cker: Andy Warhol and The Rolling Stones*, August 12, 2005–January 8, 2006.

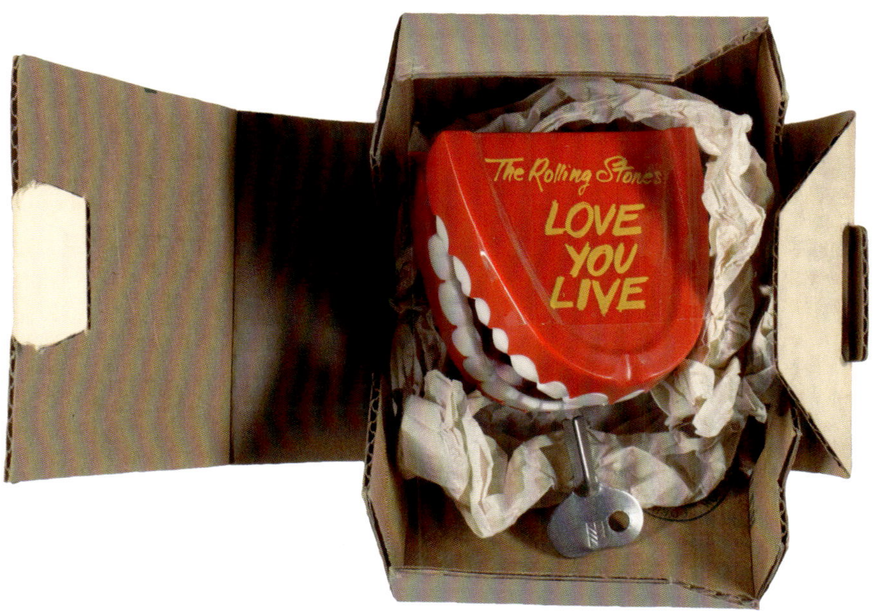

Loose Lips

Jagger appeared on the cover of Warhol's *Interview* magazine at least six times between 1969 and 1987 and was interviewed four times; in only one interview is he on his own without his wife or other friends.[1] Jagger made his first cover appearance in the publication's second issue, in the autumn of 1969. This image has the appearance of an advertisement for Jagger's then-current film, *Performance*, directed by Nicholas Roeg. The same is true of the rock star's two subsequent cover appearances, featuring Jagger in his roles in Jean-Luc Godard's *One Plus One* and Tony Richardson's *Ned Kelly*, respectively.[2] None of these issues includes an interview with Jagger, but they do feature brief reviews of the films.

Three of the covers were designed and painted by Richard Bernstein; he worked directly on the original photo, printed at the actual size of the magazine. Another cover, from December 1977, shows Ara Gallant's photo of Jagger dressed as Santa Claus, with supermodel Iman (who later married rock star David Bowie) and Paul von Ravenstein. Peter Strongwater's portrait of Jagger is on the August 1981 cover, and Albert Watson is responsible for the image from the February 1985 issue. For the first of the interviews, in September 1972, Jagger did not appear on the cover—that distinction went to actress Anjelica Huston, because both she and her father, the great film director John Huston, were each interviewed separately in the issue, and Jagger had already been on the cover three times.

Jagger appears relaxed throughout the first three interviews, possibly because Warhol was present, in addition to band members and/or his wife. In the longer, fourth interview, he's one-on-one with Lisa Robinson and her much more probing questions, and in return he gives serious answers—until the end, when he is initially evasive, then emphatic, about his sexual orientation. It may be merely chance that the interview provided publicity for Jagger's first solo LP, *She's the Boss*. Throughout the conversations, Jagger shares insights on both his professional and personal life, including his experiences of raising his children, his views on politics and physical exercise, his dislike of fur coats, some favorite authors and films, and his thoughts on romantic faithfulness.

Interview, September 1972. "Mick Jagger talks to Lee Radziwill." Date not recorded.

For his first interview in Warhol's magazine, conducted by Princess Lee Radziwill, Jagger shared the spotlight with his new bride, Bianca Pérez-Mora Macías. A native of Nicaragua, she married the rock star in 1971. After a tumultuous and extremely public life, they divorced in 1979. She is now a visible antiwar and human-rights activist. Her comment on the cruelty of bullfighting in this interview presages her wider involvement in public life, which began when she organized a benefit concert for victims of an earthquake that devastated her home country a few months after the interview was published.

This conversation is extremely brief, with an ending that leaves the reader believing it was accidentally cut off. Before discussing his stage performances, Jagger mentions his interest in wildflowers that began when his grandfather gave him a series of books on the topic. Following a brief chat about early American history, he declares that the

The Rolling Stones promotional toy hopping/chattering teeth, ca. 1977

United States is "too violent," although he seems to enjoy the roadside dining. Jagger also tells of his interest in the fantastic, supernatural novels of Welsh author Arthur Machen, science-fiction movies, and his preference for Peter Cushing over Vincent Price.

All of the photos that accompanied this interview were credited to James P. Smallwitt, perhaps a pseudonym for Peter Beard, Warhol's good friend and Radziwill's then-current beau.

Interview, December 1977. "A Stones Tea." September 29, 1977.

This interview is very casual and consists mainly of Jagger's comments, but his bandmates Ronnie Wood and especially Keith Richards have a few things to say. The president of Rolling Stones Records, Earl McGrath, is also there. Warhol is with Catherine Guinness, heiress, and Victor Hugo, artist and window dresser.[3] They chat about a wide range of topics: their first meeting in the 1960s, punk rock, celebrity, children, films by Pier Paolo Pasolini and John Waters, even their hairdressers (Richards and Wood cut their own hair). Jagger reveals that he recently danced with boxing champion Ken Norton at Studio 54 and later comments on Freud's view of children's sexual awareness and what he's observed of his own child, Jade.

Interview, August 1981. "Mick Jagger: Cocktails with Jerry Hall, Charlie Watts, Bob Colacello, and Andy Warhol." June 2, 1981.

After denying that he and Warhol have ever had a conversation, Jagger talks at length about his recently halted role in Werner Herzog's film *Fitzcarraldo*, shot in Peru, and his experiences in the Amazon rainforest. They touch on many other topics, including Jagger's new home in the Loire Valley, the reggae musicians Peter Tosh and Bob Marley, and New York nightclubs. After joking that he should endorse women's tampons, Jagger notes that celebrity endorsements are much more accepted by the culture in 1981 than they were in the 1960s. This interview occurred on Charlie Watts's birthday, and Warhol gets the humorous

last word regarding the cakes provided by blonde model Jerry Hall, Jagger's lover at the time. They met in 1977, married in 1990, and divorced in 1999.

Interview, February 1985. "Mick Jagger by Lisa Robinson." Date not recorded.

This appeared around the time of the release of Jagger's first solo recording, *She's the Boss*, which was not favorably received by either his critics or his fans. Compared to the first three interviews, this one is much more revealing and interesting. Rock journalist Lisa Robinson delves deeper with her questions than Warhol, and Jagger responds likewise in speaking about his personal life, although he refrains from specific details. It's ironic that the quote chosen by the magazine for highlighting on these pages is insipid, as it's uncharacteristic of the interview as a whole: "I get really intense, and then I'll become casual.... Or I'll be casual, and then I'll get intense and then casual."[4] Jagger goes on to provide more detail about his child-rearing experiences, including meeting the boys that his oldest daughter, Jade, has recently dated, and his personal romantic experiences, including his view of his faithfulness in a relationship, given his numerous and widely known affairs. At one point, Jagger states, "I haven't really had a heavy sexual thing with men since I was in school." After Robinson presses him to clarify, he unconvincingly tries to change course, and then cuts off the discussion with a terse "Goodbye." On other topics, Jagger briefly mentions his negative attitude toward fur coats (he considers them to be "tacky"—attention getting and a sign of immaturity). At the conclusion, Robinson raises the question of the rock star/sex symbol's age; Jagger was forty-one at the time of the interview.

Warhol, Jagger, and Stones LPs

Since their debut in 1962, the Rolling Stones have endured nearly every form of scandal in an odyssey that has been obsessively documented by the press. The Stones' sexually charged lyrics and public image have often pushed the boundaries of taste. Throughout the 1960s and 1970s, an era that is now regarded as permissive, their music and record-cover artwork were frequently censored or banned, and they were forced to self-censor song titles on at least two occasions. The lyrics of the song "Starf*cker" describe experiences with groupies, but an excerpted portion can also be applied to Warhol.

Yeah, I heard about your Polaroids,
now that's what I call obscene…
…you and me we made a pretty pair
fallin' through the silver screen.

The Archive contains forty-five of the numerous Polaroid photos that Warhol shot for the cover art for the Rolling Stones LP *Sticky Fingers* in 1971, along with three photo-stats made from the photos. One of the Polaroids plainly shows the face and torso of Glenn O'Brien, the editor of *Interview* magazine at the time. The strong sexual over-tones of the design were partly responsible for its being banned in at least two countries—Singapore (which is notorious for its strict laws and severe punishments) and Spain (which was then ruled by the dictator Francisco Franco). The Spanish substitute was designed by John Pasche and shows Phil Jude's photo of bloody-looking fin-gers emerging from a can of molasses. Spain also censored the album's song "Sister Morphine," replacing it with "Let It Rock" and printing the title as ". . .". *Sticky Fingers* was number one on the American and English charts. The zip-per in Warhol's design reveals an image of a man in under-wear that is stamped with Warhol's name and the phrase "This photograph may not be etc. etc.," borrowed from the rubber stamp on most of Billy Name's photographs. The models for the cover are thought to be Jed Johnson, Glenn O'Brien, and Corey Tippen: O'Brien is the underwear model, but exactly who is on the cover is uncertain. The designer Craig Braun worked with Warhol's concept and photos for the cover, which was nominated for a Grammy Award.

Mick Jagger and Charlie Watts worked closely with Warhol on his cover design for *Love You Live*. The idea of the Stones biting each other may be a reference to the punk aesthetic of the mid-1970s. The preprinting version of the cover shows it as Warhol originally designed it—without

words. He apparently believed that it would be recognized as a Rolling Stones album with only Jagger's image. Warhol's assistant Vincent Fremont wrote the notes after discussions with the Stones and their management. The finished version of the cover is also much more brightly colored than the original design.

Warhol's Polaroids were assembled in printed collages and printed on T-shirts and neckties. The photos were also used as publicity pictures, including both standard, glossy 8 by 10s and the more unusual method of adhesive-backed stickers arranged in a grid. A 12-foot-square, hand-painted billboard of the original cover design—without the lettering, as Warhol preferred—was installed on Sunset Boulevard in Los Angeles to promote the record. Warhol made at least eleven drawings and three acetate-and-colored-paper collages based on his photographs for *Love You Live*. Two of the collages were used for the album-cover art: Jagger biting the hand of his daughter Jade, and an image of the band members biting each other. Four Polaroids from the same shoot, used for the inside cover of the full-length record, were also reproduced for the promo-tional EP sleeve and picture disk (1977).

Correspondence shows there was an unrealized com-mission in 1969 for Warhol to create the cover of *Through the Past, Darkly (Big Hits Volume 2)*. Jagger writes that he is sending materials to be used in the design. These items may have included an early photo of the Stones piled onto a bench (ca. 1962; marked in Warhol's handwriting to be enlarged to the width of an LP cover) and a photo of the band (ca. 1964). An image of Warhol—holding the same photo—dates to the time of Jagger's letter. The Stones eventually rejected Warhol's design in favor of another art-ist's; one of Warhol's former assistants recalled Warhol's anger when he first saw the completed album and claimed that his idea had been stolen. The photographer of the completed cover is Ethan Russell, who also shot the pic-ture sleeve for *Honky Tonk Woman* and LP covers for the Beatles (*Hey Jude* and *Let It Be*) and The Who (*Who's Next*).

In addition to contributing to the Stones' album art-work, Warhol had his own personal collection of Rolling Stones materials: the LPs *12 × 5* (1964), *Aftermath* (1966), *Got Live if You Want It!* (1966), *Between the Buttons* (1967),

Beggars Banquet (1968), and *Some Girls* (1978); and the 45-rpm single *You Can't Always Get What You Want / Honky Tonk Woman* (1969). Warhol's library featured books on the Stones, and his papers include a 1983 letter from Jagger asking for Warhol's assistance with his autobiography.

The Rolling Stones managed to make it into Warhol's artwork, as well. On several of the personal recordings that Warhol taped in 1965, the Stones' "(I Can't Get No) Satisfaction" is heard on the Factory's sound system. The soundtrack of the film *Vinyl* (1965), Warhol and writer Ronald Tavel's adaptation of Anthony Burgess's *A Clockwork Orange*, includes the Stones' song "The Last Time." David Bailey, known for taking iconic photographs of the band, states that he and Warhol negotiated for the movie rights to Burgess's novel and wanted to involve the Stones, but their manager, Andrew Oldham, wanted too much money. Warhol asked Tavel to adapt Burgess's book, which became *Vinyl*, but Stanley Kubrick officially brought *A Clockwork Orange* to the screen in 1971.

It's not difficult to find other references to Warhol in the Rolling Stones' imagery. Peter Corriston's cover art for *Some Girls* (1978) recalls Warhol's use of magazine ads in paintings such as *Wigs* (1961) and his unauthorized portraits of movie stars.[5] The idea came to Corriston when he was told that the title of the record would be *Lies*, one of the songs on the LP. The record's title was changed, but the cover art was kept. Several stars objected to their appearance on the original *Some Girls* cover, and the LP's removable sleeve went "under re-construction." Pictures of the band members' faces were collaged onto photos of other people, many of whom were women.[6]

Jagger has often blurred his gender: his early nickname, "Pretty Mick"; his falsetto vocals; and his prancing onstage are some examples. In addition to the obviously fake drag images on the cover of *Some Girls* (made in response to its early title, *Lies*), androgyny appears on the cover of *Goat's Head Soup* (1973), and the entire band dressed in drag in Jerry Schatzberg's photos for the single "Have You Seen Your Mother, Baby, Standing in the Shadow?" (1966). The band made a short film in which the various members assumed feminine names: Mick as Sarah, Keith as Molly, Brian as Flossie, Charlie as Millicent, and Bill as Penelope.

Coincidentally, the Stones' bassist, Bill Wyman, visited Warhol's studio on the same day that the drag photo was shot. David Bailey took the photographs for *Goat's Head Soup* and for the picture sleeve of *Jumpin' Jack Flash* (1968).

The Stones departed from blues-influenced rock and roll to record the psychedelic *Their Satanic Majesties' Request* in keeping with the mood of 1967. Michael Cooper's cover art used the 3-D lenticular medium that Warhol also used for the cover of his *Index (Book)* the same year and again for his *Rain Machine* in 1970 (see "I is for Illusions"). The Stones recording includes "Citadel," which supposedly refers to Candy Darling, the transsexual Superstar of Warhol's films, and her friend Taffy: "Candy and Taffy, I hope you both are well / Please come see me in the citadel."

The Warhol Archive contains many objects relating to the Rolling Stones' tours in the United States during the 1970s, including a large Stones banner made of felt-tip marker on cut and glued felt, from *Time Capsule 23*. The history of this object is unknown. It is a rendition of the band's famous logo but is missing the white highlights on the lips, tongue, and teeth. Because of its homemade appearance, it's quite possible that the logo was designed by fans of the band. Contrary to popular belief, the proper tongue-and-lips logo, used by the band since 1971, was not created by Andy Warhol but by John Pasche.

The Stones' tour of the United States in 1972 is documented in Robert Greenfield's book *STP: A Journey through America with the Rolling Stones* (1974). The book includes several of Annie Leibovitz's famous photos of the band. The Leibovitz contact sheets are found in the Warhol Archive, as are VIP-button passes for the tour's three New York dates. The final concert of the tour was held in New York on Jagger's birthday—celebrated with a star-studded party at which Warhol Superstar Gerri Miller emerged topless from a giant birthday cake. Both *Rolling Stone* and Warhol's *Interview* magazines covered the party in detail.

The 1972 tour was also recorded in Robert Frank's rarely seen documentary film *Cocksucker Blues* (1972). Many consider it the best film ever made about rock and roll, presenting the boredom of life on the road as well as explicit moments of sex and drug use, which the Stones wanted to keep private. After a long legal battle between the band and Frank, a judge ruled that the film could be screened only in the context of Frank's work; he must also be physically present at each screening. Frank also designed the cover for the Stones' LP *Exile on Main Street* (1972).

Bianca Jagger's signature authorized Warhol's pass for the Stones' New York concert on June 22, 1975. The band used Warhol's Montauk, Long Island, home, Eothen, as a rehearsal studio in preparation for the tour, which was documented in Terry Southern's book *The Rolling Stones on Tour* (1978). Southern wrote that Keith Richards became frustrated with invading groupies and surrounded the house with surplus landmines; Mick Jagger ordered them to be removed. Vincent Fremont, Warhol's video producer and vice president of Warhol Enterprises, recalls the time at Eothen: "My favorite memory of the Stones' rehearsals at Montauk was hearing them play 'Wild Horses,' perfecting their performance for the tour. It was magical to hear the music floating over the sea so hauntingly."[7]

The Jaggers later rented the Montauk home separately from the band. An undated note from Mick is pasted into the scrapbook that records life in the house. The scrapbook also includes press clippings of the Stones' 1972 tour and photos of Mick, Bianca, and their daughter, Jade. Warhol socialized with Jagger and his wives, Bianca Jagger and Jerry Hall, at the beach house, in New York City, in Paris, and beyond.

While at Montauk, the rock star posed for many Polaroid photographs; nearly his entire body was photographed by Warhol for a series of portraits. These works manifest the artist's fascination with the ambiguous sexuality of Jagger's rock-star image. The eye lingers on parts of the body—hips, arms, torso—seemingly transfixed. Jagger gave himself over to a game of seduction. Warhol's photographs emphasize the performer's androgyny: bare shouldered like many of Warhol's female sitters and angled in a three-quarter profile. Soon after, Warhol worked on his portraits of drag queens, *Ladies and Gentlemen* (1975), which reflect his interest in the visual expression of gender.[8] Many drawings and collages were made as studies for the Jagger prints. Instead of painting underlayers or using stencils for the undercolors as Warhol had done for other iconic portraits, he used cut- and torn-paper shapes for the multiple screens used to print elaborate undercolor effects. Both the artist and the sitter signed the editioned works.

NOTES

1. The uncertainty regarding the magazine's early issues comes from the fact that they aren't dated; some even bear the incorrect year. *Interview* was operated quite casually in its early days; Warhol stated that he published it so that he could receive free passes to the New York Film Festival. He held a press pass to the festival in 1969, and his magazine first appeared in either September or October of that year, with the festival running from September 16 to October 2.

2. *Interview* 1, no. 7 (undated), and 1, no. 8 (Spring 1970).

3. Catherine Guinness was heir to the Guinness beer fortune and worked at *Interview* magazine as a reporter. Victor Hugo was a Venezuelan-born artist and the romantic partner of fashion designer Halston; he socialized with Warhol and became a studio assistant working on the *Oxidation* paintings and modeling for Warhol.

4. Lisa Robinson, "Mick Jagger by Lisa Robinson," *Interview* 14, no. 2 (February 1985): 48–49.

5. Wigs were much more personal to Warhol, who wore a hairpiece for most of his life and was photographed in drag on several occasions (see "F is for Fashion").

6. The Reverend Jesse Jackson attacked the lyrics of *Some Girls* for being "vulgar and obscene." The record was number one on the US charts and was nominated for a Grammy as Album of the Year.

7. Vincent Freemont in telephone conversation with the author, in 2005.

8. Warhol first explored ideas of cross-dressing in work from the 1950s and again in his *Self-Portraits in Drag* of the 1980s.

Research assistance for this chapter was provided by Archive interns Alex Mantakounis, Katy Plump, Roxana Raska, and Bill Zollinger, and additional thanks go to Alex Brunelle, Julie Chill, Brett Day, John Fetkovich, Vincent Fremont, Earl McGrath, and Jay Reeg. New object research provided by Matt Gray.

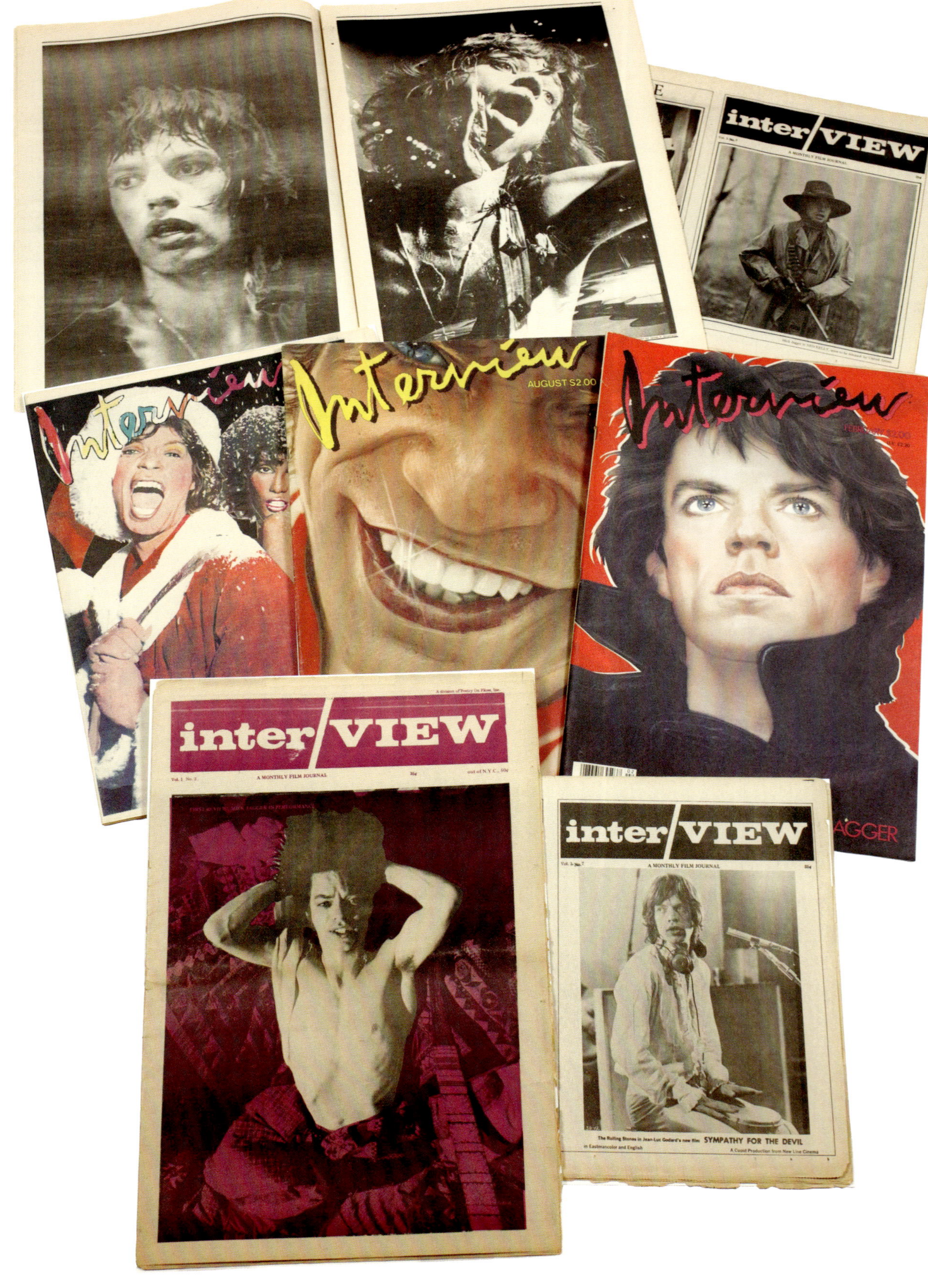

Interview magazines featuring Mick Jagger

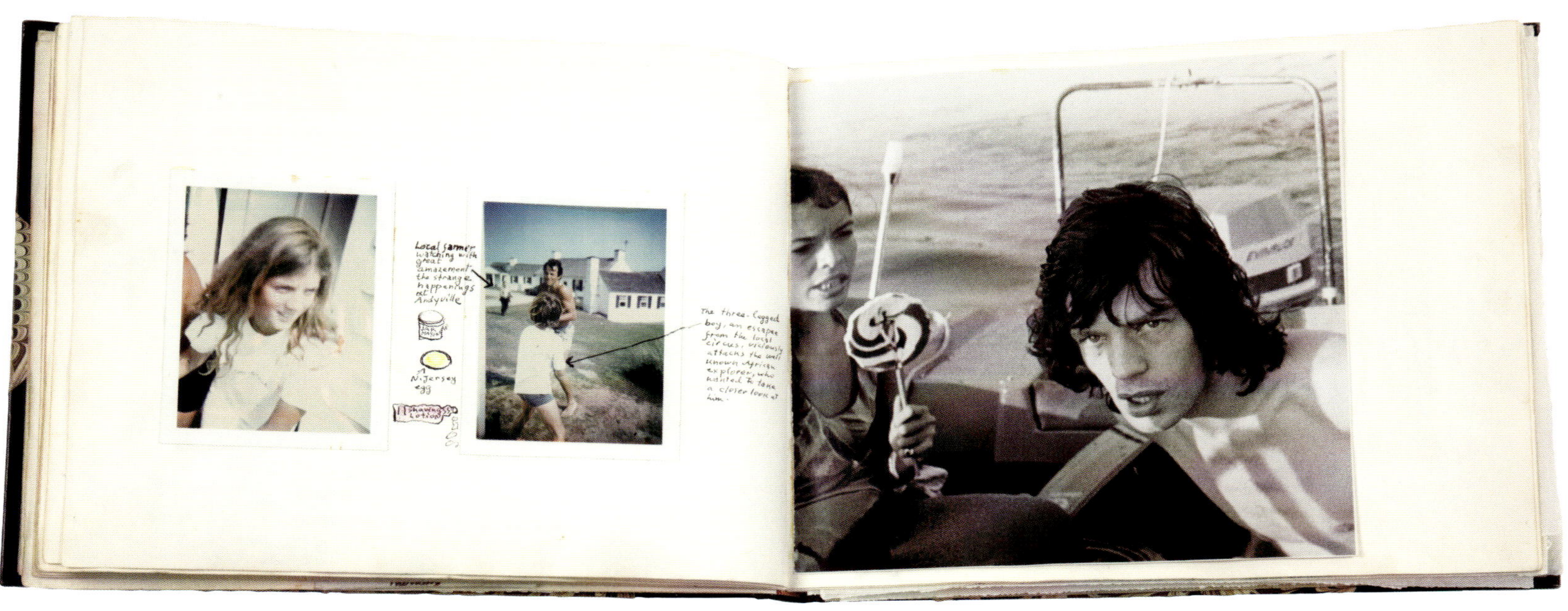

Two spreads from Warhol's Montauk scrapbook, 1972–78, with Kennedy children, Bianca and Mick Jagger, and note from Jagger to Warhol

159

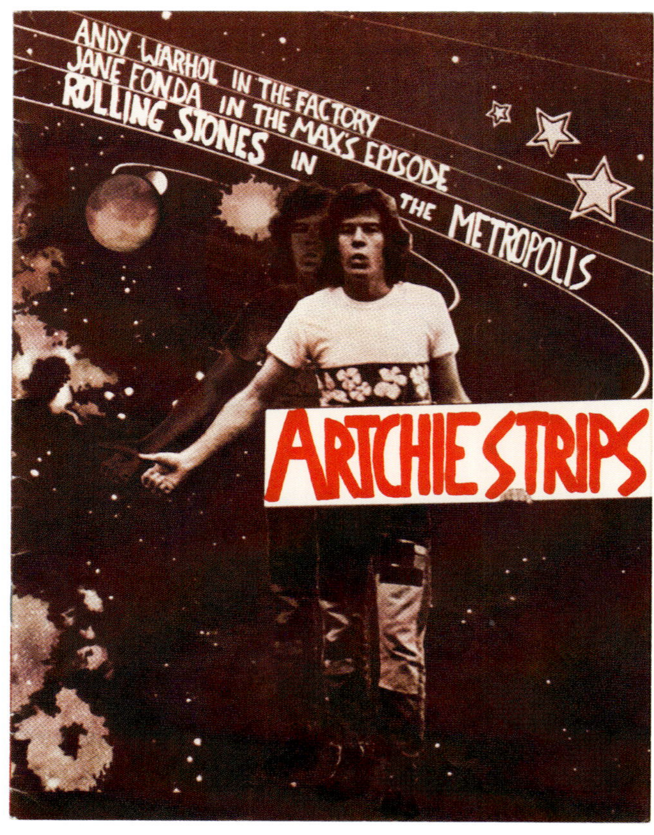

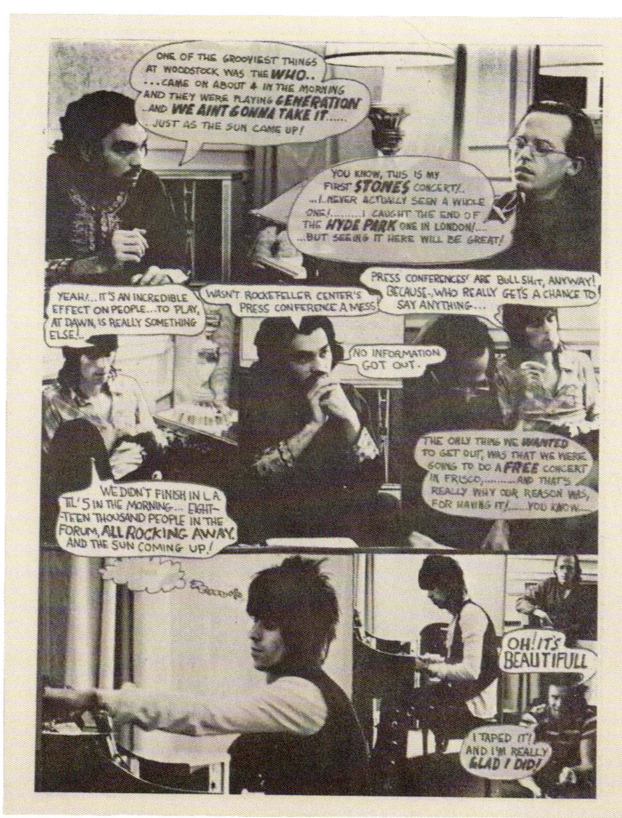

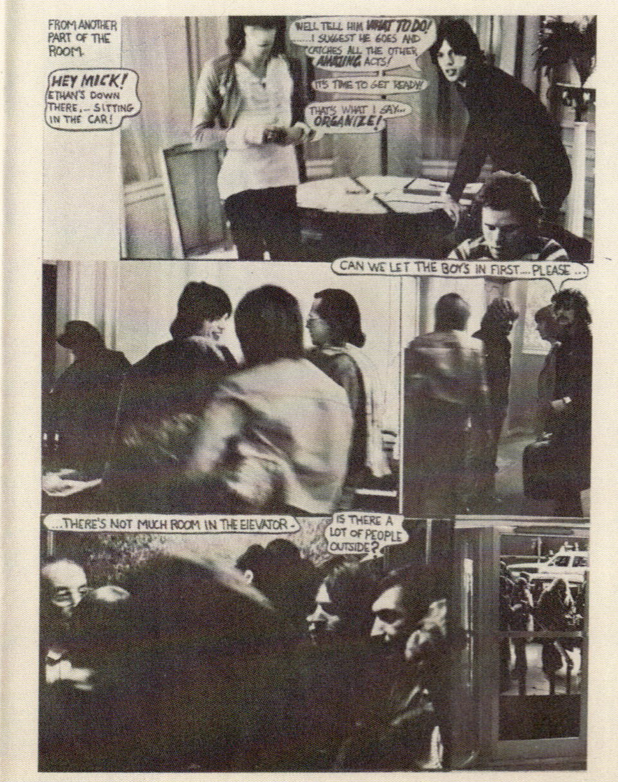

Cover and interior pages of *Artchie Strips*, featuring the
Rolling Stones, 1970

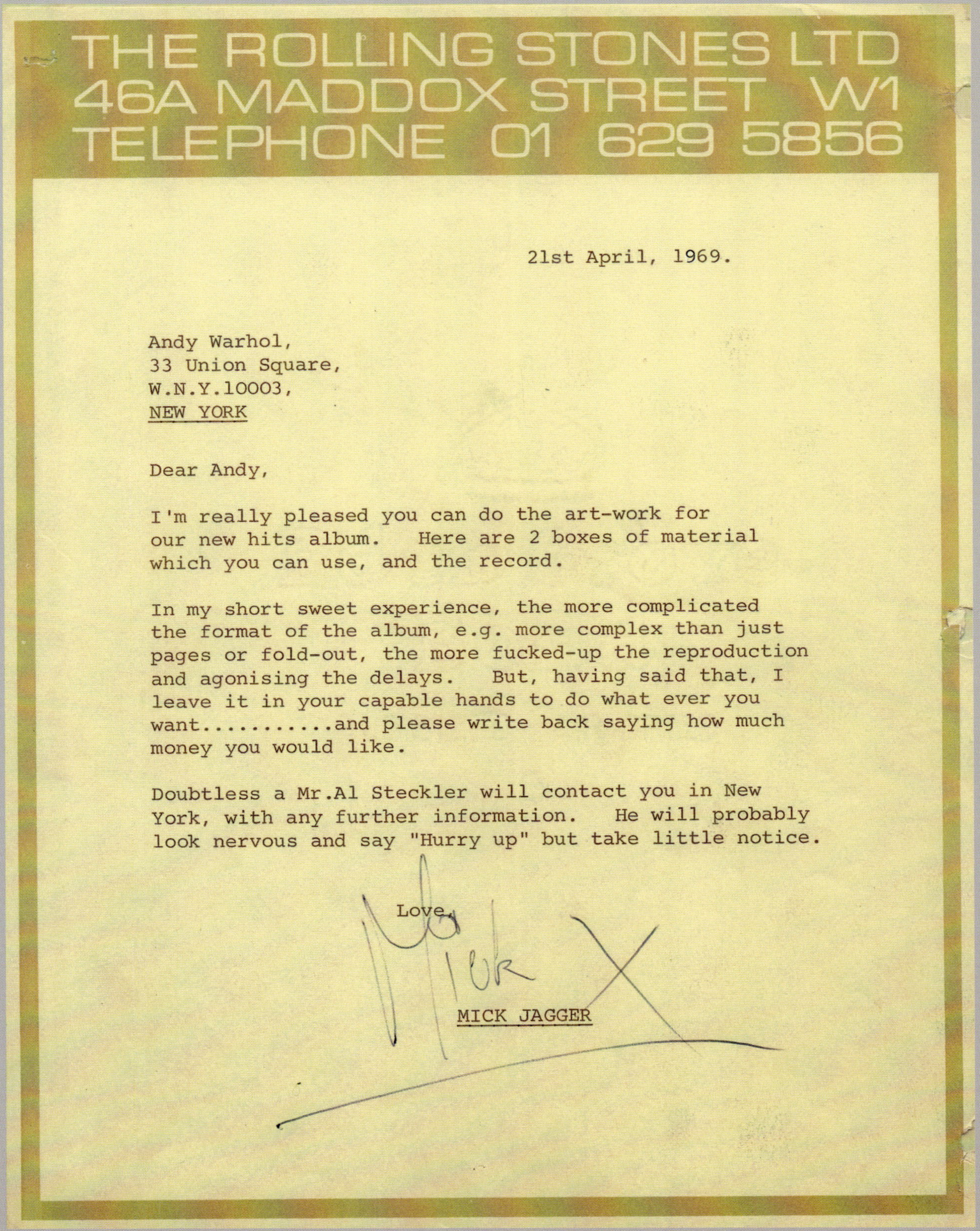

21st April, 1969.

Andy Warhol,
33 Union Square,
W.N.Y.10003,
NEW YORK

Dear Andy,

I'm really pleased you can do the art-work for
our new hits album.   Here are 2 boxes of material
which you can use, and the record.

In my short sweet experience, the more complicated
the format of the album, e.g. more complex than just
pages or fold-out, the more fucked-up the reproduction
and agonising the delays.   But, having said that, I
leave it in your capable hands to do what ever you
want..........and please write back saying how much
money you would like.

Doubtless a Mr.Al Steckler will contact you in New
York, with any further information.   He will probably
look nervous and say "Hurry up" but take little notice.

Love,

MICK JAGGER

Letter from Mick Jagger to Warhol, April 21, 1969

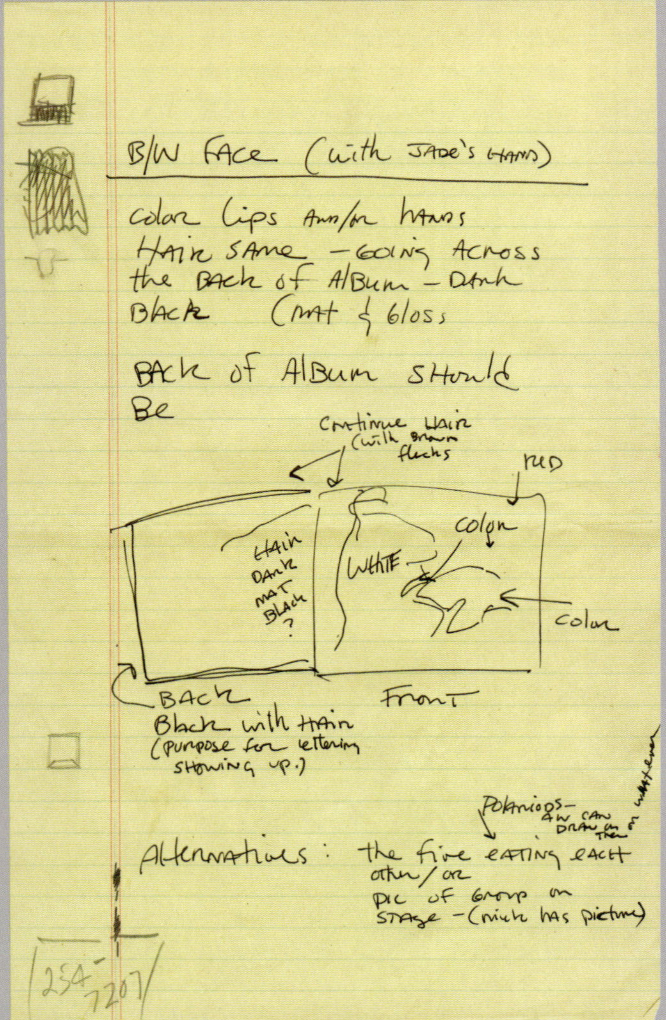

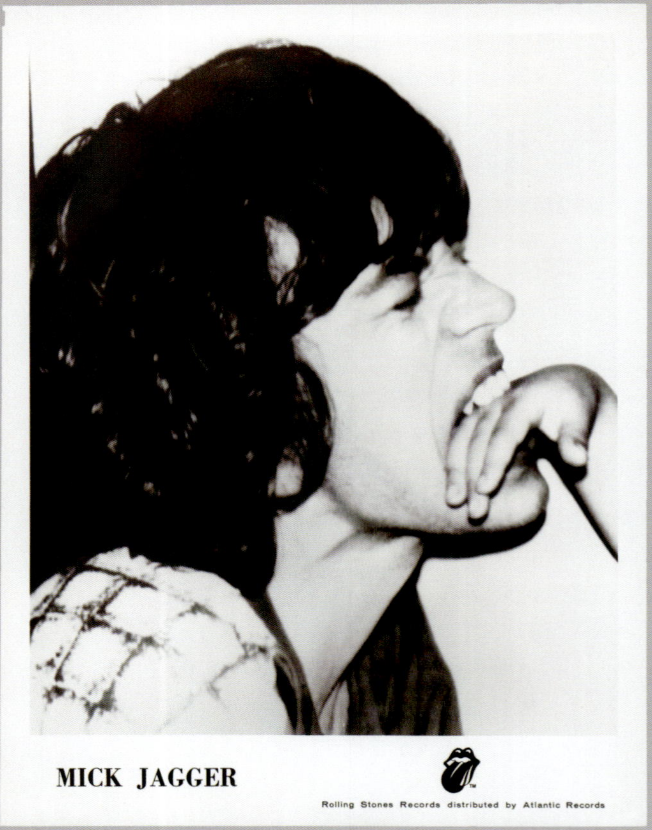

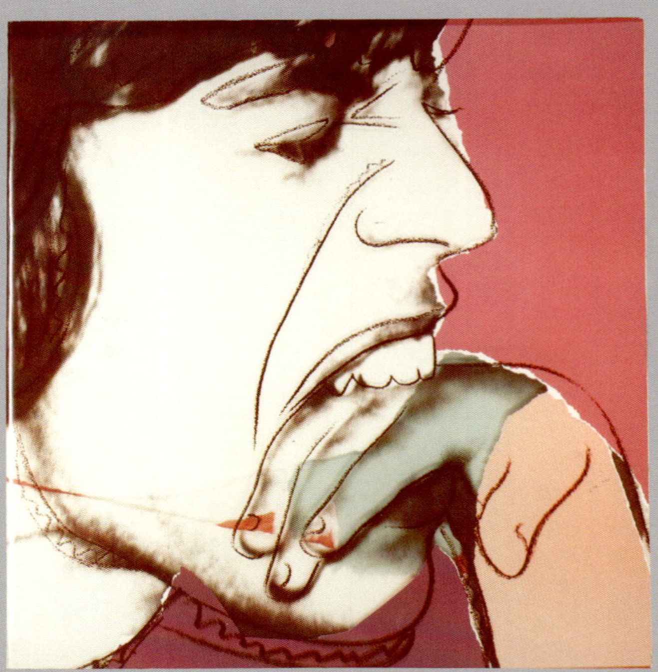

Design notes by Vincent Fremont, from the phone call in which the band's concerns about the initial design were relayed, 1976–77

Andy Warhol, *Mick Jagger*, ca. 1977; maquette of *Love You Live* by the Rolling Stones

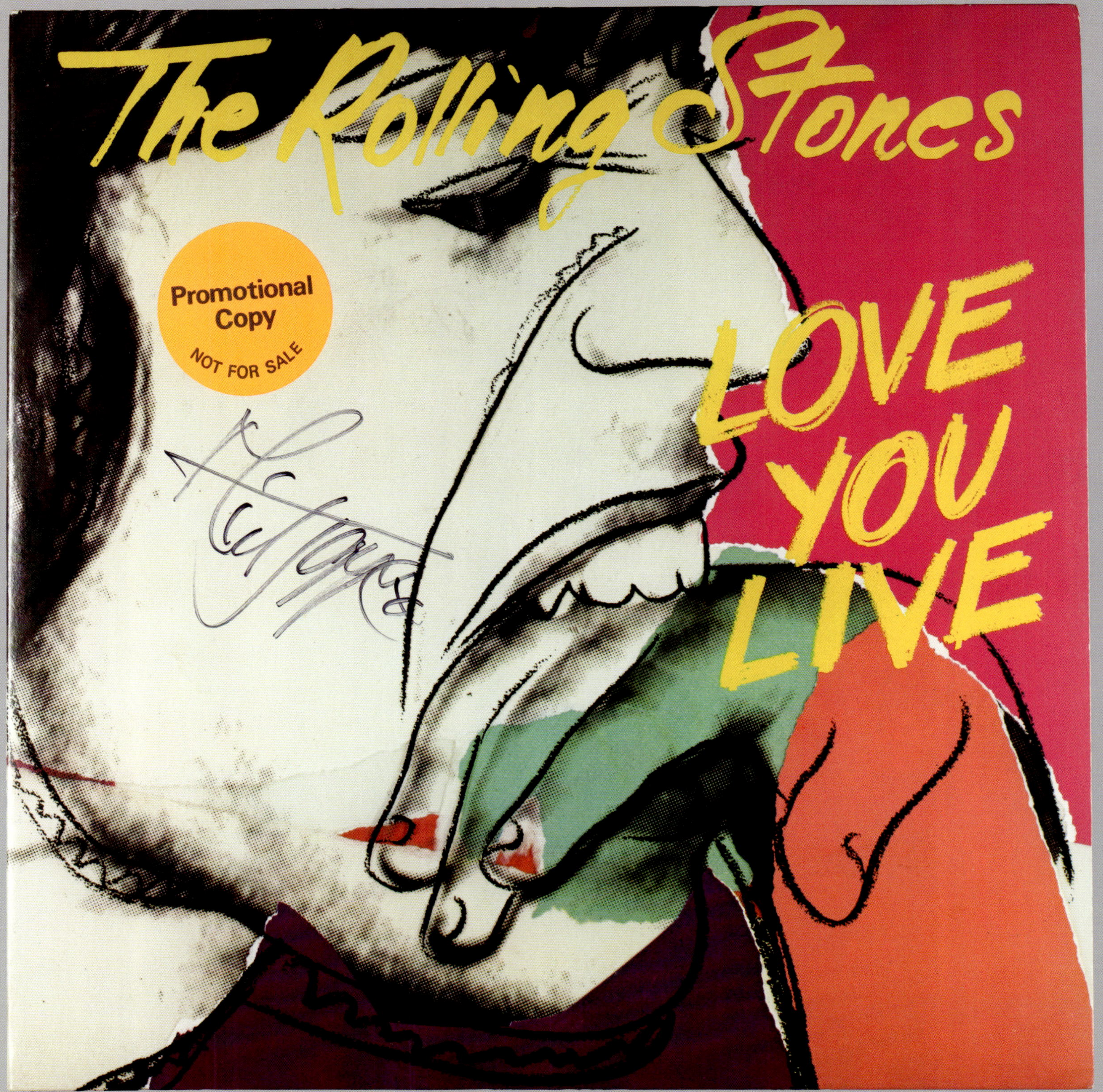

Signed promotional copy of *Love You Live* by the Rolling Stones, 1977

L is for LOOSE LIPS & LPs

164

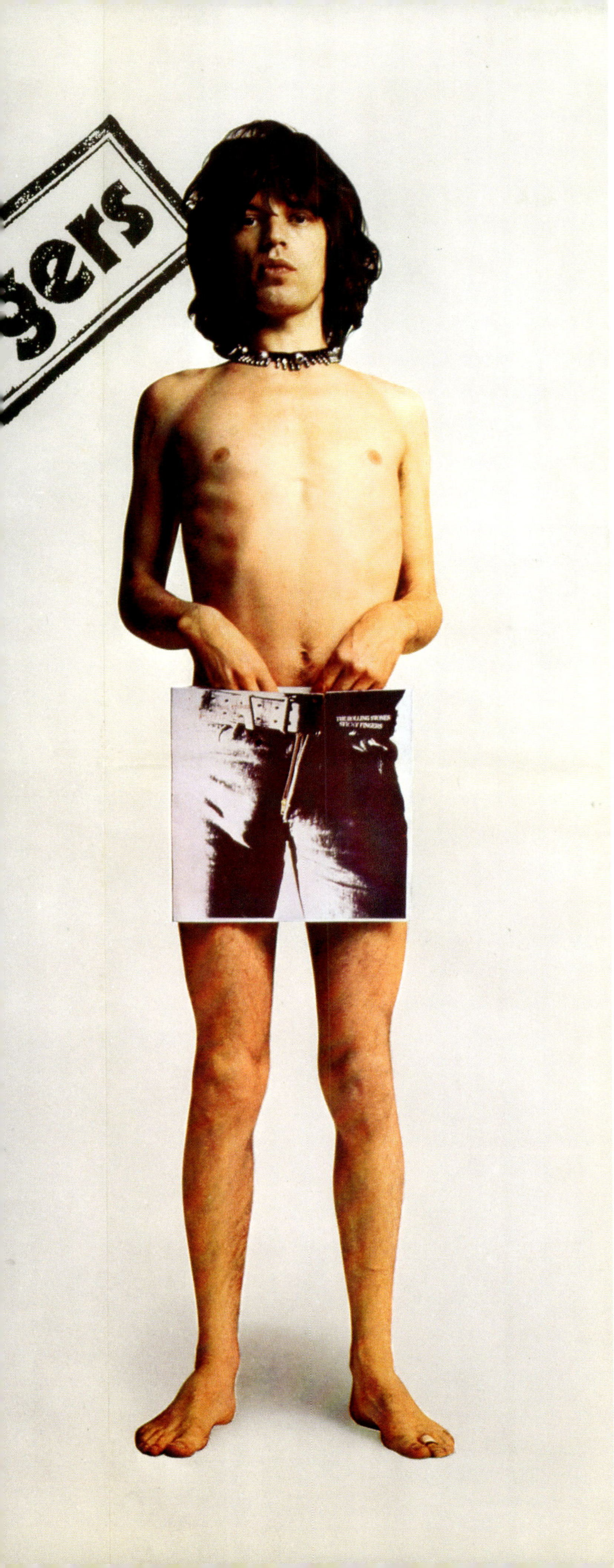

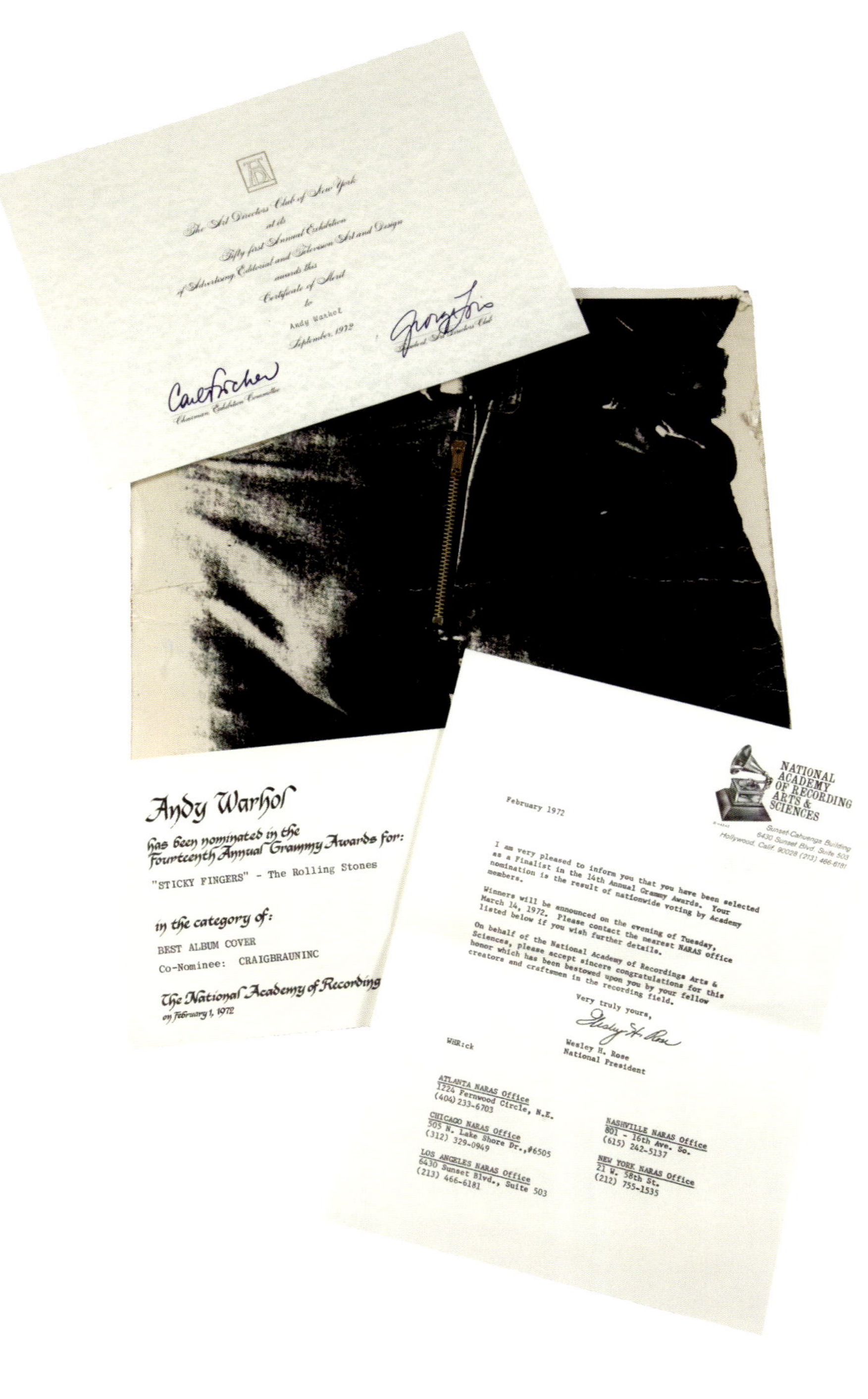

Promotional poster for *Sticky Fingers* by the Rolling Stones, 1971

Sticky Fingers by the Rolling Stones, 1971, with accolades to Warhol
for the album design, 1972

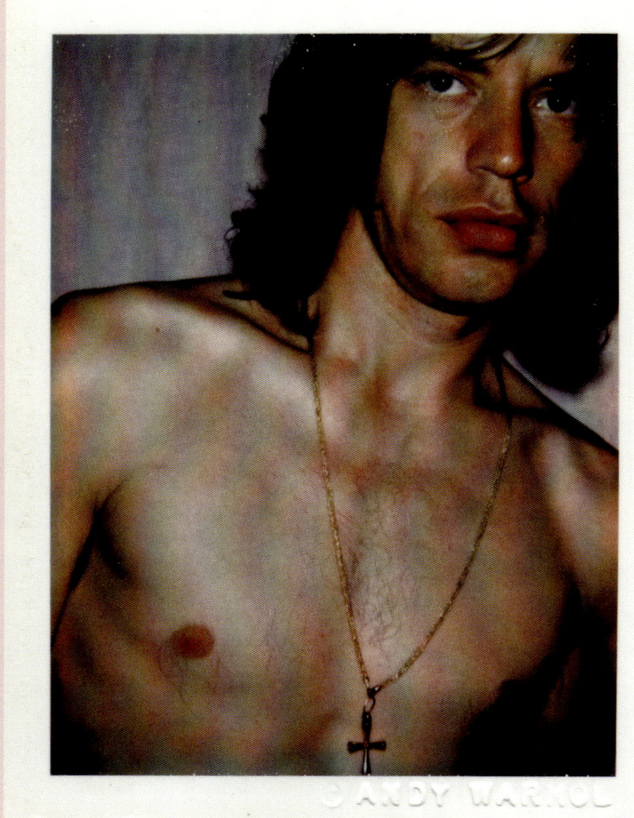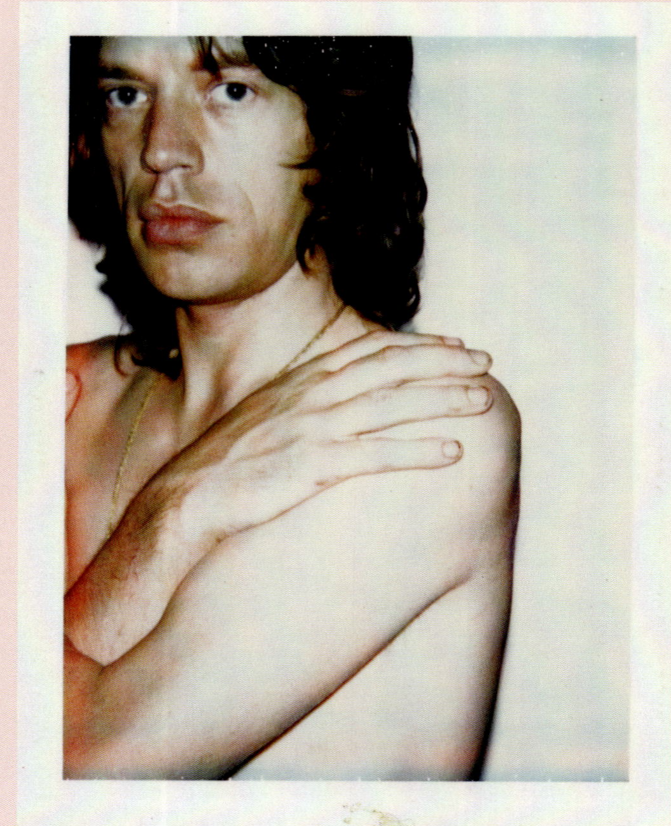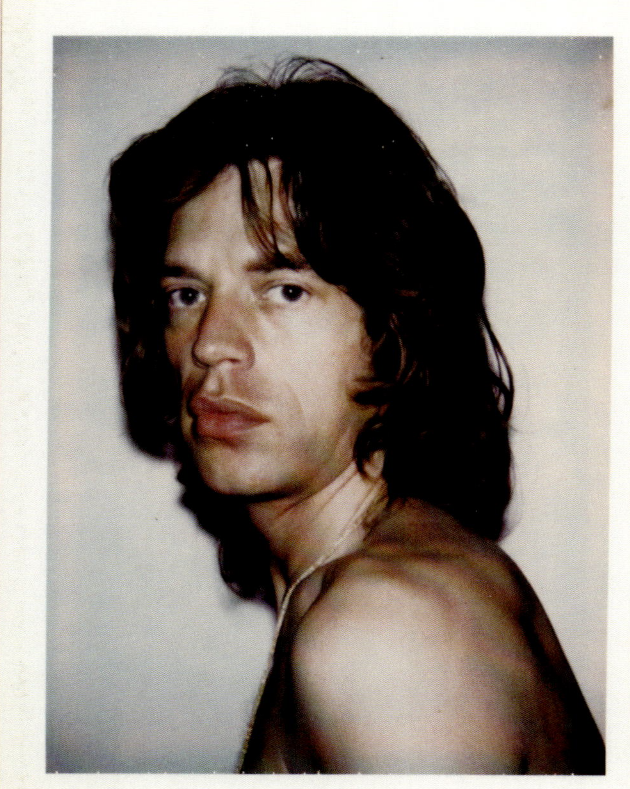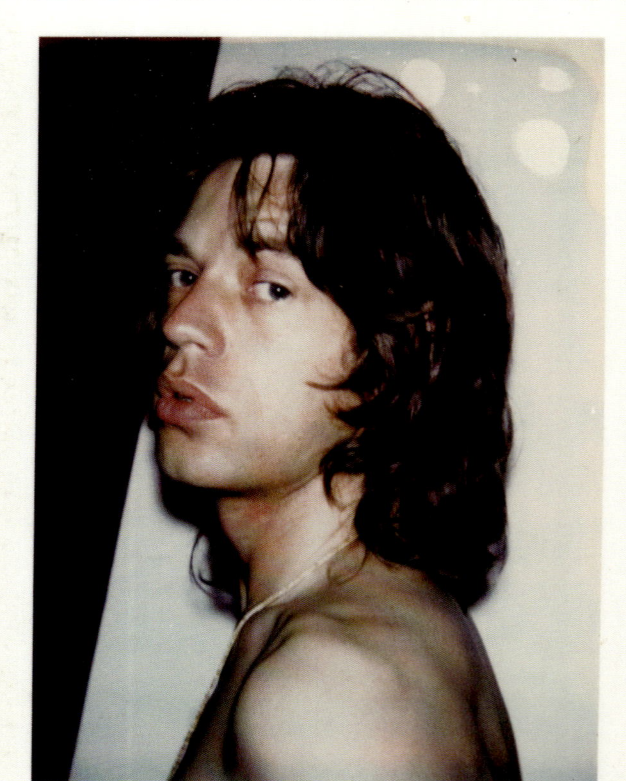

Andy Warhol, *Mick Jagger* (four Polaroids), ca. 1975

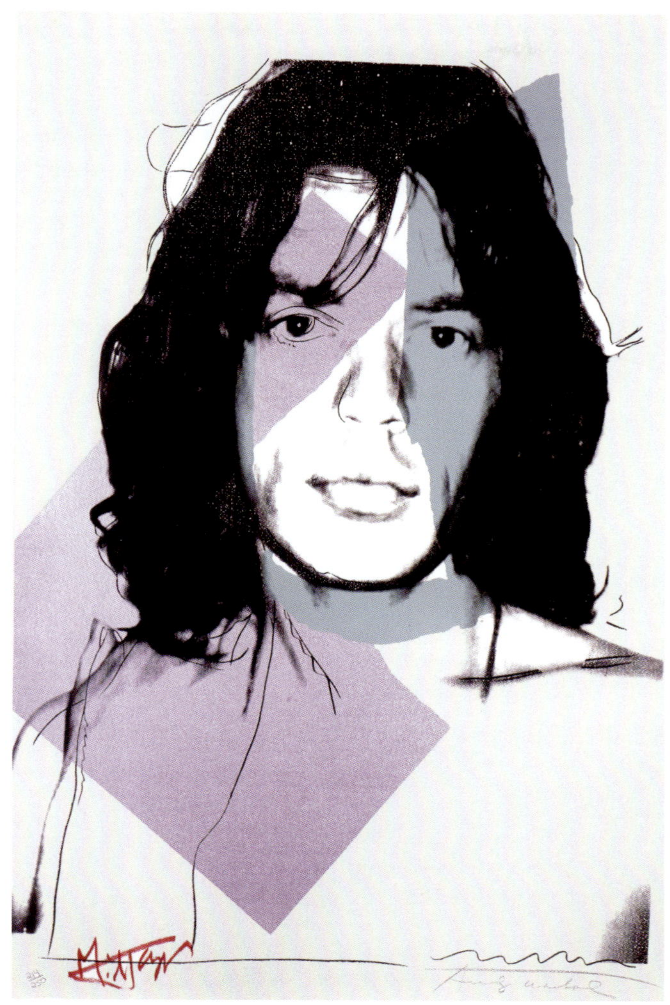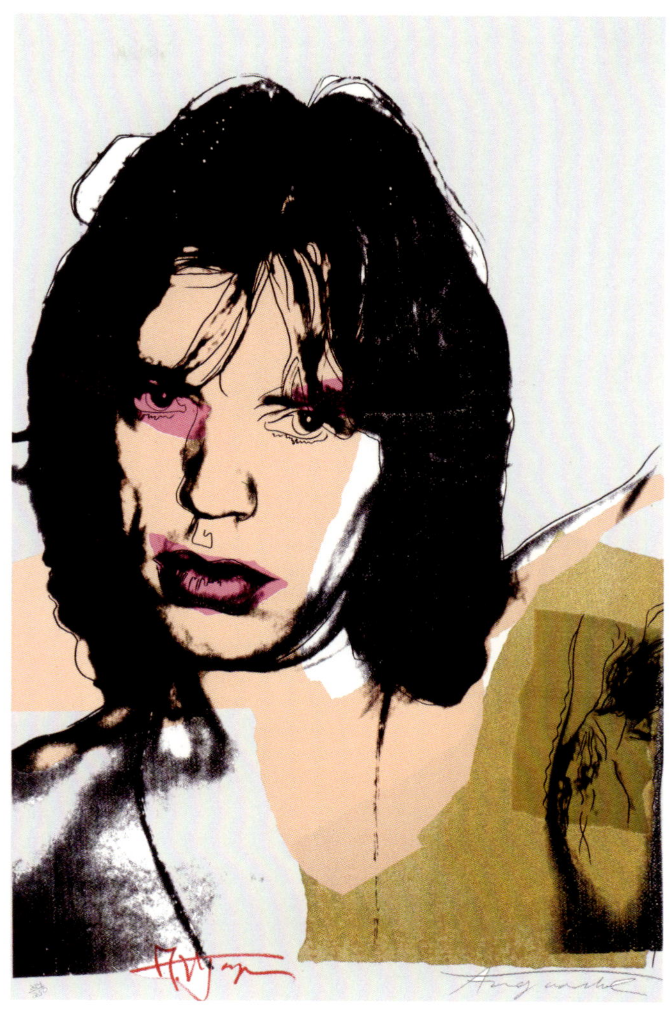

Andy Warhol, *Mick Jagger* (two prints), 1975

Ever quick with satirical comedy, the gentle, pleasure-seeking Taylor Mead became Warhol's friend in the early 1960s and circled in and out of Warhol's orbit while inhabiting his own offbeat universe, as evidenced in his note to Warhol: "Dear Andy I'm glad you're becoming famous, so am I." The sentiment seems to drip with irony, because by 1967 (the year the note was written), both Mead and Warhol had already snared that elusive, shiny object of fame. Warhol had been recognized since the 1950s for his graphic art and since the early 1960s for his Pop paintings of movie stars and consumer goods, as well as his avant-garde films. Mead gained fame as likely the first star of the "underground" New American Cinema, appearing in Ron Rice's *The Flower Thief* (1960) before joining Warhol's circle.

Mead met Warhol in the summer of 1963, when Henry Geldzahler took him along on a visit to Warhol's home on Lexington Avenue.[1] Mead and Warhol both performed in front of the camera in an early black-and-white film that could quite possibly have been shot by Geldzahler during this visit. They became fast friends. By September, Mead was invited on a road trip from New York to California with Warhol and others. Mead worked creatively as a

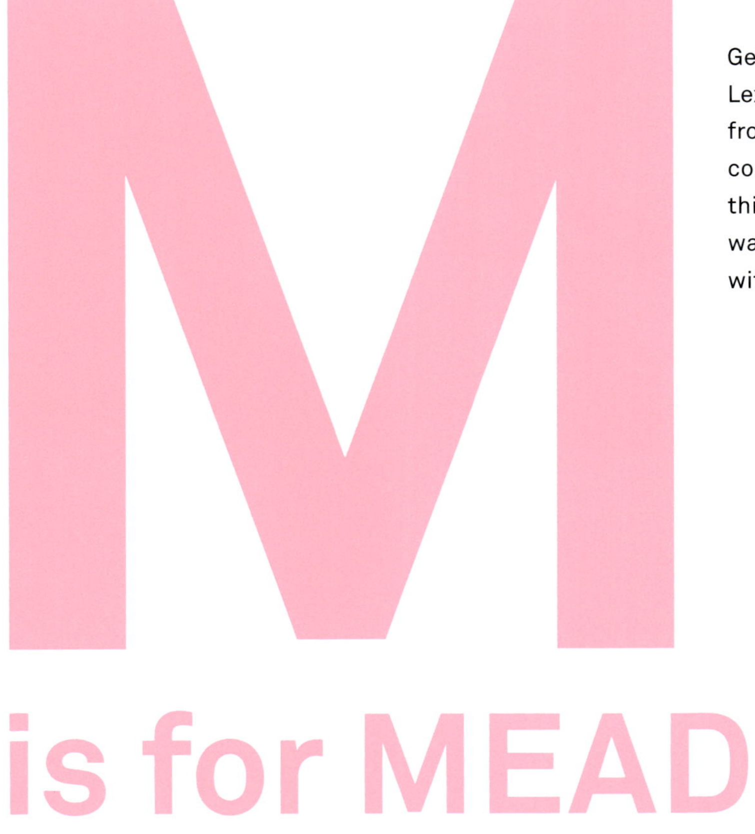

M
is for MEAD

This chapter is based on the exhibition *Taylor Mead*, in the Archives Study Center, November 10, 1999–April 30, 2000.

performer and writer from the mid-1950s until his death on May 8, 2013.

A New Year's Eve baby, Mead was born in Detroit in 1924. His well-to-do family lived in Grosse Pointe, where his father was chairman of the Michigan Democratic Party and his mother was a beautiful socialite. When his parents divorced, Taylor was sent to live with grandparents in Ohio. To escape, he stowed away on a bus and rode for miles before being discovered and returned safely to his family. Like Warhol, he loved Hollywood films and movie stars, especially Charlie Chaplin, Bette Davis, Greta Garbo, Buster Keaton, and Irene Dunne, who he thought resembled his beloved mother.

After graduating from the Loomis School in Connecticut, he joined the Pasadena Playhouse in California, where he studied the work of George Bernard Shaw. Mead then left to volunteer for World War II. He was declared unfit for the military because he was gay, although this was not cited as the official reason. Returning to Detroit, he enrolled in Wayne State University for a short time and in art school for "a day." He worked briefly as a broker in training at Merrill Lynch, a job his father had secured for him, and then was off again. In the unacknowledged mode of the beatnik, he hitchhiked around the country off and on for about ten years. Inspired by his experiences as a young gay man on the road, he began jotting down short poems and one-liners. In the course of his travels, he was arrested about twelve times, "just on general principles." His ensuing jail time "contributed to [his] feeling of being an outsider."[2]

In San Francisco in the late 1950s, he discovered the coffeehouse scene of the Beat poets and began to publicly read his work at the Co-Existence Bagel Shop. Filmmaker Ron Rice met Mead at one of his readings and, inspired by Robert Frank and Alfred Leslie's recent film, *Pull My Daisy* (1959), starring Allen Ginsberg and narrated by Jack Kerouac, made *The Flower Thief*. The film was enthusiastically received by audiences and the press. Mead, whose performance as the childlike picaresque hero wandering around North Beach with his teddy bear earned him almost mainstream recognition, became the first underground movie star.

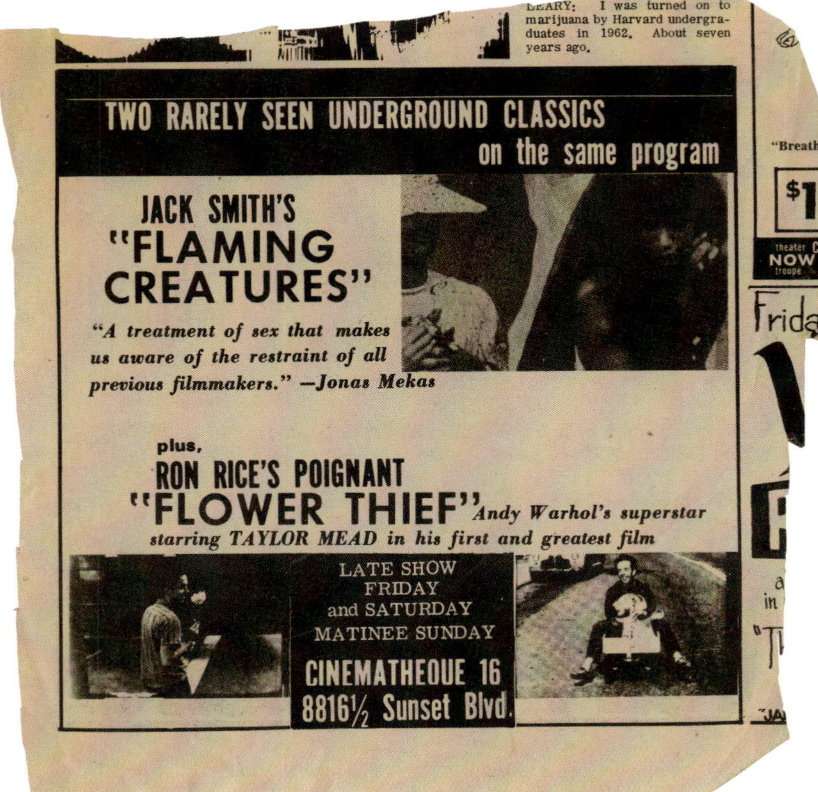

Soon after, he played a multitude of characters in films by Vernon Zimmerman, including *Lemon Hearts* (1960) and *To L.A.…with Lust* (1961).[3] Later in 1961, Mead worked on two films with Bob Chatterton in Los Angeles before moving to New York City, where he was reunited with Rice to star with Jack Smith in *The Queen of Sheba Meets the Atom Man* (1963). The first volume of his one-liners and poems written during his cross-country travels, *The Anonymous Diary of a New York Youth*, was published in 1961.

In New York, he found more audiences for his confrontational poetry readings at cafés such as the Gaslight, the Fat Black Pussy Cat, and Epitome. "We would read our wildest stuff and try to drive out the customers," said Mead.[4] In September of 1963, Mead drove from New York to California with Warhol, Wynn Chamberlain, and Gerard Malanga to attend the opening of Warhol's second Pop exhibition at the Ferus Gallery in Los Angeles, a show of his *Elvis* and *Liz* paintings. While there, he played the title character in Warhol's unusual early send-up of Hollywood films, *Tarzan*

Newspaper advertisement for *Flaming Creatures* by Jack Smith and *Flower Thief* by Ron Rice starring Taylor Mead, late 1960s *and Jane Regained…Sort Of* (1964), cavorting around Southern California with Naomi Levine (as Jane) and Dennis Hopper. Mead also edited the footage and the soundtrack.

In the summer of 1964, at the height of the underground film movement in New York, a conventional filmmaker wrote a letter of complaint to the *Village Voice* about its championing of "films shot without cameras, films shot without lenses, films shot without film, films shot out of focus, films focusing on Taylor Mead's ass for two hours."[5] Mead replied, "Andy Warhol and I have searched the archives of the Warhol colossus and find no 'two-hour film of Taylor Mead's ass.'"[6] To rectify the situation, that film was shot in Warhol's Factory that very month.

A double bill of plays by Frank O'Hara and LeRoi Jones (later known as Amiri Baraka) and starring Mead ran briefly at the Writers' Stage in 1964. O'Hara's *The General Returns from One Place to Another* featured Mead as a campy General MacArthur, arriving in Manila and ordering every inch of the palace marble to be "shining like snow in the Arctic." In Jones's play *The Baptism*, Mead played a gay Satan. The performances were a huge success, but Jones declined to transfer his work to a more established venue. Despite the short run (only four performances), Mead won an Obie award for his work in *The General Returns*.

After the sudden death of Ron Rice in December and the disappointment of *The Baptism*, Mead decided to try his luck in Europe. He stayed for three years, moving among Rome, Paris, Greece, Istanbul, Stockholm, and Amsterdam. He traveled light: a knapsack, an air mattress, and a movie camera. A lack of funds forced him to shoot his European travel film, *Home Movies*, one frame at a time. While in Europe, he made several films with Jean-Jacques Lebel. Before these could be shown at Lebel's Third Festival of Free Expression in Paris in May 1966, at the Théâtre de la Chimère, they were censored and destroyed by the film lab because they contained nudity. The following year, Mead attended a screening of Warhol's newest film, the double-screen epic *Chelsea Girls* (1966). Mead's reaction to the film was "I've been in *La Dolce Vita* land too long. *Chelsea Girls* is the real thing. I'm coming home."[7]

Upon Mead's return to America, Warhol cast him in four films in fairly quick succession: *Imitation of Christ* (1967),

The Nude Restaurant (1967), *Lonesome Cowboys* (1968), and *San Diego Surf* (1968). Amid all of this activity, Mead saved Warhol's life. One terrifying day, an unknown man entered the Factory with a gun and demanded $500, which he claimed was owed to him, and then played a horrifying game of Russian roulette with Paul Morrissey, Billy Name, Patrick Tilden-Close, and about five other Factory Superstars. He actually fired one shot, but it was aimed at the ceiling. As the intruder began to focus his attention on Warhol, Mead jumped on his back, and then ran to the window and screamed for help. The now off-balance gunman immediately left the building and drove off in a waiting car. The police refused to believe the incident wasn't a publicity stunt. Around the same time, Mead appeared in the play *Conquest of the Universe*, directed by John Vaccaro at the Playhouse of the Ridiculous. Surrounded by other stars of the underground, including Mary Woronov and Beverly Grant, he was described by Stefan Brecht as "magnificent, the best thing in the show, as good a technician now, or almost, as [Zero] Mostel or [Bert] Lahr."[8]

Mead estimated that he appeared in 130 films in all, including *Babo 73*, by Robert Downey Sr.; *Hallelujah the Hills*, by Adolfas Mekas; *Midnight Cowboy*, by John Schlesinger; *Brand X*, by Wynn Chamberlain; *One Plus One*, by Jean-Luc Godard; *Cleopatra*, by Michel Auder; *Buster's Bedroom*, by Rebecca Horn; and *Coffee and Cigarettes*, by Jim Jarmusch. He was featured in the role of a priest in Penny Arcade's live performance *Bitch! Dyke! Faghag! Whore!* He also appeared on television programs such as *The Tonight Show* with Johnny Carson and *Saturday Night Live*. In 1986 Hanuman Books published *Son of Andy Warhol*, a volume of Mead's writing, as part of its series of miniatures.[9] In the late 1990s, he hosted a weekly live program on the Internet, *The Convertible Taylor Mead*, and completed the huge manuscript for his still-unpublished autobiography, also titled *Son of Andy Warhol*. Another book, *A Simple Country Girl*, was published in 2005.

The Andy Warhol Museum fêted Mead with a festival of ten of his films throughout November and December 1999, including a screening of *Taylor Mead's Ass*, which had recently been restored; Mead introduced the film and answered audience questions afterward. Mead continued

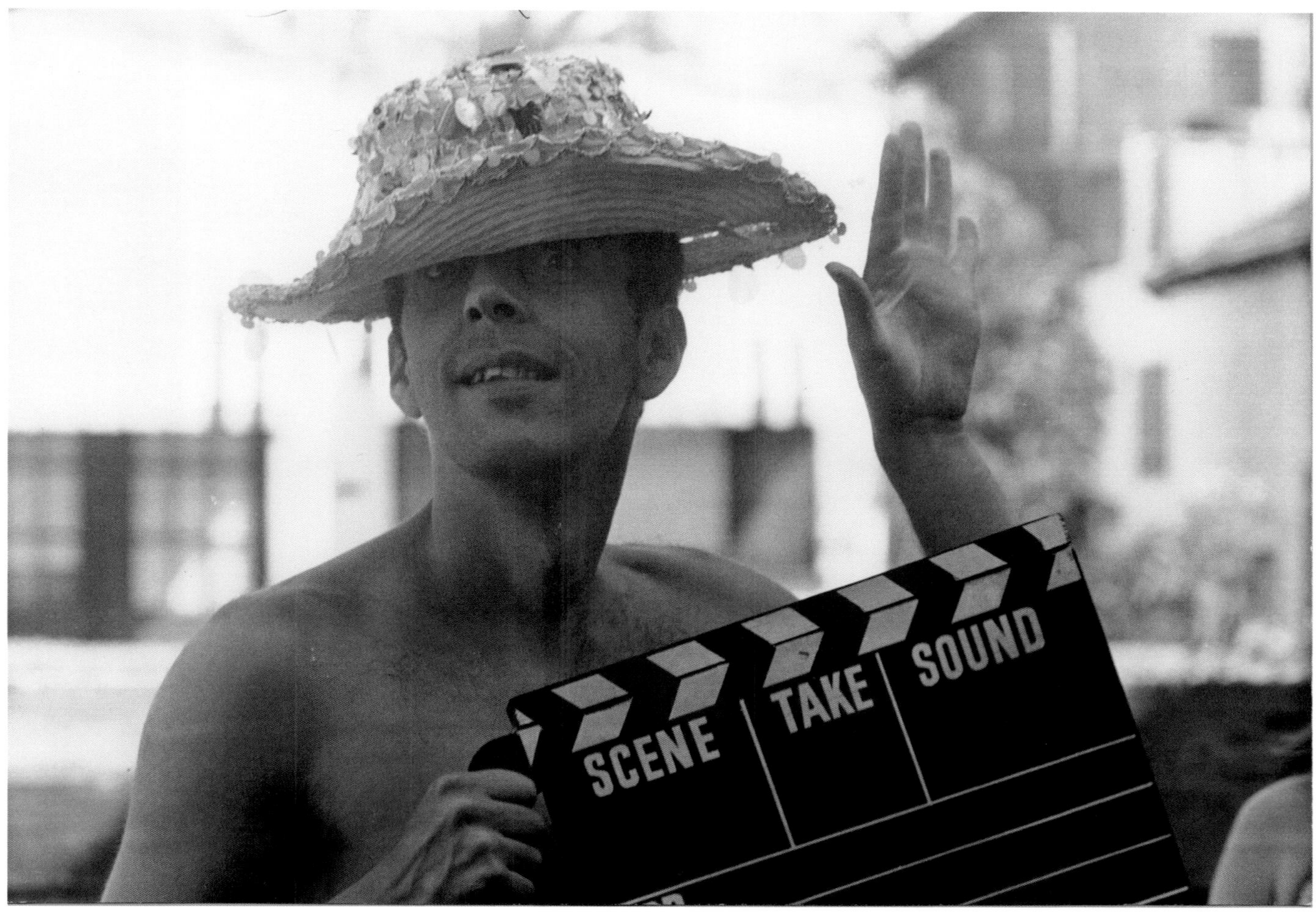

giving poetry readings, primarily at the Bowery Poetry Club. In October 2012, he made his last public appearance with a Warhol film. He delivered the introduction for the New York premiere screening of *San Diego Surf*, which features one of his most brilliant performances. In a brief interview published in advance of the screening, he reminisced about the filming with a statement that describes his life and creativity: "I could improvise forever. Andy just let me loose."[10]

NOTES

1. Callie Angell, *Andy Warhol Screen Tests: The Films of Andy Warhol; Catalogue Raisonné* (New York: Abrams, 2006), 1:126.

2. Steven Watson, *Factory Made: Warhol and the Sixties* (New York: Pantheon, 2003), 41.

3. In 1962 Zimmerman received the Rosenthal Award for young directors for *Lemon Hearts*.

4. Interview with Taylor Mead by Steven Watson, February 18, 1998.

5. Watson, *Factory Made*, 165.

6. Ibid.

7. Interview with Mead by Watson.

8. Stefan Brecht, "The Conquest of the Universe," *The Drama Review: TDR* 12, no. 3 (1968): 183–85.

9. Hanuman Books published artists' and poets' writings in editions that were identical in format; modeled after Indian prayer books, the trim size was 3 by 4 inches.

10. Christopher Bollen, "New Wave Cinema," *Interview* (November 29, 2011), https://www.interviewmagazine.com/film/san-diego-surf-warhol.

Steven Watson and Penny Arcade assisted with material featured in this chapter.

Photographer unknown, *Taylor Mead Holding a Director's Slate*, 1968

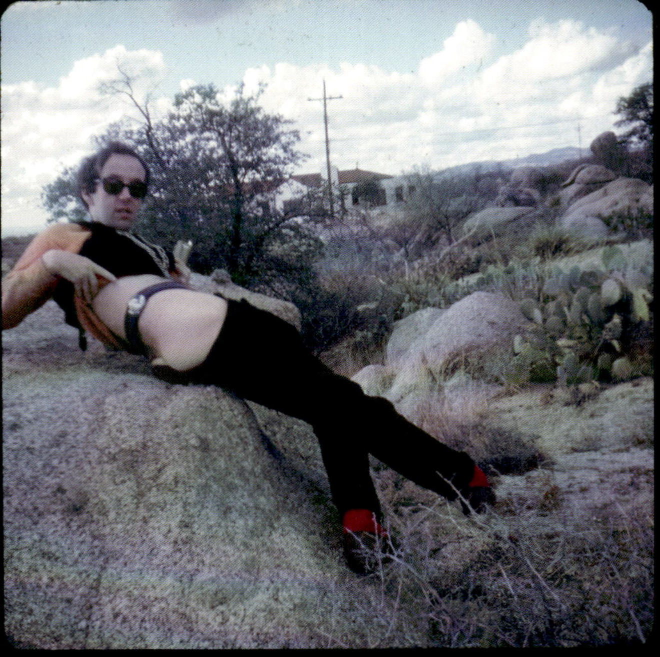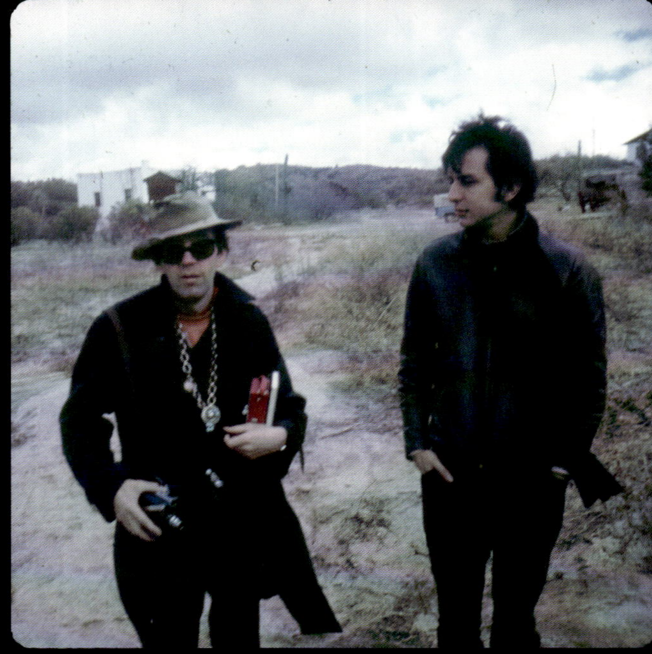

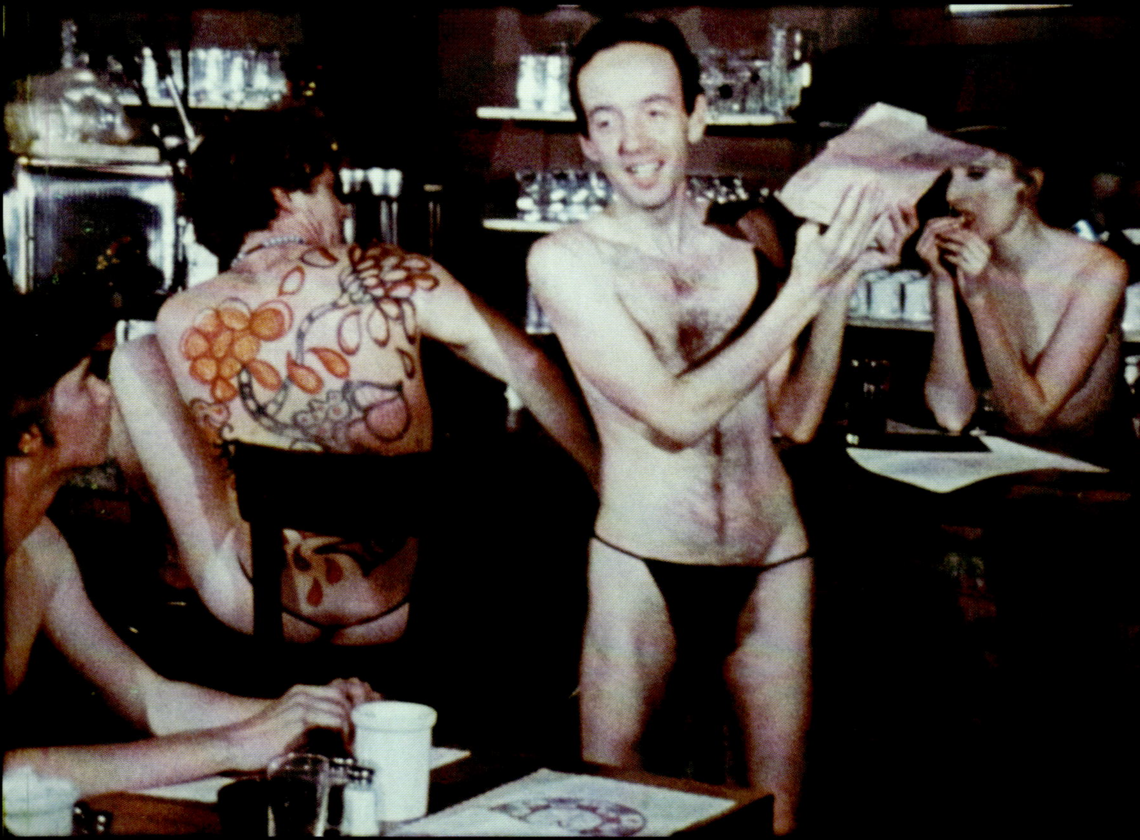

Photographer unknown, slides of Taylor Mead and Taylor Mead with Fred Hughes, 1968

Taylor Mead in film still from Andy Warhol's *The Nude Restaurant*, 1967

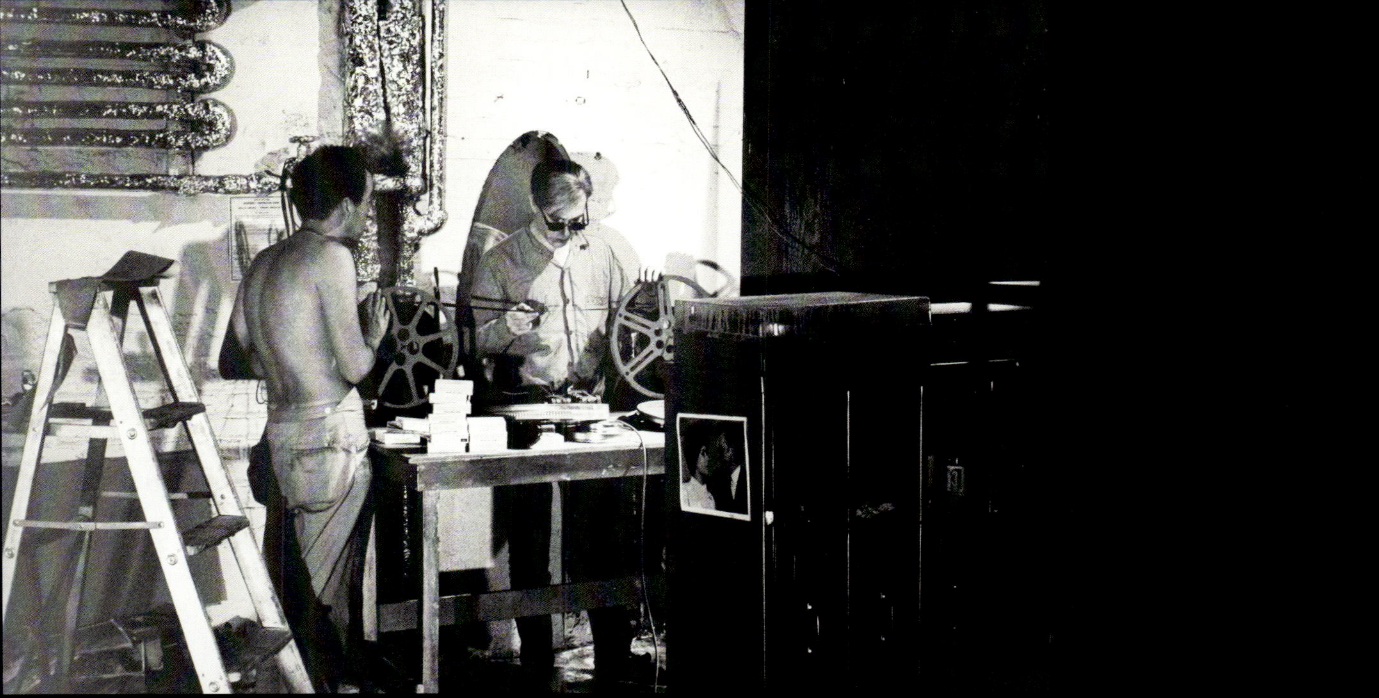

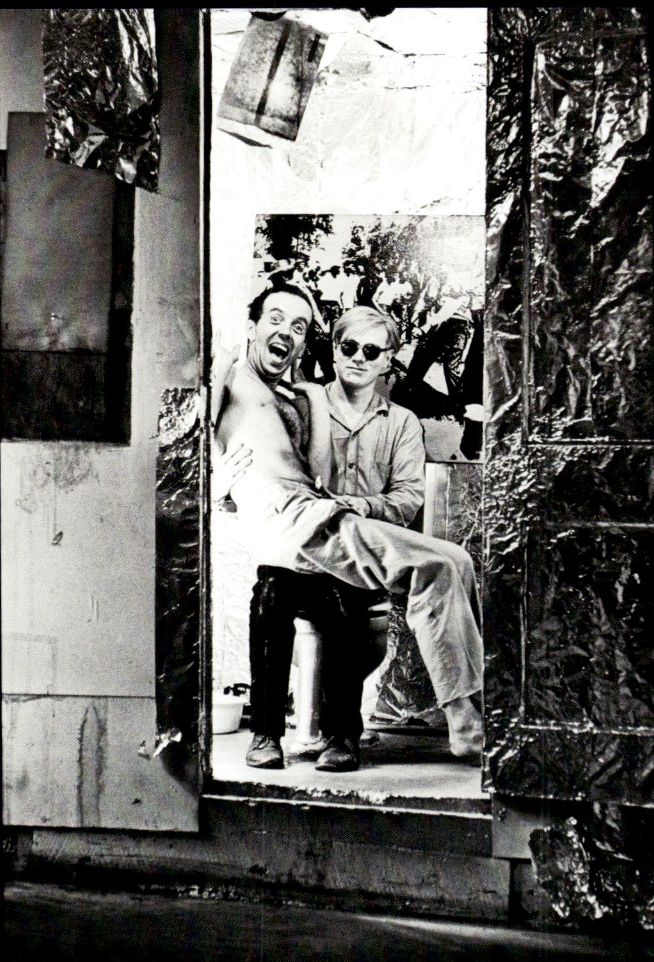 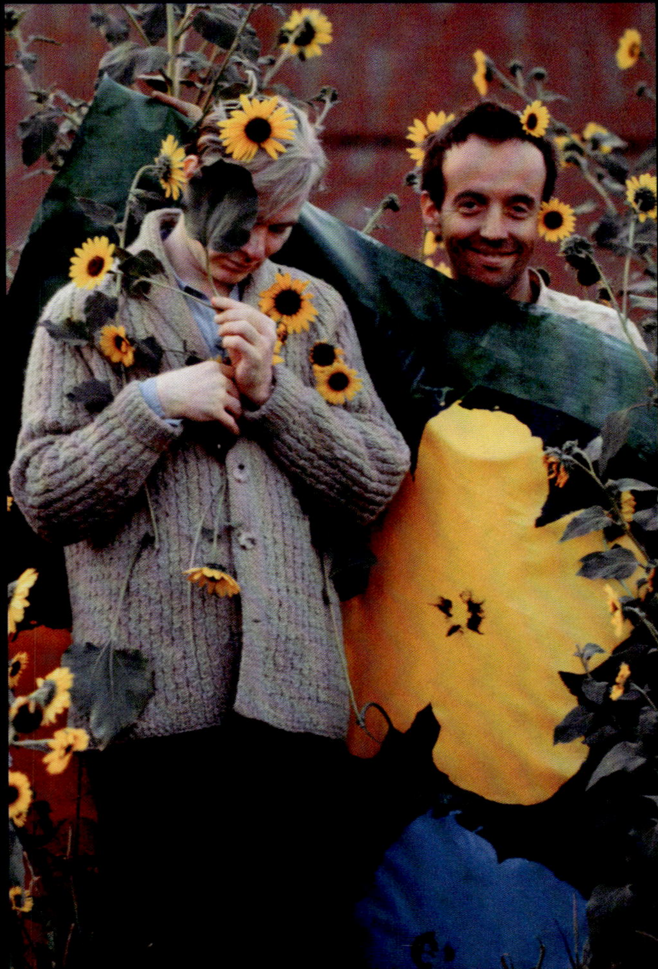

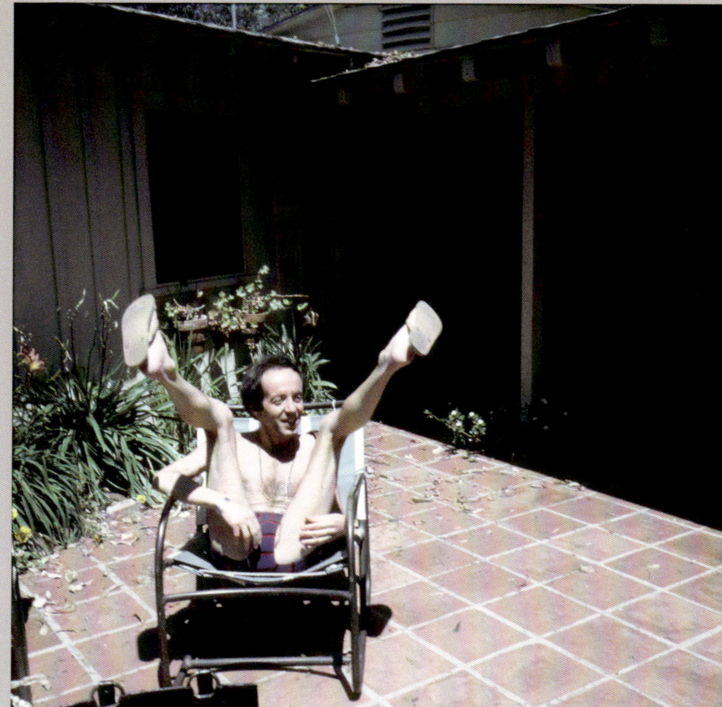

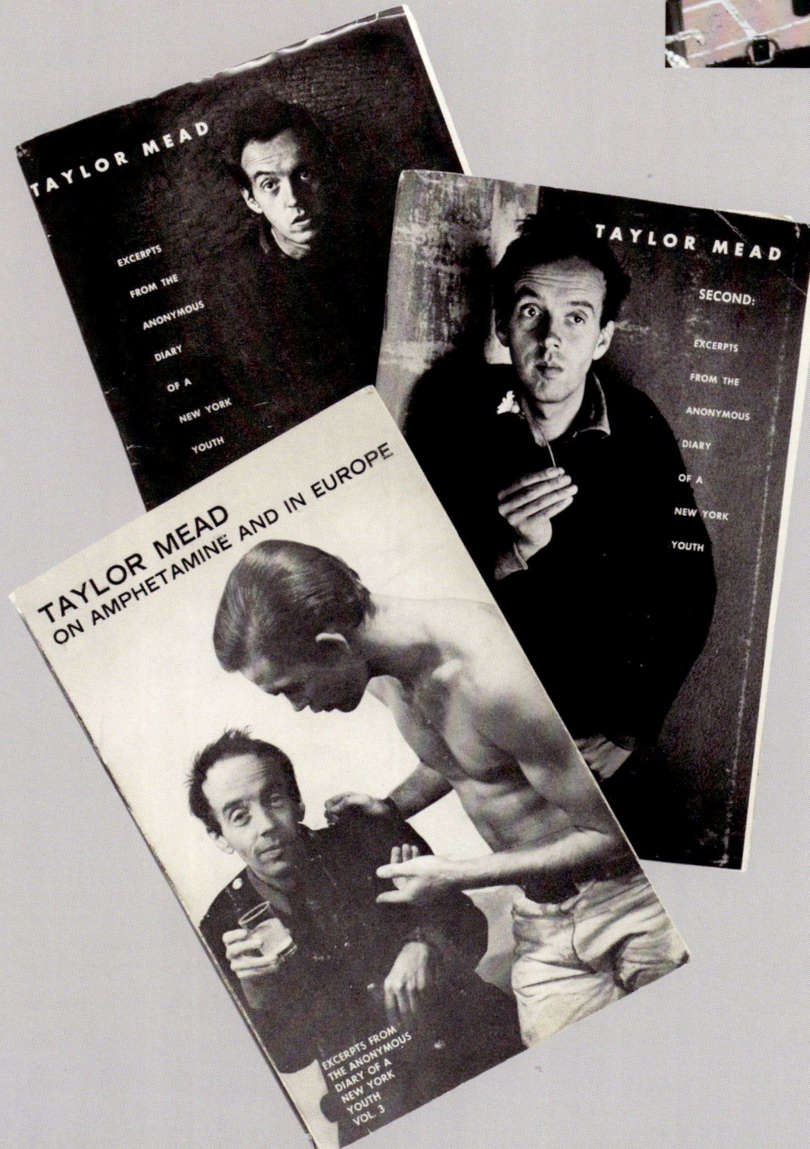

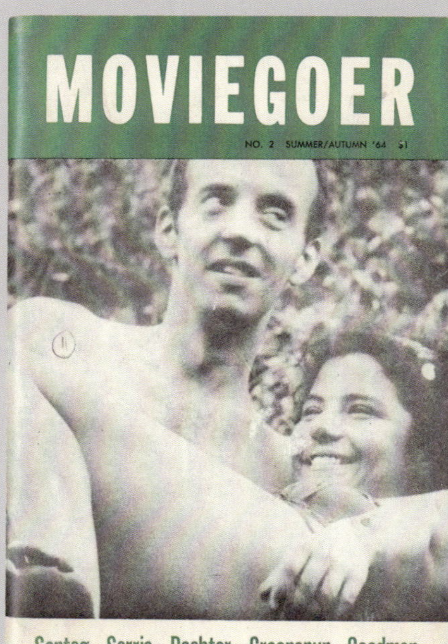

Books by Taylor Mead, *Excerpts from the Anonymous Diary of a New York Youth*, 1961; *Excerpts from the Anonymous Diary of a New York Youth*, 1962; *Taylor Mead on Amphetamine and in Europe*, 1968

Photographer unknown, *Taylor Mead*, 1968

Taylor Mead on the cover of *Moviegoer*, Summer–Autumn 1964

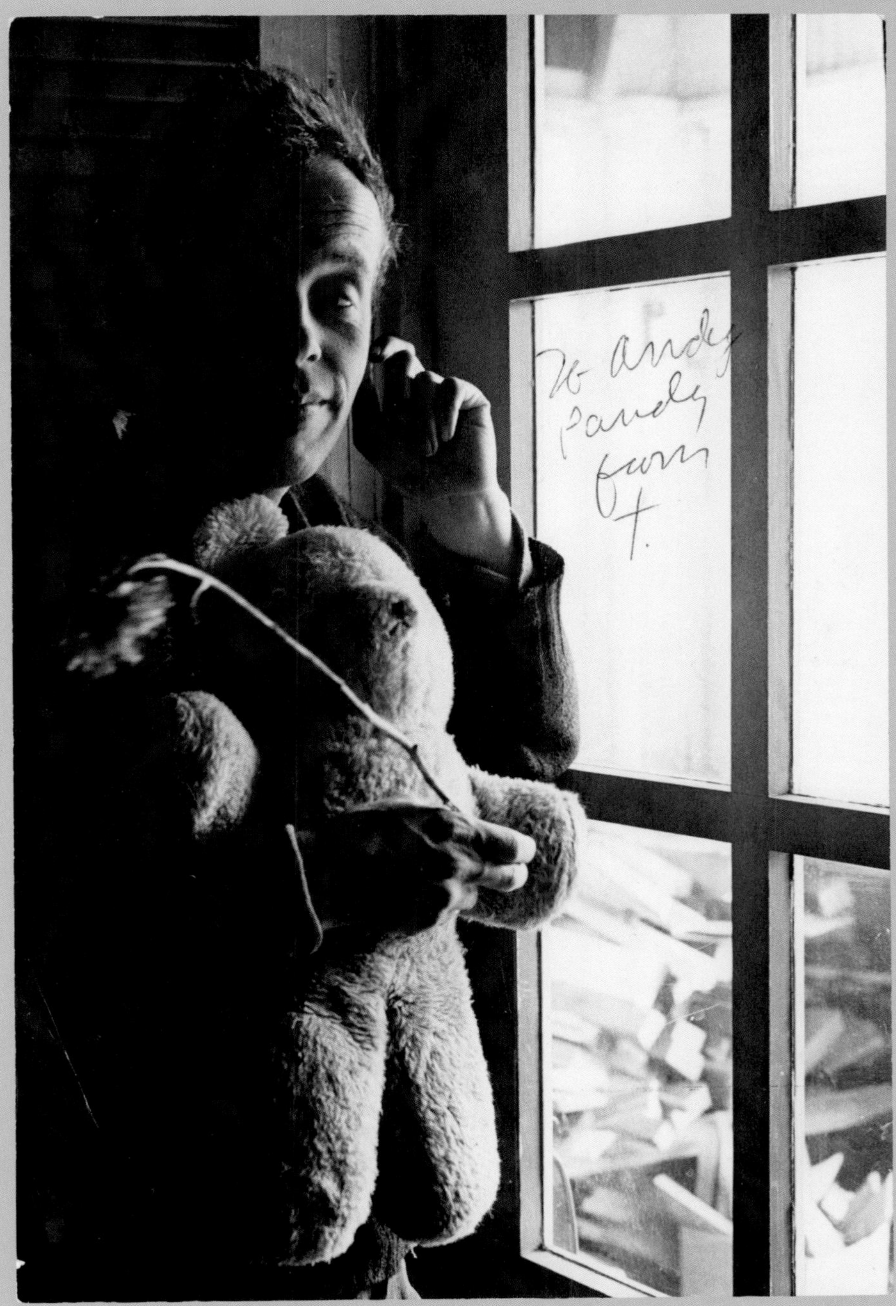

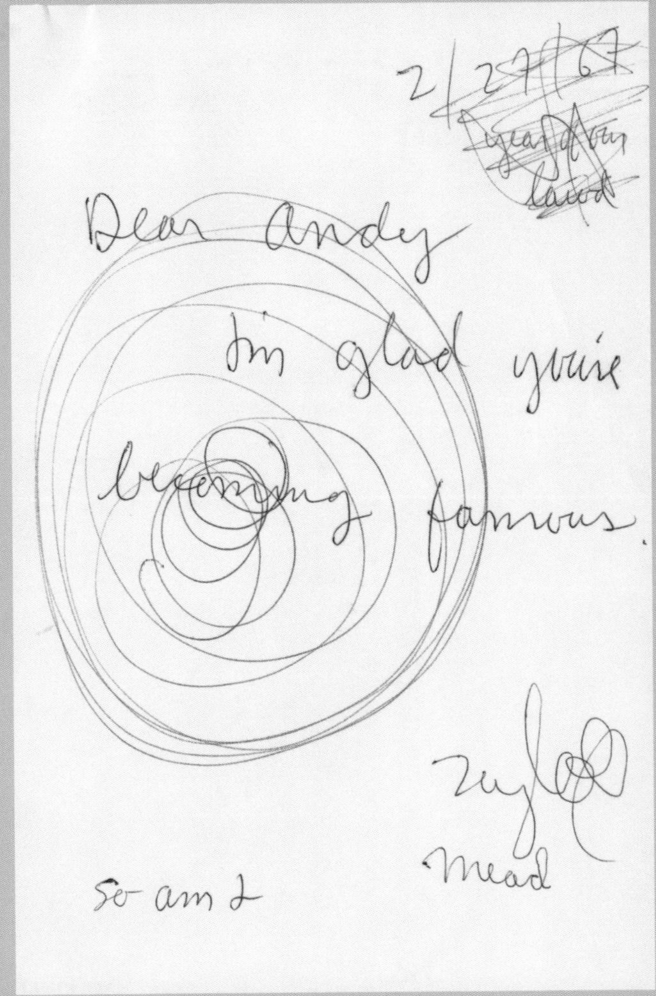

Photographer unknown, *Taylor Mead*, 1960s, inscribed by Mead to Warhol

Letter from Taylor Mead to Warhol, posted February 27, 1967

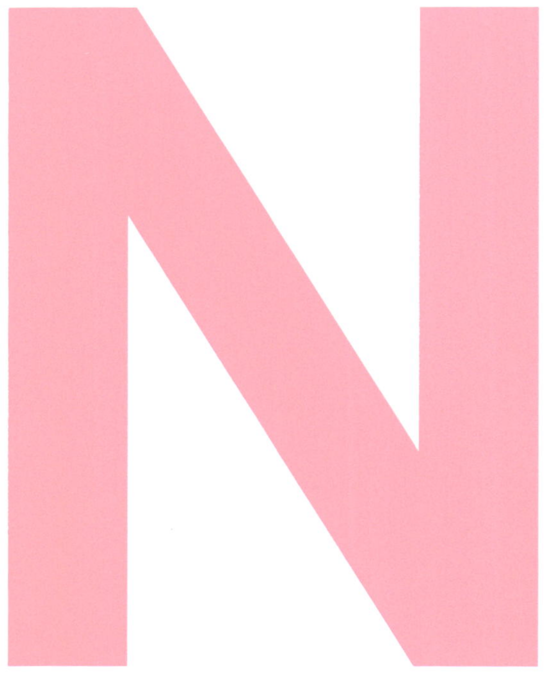

Andy Warhol loved parties. He was invited to many in New York, London, and Paris, and went to more elsewhere during his travels. Whether celebrating a birthday, a new exhibition, a book, a fashion line, or a dance or theater company, a party was happening somewhere seemingly every night, and he went to at least one on most nights. Parties in New York were said to take on a special mood when he was there: he was so identified with New York's nightlife that no party started until Warhol arrived. He entwined these celebrations with the prosperity of his fortunes. He nearly always went out with a close associate from his studio whose role was initially to entertain and chat up existing clients, or to engage with likely prospects for a portrait commission, or to meet current and rising stars for a feature in *Interview*, which might also lead to being a guest on *Andy Warhol's Fifteen Minutes* television show, or to a portrait or another venture. This strategy gave Warhol time to catch up with old friends before briefly stopping by to meet the new prospects and help seal a deal.

By the late 1970s, keeping track of this busy schedule was accomplished in part by maintaining large journals, one book for daytime events (often including lunches that

N
is for NIGHTLIFE

This chapter was created from newly catalogued archival materials relating to Warhol's social life.

the Warhol Studio was hosting for a client) and a separate book for evening appointments. Warhol received invitations in the mail to most parties, and those he expected to attend were stapled into the journal, often covering other stapled invitations and more that had been received by telephone and written onto the page. Warhol was invited to a wide variety of cultural events, and the number of invitations makes the journals physically impossible to close. Warhol was unable to attend every party to which he was invited, and the invitations for those he decided not to attend were placed into his *Time Capsules*; perhaps he wanted to have a reminder of the event even though he wasn't going, just to know that it was happening and that some of his friends might be going. He may have wanted to keep a record of missed events, as they could be important in the near future. To stay informed and up-to-date, he would need to know who attended, and with whom, and what they wore, and what they said. Because of his endless curiosity, the museum now has a great paper record of parties and other events, both those he had an interest in and those he did not. Often the journals can be cross-referenced against Warhol's published *Diaries* for

his perspective on the parties he attended and who accompanied him, but not always. For example, many of the exciting events in his 1982 journal are not discussed in the *Diaries*, leaving us to imagine what might have occurred.

The night planner from 1982 is crammed with assorted invitations ranging from concerts and performances to teas and gala dinners. Warhol was asked to a concert by the British rock band Duran Duran at midnight on July 2 at the Peppermint Lounge. Nick Rhodes, keyboardist and founding member of the band, visited the museum years later and shared how important Warhol had been to the band's early success and how generous he was to them. Objects and photographs in the Archive document this friendship.

Later that month, Warhol was invited to the Broadway musical *Best Little Whorehouse in Texas* on July 22. This run of the popular bawdy musical closed two nights later. The movie version with Dolly Parton had its US premiere on July 23, but Warhol's journal doesn't specify whether it was the stage or screen version to which he was invited. Warhol created a portrait of Parton in 1985, and she is mentioned numerous times in his *Diaries*. On July 23, Earl Blackwell was hosting a tea party. Blackwell ran a company that

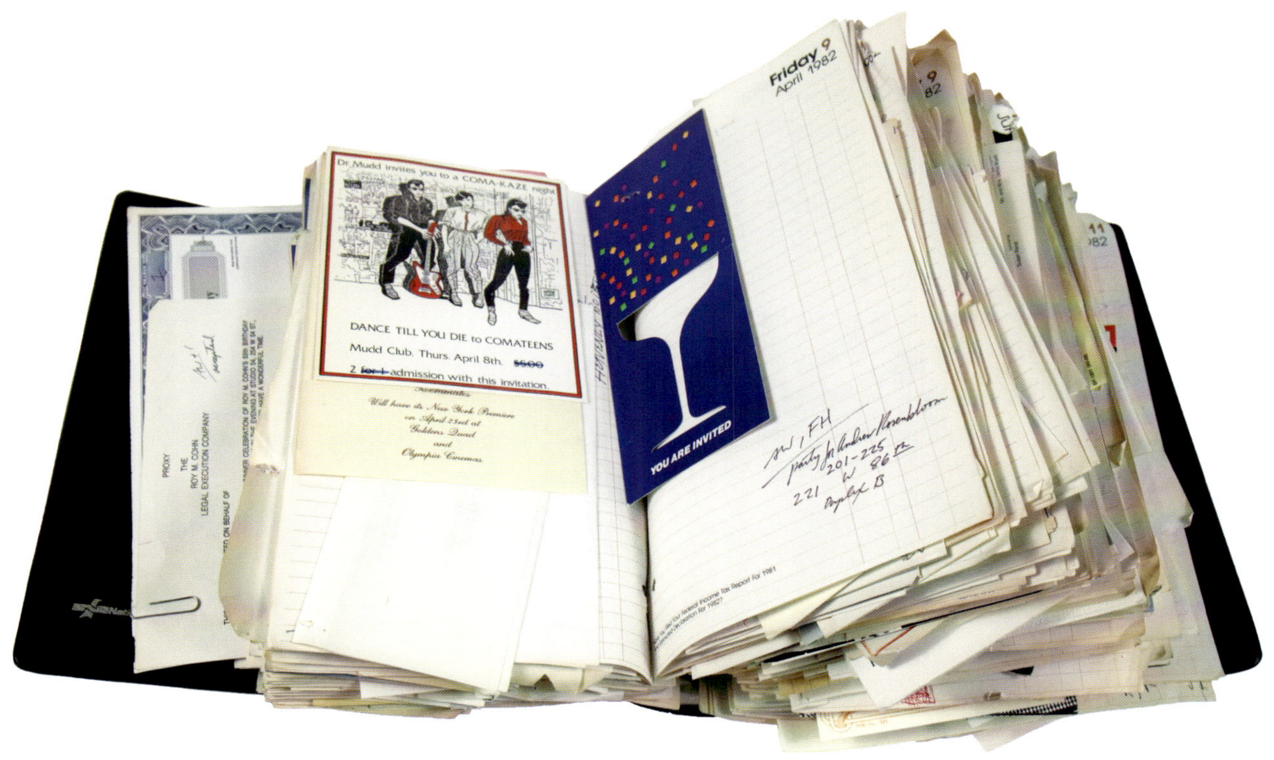

Warhol's night planner, 1982 (with various views on following pages)

tracked celebrities, and Warhol would have enjoyed this affair for the gossip. Blackwell organized and hosted famous parties, balls, and events, including Marilyn Monroe's "Happy Birthday" rendition to "Mr. President" in 1962 at Madison Square Garden. Warhol had four tickets and backstage passes for the concert by rock star Billy Squier at the same venue on July 24. This concert was on the tour promoting *Emotions in Motion*, Squier's new LP with cover art by Warhol.

On September 9, New York City Mayor Ed Koch opened the First Soho Arts Festival with "A Gala Supper" in honor of Salvador Dalí at the Greene Street Café, a jazz supper club. After artists discovered the vast interior spaces of the historic nineteenth-century cast-iron factory buildings of SoHo in the 1960s and 1970s and prevented them from being demolished (to allow for a planned highway), the area was the city's downtown center of commercial art galleries prior to their move to much larger spaces in Chelsea in the 1990s. The title of the SoHo celebratory dinner played on the name of Dalí's wife and muse, Gala. Per the *Diaries*, Warhol invited Ed Koch to lunch multiple times, but the mayor always canceled. Warhol was invited to Gracie Mansion as a guest of the mayor to celebrate artist Alice Neel's birthday earlier that year, on March 29, and rubbed elbows with the mayor again during a celebration of the Brooklyn Bridge centennial in 1983, which featured a fantastic display of fireworks. Warhol's print *Brooklyn Bridge* (1983) was commissioned for this anniversary celebration and was reproduced on all the brochures and posters announcing the event.

Warhol's most frequent party companion in 1982 was Bob Colacello, editor of *Interview* and coauthor of many of Warhol's books, among other roles that included portrait commissions. He also went out with his business managers, Vincent Fremont and Fred Hughes. After Colacello left *Interview* for *Vanity Fair* in 1983, Warhol's "dates" widened to include Benjamin Liu, Paige Powell, and others.

Warhol's social calendars, photographs, and ephemera confirm in great quantity his celebrity in New York nightlife, but at the end of the evening, he did not invite the party back to his place. Aside from maids and maintenance workers, very few people were ever welcomed into his 57 East 66th Street town house on Manhattan's Upper East Side. And for someone who documented the world around him, in every medium—photos, films, tape recordings, scrapbooks, drawings, paintings, prints—it is astonishing how little visual evidence in the Archive documents his private home. There are no self-portraits taken in his exclusive rooms or photographs of his belongings. The public and private worlds of Warhol remain resolutely so.

NOTE

Additional research for this chapter was provided by Erin Byrne, Matt Gray, and Brianna Treleven. Photographic layouts designed by Becky Shock.

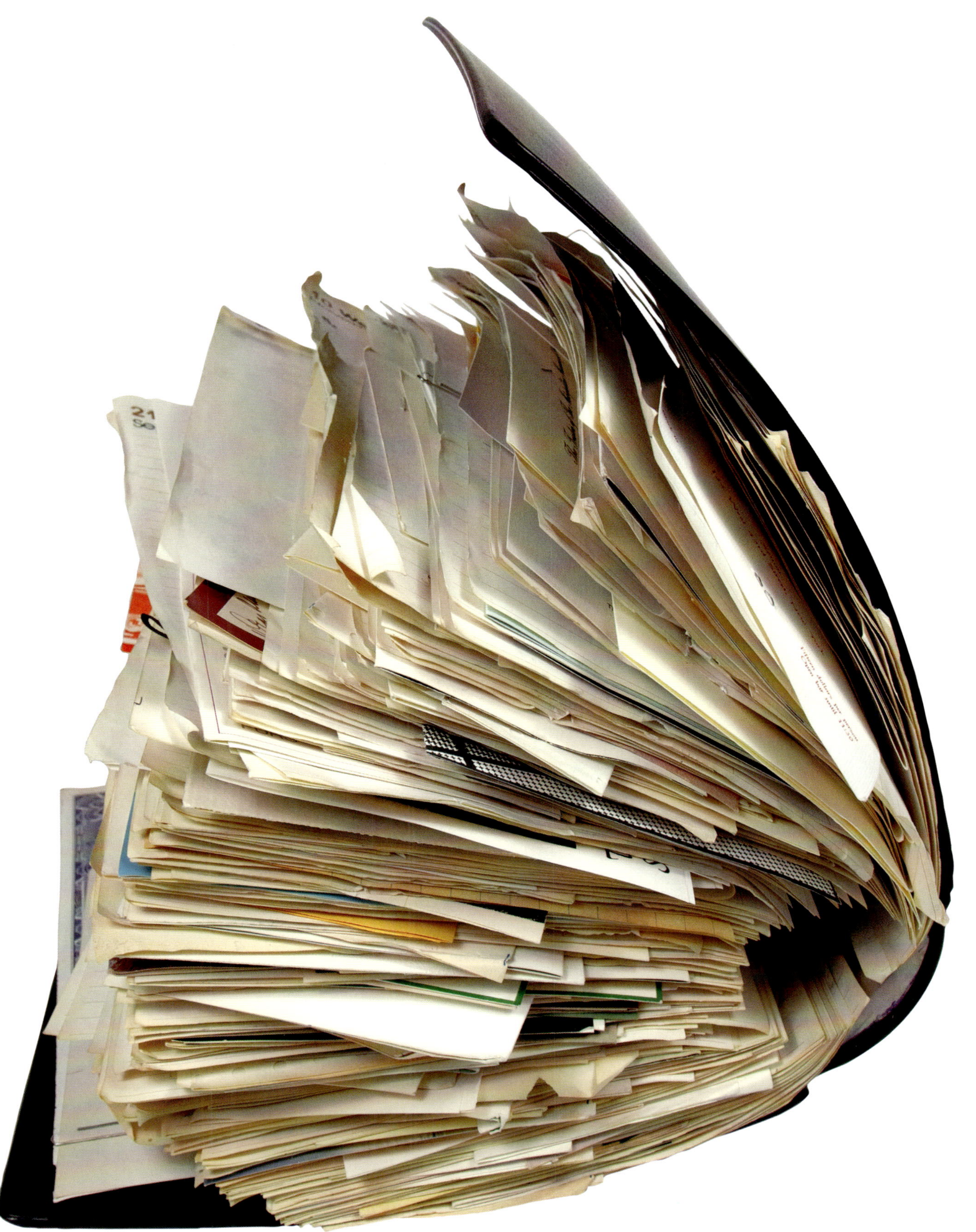

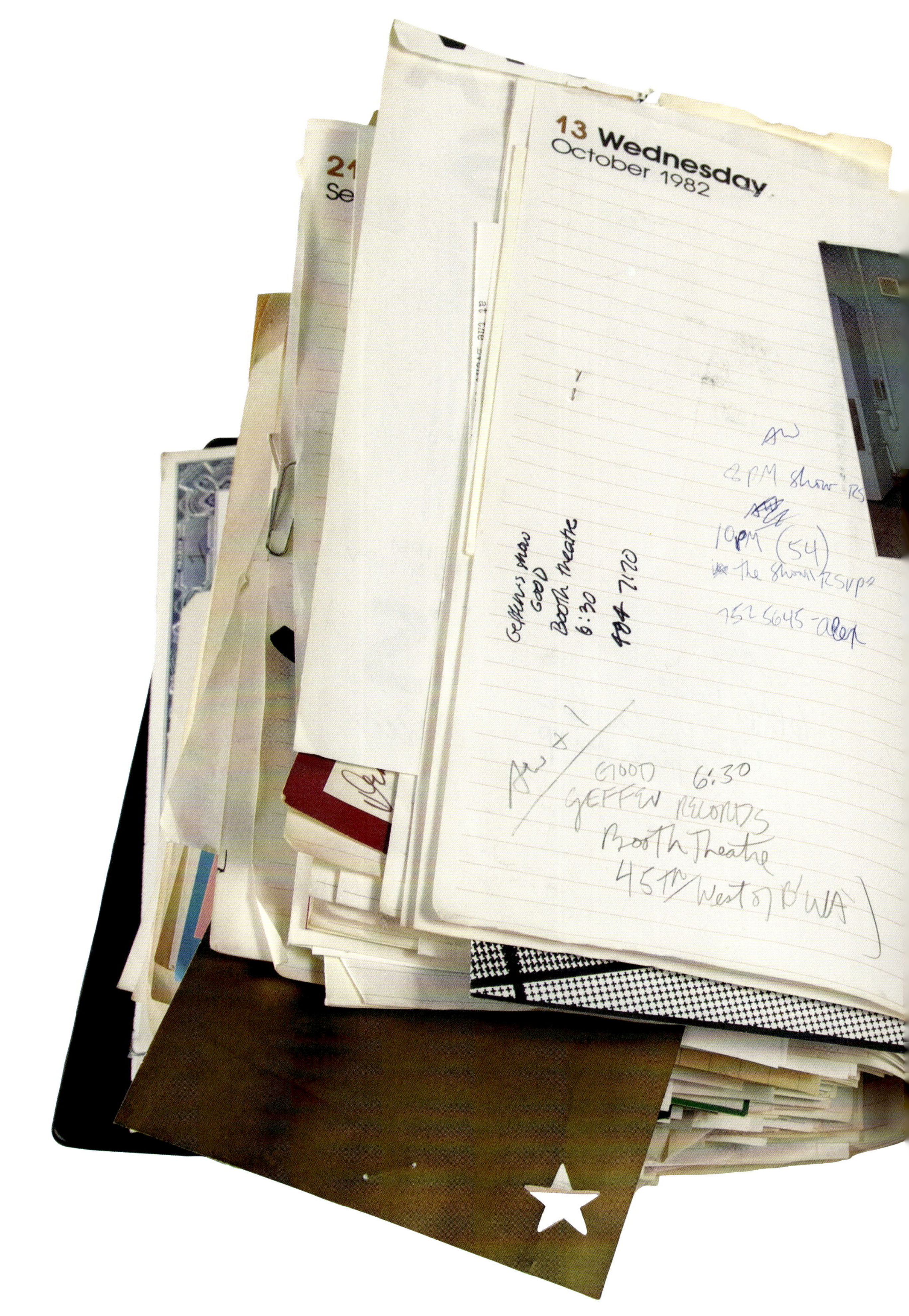
13 Wednesday
October 1982
21
Se
Geffens Man
GOOD
Booth Theatre
6:30
TDF 7:20
AW
8PM show RS
10PM (54)
the show RSVP?
752 5645 - alen
GOOD   6:30
GEFFEN RECORDS
Booth Theatre
45th West of B'WAY

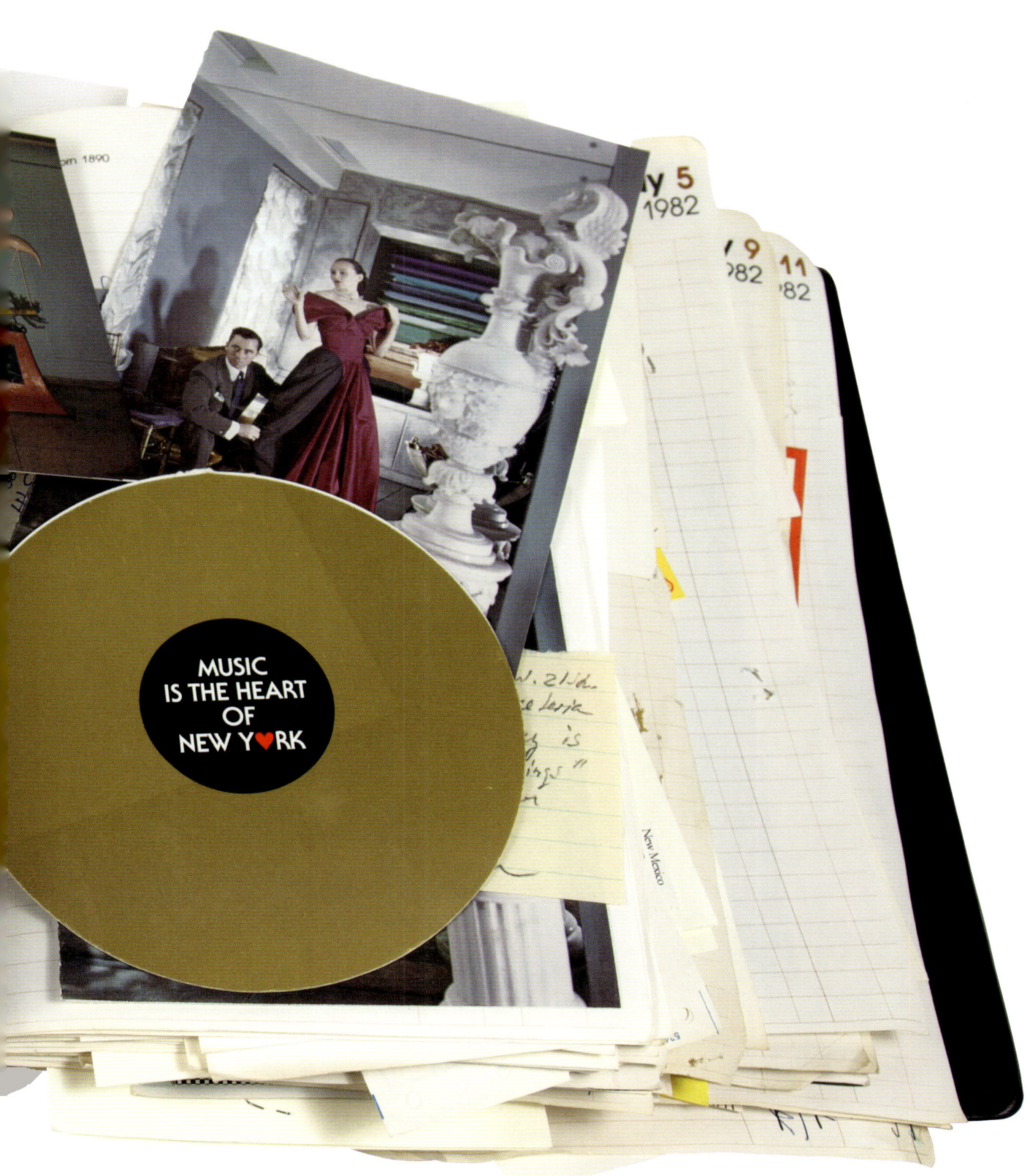
MUSIC
IS THE HEART
OF
NEW Y♥RK

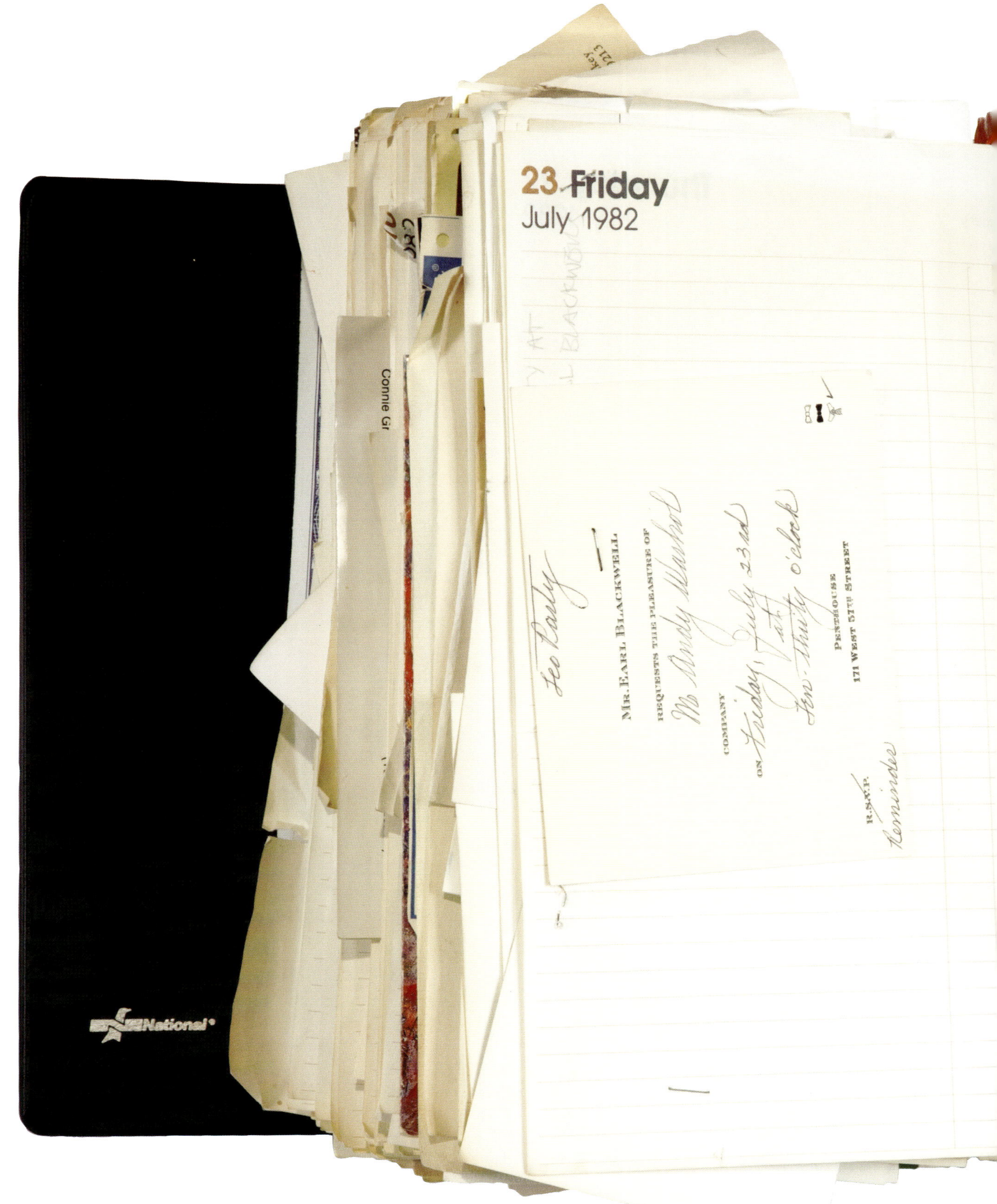
23 Friday
July 1982
Connie Gi
National
Mr. Earl Blackwell
REQUESTS THE PLEASURE OF
COMPANY
on Friday, July 23rd
PENTHOUSE
171 WEST 57TH STREET
R.S.V.P.

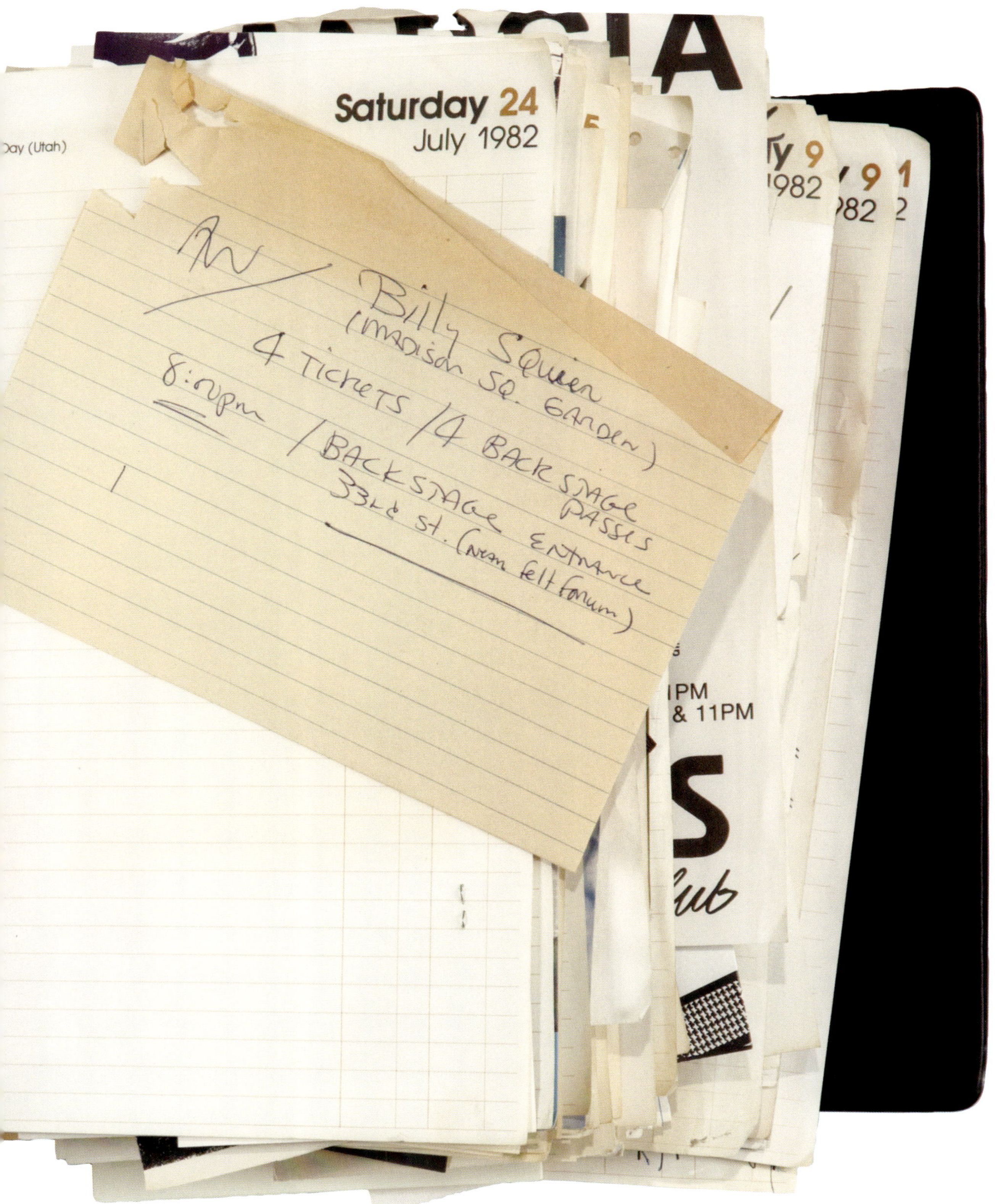
Day (Utah)
Saturday 24
July 1982
Ty 9
1982
9 1
982 2
Billy Squier
(madison sq. garden)
4 tickets / 4 Backstage
passes
8:00pm / Backstage Entrance
33rd St. (near felt forum)
1PM
& 11PM
S
Club

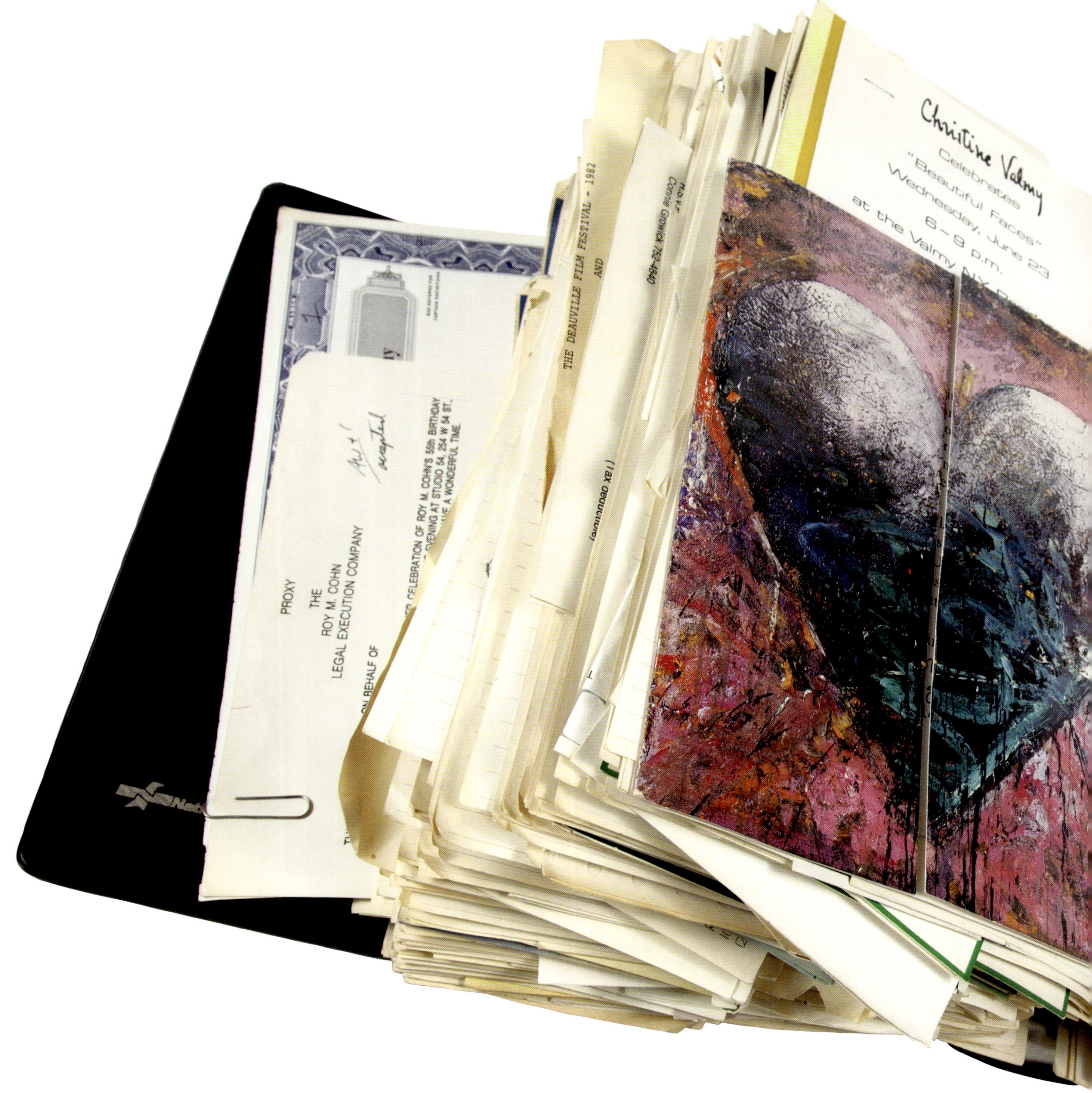

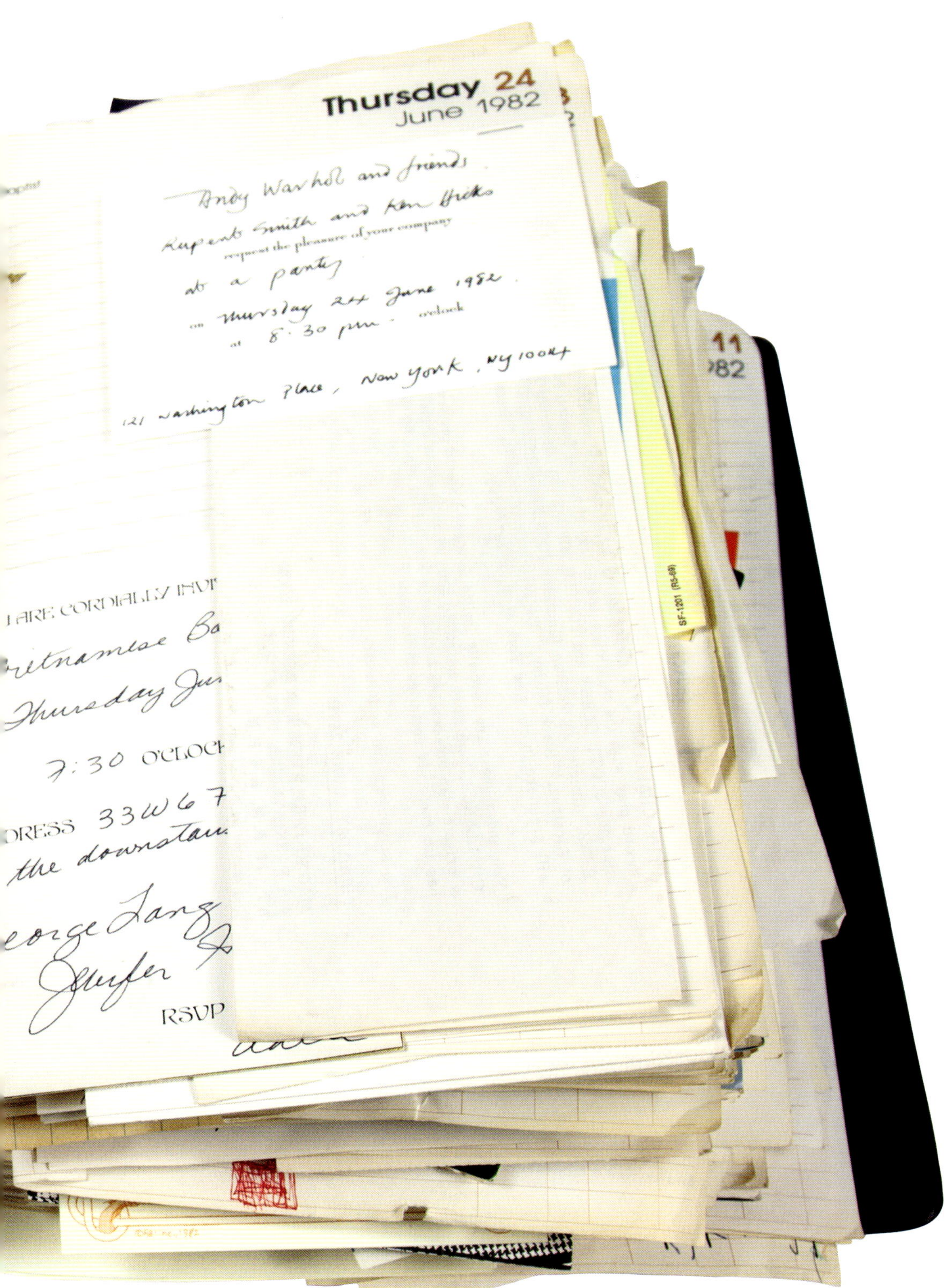
Thursday 24
June 1982

Andy Warhol and friends.
Rupert Smith and Ken Hicks
request the pleasure of your company
at a party
on Thursday 24 June 1982.
at 8:30 pm. o'clock
121 Washington Place, New York, NY 10014

ARE CORDIALLY INVIT
Vietnamese Ba
Thursday Jun
7:30 O'CLOCK
DRESS 33 W 67
the downstai
George Lang
Jenifer
RSVP

Warhol's exhibition at the Institute of Contemporary Art (ICA) at the University of Pennsylvania in Philadelphia marked one of the high points of his career as an artist in his own country. Held five-plus decades ago, October 8–November 21, 1965, it was essentially a retrospective of Warhol's Pop work.

Already celebrated throughout Europe with gallery shows in France and Germany, Warhol's work was more coolly received by an American art world accustomed to Abstract Expressionism, which in the preceding decades had been the great American contribution to art. Warhol's first one-person museum exhibition changed his standing forever, in large part due to the skills of Sam Green, the director of the ICA. Green fueled the public's interest in Warhol with novel ideas playing on the Pop concept, such as printing opening invitations on Campbell's Soup labels and as sheets of S & H Green Stamps. A wall of the gallery was covered with the Green Stamp invitations, the floors were painted silver to imitate Warhol's New York studio, and rock and roll music was played on several turntables.

The public perception of the 1965 exhibition's importance comes mainly from the near-mythic opening party, at

O
is for OPENING

This chapter is based on materials in the exhibition *Philadelphia 1965: Warhol's Public Triumph in America*, in the Archives Study Center, October 10, 1995–January 7, 1996. Additional images have been included from the photographic archive of the Institute of Contemporary Art, Philadelphia.

INSTITUTE OF CONTEMPORARY ART

UNIVERSITY OF PENNSYLVANIA

Furness Building

34th St. between Walnut & Spruce

Philadelphia

You are invited to a cocktail party

to open

an Exhibition by

ANDY WARHOL

Thursday, October 7th

5:30-7:30 P.M.

PARTY

This invitation admits two

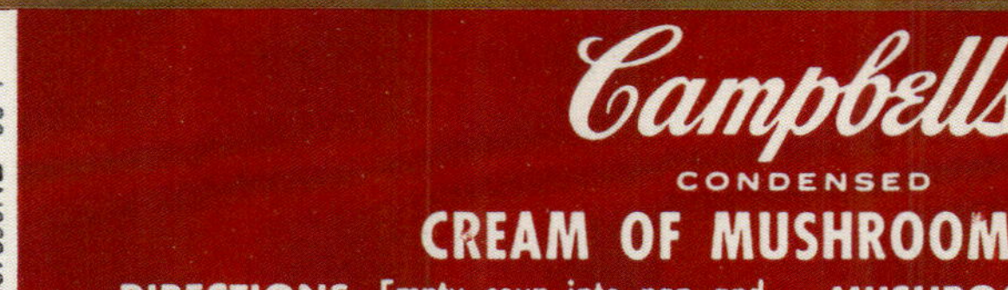

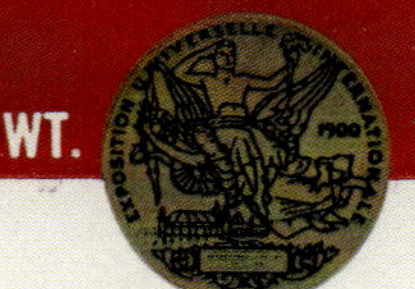

Invitation to the opening party for Warhol's exhibition at the Institute of Contemporary Art, University of Pennsylvania, October 7, 1965

which several thousand people arrived at a space designed for several hundred. The massive press preview the night before gave warning of the anticipated size of the crowd, and Green decided it was imperative to remove most of the paintings from the gallery walls to safeguard the art. The wisdom of this was proved the following evening, when Warhol arrived with his film Superstar Edie Sedgwick, Green, and others to find a mob of thousands of screaming art fans at the ICA. Sam Green remembers the scene this way: "Edie was wearing a Rudi Gernreich dress, a long thing like a t-shirt with sleeves that must have been twenty feet long…in this incredible performance…she began to let her sleeves down over the crowd like an elephant's trunk… teasing the crowd and working them up. And dancing and talking…giving interviews."[1] Warhol and his entourage were forced to climb a dead-end staircase to avoid the crush, from which they autographed Campbell's Soup cans before escaping through a hole cut into the ceiling above the stairs.

Warhol reflected on the experience in amazement. "I'd seen kids scream over Elvis and the Beatles and the Stones—rock idols and movie stars—but it was incredible to think of it happening at an *art* opening….But then, we weren't just *at* the art exhibit—we *were* the art exhibit,

we were the art incarnate."[2] Despite the chaos of the ICA opening (or maybe because of it), Warhol went on to attend more than seventy openings for his own work and hundreds of openings for friends and artists he admired. In January of 1987, just weeks before his death, Warhol flew to Milan to attend the opening of his *Last Supper* exhibition at the Palazzo delle Stelline, Milan.[3] Through excellent marketing, visitors were first instructed to view the original *Last Supper* in Santa Maria delle Grazie and then to cross the street to the gallery to see Warhol's canvases. Some estimates put the number of visitors to the Milan exhibition at thirty thousand.[4] Years later, legions of fans still make pilgrimages to Warhol openings.

NOTES

1. Jean Stein and George Plimpton, *Edie: American Girl* (New York: Grove Press, 1982), 252–53.

2. Andy Warhol and Pat Hackett, *POPism: The Warhol Sixties* (Orlando, FL: Harcourt Brace Jovanovich, 1980), 168.

3. Andy Warhol's *Last Supper* exhibition was shown at Palazzo delle Stelline, Milan, January 23–March 21, 1987.

4. "Andy Warhol's *Sixty Last Suppers*," Christie's, posted November 14, 2017, http://www.christies.com/features/Andy-Warhols-Sixty-Last-Suppers -8582-3.aspx.

After the Preview of the Warhol Exhibition at the Institute of Contemporary Art

Mr. and Mrs. Horatio Gates Lloyd

request the pleasure of
Mr. Warhol's
Mr. Malanga's
Mr. Wein's
company at dinner

on Thursday, October Seventh

at eight o'clock

R.s.v.p.

Linden
Haverford, Pennsylvania

Invitation to dinner in honor of the art opening from Mr. and Mrs. Horatio Gates Lloyd to Warhol, October 7, 1965

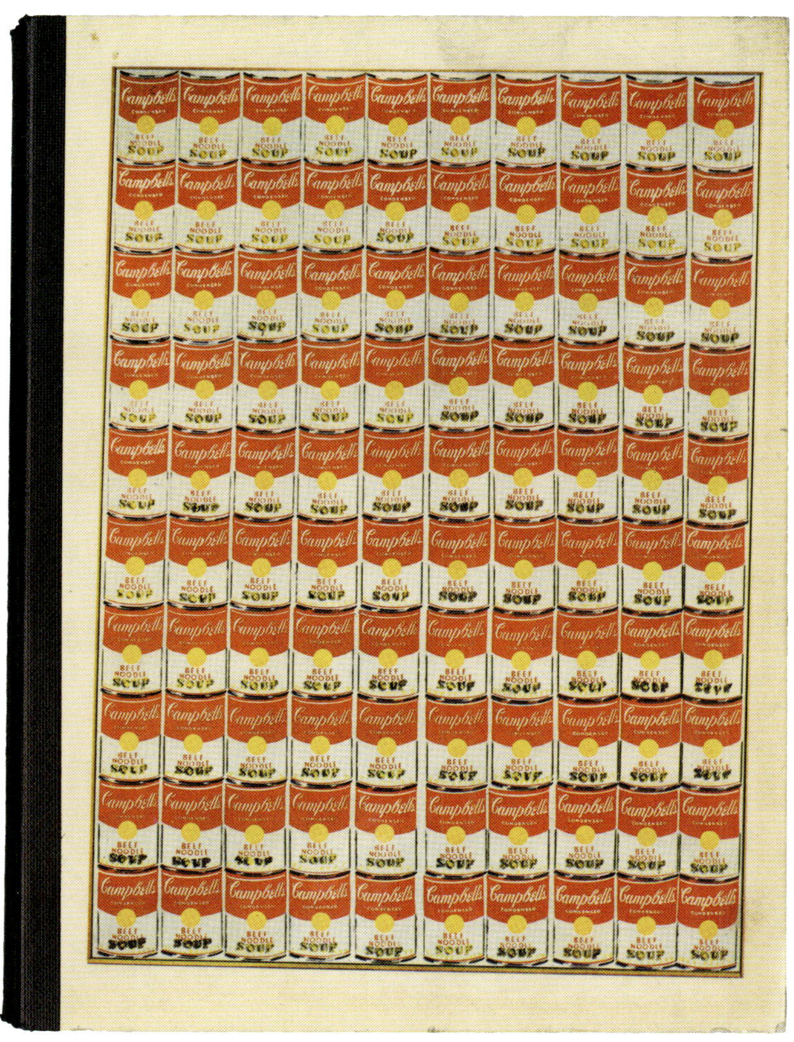

Exhibition catalogue for *Andy Warhol*, Institute of Contemporary Art,
University of Pennsylvania, 1965

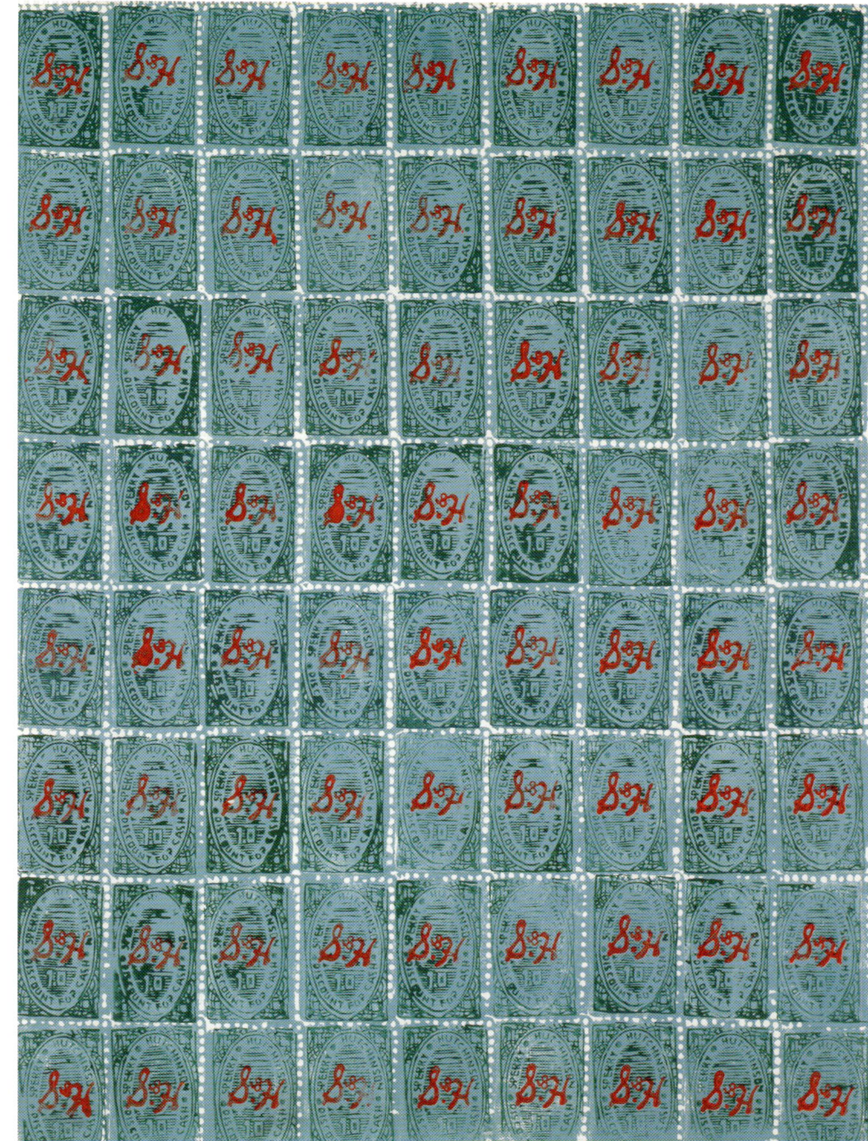

Andy Warhol, *S & H Green Stamps*, ca. 1962

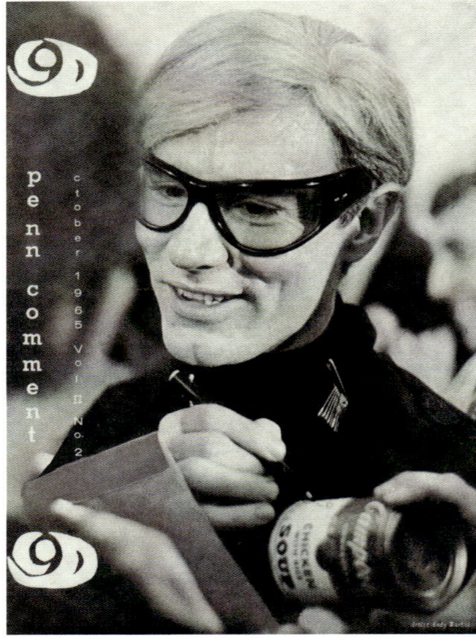

Warhol signing a soup can at the exhibition opening, reproduced on the cover of the magazine *Penn Comment*, 1965

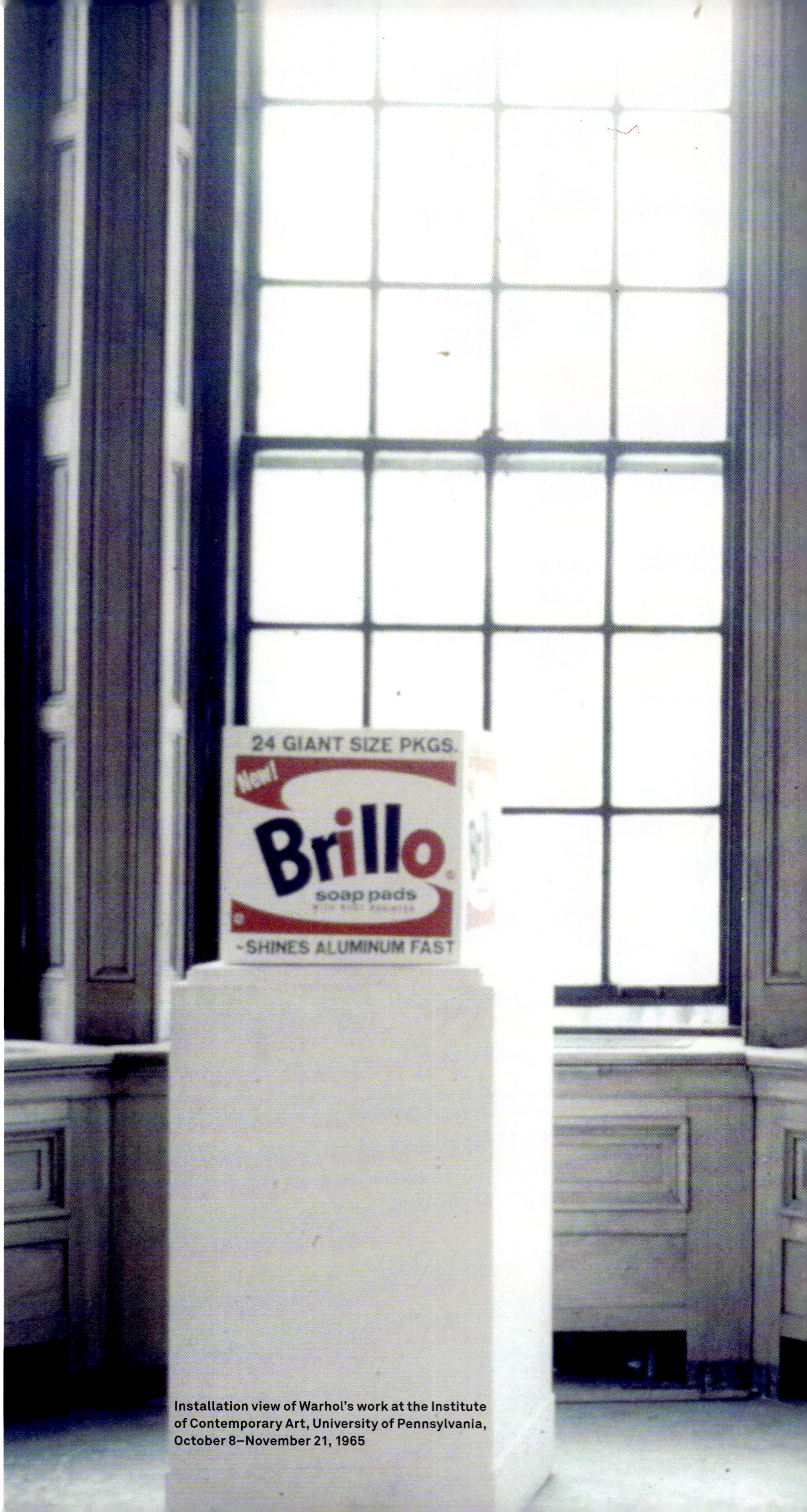

Installation view of Warhol's work at the Institute of Contemporary Art, University of Pennsylvania, October 8–November 21, 1965

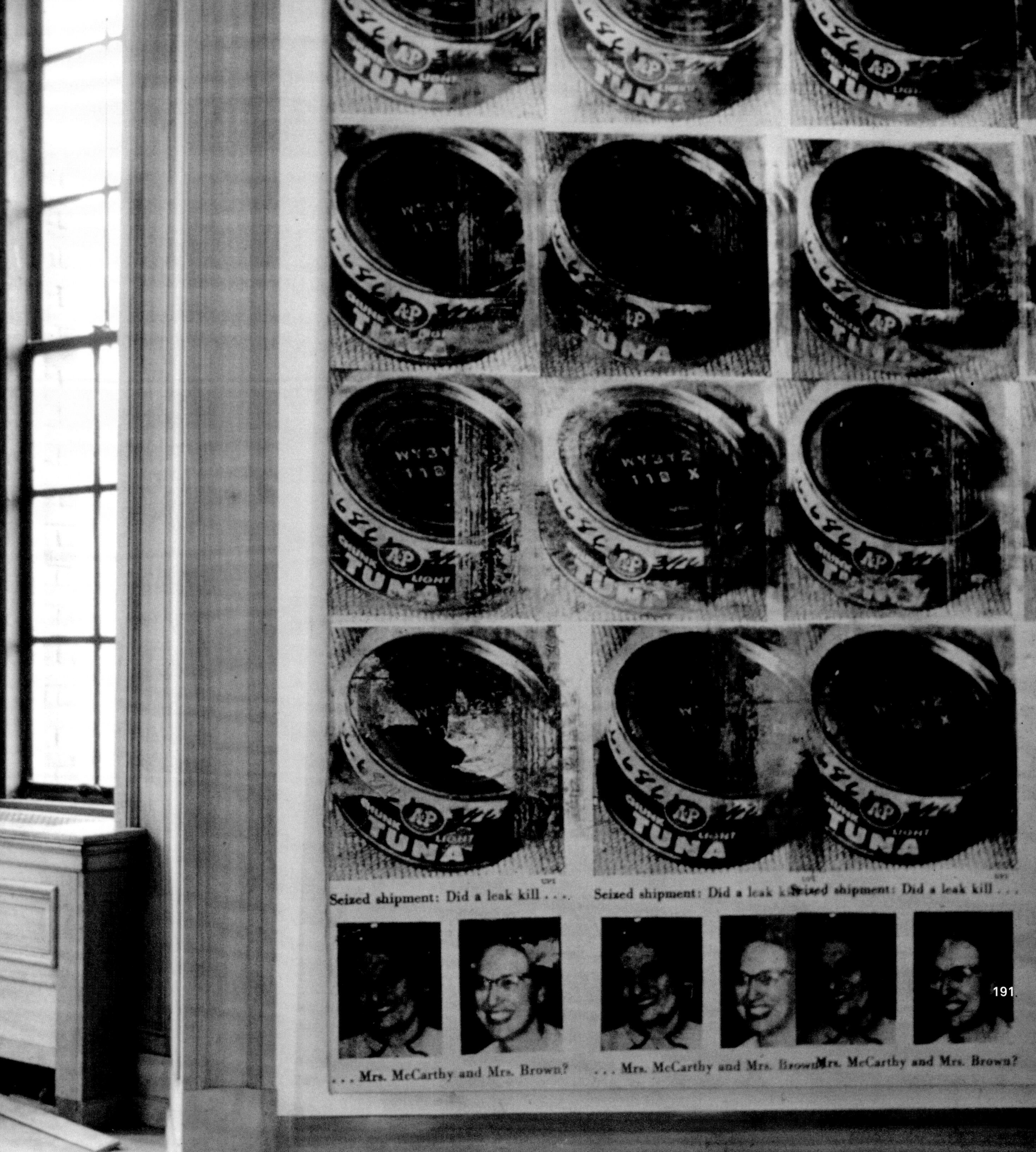

191.

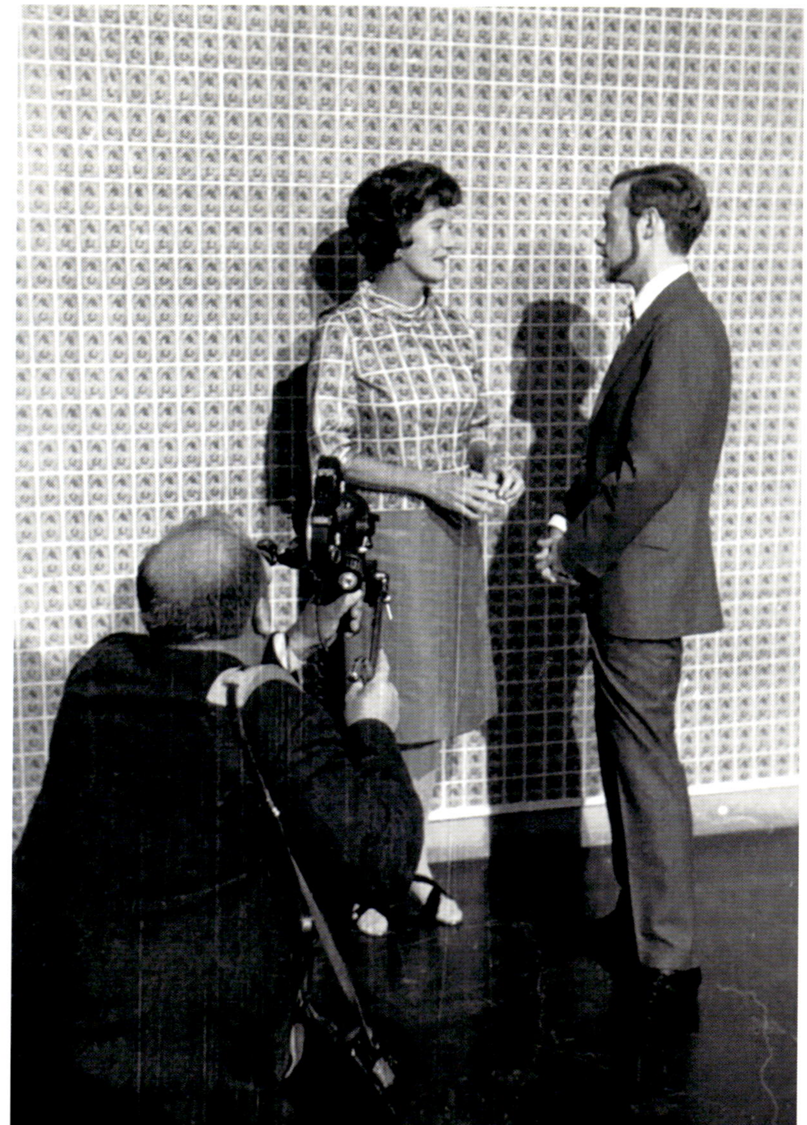

Sam Green and Mrs. Horatio Gates (Lally) Lloyd in front of S&H Green
Stamp wallpaper made for the exhibition, October 8, 1965

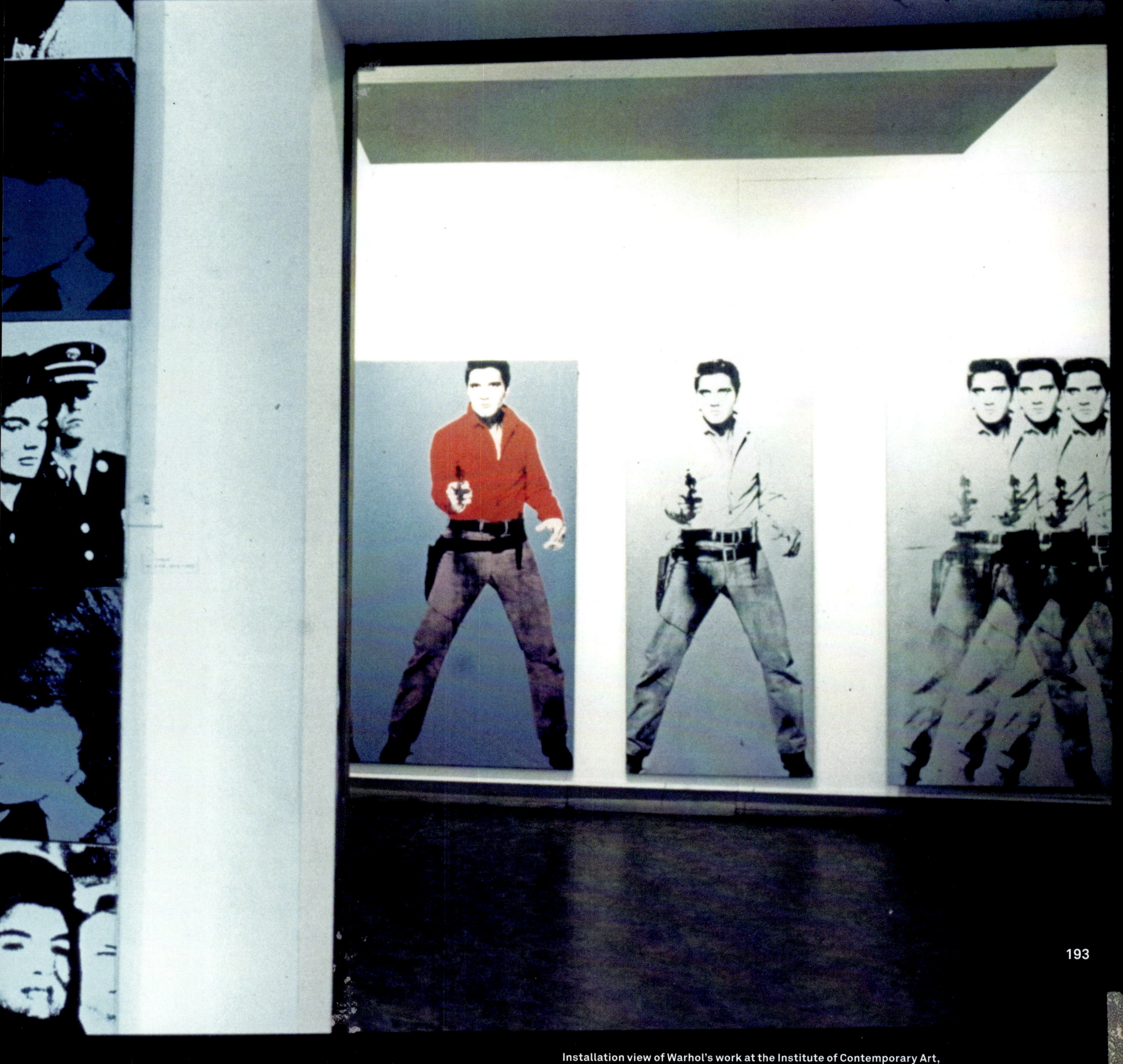

Installation view of Warhol's work at the Institute of Contemporary Art, University of Pennsylvania, October 8–November 21, 1965

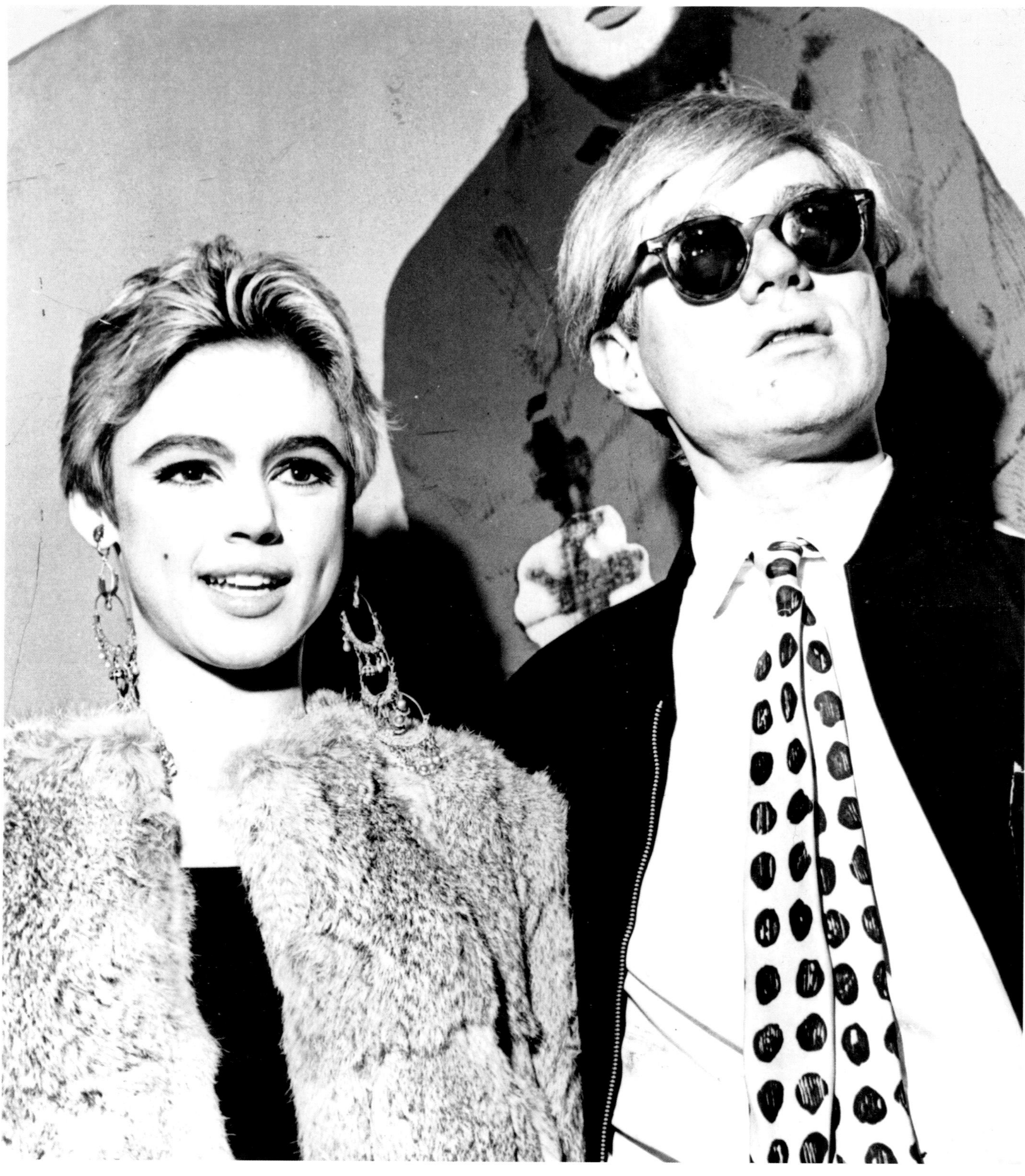

Photographer unknown, Andy Warhol and Edie Sedgwick at pre-show
party, October 7, 1965

Photographer unknown, Andy Warhol, Gerard Malanga, and
Edie Sedgwick with others on the stairs above the ICA crowd, 1965

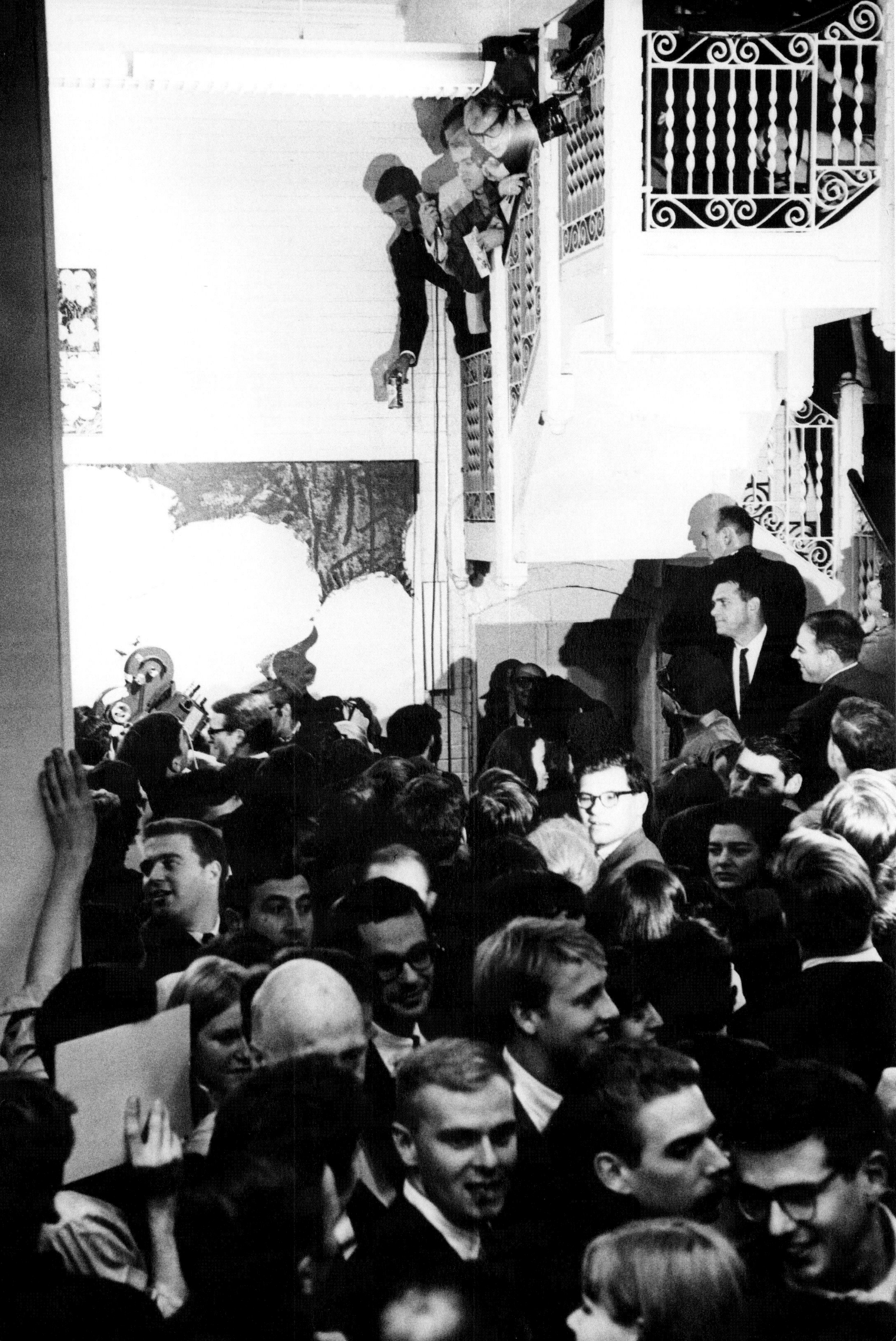

is for PHONEY

My friend is the phone.

Andy Warhol

The telephone was essential to Andy Warhol's existence, yet his family only acquired its first phone in 1943, when he was already fifteen years old. Throughout his adult life, the phone call was his favorite form of communication in both his business and personal life—he had a handful of correspondents, but he tape-recorded hundreds of his phone calls. From these recordings came the scripts for his play *Pork* (1971) and his last film, *Bad* (1976). Even his best-selling posthumous *Diaries* were "written" on the telephone. In some of his more traditional artistic endeavors, Warhol painted four large iconic homages to the phone during his early explorations of Pop Art, as well as several drawings that reference the telephone. It is fascinating to imagine how he would have utilized today's technologies; in a drawing from the early 1950s, he depicts the Bible's Three Wise Men chatting on portable phones, presumably guided by Ma Bell to Bethlehem. In 1985, with Joseph Beuys and Kaii Higashiyama, he created little-known works of telefax art for a show in Vienna. Although he experimented briefly with

This chapter is based on materials exhibited in *Really Phoney: Warhol and the Telephone*, July 9–September 19, 2004.

computers after being pursued by several young entrepreneurs, including Steve Jobs, prior to his death in 1987 Warhol had failed to access the computer networks that a small group of artists had explored for several years.

According to legend, the telephone caused Warhol to drop the final "a" from his family name in the early 1950s, when he tried to evade a $95 phone bill charged to "Andrew Warhola"—a very large sum at the time, run up by his ever-changing assortment of roommates. (Phone bills in the Archive contradict this story and indicate that the name was changed earlier.) When he moved soon after, he supposedly changed the name on his account and was off the hook, and ready for a romance—with his telephone. In *The Philosophy of Andy Warhol* (1975), Warhol writes, "I have a telephone mate. We've had an on-going relationship over the phone for six years....We don't have to worry about kids, just about extension phones."[1] His "telephone mate" was his friend Brigid Berlin (Brigid Polk); she was one of several longtime phone relationships that he maintained. Much of *The Philosophy of Andy Warhol* is in the form of a telephone conversation.

The telephone is also a prop in several of Warhol's films. Edie Sedgwick, the beautiful, tragic heiress, attempts to connect with friends over the telephone throughout the first reel of *Poor Little Rich Girl* (1965). Phone calls also play a role in *The Chelsea Girls* (1966), in which Brigid Berlin conducts her drug-dealing business over the phone while having her hair done in her hotel room. In *Eating Too Fast* (1966), a telephone call interrupts an intimate moment, but the receiver never gives it away. Warhol and Sedgwick take brief on-screen phone calls in the shadows just to the left of the equestrian star in *Horse* (1965). During the filming of Warhol's lengthy *Henry Geldzahler* (1965), Warhol deliberately walked away from the camera to make phone calls, leaving the star to fend for himself. In *Harlot*, also from 1965, Warhol's voice can be heard in the background, carrying on a phone conversation.

Warhol's most extensive cinematic use of the telephone call is his unfinished "soap opera" video project *Phoney*, from 1973. He became interested in this idea because an associate mentioned that the slang term "phony" came into being at the time that the telephone became more

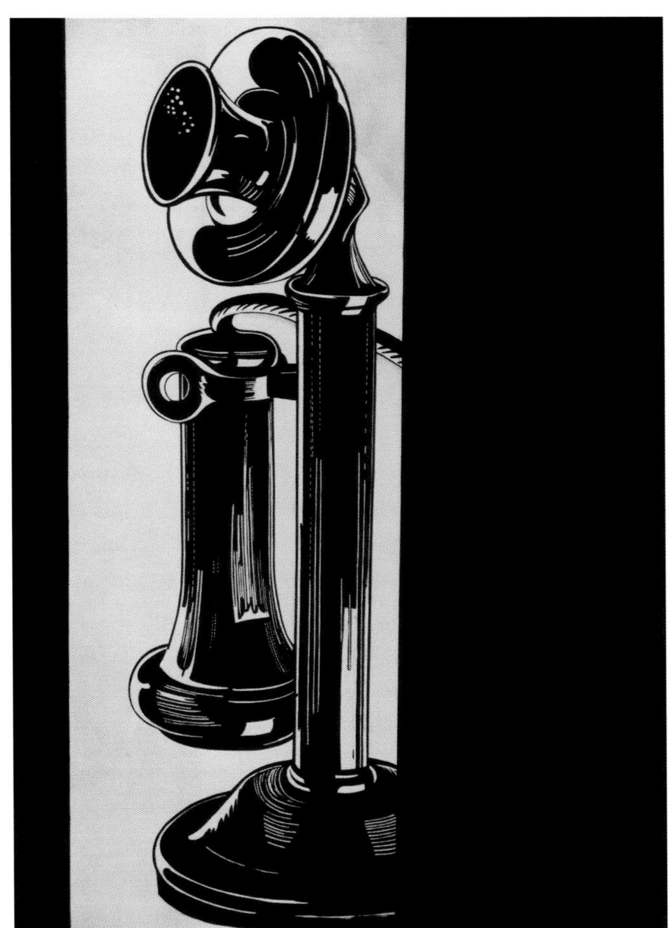

common; it was meant to describe the perceived false attitude of callers. Perhaps this was the unusual intellectual basis for Warhol's shocking coldness to his brother John when he called to tell Andy that their mother, Julia, had died. Warhol curiously recorded the conversation for posterity. Then again, maybe he truly did "want to be a machine" and avoid unpleasant, messy human emotion.[2]

The paint-smeared telephone from his studio, forty other office phones used by his employees, the enormous phone logs of Andy Warhol Enterprises, mailed-in phone messages that predate answering machines, numerous photographs of telephones, and other phone-related archival objects and works of art fill the Archive.

Andy Warhol, *Telephone [4]*, 1962

Early Years

In Warhol's teenage years, the telephone was becoming more widespread, yet it was still seen as a glamorous accessory to modern living. In 1947, Warhol's second year of college, Gian Carlo Menotti's opera *The Telephone* opened on Broadway, and it had been only four years since the Warhola family's first phone line was hardwired in their home.[3] In 1948 a famously inaccurate prediction of the US presidential election was based on the results of a telephone poll—phones were apparently not installed in many of the homes of Harry Truman's supporters.

Warhol drawings from the 1950s contain subtle and not-so-subtle references to the telephone. When Warhol drew *The Three Magi with Telephones* (ca. 1951), the closest thing in existence to a cell phone was a cumbersome military walkie-talkie. His *Dial M for Shoe (From the portfolio À la Recherche du Shoe Perdu)* (ca. 1955) references Alfred Hitchcock's classic Hollywood thriller *Dial M for Murder* (1954), starring Grace Kelly and Ray Milland. The tale of blackmail has several chilling scenes involving telephone calls.

Warhol's promotional image for his graphic-art business naturally featured his current phone number, written by his mother, Julia, in her charming style and with a hilarious spelling error, transforming the genteel "Murray Hill" phone exchange into "Murry Hell."

Pop Art

As Warhol developed his art business, the phone became ubiquitous, with businesses now relying on it, and he skillfully worked its image into his art. One of his early hand-painted Pop works depicts a monumental telephone. *Telephone [4]* (1962) is the final version of a group of large paintings of this subject. In each of the four works, the phone is turned a little bit more on its axis, so that if they were all seen side by side, they might resemble a model in motion. The source materials for these paintings were found in the Archive. Warhol seems to have borrowed them from but never returned them to the New York Public Library picture collection. These images are dated circa 1928, but the "candlestick" telephone illustrated originated as early as 1914. To create the painting (and the three slightly smaller previous versions), Warhol placed these objects in an opaque projector to enlarge them to the size of his canvas, and then traced the outlines with a pencil and painted in the shapes.

Books

The first page of Warhol's book *a: a novel* (1968) consists of a call from a pay phone, and the first words are the sounds of the dropping coins and the rotary dial (see "D is for Duchamp"). The project purportedly documents twenty-four hours in the life of Superstar Ondine (Robert Olivo), but it was based on tape-recorded conversations over a period of several months beginning in the summer of 1965. In the novel, the real-life characters are given new identities. Warhol is identified as Drella—a contraction of "Dracula" and "Cinderella"—the nickname imparted to him at the Factory. Olivo had received his nickname, Ondine, several years earlier while swimming in Brooklyn's Riis Park. It refers to the title role of a water spirit in a 1958 ballet based on Hans Christian Andersen's *The Little Mermaid*. Brigid Berlin is known as the Duchess.

Warhol's *Philosophy*, which includes provocative comments by Warhol about the telephone and many other topics, was also transcribed in part from tape recordings of phone calls. Portions of dialogue with his "business art" colleagues—Berlin, Bob Colacello, Pat Hackett, and Fred Hughes—are given in an "A to B" format. They are all compressed into the "B" of the book's subtitle, with Warhol being "A." The opening lines of the book introduce this structure:

I wake up and call B.
B is anybody who helps me kill time.
B is anybody and I'm nobody. B and I.
I need B because I can't be alone. Except when I sleep. Then
I can't be with anybody.
I wake up and I call B.

A Guide to Andy Warhol's Telephone Numbers

Warhol had a telephone answering service in the years before answering machines were common. A subscriber could call the service to receive the messages, or the operator would mail them to the subscriber. In tandem with the photo of telephones, the following chronological list of Warhol's telephone numbers throughout his career gives an idea of the size of Andy Warhol Enterprises:

MU9-4712, home/studio, 319 East 24th Street, ca. 1949–50

UN4-0120, home/studio, 74 West 103rd Street, 1950

RE4-6037, home/studio, 218 East 75th Street, 1951

MU3-0555, home/studio, 242 Lexington Avenue, 1954

AT9-1298, home/studio, 1342 Lexington Avenue, 1960

EL5-9941, Factory, 231 East 47th Street, 1964

989-9183, Warhol Enterprises, 33 Union Square West, 1968

289-8729, home, 1342 Lexington Avenue, 1968

534-0223, home, 1342 Lexington Avenue, 1968

924-4344, Andy Warhol Films, 33 Union Square West, 1969

289-8758, home, 1342 Lexington Avenue, 1970

427-6420, home, 1342 Lexington Avenue, 1970

668-2904, weekend home, Montauk, 1971

675-6790, *Interview* magazine, 33 Union Square West, 1971

668-2413, weekend home, Montauk, 1972

675-5800, *Interview* magazine, 33 Union Square West, 1974

477-2222, *Interview* magazine, 860 Broadway, 1974

475-5550, Andy Warhol Enterprises, 860 Broadway, 1979

685-1800, *Interview* magazine, 19 East 32nd Street, 1983

683-5300, Andy Warhol Enterprises, 22 East 33rd Street, ca. 1984

288-6170, home, 57 East 66th Street, 1985

Dial-A-Poem

John Giorno was Warhol's close friend from 1962 to 1964 as well as his brief lover and the star of Warhol's first film, *Sleep* (1963). In 1968 Giorno created Dial-A-Poem, in which millions of people called and listened to poetry. Dial-A-Poem was the first time the telephone was used to communicate to a large audience, launching a new era in telecommunications and mass media, and inspiring the

Dial-A-Something phenomenon: Dial-A-Joke, Dial-A-Horoscope, Dial-A-Santa Claus, Dial-A-Recipe, Dial-A-Children's Story, Dial-A-Soap, Dial-Sports, Wall Street Stock Quotations, Off Track Betting, Suicide Hotlines, Dial-Porn, Dial-Love, and more. Warhol recalled, "At the beginning of the year you could pick up your phone and Dial-A-Poem, and by June, you'd be able to even Dial-A-Demonstration—you called a number and a recording actually told you where the public protests around town were that day....John told me that it was the porno poems that got the most calls."[4]

Andy Warhol's *Pork*

Warhol's play *Pork* (1970) was performed in London and New York. Warhol's biographers have noted that it was entirely transcribed from tape-recorded phone calls, which is not true, although in one of the original transcripts used for the play, Viva is calling Dr. Timothy Leary at his hotel. Onstage, the set changes between acts were announced by the loud, persistent busy signal of a telephone.

NOTES

Epigraph: Eva Windmüller, "A Conversation with Andy Warhol," *Stern*, October 8, 1981.

1. Andy Warhol, *The Philosophy of Andy Warhol (From A to B and Back Again)* (New York: Harcourt Brace Jovanovich, 1975), 47.

2. Andy Warhol, "The reason I'm painting this way is that I want to be a machine, and I feel that whatever I do and do machine-like is what I want to do." G. R. Swenson, "What Is Pop Art? Answers from 8 Painters, Part I," *Art News* 62, no. 7 (November 1963): 26.

3. The Warhola family's first listing in the Pittsburgh telephone directory was in 1943, under the oldest brother, Paul's, name. There is no listing again until 1947, but under the name of the middle brother, John, living at the Warhola family's address.

4. Andy Warhol and Pat Hackett, *POPism: The Warhol Sixties* (Orlando, FL: Harcourt Brace Jovanovich, 1980), 321.

Photographic layouts designed by Becky Shock, Brianna Treleven, and Kristin Britanik.

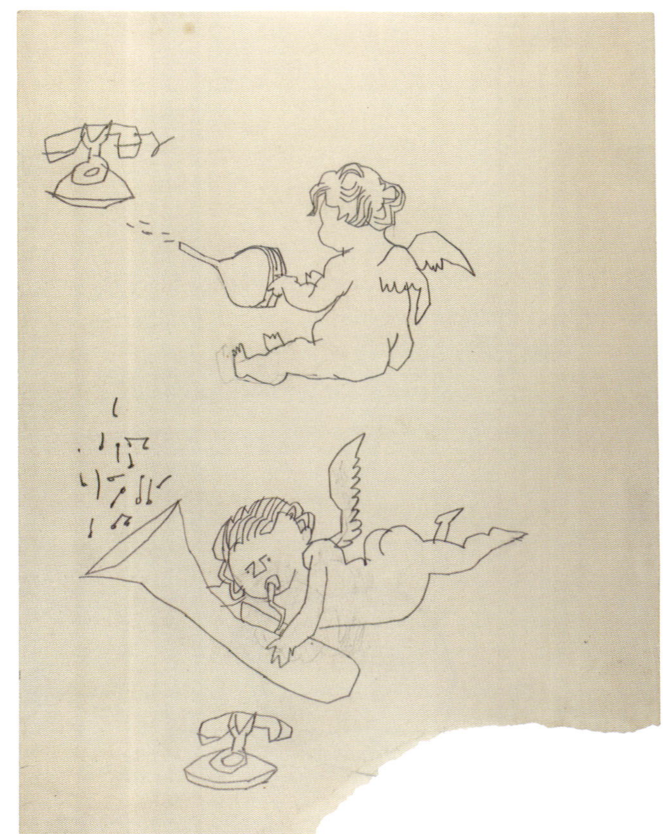

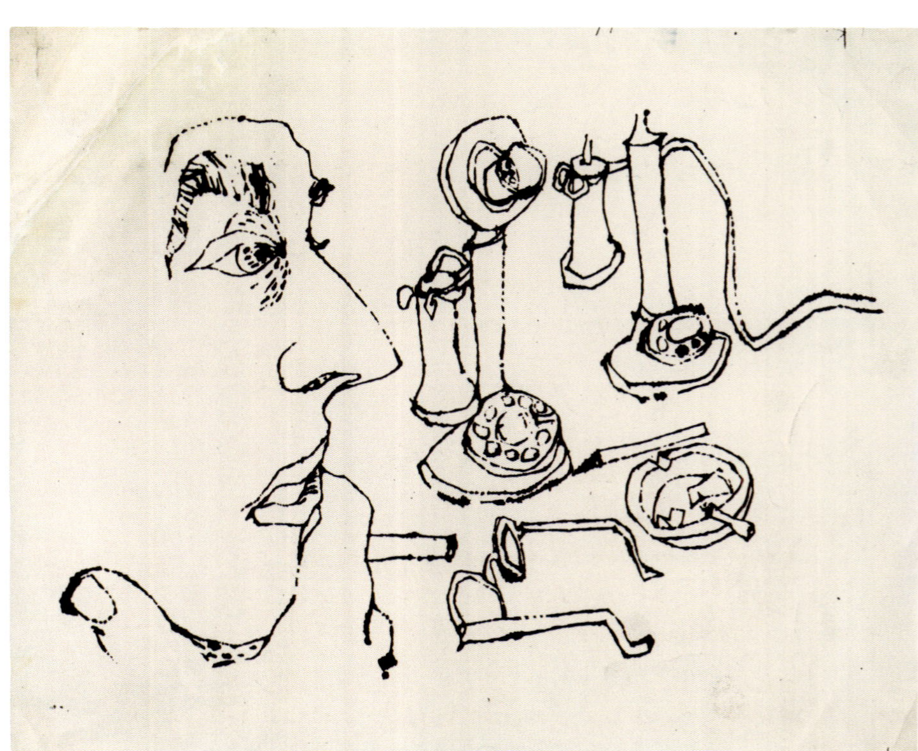

Andy Warhol, *The Three Magi with Telephones*, ca. 1951; *Two Sprite Angels with Telephones*, ca. 1950; *Man with Cigarette and Candlestick Telephones*, ca. 1950

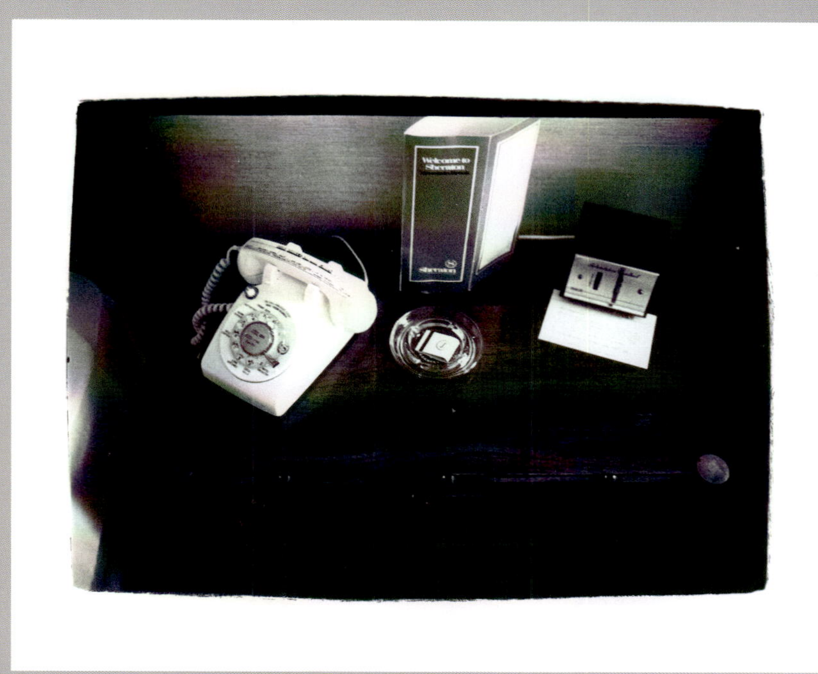

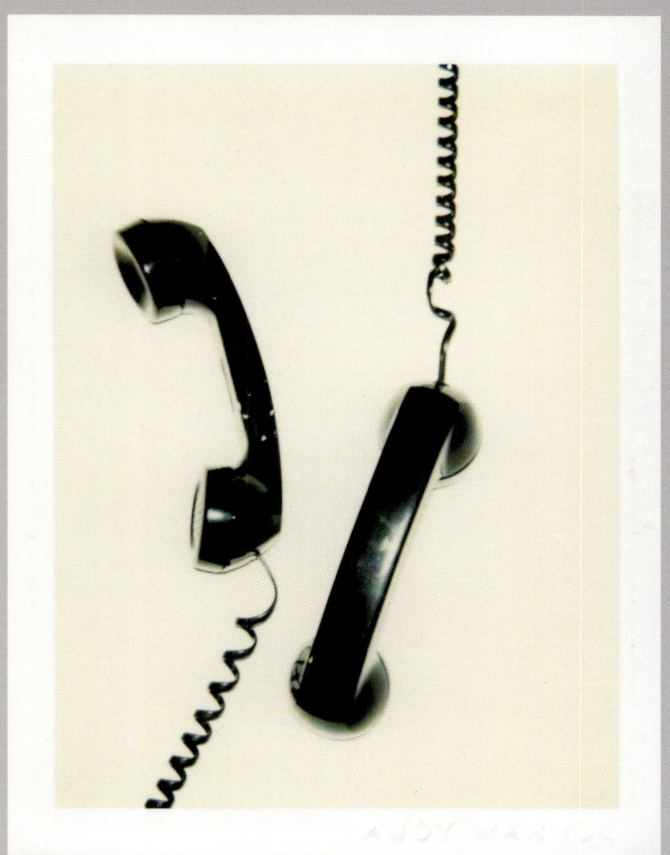

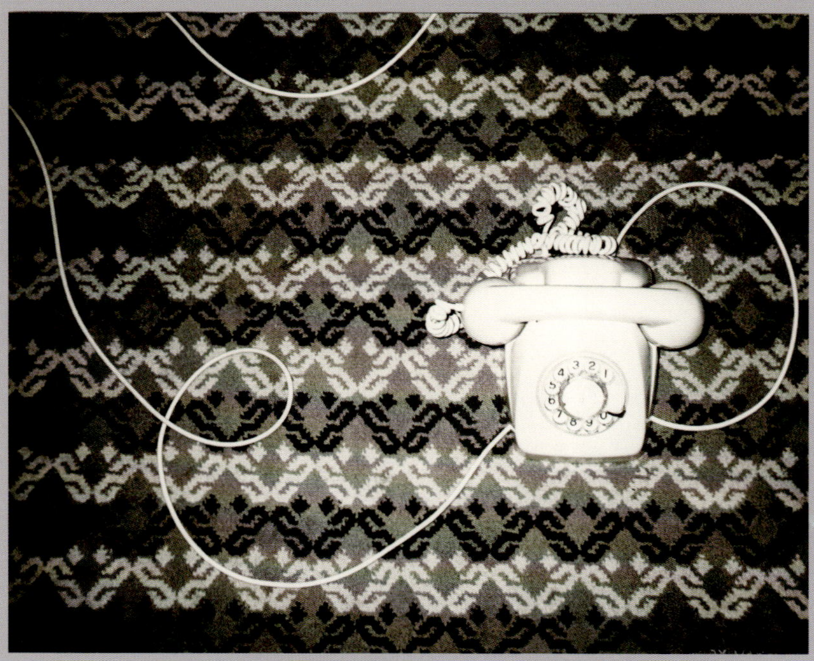

Andy Warhol, *Sheraton Hotel Bedside Table with Telephone*, 1979;
Telephones, 1980; *Telephone*, 1983

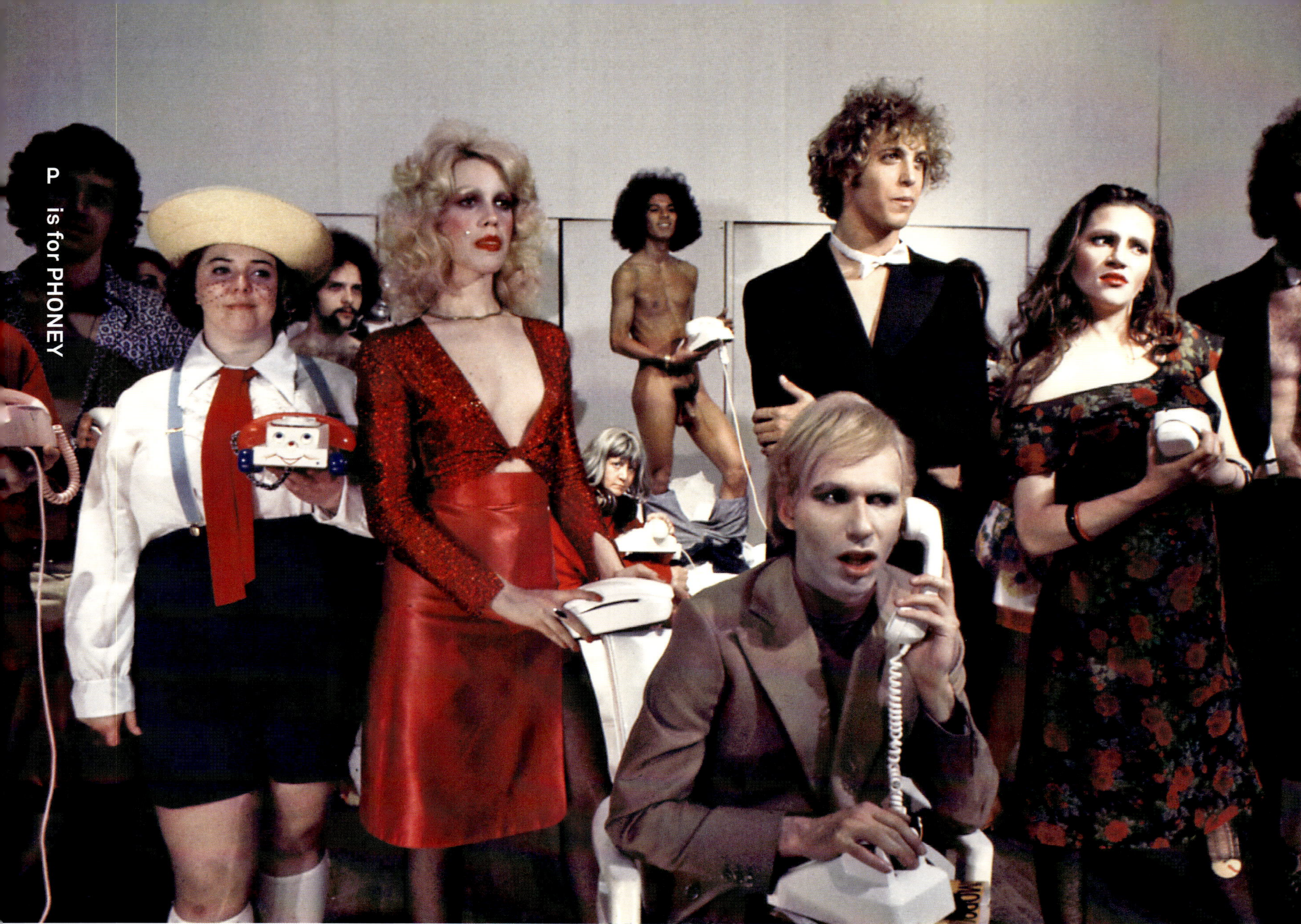

202

Jack Mitchell, *Cast of Andy Warhol's "Pork," 1971* (Tony Zanetta as
"B. Marlowe," a character based on Warhol, is seated in the foreground
holding a white telephone), reprinted 2005

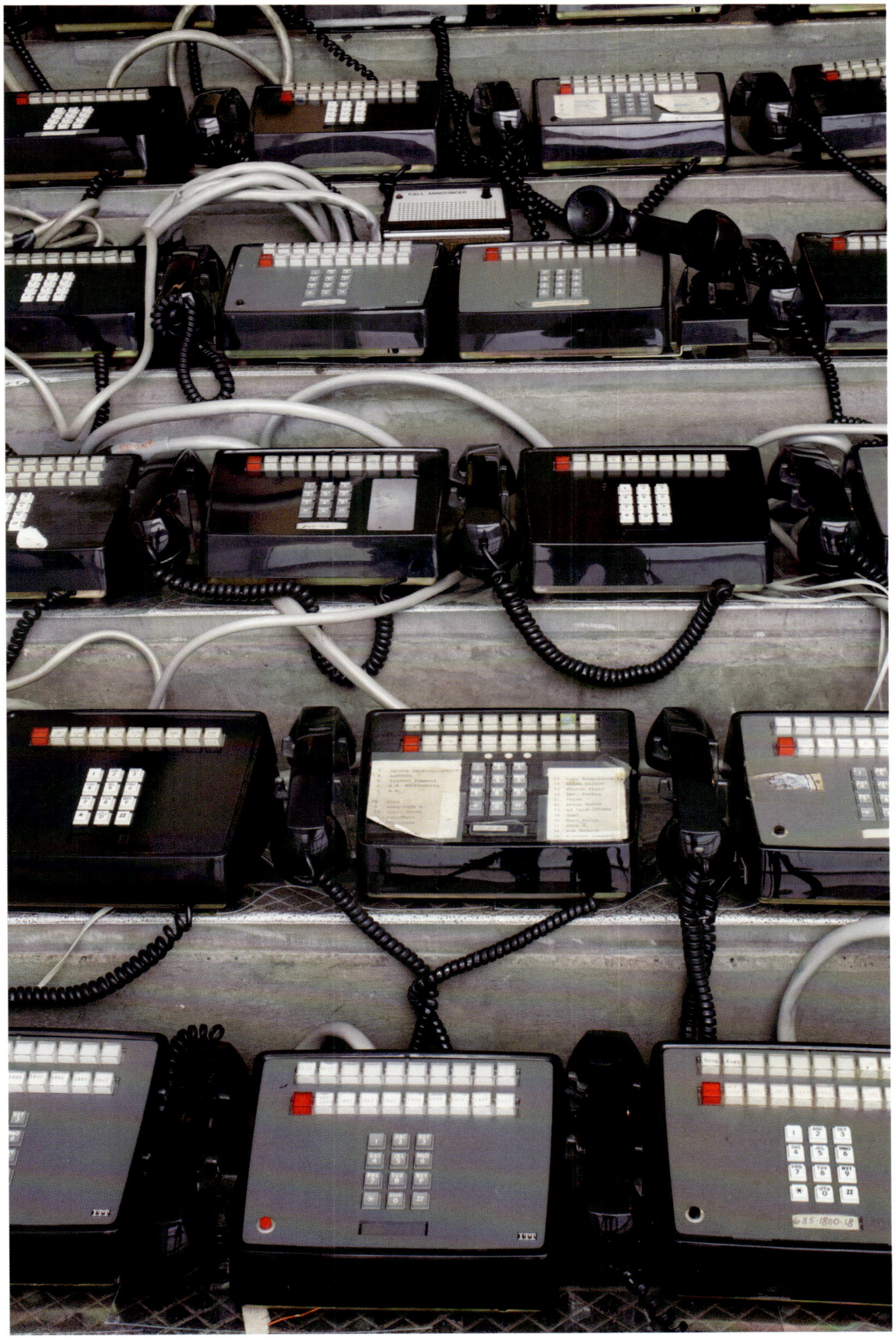

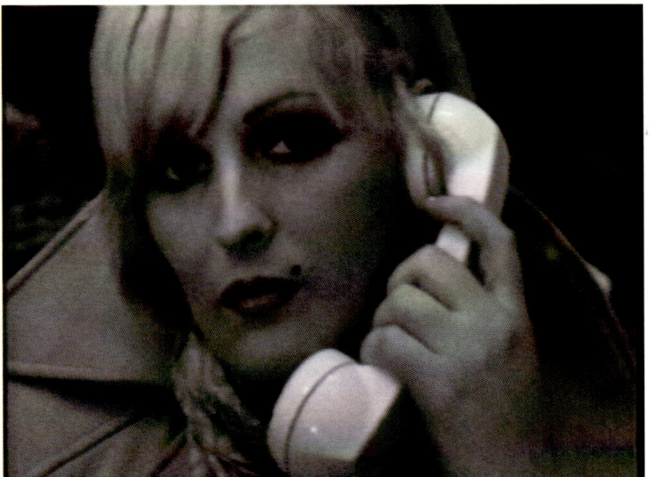

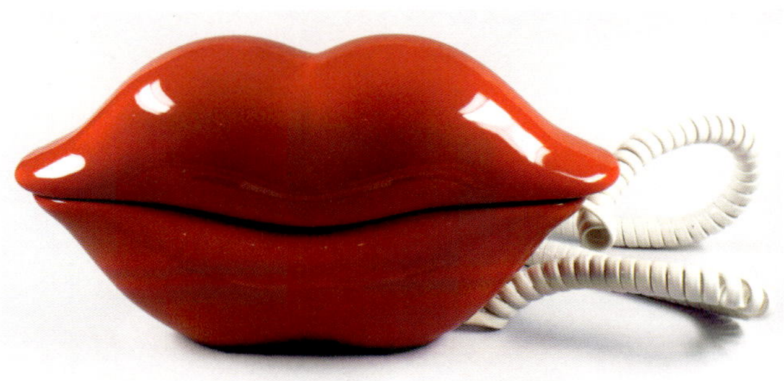

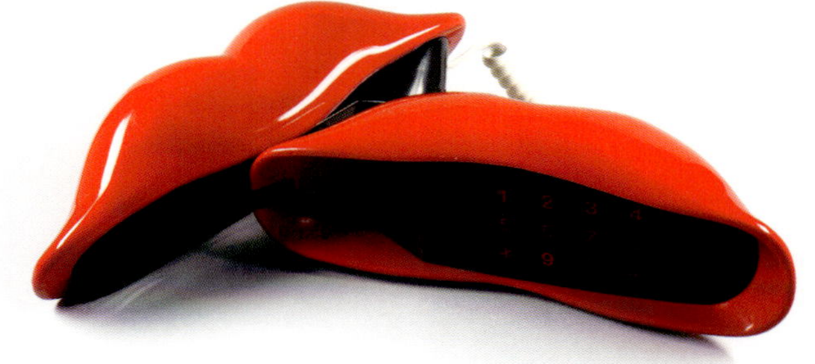

Office telephones for the staff at the Factory, 1980s

Andy Warhol and Vincent Fremont, film still of Candy Darling in *Phoney*, 1973

TeleQuest Hot Lips telephone in Warhol's collection (closed and open), 1980s

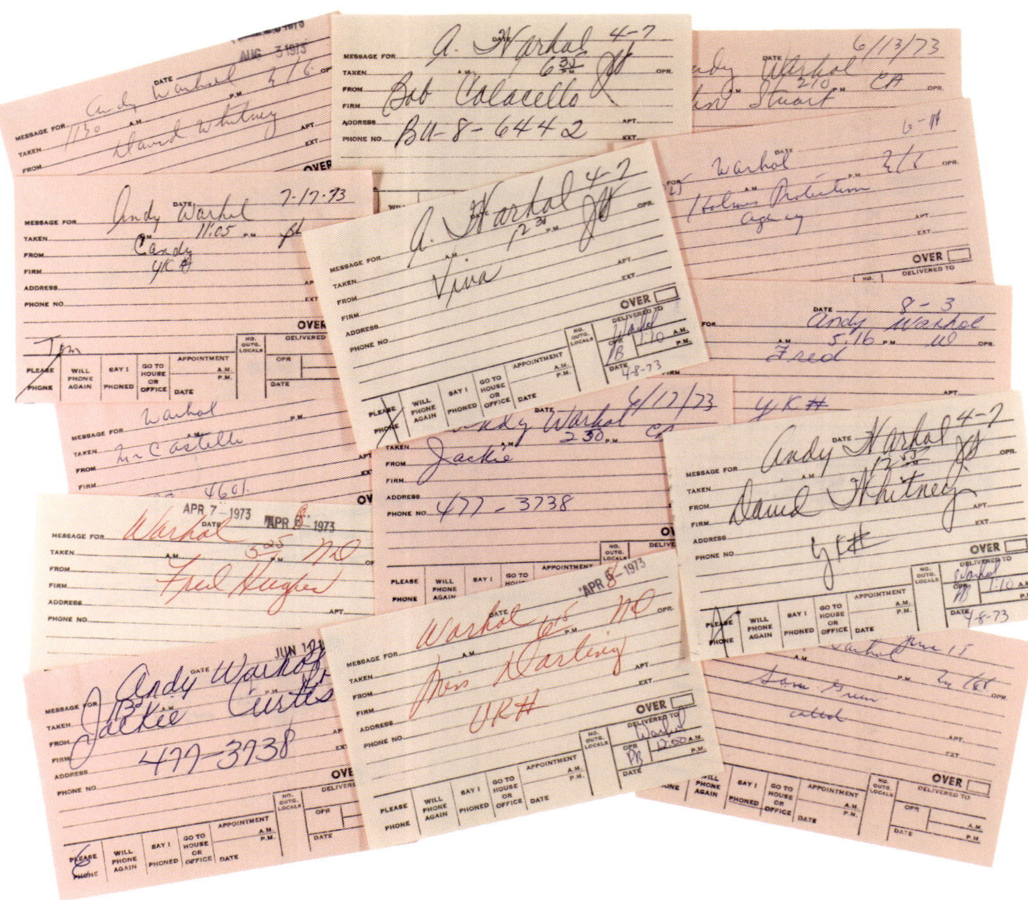

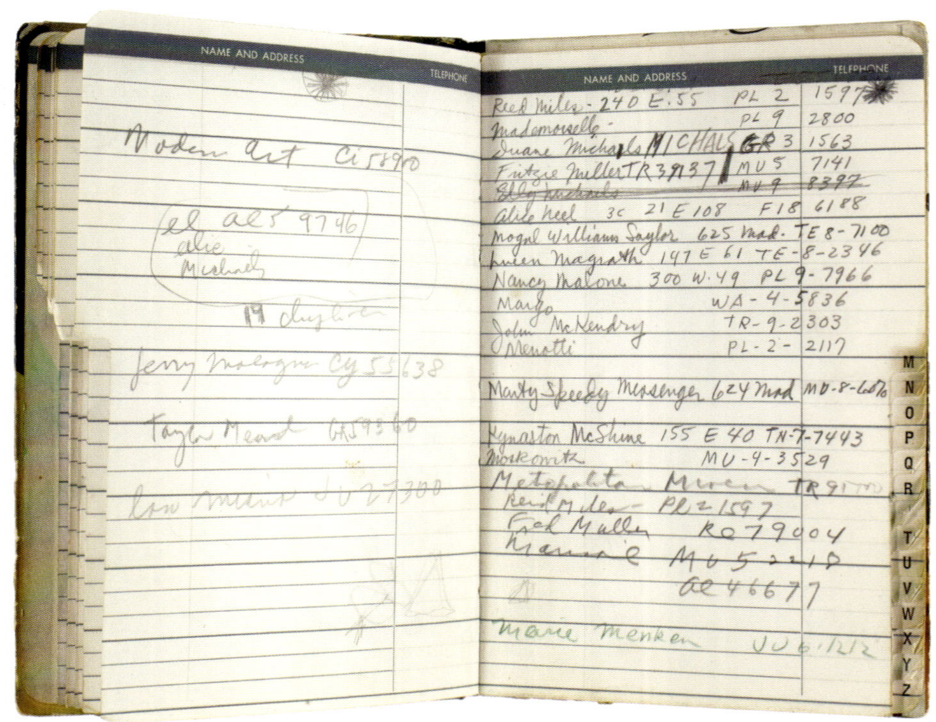

Invoice from New York Telephone to Warhol, posted November 6, 1967

Selection from hundreds of telephone messages for Warhol, April–August 1973

Warhol's address book, 1962–65

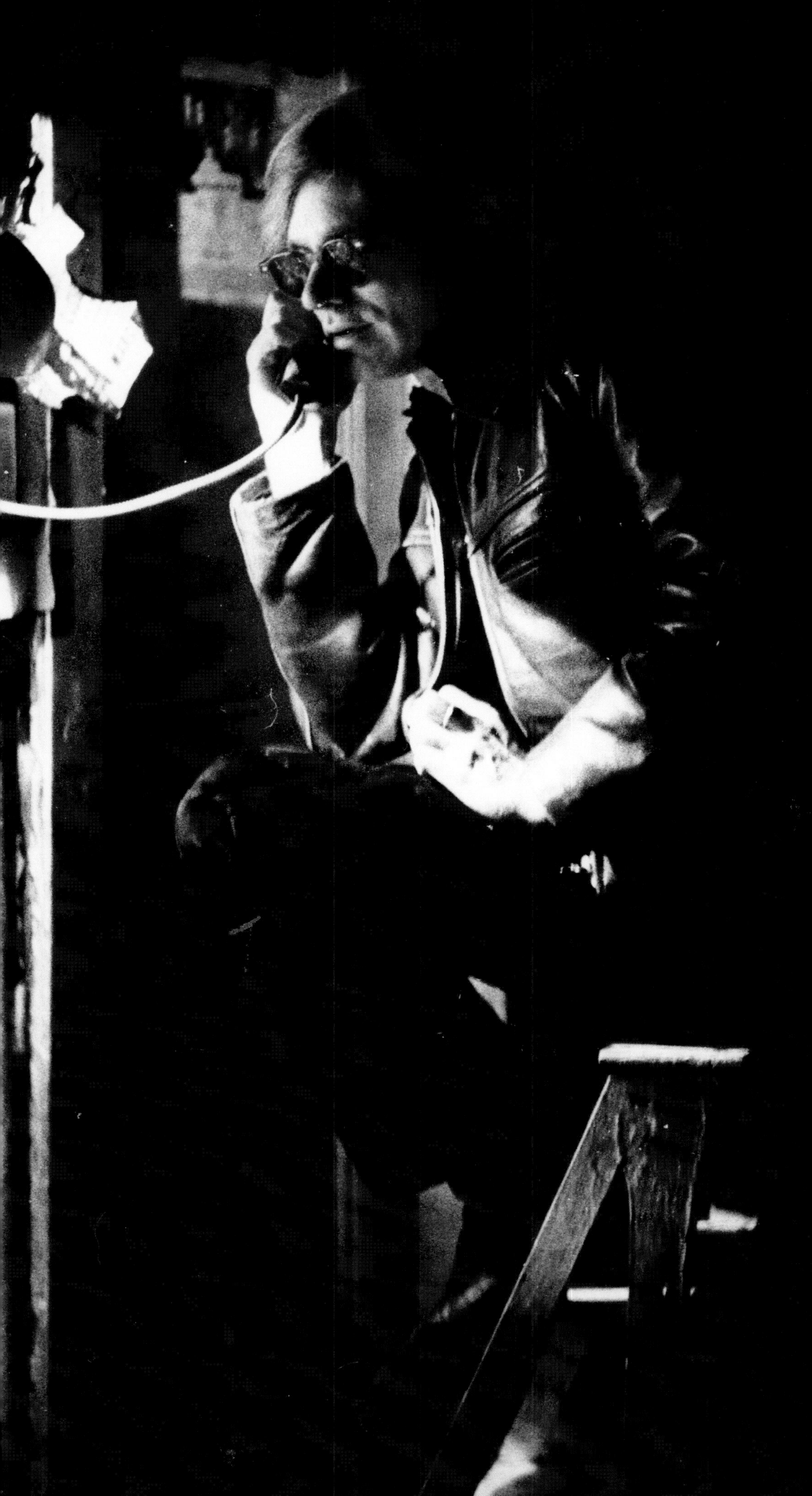

Photographer unknown, *Andy Warhol on the Payphone in the Factory*, 1966

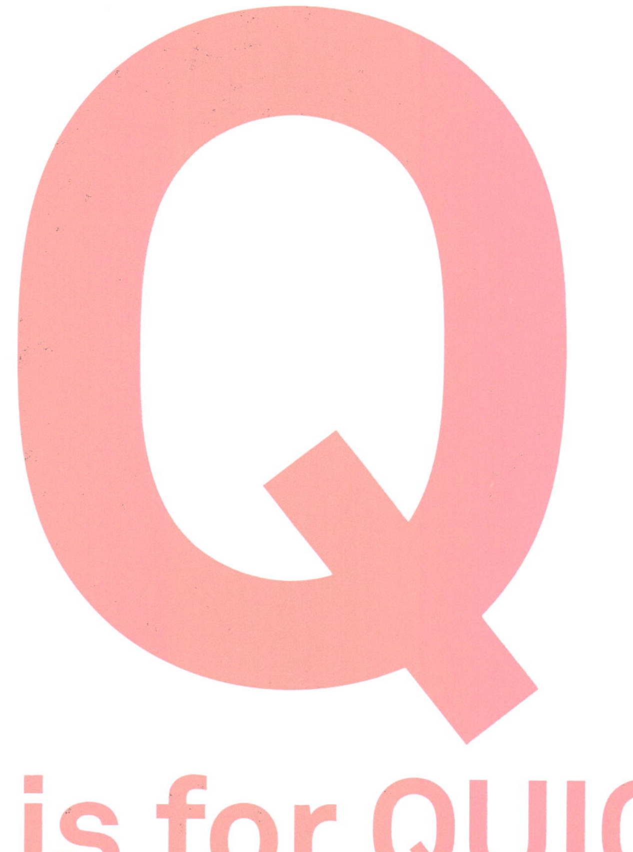

Hundreds of fans, friends, and family members expressed hopes for Warhol's quick recovery from the serious wounds he suffered when Valerie Solanas shot him in his office on June 3, 1968. His convalescence was anything but quick. Warhol spent six and a half weeks in the hospital before he could go home. The concern for Warhol was immediate. Telegrams and other messages began to arrive on that very afternoon from filmmakers Willard Maas and Marie Menken, photographer Richard Avedon, model Penelope Tree, comedian Monti Rock III, art director Ruth Ansel, and dancer Steve Paxton, among many others. The outpouring of well-wishes continued for months and eventually filled an entire *Time Capsule*. The news, gossip, and emotion shared in this correspondence are unusual in the *Time Capsules* and reflect the extreme privacy necessary for Warhol's recovery, as most of this information would previously have been conveyed by telephone or face-to-face.

Warhol met Solanas in the summer of 1967, and he gave her a part in his film *I, a Man* (1967), portraying a lesbian who embarrasses Tom Baker, the film's star. The previous year Solanas had written an article, "A Young Girl's Primer on How to Attain to the Leisure Class," describing the

is for QUICK

This chapter is a compilation of texts and images from two exhibitions, *Valerie Solanas*, June 3, 1998–November 7, 1999, and *Time Capsule 4*, July 5–November 3, 2002.

street life of a panhandling prostitute, that was published in *Cavalier* magazine under an alternative title.[1] Solanas also wrote the "SCUM Manifesto," a twenty-one-page rant against male-dominated society. SCUM is the acronym for the Society for Cutting Up Men, of which Solanas was the founder and sole member. She sold the manifesto on the street and advertised SCUM meetings, although it's not known whether anyone attended them. In the spring of 1967, Solanas had a disastrous experience as a guest on a local New York television program, *The Alan Burke Show*. Burke baited her and ridiculed lesbianism when she began to present her philosophy. The show ended violently with a physical struggle between the two and Solanas being thrown out of the studio by a security guard. In August she offered Warhol a script for a film called *Up Your Ass*. Warhol originally thought she was a police officer attempting to entrap him on pornography charges. When he failed to return the script, she became upset, believing that Warhol wanted to film the work without paying her, although it's more likely that he had just misplaced the script.

Around the same time Solanas also met Maurice Girodias, publisher of Olympia Press, who had agreed to publish a novel of her life experiences. He had read her play and thought it was "rather clever…amusingly wild."[2] A contract was signed in August 1967, but Solanas couldn't produce a manuscript. Over time she convinced herself that Warhol and Girodias were in collusion against her, that Warhol badly wanted to film her script but wouldn't pay her, and that Warhol's discussions with her were really calculated attempts to steal her work. Pushed to the edge by her paranoid beliefs, she sought a resolution. Early in the afternoon of June 3, 1968, Solanas walked to Girodias's Gramercy Park office, but Girodias was not in. She then went to Warhol's Union Square studio but was told by filmmaker Paul Morrissey that Warhol wasn't in, either. She waited on the street for him. Warhol was shopping that day and tried to visit a friend in the neighborhood, but the friend wasn't home.

At about 4:30 p.m., when Warhol entered the elevator with his friend Jed Johnson, Solanas rode up with them to the sixth-floor studio. Warhol was on the telephone with the actress Viva when Solanas suddenly pulled a gun and

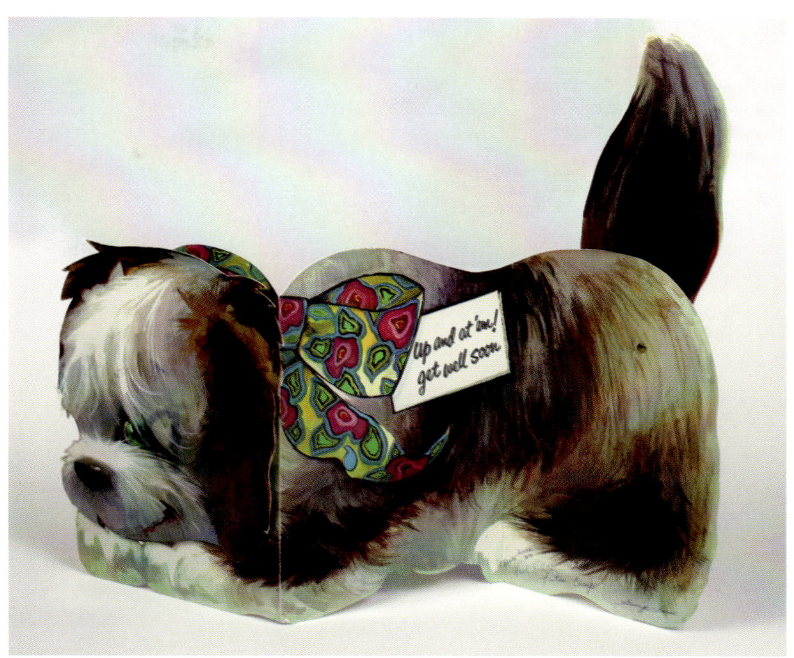

shot him. Only a single .32 caliber bullet of the four she fired hit his body, but its damage was severe. Solanas also wounded the English art critic Mario Amaya, whom she shot at twice, with one bullet entering above his left hip and narrowly missing his spinal cord. She also aimed her gun at Warhol's associate Fred Hughes, who pleaded for his life. As if on cue, the elevator doors opened behind her, and she left the scene of her crimes. Photographer Billy Name ran to Warhol from his darkroom and wept as he held Warhol's head.

Warhol and Amaya were taken by ambulance to nearby Columbus Hospital, where Warhol was supposedly pronounced dead. Amaya claims that he told doctors the identity of their dying patient and demanded that they save his life. With the help of a surgical team and twelve units of blood, Dr. Giuseppe Rossi was able to revive Warhol. The surgery spanned five hours to repair his damaged lungs, esophagus, spleen, liver, diaphragm, and colon. Warhol's brothers arrived from Pittsburgh, joining their mother, Julia, and Billy Name, Viva, Ultra Violet, Gerard Malanga, and others at the hospital. The Archive contains a hospital card

Dog-shaped card from the California cast of *Bike Boy* to Warhol, 1968

with a note from Viva and Gerard to Warhol's brothers instructing them to meet up later at Max's Kansas City.

Three hours after the shootings, Solanas surrendered to a traffic cop near Times Square. She possessed two handguns: a .32 automatic and a .22 revolver. The press reported that she told the officer, "The police are looking for me. I am a flower child. He had too much control over my life."[3] At the 13th Precinct station she was to be booked for "felonious assault and possession of a deadly weapon," but the crush of reporters made it impossible, and instead the press interviewed her. Solanas happily answered the media's questions as the cameras fired. "I have a lot of very involved reasons. Read my manifesto and it will tell you what I am."[4] After the reporters left, she was booked and sent to Bellevue Hospital for psychiatric examination.

At her June 4 arraignment, Solanas initially refused the court-appointed lawyers, insisting that she could defend herself. She demanded to be heard by the judge, and he agreed to hear her. "I was right in what I did!" she shouted. "I have nothing to regret. I feel sorry for nothing. He was going to do something to me which would have ruined me. It was reported in the papers that my motive was that Andy wouldn't produce my play. It was for the opposite reason. He has a legal claim to all my works. He had me tied up lock, stock, and barrel. It's not often that I shoot somebody. I didn't do it for nothing."[5] The judge ordered that this self-incriminating statement be struck from the legal record. Solanas was charged with two counts of attempted murder and one count of possessing dangerous weapons and was forced to accept legal counsel. In December she was released from custody when a friend, Geoffrey LeGear, posted her $10,000 bail. In a long letter LeGear wrote to Warhol that month on Solanas's behalf, he tried to transfer her guilt to the artist. Soon after, Warhol apparently received a phone call at home from Solanas, demanding that he drop the charges against her and pay for her manuscripts. He received mail with similar demands.

On June 9, 1969, Solanas was sentenced to three years in the New York State Prison for Women in Bedford Hills, including the six months already served in mental hospitals. The maximum penalty for her crimes was fifteen years. At her sentencing, Solanas stated, "I didn't want to kill him. I just wanted him to pay attention to me. Talking to him was like talking to a chair."[6] Solanas continued to write to Warhol while incarcerated and occasionally made phone calls to the Factory, still trying to reach him. Warhol recalls one such phone call in *POPism*: "When I called people up and they heard my voice for the first time since the shooting, sometimes they'd start to cry. I was very moved to see that people cared about me so much, but I just tried to get everything back to a light, gossipy level as quickly as possible. . . . As for Valerie, as far as we knew she was still in jail. Then on Christmas Eve '68, I answered the phone at the Factory and almost fainted when I heard her voice demanding that I drop all criminal charges against her, pay her twenty thousand dollars for all the manuscripts she'd ever written, put her in more movies, and—she capped the list with every lunatic's biggest dream—get her booked on the Johnny Carson show."[7] Warhol never replied to any of her communications.

Superstars

A grouping of correspondence was sent by Warhol's close associates and his Superstars, many of whom acted in his films. Included are two notes from Pepper Davis, who appeared in *The Chelsea Girls* (1966); a letter from Nathan Gluck, Warhol's assistant in the 1950s; notes from Anne Wehrer, a star of the Warhol film *Bike Boy* (1967); a collection of eighteen letters from Fred Hughes, the executor of Warhol's estate upon his death in 1987; a letter and fifteen postcards from Viva, the lead in most of Warhol's films of this period; two identical telegrams from Candy Darling, the legendary transsexual actor; and a note from the influential rock band the Velvet Underground. Warhol also received some brightly decorated cards from Brigid Berlin (Brigid Polk), a star of *The Chelsea Girls* and Warhol's close friend of twenty years; a letter addressed to "Maestro" from his former boyfriend Philip Fagen in Malaysia; illustrated letters from Naomi Levine, star of *Tarzan and Jane, Regained . . . Sort Of* (1964); and notes from Ultra Violet, a star of *I, a Man* (1967), and Ingrid Superstar, of *The Chelsea Girls*. Also included are notes from writer David Bourdon, who later wrote the definitive biography of Warhol; a huge dog greeting card from the "California Cast of *Bike Boy*"; several letters from his assistant Gerard Malanga; five letters from his soon-to-be live-in companion, Jed Johnson, and one from Jed's twin, Jay, with a collage; and notes from Linda Bentley, aka Vera Cruz.

Artist Friends

Warhol received numerous get-well cards and letters from people outside of his intimate Factory circle. Some of them, like photographer Deevy Jane Greitzer, writer Nelson Lyons, and artist Ray Johnson, were his friends. Many of them were well-known, or would soon become well-known, players in the New York art scene. *Time Capsule 4* contains a note from Ivan Karp, Warhol's art dealer at the prestigious Leo Castelli Gallery; an embroidered card and telegram from Pop artist Roy Lichtenstein and his wife, Dorothy; a Bit-o-Honey wrapper from Al Hansen, Fluxus artist (see "U is for Underground"); and correspondence from sculptor Claes Oldenburg, painter Joe Brainard, sculptor Marisol Escobar, filmmaker Lil Picard, critic Gene Swenson, curator Sam Wagstaff, art dealer Holly Solomon, curators David Whitney and David White, and conceptual artist Joseph Kosuth. The Campbell's Soup–label get-well card is from Miles White, a very successful art director for Broadway shows. Ethel and Robert Scull sent a letter on their blue personal stationery. Robert Scull was a New York City taxicab mogul and Pop Art collector who hired Warhol to make a portrait of his wife, Ethel—possibly Warhol's first commissioned portrait. Herbert Muschamp, future author and architecture critic for the *New York Times*, was just out of college when he sent Warhol the drawing of flowers. Muschamp was also one of hundreds of subjects who appeared in Warhol's *Screen Test* films (1964–66).

Fans

An enormous amount of fan mail was also sent to Warhol. The degree of his personal involvement with fans ranged from those he never met to those with whom he corresponded and became friends. During his hospitalization and recovery in 1968, copious amounts of fan mail came to the hospital.

Some fans, such as Bill Simons of Crystal Lake, Illinois, sent handmade envelopes and cards created from colorful magazine illustrations. One features an image of shoes—one of Warhol's favorite items—and a paragraph about the career of fashion designer Bill Blass. Simons's foil card is etched with the following message: "A word of sunshine, a touch of the Factory." Roberta Bernstein, chair of the Art Department of the State University of New York at Albany since 1994, began corresponding with Warhol as a student in Amherst, Massachusetts. A black-and-white photograph of her with the artist, postcards from New England, and numerous letters are among the items she sent. Poet Charles Henri Ford and his sister Ruth sent a postcard from Greece and a card from Dijon, France, both on the theme of pansies. Ford published *View*, an important art magazine that promoted the work of Joseph Cornell, Marcel Duchamp, and others in the 1940s. Cincinnati attorney Robert Schwartz mailed the "Living Letters" tape, one of a series of audiotapes and letters he sent to Warhol, and some snapshots of the artist with fans. Lance Loud began a long correspondence with Warhol as a young teenager. His letter is on orange paper (see "S is for Stamp"). Actor Jon Voight sent a blurry, sepia-toned Polaroid photo of himself starring in *Midnight Cowboy*, which was filmed around that time. Warhol's friend and Superstar Viva was also in the film, and it is thought that she encouraged Voight to send a picture that Warhol would enjoy (see "V is for Viva").

Family and Religious Materials

Warhol's family, mainly from the Pittsburgh area, sent him many cards and letters of encouragement throughout his recovery period. His elementary school–aged niece and nephew wrote letters about their school activities. A cousin from Butler, Pennsylvania, enclosed a personal photograph with her letter. Cards decorated with images of religious icons informed him of divine liturgies offered on his behalf.

Warhol attended Byzantine Catholic Church services throughout his life; his mother had instilled the importance of religion during his childhood. Some fans, however, assumed he was not a religious person and sent information on their respective faiths. Certain religious materials were intended to attract him to a specific faith, while others were meant to help him cope with his recent attack and injury. Warhol received a diverse group of religious cards and tracts, from information on multiple denominations of Christianity to a card from the Hare Krishna, an India-based cult that became extremely popular in the flower-power era of the late 1960s.

Several Catholics sent him Green Scapular icons, a small piece of decorated cloth that is said to help influence nonbelievers to convert. A woman in a Spokane, Washington, nursing home mailed Warhol pamphlets about the Unity faith, a little-known Christian denomination, along with many pages of sermons addressing various acts of immorality. The majority of religious materials he received offered words of comfort and peace.

NOTES

1. Valerie Solanas, "For 2 c: Pain, the Survival Game Gets Pretty Ugly," *Cavalier* 16, no. 157 (July 1996): 38–40, 76–77.

2. Sarah Warner, *Acts of Gaiety: LGBT Performance and the Politics of Pleasure* (Ann Arbor: University of Michigan Press, 2012), 61.

3. Frank Faso, Martin McLaughlin, and Richard Henry, "Andy Warhol Wounded by Actress," *Daily News* (New York), Tuesday, June 4, 1968, 3.

4. Howard Smith, "The Shot That Shattered the Velvet Underground," *Village Voice* (New York), Thursday, June 6, 1968, 54.

5. Frank Faso and Henry Lee, "Actress Shouts at Judge: Was Right in What I Did!" *Daily News* (New York), Wednesday, June 5, 1968, 3.

6. "Actress Gets 3 Years in Warhol Shooting," *Daily News* (New York), June 10, 1969, 3.

7. Andy Warhol, *The Philosophy of Andy Warhol (From A to B and Back Again)* (New York: Harcourt Brace Jovanovich, 1975), 355–60.

Photographic layouts designed by Becky Shock.

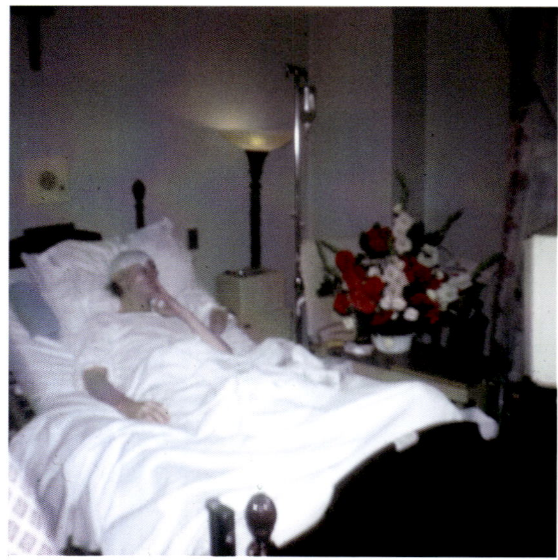

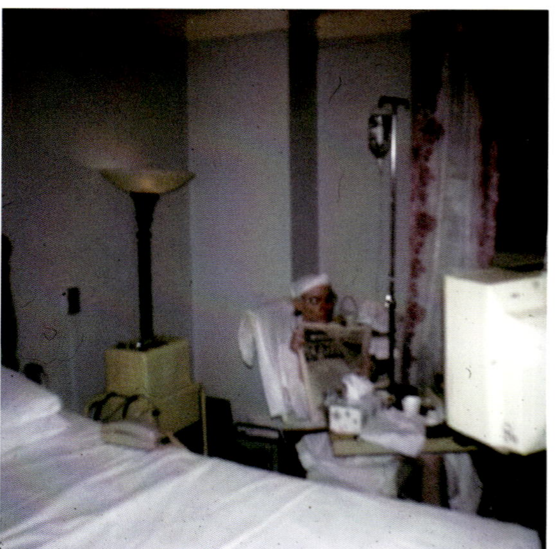

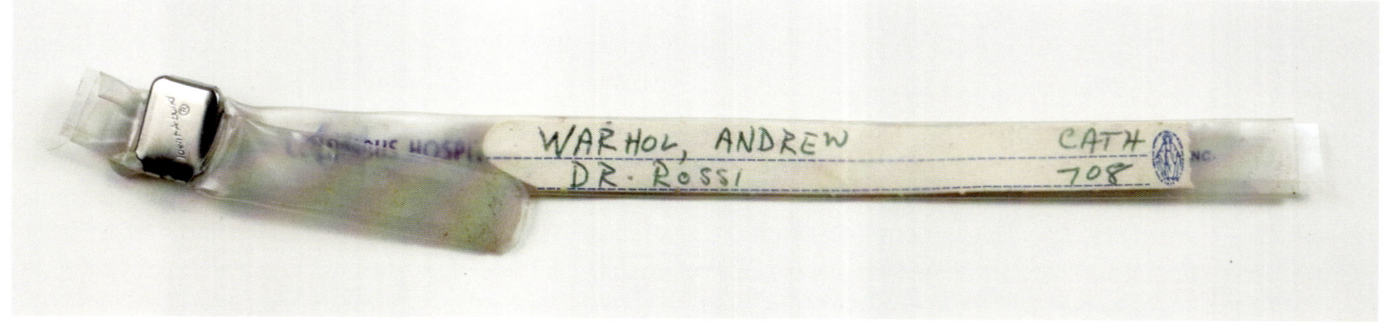

Warhol's hospital bracelet from Columbus Hospital, New York, 1968

Photographic slides of Warhol at Columbus Hospital, New York, 1968

June 14. 1968

Dear Andy,

I do hope you are feeling better. What a ghastly
thing to have happened -- I am still recovering from the
shockof it all. I had to go to the grand jury and swear
a complaint for attempted murder against that beastly girl,
but no doubt she will spend the rest of her life in a loony-bin.

The worst thing about it all was the misquoting in the
newspapers, saying things I never said, getting the story hope-
lessly confused, etc etc.

My wounds are healing as well as can be expected (two
beautiful holes in the back) and I understand you are doing fine
as well. But its an event I will never forget.

much love as always

Mario

PS We're going ahead with the exhibition and as soon
as you are better I will write you all about it.

**Letter from Mario Amaya, who was also injured by Valerie Solonas,
to Warhol, June 14, 1968**

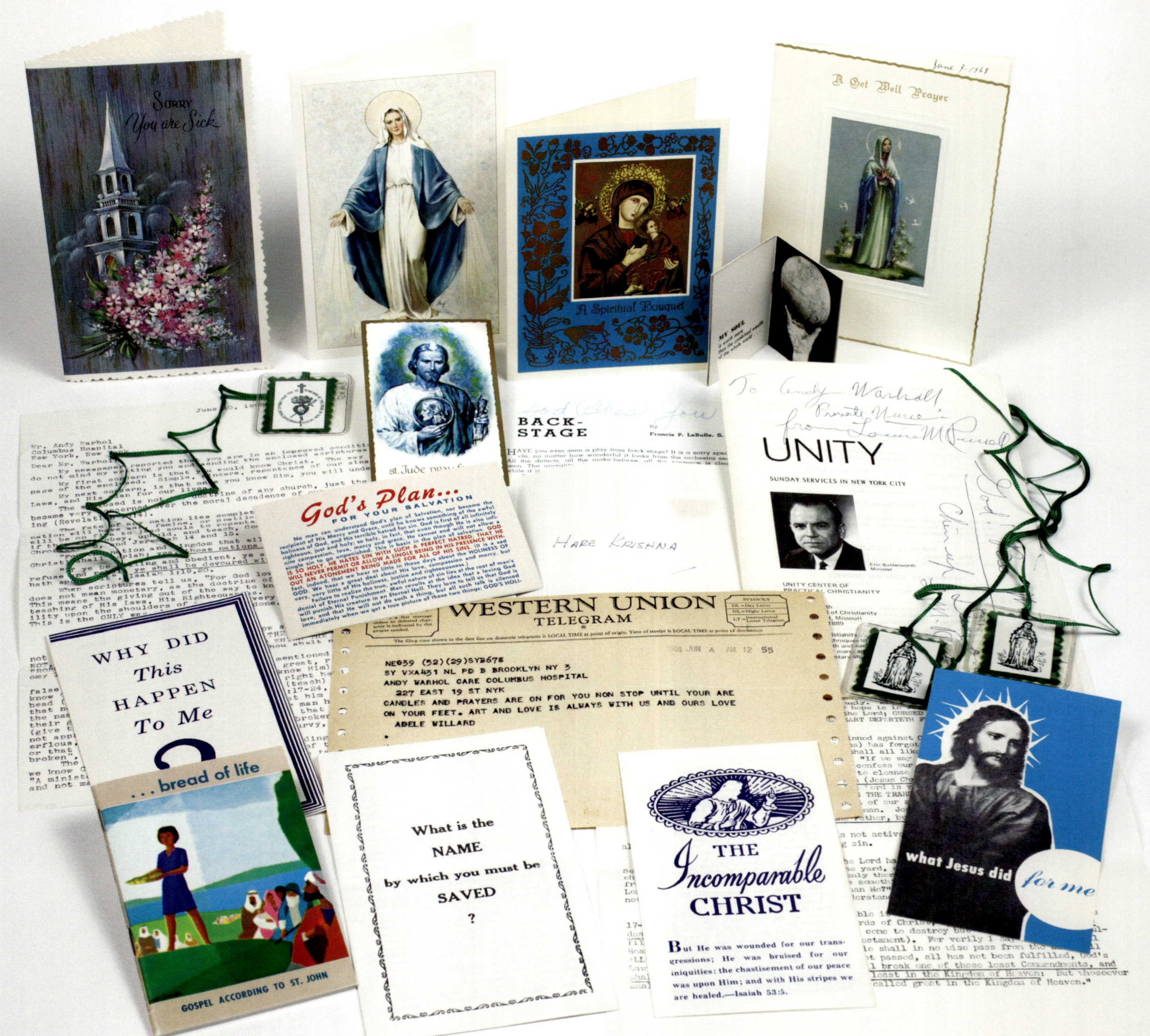

Group of religious get-well cards and correspondence addressed
to Warhol, 1968

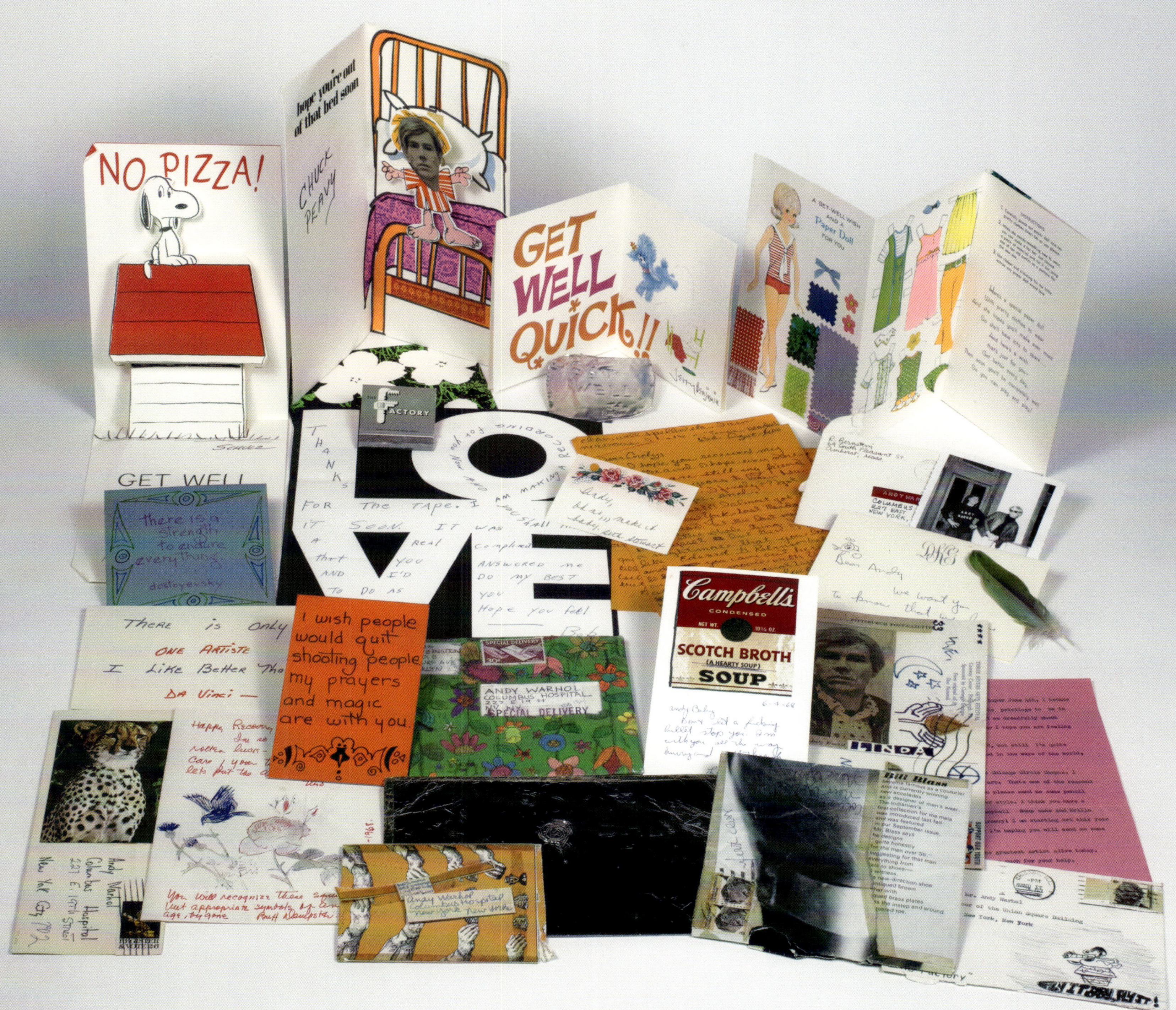

Group of get-well cards and correspondence from Warhol's fans, 1968

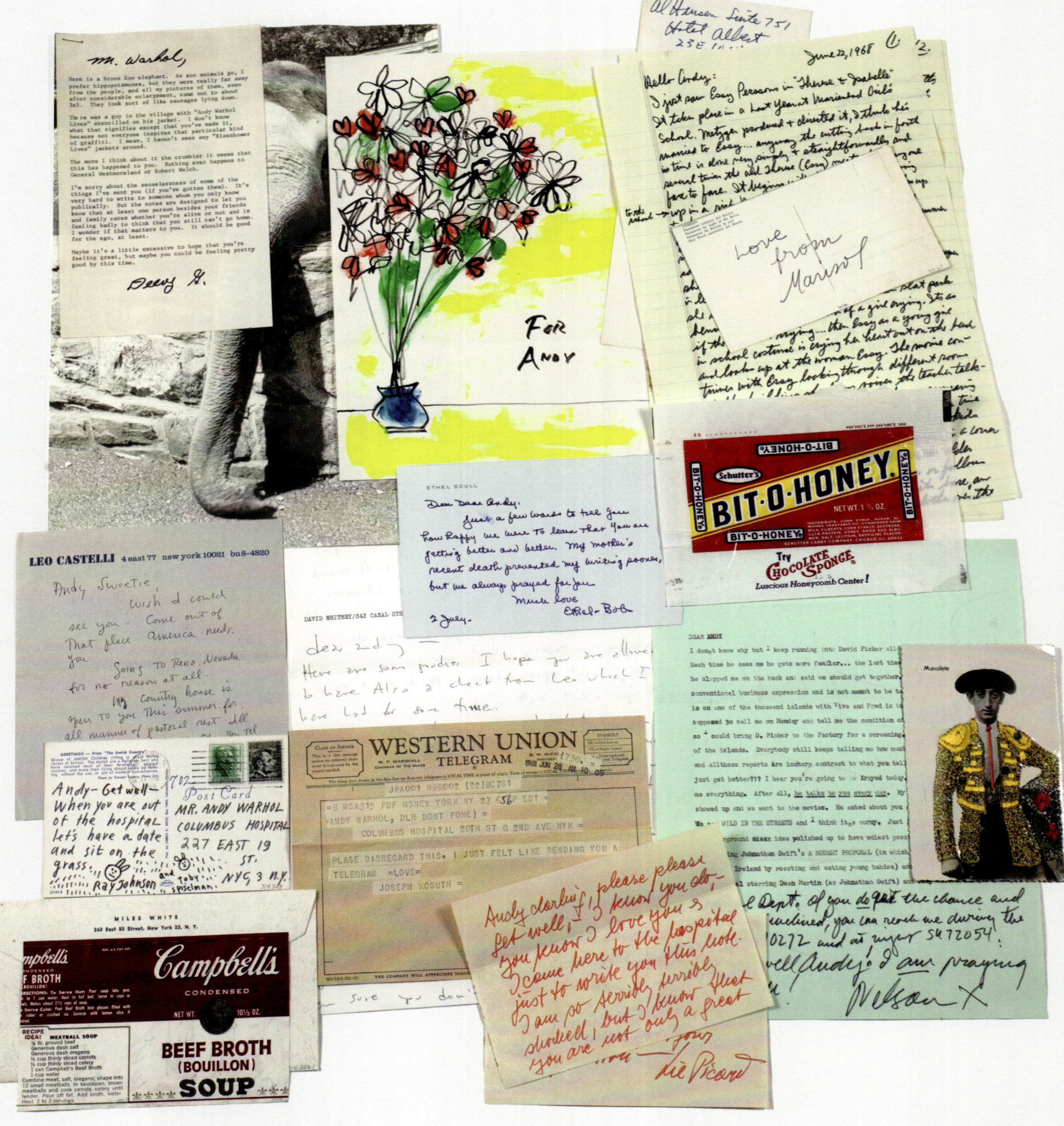

Group of get-well cards and correspondence from Warhol's artist
friends, 1968

DEAR UNCLE Andy,

How ARE you doing today? Tell Pauly he got called for two Jobs. For Duquesne Brewery And as a cashier At the meadows. A Monk gave daddy this prayer card For you. When Are you going home. Marty is very bad And he's going in second grade And im going in to Fourth grade. do you want me to come to visit you?

Love
Madalen Warhola

No. S8-113
Mother of Perpetual Help

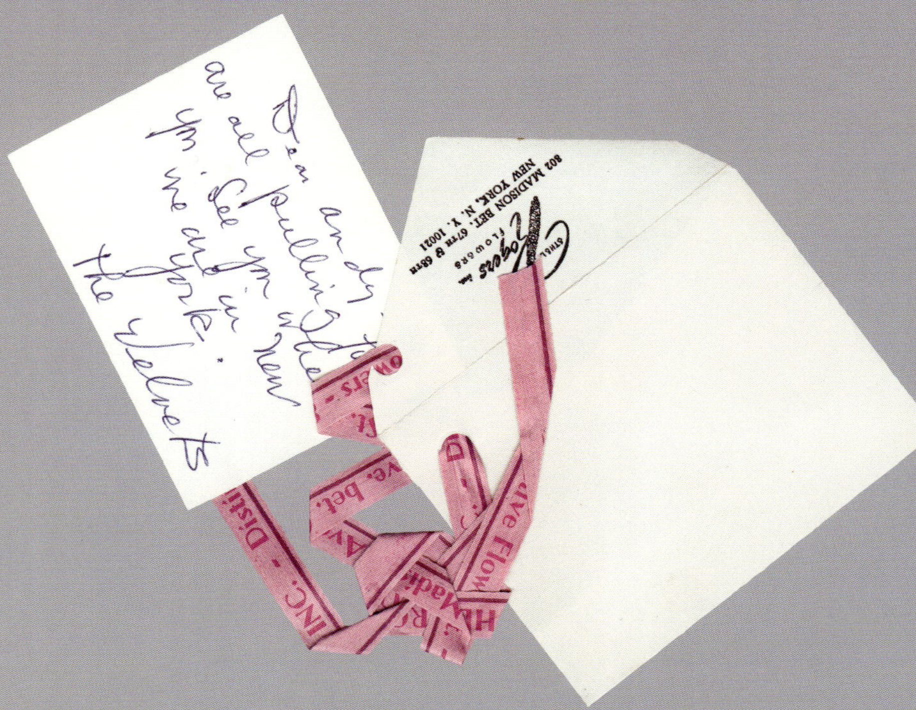

195___

COLUMBUS HOSPITAL O.P.D.

227 East 19th Street

Between 2nd & 3rd Ave.

has been successfully vaccinated on

Paul Warhol

___________ M. D.

Paul and John — Warhola
We are at
May's Kansas City
Restaurant — Park Ave
So. between 17th & 18 St.
Ph: CA 8-2080 — Viva and
Gerard

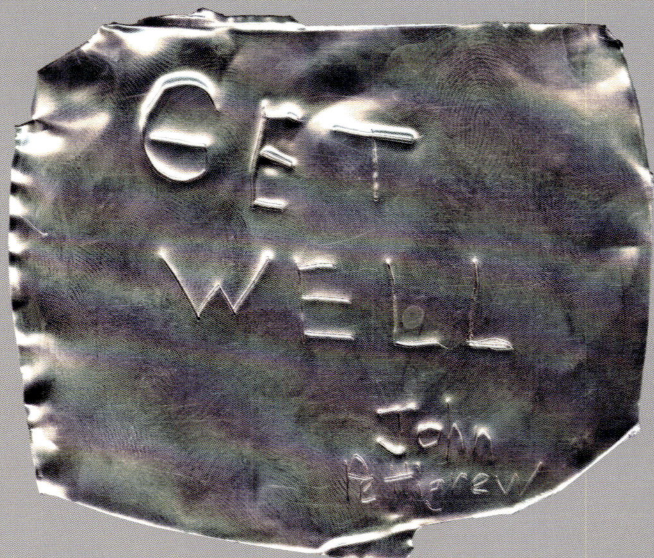

215

Card from niece Madalen Warhola to Warhol, June 26, 1968

Scrap metal with get-well message inscribed by Chuck Peavy, 1968

Flower delivery card from "the Velvets" to Warhol, 1968

Handwritten note on the back of a Columbus Hospital card from Viva and Gerard Malanga to Warhol's brothers John and Paul, directing them where to meet them in the aftermath of the shooting, 1968

In the summer of 1963, Andy Warhol hired Gerard Malanga as his painting assistant, and Malanga quickly became an important figure in Warhol's studio, the Factory. He also created his own art, film, and poetry. Warhol's Archive holds many original documents that together describe an event that nearly landed his assistant in prison for art forgery in 1968.

By 1967 Malanga's own creative reputation was becoming established, and his film *In Search of the Miraculous* was accepted into the Bergamo Film Festival in Italy. In September he flew to Europe on a one-way ticket, believing that Warhol had promised to send him the money for his return. Following the film screening in Bergamo, Malanga still needed money to fly home. He received no response to his pleas, possibly because Warhol was far away from New York, shooting films in Arizona and California. Undeterred, Malanga decided to make a new film in Rome, where he was visiting friends. He developed a scheme to pay for it by selling paintings based on news photos of the corpse of Che Guevara. The hero of the Cuban Revolution had recently been killed in Bolivia, adding to his romanticized aura as a martyr. Malanga planned to paint and silkscreen

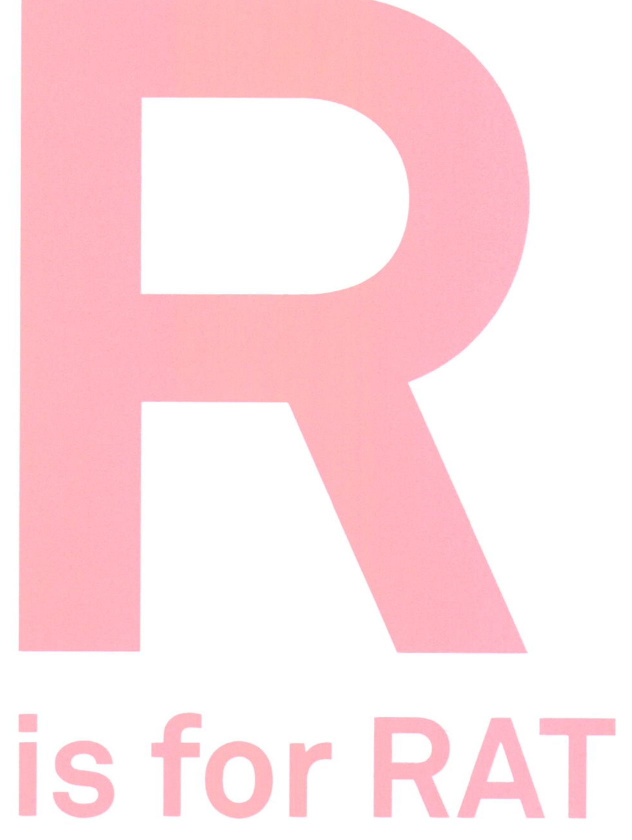

R
is for RAT

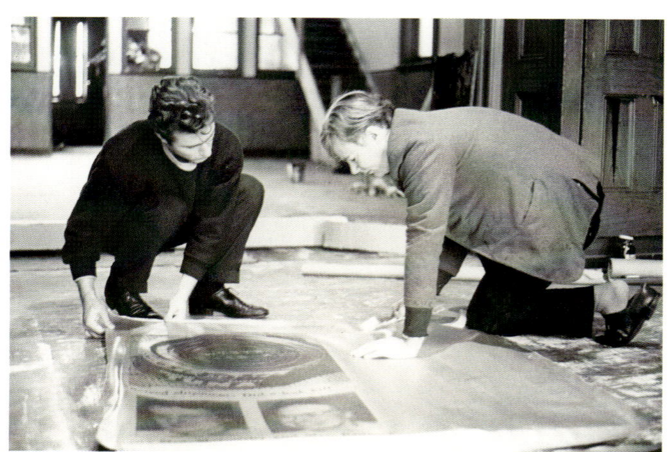

This chapter is a compilation of texts and images from the exhibition *"Trapped like a Rat in Rome": The Che Guevara Episode*, December 16, 2005–August 6, 2006.

the works in the manner of Warhol and to sell them as Warhol's own art. In his letters to Warhol, Malanga is clear about his intentions, acknowledging that he is breaking the law and therefore requires the artist's cooperation. He mailed a sample of the proposed work to his boss and repeatedly asked for approval, but when no direct answer was received, Malanga went ahead with his plan anyway, optimistically misinterpreting a lack of response from Warhol as permission.

Malanga made two large paintings on canvas of the Cuban revolutionary (one version in green and red on a blue ground, the other in blue and yellow on silver), and about twenty smaller works on paper; in one letter, he noted that the red painting was destroyed "because the paint was too thin." Malanga arranged to have them shown at Galleria La Tartaruga, one of the most established galleries for contemporary art in Rome. The gallerist, Plinio de Martis, was preparing to retire from business and was excited to have scored a final coup. De Martis needed to ensure that he was permitted to sell the art, and he contacted Warhol's main art dealer, Leo Castelli, in New York. Castelli mentioned the works to Warhol, who apparently then exposed Malanga. By that time, De Martis had already paid Malanga a small advance on two occasions; rather than receiving full payment, Malanga was now threatened with imprisonment.

Oddly, the Rome exhibition was scheduled to open on February 10, the same day as Warhol's big show at Stockholm's Moderna Museet, which Warhol attended. Eight days later, Warhol sent De Martis a telegram, falsely stating that the *Che* works were his own, but that Malanga wasn't authorized to sell them, saving him from imprisonment. Warhol delayed his reply to De Martis's later request (of February 27) for "adjustments," perhaps attempting to find a solution but compounding Malanga's anxiety. It isn't precisely clear how the story played out, but sometime between March 11 (the date of his last-known letter to Warhol and the artist's manager, Paul Morrissey) and April 19 (when his passport apparently expired), Malanga received money for the publication of his poems and flew home. He was not enthusiastically welcomed back to the Factory, but after the near-fatal shooting of Warhol in June,

Malanga continued to work for Warhol until mid-1970. Several years later, Warhol received two snapshots of the silver *Che* painting from one of his then-current Italian gallerists, along with a large fragment that was cut from the forged work, thus destroying it.

It's impossible to say why Warhol didn't reply to Malanga and possibly prevent the events from unfolding, or why Malanga chose to construe his boss's silence as approval for his project. Likewise, it's hard to say why Warhol never chose Guevara or another Cuban revolutionary, such as Fidel Castro, as a subject for his paintings. He didn't shy away from political subject matter and portrayed many such figures from the United States. He also later made portraits of Mao Tse-tung and Vladimir Lenin, as well as a series of *Hammer and Sickle* paintings; and Communism had indeed been a subject for his work in the late 1940s, while he was still a student. On the other hand, he also never made portraits of the American civil rights leaders of the 1960s, such as the Reverend Martin Luther King Jr. or Malcolm X. The nearest that he came were his large series of *Race Riot* paintings of 1964, and a unique drawing of a newspaper front page reporting a knife attack on King in 1958.

Perhaps Warhol felt that these men were too controversial and that portraying them might lead to attacks on his career or himself. It may simply have been a matter of timing and business, because in that same year Warhol had completed a suite of prints, titled *Flash—November 22, 1963*, on the assassination of John F. Kennedy. An astute businessman, Warhol may have perceived a conflict in his market, perhaps fearful that the *Flash* publisher, Racolin Press, would see reduced sales of his portfolio if Warhol were also painting a martyred revolutionary as well as the revered—almost saintly—figure of the slain American president. Like Warhol and his family, the Kennedys were of the Catholic faith, and that fact may also have played a part in his hesitation. It's also quite possible that he merely believed—or was advised by his managers Fred Hughes and Paul Morrissey—that he would be unable to sell paintings of radical figures to the wealthy patrons he was hoping to lure.

Edward Wallowitch, *Gerard Malanga and Andy Warhol ("The Tunafish Disaster")*, 1963, reprinted 1988

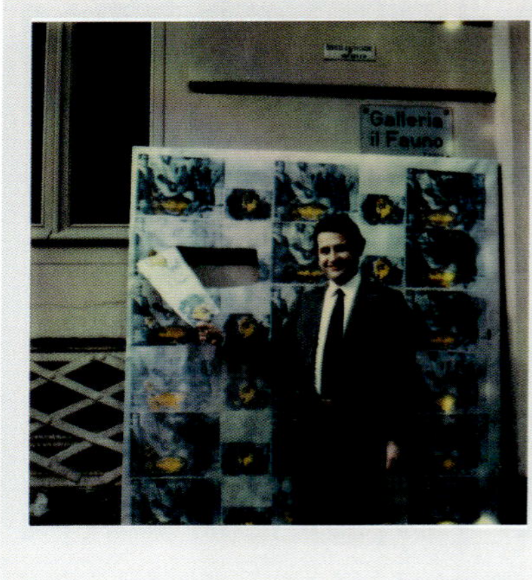

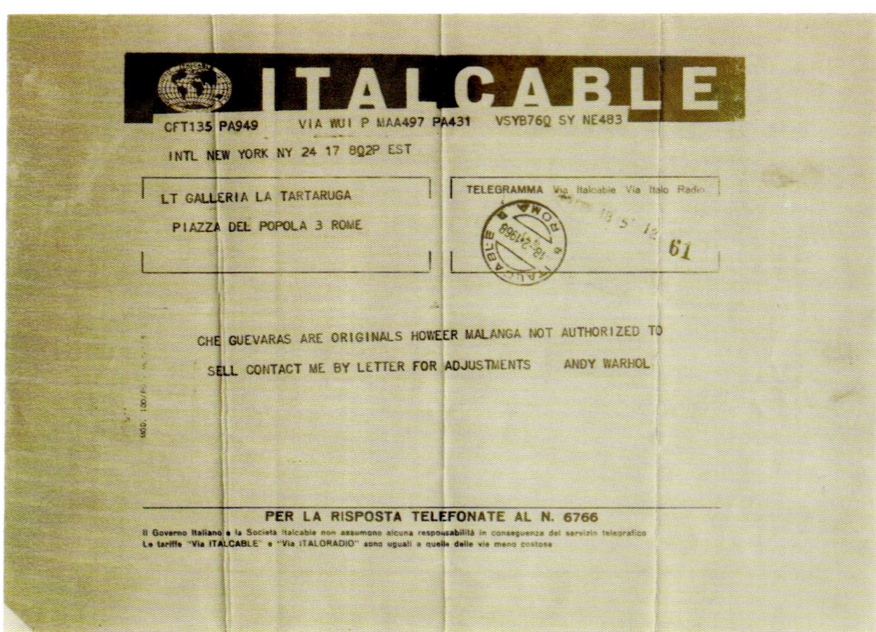

ITALCABLE

CFT135 PA949   VIA WUI P MAA497 PA431   VSYB76Q SY NE483
INTL NEW YORK NY 24 17 802P EST

LT GALLERIA LA TARTARUGA

PIAZZA DEL POPOLA 3 ROME

TELEGRAMMA Via Italcable Via Italo Radio

CHE GUEVARAS ARE ORIGINALS HOWEER MALANGA NOT AUTHORIZED TO

SELL CONTACT ME BY LETTER FOR ADJUSTMENTS   ANDY WARHOL

PER LA RISPOSTA TELEFONATE AL N. 6766

Il Governo Italiano e la Società Italcable non assumono alcuna responsabilità in conseguenza del servizio telegrafico
Le tariffe "Via ITALCABLE" e "Via ITALORADIO" sono uguali e quelle delle vie meno costose

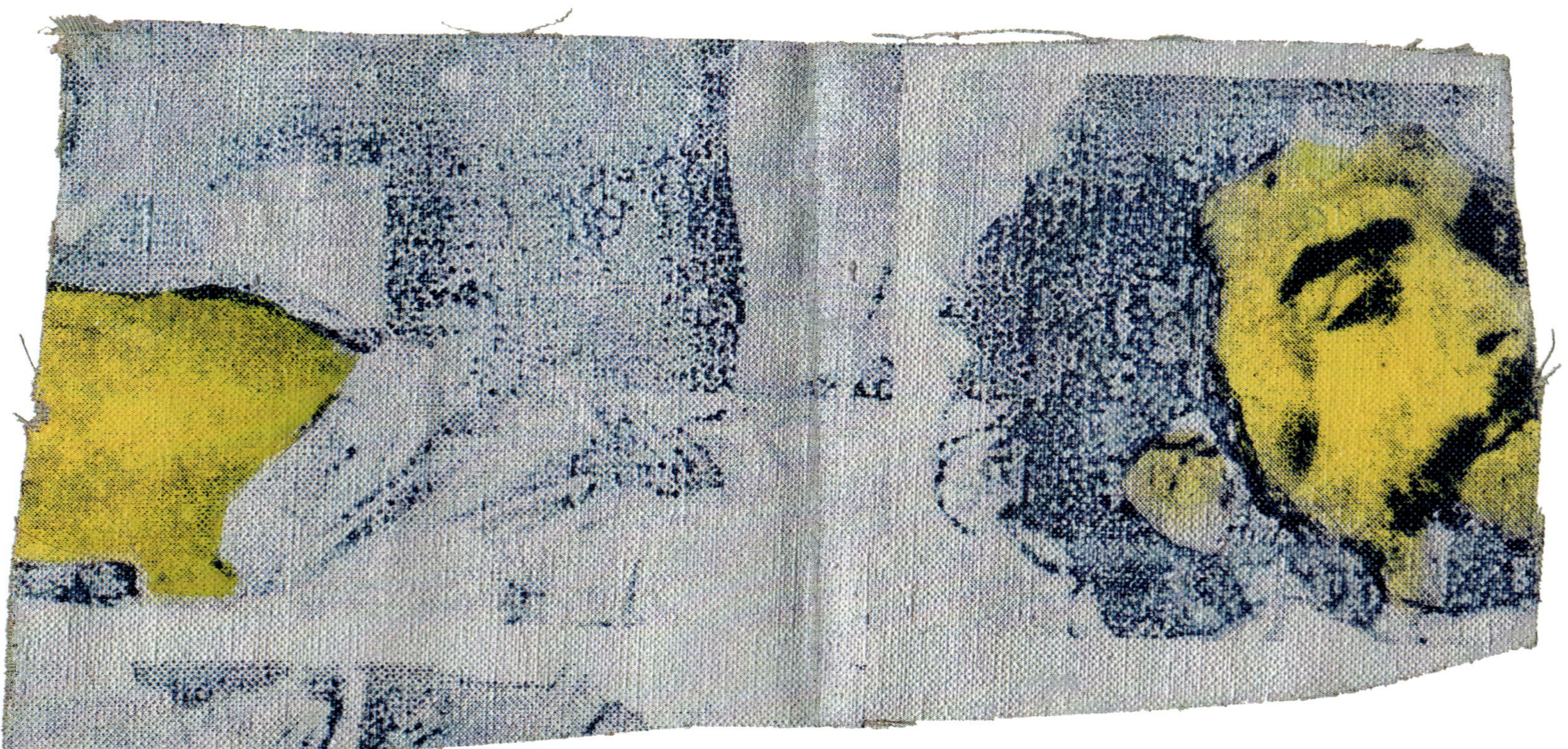

Polaroid of forged painting after it was destroyed, 1968

Gerard Malanga, piece of Che Guevara canvas, 1968

Telegram from Warhol to Galleria La Tartaruga, February 18, 1968

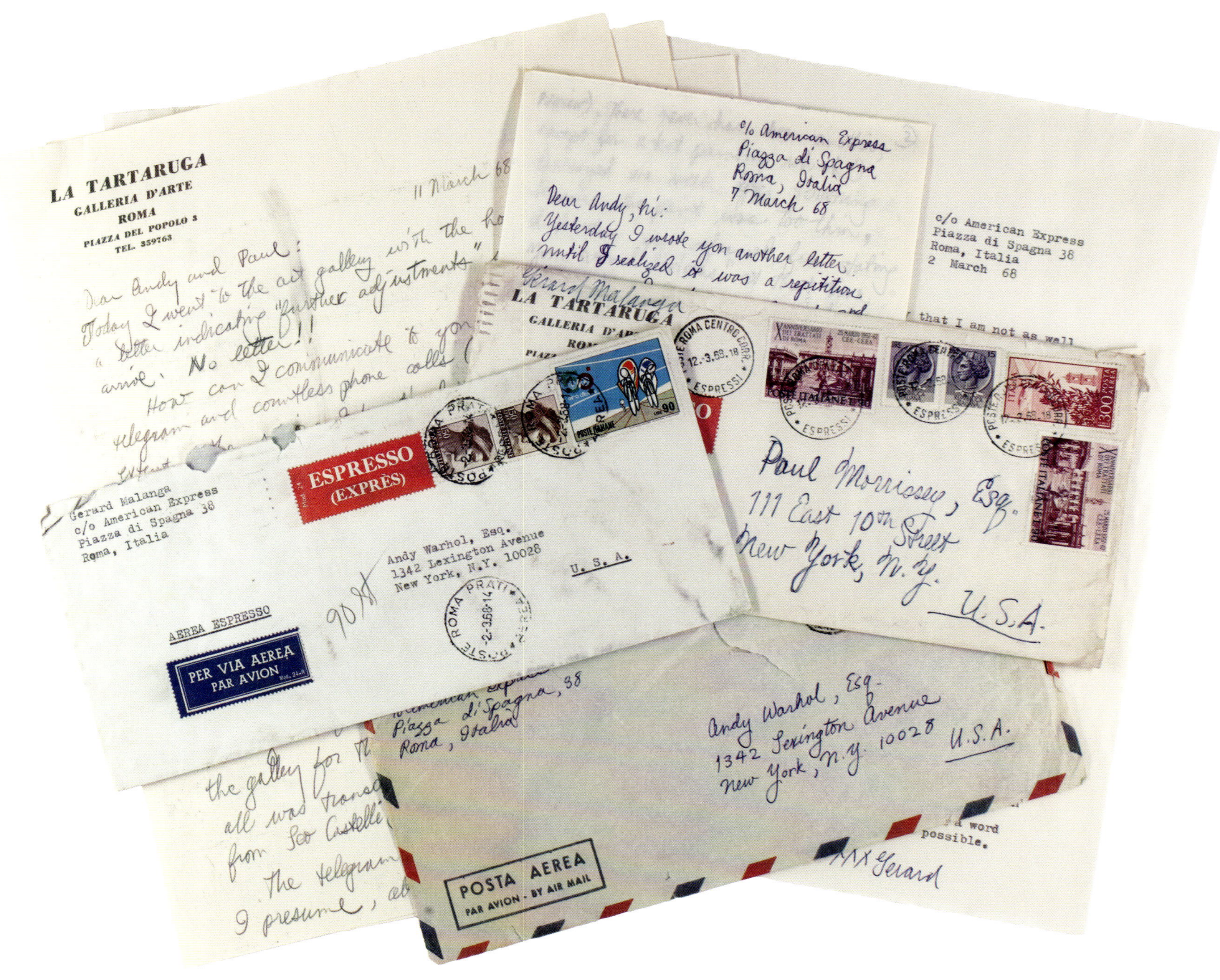

**Correspondence from Gerard Malanga to Warhol and Paul Morrissey,
March 2–11, 1968**

Throughout the history of the post, people have chosen to mail special objects to their friends, lovers, and pen pals, even if just a photo or a customized envelope. Correspondence is inherently personal—an uninterrupted dialogue between sender and recipient—and Warhol received a dizzying amount of mail in his lifetime, from both close friends and complete strangers. Likewise, Warhol inundated Truman Capote with mail when the artist first moved to New York City. Correspondence accounts for the largest part of the museum's archival holdings, ranging from little-known works of art to ephemera, and a unique assortment of correspondence and mail art from artists, friends, and fans of Warhol.

Mail Art

Beginning in the 1950s, the collage artist Ray Johnson—a good friend of Warhol—began to disseminate his art through the mail, and a new field of creativity commonly known as correspondence art, or more simply mail art, was invented. An early example of this is an ink drawing sent to Warhol by Johnson in 1956, playing on Warhol's shoe fetishism.

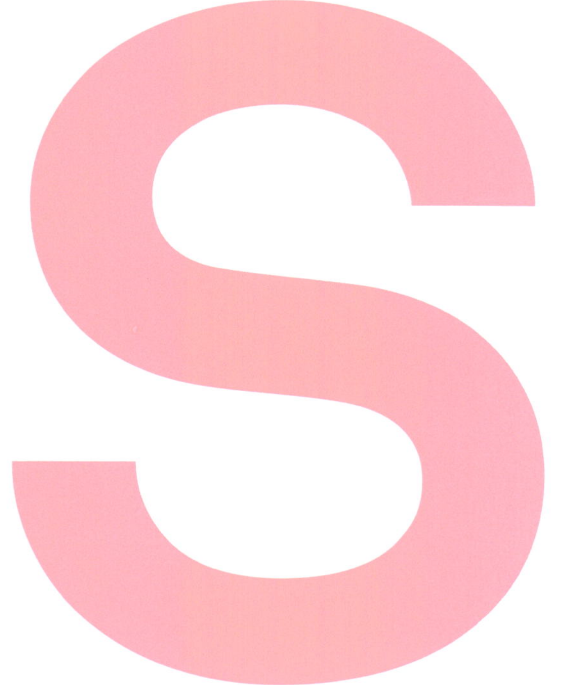

S
is for STAMP

This chapter is adapted from materials in two exhibitions, *Warhol Goes Postal: Stamp Out Now!*, July 12–August 18, 2002, and *Dear Andy: Fan Mail from the Archives*, October 15, 1996–February 2, 1997, in the Archives Study Center.

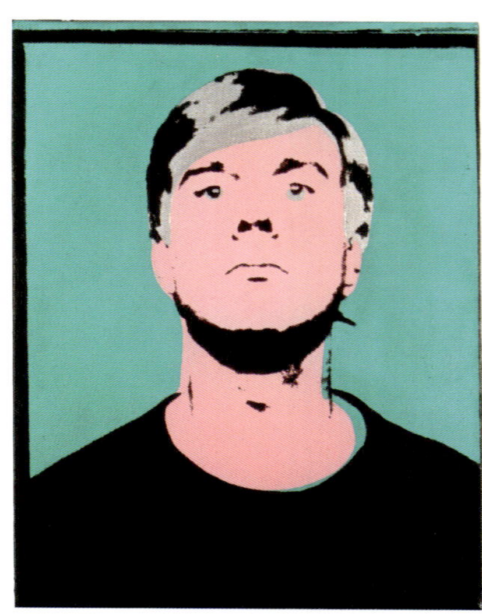

Johnson's iconoclastic performance art and mailing activities usually occurred under the informal auspices of the New York Correspondance School, a deliberate misspelling that revealed Johnson's approach to his work: a waltz of art through the postal system. The Archive contains many of Johnson's mail art works sent to Warhol. One has instructions to be resent to the actor Dennis Hopper, who acted in Warhol's films, and another to be sent to the avant-garde artist George Brecht. Warhol, however, did not forward the mailings; consequently, the museum still has these works by Johnson.

In that same year, Johnson began creating *A Book about Death*. The pages were mailed individually to subscribers; no one is known to have received a complete copy. Warhol received at least two pages, which were dedicated to him and mimic a page of postage stamps. Another work in the Archive is from Johnson's series *Droppings* (1968), in which he announced the expulsion of various people from the Correspondance School. This work was initially sent to Warhol Superstar Ultra Violet, with instructions for her to resend it to Warhol. She did. Johnson's *Untitled Mailing (Bob Dylan and Lyndon Johnson)* (1969) merited special preservation by Warhol, who had it framed.

Creative Correspondence

Warhol also received many artistic mailings from Peter Beard, a photographer of fashion and of the wildlife of Kenya. Warhol met Beard in about 1970, and their ensuing friendship took several forms. They socialized together at the nightclub Studio 54, and Warhol published not only Beard's photographs in *Interview* but also occasional film reviews and interviews. For several weeks in 1970, they kept a schedule of meeting in a hotel to work together on collages and on a daily writing project partly derived from Beard's diaries. This may have been the inspiration for Warhol's own *Diaries*, started in about 1972. Beard's diaries are extremely visual and tactile: massive, bound collages of rocks, feathers, snakeskin, and dried animal blood, combined with his photos, cultural ephemera, and daily notes. Beard's obsessive diaries are mirrored somewhat in his correspondence to Warhol in the early 1970s. Filled with observations of wild, jet-set life and African flora and fauna, the letters' margins contain doodles of strange faces and sinking ships, as well as reminders of his property, Hog Ranch: a desiccated scorpion, a clutch of feathers, and the label from a bottle of Tusker beer.[1]

Warhol's voluminous correspondences with young fan Lance Loud and friends Dudley Huppler and Tommy Jackson, as well as mail that he sent to his mother, represent the slightly more prosaic aspect of his postal correspondence. In his 1956 postcards, sent during his travels around the world, Warhol writes nothing of the adventure but briefly reassures his mother, "I'm OK."

The Archive contains a series of postcards printed with drawings by Huppler (ca. 1954–55). Warhol appears to have corresponded with Huppler for many months before they actually met. In his letters, Huppler, who attended the artist's colony Yaddo in Saratoga Springs, New York, in 1955, states that he is a self-taught artist who has met George Platt Lynes, Marianne Moore, and Katherine Anne Porter. He talks about his young nieces, his award-winning cakes, his experiences in Europe, and his admiration for Warhol's art, especially the artist's brilliant use of color. Four letters from Huppler (1954–55) each contain more than just a letter—a valentine made by his nieces, an original drawing, a sand dollar, and a humorous newspaper clipping. Huppler often decorated his envelopes as well. One of these features a drawing of Warhol's initials set inside a pair of eyeglasses similar in style to those that Warhol wore at the time.

Warhol received at least forty-eight postcards and letters from Tommy Jackson between 1950 and 1954. The collection of cards shows that Warhol initiated the correspondence, first sending a card typed in black. Jackson's reply was typed on the same card in green. Through the addresses on this series of postcards, three of Warhol's frequent changes of address during this relatively unsteady period of his life have been identified.

Lance Loud wrote many long letters to Warhol, starting in 1967 as a sixteen-year-old fan. These letters are personal and revealing, and Warhol wrote back. Eventually the fan-turned-friend talked to Warhol on the phone, and the two even exchanged clothing in the mail. Loud's family became well known in 1973, when their lives were filmed for the groundbreaking PBS program *An American Family*, the first reality TV show. Viewers saw Loud's parents' marriage disintegrate and witnessed Lance come out as gay. He later had a successful career as a journalist.

Art and Stamps

Warhol's art collection contained little-known works related to the post, including an untitled wall filled with hundreds of tiny blue portraits of George Washington that were carefully cut from canceled stamps by Johnny Dodd in the 1960s. Dodd was a theatrical lighting designer for small stage productions in New York at that time. He was a friend of Billy Name, the lighting designer who decorated Warhol's Silver Factory. Viewers of this repetitive and obsessive work could mistake it as a product of amphetamine use; however, unlike many of the members of Warhol's entourage in those years, Dodd was not a speed user.[2]

Stamps are a Pop subject represented in Warhol's oeuvre. In 1962 he created a series of paintings using a hand-carved rubber stamp based upon an actual airmail stamp at the time. He printed the canvas with irregular grids. The rubber stamps used for these works and for *Red Airmail Stamp* (1962) are in the Archive. In 1979 he created a print designed for the first-day cover of a United Nations stamp. This work was commissioned to raise funds to support the United Nations Disaster Relief Organization. Buyers of the print also received a cachet, or first-day cover envelope, printed with a miniature reproduction of this work, along with the newly issued postage stamps. Papers related to this project include a letter dated January 26, 1979, from Annabelle Wiener, director of the World Federation of United Nations Associations, thanking Warhol for his design and inviting him to a luncheon at the Interpex philatelist convention to celebrate his work for the United Nations.

The typical stamp collector prizes the uncanceled sleeve of stamps such as those given out at the philatelist convention. Warhol's own "stamp collection" (as he thought of it), however, consists of thousands of canceled stamps from all over the world, carefully ripped from the original envelopes and saved in manila envelopes. These collections are sprinkled throughout the *Time Capsules*.

Warhol Honored with Stamps

Beginning in March 1987—a month after Warhol's death—Michel Hosszú, a Hungarian artist working in France who makes his own postage stamps, designed and published "bootleg" Warhol postage stamps, which he apparently used on his correspondence for a year. The stamps were featured on an envelope addressed to Warhol's executor, Fred Hughes, containing a letter from Hosszú describing his project and a letter from his art dealer to Hughes. A framed set of six of these artist's illegal stamps are in the Archive. These Warhol stamps, like all of Hosszú's work, are hand-printed, as the off-register printing attests. In a common error, probably due to Warhol's own misinformation, Hosszú incorrectly identifies Warhol's date of birth as 1930, rather than 1928.

On August 9, 2002, the US Postal Service released an official Andy Warhol first-class postage stamp. The design for the stamp is a self-portrait painting by Warhol from the museum's collection that was based on a photobooth photograph. The postage stamp is slightly smaller than the original photograph.

NOTES

1. Beard has lived on Hog Ranch since 1962 as well as on Long Island, NY. His move to Africa and his life's work are inspired by the work of the Danish author Karen Blixen (Isak Dinesen), best known for *Out of Africa*. Beard's experiences hunting crocodiles in the name of science led to his later environmentalism, protesting a massive die-off of elephants in Kenya's Tsavo National Park.

2. Conversation with scholar Gerard Forde and archivist Erin Byrne, November 29, 2018.

Additional research for this chapter was provided by Erin Byrne. Photographic layouts designed by Becky Shock.

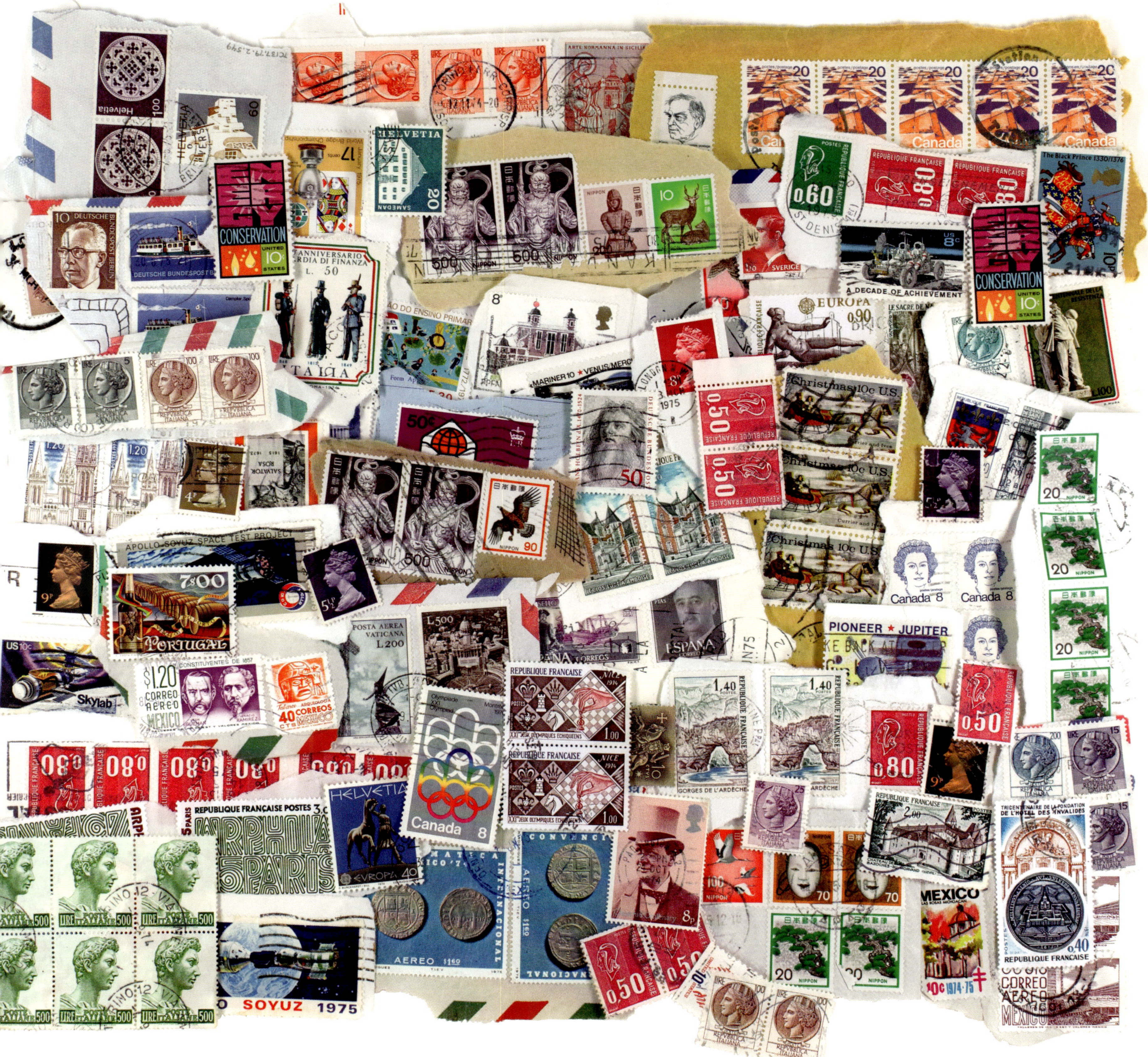

Canceled stamps collected by Warhol from *Time Capsule 137*, 1974–76

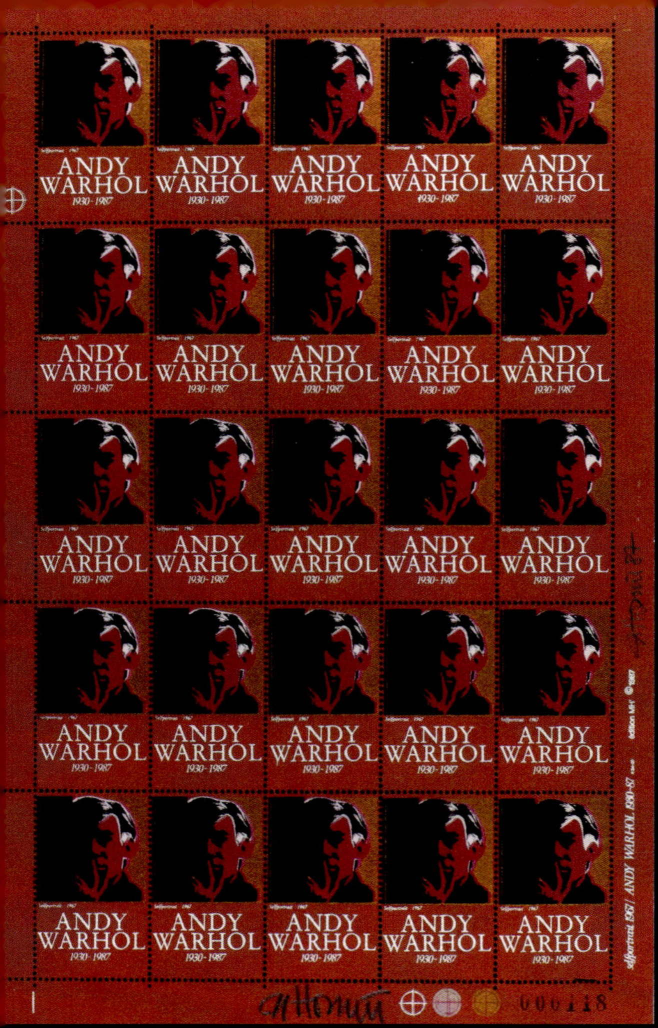

Michel Hosszú, *Homage to Andy Warhol Stamp Sheet*, 1987

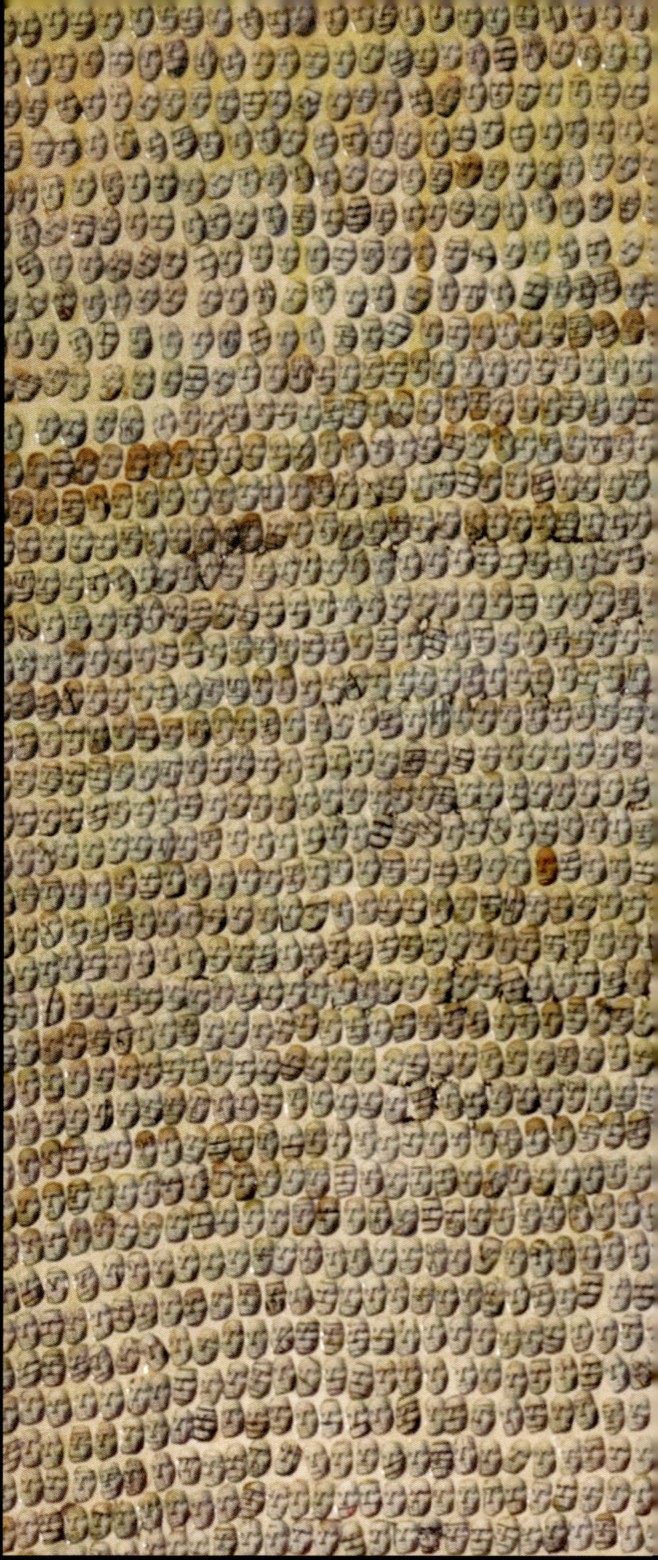

Johnny Dodd, *Untitled* (six postage stamp panels, detail), 1964

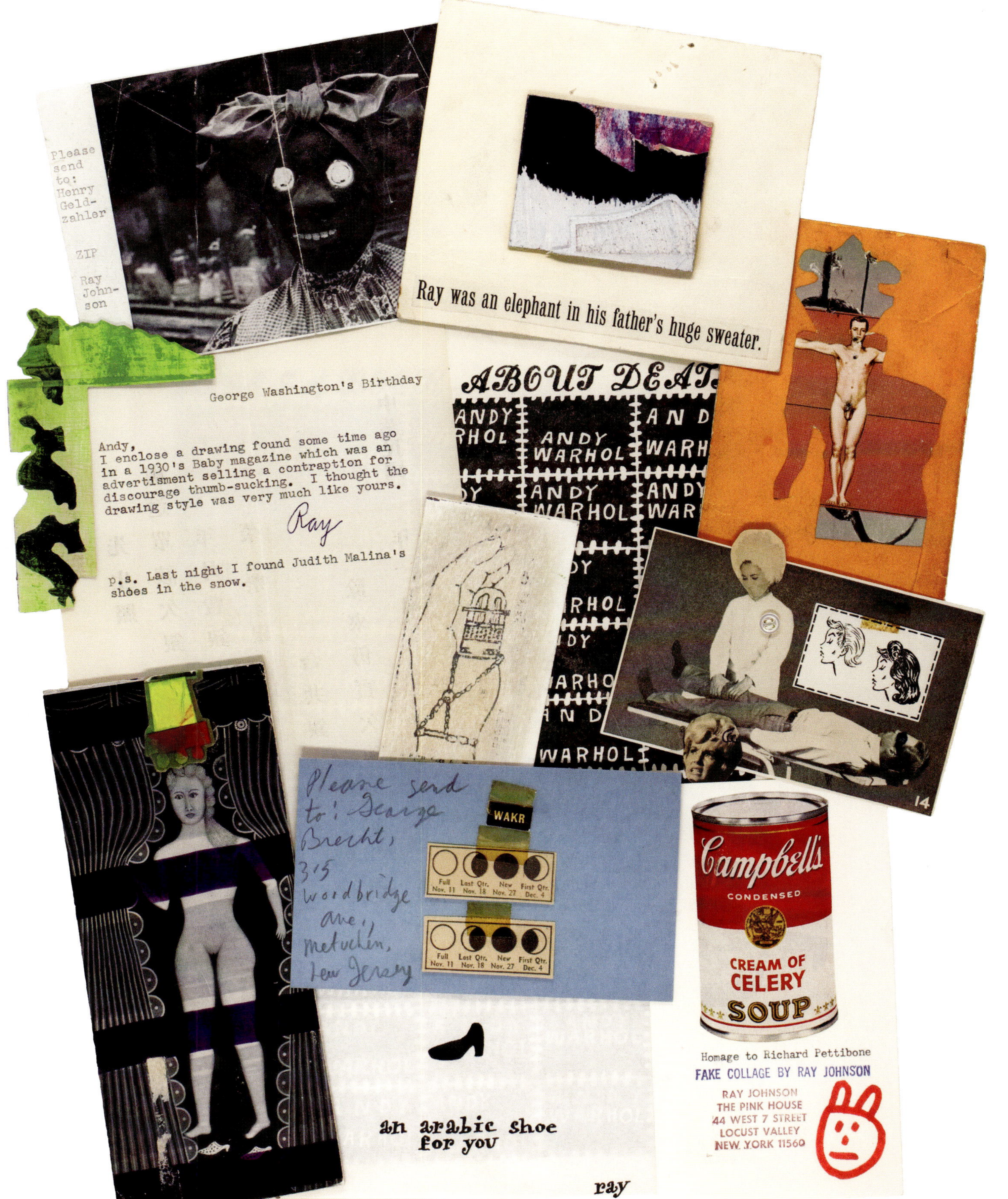

Selection of mail art sent to Warhol by Ray Johnson, 1956–69

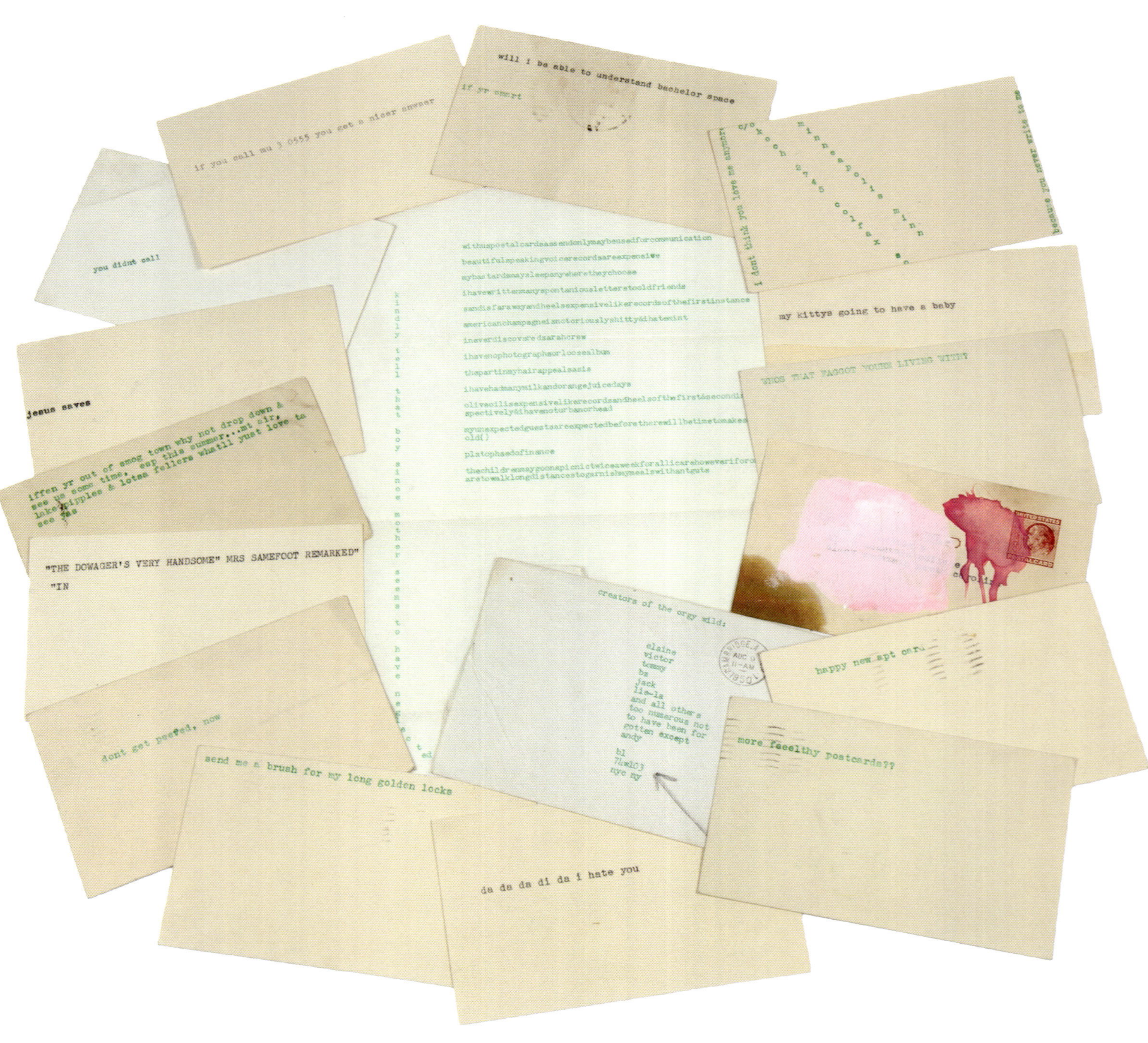

Selection of correspondence from Tommy Jackson to Warhol, 1950–54

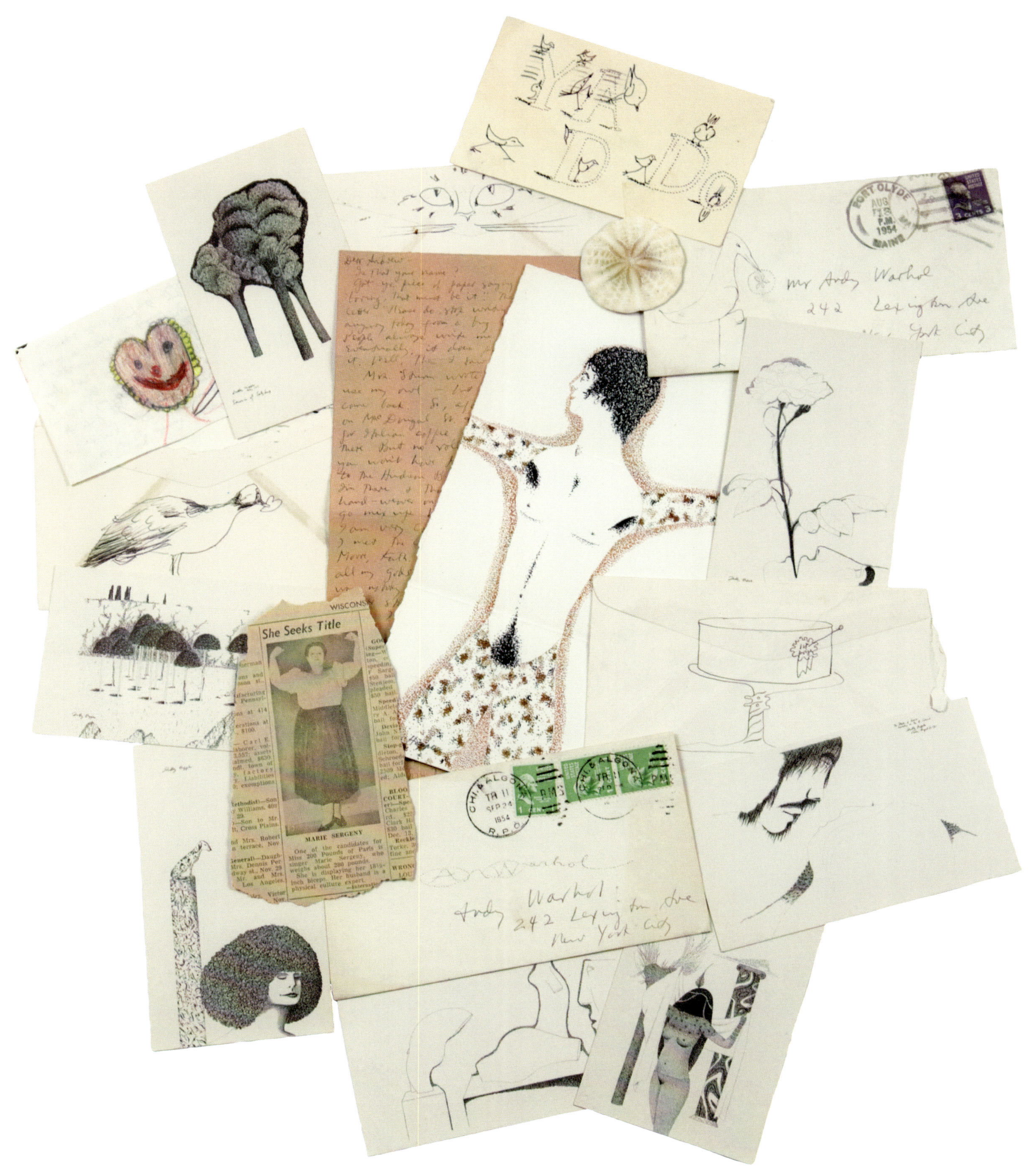

Dudley Huppler illustrations sent to Warhol, 1954–55

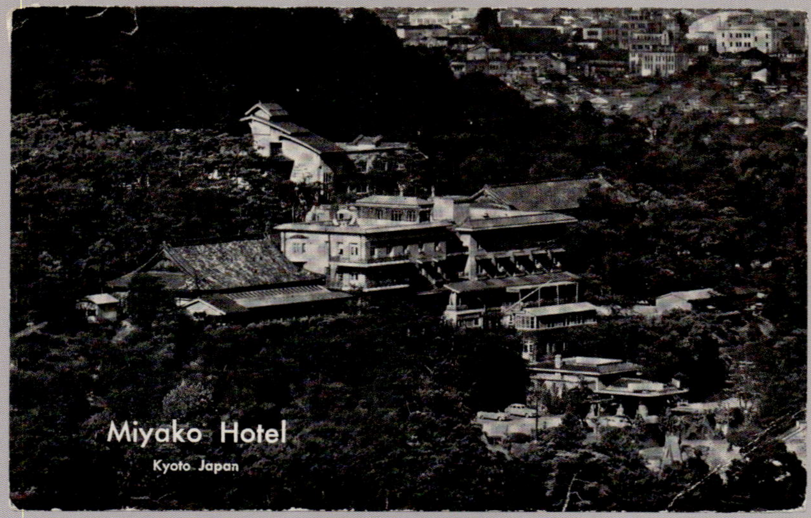

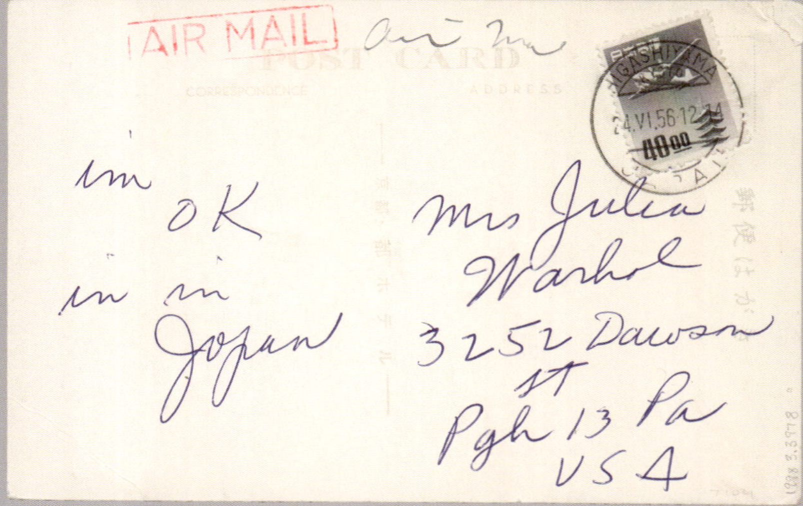

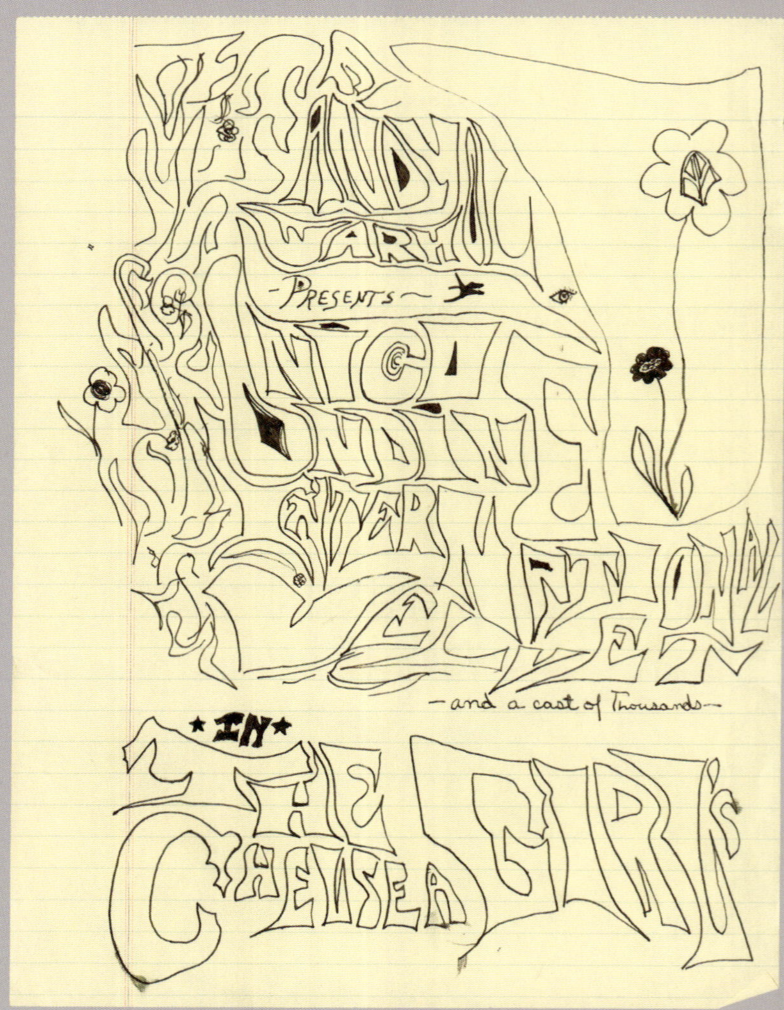

Postcard from Warhol to Julia Warhola, posted June 24, 1956, Higashiyama, Japan (front and back)

Letter from Lance Loud to Warhol, ca. 1967

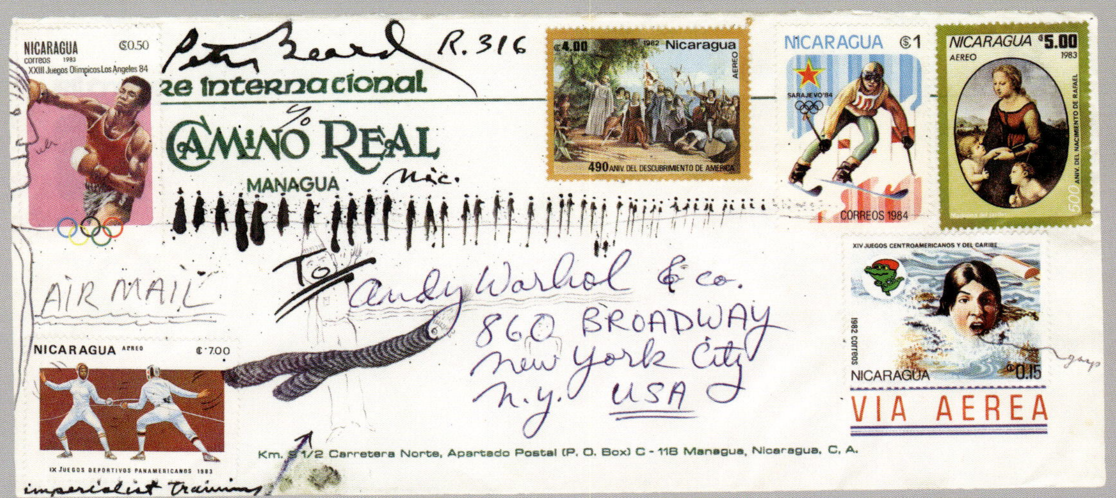

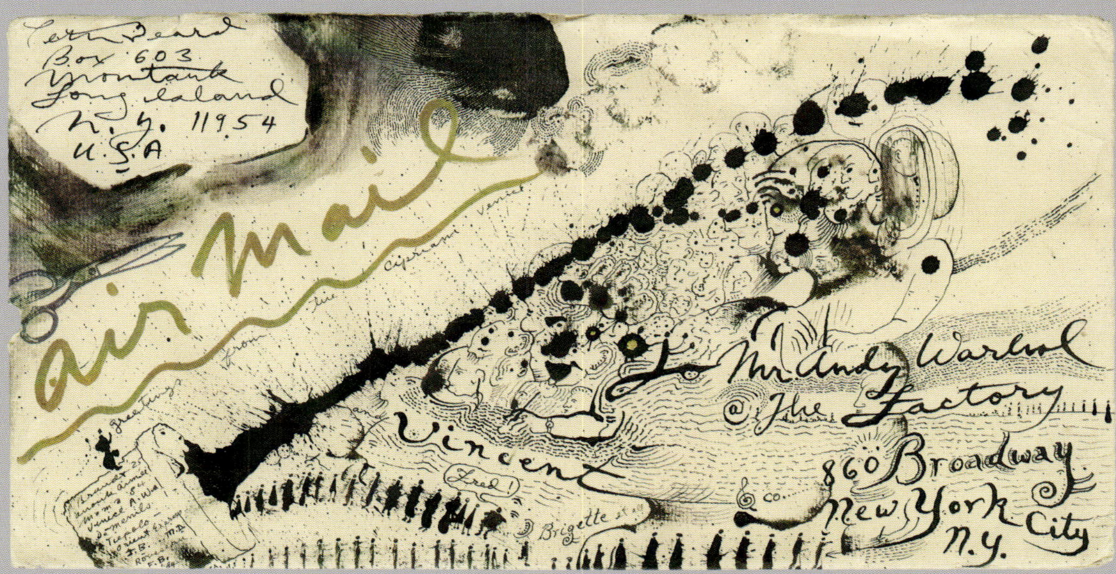

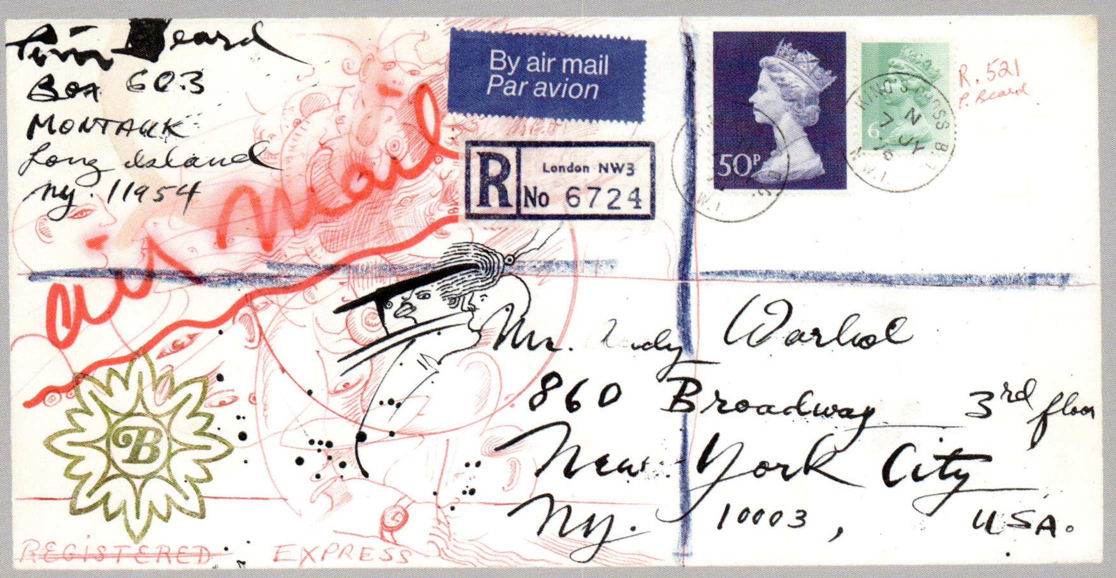

Decorated envelope from Peter Beard to Andy Warhol & Co.,1984

Decorated postcard from Peter Beard to Warhol, posted April 6, 1983, Venice

Decorated envelope from Peter Beard to Warhol, posted July 7, 1976, London

In the 1968 satirical film *I Love You, Alice B. Toklas!*, middle-aged lawyer Harry Fine (played by Peter Sellers) argues with his beautiful hippie girlfriend, Nancy (Leigh Taylor-Young), about an evening's entertainment. Newly liberated Harry wants to stay home and share a bubble bath with Nancy in his wood-paneled apartment, which has just been redecorated with hookahs, saris, bead curtains, and a psychedelic mural featuring solarized portraits of the Beatles, circa *The White Album*. Nancy, eager for a new experience, wants to see the latest Warhol film, *Mondo Teeth*. The couple discusses that it's alleged to be six hours of teeth, both human and animal, with the screen divided into thirty-two parts, one for each tooth in a normal set of human choppers.

Although Warhol never really made a film about teeth, he was very interested in them, as evidenced by his collection of dental models, some of which had been used as teaching aids in dental schools. In the July 28, 1982, entry in his *Diaries*, Warhol records that he bought the teeth at a store on 21st Street in Manhattan that his assistant Jay Shriver had discovered. He doesn't state a reason for purchasing them, noting that he paid $484 for the collection and that he wanted a "giant-size" set of antique aluminum

T

is for TOOTH FAIRY

This chapter is adapted from the exhibition *Tooth Fairy: Andy Warhol's Collection of Dental Models*, in the Archives Study Center, February 7–July 7, 2003.

teeth. It may be that Warhol's choice of words was not clearly interpreted by his recorder, Pat Hackett, and he was referring to the large collection of teeth that you see here; however, the large aluminum models he mentions were not published in the catalogue of his estate auction and have yet to be discovered in the Archive. In any event, upon leaving the store, Warhol says that he and Shriver "carried the big teeth in the rain. That was fun."

In another emblematic film from the 1960s, *The Graduate*, directed by Mike Nichols, Dustin Hoffman's character, Benjamin Braddock, a recent college graduate soon to be seduced by Anne Bancroft's "Mrs. Robinson," receives a famous single word of advice regarding his future: "Plastics." Dental schools began to use plastics in their teaching models as early as the 1940s; therefore, the primarily metal composition of these replica teeth dates them to at least that era, and probably earlier. Those with the brilliant chrome-like finish seem to be made of injection-molded plastic. The cast-metal life-size teeth may date to 1917, since that is the year that the manufacturer, Columbia Dentoform Corporation, started in the business.

Many of the life-size sets have several teeth that can be separated from the gum. Some of these are attached to the metal gum by small setscrews; others simply rest in holes in the gum. The more realistic-appearing models that consist of hinged upper and lower jaws are known as "manikins" and were intended to be placed in life-size models of heads on which dental students honed their skills. Some of this type include details such as a flexible plastic tongue, which will give way to any pressure applied by an errant dental tool. One of the manikins has a clear plastic tooth; others have combinations of ivory-colored plastic and metal. The large set of plaster upper and lower teeth may have been intended for use in a large classroom so that all of the students could see the model. The extremely large set of five loose plaster teeth with a matching plaster gum may have also been designed for such a situation, or they may have been hand-carved by a student. This is still a common practice for students of dentistry, helping them to become familiar with the forms and shapes of the objects of their profession. It's not clear whether the life-size models were cast from actual teeth or carved and then cast in

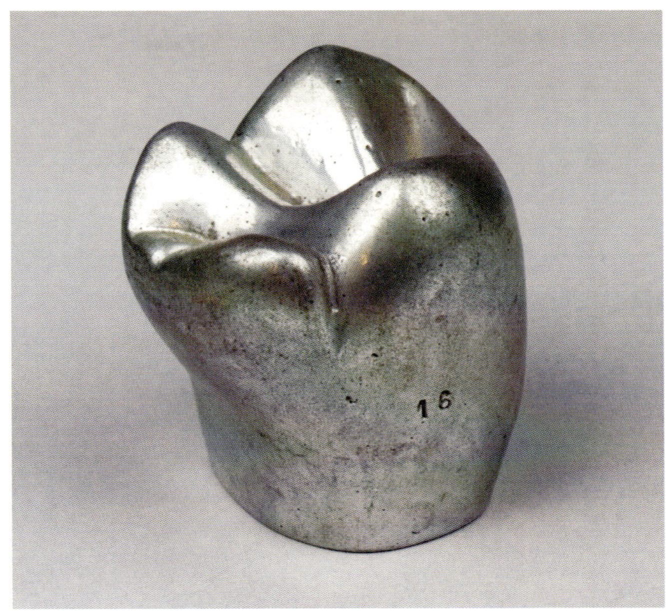

metal, but many of them appear extremely realistic and precisely detailed.

These models were a great improvement over the first models used. In the 1840s, Emiline Roberts Jones, the first professional woman dentist in the United States, practiced on extracted real human teeth. Advances in model-making technology have eliminated much of the need to use living patients for training, and many state boards of certification have worked toward the exclusive use of replicas by students. Plastic life-size models that include complete internal tooth details, such as the pulp and nerve, allow students to accurately practice serious procedures.

Warhol's library features many books, pamphlets, and other published materials pertaining to human anatomy, especially deformities and corrective surgery. Warhol used many of these publications as source material for artworks, and he also made photographs of some of these dental models. A six-page price list from Columbia Dentoform dated June 1982 was found among the models and appears to match only a very few of those that Warhol acquired. The handcrafted nature of the antique dental models, their obscurity outside the medical profession, and their relationship to Warhol's ongoing interest in

Dental model, ca. 1982

human anatomy could be among the reasons for his attraction to them.

Warhol did focus his creative attentions on teeth—actually, false teeth—in both his early Pop and later hand-painted paintings. *False Plate* (1961) was based on a small magazine advertisement for false teeth. In the mid-1980s, Warhol again worked with an image of dentures and produced several paintings in which the image appears. His series of *Skulls* from 1976 provides an example of his interest in the broader category of human anatomy.

A dental reference is found in Warhol's prints of *Saint Apollonia*, created in 1984. Apollonia was a Christian martyr who was burned alive after having had her teeth smashed by a mob in Alexandria in the third century AD. For her suffering, she is now regarded by Roman Catholics as the patron saint of toothaches. She is always portrayed holding a tooth in a set of pincers, and Warhol follows this convention, basing his work on a fifteenth-century painting attributed to the studio of the great Italian Renaissance master Piero della Francesca, now in the National Gallery of Art in Washington. The metal teeth also recall a work by the artist Jasper Johns, whose art prefigured Warhol's generation of Pop artists, and whom Warhol very much admired. His small sculpture *The Critic Smiles* (1959) is a sculpted model of a toothbrush set on a plinth, its bristles replaced by four chunky molars.

A more tangential way to view these replicas is through another Christian reference with which Warhol was certainly familiar: the Bible's description of Judgment Day with the phrase "wailing and gnashing of teeth." Warhol himself underwent several judgment days during his college career at Carnegie Tech. At the end of each semester, a "judgment day" was held in which the work of each student was displayed for review by the faculty. Warhol is said to have squeaked by each time by a narrow majority of favorable comments.

Although he never made the *Mondo Teeth* film discussed in the Peter Sellers movie, Warhol's camera on occasion did zoom in on his actors' mouths, as in his four-minute film *Screen Test: John Cale's Lips* (ca. 1965–66), and he's well-known for the extreme duration of several of his films, along with his pioneering use of the multiscreen technique. The writers of *I Love You, Alice B. Toklas!*, Paul Mazursky and Larry Tucker, may also have been familiar with the work of several other filmmakers of the era on a similar theme, including two associated with the Fluxus movement. In 1966 artist Mieko Shiomi made a film of close-ups of teeth titled *Disappearing Music for Face* that was based on her earlier performance piece from 1964 of the same name. The performers were to "change gradually from a smile to a smile," with a presumably blank expression in between. In 1968 another Fluxus artist, Yoko Ono, created *Film No. 5 (Smile)*, which stars her celebrity lover and later husband, John Lennon. She had initially intended the film to last four hours but decided on fifty-two minutes. In the film, Lennon sticks out his tongue, raises his eyebrows, purses his lips, and smiles twice—all in extreme slow motion. The scenario for another, unrealized film by Ono was to be "a smiling face snap of every single human being in the world." A third related film is Icelandic artist Gudmundur Erro's 1967 *Grimaces*. This film shows the faces of hundreds of contemporary artists, including Warhol, each making a contorted facial expression.

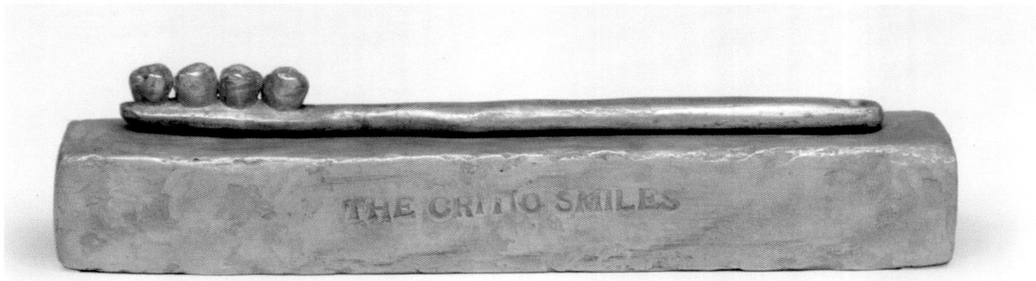

Jasper Johns, *The Critic Smiles*, 1959

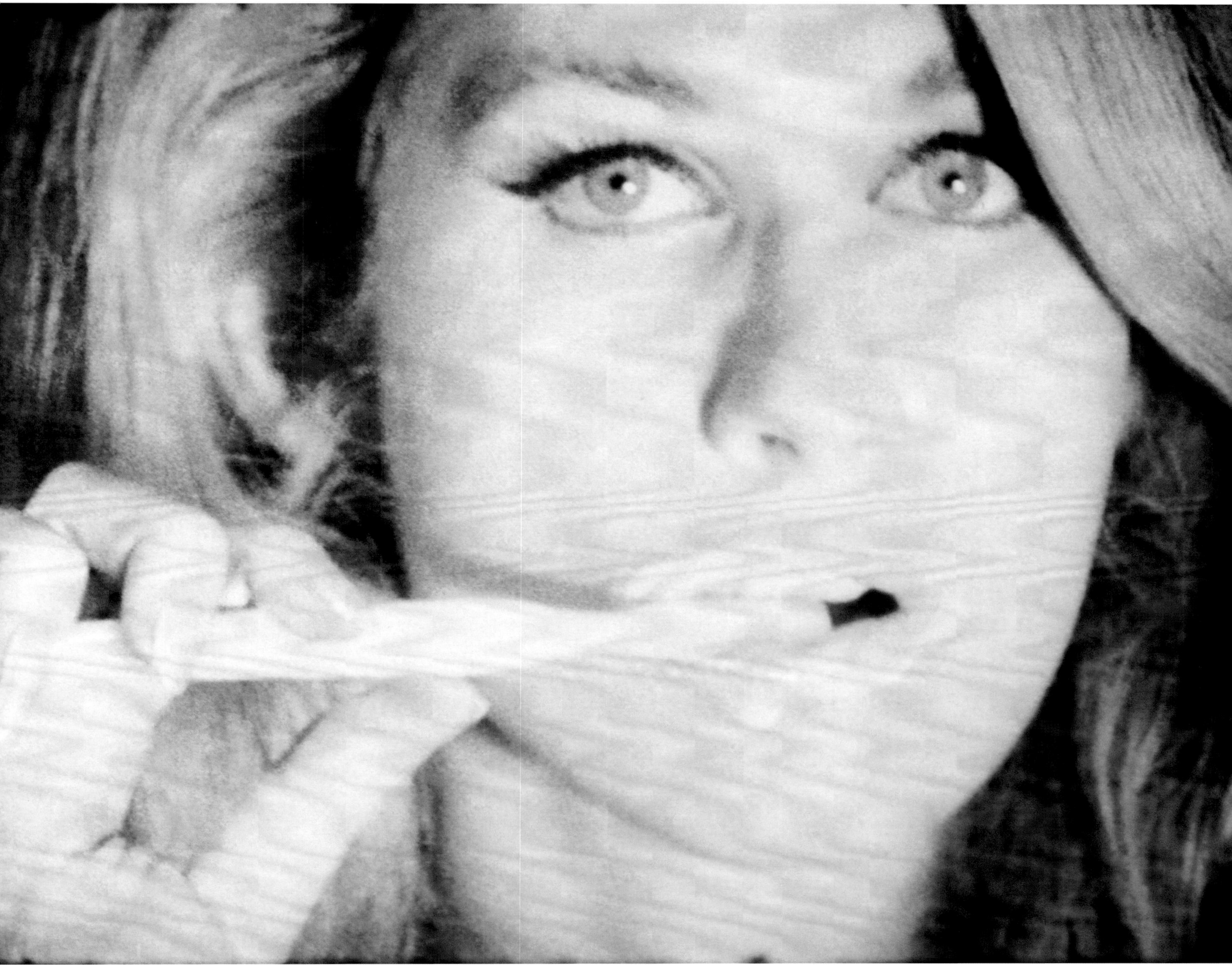

Andy Warhol, *Screen Test: Jane Holzer (Toothbrush) [ST147]*, 1964

234

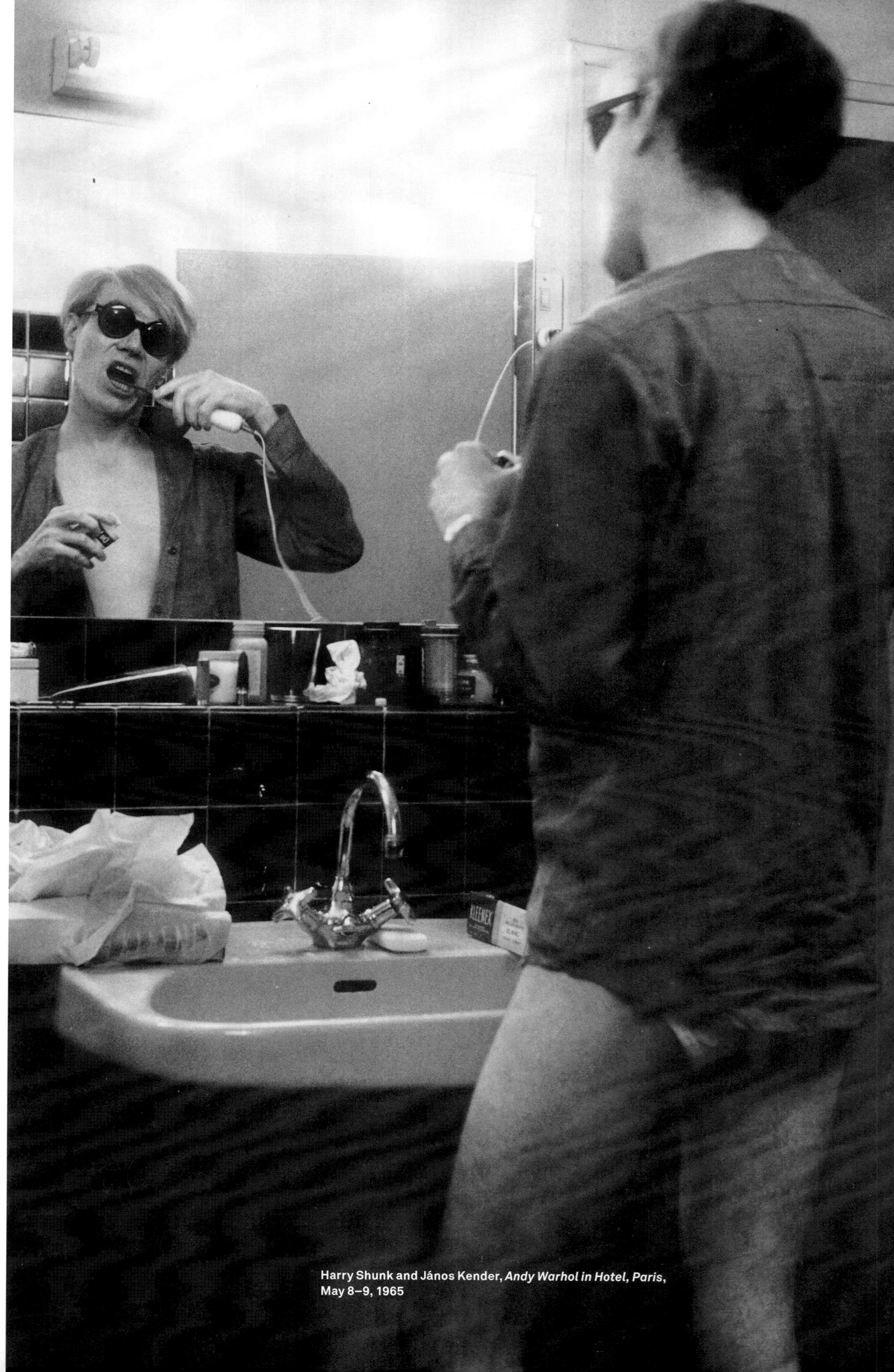

Harry Shunk and János Kender, *Andy Warhol in Hotel, Paris,*
May 8–9, 1965

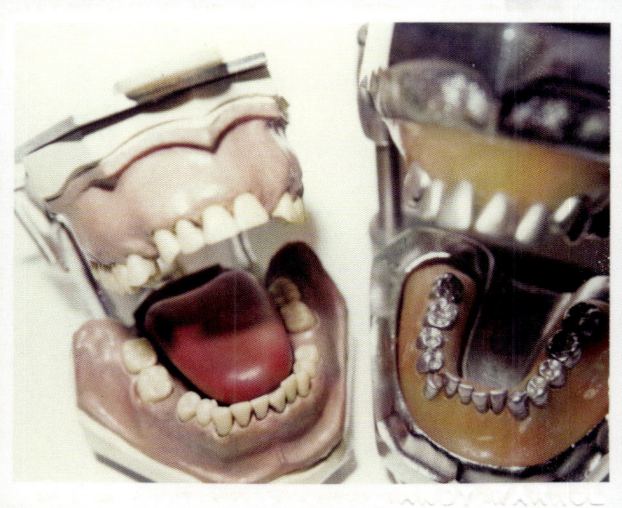

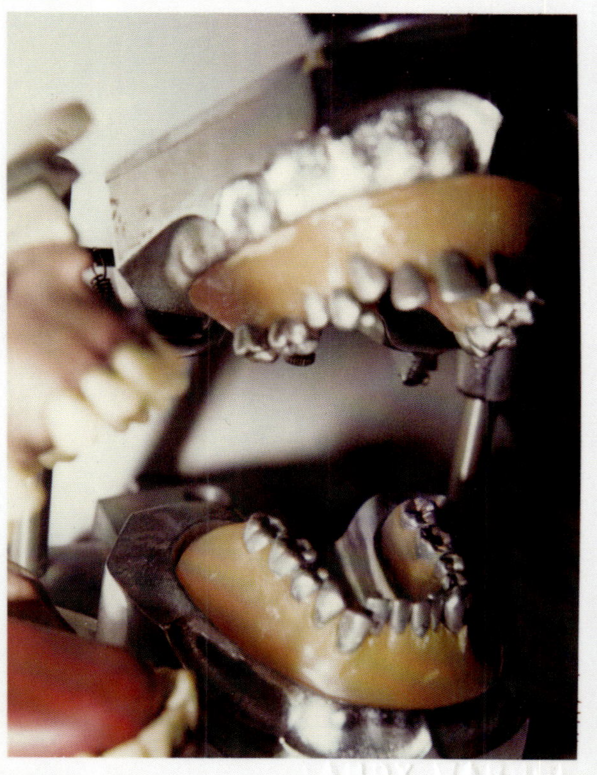

Andy Warhol, *Dental Molds* (two Polaroids), 1982–83

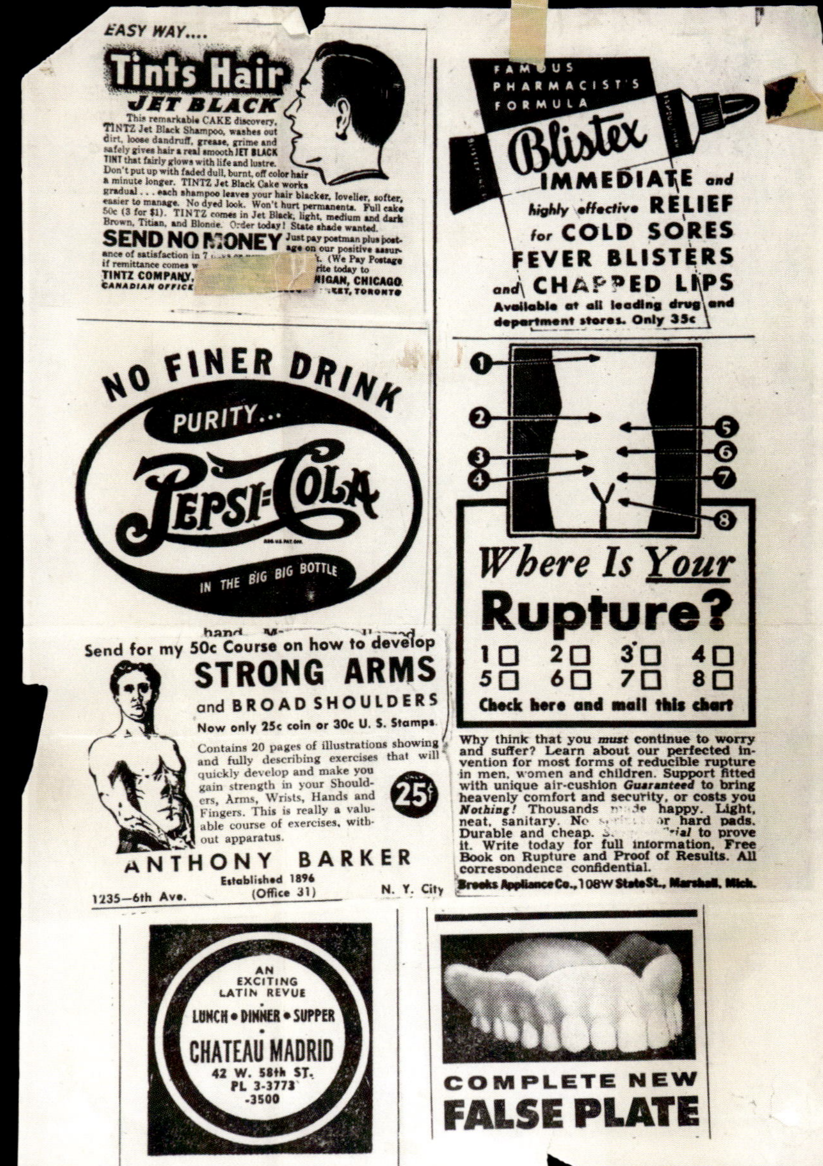

Andy Warhol, *Photostat (Advertisement Collage)*, ca. 1961, which includes
source imagery for *False Plate*, ca. 1961

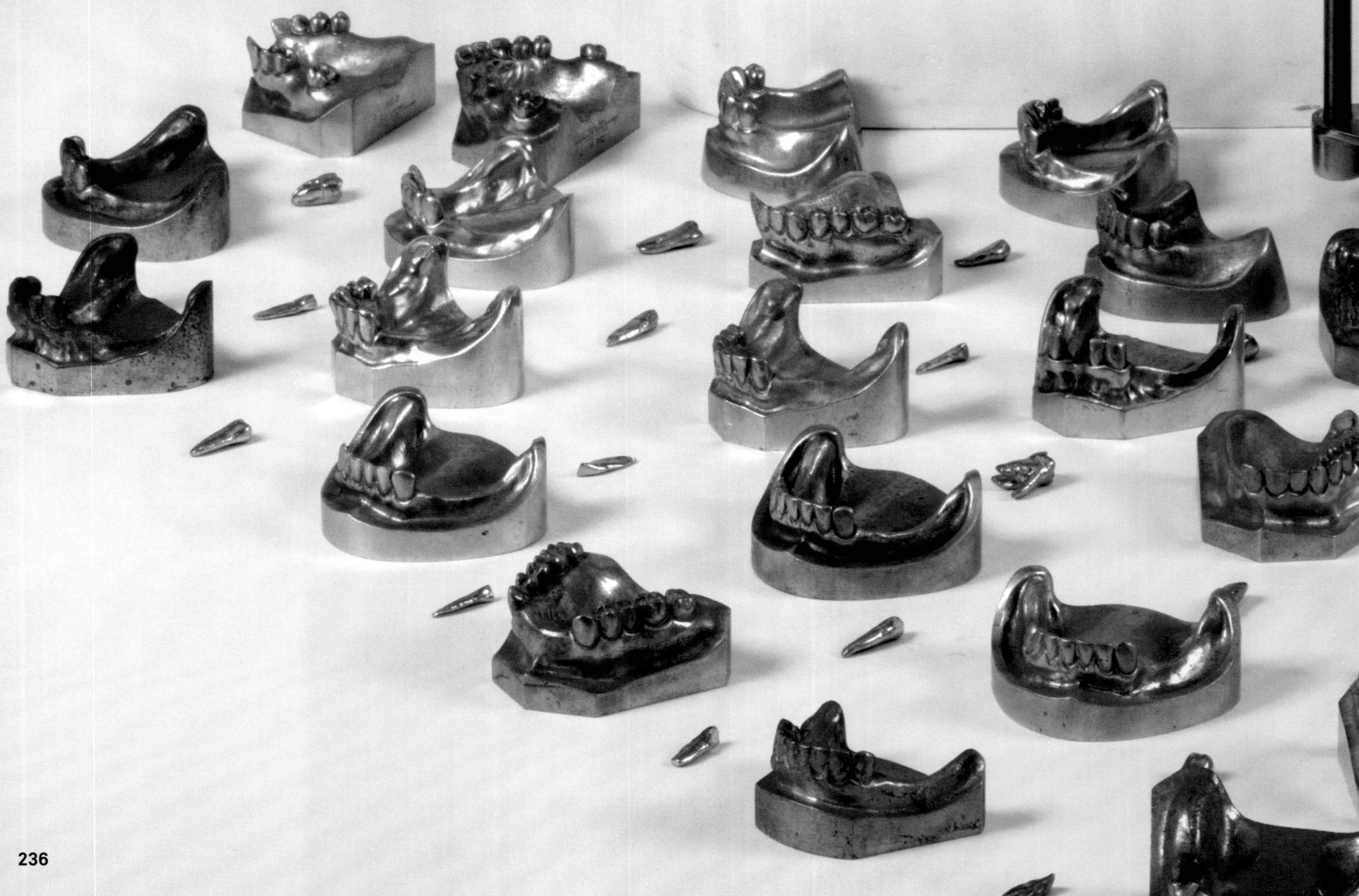

Warhol's collection of dental molds and models, ca. 1982–85

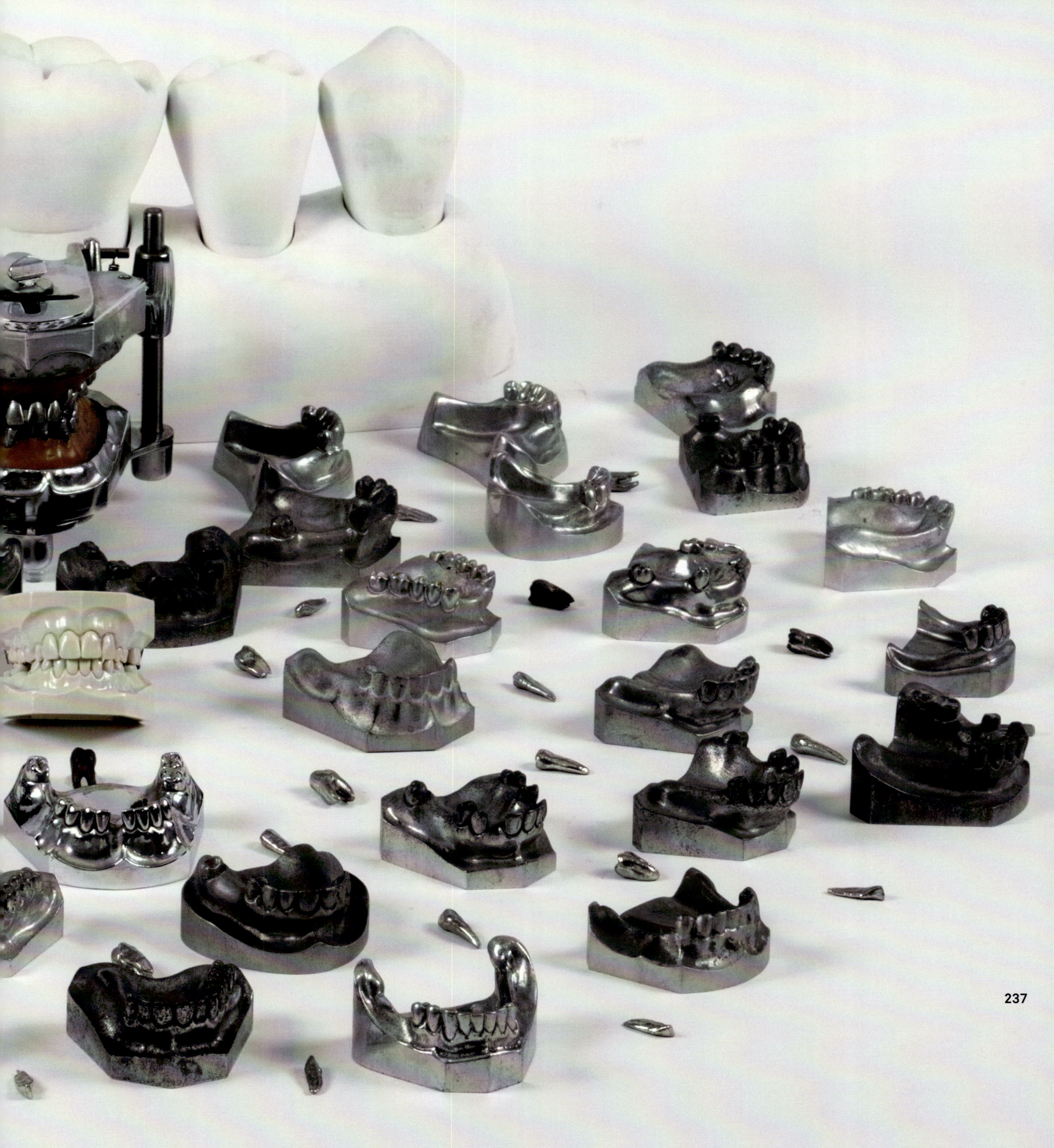

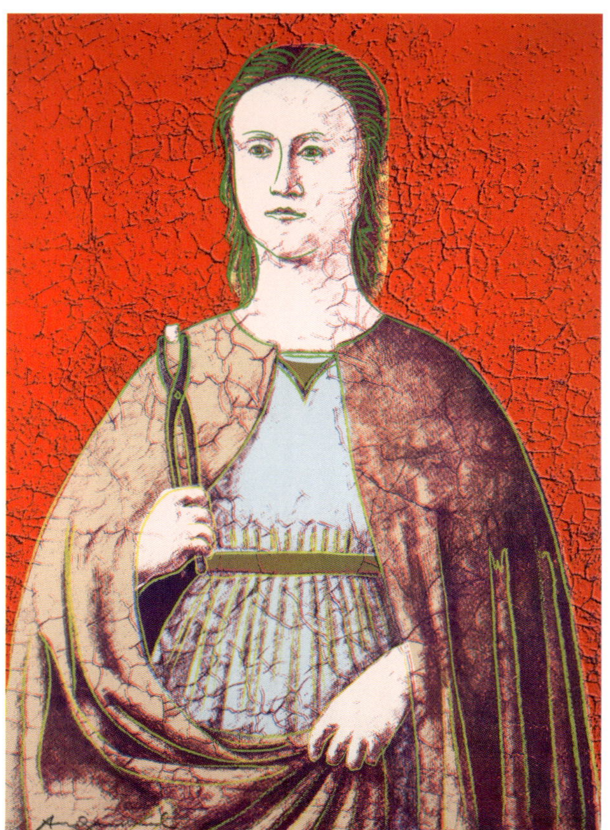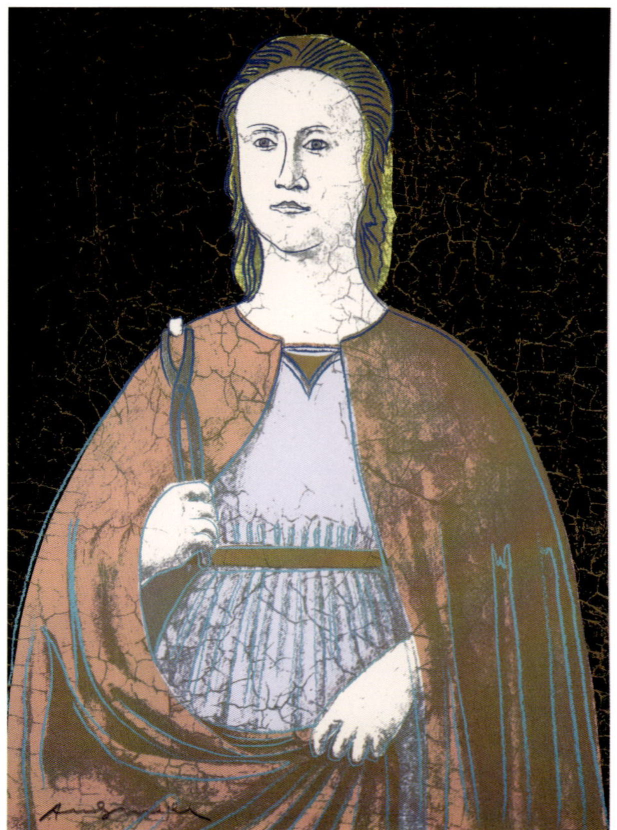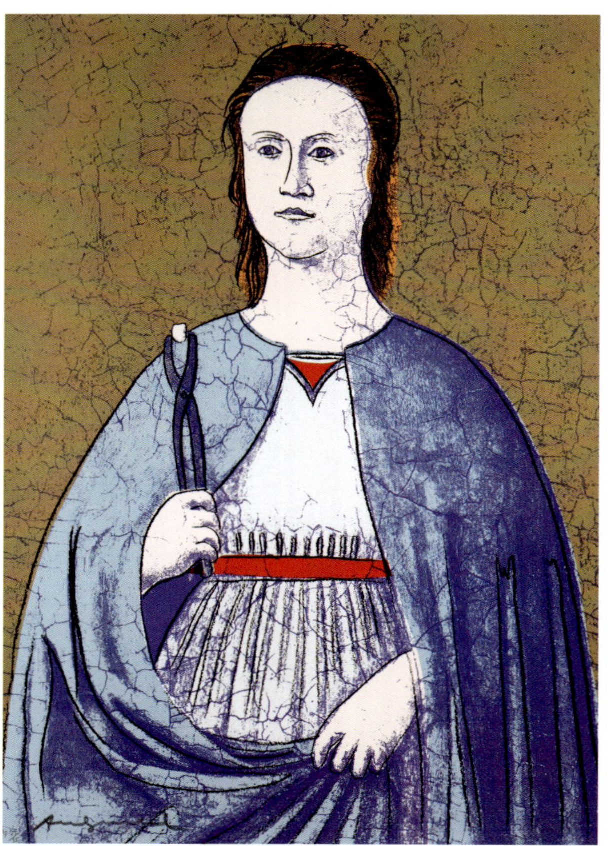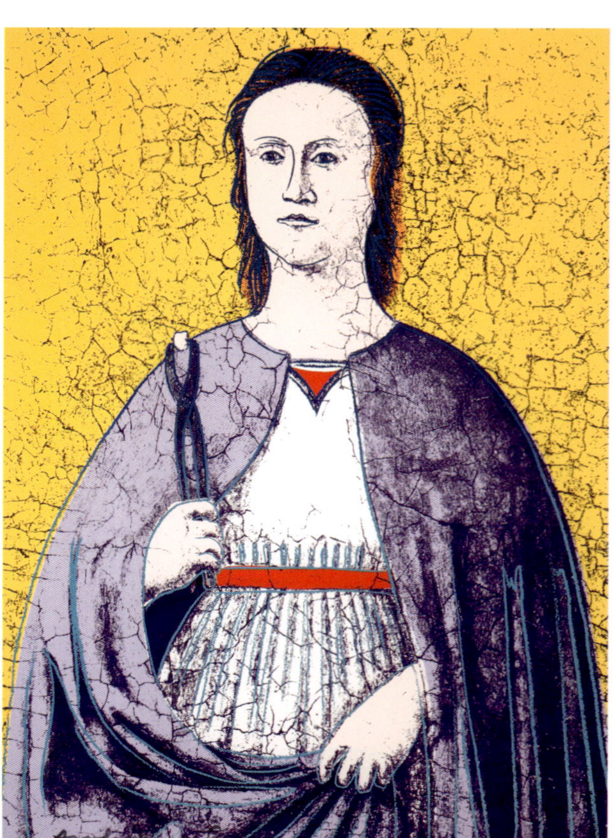

Andy Warhol, *Saint Apollonia*, 1984

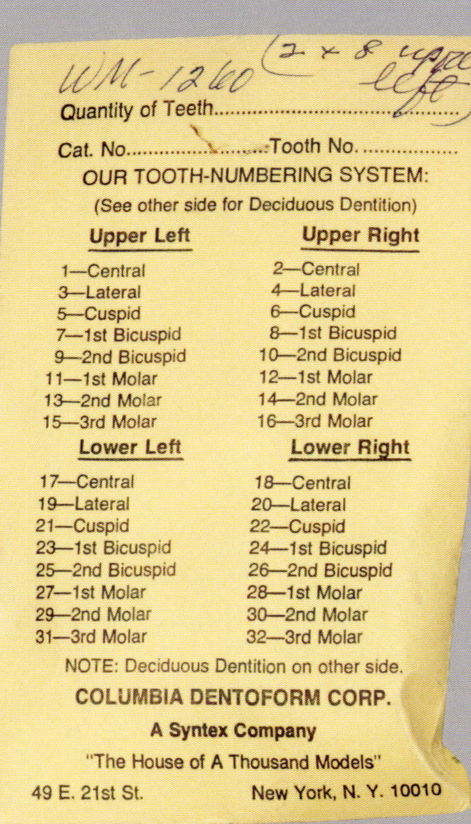

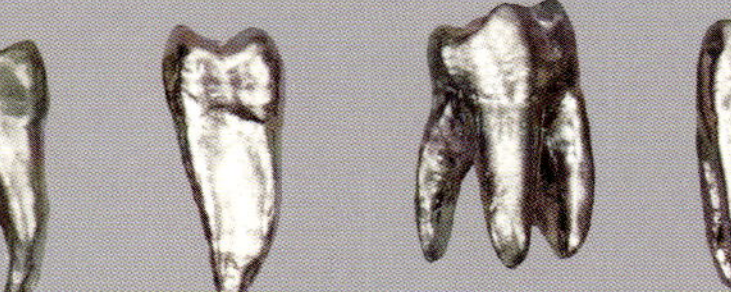

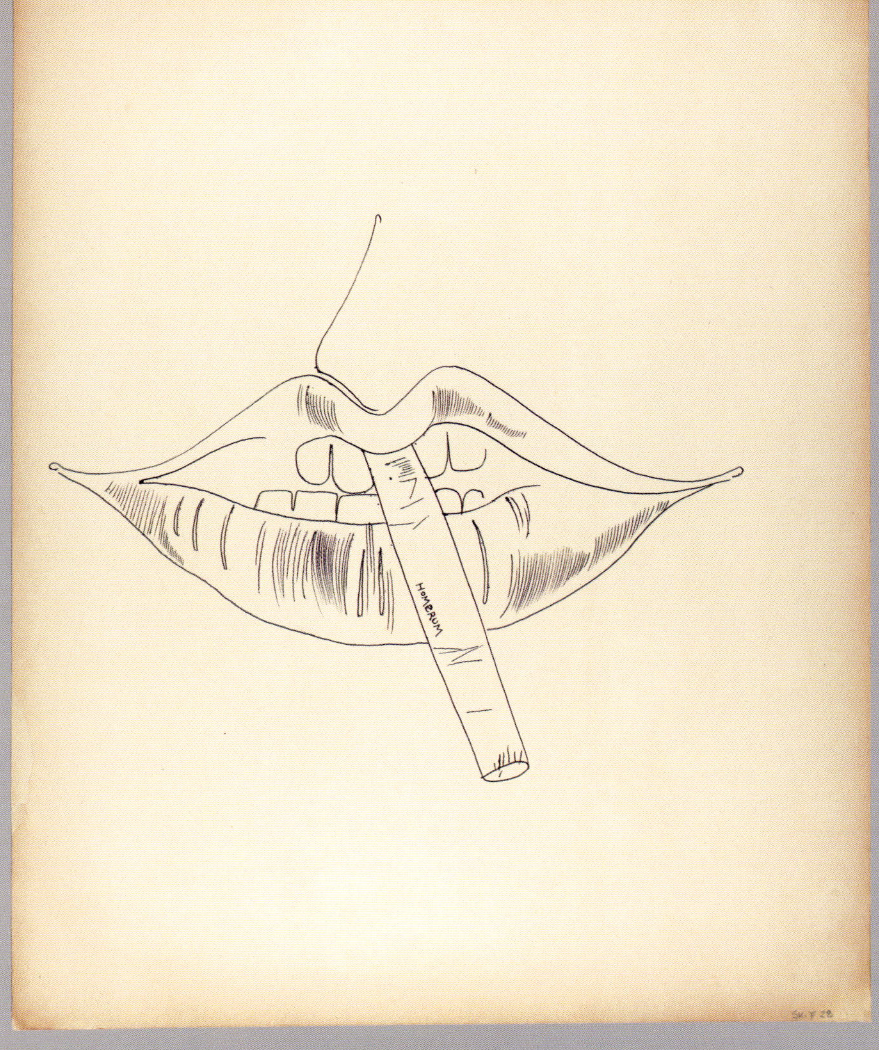

Dental models from Columbia Dentoform Corp., ca. 1982

Andy Warhol, *Lips and "Home Rum" Cigarette*,
drawing in sketchbook, 1950s

The alternative press of the 1960s, popularly known as the underground press, covered the entire range of issues and themes of this vibrant and turbulent era. Free speech and freedom of expression struggled to blossom after being stifled by the repressive depths of the Cold War 1950s and took up the challenges issued by the Beat poets. Violent conflict frequently erupted over racial segregation, the morality and legality of the United States' military involvement in Vietnam and Cambodia, the use of psychedelic drugs, sexual orientation, and promiscuity. Real and would-be revolutionaries, poets, artists, cartoonists, and high-school students actively engaged in the publication of journals, pamphlets, and newspapers that reflected the values of the new counterculture. The Warhol Archive contains hundreds of these publications, attesting to the artist's far-reaching curiosity and engagement with journalism, history, and alternative views.

International and National

The underground press was international in scope. London was home to the satiric *Oz* (1963–73); the *International*

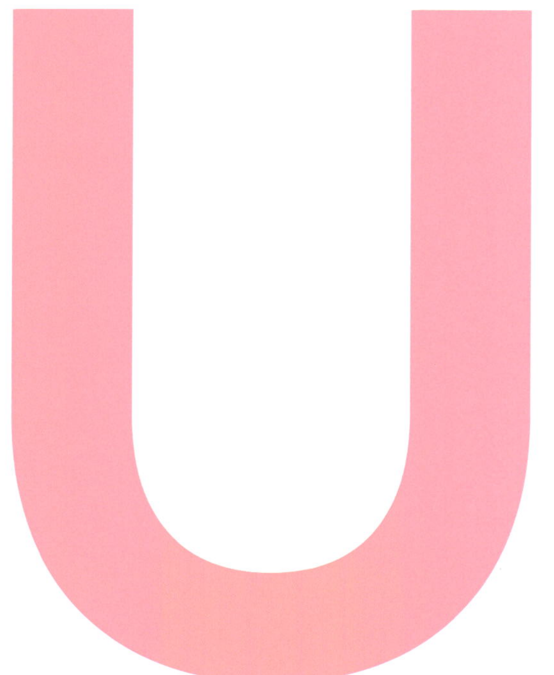

U
is for UNDERGROUND

This chapter features materials exhibited in *The 1960s Underground and Alternative Press*, in the Archives Study Center, July 26–October 15, 2000.

Times; and *Black Dwarf*, which covered politics. Paris had *Actuel*; Stockholm had *Puss*; Amsterdam had *Om*; and Buenos Aires, *Eco Contemporáneo*. *Hotcha* was published in Zurich and gave rise to *Gorps Underground Comix* in 1969, which included work by the Swiss brothers Anton and Peter Suter, Robert Crumb, and others. Most of the papers in the United States were members of the Underground Press Syndicate (UPS), founded in 1966 by Walter Bowart and Allen Katzman of the *East Village Other*. By mid-1969 the organization included about five hundred papers, printing between two and four million copies. UPS helped its members share articles and provided legal assistance in its many battles against censorship.

In Seattle, the alternative newspaper of note was the *Helix*. Predating it was the *Eclectic*, one of the high-school papers, done in mimeographed form. California was one of the most active alternative-publishing states. Los Angeles had several papers, including *Open City* and *Free Press*. The *Free Press* began its life as the *Faire Free Press*, published on the occasion of the Renaissance Pleasure Faire in Los Angeles in 1964. It had the look of a days-of-yore broadside, but the actual content differed. Articles truly of the moment included one on a local cinema recently ordered closed for screening Kenneth Anger's *Scorpio Rising* and another on Joan Baez's refusal to pay Vietnam-bound taxes. The *Free Press* would become one of the most enduring and lucid of the alternative papers. The Bay Area was also home to several papers, the *Berkeley Barb*, *Berkeley Tribe*, and *Oracle* among them. The circulation of the *Barb* grew to eighty-five thousand by July 1969. It was editorially opposed to the violence occurring in the nation, while the *Tribe* urged readers to fight. The *Oracle* was perhaps the most visually interesting of all of the papers, with psychedelic artwork by Rick Griffin, who designed many of the well-known posters and albums for the San Francisco music scene.

In Texas, the offices of Houston's *Space City* were bombed, and the Austin *Rag* was censored by its printers, who put black boxes over offending content. *Dallas Notes* was published and edited by Stoney Burns. Burns was arrested dozens of times, the first soon after he published a story about a congressman who was arrested for drunk driving after he hit a car full of soldiers. Burns was sentenced to ten years in prison for a minor drug charge denounced by the American Civil Liberties Union.

The *Fifth Estate* was the primary alternative publication in Detroit, which also had the *Sun*, edited by artist Gary Grimshaw and poet John Sinclair. Previously, Sinclair had produced *Guerilla* in his Artists' Workshop. His *Poem for Warner Stringfellow*, about a Detroit police lieutenant who harassed him for years, was published in the second issue of *Other Scenes*. The first issue of the *Sun* (April 1967) includes an interview with avant-garde jazz musician Sun Ra and discusses the alleged effects of smoking banana peels. Sinclair established the White Panther Party and hoped to unite the energy of rock music (mainly that of Detroit's MC-5) with political and cultural revolution. William Leach, a Black Panther writer for Detroit's *Inner City Voices*, denounced his view.

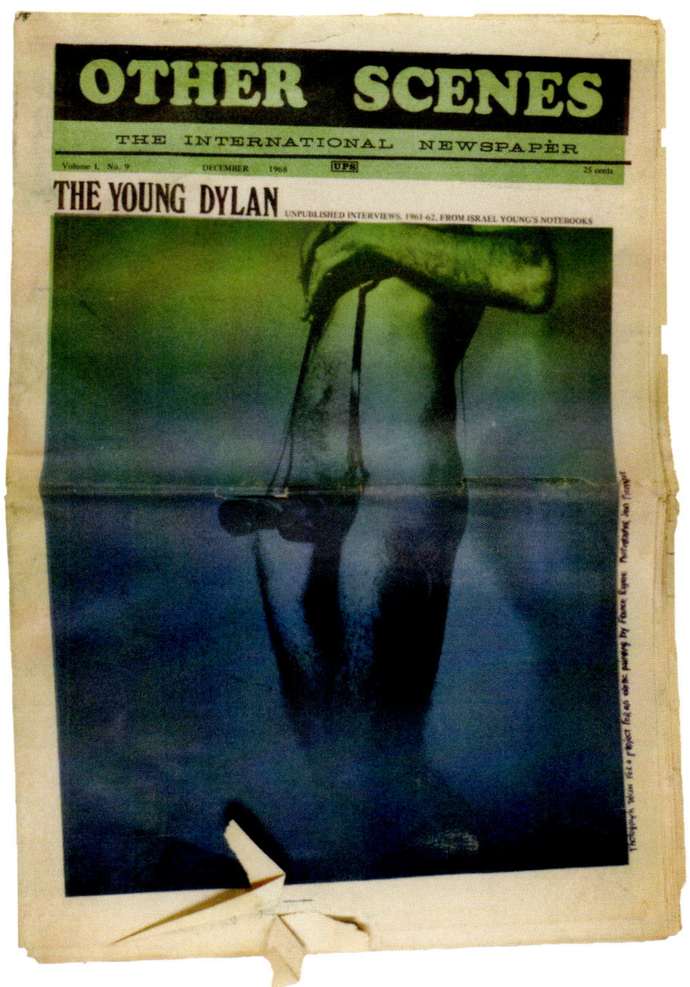

John Wilcock, *Other Scenes*, December 1968

The *Phoenix* covered the counterculture in Boston, while the *Avatar* published poetry and espoused the personal philosophy of its editor, Mel Lyman, the leader of a Roxbury cult-of-personality commune.

New York City

Perhaps the original underground paper was based in New York. In 1958 Paul Krassner, a satirical writer for *Mad* magazine, and Steve Allen, a comedian, founded the *Realist*. Krassner's no-holds-barred coverage, mostly satirical but also well-researched news reports, lampooned and intentionally offended every sensibility, including the radical left. It eventually claimed a circulation of one hundred thousand.

The largest alternative paper in New York City, the *East Village Other* (*EVO*), was more radical than the *Village Voice*, which itself had supplanted the *Villager* soon after it began publishing late in 1955. Walter Bowart, a native Oklahoman, had arrived in New York as a painter and tended bar at Stanley's, the East Village artist's hangout. He founded *EVO* during the newspaper strike of 1965. As a devotee of media theorist Marshall McLuhan, Bowart saw *EVO* more as a television show than as a newspaper.

EVO's news editor, youthful veteran journalist John Wilcock, an expatriate Briton, wrote a column titled "Other Scenes." When Bowart refused to print a story about Andy Warhol's film *Chelsea Girls* (1966), Wilcock left to freelance his column, and he continued to write travel guides for Arthur Frommer. While living near Los Angeles in 1967, he collaborated with the staff of the *LA Free Press* to produce a small six-page newsletter edition of *Other Scenes*, with a New York City mailing address. Several issues were published from Los Angeles, and others followed Wilcock's travel-writing itinerary. Soon the newsletter became a New York–based international underground newspaper, and then adopted a magazine format. In 1969 Wilcock was one of four cofounders of *Interview* magazine, along with Andy Warhol.

Fact was a quarterly journal with satirical commentary about society and politics, notable for being sued by Barry Goldwater for the issue titled "The Unconscious of a Conservative: A Special Issue on the Mind of Barry Goldwater."[1] The publisher, Ralph Ginzburg, was also responsible for *Avant Garde* and *Eros*, a fairly tame erotic magazine. In 1966 the Supreme Court, encouraged by a Catholic priest, upheld Ginzburg's five-year prison sentence for publishing and distributing obscene materials in *Eros*. Opinions expressed in the magazine would have run afoul of the Catholic Church, such as the stance that women should have extramarital affairs when they are sexually dissatisfied with their husbands.

Rat debuted on March 4, 1968, and soon printed insider reports of the student takeover of buildings at Columbia University, revealing the university's involvement in war-related research. The following year, the paper became a battleground for feminism. Most of the underground papers were male-dominated, but the *Rat* had a significant number of female staff. They objected to much of the editorial content and published their own issue that included Robin Morgan's "Goodbye to All That," a diatribe against male domination of the counterculture. Within a few months, *Rat* was theirs, and more feminist papers were launched in Berkeley; Washington, DC; and elsewhere.

Sexuality

Many of the underground papers were losing advertising and circulation money by 1969 and began to rely financially on personal sex ads that mainstream papers refused to print. Other publishers went further, publishing papers exclusively about sex.

Al Goldstein founded *Screw* magazine in 1968. Its appearance was largely responsible for the decline of the other papers, and its circulation quickly rose to 150,000. Unafraid of censorship, *Screw* soon inspired competitors who tried to follow Goldstein's example. The *East Village Other* began to publish *Kiss* in April 1969. It sought to be beautiful and sensual, but a former *EVO* staff member later recalled it as cheap, ugly porn. *Pleasure* was published independently by *Rat*'s business manager and enjoyed success as "the newspaper you can read with one hand." It appealed to all sexual proclivities. Another title in this grouping was the *New York Review of Sex and Politics*.

In 1947 *Vice Versa* was published in Los Angeles by a woman under the pseudonym of Lisa Ben. Each copy was of necessity individually hand-typed, stapled, and distributed face-to-face in lesbian bars. This underground activity marked the birth of the lesbian and gay press in America. Also in Los Angeles, in 1953, the Mattachine Society produced the premier issue of *ONE*, the first publication for gay men. It won a landmark Supreme Court case in 1958, which reversed two lower courts' decisions that its content—the subject of homosexuality—was obscene. This followed several years of intense scrutiny and interrogation of the magazine and its writers by the FBI.

The Stonewall Riots in Greenwich Village in June 1969, a watershed event in the gay-rights movement in America, were covered derisively by the mainstream press. Dick Leitsch, writing in the *Los Angeles Advocate*, the first gay newspaper in America, founded in 1967, covered the events objectively and in detail. Six months after Stonewall, *GAY*, published by *Screw*'s Al Goldstein, appeared on newsstands in New York. It was edited by Lige Clark and Jack Nicols, the authors of *Screw*'s gay column, "Homosexual Citizen," which had reported Stonewall with enthusiasm.

In 1967 the launch of *Rolling Stone* magazine revolutionized music journalism. Baron Wolman, who had been *Rolling Stone*'s first chief photographer, drew on his experience documenting musical culture to start the fashion magazine *Rags*, in 1970. Unlike *Vogue* and *Harper's Bazaar*, which reviewed the latest high-fashion styles, *Rags* focused instead on the newest street styles and countercultural aesthetics. The issue in the Archives, issue 3 from August 1970, has an illustrated article about the Cockettes, a psychedelic theater troupe that included gay and trans members and frequently challenged gender/sexuality norms.[2] The art director of *Rags* was Barbara Kruger, who later came to prominence as an artist in the 1980s.

Artists' Newspapers

At the same time, artists also began to publish visual broadsides and newspapers describing their interests. One of the first was by Fluxus, a loosely organized avant-garde collective under the leadership of George Maciunas. Based in New York City, the group included many artists in Europe and Japan in its performances, writings, and object making. The newspaper *cc Valise eTRanglE* was the third issue of *cc V TRE*, which began as a collage of random clippings assembled in the form of a newspaper.

Newspaper, a large-format paper, appeared in April 1969 and included two reproductions of works by William Blake, the nineteenth-century British visionary, as well as contemporary artists Richard Avedon, Sheyla Baykal, Peter Hujar, Gerald Laing, and Lucas Samaras, among others.[3] Each artist had a full page or two, each of which was devoted to a single work. The paper lasted for at least two issues. *Ark* is similar in style to *Newspaper* but predates it by one year. Little-known works by Andy Warhol are reproduced in one of the issues: high-contrast photographic images of an unsalted butter wrapper and what appears to be a Venus-brand sponge. Other artists in this issue include William T. Wiley, Peter Hujar, Diane Arbus, Joseph Raffael, Richard Avedon, and John Chamberlain.

Poetry, Journals, and Artists' Books

From pop-ups to flip-books, from poetry to song, and from rallying cry to manifesto, the underground press materials collected by Warhol pushed boundaries with audacious content and innovative design. The majority of the works were written, edited, or published by artists and creative friends of Warhol.

The history of independent publishing of poetry and art in America began with Walt Whitman's *Leaves of Grass* in 1855. Almost a century later, the inexpensive mimeograph and offset-lithograph printing processes sparked a revolution in self-published and small-press works, a literary underground with centers in New York and San Francisco, and some in more remote locations. Avant-garde artists and writers were able to experiment as never before with new printed forms of expression and could reach audiences beyond poetry readings and art galleries without the formalities and censorship of the publishing business. After Whitman, the lineage continued with the "little magazines" and the work of William Carlos Williams and Gertrude Stein, whose *Geography and*

Plays (1922) was republished in 1968 by Dick Higgins's Something Else Press.

Higgins scored numerous performances as a member of Fluxus who embraced their aesthetic of celebrating the commonplace. In his work with Fluxus, he experienced the breakdown of traditional art forms, which led him to invent the term "intermedia" to describe work done between various media. He likely started Something Else out of dissatisfaction with the sporadic nature of Fluxus's publishing ventures. Something Else publications include Diter Rot's *246 Little Clouds* (1968), which reproduces Rot's handwritten text superimposed over photographic collages of his drawings. Emmett Williams's *Sweethearts* (1967) is a book-length, one-word ("sweethearts") poem in flip-book form, in which the letters disperse from page to page to create the illusion of motion. The cover of *Sweethearts* is taken from Marcel Duchamp's *Fluttering Hearts*, a magazine cover from 1936.

Something Else also published Great Bear Pamphlets, including Al Hansen's *Incomplete Requiem for W. C. Fields* and *Manifestos*, both in 1966. Hansen's *Requiem* is dedicated to his daughter, Bibbe, who appeared in Warhol's films and is the mother of Beck, the contemporary pop musician. *Manifestos* presents sixteen declarations of purpose, mostly by Fluxus artists but also including Allan Kaprow, creator of Happenings, and John Giorno, star of Warhol's first film, *Sleep*, in 1963.

Among other Fluxus-related works in the Archive are two printed scrolls: *Yam Festival Newspaper*, edited by George Brecht and Robert Watts for their proto-Fluxus Yam Festival in May 1963, and *Fluxus Preview Review*. Many of the Fluxus artists had previously studied with composer John Cage at the New School in Greenwich Village. Cage's interest in chance operations and other nontraditional approaches to music, including his famous "silent" work for piano, *4'33"*, derived from his experiences at North Carolina's celebrated tiny hotbed of the avant-garde, Black Mountain College. Warhol's friend Tommy Jackson studied typography there in 1951 and mailed a copy of his *Babel 1* to Warhol in New York. The letterpress publication consists of a single twenty-line poem, "La Vie Entre les Gadarenes (Infinity First, Not Last)," by Jonathan Williams, also a Black Mountain attendee and himself the publisher of the *Jargon Society*.

Another Black Mountain artist, Ray Johnson, coedited the *Sinking Bear* in New York with Billy Linich (Billy Name) and Soren Agenoux. All three were close acquaintances of Warhol. They collected statements and thoughts from their daily lives, broke them into fragments, and interspersed them throughout the small mimeographed pages in a stream-of-consciousness manner. The *Sinking Bear* was created as an alternative to the *Floating Bear*, another mimeo journal on which Linich also worked. Edited by LeRoi Jones (later Amiri Baraka) and Diane di Prima, it functioned as a vehicle for the quick delivery of new works. Among the poets and artists it published were Wallace Berman, Robert Creeley, Ray Johnson, Charles Olson (the founder of Black Mountain), and Philip Whalen. Painter Alfred Leslie designed the humorous cover of issue 28 of the *Floating Bear* (1963). Jones and di Prima were arrested for obscenity for issue 9 in 1961, but the trial jury failed to reach a verdict.

Also in frequent trouble with the law was Ed Sanders, an important link between the Beats and the hippies, and editor/publisher of *Fuck You: A Magazine of the Arts*, which appeared in thirteen multihued mimeo issues from 1962 to 1965. His Fuck You Press also published W. H. Auden's *The Platonic Blow*, a bootleg version of the final *Cantos* of Ezra Pound, and work by Carol Bergé, Ted Berrigan, William S. Burroughs, Allen Ginsberg, D. H. Lawrence, and Ron Padgett, among others. A frame from Warhol's notorious film *Couch* provided the cover art for the February/March 1965 issue. These publications and others were available from Sanders's Peace Eye bookstore. Sanders was also a cofounder of the Fugs, the resident satirical folk-rock band of the Lower East Side, and published *The Fugs Songbook*. Throughout all of his work, Sanders maintained an attitude of radical exploration and expression regarding sex and drugs. Lawrence Ferlinghetti's City Lights published Sanders's *Poem from Jail* in 1963, originally written on thirty sheets of toilet paper while he was incarcerated for protesting nuclear weapons in 1961. He was arrested for obscenity in 1966 when police who were called to investigate a break-in at the Peace Eye confiscated his publications, including titles such as *Fuck God in the Ass* and the *Marijuana Newsletter*. In 1967 Sanders graced the cover of *Life* magazine.

Ted Berrigan's New York mimeo, *C: A Journal of Poetry*, commenced publication in 1963. Berrigan had come to New York from Tulsa, Oklahoma, with three creative friends, Joe Brainard, Dick Gallup, and Ron Padgett, all of whom had previously worked with him on Padgett's *White Dove Review*. C Press published works by William S. Burroughs, Joe Ceravolo, Alice Notley, and others, as well as Berrigan and Padgett. Berrigan and Padgett also produced collaborative works, while Brainard frequently provided the cover art. Warhol designed two covers of *C* including, for the Edwin Denby issue, silkscreened images of Denby and Gerard Malanga, Warhol's assistant, kissing. Malanga's poetry frequently appeared in Lita Hornick's *Kulchur*, Anne Waldman and Lewis Warsh's *Angel Hair*, and Waldman's *World*, which was part of the Poetry Project at St. Mark's Church.

The books by Rot and Williams are artists' books, a medium that began to be an important means of expression by 1950, though the form can be traced back to William Blake's works of the 1780s to the 1820s. In the 1960s Ed Ruscha produced several important contemporary artists' books, including *Gas Station* (1963) and *Royal Road Test* (1967).[4] The latter, a hilarious deadpan parody of official scientific and government reports, documents the destruction of an old typewriter as it is hurled from the window of a Buick LeSabre speeding down a desert highway. Warhol's contribution to the medium was his *Index (Book)* of the same year, which features many pop-ups used in children's books (see "I is for Illusions").

NOTES

1. "The Unconscious of a Conservative: A Special Issue on the Mind of Barry Goldwater," *Fact* 1, no. 5 (September/October 1964).

2. The Archive contains artistically decorated correspondence to Warhol from the Cockettes.

3. *Newspaper* was also titled *No Word Newspaper*.

4. Per Blake Gopnik, Ruscha gave *Gas Station* as a gift to Warhol during a visit to the Factory in 1963, and Warhol loved the book.

Additional research for this chapter was provided by Brianna Treleven.

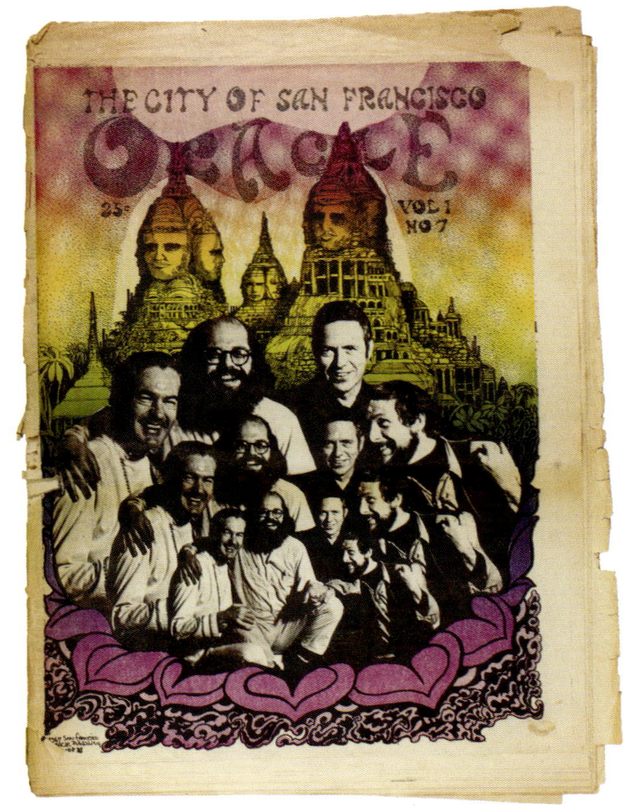

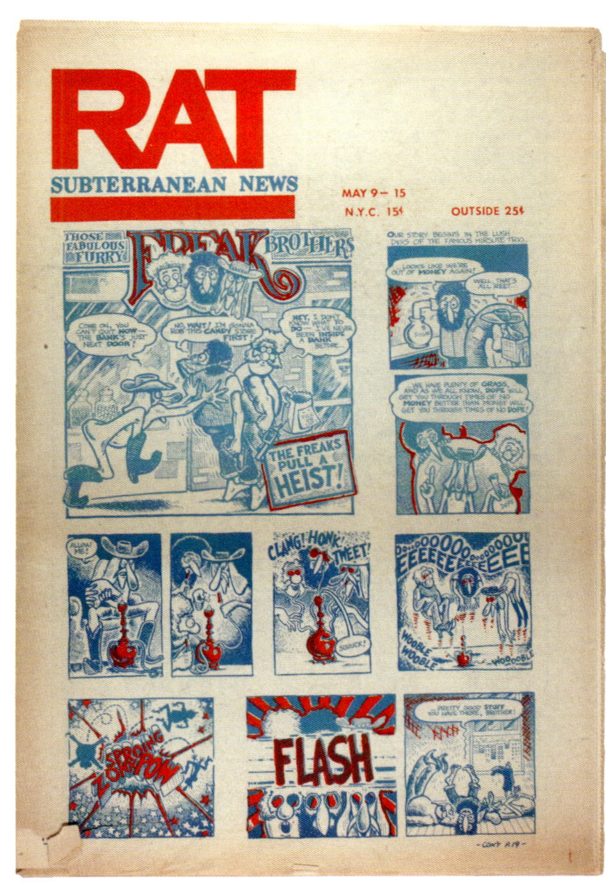

Oracle, April 1967

Rat, May 9–15, 1969

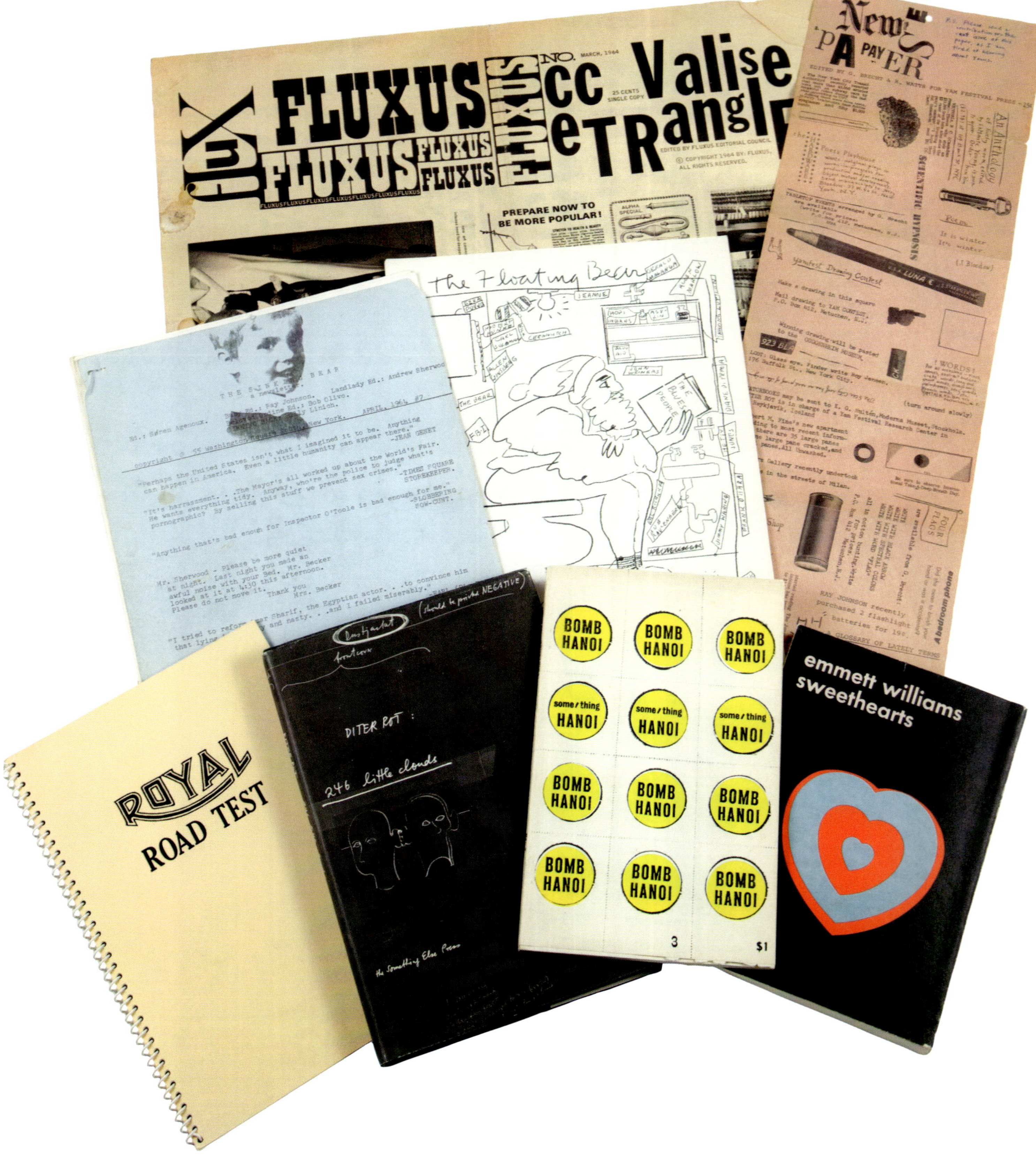

246

Eight of Warhol's many artists' books and publications, 1963–68

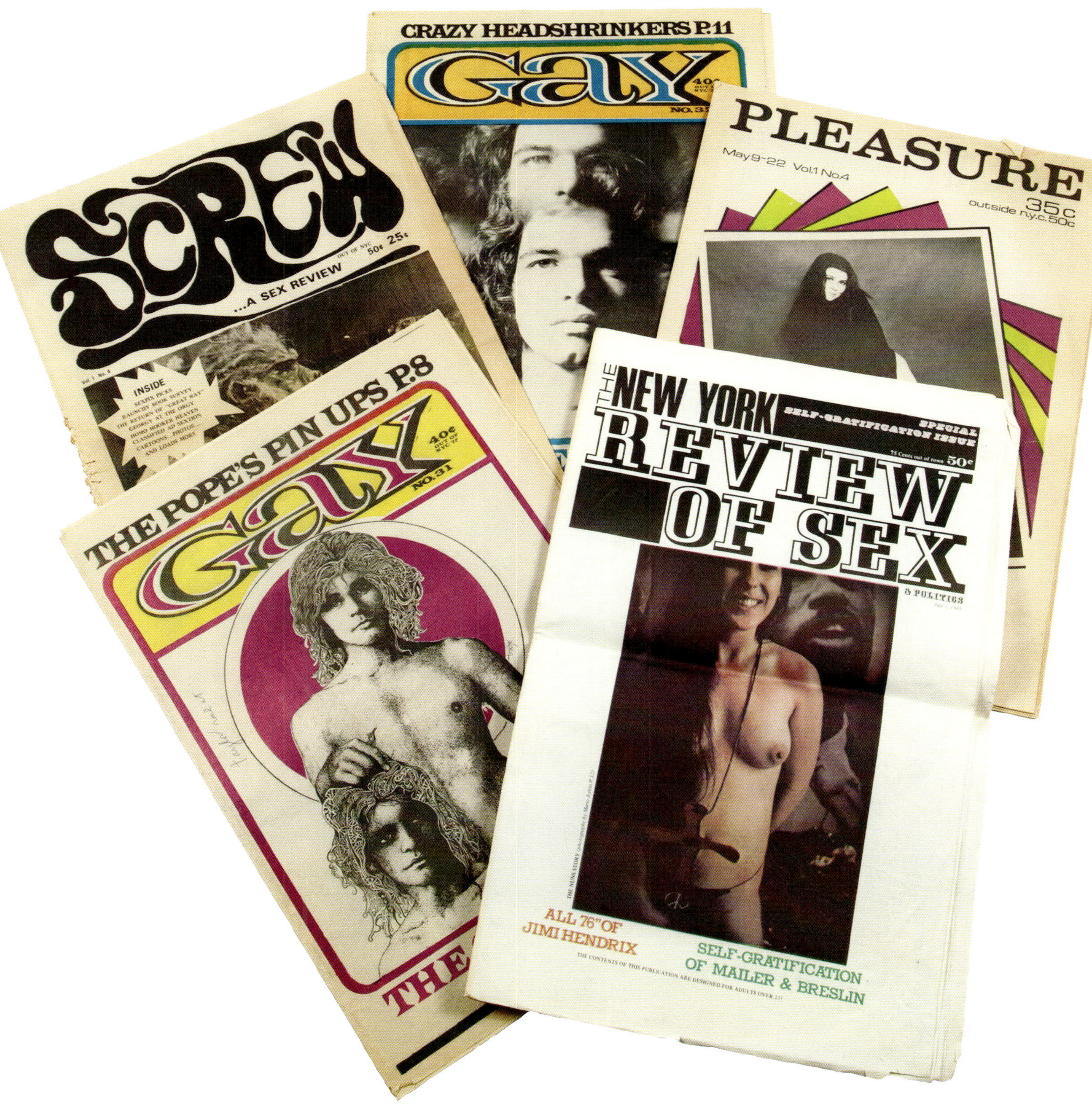

Five of Warhol's many underground publications related to sexuality, 1969–70

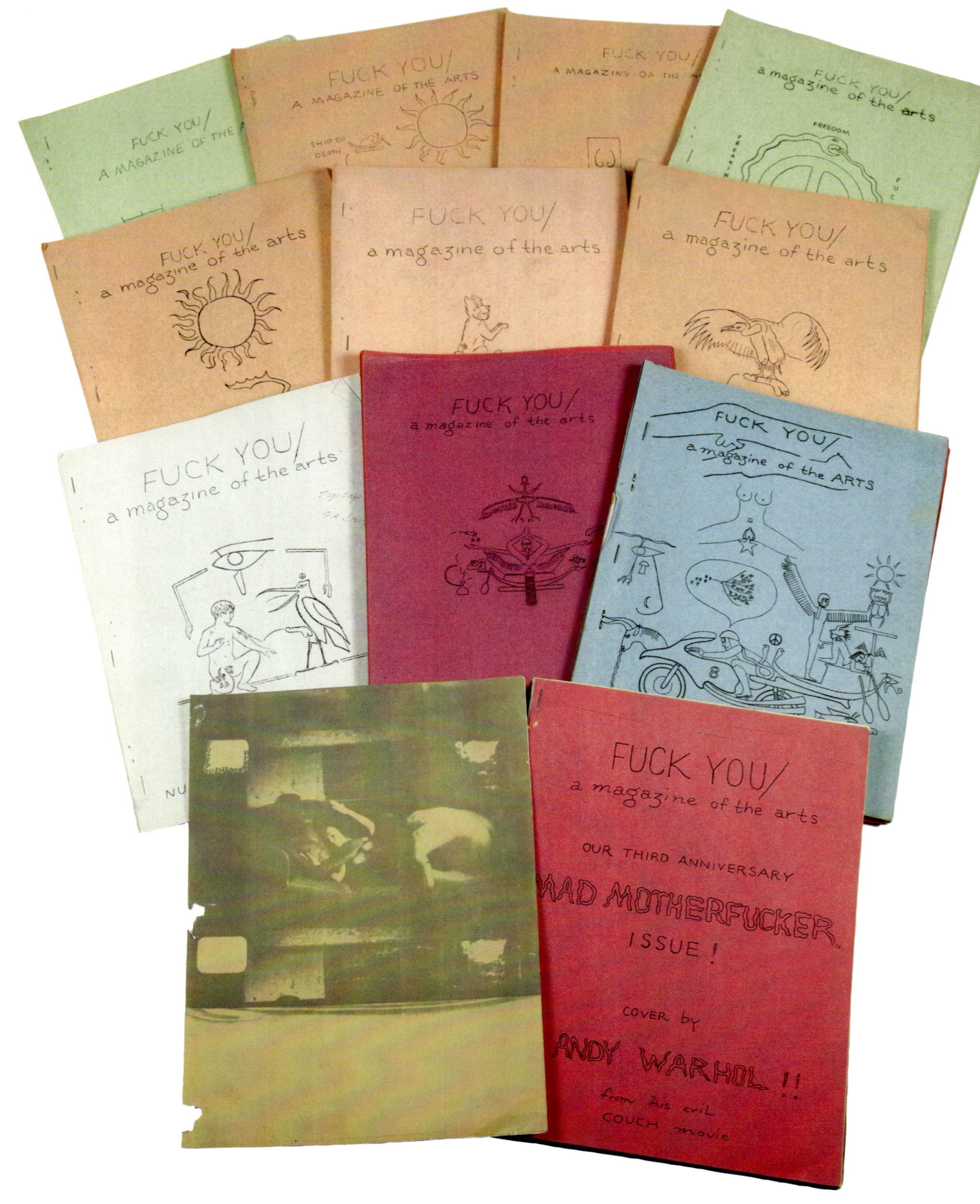

Warhol's collection of *Fuck You: A Magazine of the Arts*, 1962–65

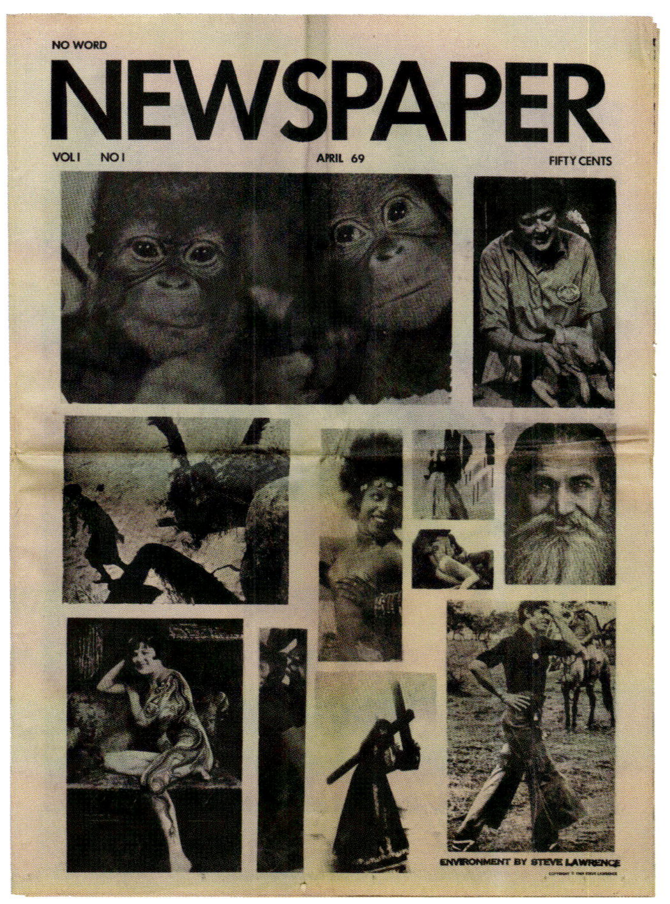

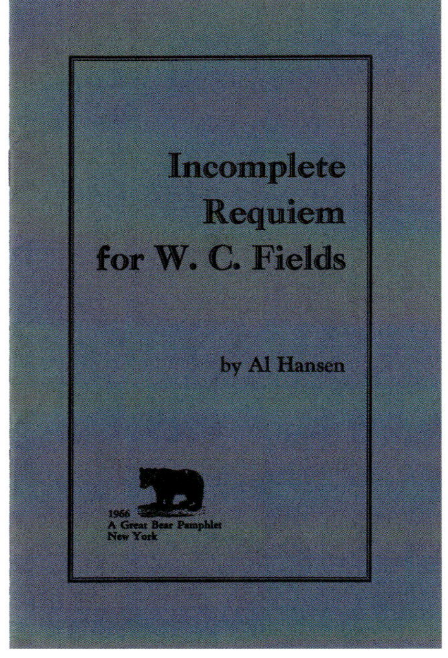

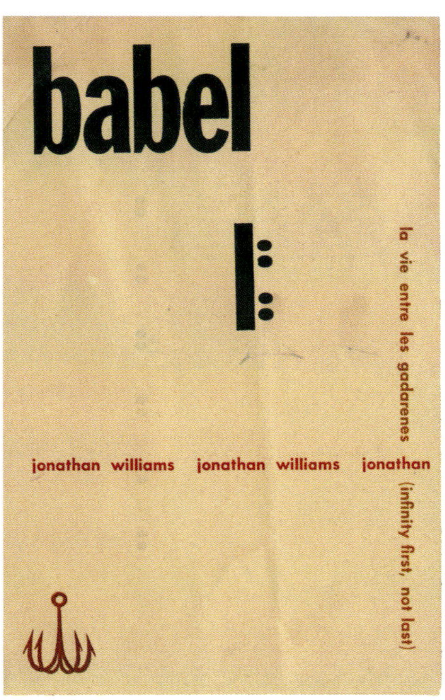

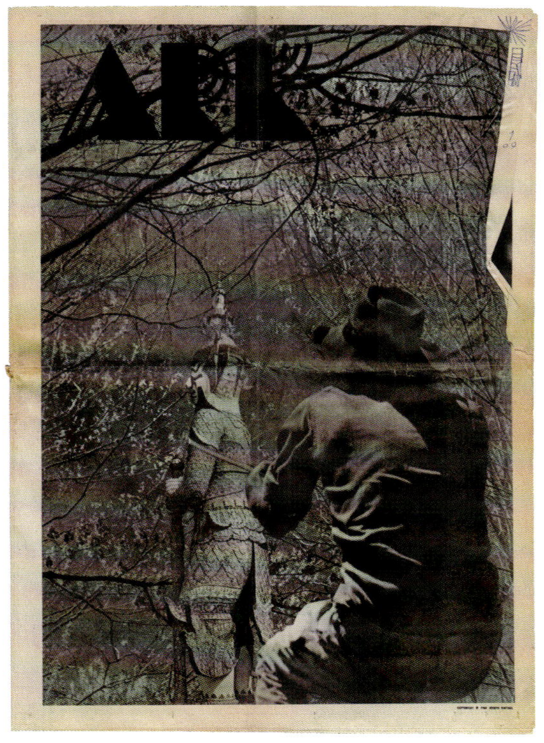

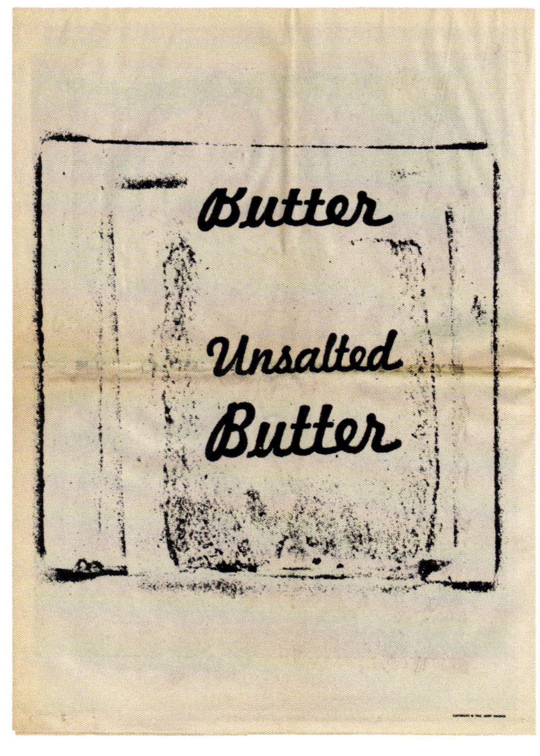

Steve Lawrence, *Newspaper*, April 1969

Steve Lawrence, *Ark*, 1968

Al Hansen, *Incomplete Requiem for W. C. Fields*, 1966

Babel I, 1951

Andy Warhol, *"Unsalted Butter,"* 1968, artwork created for *Ark* magazine

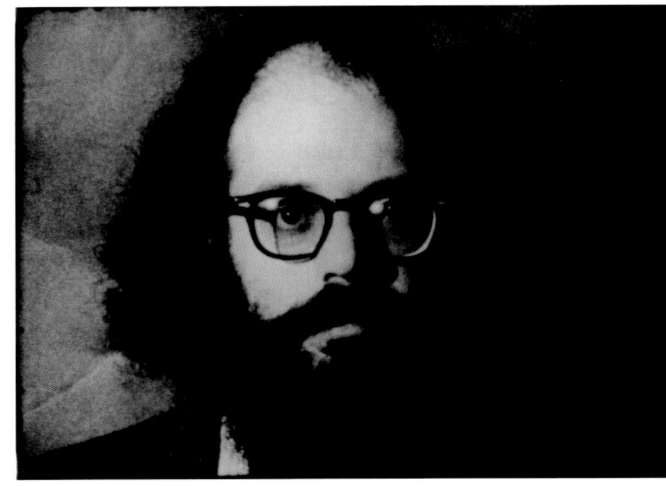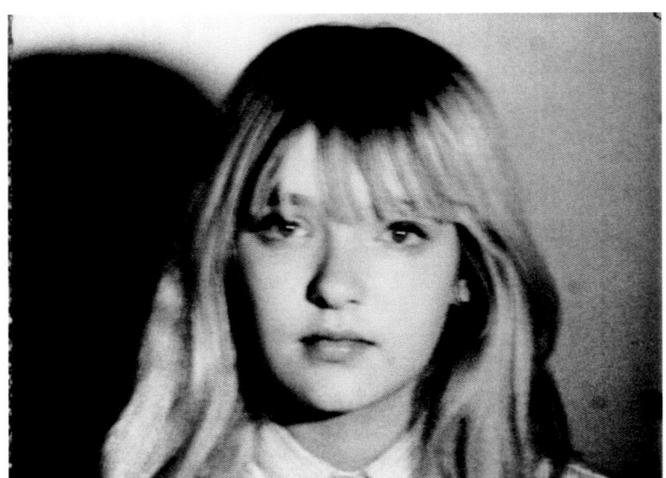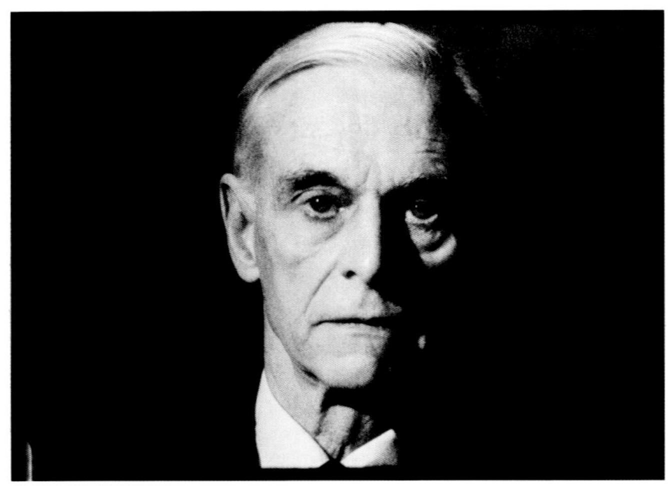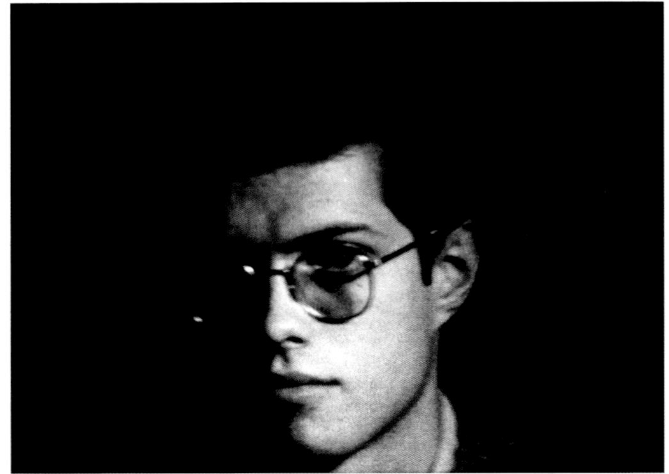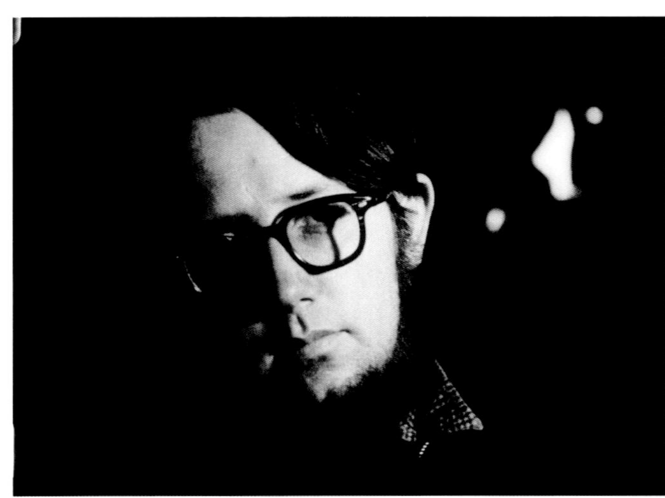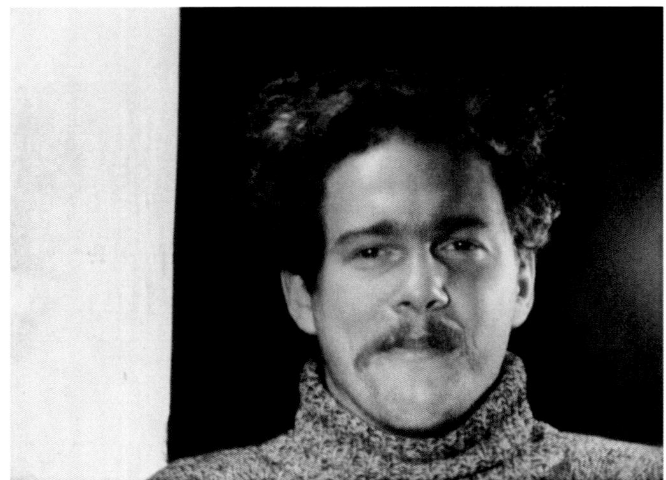

Andy Warhol, (top) *Screen Test: Allen Ginsberg [ST115]*, 1966; *Screen Test: Bibbe Hansen [ST128]*, 1965; (middle) *Screen Test: Edwin Denby [ST75]*, 1964; *Screen Test: Ron Padgett [ST251]*, 1964; (bottom) *Screen Test: Ted Berrigan [ST22]*, 1964; *Screen Test: Ed Sanders [ST294]*, 1964

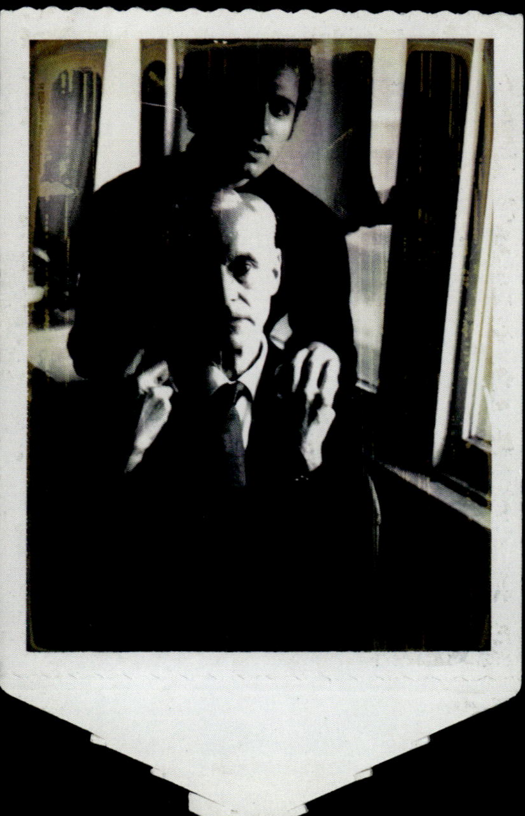

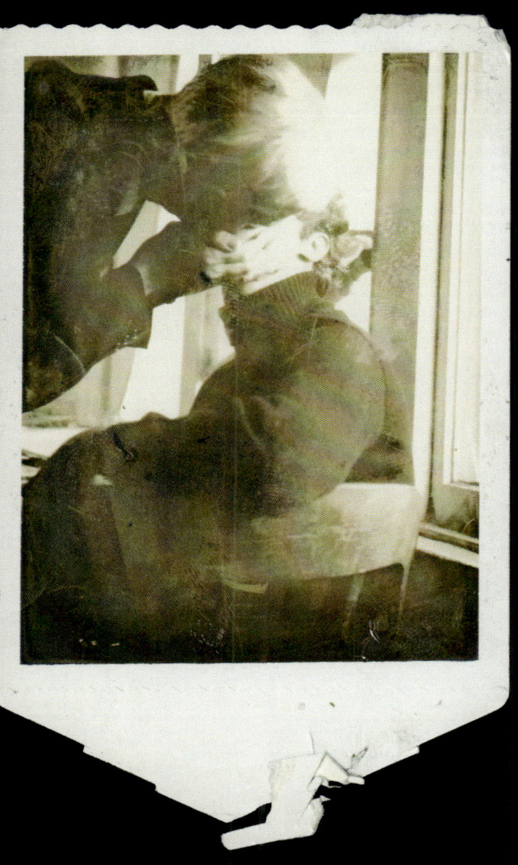

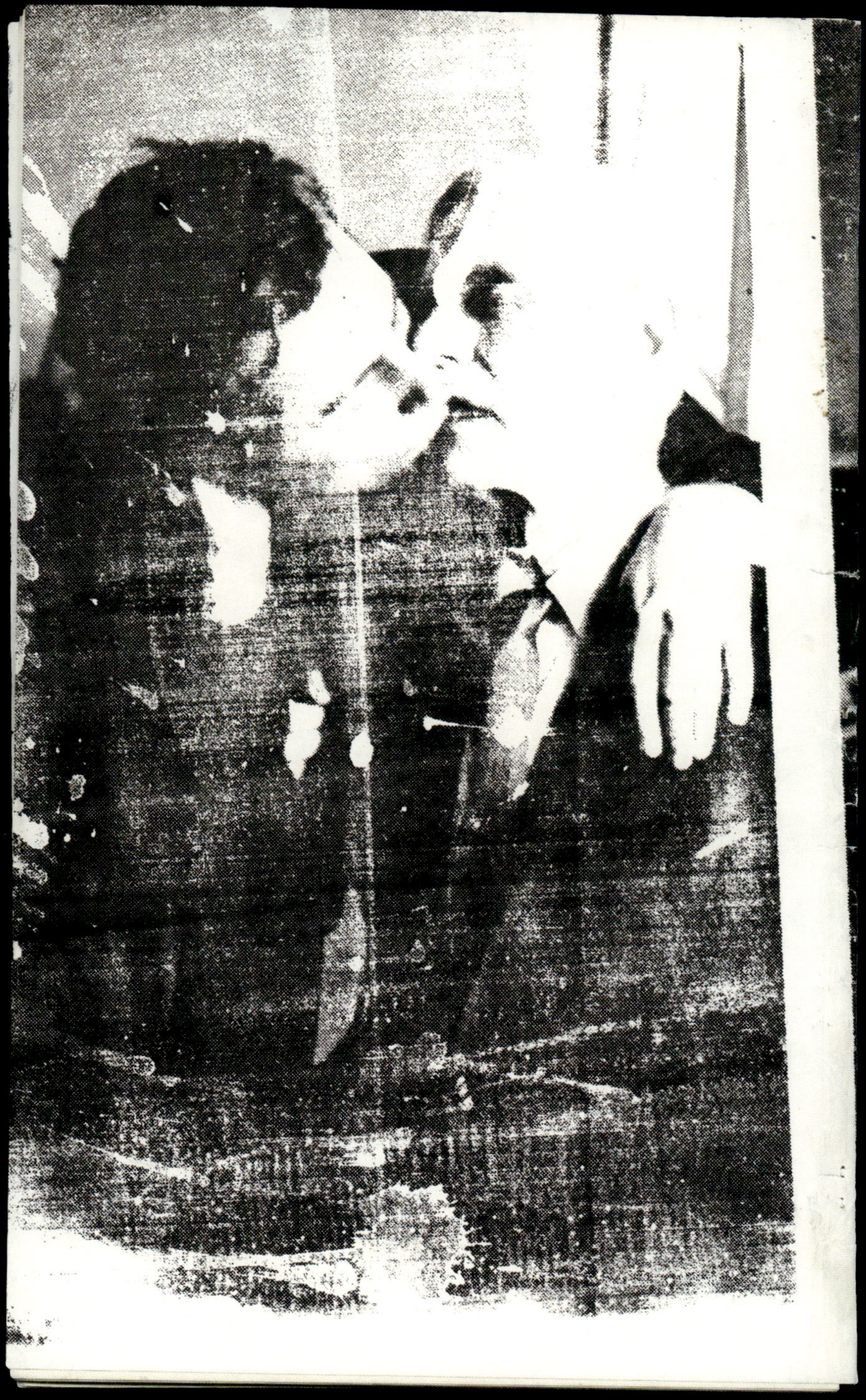

Andy Warhol, *Gerard Malanga and Edwin Denby* (two Polaroids), 1963

Warhol photograph on cover of *C: A Journal of Poetry*, September 1963

251

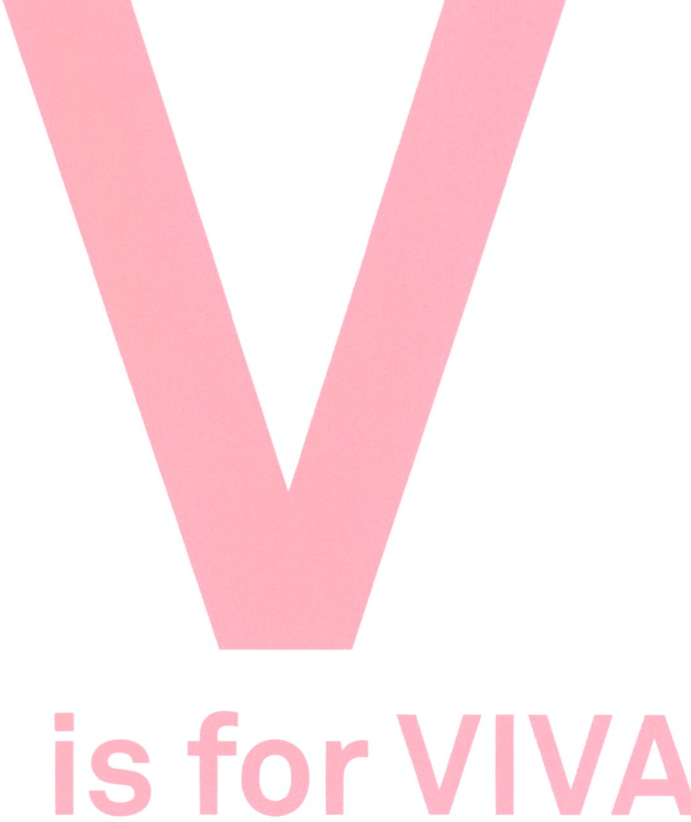

"I thought she had all the qualities—plus the magic—
that could make a woman into a true star."[1] Janet Susan
Mary Hoffmann (also known as Susan Hoffmann and later
Viva) developed her wit and verbal skills in convent
schools and at the Sorbonne; they matched her physical
beauty, which earned her a brief career as a fashion
model. Both talents were celebrated in Warhol's films.
Viva was very likely his greatest comic actress. Starting
with her first role in Warhol's *Loves of Ondine* (1967), she
went on to star in five more Warhol films and worked with
directors John Schlesinger (*Midnight Cowboy* [1969]),
Agnès Varda (*Lion's Love* [1969]), Woody Allen (*Play It
Again, Sam* [1972]), and Wim Wenders (*The State of Things*
[1982]), among others. In 1970 her acting career was
honored by the Cinémathèque Française in Paris.

Although Viva had met Warhol briefly a few times previously, she began working with him after she chanced
upon him at a party given by Betsey Johnson, who was
engaged to John Cale at the time. Warhol recalled, "Maybe
it was hearing about our having so many girls in a movie
for a change that gave Viva the idea that she'd like to be in
our next one, because she cornered me at Betsey's party

is for VIVA

This chapter features newly discovered and catalogued
archival materials related to Viva, as well as materials
that were on display in the exhibition *Viva Viva!!!*, in the
Archives Study Center, May 3–July 23, 2000.

and asked me if she could be. This was only the third time I'd ever had a conversation with Viva. She'd come over and introduced herself to me at some art opening around '63, when she was living with a photographer and trying to become a fashion illustrator. I don't know what we talked about then—art, maybe (she knew a lot of artists)."[2] Warhol appreciated attractive people with ideas: "She had a face that was so striking…and I was impressed with all the references she kept dropping to literature and politics."[3]

Viva described that same meeting with Warhol: "Andy was at this party. I screwed up my courage and asked him if I could make a movie. I thought I'd make a few Warhol movies and become a big Hollywood star—starting at the bottom, with Andy my first step toward my ultimate, incredible glory and fame and riches and stardom. Andy said, 'If you want to take off your blouse, you can make a movie tomorrow. If you don't want to take it off, you can make another one.' I was afraid if I didn't take off my blouse that very next day he would forget me completely. So I put these round Band-Aids on my nipples and took off my blouse. They loved me; they all thought it was an incredible acting technique they were seeing."[4] The film, shot in August 1967, was *Loves of Ondine*, one of Warhol's "sexploitation" features designed to capitalize on the relaxing censorship code. That month she also acted in *Bike Boy*, a sex comedy, which featured Joe Spencer, a member of a motorcycle gang who attempts to fit in with the sophisticated and savvy Warhol Superstars. *The Nude Restaurant*, filmed in New York in October 1967 at the Mad Hatter restaurant, was another in the series of Warhol's sex comedies, again featuring Viva, this time with Taylor Mead (see "M is for Mead").

Audiences were captivated by Viva, and her obvious intelligence was unusual for actors of the time. Warhol was so impressed with Viva that he took her along on a college lecture tour organized by the American Program Bureau. Warhol was not a great conversationalist, whereas he referred to Viva as "a talker." Her talents balanced Warhol's inadequacies, self-perceived or otherwise, and they became close on the tour. "We all loved Viva; we'd never seen anything like her, and from then on, it was just taken for granted that she'd be in whatever movie we did. She

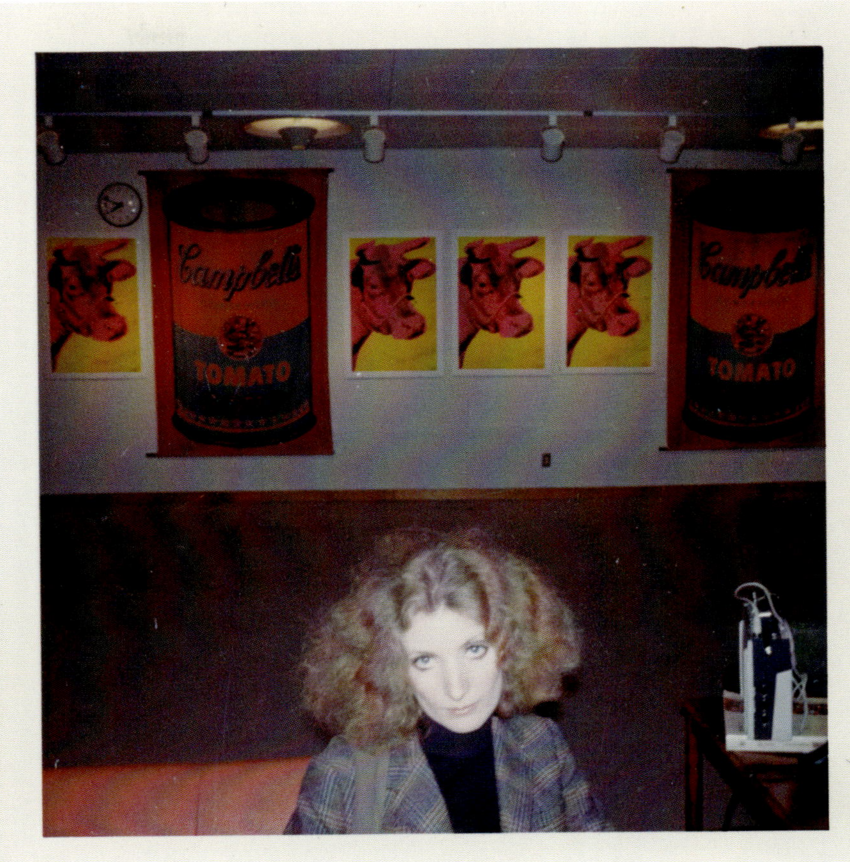

was funny, stylish, and photogenic—and she gave great interviews."[5] Mid-tour, because of his stage fright and discomfort with his physical appearance, Warhol sent Allen Midgette, one of the Superstars, to impersonate him. The charade caused a scandal when it was discovered, and Warhol was required by contract to complete the tour.

In January of 1968, Viva flew to Arizona with Warhol to film *Lonesome Cowboys*, a foray into the Western genre with a loose *Romeo and Juliet* theme. Their entourage consisted of almost twenty people, including costars Julian Burroughs (who was also in *The Nude Restaurant*), Joe Dallesandro, Eric Emerson, Tom Hompertz, Taylor Mead, Louis Waldon, and drag star Frances Francine, who played the sheriff. They filmed at Old Tucson, an old Hollywood movie set and theme park, while the tourists looked on.

253

Photographer unknown, *Viva with Andy Warhol's Art*, ca. 1968

They also shot at the dude ranch where the whole crew was staying. Viva exhibited her religious upbringing by chanting hymns in Latin while trying to seduce Tom Hompertz. As a fellow Catholic, Warhol appreciated Viva's opinions on religion: "She would give us all long speeches about what was wrong with the Catholic Church—putting down every nun she'd ever known, every priest, every bishop, right up to the Pope—but she always claimed that there was one good thing about being brought up strict: when you finally did go out and do the things you'd never been allowed to do, they thrilled you a lot more."[6] The local officials in Oracle, Arizona, were not so entertained by the invasion of New Yorkers and called the FBI to keep tabs on the Warhol production.[7]

In early February, shortly after returning to New York from Tucson, Warhol, escorted by Paul Morrissey and Viva, attended his first major non-US retrospective at the Moderna Museet in Stockholm. "Those months between August…and February…Viva and I were inseparable—we made movies, gave lectures, and did interviews and photography sittings together. She seemed like the ultimate superstar, the one we'd always been hoping to find: very intelligent, but also good at saying the most outrageous things with a straight-on beautiful gaze and that weary voice of hers."[8]

Setting up another rather unusual scenario for Viva and the Superstars, Morrissey and Warhol traveled in May 1968 to La Jolla, California, to shoot a surfing movie with a cast that couldn't surf. *San Diego Surf* featured Joe Dallesandro, Nawana Davis, Eric Emerson, Tom Hompertz (the only actual surfer in the cast), Taylor Mead, Ingrid Superstar, Viva, Louis Waldon, and others. A Warholian takeoff on the beach-party films that were popular at the time, its loose narrative concerns a hilarious but unhappily married couple (Mead and Viva) with a baby who rent an extra beach house to a group of surfers.

Soon after they returned to New York from California, Viva telephoned Warhol and was in conversation with him when Valerie Solanas shot him in the chest on June 3, 1968 (see "Q is for Quick"). In the aftermath of the trauma, Viva visited Warhol's mother (who lived with him) almost every day and sent Warhol numerous letters and get-well cards in the hospital. While Warhol was hospitalized she appeared in John Schlesinger's *Midnight Cowboy*, which was being filmed in New York. To lift his spirits, Viva sent him postcards from her family home in the Thousand Islands and progress reports from the movie.

Warhol and Viva did not make a film together again after she married the filmmaker Michel Auder, with whom she had a daughter, Alexandra. Viva and Auder later divorced, and she had another daughter, the actress Gaby Hoffmann, with Anthony Herrera, in 1982. Viva has authored two books, *Superstar* (1970) and *The Baby* (1975), and has written for the *Village Voice* and other newspapers. She is also a painter. Warhol photographed Viva with Brigid Berlin (Brigid Polk) in 1981 during the former's pregnancy, but there are few mentions of their getting together and socializing during the 1970s and 1980s. Warhol recalls becoming sad while packing for a move out of 860 Broadway in 1984, finding old pictures of "Viva and twenty of us. Before I was shot. We really were the only freaks there."[9]

NOTES

1. Andy Warhol and Pat Hackett, *POPism: The Warhol Sixties* (Orlando, FL: Harcourt Brace Jovanovich, 1980), 266.

2. Ibid., 228.

3. Ibid., 229.

4. Viva in Jean Stein and George Plimpton, *Edie: American Girl* (New York: Grove Press, 1982), 220–21.

5. Warhol and Hackett, *POPism*, 231.

6. Ibid., 267.

7. A series of Ektachrome slides from the Archive were recently discovered and show Warhol, Viva, Taylor Mead, and others posing for the camera on the set of *Lonesome Cowboys*.

8. Warhol and Hackett, *POPism*, 267.

9. Andy Warhol and Pat Hackett, eds., *The Andy Warhol Diaries* (New York: Hachette Book Group, 1989), 592.

Additional research for this chapter was provided by Geralyn Huxley.

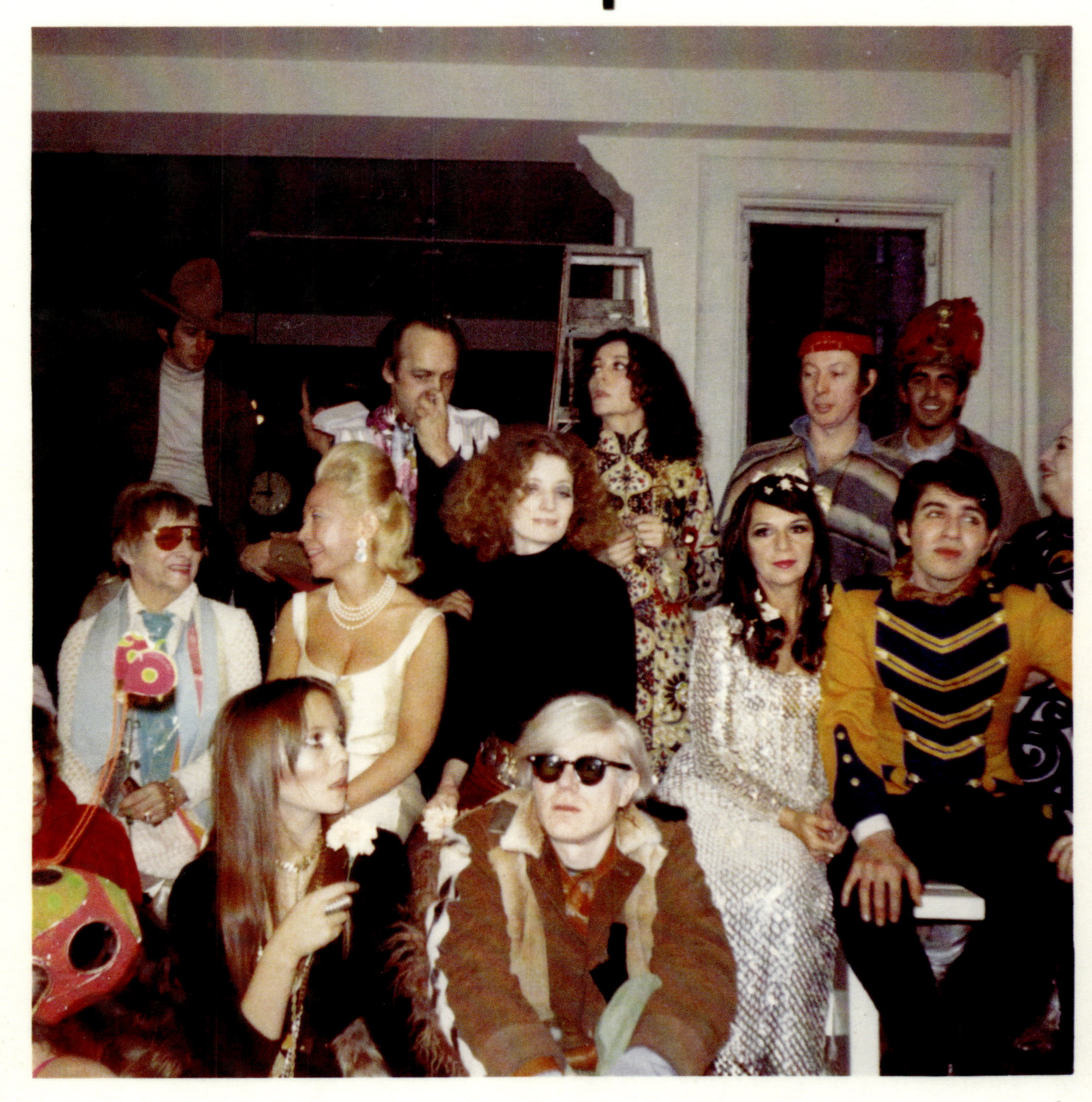

Photographer unknown, *Andy Warhol, Penelope Tree, Lita Hornick, Viva, Fred Hughes, and Ultra Violet*, 1968

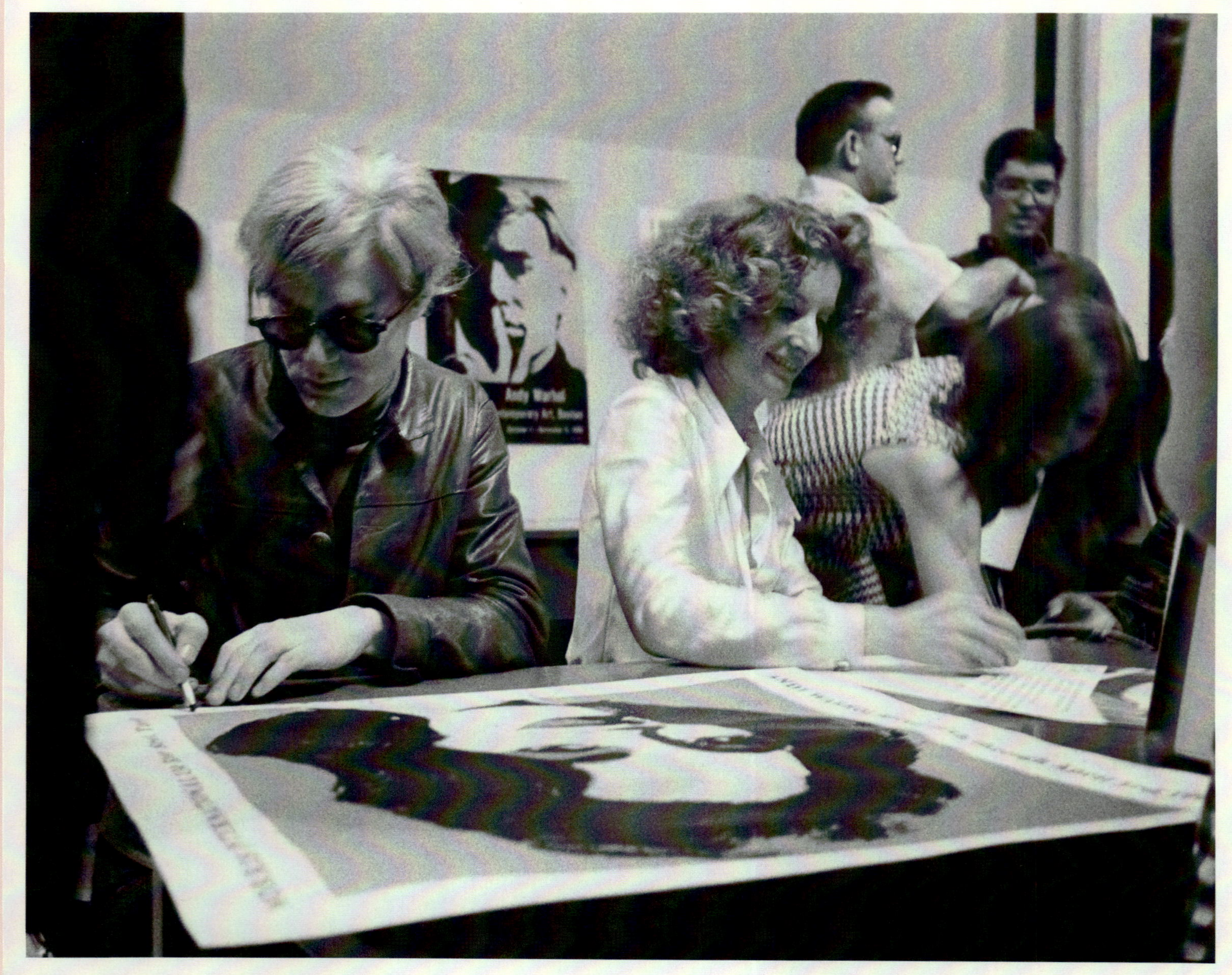

Hickey & Robertson, *Andy Warhol and Viva in Houston*, 1968

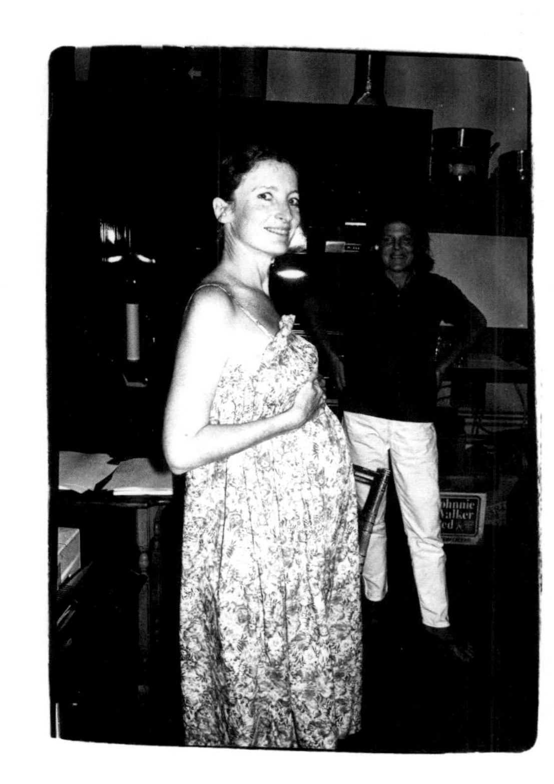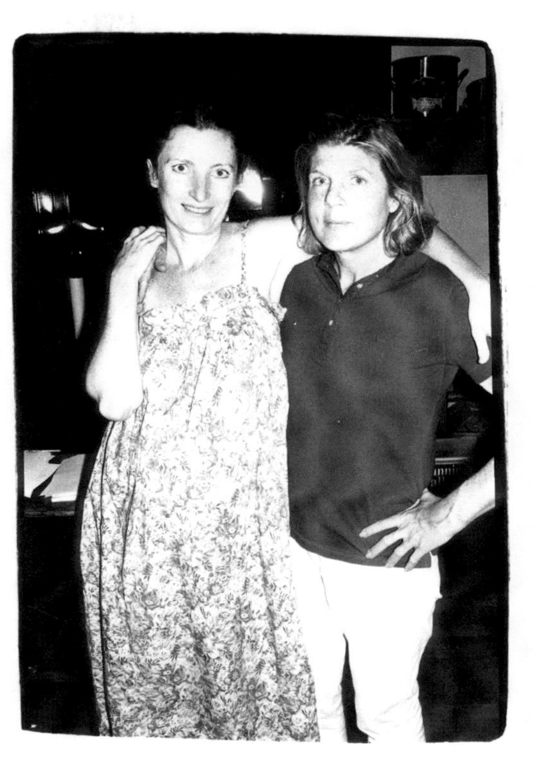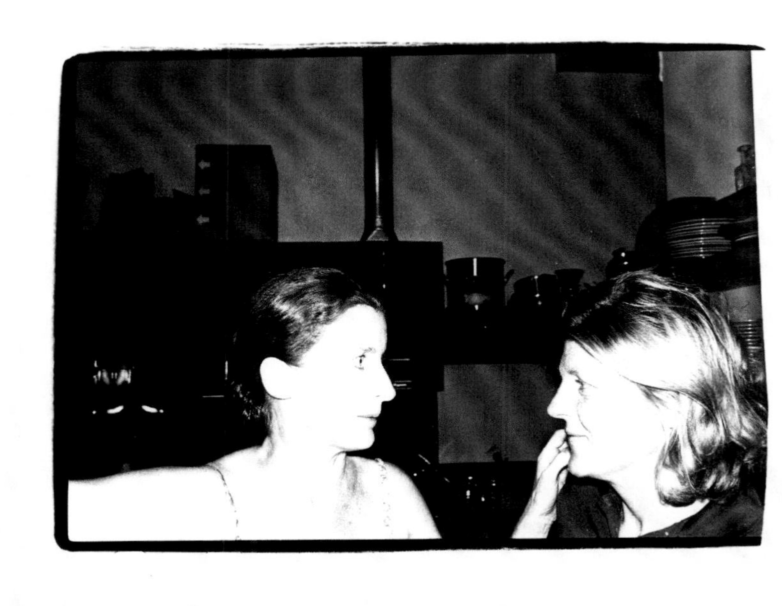

Andy Warhol, *Viva, Viva and Brigid Berlin, Viva and Brigid*, all ca. 1981

257

Fruchter: North Vietnam — pp. 31-35

the village Voice

15c

15c in New York; 20c elsewhere
Copyright © 1968 The Village Voice Inc.

THE WEEKLY NEWSPAPER OF NEW YORK

Vol. XIII, No. 19 ● New York, N. Y. ● Thursday, February 22, 1968

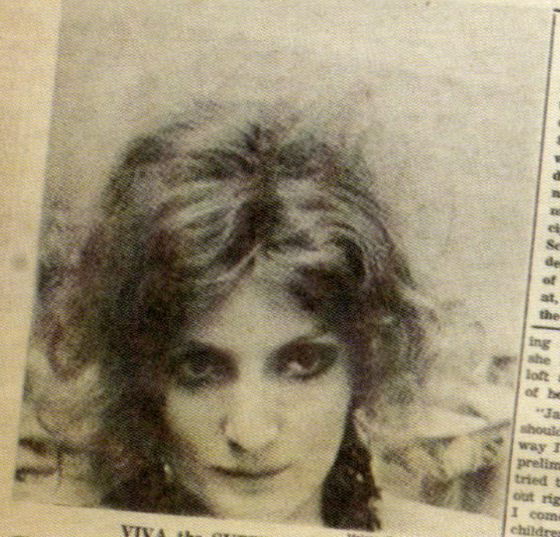

VIVA the SUPER SUPERSTAR
Voice: Fred W. McDarrah

Andy's Juliet

Viva of the Visions: A Scar is Borne

by Sally Kempton

Andy Warhol's actors—the temptation is to refer to them as "Andy's People," as if they were characters in a television serial of that name—have certain essential qualities in common. Most of them are beautiful. Most of them appear by now to be somewhat larger than life size, if only because one has seen them blown up on movie screens. And most of them are a little desperate. Warhol's best superstars are monologists, marathon monologists, and there is always an edge of hysteria in their talk, as if an interruption would release in them some fearful depression. If their talk is self-exploitive, it is also self-generative, for in talking they create themselves again and again.

One remembers Bridget Polk in "Chelsea Girls" lying on a couch like a Westchester matron in hippie disguise, cataloguing her stock of drugs. Or Joe Spencer in "Bike Boy" playing rigorous verbal games with six different girls as though only by sparring could he avoid actually having to make love to them. But particularly, one remembers Viva. Whether she is putting on Joe Spencer in "Bike Boy" or talking non-stop in "Nude Restaurant" about the priest who tried to seduce her, she is in

some essential way the ultimate Warhol Woman.

Viva is extremely beautiful. She is of medium height, very thin, with a presence which appears mysterious and commanding on screen. She has a face like Garbo and Dietrich, bony and classically well-defined. Her eyes are enormous. She has blonde curly hair and a small rather thin-lipped mouth. The mouth is incongruous: there is an Irish Catholic nun in her lips.

Her personality style, on screen and off (for most Warhol People there is no distinction), is recognizably akin to the anti-heroines of so much minor 20th century literature. Like Sally Bowles and Holly Golightly, she is a sexual rebel, a refugee from a rigidly oppressive background. Like them, she is charming, childlike, and perceptibly lost. Like them, she makes sagas out of her life.

When I met her one afternoon a couple of weeks ago, she was sitting around Warhol's new, half-decorated Factory, telling the saga of her troubles with the passport office. The group was supposed to go to Sweden for a museum opening the next day and she had lost her passport. It had taken a harrowing effort to get it back. People drifted into the Factory as she talked and she told the story to each new arrival until, 'hav-

Continued on page 51

On Bundy Report

The Parent-Teachers Association of P. S. 116, 210 East 33rd Street, will sponsor a community meeting on the Bundy report on Thursday, February 29, at 8 p.m. Members of the panel will be Bronx Borough President Herman Badillo; State Senator Whitney North Seymour, Jr.; Roxee Joly, principal of Julia Richman High School; Abe Levine, vice-president of the United Federation of Teachers; and Richard Maat, director of publications for the Ford Foundation.

ing exhausted its possibilities, she led me to the back of the loft and began to tell the story of her life.

"Jakov Lind once told me I should write a story just the way I talk," she said by way of preliminary. "So I sat down and tried to do it but it didn't come out right on paper. Let's see. . . . I come from a big family—10 children. I'm the oldest. I was brought up by the nuns, grade school, high school. I went to Paris with the nuns. I was studying at the Sorbonne and I would run home every night to the convent at Neuilly. Then I had my first nervous breakdown. I began having these Christ-religion-sex obsessions. I thought I was really flipping out. I went to the head nun and told her about it, and she sent me to this Irish Catholic priest. So I went to the priest and I told him all my obsessions. I told him, 'I keep having these visions, I'm scared to go to church.' You see, I'd never heard of anything like that then. Now, of course, I realize it's pretty normal, in fact I realized the whole Last Supper is probably a sex thing. No, not a symbol, I mean they actually did it. Like Alan Midgette says, 'what do you think they lived on all those 12 days? I mean the blood and flesh was really blood and flesh, right?'

"So anyway, the priest says, 'It's worse than I thought, you need a psychiatrist.' So they send me to the hospital and they check me out and find out I'm perfectly all right. They said I should take a vacation with a trusted friend. I said, I don't have one. They said take a vacation anyway. So when school was out I went to Germany. But I kept seeing nuns everywhere I went. Nuns walking with little girls—all over the place. Anyway, that was my first nervous breakdown.

"My parents are real reactionaries, pro the war, voted for Goldwater. They sent me to the nuns so I wouldn't become an atheist and a communist. Joe McCarthy was their big hero. I used to have to stay home from school and watch the hearings

Continued on page 51

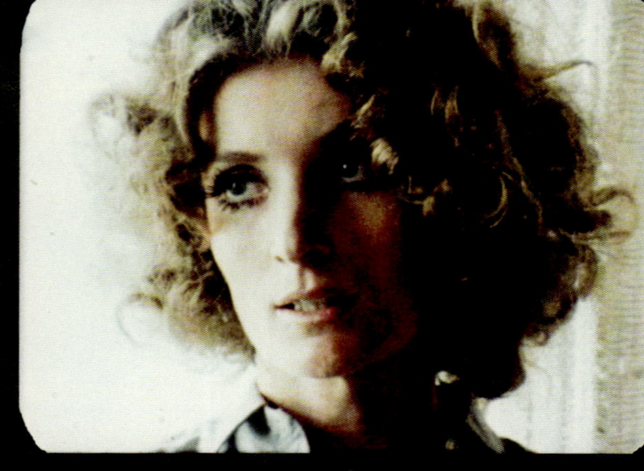

SENATOR McCARTHY came to New York last week to be seen by his supporters. He was given a friendly reception, but failed to turn his campaign into a crusade. A McCarthy backer who met him in the course of his day in the city remarked wryly, "I guess what we're all looking for is a demagogue." The Senator is speaking to Councilman Koch.
Voice: Fred W. McDarrah

Soldiers Doubt War

Catch 23: No Meditation In a Martial Society

by Jack Newfield

COLUMBIA, South Carolina. This characterless state capital, where General Westmoreland was born, and where Dr. Howard Levy was court-martialed, experienced an obscure but perhaps prophetic demonstration against the Vietnam war last Tuesday night. About 30 uniformed soldiers tried to hold a "meditation" to express their "doubts" about the war at the inter-faith chapel on the 36,000-man Fort Jackson army base. Military police barred the entrance to the chapel, and forcibly took five of the soldiers into custody. Two of them now face court-martial.

The event did not make much impact on the media, partially because the Fort Jackson Public Information Office pretended ignorance to inquiring reporters. Also, the protestors do not fit any of the existing stereotypes, are anonymous, and have no access to mimeograph machines. But what they did is as portentous—and as invisible—as the

first civil rights sit-in, staged in Greensboro, North Carolina, eight years ago this month.

Ordinary, unpolitical soldiers, trapped inside the hermetic military machine, with nothing in their environment to reinforce their doubts, are beginning to rebel against their regimented fate. Two privates—Denis Adelsberger and Robert Mears—are being held under maximum security guard at Fort Gordon, Georgia, for refusing, in protest against the war, to wear their uniforms. Private George Davis voluntarily returned from AWOL to refuse a direct order to go to Vietnam, and is now in the stockade at the Presidio. An underground anti-war newspaper, written by soldiers, is being distributed clandestinely at Fort Ord. The paper, called "The Soldier's Manual of Free Thinking," notifies its readers that "this paper is written on Army machines, with Army ink, on Army paper." The Pentagon officially admitted last week that desertion convictions in the

Continued on page 56

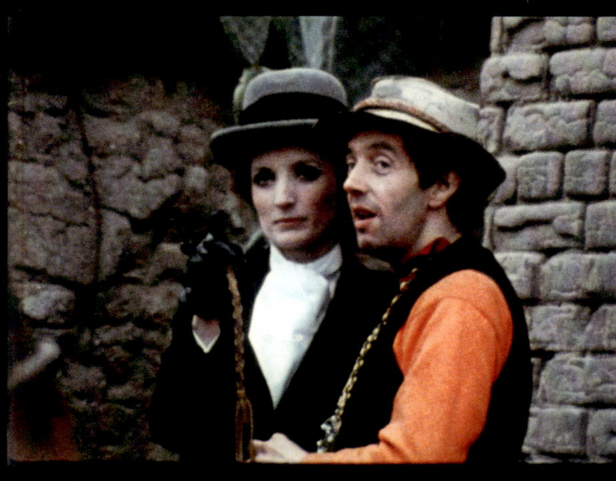

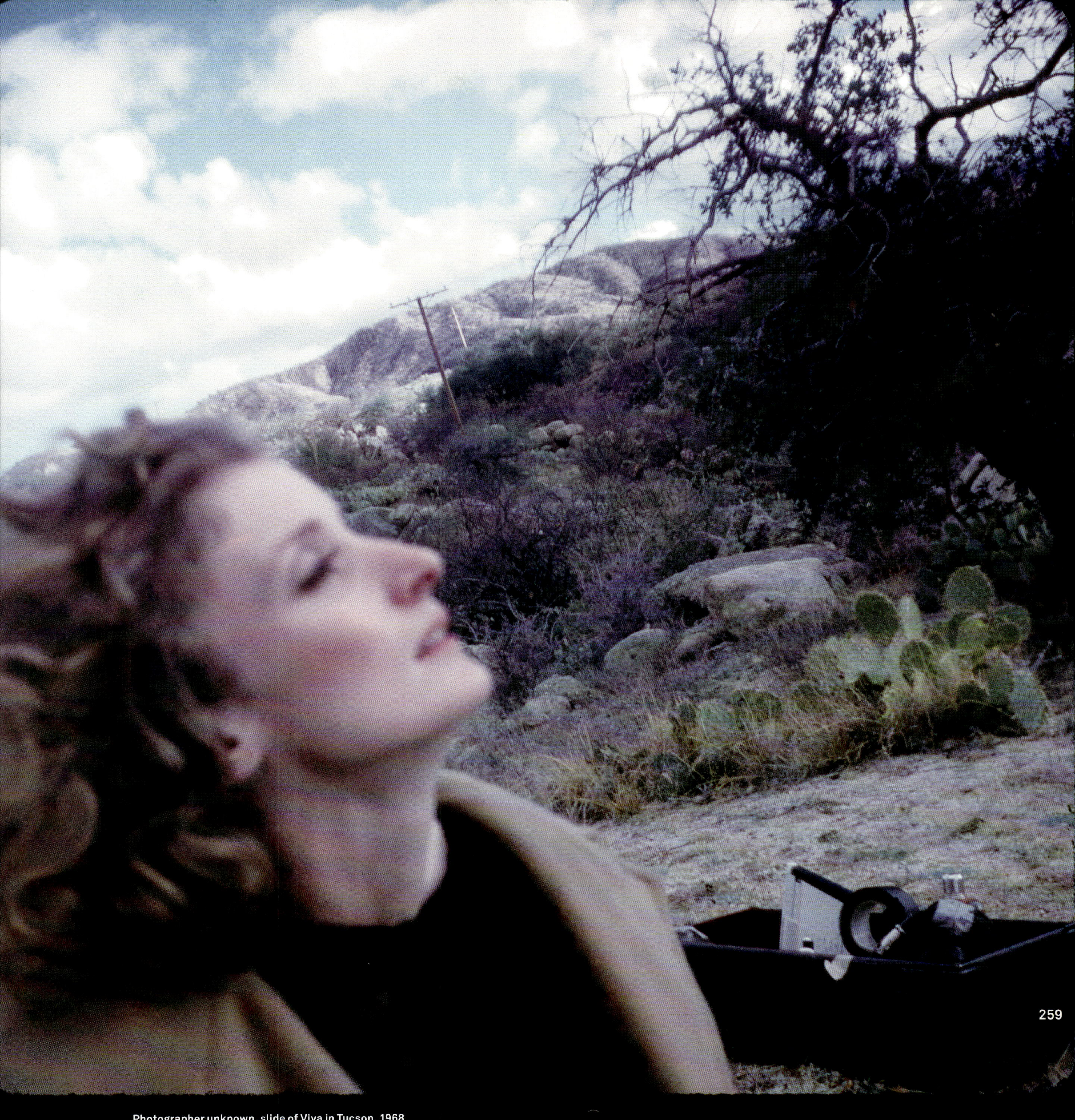

Photographer unknown, slide of Viva in Tucson, 1968

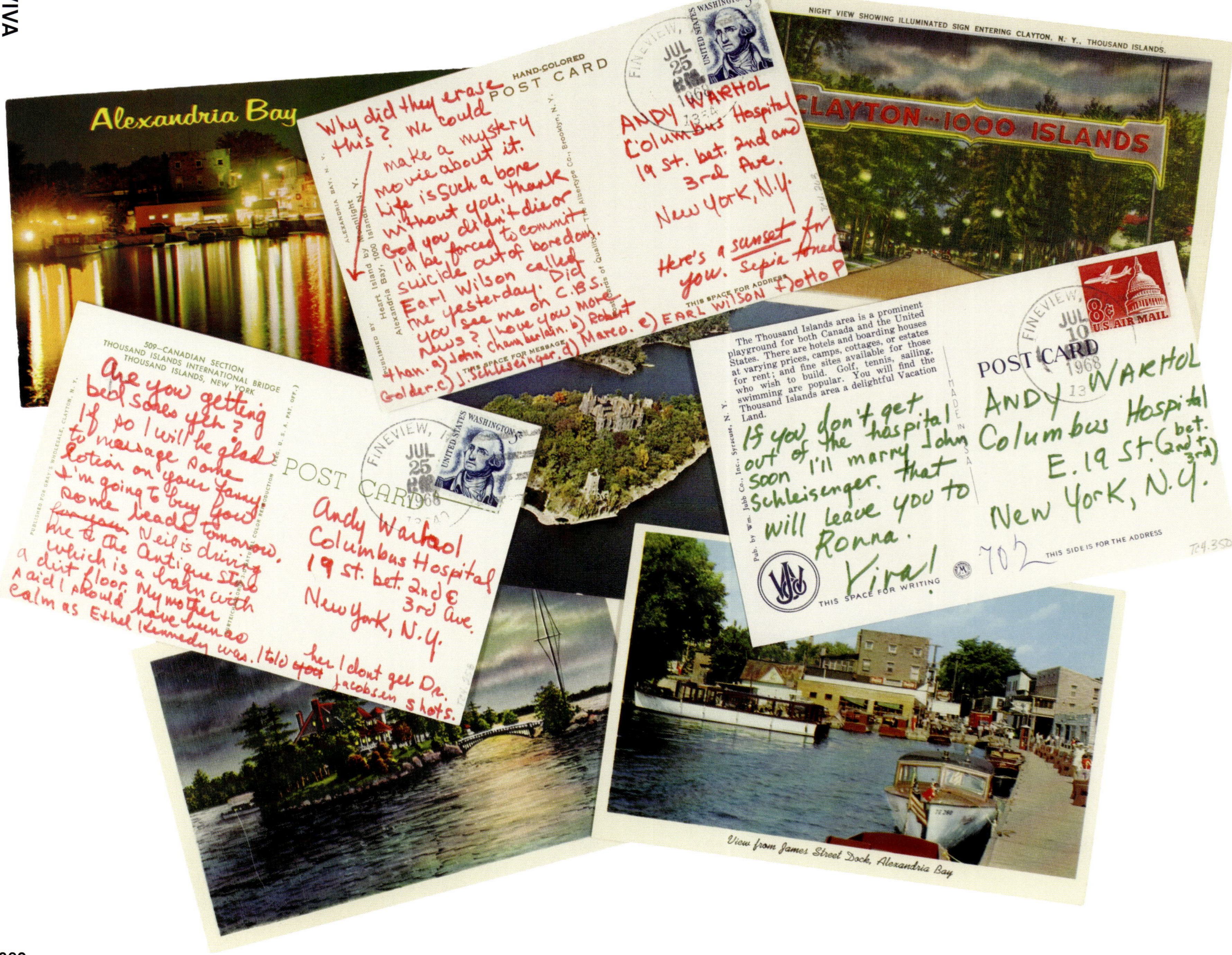

Postcards sent from Viva to Warhol in the hospital, 1968

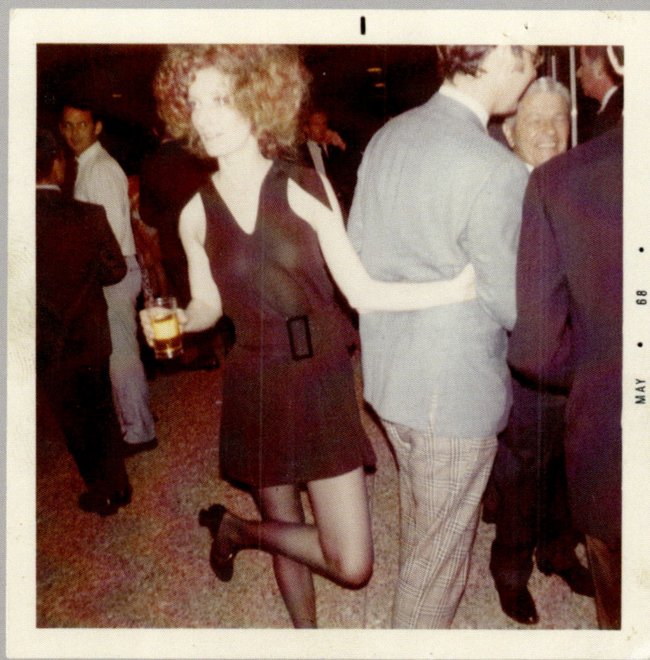
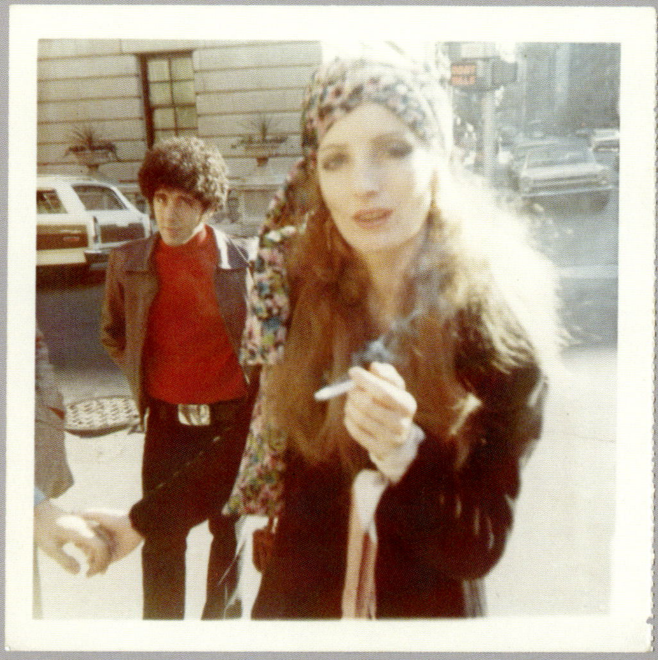
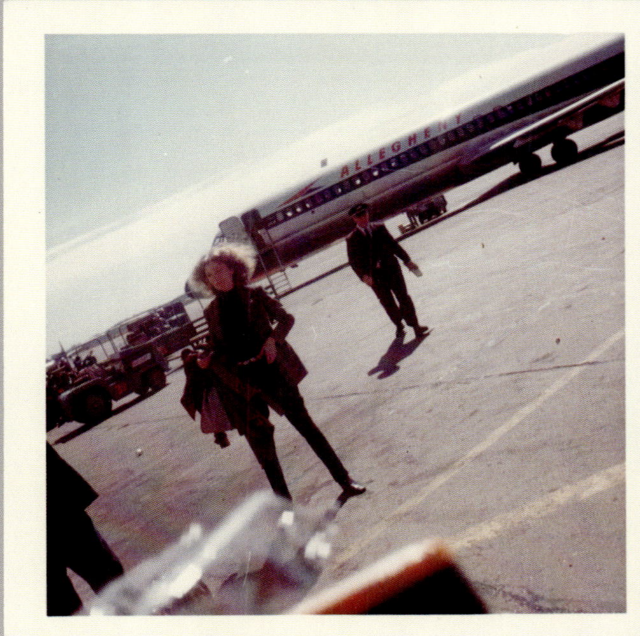
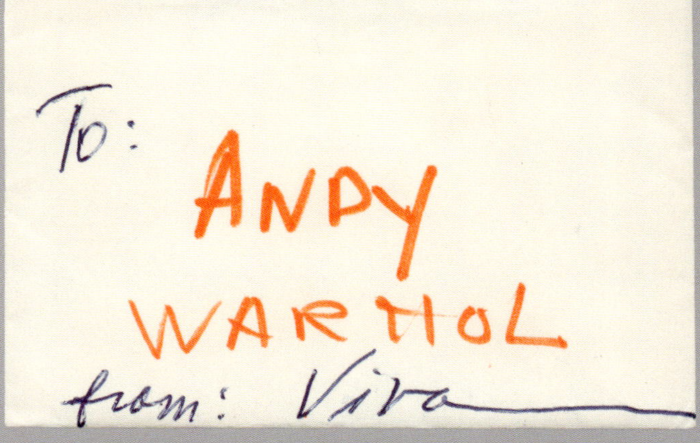

Photographer unknown, *Viva in Black Dress*, 1968; *Viva Holding a Cigarette*, 1968; *Viva on Airport Tarmac*, ca. 1968

Small envelope from Viva to Warhol during his stay in the hospital containing a note regarding Viva's visit to Julia Warhola, 1968

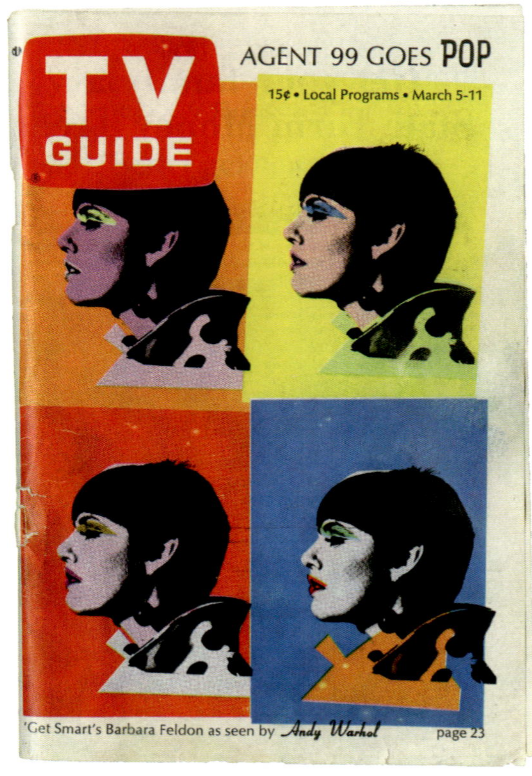

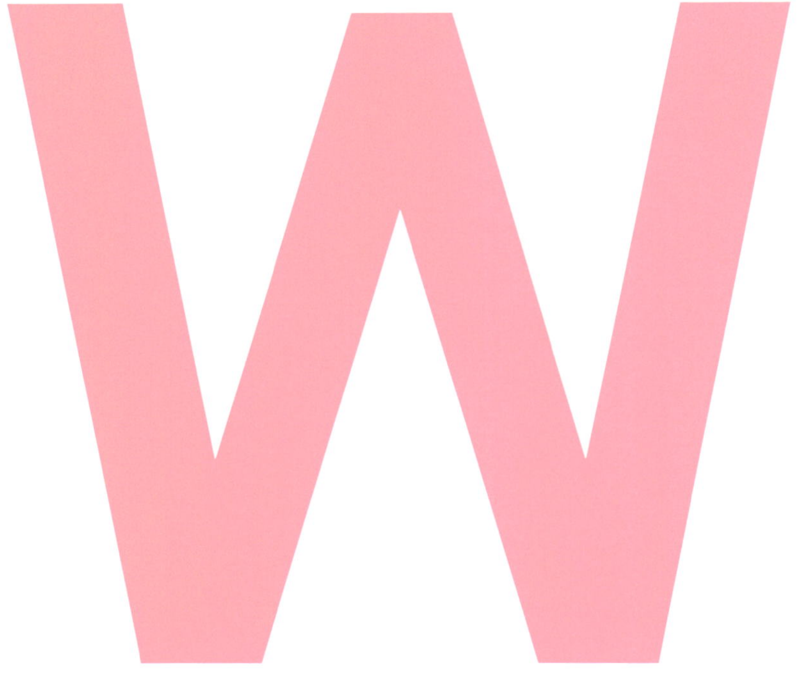

W

is for WIRETAPPING

The materials in this chapter were featured in the exhibition
Buggin': Taps for Justice, in the Archives Study Center,
October 7, 2006–July 1, 2007.

Andy Warhol was fascinated with wiretapping and current events in America that related to such espionage. He painted portraits of Supreme Court Justice Louis Brandeis, who wrote a brilliant opinion opposing wiretapping, although in the minority. Warhol's portrait of Brandeis was part of a larger series titled *Ten Portraits of Jews of the Twentieth Century* (1980). Warhol later completed a portrait of Richard Nixon shortly before his presidency ended due to the Watergate scandal, much of which hinged on Nixon's self-incriminating tape recordings of his conversations. Warhol himself made more than three thousand tape recordings of his life; several of his friends also engaged in this activity. For them, it was only a game, the goal being to get a "good tape." The legality of wiretapping and electronic eavesdropping was hotly debated during Warhol's lifetime. Some of the milestones of legal precedence, and the public discourse surrounding them, related directly to his own creative activities.

Louis Brandeis was one of the most influential and respected Supreme Court Justices in US history. He served on the Supreme Court from 1916 until 1939. In his dissenting opinion in *Olmstead v. United States*, written in June 1928, just weeks before Warhol was born, Brandeis argued, as he had prior to his Supreme Court nomination, that the Fourth and Fifth Amendments to the Constitution protected a "right of privacy." He called it "the most comprehensive of rights and the right most valued by civilized men":

The evil incident to invasion of the privacy of the telephone is far greater than that involved in tampering with the mails. Whenever a telephone line is tapped, the privacy of the persons at both ends of the line is invaded, and all conversations between them upon any subject, and although proper, confidential, and privileged, may be overheard. Moreover, the tapping of one man's telephone line involves the tapping of the telephone of every other person whom he may call, or who may call him. As a means of espionage, writs of assistance and general warrants are but puny instruments of tyranny and oppression when compared with wiretapping.[1]

Brandeis's opinion was later influential in a 1967 Supreme Court ruling (known as *Katz*), which effectively reversed *Olmstead*'s permission to wiretap.

Wiretapping may have initially appeared in popular culture in the comic strip *Dick Tracy* (June 1932) and the movie *I've Got Your Number* (1934). The James Bond books and films that emerged in the 1950s included fantastic eavesdropping devices. In *From Russia With Love*, 007 used a phone-bug detector when inspecting his Istanbul hotel room. Bond inspired several TV shows of the 1950s and 1960s: *Dragnet*, *I Spy*, *The Man from U.N.C.L.E.*, and *Get Smart*. Warhol's portrait of *Get Smart*'s Barbara Feldon (as Agent 99) appeared on the cover of *TV Guide* in 1966. A brief list of *Get Smart* gadgets includes the magic ear, the ice-cube mic, the fly mic, the martini-and-olive radio, the Fudgsicle mic and transmitter, and the coffee-and-donut radio.

Warhol's own collection of International News Photos document eavesdropping equipment and the use of wiretapping in the 1950s, as in "Z.1108389 / Mayor William O'Dwyer, pipe in hand, casts a quizzical eye over equipment allegedly used—or ready to be used—in tapping phones of high city officials. Police Commissioner O'Brien is on the right. (SM-3-12-49)" and "1282060 / Electronics expert Bernard Spindel gives Emanuel Celler, of the House Judiciary Comm., a 1st hand lesson in the powers of wire-tapping. May 1955 / Washington."

Popular magazines debated the legality of such spying. In "The Case Against Wire Tapping," in *Look* magazine (1949), James Lawrence Fly argues that electronic spying has resulted in the devastation of many American liberties.[2] He points out that our own government is a primary violator of our democratic freedoms, as the FBI is the most extensive wiretapper in the country—and despite the fact that wiretapping is federally outlawed, a ruling upheld by the Supreme Court as applicable for government agents as well as private citizens. Fly blames the government not only for its own illegal use of wiretapping but also for its failure to enforce federal and state laws against electronic surveillance. In addition, Fly writes, officially authorized wiretaps are quite frequently used in investigations of minor crimes such as gambling, bookmaking, and prostitution—all common fields for blackmail and extortion. All in all, "wire-tapping promotes far more crime than it suppresses."[3] According to Fly,

TV Guide, March 5, 1966, with cover and interior art by Warhol depicting actress Barbara Feldon in her role as Agent 99 on the TV comedy *Get Smart*

electronic spying is so easy and secretive that it is assumed to be everywhere and inevitable.

In "The Big Snoop," in *Life* magazine (1966), John Neary reveals the increasing popularity and ease of electronic spying, both by government and police officials as well as by private citizens.[4] In addition, electronic spying equipment is constantly developing, improving, and shrinking—Neary depicts one transmitter the size of a postage stamp. As these devices—transmitters, mikes, amplifiers—become smaller and easier to hide, protecting the individual's legal right to privacy becomes an increasingly difficult task. This task is further complicated, Neary points out, by the ineffectiveness of federal and state laws limiting the use of wiretapping.

In a 1962 article, Senator Edward V. Long describes the problems of wiretapping in the United States, especially with regard to its violation of the Fourth Amendment to the Constitution.[5] He objects to then–Attorney General Robert F. Kennedy's wish to wiretap suspected members of organized crime. Long recounts at length the history of wiretap legislation and notes that it was repeatedly voted down by Congress during World War II and the Cold War, although it was secretly approved by the Justice Department and the FBI.

Alan F. Westin's book *Privacy and Freedom* prompted privacy legislation in the United States and helped launch global privacy movements in many democratic nations in the 1960s and 1970s. In a September 17, 1967, review of the book, Walter Goodman notes that Westin believes that the Supreme Court is "on the verge of a major ruling in defense of privacy," and exactly two months later it announced the decision in *Katz*.[6] Attorney General Ramsey Clark had also recently issued a regulation forbidding nearly all wiretapping, except in matters of national security. In signing the Omnibus Crime Bill of 1968, President Lyndon Johnson stated that Congress had moved close to his goal of banning all wiretapping and eavesdropping, except where national security was involved, "and then only under the strictest of safeguards."[7]

In 1972 Warhol was commissioned to create a print to support the presidential campaign of Senator George McGovern. Created in a numbered edition of 250, it raised a considerable sum of money for President Richard Nixon's opponent, although McGovern lost in a landslide. Those facts, combined with Warhol's decision to portray Nixon in a ghoulish manner with blue-green skin and yellow eyes and lips, rather than feature an image of McGovern—or any of his issues—reflect the artist's great antipathy for the incumbent president. In the years leading up to this campaign Warhol had been audited by New York State for his 1968 tax return, and although he was cleared in 1971, the episode caused much stress.[8] In an unsupported statement, one of the artist's biographers claims that Warhol was also included on Nixon's notorious "Enemies List."[9] This infamous list of powerful American citizens was revealed during the congressional investigation in 1972. The hearings also revealed that Nixon, like other presidents before him, was secretly tape-recording his phone calls and meetings. One of these tapes later proved that he was aware of the break-in and eavesdropping in the Watergate scandal. Although Nixon won by a wide margin, the 1972 election marked the beginning of his downfall.

The Watergate scandal became public on June 17, 1972, with the arrest of five burglars who broke into the Democratic National Committee headquarters at the Watergate Hotel in Washington, DC. The men were returning to fix broken wiretaps that they had installed during a previous break-in. When they were arrested at 2:30 a.m., one was carrying a White House pass. The ensuing revelations eventually led to President Nixon's resignation. All the major news sources, including *Newsweek*, focused on Nixon's fight against impeachment. *Newsweek* covered his attempt to regain public support only sixteen months after his reelection, and his slow retreat into privacy following continuous accusations. It reported his efforts to illegally filter and withhold subpoenaed tapes, transcripts, and documents, as many of his trusted colleagues were charged, tried, and sentenced. In the cover issue "The Eleventh Hour," the magazine covered the charges against Nixon: obstruction of justice, abuse of power, and contempt of court.[10] The need for impeachment became inevitable to all but Nixon, who sat in his office playing and replaying hours of taped conversations. As others discussed the option of resigning with amnesty for Nixon, he continued to

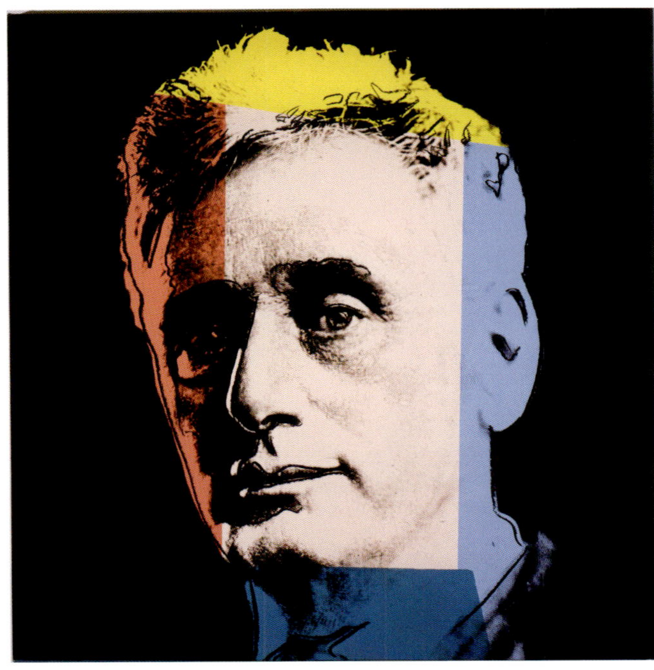

deny his own guilt until August 5, 1974, when "the smoking gun" tapes were released. Four days later, Nixon resigned from office.

Warhol made thousands of tape recordings, including of phone calls and other experiences in his life. Many were made specifically for his books, such as *a: a novel* (1968), but others were done simply to document his life. His friends were aware of his privacy-flouting habit, and several of them also made tapes of their conversations, but reading the transcripts of them now gives us the experience of eavesdropping. In *Andy Warhol's Exposures* (1979), he wrote, "Watergate frightened me: I didn't know whether Nixon copied me or I copied Nixon. I had to stop taping for a while. But I started again because *my* Rose Mary Woods didn't have anything to do."[11]

Rose Mary Woods was Nixon's secretary; one of her duties was transcribing the White House tapes. In a bizarre twist to the Watergate scandal, one of Nixon's tapes included a mysterious gap of 18 1/2 minutes, for which Woods accepted the blame, claiming that she had been transcribing the tape when she was startled by the

phone and unintentionally erased the segment by pressing the recorder's foot pedal as she talked. However, when asked to replicate her position during the accident, she had to stretch out in her chair to an extreme length to reach both the foot pedal and the telephone. That she could have held this awkward position for 18 1/2 minutes was preposterous, and it is widely believed that the segment was erased deliberately. Other governmental abuses of wiretapping were revealed by extensive Senate investigations in the 1970s, leading to the Foreign Intelligence Surveillance Act (FISA) in 1978, requiring that warrants be issued for surveillance.

NOTES

1. Olmstead v. United States, 277 U.S. 438, 476 (1928), no. 493, decided June 4, 1928.

2. James Lawrence Fly, "The Case Against Wire Tapping," *Look* 13, no. 20 (September 27, 1949): 35–40.

3. Ibid.

4. John Neary, "The Big Snoop," *Life* 60, no. 20 (May 20, 1966), 38–47.

5. Edward V. Long, "Wire Tapping: The Silent Intruder," *The Nation*, July 14, 1962, 6–9.

6. Walter Goodman, "Snooping," *New York Times Book Review*, September 17, 1967, section 7 (review of *Privacy and Freedom*, by Alan Westin [New York: Atheneum, 1967]), 1, 59.

7. Lyndon B. Johnson, "Statement by the President Upon Signing the Omnibus Crime Control and Safe Streets Act of 1968," June 19, 1968; Gerhard Peters and John T. Woolley, The American Presidency Project, http://www.presidency.ucsb.edu/ws/?pid=28939.

8. Previous biographers have stated that the *Vote McGovern* poster caused the IRS to audit Warhol. Documents in the Archive have not been found to confirm the IRS audits but do confirm that Warhol was audited for his 1968 New York state return, prior to the political poster commission. The FBI also investigated Warhol in 1968 and created a file on the artist in response to complaints of possible "transportation of obscene material" during the shooting of *Lonesome Cowboys* in Arizona (see "V is for Viva").

9. Bob Colacello, *Holy Terror* (New York: Cooper Square Press, 2000), 164.

10. "The Eleventh Hour," *Newsweek*, August 12, 1974.

11. Andy Warhol, *Exposures* (New York: Grosset & Dunlap, 1979), 144. Warhol's "Rose Mary Woods" was Pat Hackett, who functioned as his secretary, editor, and diary-confessor; Colacello, *Holy Terror*, 164.

Research assistance for this chapter was provided by Archives interns Jessica Bitely, Addie Byrum, and Kathleen Garman.

Andy Warhol, *Ten Portraits of Jews of the Twentieth Century: Louis Brandeis*, 1980

The New York Times Book Review

SEPTEMBER 17, 1967   SECTION 7

Snooping

PRIVACY AND FREEDOM. By Alan F. Westin. 487 pp. New York: Atheneum. $10.

By WALTER GOODMAN

BY now, quite a number of us have experienced and all of us have heard about the postwar intrusions into corners of our lives which were once considered nobody else's business. Young children have discovered via U.N.C.L.E. and 007, as their parents have discovered through Congressional hearings, magazine articles and books with scary titles, the astounding array of late-model devices that make spying easy, economical and exceedingly difficult to detect.

The impact of these gadgets provides the inspiration for Alan Westin's admirable report. Mr. Westin, who is director of the Center for Research and Education in American Liberties at Columbia University, does not have much to add to previously published details of how the devices work, but the facts gain force from his dispassionate recital, and he goes beyond them to suggest how rampant technology, whose benefits we cannot be expected to abjure, may be brought under control.

Control would be a less difficult matter if the snoops were merely vicious persons bent on vile purposes: private eyes checking up on adulterers, gossip columnists gathering their tawdry items, blackmailers, blacklisters and the like. But in fact, as Mr. Westin shows, the great assault on our privacy comes from persons with respectable, if not impeccable, motives. They include security officials entrusted with the nation's safety, civil servants attempting to carry forward ambitious programs in the fields of health, education and welfare, sociologists gathering the raw materials for an under-

MR. GOODMAN is the author of "All Honorable Men: Corruption and Compromise in American Life," and is completing a book on the House Un-American Activities Committee.

standing of the problems that oppress our society, and psychologists seeking insights into how the mind works and, incidentally, how it may be made to work "better." There are inevitable value judgments here: we can agree that it is bad when segregationists snoop on civil rights workers . . . but is it bad when liberals snoop on workers for the radical right? The prevailing enthusiasm for collecting information, in conjunction with the celebrated innovations that make collecting a snap, has created a potential for prying most unbecoming to a free country.

"Privacy and Freedom" was sponsored by the Association of the Bar of the City of New York, with an assist from the Carnegie Corporation, and the weight of those institutions can be felt in a stiffness and repetitiveness that I have not encountered before in Westin's numerous works. What it lacks in elegance, however, the book makes up in substance. Not the least of its accomplishments is that it brings together the several species of threats to privacy that other, less diligent, if more facile writers have considered singly. There is physical surveillance — notably wiretapping, eavesdropping and picture-taking, which have benefited so spectacularly from technological progress. There is psychological surveillance — lie detectors, intimate questions about sex and God on employment forms, subliminal advertising and other perversions of the psychologist's skills, with mind drugs and the manipulation of brain waves coming soon. And there is data surveillance, not so well publicized as the others, but with unlimited promise of mischief as the facts and figures of every citizen's life are brought together by prodigious computers, all memory and no heart, for ready scrutiny. Doubtless all of these tools will be used to apprehend despicable criminal types, but they bode no good for unorthodox opinions or eccentric behavior of any sort.

Mr. Westin describes with care the various methods of prying, and it is hardly possible to go through his pages without an uneasy sense of being observed from afar. Unless you are in a position to fight technology with technology, there is no escape. He reviews the extent of these methods' use (businessmen listening in not only on their employees and their competitors, but on their customers, too) and suggests soberly, yet unnervingly, how they may be used tomorrow. He analyzes the public's increasingly critical attitude toward snooping in response to the periodic exposés. He acquaints us with the steps taken up to now to handle the situation—a hodgepodge of largely ineffectual regulations regarding physical surveillance and virtually nothing regarding psychological and data surveillance.

And in the valuable final section of his long book, he suggests the administrative and legislative forms that controls might (and in his opinion should) take. He emphasizes the need for explicit rules governing police eavesdropping—making it permissible, for example, to tune in on kidnappers but not on suspected homosexuals. He calls for a review board on behalf of citizens to check on official adherence to the laws, officials not (Continued on Page 59)

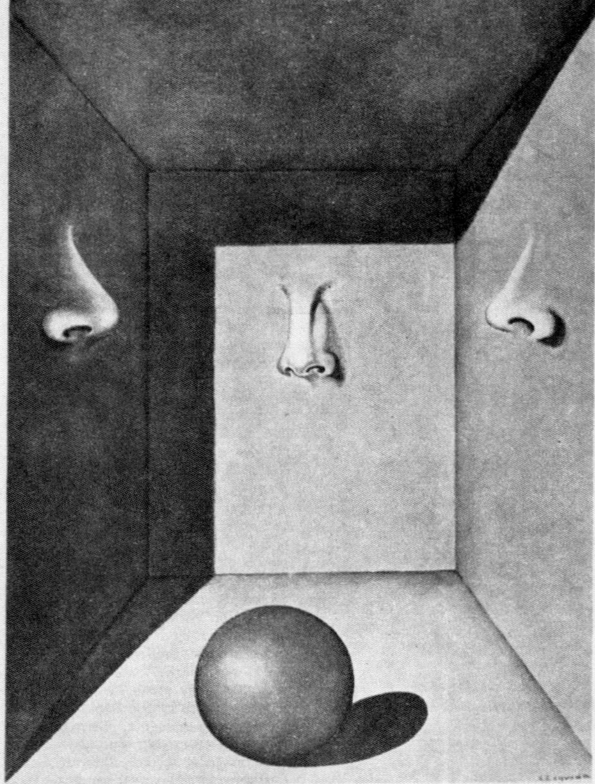

Painting by Xavier Esqueda.
Courtesy The Contemporaries.

"Snooping" by Walter Goodman, *New York Times Book Review* (review of *Privacy and Freedom* by Alan F. Westin), September 17, 1967

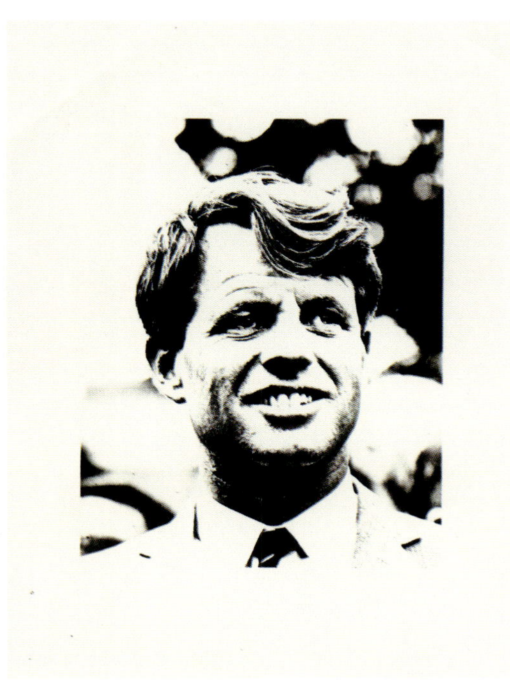

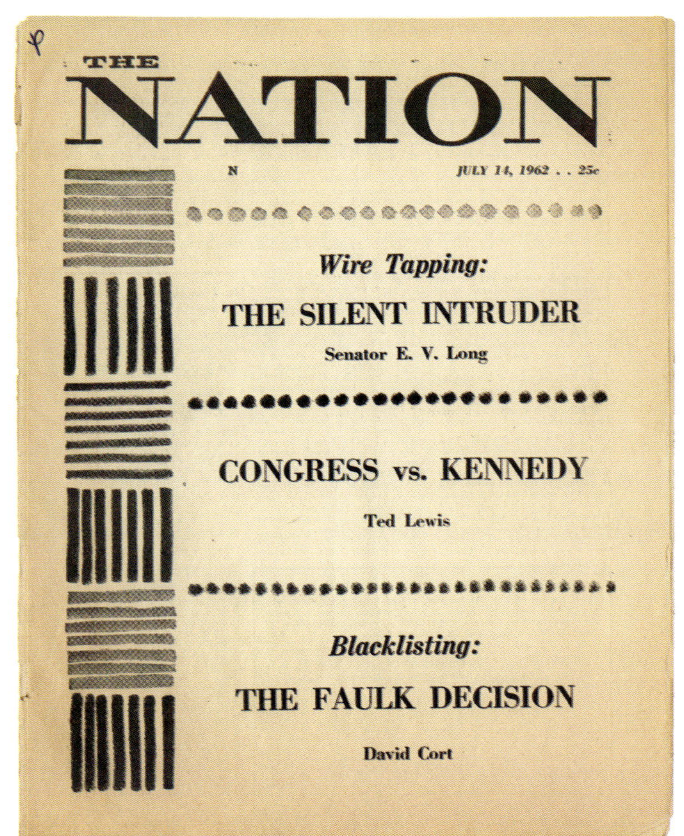

THE
NATION

N   JULY 14, 1962 .. 25c

Wire Tapping:

THE SILENT INTRUDER

Senator E. V. Long

CONGRESS vs. KENNEDY

Ted Lewis

Blacklisting:

THE FAULK DECISION

David Cort

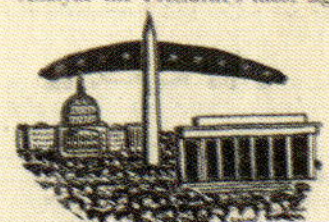

Photographer unknown, *Robert F. Kennedy*, ca. 1968. Source image for an extant silkscreen print meant to be part of Warhol's *Flash* portfolio. Warhol changed his mind when Kennedy was assassinated June 5, 1968.

The Nation, July 14, 1962, front page and interior spread of article "Wire Tapping: The Silent Intruder" by Edward V. Long

W

is for WIRETAPPING

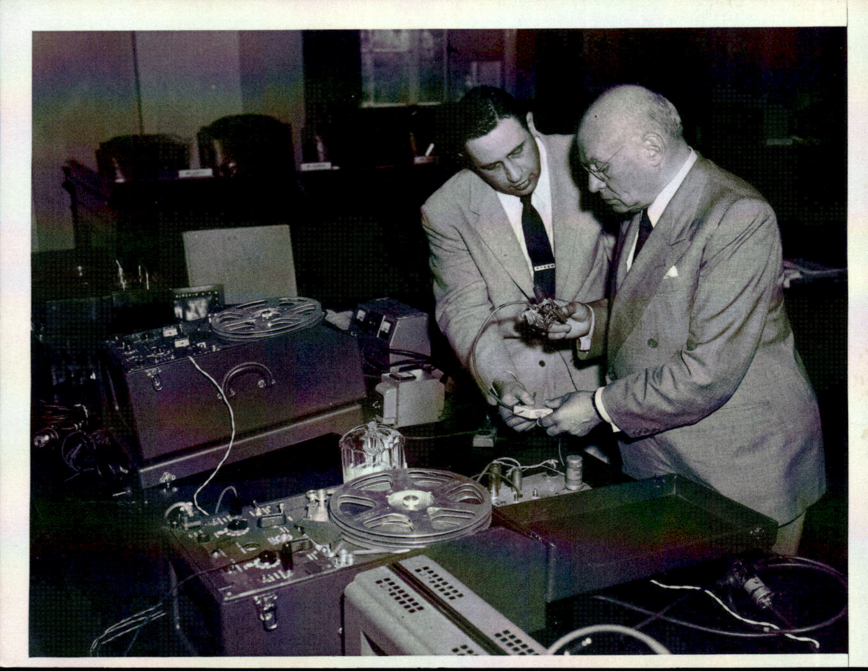

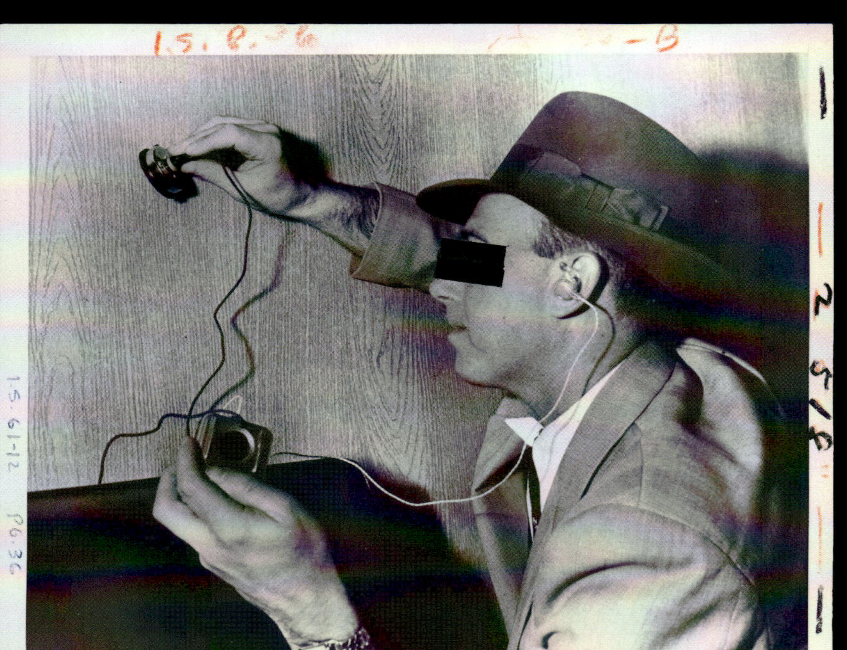

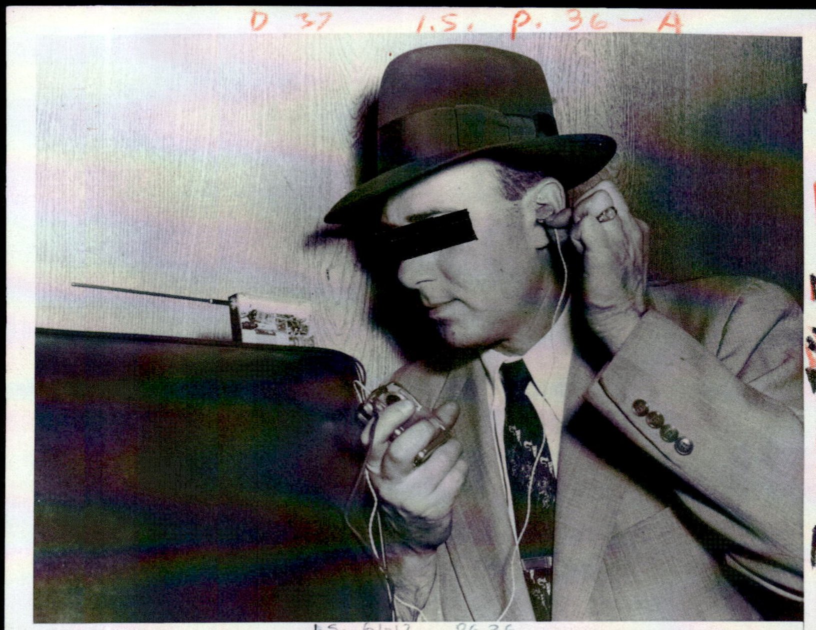

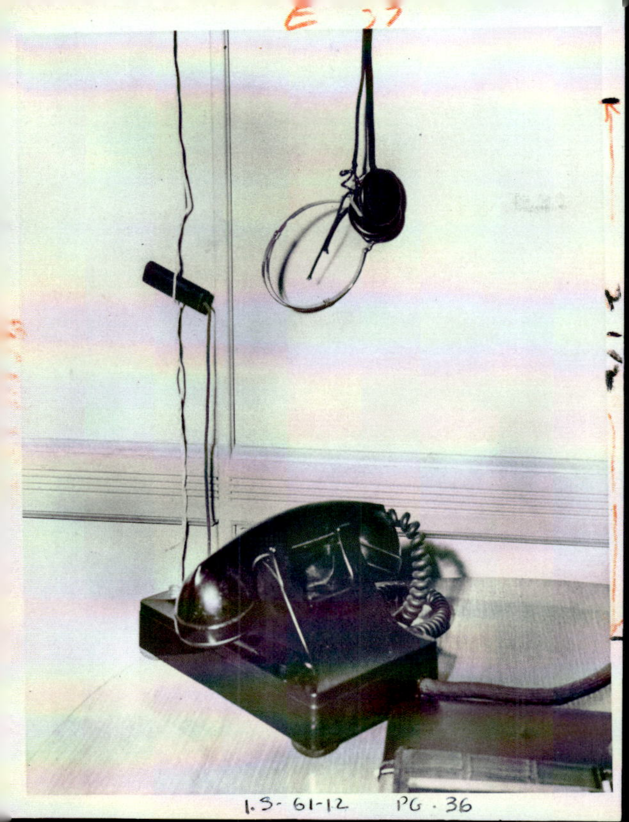
E 37
I.S. 61-12   PG. 36

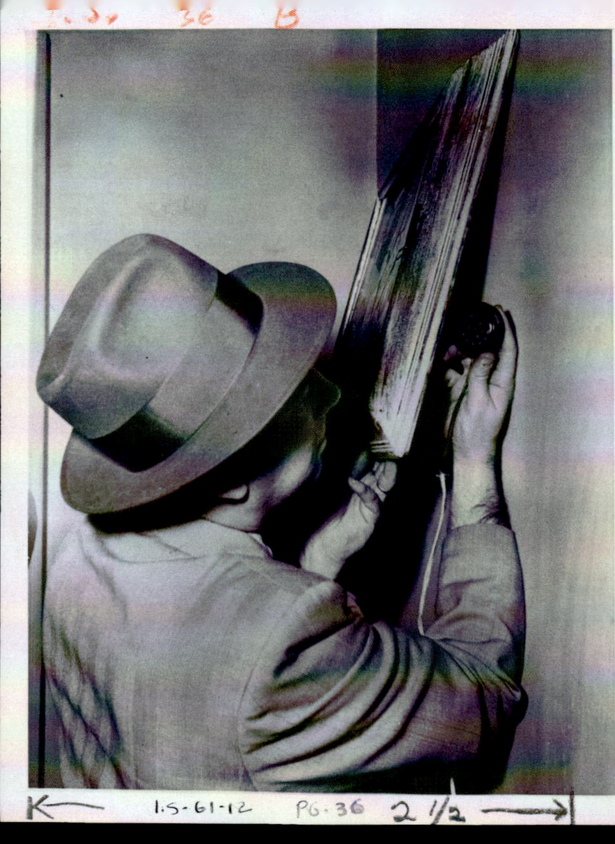
36   B
I.S. 61-12   PG. 36   2 1/2

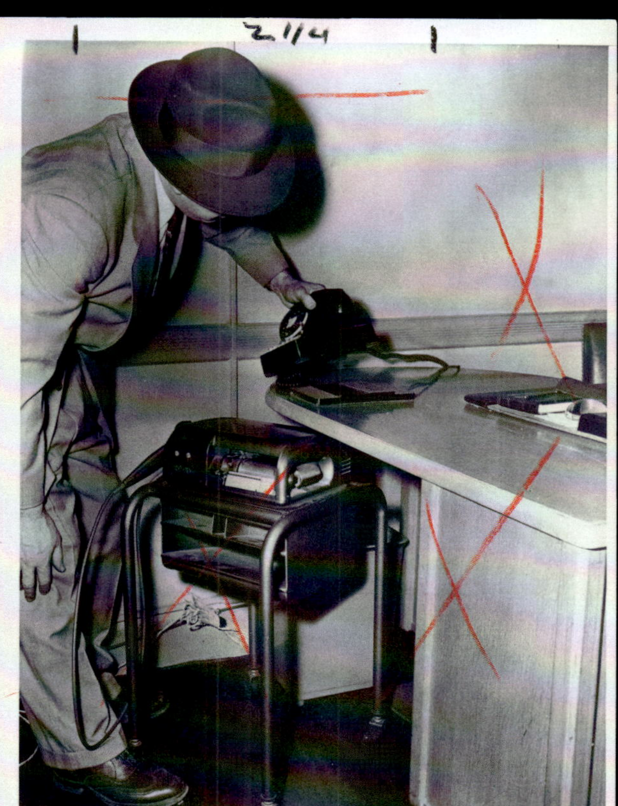
2 1/4
I.S. 61-12   PG. 66

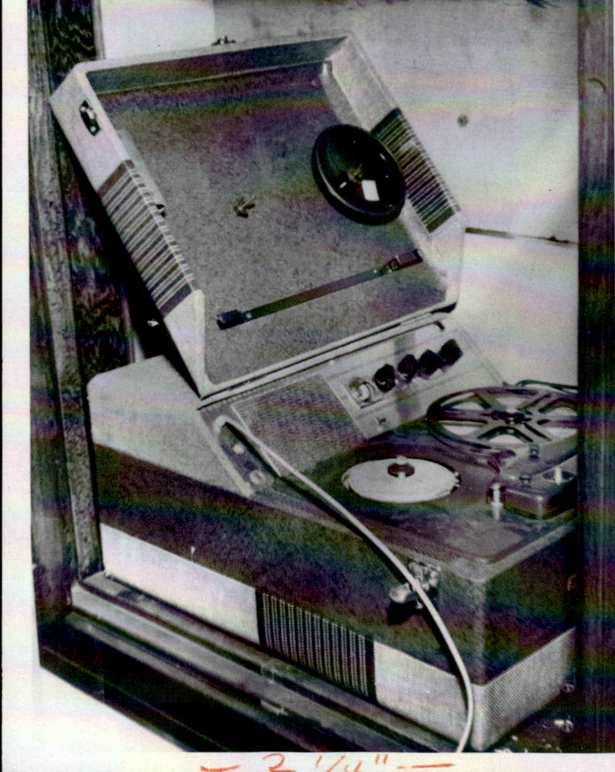
E 37
2 1/4"

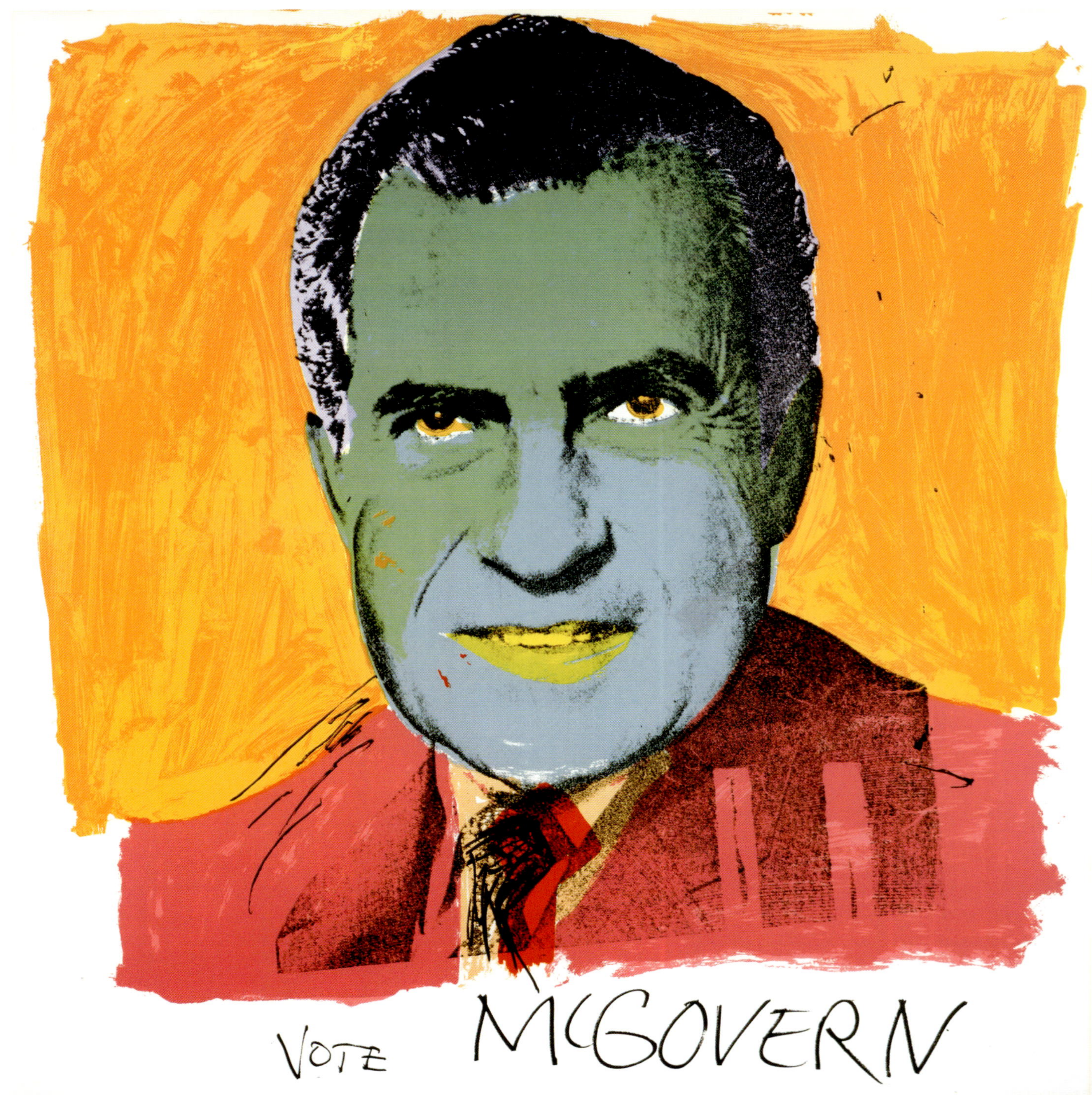

Andy Warhol, *Vote McGovern*, 1972

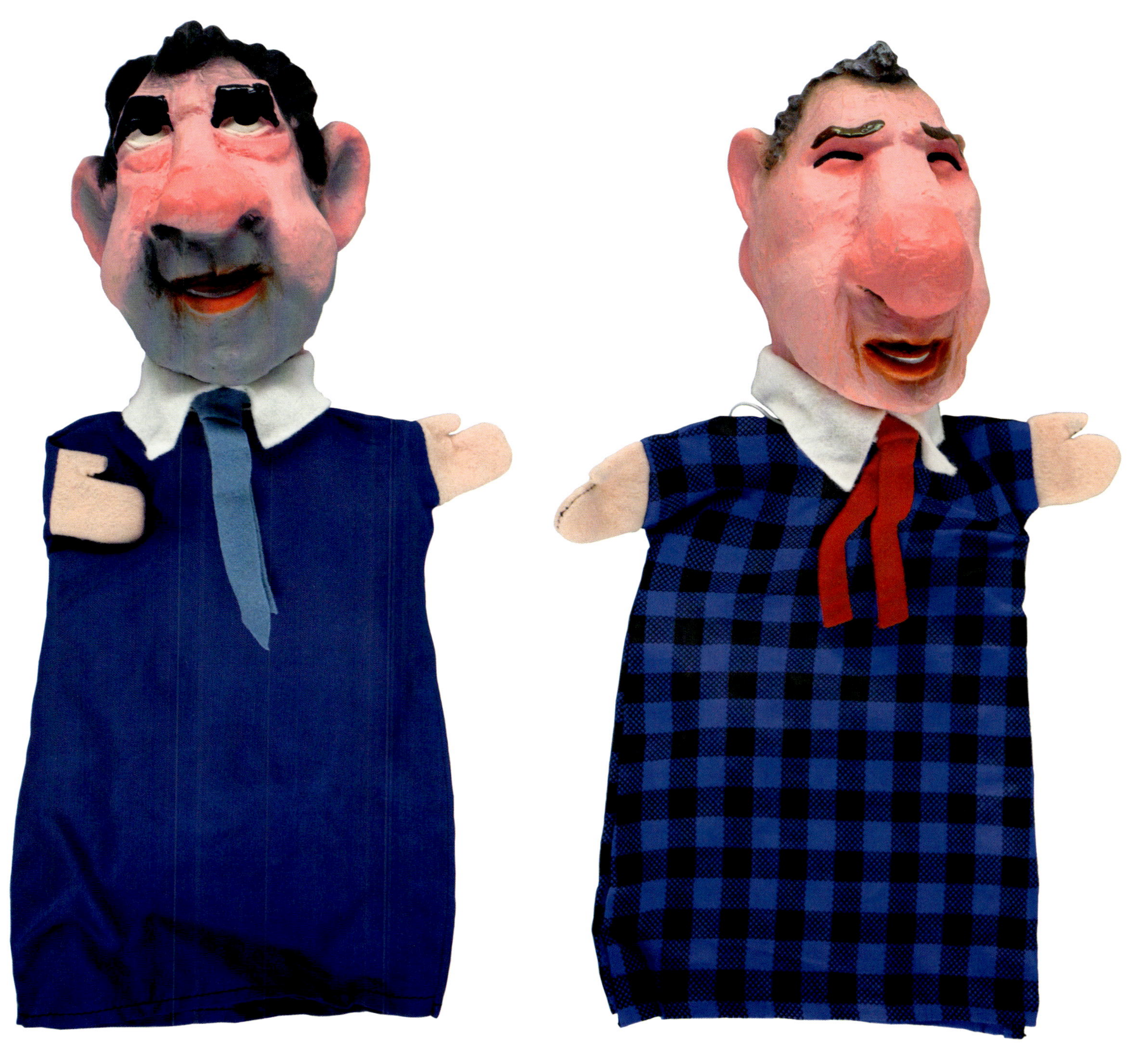

Rick Meyerowitz, Richard Nixon and Spiro Agnew hand puppets, 1970–71

In the late 1960s, the issue of showing explicit sexuality in films and publications was a heated topic in the United States. *Time Capsule -10* presents some of the visual manifestations of this cultural back-and-forth surrounding pornography and sexually explicit art. Warhol's film work repeatedly challenged the so-called "Hayes Code," which had carefully censored content in Hollywood films since 1934. This censorship eliminated all nudity and most verbal references to sexuality. Platinum blonde Jean Harlow (whose elegant black silk gown is in *Time Capsule 67*) was one of the last great stars whose daring roles resulted in the prudishness of the Hayes Code.

The brilliant African American entertainer Josephine Baker, renowned for her erotic dancing, was another of Warhol's favorite "retro" stars. Warhol collected large-scale photographs of Baker, whose frenzied sexuality was more appreciated in Paris than in the race-conscious United States. She was an overnight sensation in Paris when she first performed there in 1925. When she returned to New York to perform in 1936, it was a disaster, apparently due to the racial bigotry of the critics. She returned to Paris a year later and did not perform again in the United States until

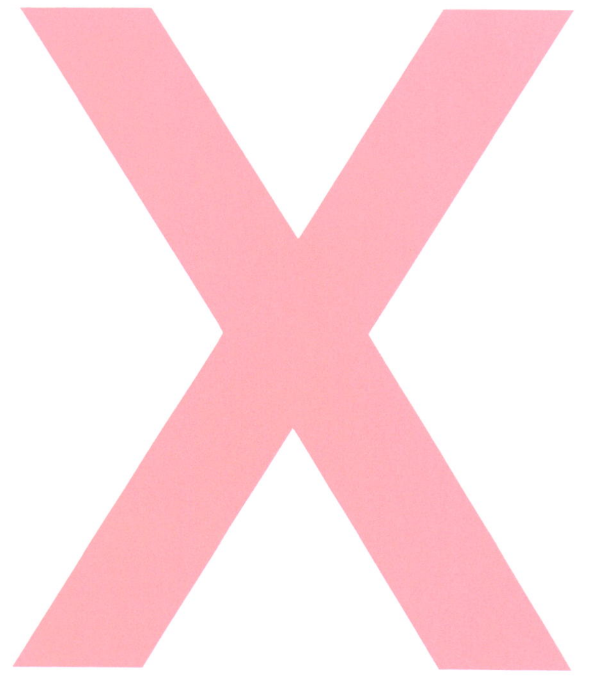

is for X-RATED

This chapter is based on materials in *Time Capsule -10* that were part of a larger exhibition, *Andy Warhol's Time Capsules*, September 27, 2003–May 8, 2005.

shortly before her death in 1975. Warhol's former employee and later biographer, Bob Colacello, wrote that they attended Baker's comeback, which was "a hit," but doesn't provide any further details.[1] This was likely in June 1973, during a series of sold-out shows at Carnegie Hall in New York, which earned Baker standing ovations.[2]

Additional content in *Time Capsule -10* is devoted to Warhol film productions of the late 1960s and early 1970s and comprises numerous reviews of Warhol's films *Blue Movie* (1969), *Trash* (1970), and *Women in Revolt* (1971). *Women in Revolt* was originally titled both *P.I.G.S.* (for "Politically Involved GirlS") and *Sex*, which may have been an homage to Mae West, who wrote a play of the same name that landed her in jail in 1926. The Warhol film satirizes the women's liberation movement and features transgendered Superstars Jackie Curtis, Candy Darling, and Holly Woodlawn.

Blue Movie was seized by government authorities soon after it premiered in 1969, and courts declared it to be obscene. Like most Warhol films, the entire film consists of unscripted dialogue between its stars, Viva and Louis Waldon. They discuss Catholicism and the war in Vietnam and make small talk as they enjoy casual afternoon sex. In response to the government's actions, Warhol published the dialogue and many frame enlargements in a paperback-book version of the film. The book is from a series published by Barney Rosset's Grove Press. These books provided access to the content of censored films, as the legal definition of obscenity in books differed from that in films. This subject was frequently argued in court by Grove Press, perhaps most successfully in 1959, in regard to D. H. Lawrence's *Lady Chatterley's Lover*, written three decades earlier (in 1928, the year of Warhol's birth). Warhol also chose a frame from *Blue Movie* to be made into a silkscreen print. A conversation in which Warhol, Billy Name, and Warhol's editor at Grove Press, Arnold Leo, discuss *Blue Movie* and other erotic films of the period was published in 1968. The film was shown in Frankfurt in 1971.

Many of Warhol's films could be considered pornographic comedies. They featured male sex objects, male prostitution, and transgendered characters. Joe Dallesandro starred in both *Flesh* (1968) and *Trash* (1970), and his body

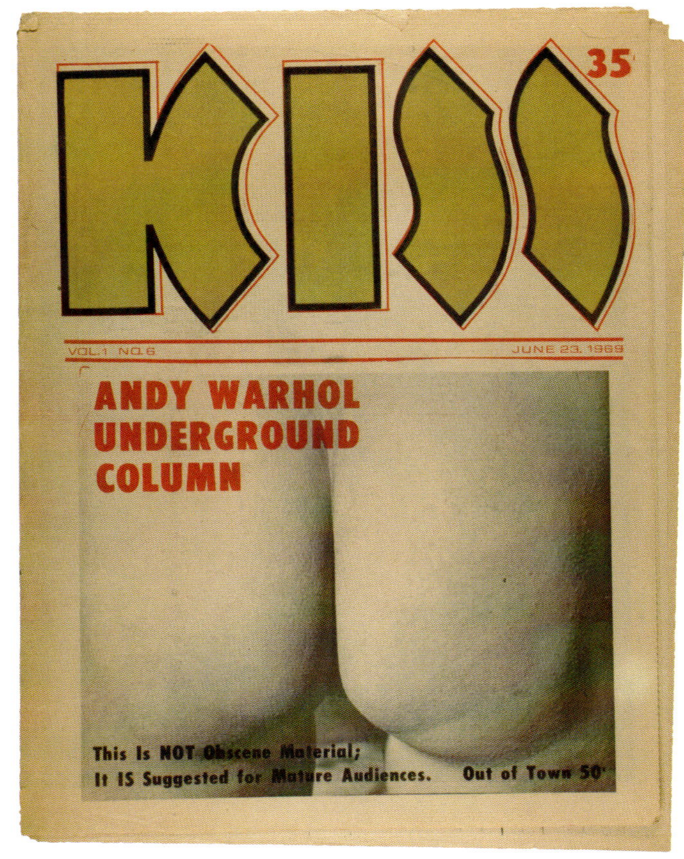

was the center of the camera's erotic attention throughout much of these films.[3] Paul Morrissey shot and edited both films, which were funded by Warhol and promoted with Warhol's name. *Flesh* tells the story of a hustler who pays for his wife's lover's abortion by turning tricks. There are several nude scenes with Dallesandro. The film was confiscated by the police when it was shown in London in 1970. In *Trash*, Dallesandro plays a heroin addict. The film follows him and his girlfriend, played by Holly Woodlawn, through a single day filled with lies, arguments, an overdose, and sexual impotency. The newspaper ads for *Trash* feature the muscular Dallesandro bare to the waist.

The *Time Capsule* also contains a notebook for Paul Morrissey's film *Blood for Dracula*, starring Udo Kier and produced by Andy Warhol and Carlo Ponti in 1973. It was made simultaneously with *Flesh for Frankenstein* in Italy,

Kiss newspaper, June 23, 1969, with "Andy Warhol Underground Column"

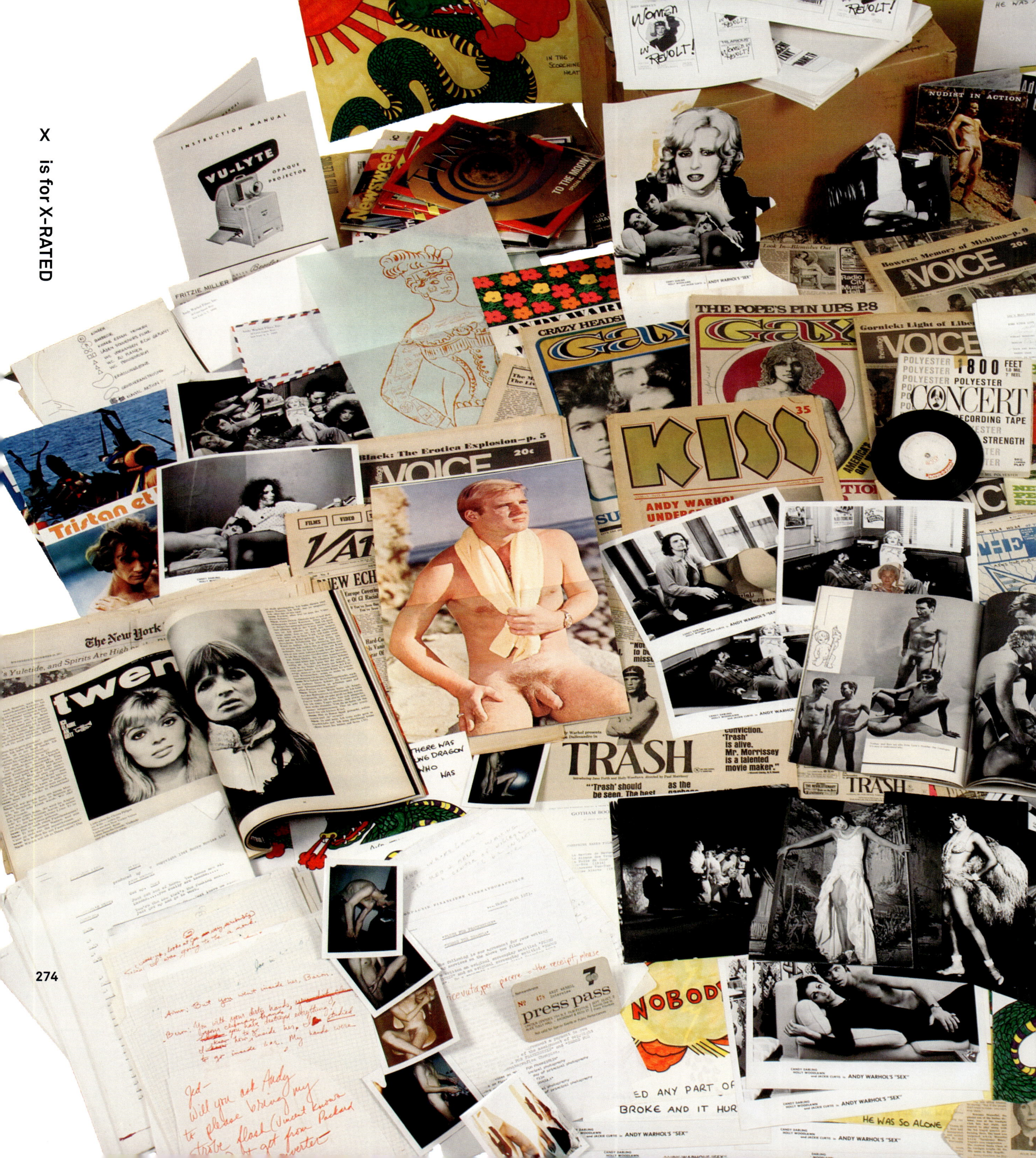

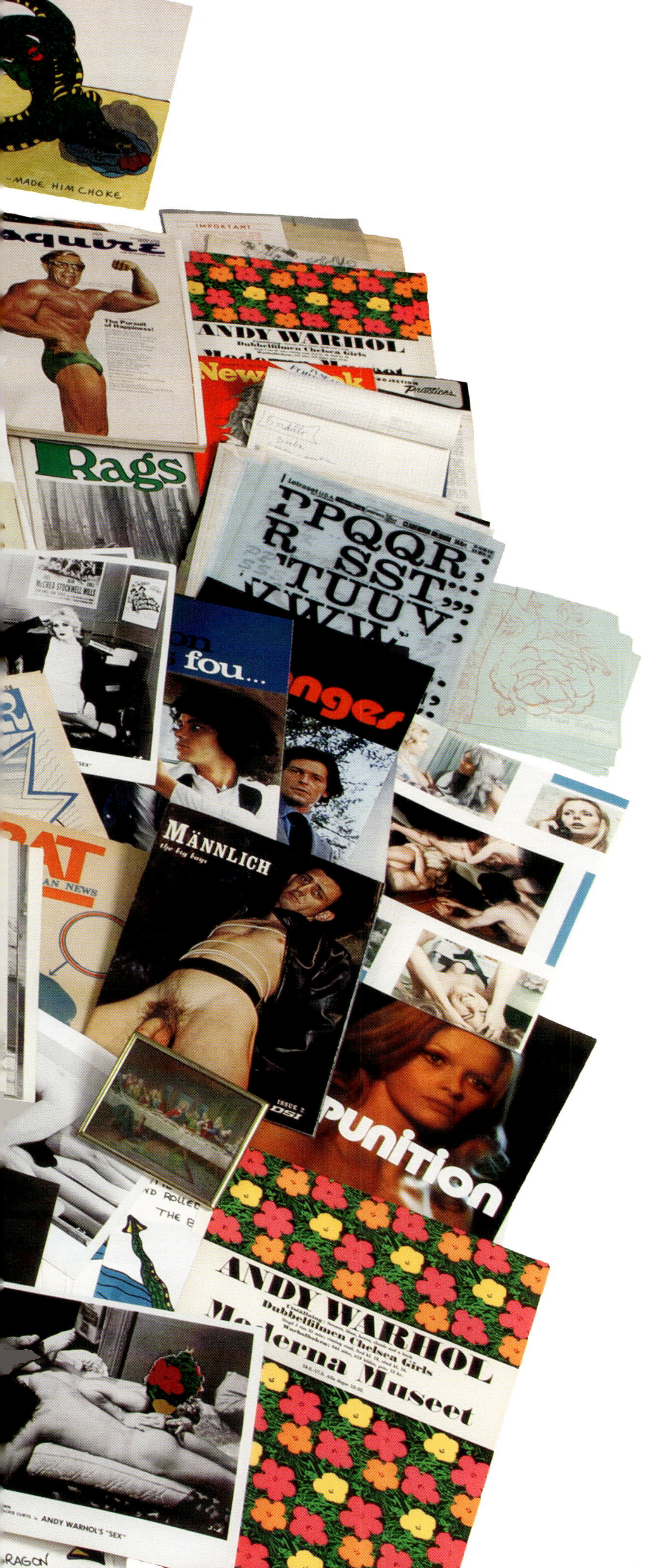

with a nearly identical cast. Both films were shot in 3-D (see "I is for Illusions"). Additional notes were kept for *Flesh for Frankenstein*'s scenes, starring Kier and Arno Juerging. These handwritten missives reveal both sexually explicit and violent content.

Warhol's collection of porn and gay magazines is strewn throughout the Archive, but *Time Capsule -10* contains quite a few. Polaroid photos of an unidentified nude man (ca. 1969) represent examples of Warhol's habitual practice of photographing and drawing willing nude subjects. Polaroids such as these eventually became the source material for Warhol's 1977 series *Torsos* and *Sex Parts*.

NOTES

1. Bob Colacello, *Holy Terror* (New York: Cooper Square Press, 2000), 193.

2. John S. Wilson, "Josephine Baker Sings, Talks, Dances and Captivates," *New York Times*, June 7, 1973, 56.

3. Stephen Koch, *Stargazer: Andy Warhol's World and His Films* (New York: Praeger, 1973), 49–50.

Photographic layouts designed by Becky Shock and Brianna Treleven.

275

The contents of Andy Warhol, *Time Capsule -10*, 1939–73

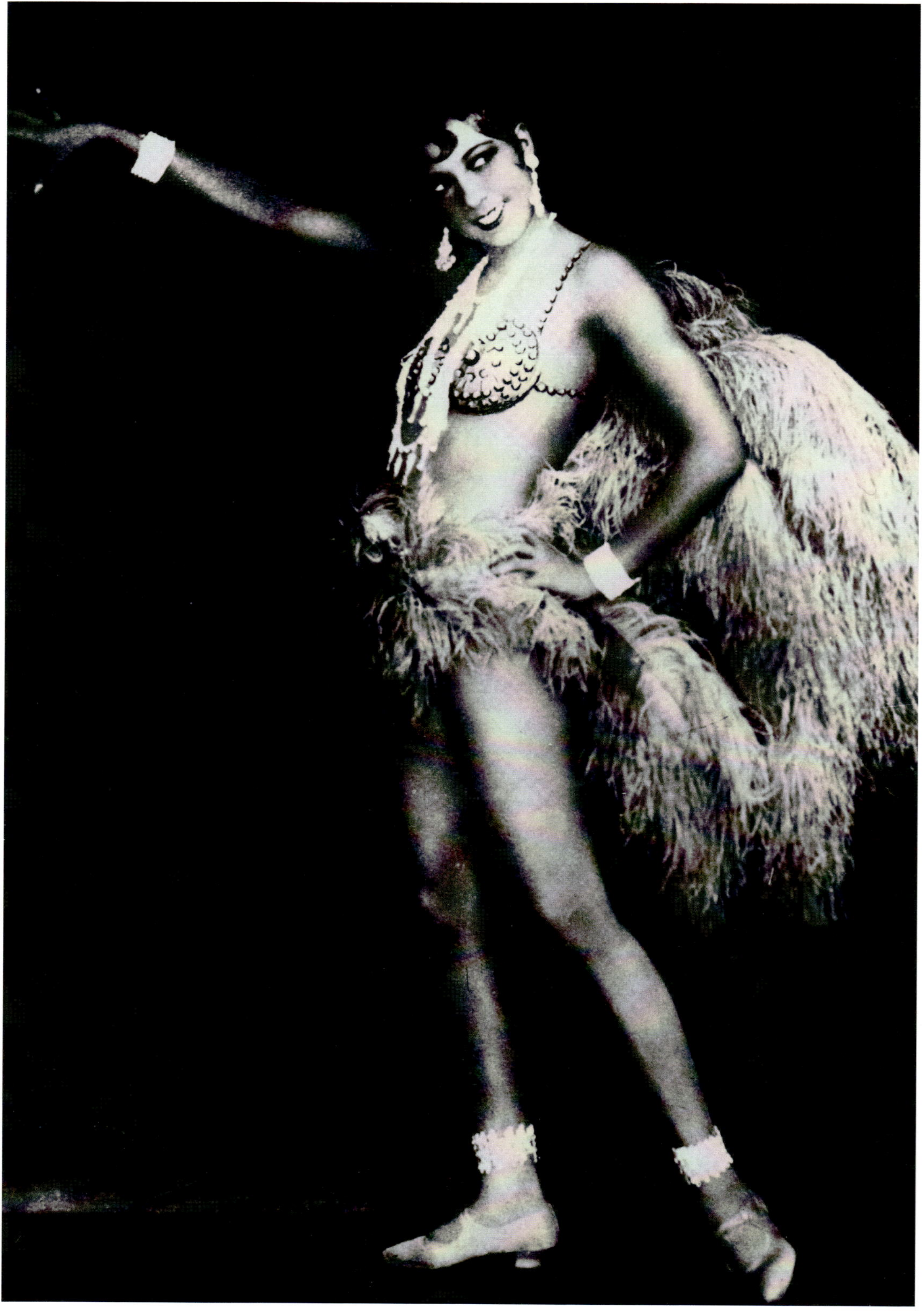

Photographer unknown, *Josephine Baker*, ca. 1938

Photographer unknown, *Josephine Baker*, ca. 1924–25

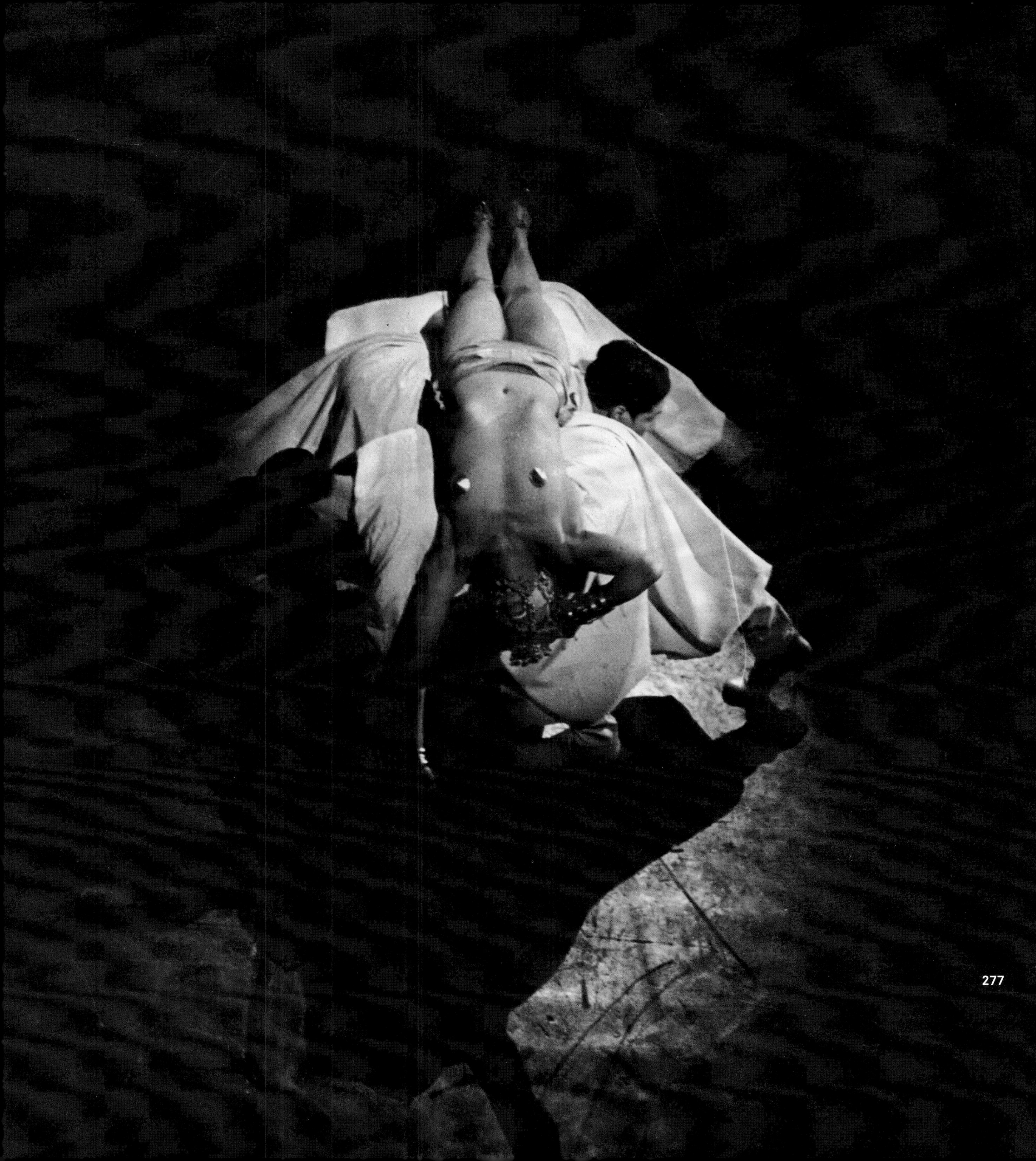

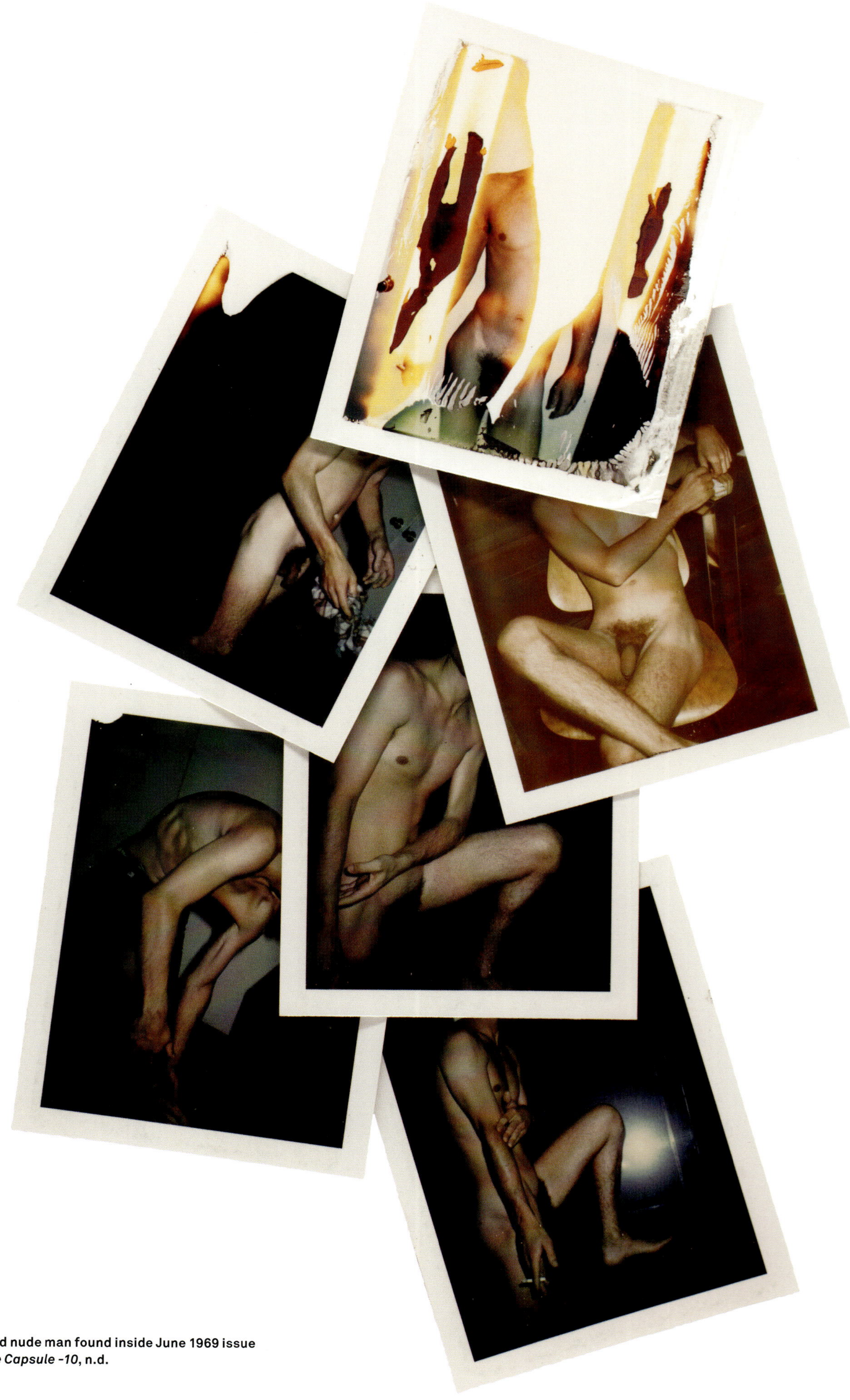

278

Six Polaroids of unidentified nude man found inside June 1969 issue
of *Film* magazine from *Time Capsule -10*, n.d.

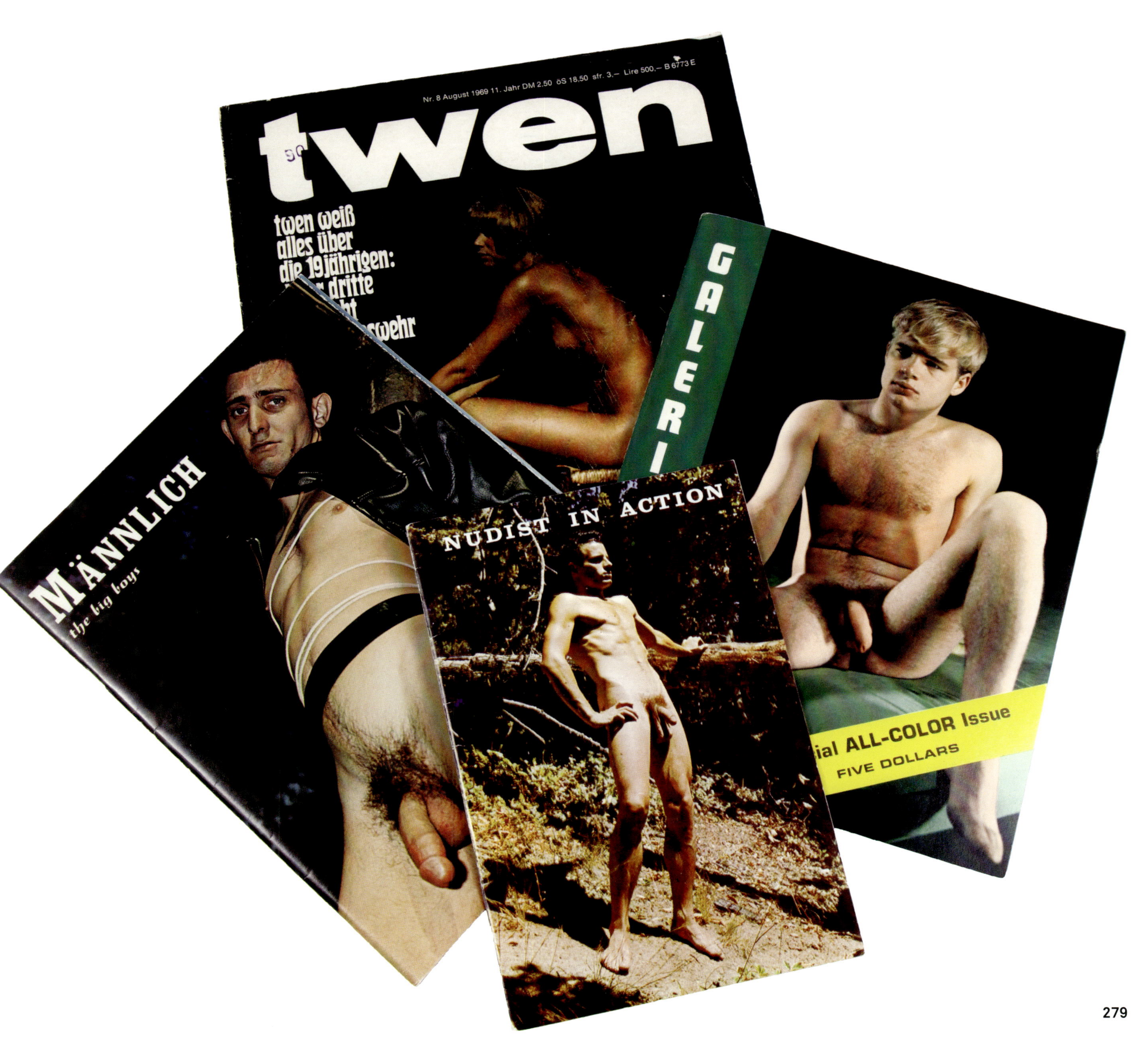

Magazines from *Time Capsule -10*, 1967–69

Y

is for YVES

Andy Warhol frequently traveled to Paris for exhibition openings, film screenings, and social events, and he made many French contacts. Among these, quite a few were named Yves. The Archive contains material relating to four whom Warhol admired, collected, and befriended: painters Yves Tanguy and Yves Klein, jeweler Yves Piaget, and fashion designer Yves Saint Laurent.

As a student in Pittsburgh in the 1940s, Warhol was exposed to the work of many prominent creative minds of the era through the ambitious exhibition program of Betty Rockwell's modern art gallery, Outlines. Figures exhibited included John Cage, Maya Deren, Buckminster Fuller, and László Moholy-Nagy, as well as some of the most important French artists of the time, among them Eugène Atget, Marcel Duchamp, and André Lhote. During this time, Warhol also paid his first visit to New York City, traveling with fellow students to take in the art museums and galleries. It is not known when exactly Warhol acquired a copy of a double issue of *View*, from May 1942, which featured the artists Yves Tanguy and Pavel Tchelitchew, but his admiration of these artists spanned decades.[1] The journal coincided with their respective exhibitions at the Pierre

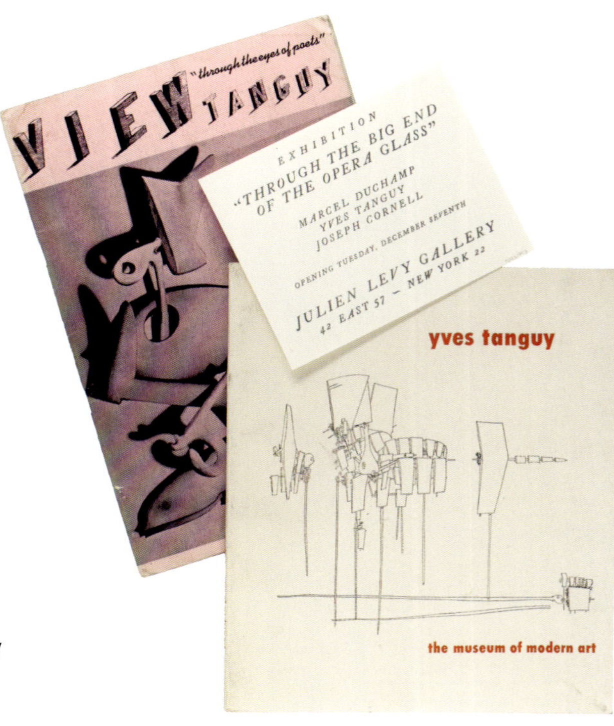

This chapter is based on both exhibited and newly catalogued materials in the Archive.

Matisse Gallery and the Julien Levy Gallery and was printed with two covers, one upside down.[2] Warhol sought out or had encounters with several other figures in the Surrealist movement, most notably Salvador Dalí, as well as artists in the US-based branch of Surrealism, such as Joseph Cornell, Leonor Fini, and Charles Henri Ford. In 1955, only a few months after Tanguy's death, the Museum of Modern Art exhibited a range of paintings by the artist. Warhol most likely attended the exhibition and acquired the accompanying catalogue; it would become one component of the Pop artist's largest serial artwork, when it was placed into *Time Capsule 15*.

Warhol contemporary Yves Klein was known as "Yves le monochrome" for his single-hued painting palette. Klein developed and patented an intense blue pigment called International Klein Blue. Warhol owned two relatively small paintings by Klein dating from the mid-1950s.[3] The addition of a blank canvas to many of Warhol's grid paintings may have been inspired by Klein's paintings; at the least, Klein served as a precedent for paintings consisting of a single color, lacking imagery of any sort.[4] In 1961 Klein made his New York debut at the Leo Castelli Gallery, where he met Warhol. Warhol's Archive contains an invitation to the wedding of Klein and Rotraut Uecker in 1962, although Warhol probably did not attend the ceremony in Paris.

After reaching the heights of the art world, Warhol did attend gala fundraisers and society events with the French watchmaker and jeweler Yves Piaget. Warhol revered celebrity and luxury, and both qualities were harnessed in the Piaget brand. Invitations to the elegant events thrown by the Piaget company were sought after, with powerful and beautiful VIPs in attendance. One such event, the 1983 Piaget Polo World Cup, became the basis for an entire episode of *Andy Warhol's T.V.*, with Warhol videotaping the associated picnics and parties. The glamor didn't end there; afterward, the event was celebrated in New York City with a formal ball and parties at Studio 54 and Regine's. The memories from one of these nights were captured in the photographs from *Time Capsule 361*, which in a sign of friendship were mailed directly to Warhol from Piaget himself. There were no less than ten Piaget watches in Warhol's collection when he died.

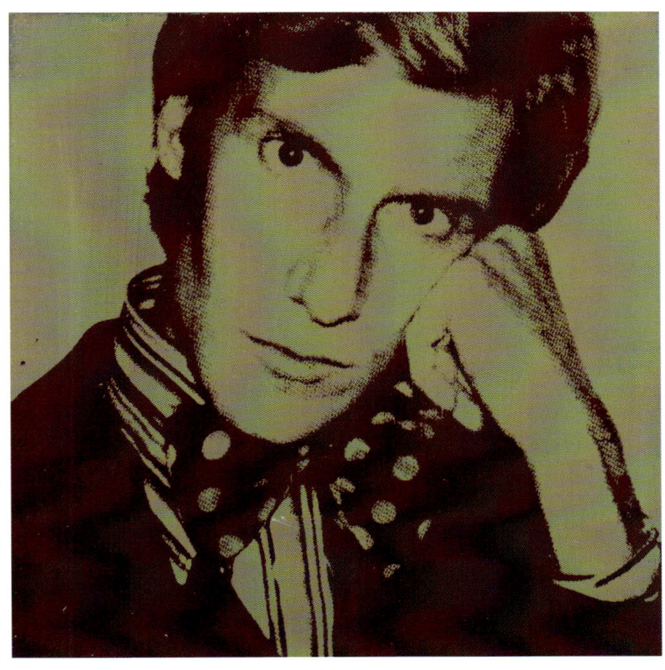

Yves Saint Laurent, or YSL, was likely the most important Yves for Warhol; the two men had a long and very close friendship, both socially and professionally. Warhol painted YSL's portrait in 1972 and received from Saint Laurent a note stating that he loved the portrait and that any rumors he may have heard to the contrary were false. Warhol received autographed posters of original art that Saint Laurent made every New Year for the occasion. He owned many of YSL's safari jackets and a navy-blue blazer, plus other clothing by the designer, including at least one ladies' haute-couture outfit (see "F is for Fashion"). Warhol also painted a portrait of Moujik, the French bulldog owned by YSL and his partner, Pierre Bergé. This painting was the impetus for Warhol's series of portraits *Cats and Dogs* (1976). After Saint Laurent passed away in 2008, Bergé was entrusted with the sale of his estate, which included numerous masterpieces of art and design from many periods and styles. Bergé said that the only objects he could not bear to part with were Warhol's portraits of his late friend, and they were not included in the estate auction.

Andy Warhol, *Yves Saint Laurent*, 1972

NOTES

1. In 1978 Nathan Gluck recalled selling many copies of *View* to Andy, as he was downsizing his library. Patrick S. Smith, *Andy Warhol's Art and Films* (Ann Arbor, MI: UMI Research Press, 1986), 322.

2. Created by Charles Henri Ford, *View* ran from 1940 to 1947. Ford often partnered with galleries, publishing a new issue of *View* that would double as a catalogue for their exhibitions. The Tanguy exhibition was at the Pierre Matisse Gallery, April 21–May 9, and the Tchelitchew exhibition was at the Julien Levy Gallery, April 21–May 18. Four additional clippings regarding the Tanguy and Tchelitchew exhibitions from unidentified newspapers were found inside Warhol's copy in the Archive.

3. These paintings by Klein are pictured in the Sotheby's catalogue for Warhol's estate sale.

4. Warhol created many works with multiple gridded canvases. Some of these screenprinted works were partnered with one or more blank canvases of the same size, painted the same solid color as the ground of the others— often silver, but also red, blue, or another single hue. Examples include *Mustard Race Riot* (1963), *Orange Car Crash Fourteen Times* (1963), and the original installation of *Thirteen Most Wanted Men* on the exterior of the New York State Pavilion of the New York World's Fair in 1964.

Additional research for this chapter was provided by Erin Byrne. New object research provided by Brianna Treleven.

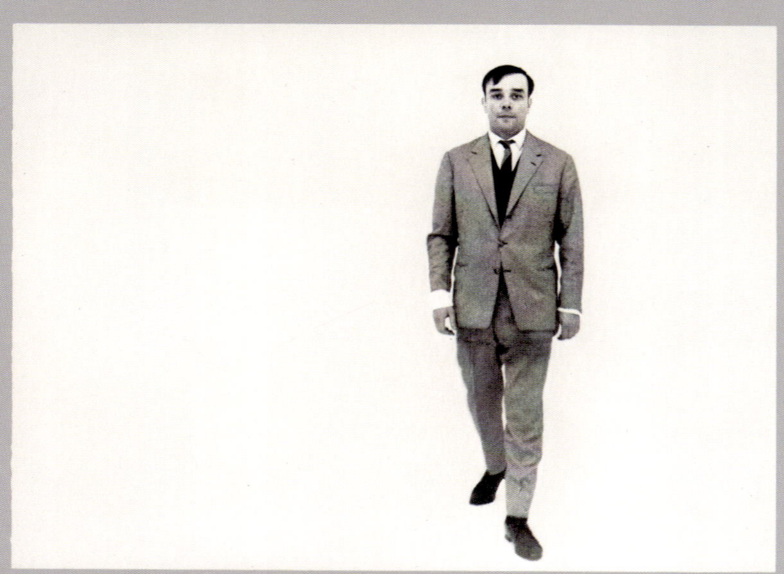

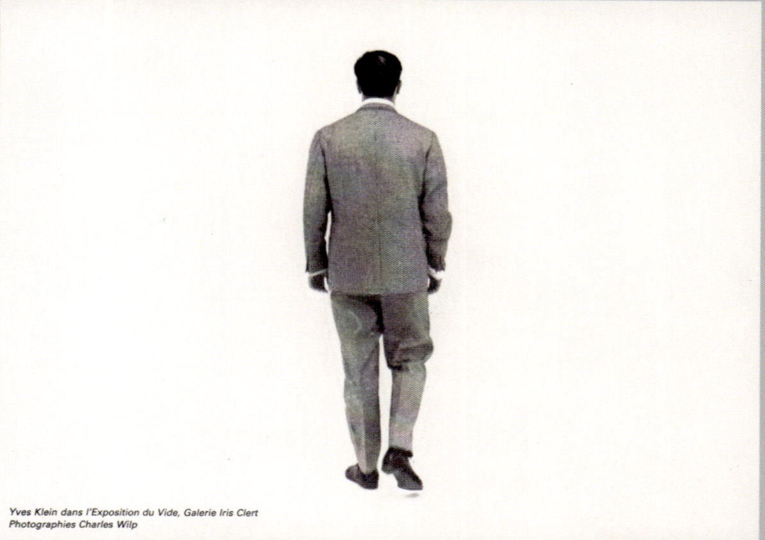

Yves Klein dans l'Exposition du Vide, Galerie Iris Clert
Photographies Charles Wilp

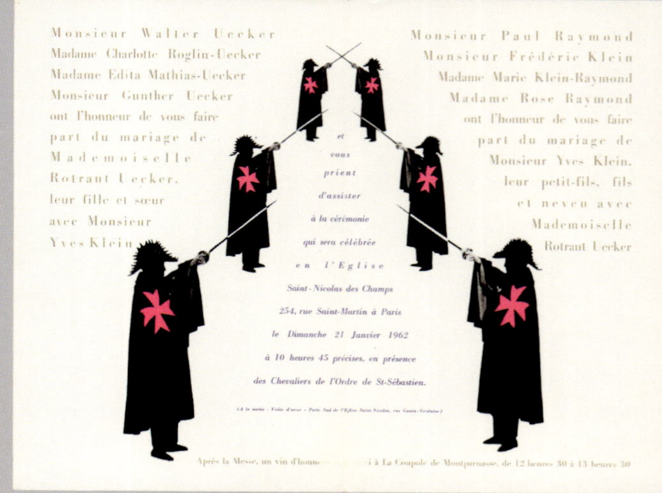

Invitation to Yves Klein exhibition opening at Centre Georges Pompidou, March 1, 1983 (front and back)

Invitation to wedding of Yves Klein and Rotraut Uecker, January 21, 1962

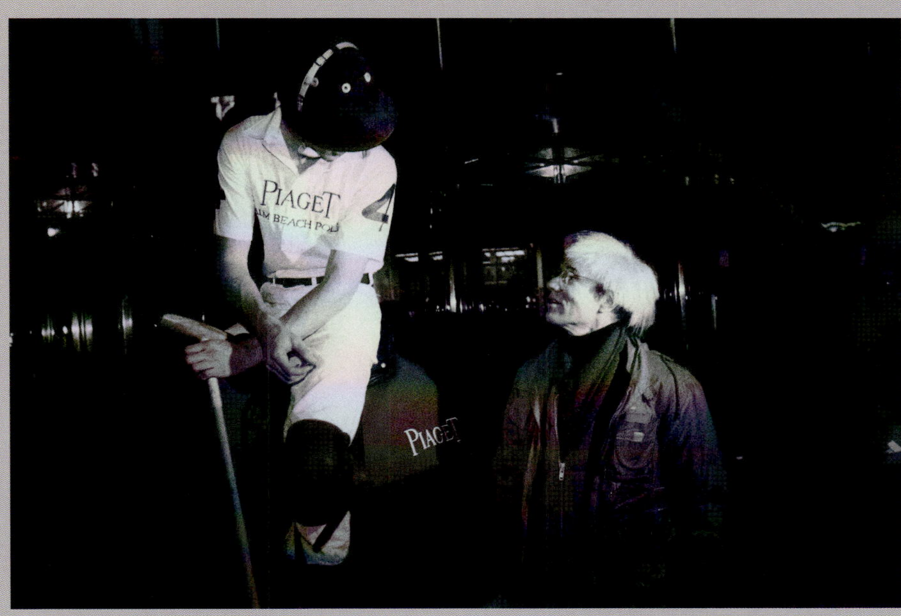

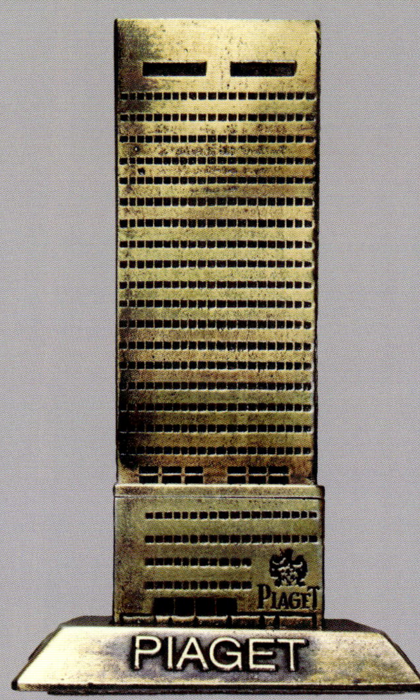

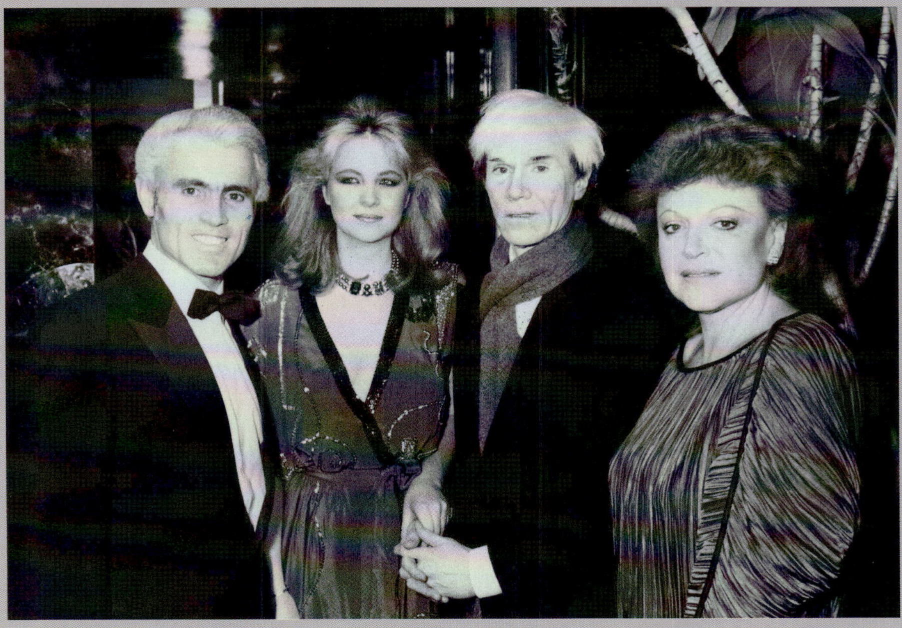

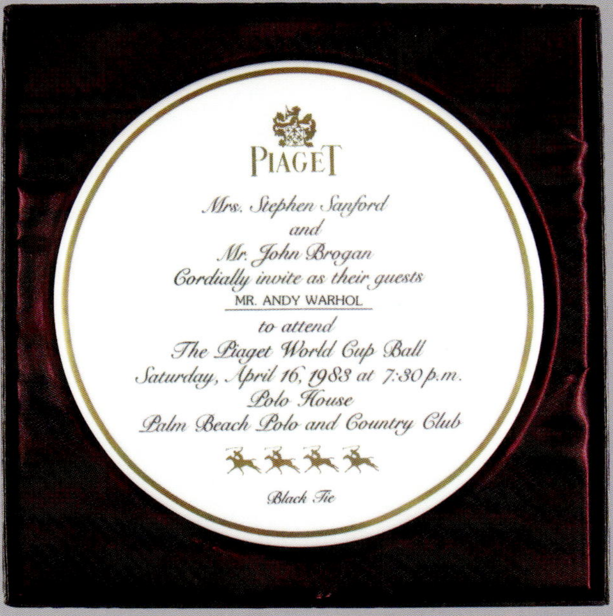

Photographer unknown, *Andy Warhol and Unidentified Piaget Polo Jockey and Horse*, 1984

Photographer unknown, *Yves Piaget, Cornelia Guest, Andy Warhol, and an Unidentified Woman at the Piaget Polo World Cup Palm Beach*, 1983

Piaget building paperweight, June 21, 1979

Boehm porcelain invitation to the Piaget World Cup Ball, April 16, 1983

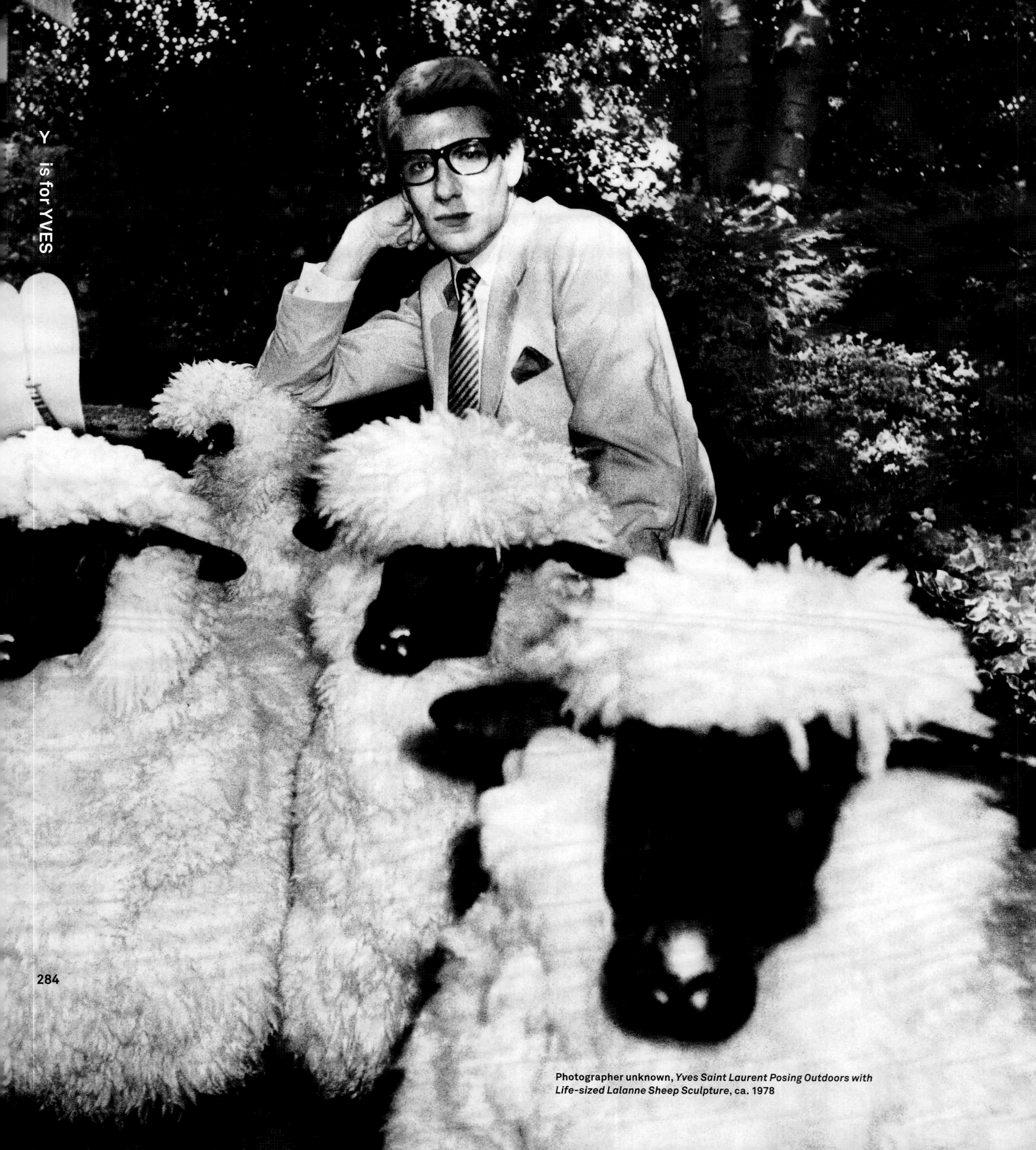

Photographer unknown, *Yves Saint Laurent Posing Outdoors with Life-sized Lalanne Sheep Sculpture*, ca. 1978

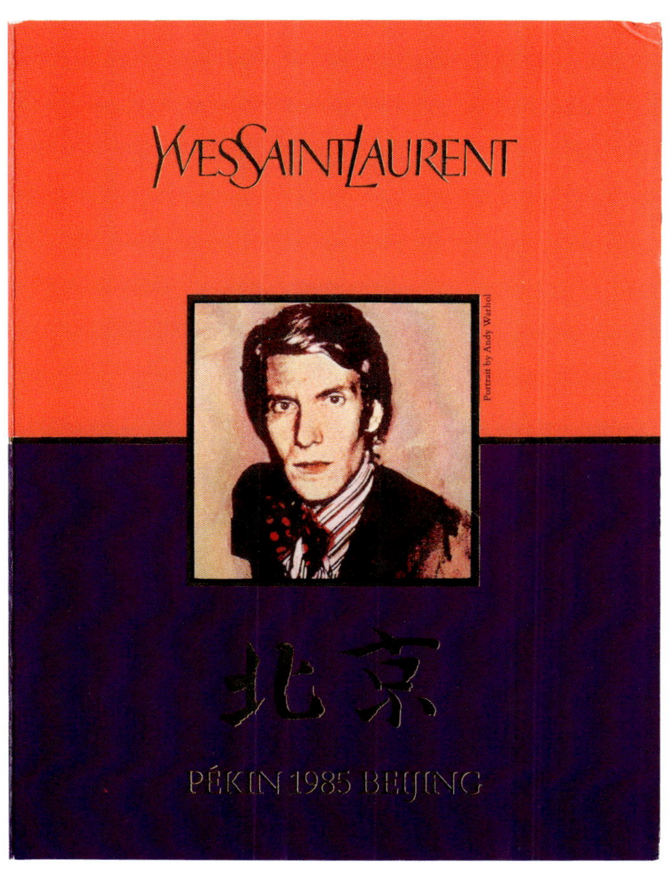

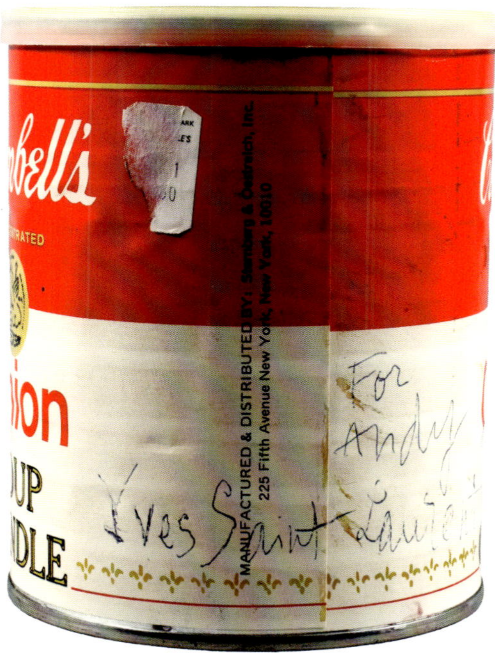

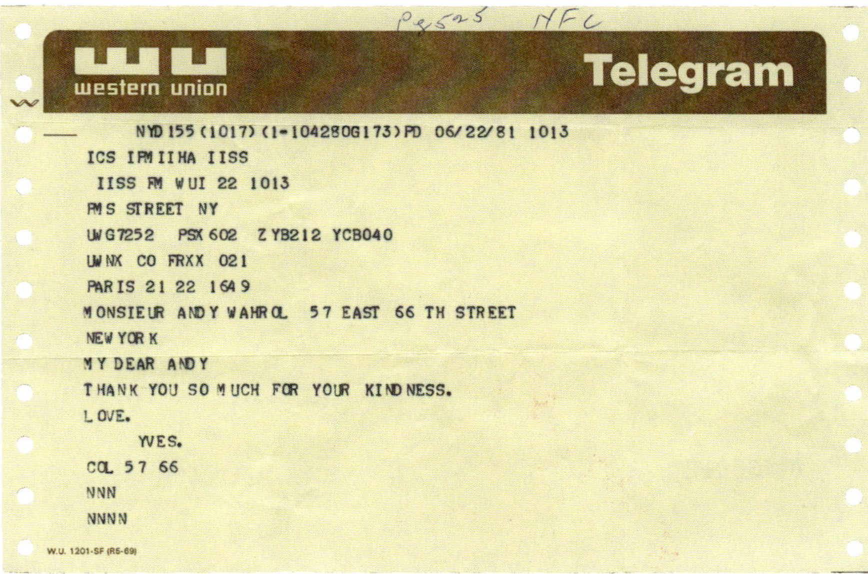

(clockwise from top) Note from Yves Saint Laurent to Warhol, ca. 1972; Telegram from Yves Saint Laurent to "Monsieur Andy Warhol," June 22, 1981; Invitation for first New York showing of Yves Saint Laurent's Haute Couture collection sent to Warhol, November 5, 1974; Campbell's Onion Soup candle signed "for Andy—Yves Saint Laurent," 1970–75; Announcement for retrospective exhibition of Yves Saint Laurent at the Palace of Fine Arts, Beijing, May–July 1985

There is much evidence that Warhol was unhappy with his physical appearance, yet he left behind an incredible number of images of himself. He created many self-portraits beginning in his youth and allowed himself to be painted, photographed, filmed, and videotaped throughout his life. Some of these he changed to make his image more flattering. His childhood photos show him to be sweet looking, but his late adolescence changed his facial features. In the 1950s, during his early twenties, Warhol started to lose his hair and wore a small hairpiece to hide this problem. Some years later, this became a trademark wig.

In the mid-1950s, Warhol had minor corrective surgery on his bulbous nose, although it wasn't terribly successful. His series of *Before and After* paintings (1961–62) addresses this desire to change his appearance. "At one time the way my nose looked really bothered me—it's always red—and I decided that I wanted to have it sanded....I went to see the doctor and I think he thought he'd humor me, so he sanded it, and when I walked out of St. Luke's Hospital I was the same underneath, but I had a bandage on."[1] Prior to the surgical treatment, Warhol made cosmetic alterations to a number of photos. The portrait of

Z

is for ZOMBIE

This chapter is based on an exhibition titled *Warhol and Disguise*, in the Archives Study Center, August 24, 2002–January 26, 2003.

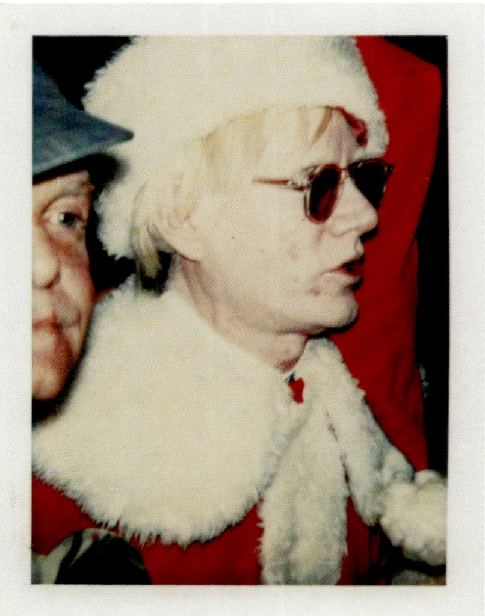

Warhol by the Melton-Pippin studio (ca. 1952) was subtly modified by Warhol with a pencil to make his large, round nose appear more slender. Warhol also altered his 1956 passport photo to correct his thinning hair and his nose.

Edward Wallowitch made a series of photographs of Warhol in 1957 that artistically modified his appearance with projections. In one photo, Warhol's profile is distorted by the image of a girl's face superimposed onto his at an odd angle. The juxtaposition and morphing of faces causes a discomforting view with multiple features. Little is known about Wallowitch's photograph taken at another sitting in the 1950s, of Warhol dressed as a clown.

While he worked very hard to improve his looks, Warhol's image became recognizable throughout American culture by the 1960s. It was imitated by anonymous fans and well-known friends such as the artist Roy Lichtenstein and his wife, Dorothy, who attended a costume party in the mid-1960s dressed as Warhol and Edie Sedgwick, the star of many of his films and his "Girl of the Year" for 1965 (see "E is for Edie").

Warhol was hired for a college lecture tour in 1967. He decided to split his fee with his handsome Superstar Allen Midgette, and sent him in his place, dressed as Warhol, using talcum powder to whiten his hair and skin. The photos show Midgette onstage as Warhol and together with Warhol. After several successes, a college in Oregon discovered the ruse, forcing Warhol to repeat the tour. Warhol continued, however, to allow others to impersonate him over the phone: "One afternoon as I was silk-screening some Jackie canvases, I watched Lou [Reed] answer the phone, then hand it over to Silver George who identified himself: 'Yes, this is Andy Warhol.' That was fine with me. Everybody at the Factory did that….Anyway, it was more fun to let other people take the calls for me, and I'd sometimes read interviews with me (supposedly) that I'd never given at all, that had been done over the phone."[2]

In 1980 Warhol modeled for a robot, intended for a stage show, *Andy Warhol: A No-Man Show*. The robot was constructed, but the play wasn't produced. The following year, Warhol created a series of drag self-portraits and posed for his friend and collaborator, the photographer Christopher Makos, for Makos's portfolio *Altered Image*.

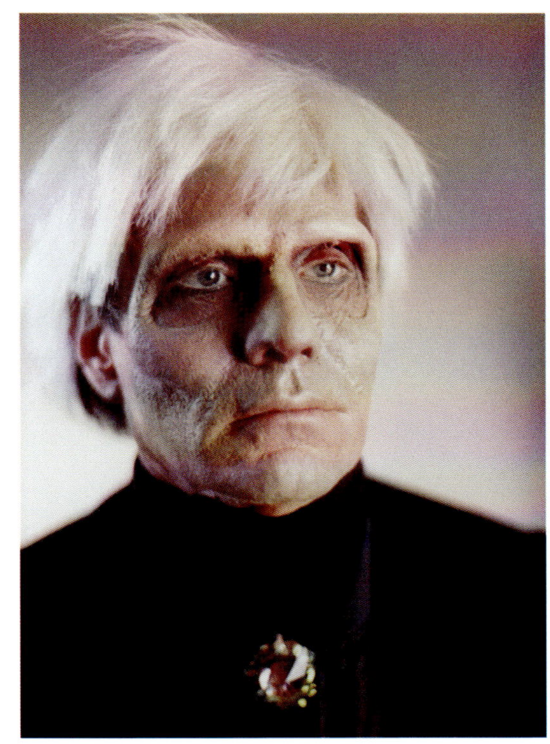

One of these photos was published in *Artforum* magazine in February 1982. In his *Philosophy* (1975), Warhol revealed, "I'm fascinated by boys who spend their lives trying to be complete girls, because they have to work so hard—double time—getting rid of the tell-tale male signs and drawing in all the female signs. I'm not saying it's the right thing to do, I'm not saying it's a good idea, I'm not saying it's not self-defeating and self-destructive, and I'm not saying it's not possibly the most absurd thing a man can do with his life. What I'm saying is, it is very hard work. You can't take that away from them."[3] Warhol had assistants capture all the "hard work" on videotape, shooting the various stages of the drag-makeup process. Quite possibly the most unlikely disguise was Warhol-turned-zombie. The makeup artist Tom Savini, famous for his work on George Romero's *Living Dead* films, dressed Warhol as a walking-dead person in 1984.

Nine months before his untimely death, Warhol undertook a series of large self-portrait works. The *Camouflage Self-Portraits* (1986) are monumental in size, some measuring over 6 feet square, and have a haunting quality from the compositional use of dense black. Each work centers on a levitating head surrounded by spiky hair and patterned with colorful camouflage. In Warhol's hands, camouflage references the military art of concealment but also reflects his personal need for cover. About earlier works, Warhol explained, "When I did my self-portrait, I left all the pimples out because you always should. Pimples are a temporary condition and they don't have anything to do with what you really look like. Always omit the blemishes—they're not part of the good picture you want."[4] After a lifetime of skin treatments, hairpieces, and

"gluing himself together," Warhol's masquerade was his only form of exposure.[5]

NOTES

1. Andy Warhol, *The Philosophy of Andy Warhol (From A to B and Back Again)* (New York: Harcourt Brace Jovanovich, 1975), 63–64.

2. Andy Warhol and Pat Hackett, *POPism: The Warhol Sixties* (Orlando, FL: Harcourt Brace Jovanovich, 1980), 250–51.

3. Warhol, *Philosophy of Andy Warhol*, 54–55.

4. Ibid., 62.

5. Andy Warhol and Pat Hackett, eds., *The Andy Warhol Diaries* (New York: Hachette Book Group, 1989), xvii.

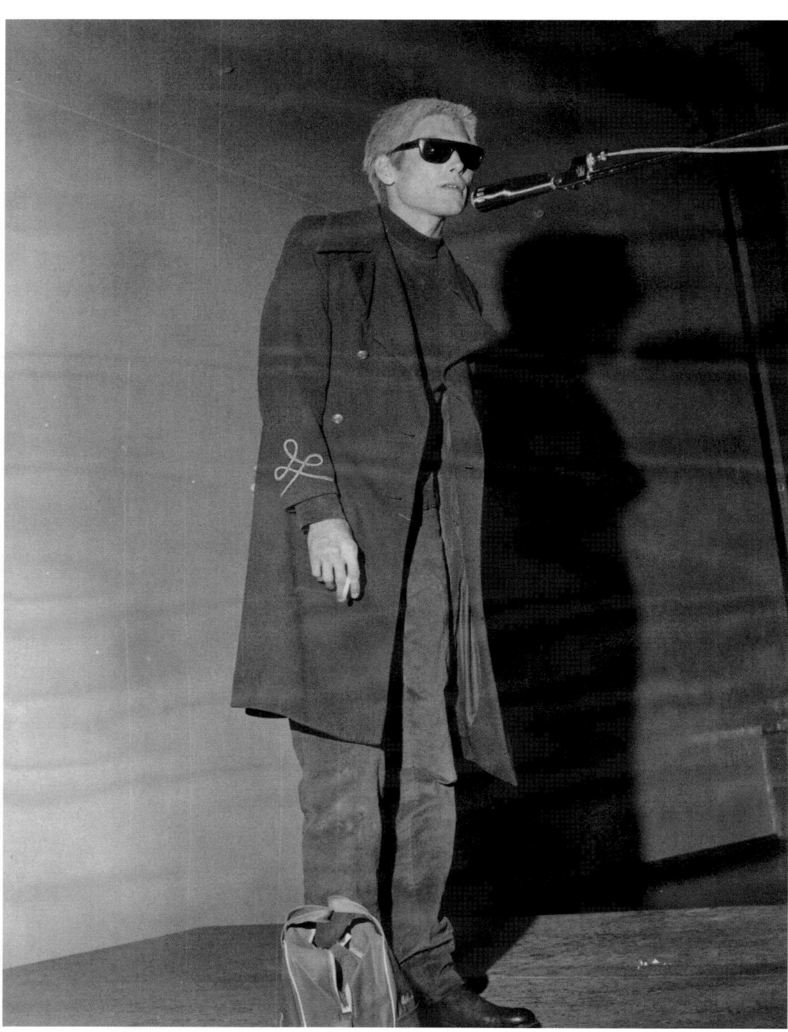

Photographer unknown, *Allen Midgette Impersonating Andy Warhol*, 1967

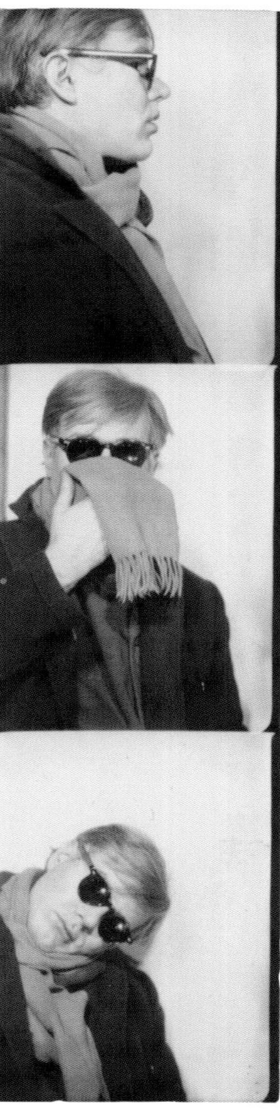

Andy Warhol, *Self-Portrait*, 1963–64

Edward Wallowitch, *Andy Warhol with Girl Projected on Face*, 1957

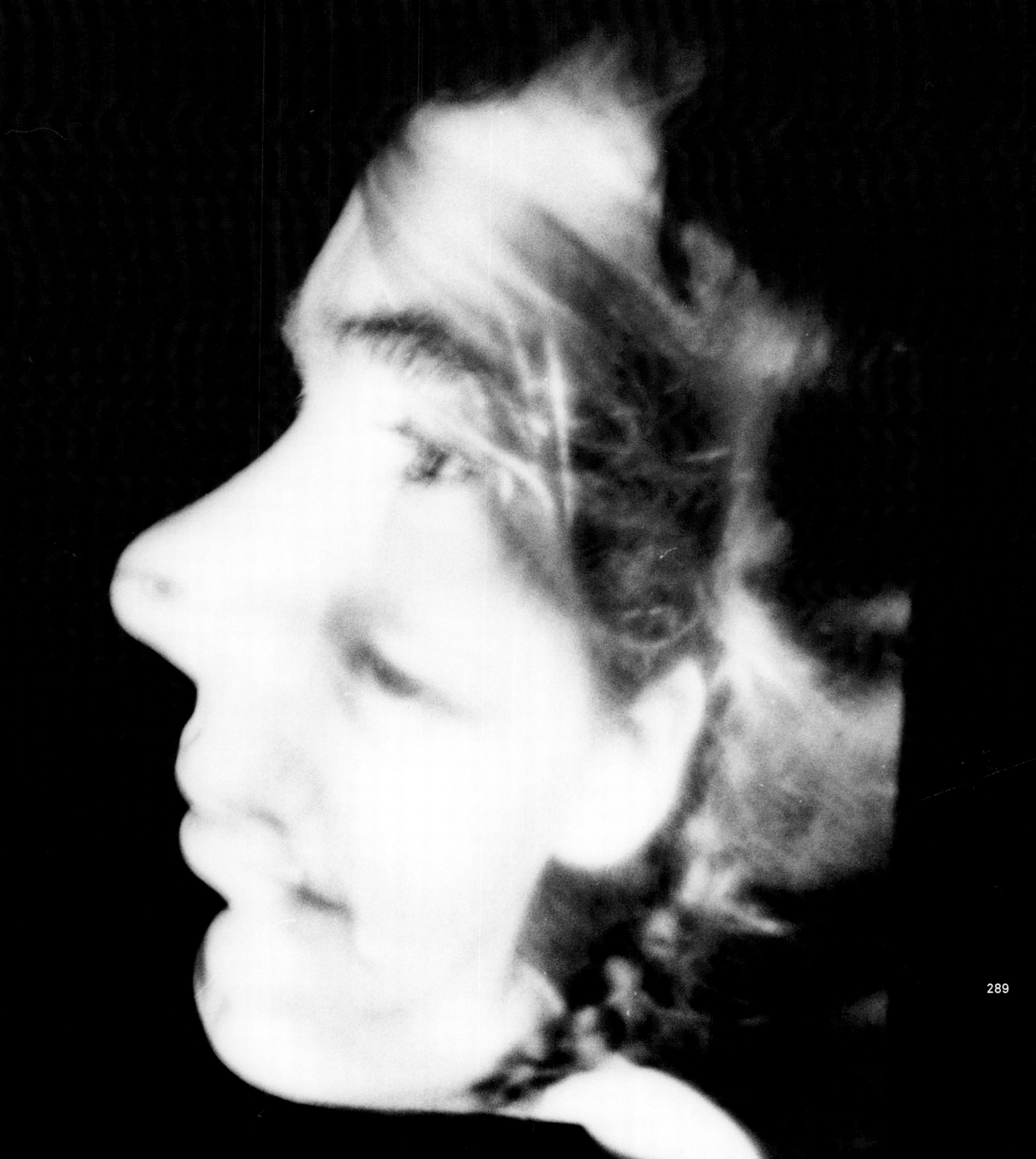

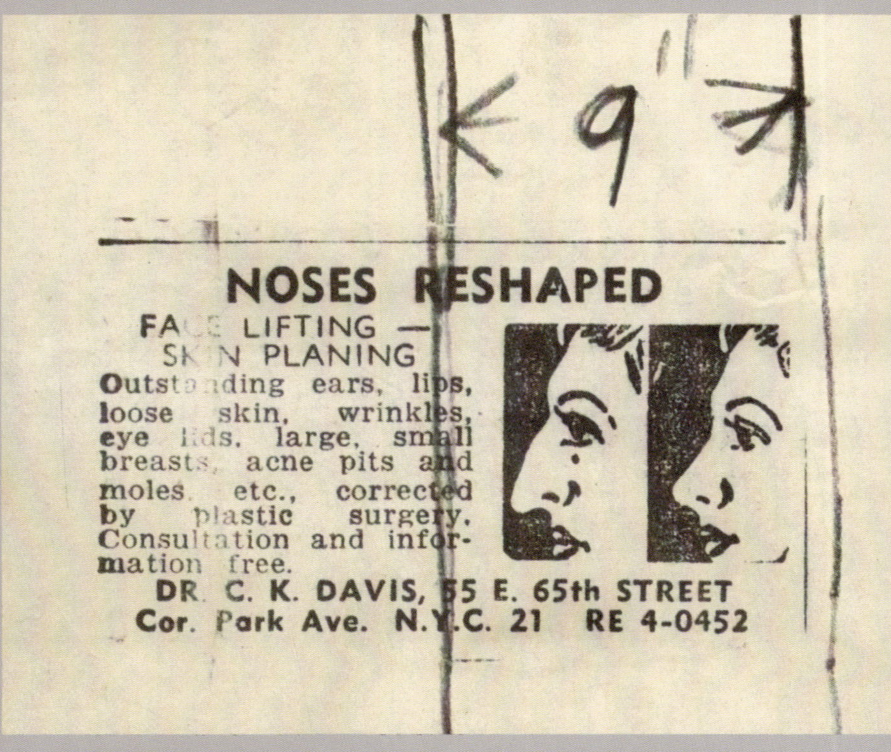

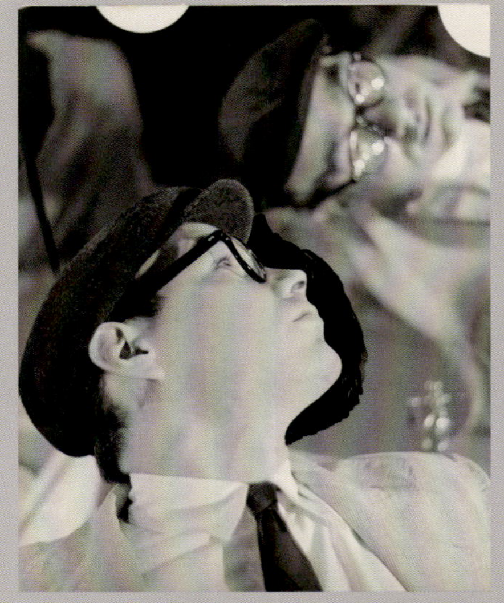

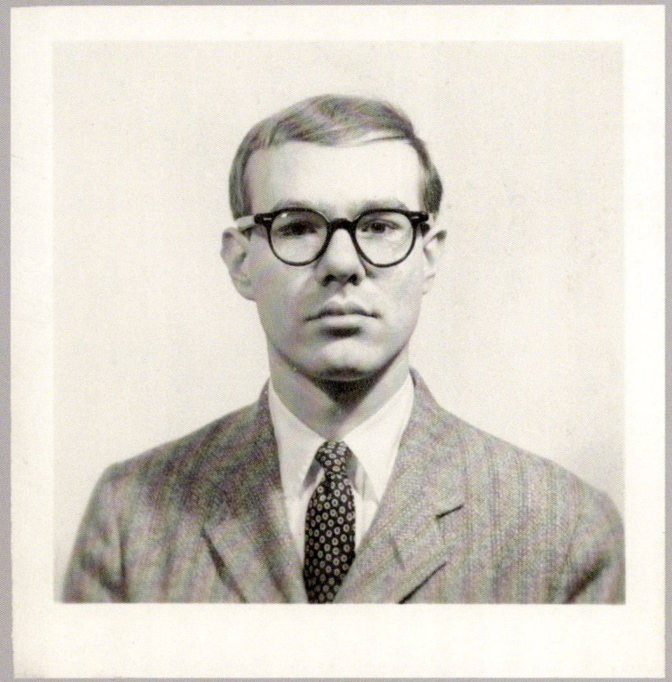

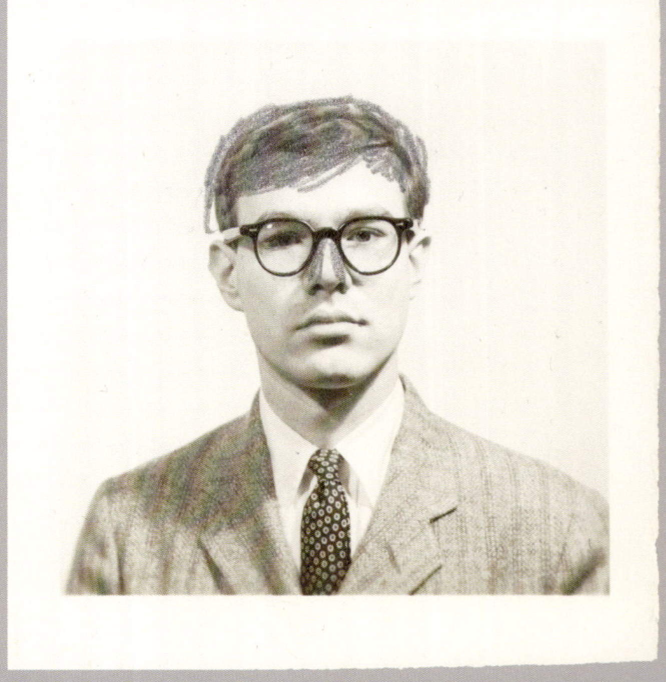

Photostat, "Noses Reshaped," 1961

Warhol passport photograph, 1956

Otto Fenn, *Andy Warhol with Altered Nose*, ca. 1952

Andy Warhol, *Self-Portrait (Passport Photograph with Altered Nose)*, 1956

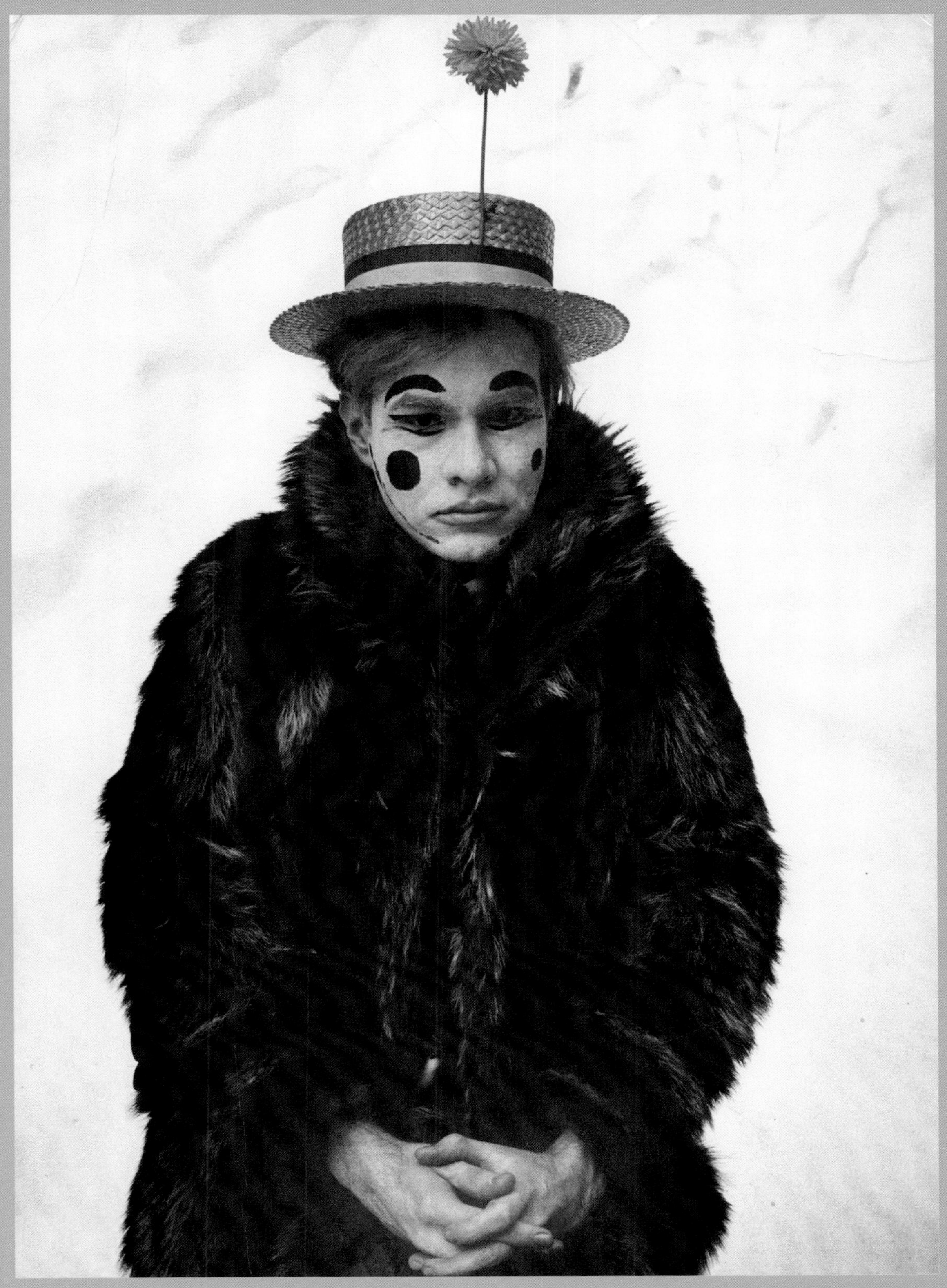

291

Edward Wallowitch, *Andy Warhol Dressed as a Clown*, 1950s

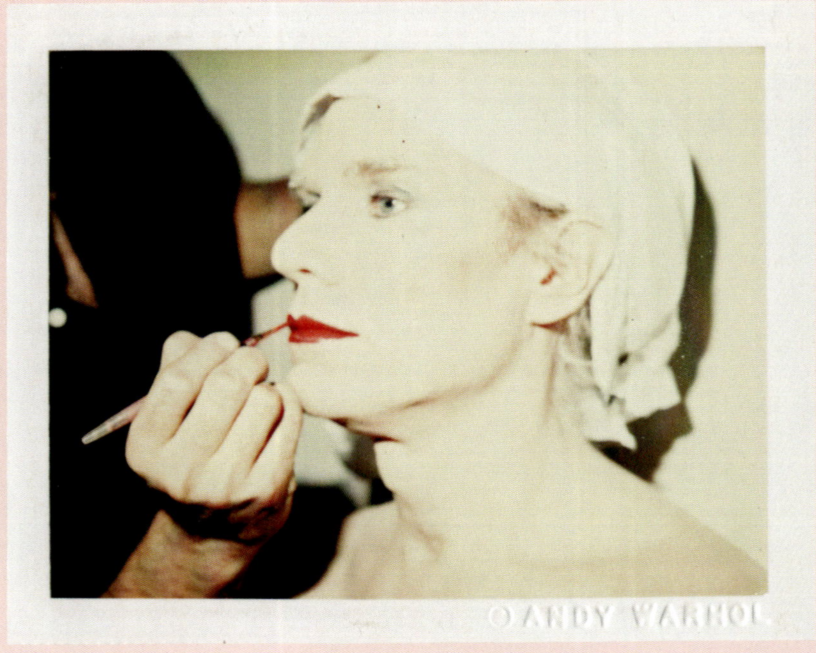

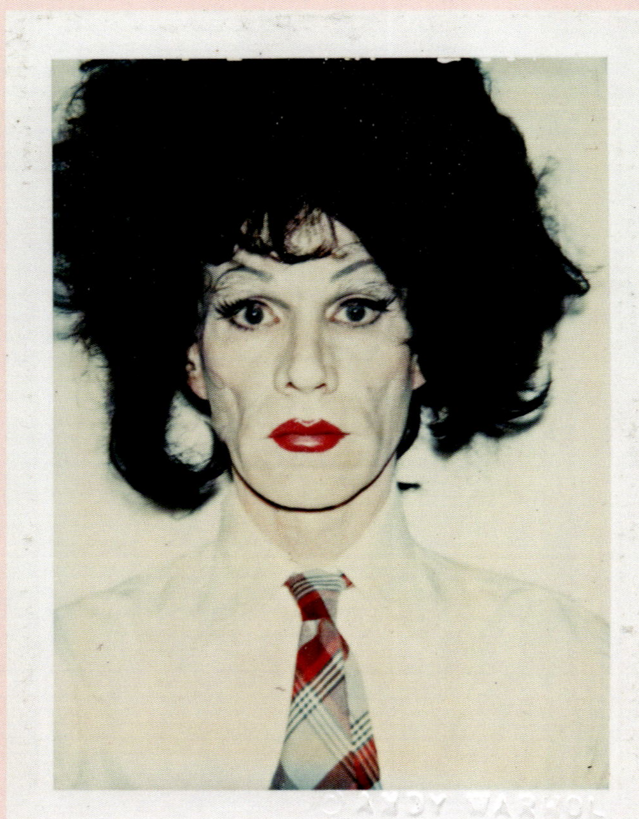

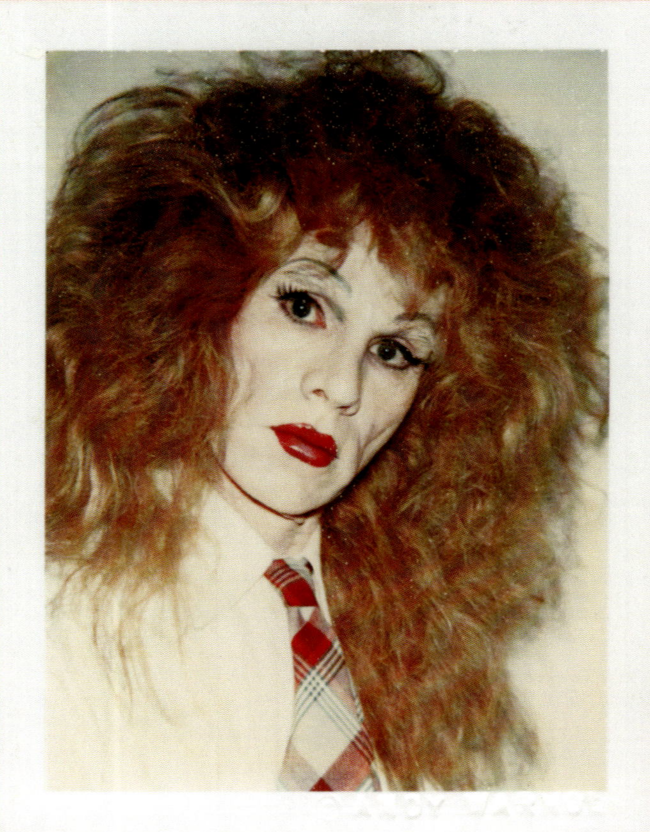

Andy Warhol, *Self-Portrait in Drag* (three Polaroids), 1981

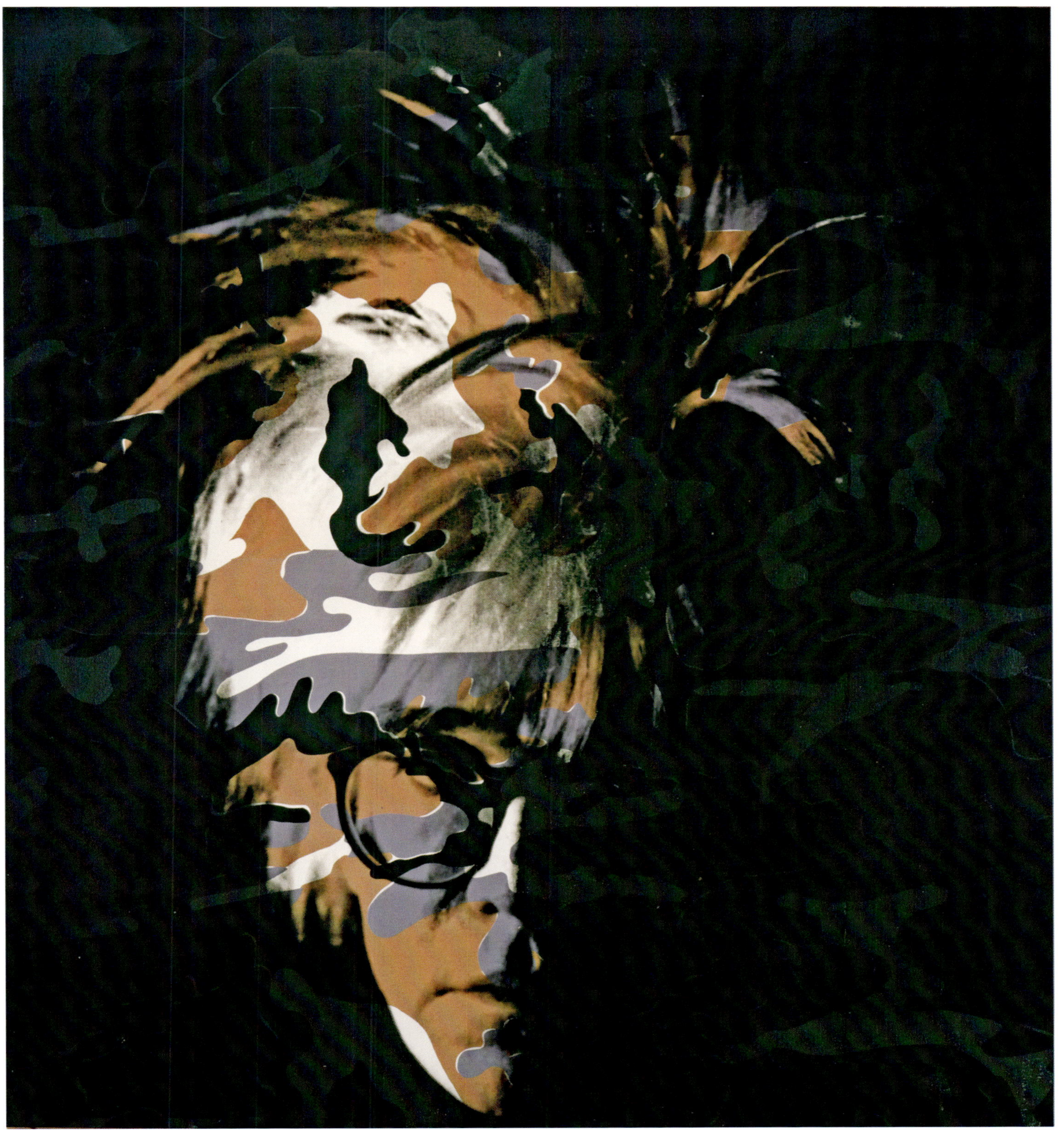

Andy Warhol, *Self-Portrait*, 1986

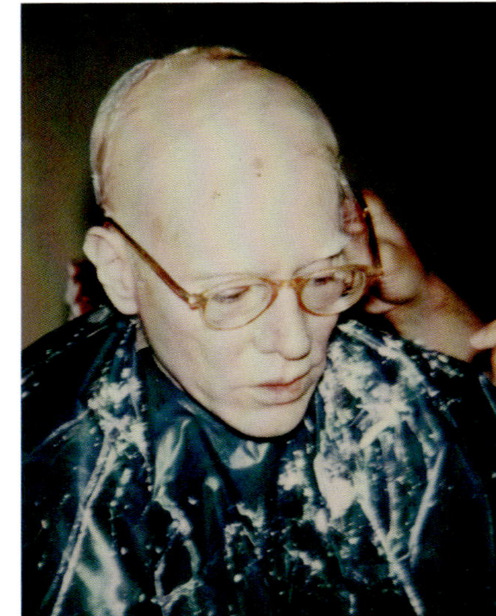

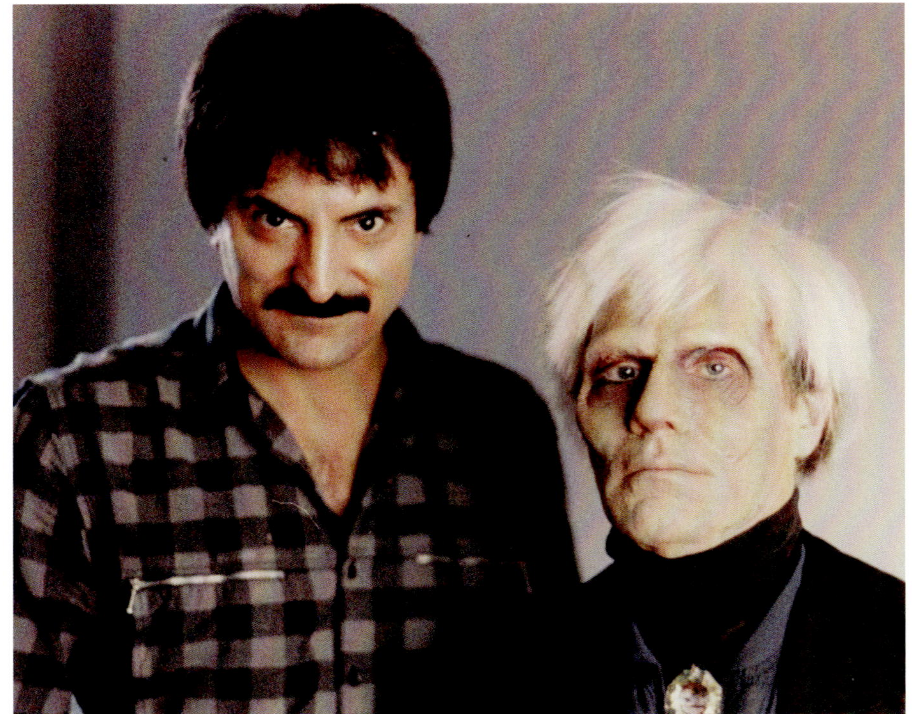

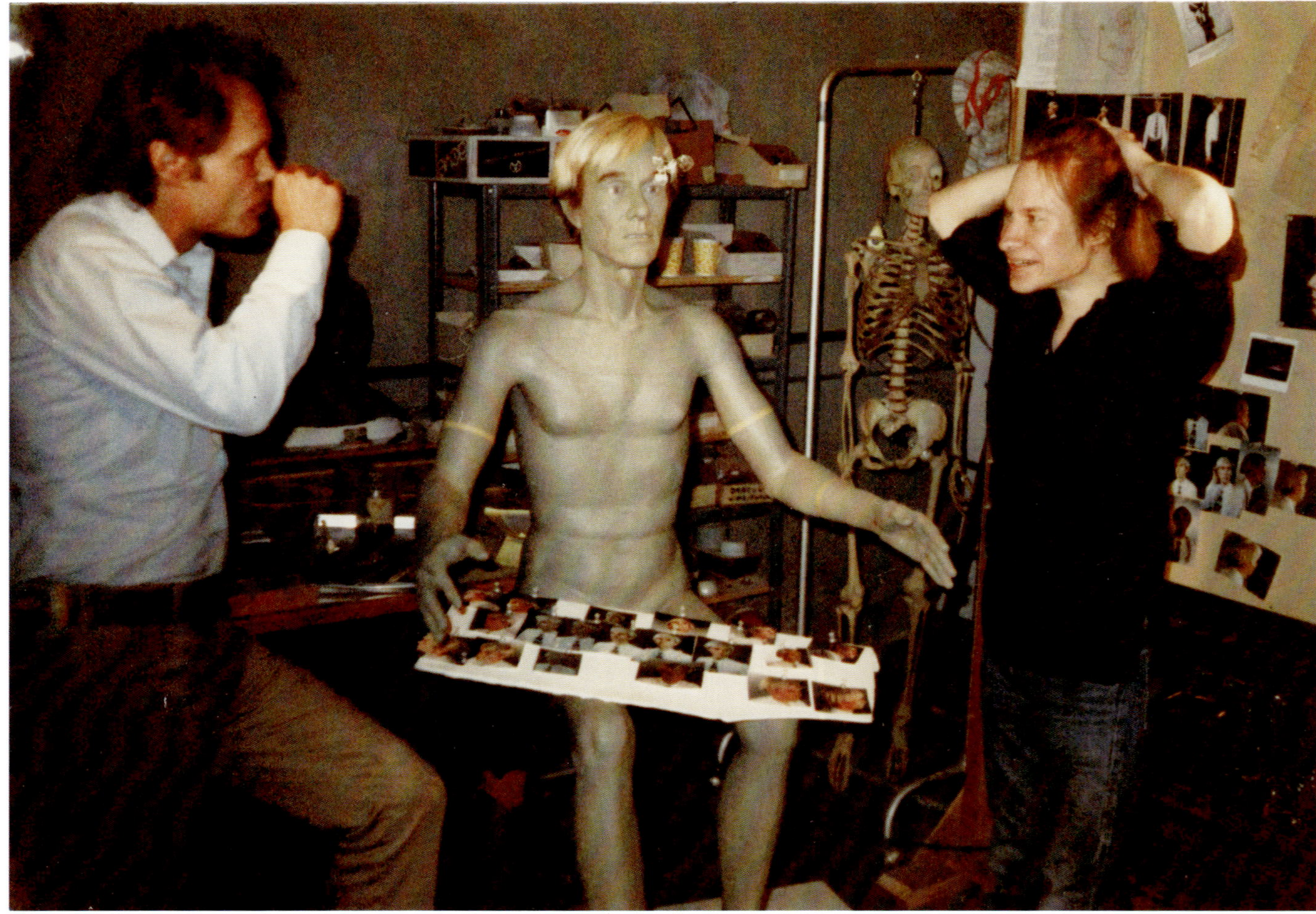

Andy Warhol, *Self-Portrait* (during the life-mask process for the Warhol robot), ca. 1982

Photographer unknown, *Unidentified Man and Woman with the Andy Warhol Audioanimatronic Robot*, ca. 1982–83

Tom Savini, *Tom Savini and Andy Warhol*, ca. 1984

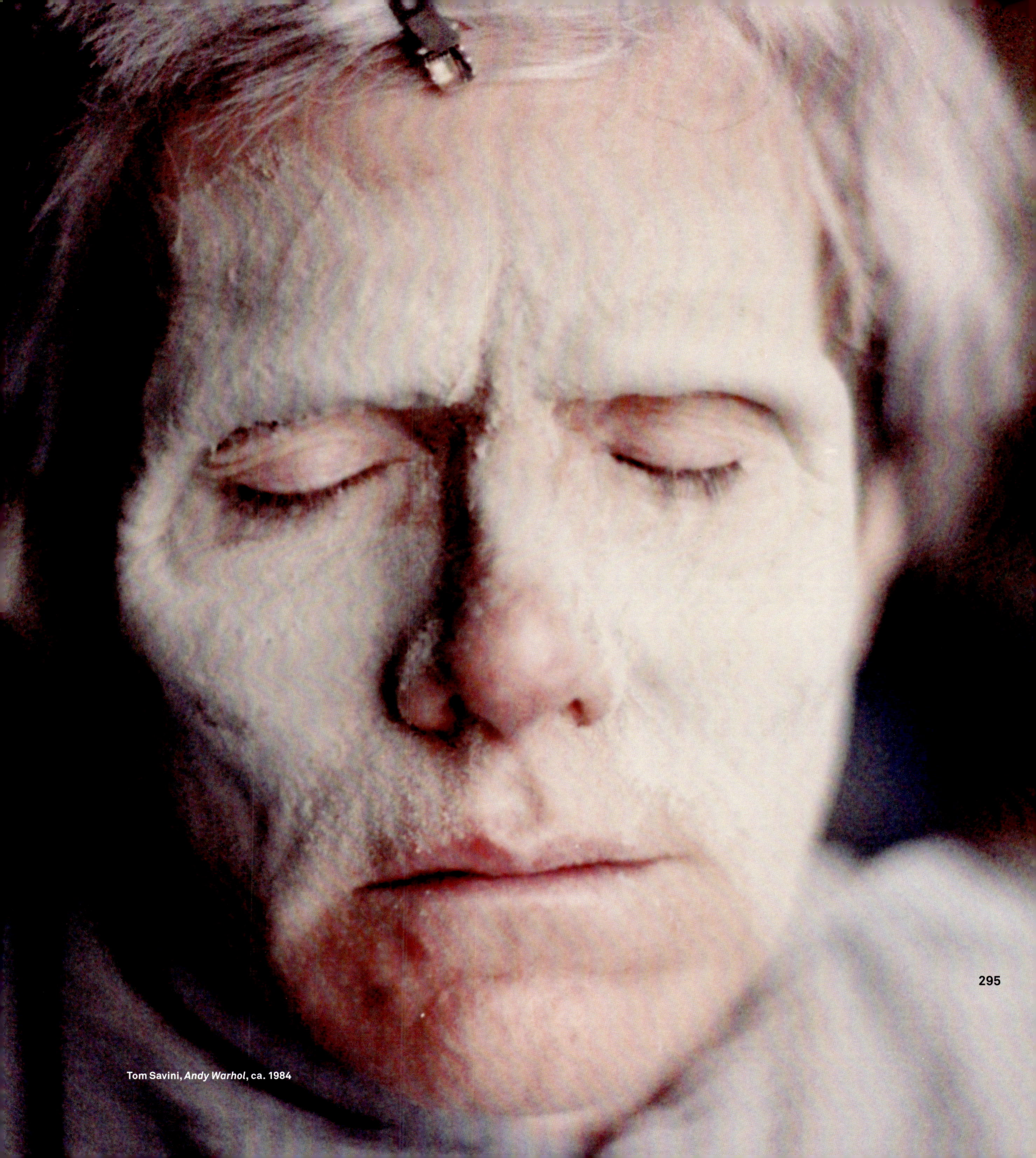

295

Tom Savini, *Andy Warhol*, ca. 1984

List of Illustrations

Unless otherwise noted, all images are from the collection of The Andy Warhol Museum, Pittsburgh; Founding Collection, Contribution The Andy Warhol Foundation for the Visual Arts, Inc. and the Dia Center for the Arts. In illustrations of grouped objects, individual materials and dimensions are not listed.

A is for AUTOGRAPH

11
Inflatable birthday cake inscribed by Yoko Ono to Andy Warhol, n.d. Plastic, 12 × 12 × 9 in. (30.5 × 30.5 × 22.9 cm). TC527.1.2

12
Plate signed by Salvador Dalí, n.d. Felt-tip marker on glazed ceramic, diameter: 6 3/4 in. (17.1 cm). 2000.2.1049

Vulcan Electric Company, electric Andy Warhol signature branding iron, n.d. Iron, electrical wiring, 13 1/2 × 5 in. (34.3 × 12.7 cm). T3657.1

13
Signed note from Robert Rauschenberg on Andy Warhol's personal stationery, ca. 1984. Felt-tip marker on printed paper, 11 × 8 1/2 in. (27.9 × 21.6 cm). TC522.113

Plaza Hotel napkin inscribed by artist and designer Erté to Andy Warhol, n.d. Felt-tip marker on linen, 20 × 24 in. (50.8 × 61 cm). 2000.2.1543

Eddie Bauer ski vest signed and dated with graffiti art and doodles by Jean-Michel Basquiat, Keith Haring, L.A. II, Liberace, Mimi, Christopher Reeve, and Kenny Scharf, 1984. Felt-tip marker on 100% nylon cloth, size (US): 36. T500

14
Birth certificate for Jean-Michel Basquiat, issued 1984. Printed ink and felt-tip marker on paper, 6 × 7 3/4 in. (15.2 × 19.7 cm). TC522.117

15
Andy Warhol, scrapbook (Eothen, Montauk), 1972–78. Mixed archival materials, closed: 8 3/4 × 11 3/4 × 1 1/4 in. (22.2 × 29.8 × 3.2 cm). 1998.3.4646

16
David Bowie, *Hunky Dory* (pre-release copy), inscribed by Bowie to Andy Warhol, 1971. Vinyl record album. 1998.3.9392.3.1a

17
The Beatles, *The Beatles Christmas Album*, inscribed by John Lennon and Yoko Ono to Andy Warhol, 1970. Offset lithograph on coated record cover stock with vinyl record album, cover: 12 3/8 × 13 in. (31.4 × 33 cm). 1998.3.6503.1a–.1c

18
Grace Jones, *That's the Trouble*, inscribed by Jones to Andy Warhol, 1976. Offset lithograph on coated record cover stock with vinyl record album, cover: 12 3/8 × 12 3/8 in. (31.4 × 31.4 cm). 1998.3.6367a–c

Warner Bros. Records, pin-back button promoting *Under Wraps* by Shaun Cassidy, ca. 1978. Printed ink on paper and metal. TC194.266.3

Menu from the Edwardian Room at the Plaza Hotel inscribed by Shaun Cassidy to Andy Warhol, ca. 1978. Printed ink and felt-tip marker on paper, elastic cord, 13 × 10 in. (33 × 25.4 cm). TC194.274

19
Photographer unknown, *Shirley Temple*, inscribed to "Andrew Warhola," 1941. Hand-colored sepia print, 10 × 8 in. (25.4 × 20.3 cm). TC61.3

Photographer unknown, *Liza Minnelli*, inscribed to Andy Warhol, 1970s. Gelatin silver print, 10 × 8 in. (25.4 × 20.3 cm). 1998.3.2725

Andy Warhol, *Stevie Wonder*, signed by Wonder, 1972. Polaroid, 4 1/4 × 3 3/8 in. (10.8 × 8.6 cm). 1998.1.2997.6

20
New York Yankees baseball cap inscribed by Bobby Murcer to Andy Warhol, ca. 1979–83. Cotton, plastic, 9 1/2 × 8 × 6 in. (24.1 × 20.3 × 15.2 cm). 1998.3.5730.1

Hockey sticks inscribed by Rod Gilbert, Ron Duguay, and Wayne Gretzky to Andy Warhol, 1978, 1982, 1983. Printed ink and felt-tip marker on wood. 1998.3.8870–.8872

21
Letter from Wayne D. Gretzky to Mr. Andy Warhol, July 7, 1983, posted July 8, 1983, Edmonton, Alberta. Typewritten with felt-tip marker signature on printed letterhead, 11 × 8 1/2 in. (27.9 × 21.6 cm). 1998.3.9584.2

22–23
Note from comedian Milton Berle to Andy Warhol, n.d. Printed ink and ballpoint pen on cardstock, overall: 5 × 8 in. (12.7 × 20.3 cm). T3622

Drinking glass signed by Nick Rhodes, ca. 1984. Felt-tip marker on glass, height: 5 in. (12.7 cm), diameter: 2 1/2 in. (6.4 cm). TC522.99

Cassette case signed by Richard James Burgess, ca. 1984. Printed ink on paper with plastic case, case: 2 3/4 × 4 1/4 in. (7 × 10.8 cm). TC522.155a–b

Hergé, *Tintin in Tibet*, inscribed by Hergé to Andy Warhol, April 27, 1972. Printed ink on paper with coated cardboard cover, closed: 12 × 9 × 3/8 in. (30.5 × 22.9 × 1 cm). TC35.2

Note from Amy Carter to Andy Warhol, late 1970s. Felt-tip marker on paper, 9 × 6 in. (22.9 × 15.2 cm). TC194.66

Place card for Mr. Andy Warhol signed by Rube Goldberg, ca. 1970–75. Typewritten ink and ballpoint pen on card, 3 × 3 1/2 in. (7.6 × 8.9 cm). TC67.88

Andy Warhol, guestbook from the Factory, ca. 1977–84. Leather, paper, ink, closed: 12 1/4 × 9 × 1 1/2 in. (31.1 × 22.9 × 3.8 cm). T714

24
Shoes ("Miss Piggy Jogger") inscribed by Halston to Andy Warhol, 1980–83. Printed ink on cardboard, suede, cotton, rubber, size (US): 8 1/2. TC471.4.1a–.3

Andy Warhol, guestbook from the Factory, ca. 1977–84. Leather, paper, ink, 12 1/4 × 9 × 1 1/2 in. (31.1 × 22.9 × 3.8 cm). T714

Note from Gianni Versace to Andy Warhol, n.d. Printed ink and ballpoint pen on cardstock, 4 1/2 × 6 1/4 in. (11.4 × 15.9 cm). TC236.119.2

25
Andy Warhol, scrapbook (Eothen, Montauk), 1972–78. Mixed archival materials, 8 3/4 × 11 3/4 × 1 1/4 in. (22.2 × 29.8 × 3.2 cm). 1998.3.4646

Calvin Klein men's underwear signed by
the designer, 1984. Felt-tip marker on cotton,
9 3/4 × 13 1/2 in. (24.8 × 34.3 cm). 2000.2.1531

B is for BOX

27
Clipping from unidentified newspaper with
excerpt from "A Psychodelic [*sic*] Sparkle,"
Tuesday, February 28, 1967. 2 3/4 × 4 1/8 in.
(7 × 10.5 cm). TC79.75

31
Group of magazines from *Time Capsule 79*,
1963–71. TC79.132, TC79.133, TC79.4a–b,
TC79.9, TC79.110, TC79.27, TC79.111,
TC79.112a–b, TC79.223

32
Financial records for various commercial
assignments completed by Andy Warhol from
Time Capsule 79, 1960–62. TC79.77, TC79.78,
TC79.79, TC79.92, TC79.70.1–.3

33
Receipts, 1964–66: Gem Electronics.
TC79.139.6; Modernage Photographic Services,
Inc. TC79.139.7; Peerless. TC79.183.13;
National Transparent Mfg. Co. TC79.183.28.2;
E.H. & A.C. Friedrichs Co. NY. TC79.139.2;
Invoice from Video Film Laboratories. TC79.34.1

Andy Warhol stationery envelope, ca. 1959.
Printed ink on paper, 4 1/8 × 9 1/2 in.
(10.5 × 24.1 cm). TC79.91

34
Andy Warhol's source materials for *Mona Lisa*
paintings, soup can stencils, and United Scenic
Artists' examination instructions for costume
design work from *Time Capsule 79*, ca. 1962–63.
TC79.50, TC79.53, TC79.95, TC79.96, TC79.161

35
RCA Victor, vinyl record jacket for Ravel, *Daphnis
and Chloe*, Boston Symphony Orchestra, with
original illustrations by Andy Warhol on interior
pages, 1955. Book board and printed ink on
paper, 12 3/16 × 12 7/8 in. (31 × 32.7 cm). TC79.145

36
Stardom 1, no. 5 (November 1959). 10 13/16 × 8 1/8 in.
(27.5 × 20.6 cm). TC79.175

Newspaper clipping sent by Jim Elliott to Andy
Warhol, posted February 13, 1963, Los Angeles.
10 1/2 × 4 11/16 in. (26.7 × 11.9 cm). TC79.190.2

Screen Stars 29, no. 9 (September 1971). Printed
ink on coated and uncoated paper, 10 13/16 × 8 1/4 in.
(27.5 × 21 cm). TC79.222

Promotional book for *Penny Serenade*, 1941.
Printed ink on coated paper, 18 1/2 × 12 1/4 in.
(47 × 31.1 cm). TC79.233a–d

Movie Life 26, no. 5 (May 1963). Printed ink on
coated paper and newsprint, 10 7/8 × 8 1/8 in.
(27.6 × 20.6 cm). TC79.137

Postcard with newspaper clipping from "Max"
to Andy Warhol, posted January 24, 1963, New
York. Ballpoint pen and newsprint on cardstock,
overall: 3 1/4 × 5 1/2 in. (8.3 × 14 cm). TC79.196

37
Contact prints of Rudolf Nureyev dancing, n.d.
Two gelatin silver photographs, each:
2 1/2 × 2 3/4 in. (6.4 × 7 cm). TC79.188a, TC79.188c

Photograph sent by Bill Wilson to Andy Warhol,
possibly the artist May Wilson. Gelatin silver
photographs, 2 7/16 × 3 3/8 in. (6.2 × 8.6 cm).
TC79.94.2

Photographer unknown, Unidentified man
drinking coffee and smoking, n.d. Photographic
negative, 1 3/8 × 9 in. (3.5 × 22.9 cm). TC79.109

Photographs sent by Billy Name to Andy
Warhol, ca. 1966. Ink on paper and gelatin silver
print, left: 2 1/2 × 2 1/2 in. (6.4 × 6.4 cm), right:
3 1/4 × 4 1/2 in. (8.3 × 11.4 cm). TC79.52.2–.3

38
Clipping from "New Faces, New Forces, New
Names in the Arts," *Harper's Bazaar* (June 1963).
Printed ink on coated paper, 11 1/2 × 6 1/2 in.
(29.2 × 16.5 cm). TC79.189

Exhibition announcement for *Andy Warhol:
The Personality of the Artist*, Stable Gallery,
New York, April 21–May 9, 1964. Printed ink on
coated paper, 13 3/8 × 9 1/2 in. (34 × 24.1 cm).
TC79.201.2.1

Photographer unknown, *Andy Warhol*, early
1960s. Polaroid, 5 1/4 × 3 1/4 in. (13.3 × 8.3 cm).
TC79.39.1

39
Group of items related to the Velvet Underground
from *Time Capsule 79*, 1966. TC79.108,
TC79.183.24, TC79.57.2, TC79.28.1–.3, TC79.114,
TC79.58

C is for CANIS MAJOR

41
Photographer unknown, Andy Warhol with
the family's dog, Lucy, and Julia Warhola at
Dawson Street, ca. 1946. Gelatin silver print,
3 3/8 × 2 1/2 in. (8.6 × 6.4 cm). 1998.3.2691

43
Andy Warhol, *"Do You See My Little Pussy,"* 1958.
Ink on Strathmore Seconds paper, and colored
graphic art paper, overall with homemade
mat: 22 × 13 3/8 in. (55.9 × 34 cm). 1998.1.1447

44
Andy Warhol, *Cats and Dogs (Maurice)*, 1976.
Acrylic and silkscreen ink on linen, 32 × 26 in.
(81.3 × 66 cm). 1998.1.202

45
Andy Warhol, *Cats and Dogs (Cecil)*, 1976.
Acrylic and silkscreen ink on linen, 40 × 50 in.
(101.6 × 127 cm). 1998.1.207

46
Julia Warhola, *Holy Cats by Andy Warhol's
Mother*, 1960. Offset lithograph on colored
paper with buckram board cover, book:
9 1/8 × 5 7/8 × 3/16 in. (23.2 × 14.9 × 0.5 cm),
each plate: 8 3/4 × 5 1/2 in. (22.2 × 14 cm).
1998.3.2429.4

47
Andy Warhol, *25 Cats Name Sam and One Blue
Pussy*, 1956. Offset lithograph and Dr. Martin's
aniline dye on paper with buckram board cover,
9 1/4 × 6 1/8 × 3/8 in. (23.5 × 15.6 × 1 cm). Gift of
George Klauber, 1998.2.9

48–49
Taxidermy lion. Animal hide, glass, life-size.
1998.3.10

50
Andy Warhol:
Dalmatian, ca. 1976–86. 2001.2.9
Pug, ca. 1984. 2001.2.4
West Highland White Terrier ("Westie"),
ca. 1976–86. 2001.2.8
Black Labrador and Golden Retriever,
ca. 1976–86. 2001.2.11
Cat, ca. 1976–86. 2001.2.5
Five gelatin silver prints, each: (left) 8 × 10 in.
(20.3 × 25.4 cm), (right) 10 × 8 in. (25.4 × 20.3 cm).

51
Andy Warhol:
Dog, ca. 1976–86. 2001.2.1
Great Dane, 1983. 2001.2.16
Great American Mutt, ca. 1976–86. 2001.2.12
Paloma Picasso and Raphael Lopez Sanchez,
1980. 2001.2.773
Four gelatin silver prints, each: 8 × 10 in.
(20.3 × 25.4 cm), (bottom right) 10 × 8 in.
(25.4 × 20.3 cm).

John Bean Studios, New York, *Sandy (Dog from
the Broadway Musical "Annie")*, 1977. Gelatin
silver print, 11 × 13 ⁷/₈ in. (27.9 × 35.2 cm).
2000.2.3286

52
Andy Warhol:
Brigid Berlin, ca. 1981. 2001.2.72
Jean-Michel Basquiat and Dog, 1984. 2001.2.571
Two gelatin silver prints, each: 10 × 8 in.
(25.4 × 20.3 cm).

Interview magazine "Santa Paws" Christmas
card, n.d. Printed ink on cardstock, 5 × 7 in.
(12.7 × 17.8 cm). T3635

53
Edward Wallowitch, *Andy Warhol in Bed with
Cats*, ca. 1957. Gelatin silver print, 10 × 8 in.
(25.4 × 20.3 cm). 1998.3.5202

Andy Warhol, *Jed Johnson*, 1973. Polacolor Type
108 Polaroid. 2001.2.1275

Photographer unknown, *Andy Warhol
Holding Archie*, ca. 1977. Polaroid, 4 × 3 ⁷/₈ in.
(10.2 × 9.8 cm). TC276.93

54
Dog collars, tags, and papers for Amos and
Archie, dachshunds owned by Jed Johnson and
Andy Warhol. 1998.3.6921.1–.2, 1998.3.7241,
1998.3.7590.1–.3, 2000.2.2586.1.1–2.4,
1998.3.7254, 1998.3.9613.2–.3, 1998.3.9613.5

55
Beige dog sweater possibly worn by Amos or
Archie. 1998.3.8227

D is for DUCHAMP

57
RSVP card from Marcel Duchamp to Andy
Warhol, April 14, 1965. Printed ink and ballpoint
pen on paper, 3 ¹/₄ × 5 ¹/₂ in. (8.3 × 14 cm).
TC25.57.3

58
Marcel Duchamp, *In Advance of the Broken Arm*,
1915/63. Readymade: snow shovel of wood and
iron, 50 × 16 ¹/₂ × 5 ³/₄ in. (127 × 41.9 × 14.6 cm).
Moderna Museet, Stockholm; Donation 1965
from Moderna Museets Vänner, NMSK 1888

Andy Warhol, *Brillo Soap Pads Box*, 1964. Silkscreen ink and house paint on plywood, 17 × 17 ×
14 in. (43.2 × 43.2 × 35.6 cm). 1998.1.706

59
Marcel Duchamp, *Fountain*, 1917/63. Assisted
readymade: porcelain urinal on its back,
13 × 16 ¹/₂ × 20 ¹/₂ in. (33 × 41.9 × 52.1 cm).
Moderna Museet, Stockholm; Donation 1965
from Moderna Museets Vänner, NMSK 1884

Andy Warhol, *100 Cans*, 1962. Casein, spray paint,
and pencil on cotton, 72 ³/₈ × 52 ³/₈ in. (183.8 ×
133 cm). Albright-Knox Art Gallery, Buffalo; Gift of
Seymour H. Knox, Jr., 1963, K1963:26

60
Andy Warhol, *Toilet*, 1961. Water-based paint on
linen, 68 ⁵/₈ × 59 in. (174.3 × 149.9 cm). 1998.1.6

Andy Warhol, *Oxidation Painting*, 1978. Acrylic
and urine on linen, 14 × 10 in. (35.6 × 25.4 cm).
1998.1.215

61
Marcel Duchamp, *Bottle-Rack*, 1914/64. The
original, lost, was carried out in Paris in 1914.
Replica under the direction of Duchamp in
1964 by the Gallery Schwarz, Milan. Galvanized
metal, 25 ¹/₄ × 9 ¹/₂ in. (64 × 24 cm). Musée
National d'Art Moderne, Centre Georges
Pompidou, Paris, AM 1986-288

Andy Warhol, *You're In*, 1967. Spray paint on
glass bottles in printed wooden crate, crate:
8 × 17 × 12 in. (20.3 × 43.2 × 30.5 cm), each
bottle: 8 × 2 ¹/₄ in. (20.3 x 5.7 cm), diameter:
7 ³/₈ in. (18.7 cm). 1998.1.789a–x

62
Marcel Duchamp, *A Poster Within a Poster
(Pasadena exhibition poster)* (detail), 1963.
Offset lithograph on paper, signed by the artist,
19 ¹/₂ × 14 in. (49.5 × 35.6 cm). TC-24.228

Andy Warhol, *Most Wanted Men No. 2, John
Victor G.*, 1964. Silkscreen ink on linen,
48 ¹/₂ × 37 ¹/₈ in. (123.2 × 94.3 cm). Founding
Collection, Contribution Dia Center for the
Arts, 2002.4.4a

63
Marcel Duchamp, *L.H.O.O.Q.*, 1919/41. Rectified
readymade: pencil on a printed reproduction,
7 ⁵/₈ × 4 ⁷/₈ in. (19.4 × 12.4 cm). Moderna Museet,
Stockholm; Donation 1975 from Ulf Linde,
MOM/2002/324

Andy Warhol, *Mona Lisa*, ca. 1979. Acrylic
and silkscreen ink on canvas, 25 × 20 in.
(63.5 × 50.8 cm). 1998.1.231

64
Marcel Duchamp, *The Bride Stripped Bare by Her
Bachelors, Even (The Green Box)*, September
1934. Box containing collotype reproductions on
various papers, overall: 13 × 11 ¹/₈ × 1 in.
(33 × 28.3 × 2.5 cm). The Metropolitan Museum
of Art, New York, NY; Anonymous gift, 2002,
2002.42a-vvvv

65
Andy Warhol, blank books, known as "trip books,"
ca. 1968. Paper with coated paper cover, overall:
7 × 4 ¹/₄ × ⁵/₈ in. (17.8 × 10.8 × 1.6 cm). TC74.1.1

66
Marcel Duchamp, *Boîte-en-valise* (*Box in a
Valise*), 1961. Mixed media, 15 × 15 × 3 ¹/₂ in.
(38 × 38 × 8.9 cm). Munson-Williams-Proctor
Arts Institute, Utica, NY; Museum Purchase,
2005.5.1

67
Marcel Duchamp, *Some French Moderns Says
McBride*, 1922. Book (18 printed cardboard
sheets, 7 photographs, bound with 3 metal
rings), 11 ¹³/₁₆ × 9 ¹/₄ in. (30 × 23.5 cm). Courtesy
Beinecke Rare Book & Manuscript Library,
Yale University, New Haven, CT

Andy Warhol, *a: a novel* (New York: Grove Press,
1968). Printed ink on paper, buckram board
cover, 9 ³/₁₆ × 6 ³/₈ × 1 ¹/₄ in. (23.3 × 16.2 × 3.2 cm).
Gift of Jay Reeg, 2012.7.3a–b

68
Exhibition list, *Marcel Duchamp 1904–1968*,
Ronald Feldman Fine Arts Ltd., New York,
November 1973. 2000.2.1606.1
Envelope, letter, invoice, and declaration of
authenticity for purchase of Marcel Duchamp
"Rotorelief" from Jon Grossbard, Everyman
Gallery, to Andy Warhol, posted February 4, 1970,
New York. 2000.2.1621.1–.4
Receipt from Macy's, New York, to Andy Warhol
Enterprises for the purchase of Marcel
Duchamp and René Magritte objects, $3,370.20,
November 25, 1969. T618

69

Pamphlets from Portable Gallery Press, Inc., New York, to Mr. Andy Warhol, posted April 29, 1965, New York. TC5.53.5, TC5.53.2

Realität, Realismus, Realität, exhibition catalogue, Von der Heydt-Museum, Wuppertal, Germany, October 28–December 17, 1972. TC90.231

70

Andy Warhol's Folk and Funk, exhibition catalogue, Museum of American Folk Art, New York, September 20–November 19, 1977. 10 × 7 in. (25.4 × 17.8 cm). T616

Marcel Duchamp, *Door: 11, rue Larrey, Paris (Porte: 11, rue Larrey, Paris)*, 1927. C-print, 98 1/2 × 39 3/4 in. (250 x 100 cm). Photoconsortium, The Israel Museum, Jerusalem, 219536

71

Marcel Duchamp, *La mariée mise à nu par ses célibataires, même (The Bride Stripped Bare by Her Bachelors, Even)*, also known as *The Large Glass*, 1915–23, replica by Ulf Linde, Henrik Samuelson, and John Stenborg, 1991–92, after the 1961 version. Oil, varnish, lead foil, lead wire, and dust on two glass panels, with wood frame, 111 3/8 × 74 3/8 in. (282.9 × 188.9 cm). Moderna Museet, Stockholm, Replik 1

Andy Warhol, *Large Kiss*, 1965. Screen print on Plexiglas in stainless steel and Plexiglas frame, framed: 63 × 42 1/2 × 9 1/4 in. (160 × 108 × 23.5 cm). 1998.1.2378

72–73

Nat Finkelstein, *Marcel Duchamp Filmed by Andy Warhol, Cordier & Ekstrom Gallery, New York City*, 1966. Gelatin silver print, 7 1/8 × 9 1/2 in. (18.1 × 24.1 cm). Museum Purchase, 1996.9.50

74

Correspondence from Marcel Duchamp to Andy Warhol, on Cordier & Ekstrom Gallery letterhead, November 10, 1965. Typewritten ink on paper, 11 × 8 1/2 in. (27.9 × 21.6 cm). TC25.60

75

Andy Warhol, *Chess Player*, 1950s. Ink, wash, and tempera on colored paper, 24 × 18 in. (61 × 45.7 cm). 1998.1.1138

76

Marcel Duchamp, *Tu m'*, 1918. Oil on canvas, with bottlebrush, safety pins, and bolt, 27 1/2 × 119 5/16 in. (69.8 × 303 cm). Yale University Art Gallery; Gift of the Estate of Katherine S. Dreier, 1953.6.4

77

Andy Warhol, *Shadows*, ca. 1978. Screen print on paper, 86 3/8 × 54 1/8 in. (219.4 × 137.5 cm). 1998.1.2545

78

Andy Warhol, *Edie Sedgwick*, ca. 1965. Photo-booth photograph, 7 7/8 × 1 5/8 in. (20 × 4.1 cm). 1998.1.2797

81

David McCabe, *Edie Sedgwick, Andy Warhol, Chuck Wein, and Gerard Malanga*, 1965, reprinted 1996. Gelatin silver print, 11 × 13 15/16 in. (27.9 × 35.4 cm). Museum Purchase, 1996.9.97

84

Stephen Shore, *Edie Sedgwick and Andy Warhol*, ca. 1965. Gelatin silver print, 8 × 10 in. (20.3 × 25.4 cm). Contribution DIA Center for the Arts, 1996.19.15

85

Andy Warhol, *Kitchen*, 1965. 16mm, black-and-white film, sound, 66 mins. 1997.4.150

86

Edie Sedgwick, *Mice*, 1963. Watercolor, ink, and graphite on paper, 9 × 12 in. (22.9 × 30.5 cm). TC64.2

Edie Sedgwick, *Landscape*, 1961. Watercolor and colored pencil on mat board, 7 3/16 × 9 3/16 in. (18.3 × 23.3 cm). TC64.1

87

Edie Sedgwick, *Sketchbook*, 1963. Graphite on spiral bound sketchbook paper, 9 1/4 × 5 1/2 × 3/8 in. (23.5 × 14 × 1 cm). TC64.3

Edie Sedgwick, *Cat with Yarn*, 1961. Graphite on paper, 8 1/2 × 5 3/4 in. (21.6 × 14.6 cm). TC64.13

88

Mental Hygiene Reeducation: Talks to Patients, ca. 1962. Leather-bound board, printed and typewritten ink on paper, 7 5/8 × 5 1/4 × 1 1/4 in. (19.4 × 13.3 × 3.2 cm). 2000.2.3156.1–.2

Pennsylvania Railroad ticket with "Edie 914 679 8094" written by Andy Warhol, ca. 1965, from *Time Capsule 79*. Printed ink on paper, 2 3/16 × 4 5/16 in. (5.6 × 11 cm). TC79.183.2

Get-well card from Edith M. Sedgwick to Mr. Andy Warhol, posted June 4, 1968, New York. Ballpoint pen on coated paper, open: 6 3/16 × 10 1/8 in. (15.7 × 25.7 cm). TC57.1.2

89

Harry Shunk and János Kender, *Andy Warhol in Hotel, Paris, with Gerard Malanga, Edie Sedgwick, and Chuck Wein*, 1965. Gelatin silver print, 7 1/4 × 9 1/2 in. (18.4 × 24.1 cm). 2000.2.3274

91

Melton-Pippin, *Andy Warhol*, ca. 1953. Gelatin silver print, overall: 2 7/8 × 2 7/8 in. (7.3 × 7.3 cm). 1998.3.5424.1

93

Andy Warhol's striped, sailor-style shirt, 1965. Machine-sewn cotton knit, nominal size (European): 3, flat: 57 × 24 in. (144.8 × 61 cm). 1998.3.6002.1

Halson turtleneck, 1985. Black cashmere and silk, size (US): unknown, flat: 31 × 57 1/2 in. (78.7 × 146.1 cm). 1998.3.7492

94

Robert J. Levin, *Andy Warhol Choosing a Bullet-proof Vest, New York City*, 1981. Carbon ink print on rag paper, 13 × 19 in. (33 × 48.3 cm). Gift of Robert J. Levin, 2015.6.13

Patrick McMullan, *Andy Warhol at the Palladium Saturday, September 14, 1985,* 1985. Gelatin silver print, 7 × 5 in. (17.8 × 12.7 cm). 1998.3.3015

95

Stephen Shore, *Andy Warhol with "Flowers,"* 1965. Gelatin silver print, 5 × 8 in. (12.7 × 20.3 cm). 1998.3.14763

Stephen Shore, *Andy Warhol*, 1965. Gelatin silver print, 5 × 8 in. (12.7 × 20.3 cm). 1998.3.14672

96–97

A selection of Andy Warhol's corsets hand-dyed in rainbow colors by Brigid Berlin, late 1960s–1980s. T3664–T3672

98

David Montgomery, *Andy in Repose*, June 1969, reprinted 2005. Piezo pigment color print on Hahnemuhle 100% photo rag paper, 35 1/16 × 22 7/8 in. (89.1 × 58.1 cm). Gift of David Montgomery, 2005.8.1

99

A selection of Andy Warhol's wigs manufactured by Paul Bochicchio Inc., 1980s. Natural and synthetic hair on dyed cloth, each: 15 × 9 × 1 1/2 in. (38.1 × 22.9 × 3.8 cm). 1998.3.6158.1, 1998.3.10814.1 (verso), 1998.3.6158.4 (verso), 1998.3.10814.1, 1998.3.10814.2, 1998.3.6158.2, 1998.3.10814.2 (verso), 2014.8.126, T3104.3

100
Photographer unknown, *Andy Warhol*, 1968.
Color transparency with printed ink on
cardboard mount, slide: 2 × 2 in. (5.1 × 5.1 cm),
transparency: 1 1/16 × 1 1/16 in. (2.7 × 2.7 cm).
2000.2.2973.1

101
Stefano Castronovo, *Jean-Michel Basquiat
Leather Jacket*, 1985. Oil and alkyd paint
on leather, length (jacket): 22 in. (55.9 cm),
length (sleeve): 22 1/2 in. (57.2 cm), collar:
15 in. (38.1 cm), waist: 34 in. (86.4 cm). T449

102
Photographer unknown, *Andy Warhol*,
1950s. Chromogenic color print, 10 × 8 in.
(25.4 × 20.3 cm). T849.7

A selection of Andy Warhol's neckties. T754,
T755, T3284.2–.4, T3284.7, T3284.9, T3284.11,
T3284.12, T3284.14, T3284.17, T3659, T3660,
T3673–T3675

Point Blank Body Armor, bulletproof vest, 1981.
Nylon, bullet-resistant material, 21 × 19 1/4 in.
(53.3 × 48.9 cm). 1998.3.8271

Photographer unknown, *Andy Warhol*, ca. 1978.
Polaroid SX-70, 4 1/4 × 3 1/2 in. (10.8 × 8.9 cm).
TC185.177.5

103
Andy Warhol's Yves Saint Laurent "safari jacket,"
white shirt, and skinny tie, 1970s. 1998.3.7066,
T3661, T3660

Black leather Calvin Klein jacket, 1980s.
1998.3.5737.5; Ford Modeling Agency softball
team sweatshirt, 1980s. T3663

104–5
Andy Warhol's cowboy boots, 1960s–1980s.
1998.3.6958.1a–b, 1998.3.6958.2a–b,
1998.3.6964.1a–b, 1998.3.6964.4a–b,
1998.3.6964.5a–b, 1998.3.7034.1a–b,
1998.3.7034.2a–b, 1998.3.7034.3a–b,
1998.3.8213.1a–b, 1998.3.8213.2a–b,
1998.3.8213.3a–b, 1998.3.8213.4a–b

G is for GRETCHEN

106
Clipping of article "Warhol, Andy :: My True Story"
by Gretchen Berg from *Los Angeles Free Press*,
March 17, 1967. 17 1/2 × 11 5/8 in. (44.5 × 29.5 cm).
TC-6.21

110
Gretchen Berg, *Andy Warhol, Summer 1966*,
reprinted 2006. Gelatin silver print, 11 × 14 in.
(27.9 × 35.6 cm). Gift of Gretchen Berg, 2006.12.4

Gretchen Berg, *Joey Freeman, Andy Warhol and
Unidentified Man, Summer 1966*, reprinted 2006.
Gelatin silver print, 11 × 14 in. (27.9 × 35.6 cm).
Gift of Gretchen Berg, 2006.12.10

111
Typescript "Interview with Andy Warhol" by
Gretchen Berg, 1967. Photocopy on paper,
9 × 12 1/16 in. (22.9 × 30.6 cm). TC14.41.2.2–.7

H is for HEADLINES

113
Andy Warhol, *Time Capsule 322*, January 27,
1981–April 6, 1982, bulk 1981. Mixed
archival material, box: 10 × 14 × 18 in.
(25.4 × 35.6 × 45.7 cm). TC322

115
Jean-Michel Basquiat and Andy Warhol,
Collaboration, 1984–85. Acrylic and oil stick
on linen, 76 × 104 1/8 in. (193 × 264.5 cm).
1998.1.485

116
Andy Warhol:
Time Capsule 433, 1985, undated; bulk
November 1985. TC433
Time Capsule 465, 1983–87, undated;
bulk 1985. TC465
Time Capsule 189, 1976–78; bulk 1978. TC189
All: mixed archival material, box: 10 × 14 × 18 in.
(25.4 × 35.6 × 45.7 cm).

117
Andy Warhol:
Time Capsule 170, 1975–77; bulk 1976–77. TC170
Time Capsule 316, December 1979–
January 1981, undated; bulk 1980. TC316
Time Capsule -5, 1967. TC-5
Time Capsule 529, June 1977–July 1979;
bulk January 1978–July 1979. TC529
Time Capsule -6, 1967–68; bulk 1967. TC-6
Time Capsule 428, 1984–86, undated;
bulk June 1985. TC428
All: mixed archival material, box: 10 × 14 × 18 in.
(25.4 × 35.6 × 45.7 cm).

118
Newspaper headline "Pirates Seize Ship with
900," *Daily News*, January 24, 1961. 15 × 10 7/8 in.
(38.1 × 27.6 cm). TC29.4

Andy Warhol, *"Pirates Sieze Ship . . . ,"* 1961.
Graphite on Strathmore paper, 29 × 23 in.
(73.7 × 58.4 cm). 1998.1.2346

119
Andy Warhol, *Journal American*, ca. 1959.
Ballpoint pen on paper, 23 3/4 × 17 7/8 in.
(60.3 × 45.4 cm). Founding Collection,
Contribution Dia Center for the Arts, 2002.4.39

120
Newspaper article "Artist-Huckster Sketches
Customers and Wins Prize," *Pittsburgh Press*,
Sunday, November 24, 1946. 23 1/2 × 16 5/8 in.
(59.7 × 42.2 cm). 1998.3.5748.1

Village Voice 22, no. 18 (May 5, 1987).
15 1/8 × 12 × 3/8 in. (38.4 × 30.5 × 1 cm).
Gift of Darren Port, 2004.6.23

121
Jean-Michel Basquiat, Francesco Clemente, and
Andy Warhol, *Collaboration*, ca. 1984. Acrylic,
oil stick, collage, and paper on canvas, approx.
83 × 52 × 39 in. (210.8 × 132.1 × 99.1 cm), painting
on paper, 23 × 16 in. (58.4 × 40.6 cm), red canvas,
17 × 22 × 2 1/2 in. (43.2 × 55.9 × 6.4 cm), blue
canvas, 24 1/2 × 22 × 2 1/2 in. (62.2 × 55.9 × 6.4 cm).
1998.1.792a–d

I is for ILLUSIONS

122
Marcel Duchamp, *Rotorelief*, 1965. Six offset
lithographs on cardboard, each disc: 7 7/8 in.
(20 cm). Base: metal, velvet, plywood, electric
motor, magnets, 14 3/4 × 14 3/4 × 3 1/4 in.
(37.5 × 37.5 × 8.3 cm). 2001.2.2255a–j

125
Anaglyphic illustration of beach scene, 1950s.
Offset lithograph on paper, 7 5/8 × 5 3/8 in.
(19.4 × 13.7 cm). 1998.3.4520

Brownie Manufacturing Co., die-cut anaglyph
3-D eyeglasses, 1950s. Cellophane and printed
ink on cardboard, 1 1/2 × 5 in. (3.8 × 12.7 cm).
TC79.185.1

126
Holmes-type wood and aluminum stereoscope
with seven different stereo cards. 1998.3.7140.4,
2000.2.2460.25, 2000.2.2460.13, 2000.2.2460.15,
2000.2.2460.4, 2000.2.2460.30.2, 2000.2.2460.24,
2000.2.2460.27

Five stereo cards depicting female impersonator
Sam Burg, n.d. T3568–T3571, T3573

127
Ronnie Cutrone, *3-Dimensional Tour of Andy
Warhol's New York*, 1975. Printed ink on
paper and cardboard, plastic slide viewer, box:
7 1/4 × 11 1/4 × 2 in. (18.4 × 28.6 × 5.1 cm),
packet: 10 1/2 × 7 3/4 in. (26.7 × 19.7 cm), viewer:
7 × 4 × 1 1/2 in. (17.8 × 10.2 × 3.8 cm).
TC-9.1.1a–.4

Marks Polarized Corporation, Polarator lenses, 1970s. Metal and glass, each: 6 3/4 × 6 3/4 × 8 in. (17.1 × 17.1 × 20.3 cm). T3637.1–.7

Lobby card for *Andy Warhol's Frankenstein*, aka *Flesh for Frankenstein*, directed by Paul Morrissey, 1974. Offset lithograph on heavy-weight paper, 11 × 13 7/8 in. (27.9 × 35.2 cm). Museum Purchase, 2009.5.2

128
Jason Arthur Sapan, *Andy Warhol*, 1977. Hologram on acetate, 9 1/2 × 19 1/8 in. (24.1 × 48.6 cm). 1998.3.3.1–.2

129
Andy Warhol, *Statue of Liberty*, 1962. Silkscreen ink and spray paint on linen, 80 × 61 in. (203.2 × 154.9 cm). 1998.1.138

Andy Warhol, *Album of a Mat Queen*, 1962. Silkscreen ink and graphite on linen, 21 × 17 in. (53.3 × 43.2 cm). 1998.1.137

130
Arthur Rothstein, *Untitled (Bust of Edison with Five Inventions)*, 1964. Lenticular print, 4 × 4 3/4 in. (10.2 × 12.1 cm). 1998.3.4240

Andy Warhol, *Andy Warhol's Index (Book)*, 1967. Offset lithograph on paper, lenticular photograph on buckram board cover and printed ink on plastic bag, 11 3/4 × 9 1/4 × 5/8 in. (29.8 × 23.5 × 1.6 cm). 1998.3.2457.4

Group of six different lenticular prints. TC30.78.10, TC30.78.3, TC30.78.6, TC56.40, TC63.34.2, TC61.7

131
Andy Warhol, *Rain Machine (Reconstruction of Los Angeles Version 1/2)*, reconstruction by Maurice Tuchman and Martin Beck, 1988. Mixed media and xerographic prints, 107 × 248 × 69 in. (271.8 × 629.9 × 175.3 cm). Anonymous gift, 1991.1

J is for JULIA

133
Julia Warhola's passport, 1920. Ink on paper and gelatin silver print, folded: 7 × 4 3/8 in. (17.8 × 11.1 cm). TC522.118.4

135
Julia Warhola's birth certificate, issued 1953. Ink on paper, 11 5/8 × 8 1/4 in. (29.5 × 21 cm). TC522.118.6

Marriage certificate for Julia and Andrei Warhola, May 24, 1909. Ink on paper, 8 1/4 × 11 3/4 in. (21 × 19.8 cm). TC522.118.7

Julia Warhola's certificate of naturalization, 1942. Ink on paper and gelatin silver print, 8 × 10 in. (20.3 × 25.4 cm). TC522.118.3

136
Photobooth strip of Julia Warhola, ca. 1960s. 4 × 1 9/16 in. (10.2 × 4 cm). T3335.2

136–37
Selection of Julia Warhola's hats. TC-27.123–.126, TC-27.128

138
Molded candy marzipan lamb, n.d. Molded marzipan with gold foil and cloth ribbon on printed cardboard, 3 1/8 × 3 1/2 × 5 5/8 in. (7.9 × 8.9 × 14.3 cm). TC-27.140

Hand-colored photograph of Julia Warhola, n.d. Heavyweight cardstock and hand-colored photograph, 9 × 7 in. (22.9 × 17.8 cm). T615.2

Czechoslovakian-style floral pattern scarf, n.d. Printed ink on woven dyed rayon, 26 × 28 5/16 in. (66 × 71.9 cm). TC-27.121

139
Group of religious objects owned by Julia Warhola, 1960s. 1998.3.5890.1, TC20.29a–b, TC20.14.4, TC20.53.1, TC20.5.1, 1998.3.8245.4a–c, 1998.3.8245.5, 1998.3.8245.6, 1998.3.8245.1, 1998.3.5896, TC20.53.13.3, 1998.3.8245.2–.3

140
Julia Warhola, *Cat with a Hat Reclining on a Hat*, n.d. Ink on Strathmore paper, 6 1/4 × 8 1/4 in. (15.9 × 21 cm). 1998.3.1845

Julia Warhola, *Cat with a Hat*, n.d. Ink on Strathmore paper, 12 3/8 × 8 7/8 in. (31.4 × 22.5 cm). 1998.3.1817

Julia Warhola, *Mary Lou Warhola and George Warhola*, n.d. Ink on ivory paper, 6 7/8 × 6 7/8 in. (17.5 × 17.5 cm). 1998.3.1954

141
Prestige Records, vinyl record jacket for *The Story of Moondog*, with calligraphy by Julia Warhola, ca. 1957. Offset lithograph on coated paper, 12 × 12 in. (30.5 × 30.5 cm). 1998.3.3532

Andy Warhol, *"I Love You So,"* 1950s. Ink, graphite, and Dr. Martin's aniline dye on paper, 10 × 12 1/4 in. (25.4 × 31.1 cm). 1998.1.1393

Letraset of Julia Warhola's handwriting, ca. 1963. Dry-transfer lettering on plastic sheet, 10 1/4 × 15 in. (26 × 38.1 cm). 1998.3.1998.1

K is for KRONK

143
Note from Billy Name to Andy Warhol, 1960s. Felt-tip marker on blue paperboard, 4 × 7 in. (10.2 × 17.8 cm). T3341

145
Andy Warhol, *Haircut (No. 1)*, 1963. 16mm, black-and-white film, silent, 27 mins. 1997.4.50

146
Grouping of correspondence, with drawings and poems given to Warhol by Billy Name, 1960s. T521, 1998.3.9054.1–.2, TCFilm.2.9h, TC92.20

147
Michael (Felix) Katz, *Billy (Name) Linich on a Rooftop in New York*, ca. 1964. Gelatin silver print, 3 7/16 × 9 7/8 in. (8.7 × 25.1 cm). T3507

148
Program for the I.F.B.B. Mr. New York Contest and Variety Show, May 25, 1963. Printed ink on coated paper, 9 1/8 × 6 1/8 in. (23.2 × 15.6 cm). TC79.85

149
Billy Name, nineteen astrology charts cast at the Factory in 1968, including charts for Nico, Ondine, and the day Andy Warhol was shot. Printed ink and felt-tip marker on paper, each: 11 × 8 1/2 in. (27.9 × 21.6 cm). TC3.71.1–.5

150
Andy Warhol, *Screen Test: Billy Linich [ST193]*, 1964. 16mm film, black and white, silent, 4.4 mins. at 16 frames per sec. 1997.4.113.193

151
Note from Billy Name to Andy Warhol, ca. 1969. Felt-tip marker and printed ink on coated paper, 9 × 8 1/2 in. (22.9 × 21.6 cm). TC94.146

L is for LOOSE LIPS AND LPs

153
The Rolling Stones promotional toy hopping/chattering teeth, ca. 1977. Printed ink on plastic with metal components and key, box: 3 1/2 × 3 1/2 × 2 in. (8.9 × 8.9 × 5.1 cm), toy: 2 1/2 × 2 1/2 in. (6.4 × 6.4 cm), key: 1 1/2 × 1 in. (3.8 × 2.5 cm). TC181.169.12.1–.3

158
Interview 1, no. 2 (1969); 1, no. 8 (1970); 7, no. 12 (December 1977); 11, no. 8 (August 1981), Gift of Mark W. Van Sweringen; 15, no. 2 (February 1985); 1, no. 7 (1970); no. 25 (September 1972). 1998.3.11251, 1998.3.14814, 1998.3.2577, 1999.5.5, 2001.4.2, 1998.3.14815, 1998.3.2480.1

159
Andy Warhol, scrapbook (Eothen, Montauk), 1972–78. Mixed archival materials, 8 3/4 × 11 3/4 × 1 1/4 in. (22.2 × 29.8 × 3.2 cm). 1998.3.4646

160
Artchie Strips, featuring the Rolling Stones, 1970. Printed ink on coated paper and newsprint, 10 × 8 in. (25.4 × 20.3 cm). TC137.95

161
Letter from Mick Jagger to Andy Warhol, April 21, 1969. Typewritten on printed letterhead with ballpoint pen signature, 10 × 8 in. (25.4 × 20.3 cm). 1998.3.5519.68.1

162
Design notes by Vincent Fremont, 1976–77. Graphite and felt-tip marker on lined, colored paper, 12 1/2 × 8 in. (31.8 × 20.3 cm). TC157.1.2

Andy Warhol, *Mick Jagger*, ca. 1977. Gelatin silver print, 10 1/8 × 8 in. (25.7 × 20.3 cm). TC175.179.5

Andy Warhol, maquette of *Love You Live* by the Rolling Stones, 1976–77. Offset lithograph on coated record cover stock, cover: 12 3/8 × 12 3/8 × 1/4 in. (31.4 × 31.4 × 0.6 cm). TC157.1.1

163
The Rolling Stones, *Love You Live* (signed promotional copy), 1977. Offset lithograph on coated record cover stock with vinyl record album, 12 1/4 × 12 1/4 in. (31.1 × 31.1 cm). TC181.169.2.1a–.2b

164–65
Promotional poster for *Sticky Fingers* by the Rolling Stones, 1971. Offset lithograph on coated paper, 12 1/4 × 12 1/4 in. (31.1 × 31.1 cm). TC82.71

165
The Rolling Stones, *Sticky Fingers*, 1971. 2014.8.71a–b
Art Directors Club of New York certificate of merit to Andy Warhol, 1972. TC90.243.3
Nomination card for Best Album Cover in the 14th annual Grammy Awards, February 1972. TC46.58.3
Letter from the National Academy of Recording Arts and Sciences to Andy Warhol, February 1972. TC46.58.2

166
Andy Warhol, *Mick Jagger*, ca. 1975. Four Polacolor Type 108 Polaroids, each: 4 1/4 × 3 3/8 in. (10.8 × 8.6 cm). 1998.1.2995.16, 1998.1.3003.1–.3

167
Andy Warhol, *Mick Jagger*, 1975. Two screen prints on Arches Aquarelle (Rough) watercolor paper cut from a roll, each: 43 1/2 × 29 in. (110.5 × 73.7 cm). 1998.1.2412.1, 1998.1.2412.4

M is for MEAD

169
Newspaper advertisement for *Flaming Creatures* by Jack Smith and *Flower Thief* by Ron Rice starring Taylor Mead, late 1960s. 7 1/2 × 7 1/2 in. (19.1 × 19.1 cm). TC7.369

171
Photographer unknown, *Taylor Mead Holding a Director's Slate*, 1968. Gelatin silver print, 6 3/4 × 9 15/16 in. (17.1 × 25.2 cm). 1998.3.4982

172
Photographer unknown, slides of Taylor Mead and Taylor Mead and Fred Hughes, 1968. Two color transparencies with printed ink on cardboard mount, each slide: 2 × 2 in. (5.1 × 5.1 cm). 2000.2.2973.10–.11

Andy Warhol, *The Nude Restaurant*, 1967. 16mm, color film, sound, 100 mins. 1997.4.88

173
William John Kennedy, *Untitled*, ca. 1964, reprinted 2010. Gelatin silver fiber print, 20 × 24 in. (50.8 × 61 cm). Gift of Kiwi Arts Group, 2013.12.80

William John Kennedy, *Untitled*, ca. 1964, reprinted 2010. Gelatin silver fiber print, 24 × 20 in. (61 × 50.8 cm). Gift of Kiwi Arts Group, 2013.12.88

William John Kennedy, *Untitled*, ca. 1964, reprinted 2012. Chromogenic color print, 39 × 27 in. (99.1 × 68.6 cm). Gift of Kiwi Arts Group, 2013.12.4

174
Photographer unknown, *Taylor Mead*, 1968. Color transparency with printed ink on cardboard mount, slide: 2 × 2 in. (5.1 × 5.1 cm). T3444

Books by Taylor Mead:
Excerpts from the Anonymous Diary of a New York Youth, 1961. 1998.3.10338
Excerpts from the Anonymous Diary of a New York Youth, 1962. 1998.3.10339
Taylor Mead on Amphetamine and in Europe, 1968. TCFilm.1

Moviegoer, no. 2 (Summer–Autumn 1964). Printed ink on paper, 8 7/8 × 6 in. (22.5 × 15.2 cm). TC-17.39

175
Photographer unknown, *Taylor Mead*, 1960s, inscribed by Mead to Andy Warhol. Gelatin silver print, 9 1/2 × 6 1/2 in. (24.1 × 16.5 cm). T937

Letter from Taylor Mead to Andy Warhol, posted February 27, 1967. Ballpoint pen on paper, 8 1/4 × 5 5/16 in. (21 × 13.5 cm). 1998.3.8338.2

N is for NIGHTLIFE

177–85
Andy Warhol's night planner, 1982. 9 × 24 × 13 in. (22.9 × 61 × 33 cm). 2000.2.1835.1

O is for OPENING

187
Invitation to the opening party for Andy Warhol's exhibition at the Institute of Contemporary Art, University of Pennsylvania, October 7, 1965. Offset lithograph on paper, 3 5/8 × 8 1/2 in. (9.2 × 21.6 cm). Gift of Samuel Adams Green, 1994.19.3.2

188
Invitation from Mr. and Mrs. Horatio Gates Lloyd to Mr. Andy Warhol, October 7, 1965, postmarked September 29, 1965, New York. Printed ink and felt-tip marker on stationery, 3 5/8 × 5 1/8 in. (9.2 × 13 cm). TC59.95.2

189
Andy Warhol, exhibition catalogue, Institute of Contemporary Art, University of Pennsylvania, 1965. Printed ink on paper, 7 3/8 × 5 × 1/2 in. (18.7 × 12.7 × 1.3 cm). TC70.20a–b

Andy Warhol, *S & H Green Stamps*, ca. 1962. Acrylic stamped on sketchbook paper, 23 7/8 × 18 in. (60.6 × 45.7 cm). 1998.1.2309

190
Penn Comment 2, no. 2 (October 1965): cover. Offset lithograph on coated paper, 11 × 8 1/2 in. (27.9 × 21.6 cm). Gift of Samuel Adams Green, 1994.19.3.1

190–91
Installation view of Andy Warhol's work at the Institute of Contemporary Art, University of Pennsylvania, October 8–November 21, 1965. ICA, University of Pennsylvania

192
Sam Green and Mrs. Horatio Gates (Lally) Lloyd in front of S&H Green Stamp wallpaper made for the exhibition, October 8, 1965. ICA, University of Pennsylvania

192–93
Installation view of Andy Warhol's work at the
Institute of Contemporary Art, University of
Pennsylvania, October 8–November 21, 1965.
ICA, University of Pennsylvania

194
Photographer unknown, Andy Warhol and Edie
Sedgwick at pre-show party, October 7, 1965.
ICA, University of Pennsylvania

195
Photographer unknown, Andy Warhol, Gerard
Malanga, and Edie Sedgwick with others
on the stairs above the ICA crowd, 1965. Gelatin
silver print, 9 1/4 × 6 1/4 in. (23.5 × 15.9 cm).
1998.3.10667.68

P is for PHONEY

197
Andy Warhol, *Telephone [4]*, 1962. Acrylic and
graphite on linen, 100 × 72 in. (254 × 182.9 cm).
1998.1.10

200
Andy Warhol, *The Three Magi with Telephones*,
ca. 1951. Graphite on Hammermill bond paper,
9 1/8 × 11 7/8 in. (23.2 × 30.2 cm). 1998.1.1600

Andy Warhol, *Two Sprite Angels with Telephones*,
ca. 1950. Graphite on bond paper, 11 × 8 1/2 in.
(27.9 × 21.6 cm). 1998.1.1604

Andy Warhol, *Man with Cigarette and
Candlestick Telephones*, ca. 1950. Positive photo
print on sensitized paper, 11 1/8 × 13 7/8 in.
(28.3 × 35.2 cm). 1998.3.3444

201
Andy Warhol, *Sheraton Hotel Bedside Table with
Telephone*, 1979. Gelatin silver print, 8 × 10 in.
(20.3 × 25.4 cm). 2001.2.253

Andy Warhol, *Telephones*, 1980. Polacolor 2
Polaroid, 4 1/2 × 3 1/2 in. (11.4 × 8.9 cm).
2001.2.1593

Andy Warhol, *Telephone*, 1983. Gelatin silver
print, 7 15/16 × 10 in. (20.2 × 25.4 cm). 2001.2.980

202
Jack Mitchell, *Cast of Andy Warhol's "Pork," 1971*,
reprinted 2005. Hi-res, color photo scan from an
original color slide. Gift of Jack Mitchell, 2005.7.1

203
Office telephones for the staff at the Factory,
1980s

Andy Warhol and Vincent Fremont, *Phoney*, 1973.
Half inch reel-to-reel videotape, black and white,
sound, 48 mins. 1997.4.336

TeleQuest Hot Lips telephone, 1980s. Plastic
with metal components, 4 × 8 1/4 × 2 1/2 in.
(10.2 × 21 × 6.4 cm). 1998.3.11081.2

204
Invoice from New York Telephone to Andy
Warhol, posted November 6, 1967, New York.
Printed ink and ballpoint pen on paper,
3 1/2 × 8 1/2 in. (8.9 × 21.6 cm). TC-2.198.2

Selection from hundreds of telephone
messages for Andy Warhol, April–August 1973

Andy Warhol's address book, 1962–65. Printed
ink on paper with graphite inscriptions and
printed, coated board covers, 7 3/4 × 5 1/4 × 3/8 in.
(19.7 × 13.3 × 1 cm). TC36.6

205
Photographer unknown, *Andy Warhol on the
Payphone in the Factory*, 1966. Gelatin silver
print, 9 3/16 × 6 15/16 in. (23.3 × 17.6 cm).
1998.3.10859.2

Q is for QUICK

207
Card addressed from the California cast of
Bike Boy to Andy Warhol, postmarked June 13,
1968, San Lorenzo, CA. Ballpoint pen and felt-tip
marker on paper and printed ink on coated paper,
unfolded: 13 1/2 × 26 in. (34.3 × 66 cm). TC4.1.2

210
Two photographic slides of Andy Warhol at
Columbus Hospital, New York, 1968. Color
transparency with printed ink on cardboard
mount, slide: 2 × 2 in. (5.1 × 5.1 cm),
transparency: 1 1/16 × 1 1/16 in. (2.7 × 2.7 cm).
T3446, T3447

Hospital bracelet for Andrew Warhol at
Columbus Hospital, New York, 1968. Printed ink
and ballpoint pen on paper inside plastic holder
and metal clasp, 3/4 × 7 1/8 in. (1.9 × 18.1 cm).
TC61.10

211
Letter from Mario Amaya to Andy Warhol, June
14, 1968, London. Ballpoint pen and typewritten
ink on paper, 10 × 8 in. (25.4 × 20.3 cm). TC4.14.2

212
Group of religious get-well cards and
correspondence addressed to Andy Warhol,
1968. TC4.234.2, TC4.276.3, TC4.276.5, TC4.64,
TC4.101.2, TC4.149, TC4.182.1, TC4.187.2,
TC4.191.2, TC4.215.2–.3, TC4.275.2, TC4.418,
TC4.79.2, TC4.79.4.1a, TC4.152.2, TC4.214.3,
TC4.214.5, TC4.280.7–.8

213
Group of get-well cards and correspondence
from Andy Warhol's fans, 1968. TC4.245,
TC4.179.2, TC4.177.2, TC4.32.2, TC4.42.2, TC4.44,
TC4.66.2, TC4.83.2, TC4.117.2–.3, TC4.121.2,
TC4.128.1–.2, TC4.137.2, TC4.138, TC4.199.1–.2,
TC4.206, TC4.210.2, TC4.213.2, TC4.242.2,
TC4.328.2, TC4.329.1a–.2, TC4.330.2, TC4.331.1,
TC4.332.2, TC4.322.3

214
Group of get-well cards and correspondence
from Andy Warhol's artist friends, 1968. TC4.7.2,
TC4.122.2, TC4.314.2, TC4.346.2, TC4.143.2a–b,
TC4.398, TC4.246.3, TC4.204.2, TC4.226.1–.2,
TC4.82.1–.3, TC4.167, TC4.348, TC4.155.3

215
Prayer card from Madalen Warhola to Andy
Warhol, posted June 26, 1968, Clairton, PA.
Ballpoint pen on coated paper, 8 1/4 × 5 1/2 in.
(21 × 14 cm). TC4.234.2

Flower delivery card from "the Velvets" to Andy
Warhol, ca. 1968. Ballpoint pen and printed ink
on paper, 4 1/2 × 5 in. (11.4 × 12.7 cm). TC4.268

Scrap metal inscribed by Chuck Peavy to
Mr. Andy Warhol, posted June 7, 1968, New York.
Aluminum, 7 5/8 × 8 3/4 in. (19.4 × 22.2 cm).
TC4.177.2

Handwritten note from Viva and Gerard Malanga
to John and Paul Warhola, on the back of a
Columbus Hospital vaccination record, 1968.
Ballpoint pen, printed and carbon ink, and
graphite on paper, 3 1/2 × 5 in. (8.9 × 12.7 cm).
TC-27.59.2

R is for RAT

216
Edward Wallowitch, *Gerard Malanga and Andy
Warhol ("The Tunafish Disaster")*, 1963,
reprinted 1988. Gelatin silver print, 11 × 14 in.
(27.9 × 35.6 cm). Gift of John Wallowitch,
1997.10.21

218
Polaroid of forged painting after it was
destroyed, 1968. 4 1/4 × 3 1/2 in. (10.8 × 8.9 cm).
TC123.2.2

Photocopy of telegram from Andy Warhol to
Galleria La Tartaruga, February 18, 1968.
Photocopy on paper, 8 5/16 × 11 5/8 in.
(21.1 × 29.5 cm). TC-2.74

Gerard Malanga, piece of Che Guevara canvas,
1968. Acrylic on canvas and dye diffusion
transfer prints, fragment: 7 1/2 × 15 1/2 in.
(19.1 × 39.4 cm). TC123.2.1

219
Correspondence from Gerard Malanga to Andy Warhol and Paul Morrissey, March 2–11, 1968. Ink on paper, dimensions variable. T73271.1–.4, T3272.1–.3, T3273.1–.2

S is for STAMP

220
Andy Warhol, *Self-Portrait*, 1964. Acrylic, metallic paint, and silkscreen ink on linen, 20 1/8 × 16 1/8 × 3/4 in. (51.1 × 41 × 1.9 cm). 2002.4.20

223
Canceled stamps collected by Andy Warhol from *Time Capsule 137*, 1974–76. Single stamp, smallest: 1 × 3/4 in. (2.5 × 1.9 cm), multiple stamps, largest: 5 × 5 in. (12.7 × 12.7 cm). TC137.79.1–.2.692

224
Michel Hosszú, *Homage to Andy Warhol Stamp Sheet*, 1987. Silkscreen ink on paper, 10 3/4 × 7 1/8 in. (27.3 × 18.1 cm). 2013.19.2

Johnny Dodd, *Untitled* (six postage stamp panels), 1964. Six wood panels with postage stamps, 94 1/2 × 75 1/4 in. (240 × 191.1 cm). 2000.2.1086

225
Selection of mail art sent to Andy Warhol by Ray Johnson, 1956–69. 2001.2.2258.1–.3, TC76.195.130, T3623, TC76.195.109.1–.4, TC37.74.1a–.3, TC76.195.120, 2001.2.2248.1–.2, TC76.195.140.1–.8b, 2001.2.2265

226
Selection of correspondence from Tommy Jackson to Andy Warhol, 1950–54. Notecards typed in green ink. T3375, T3367, 1998.3.3957, 1998.3.3898, T3389, T3397.1–.2, T3368, T3382, T3374, T3395, T3384, T3379, T3370, T3383, T3396, T3393

227
Dudley Huppler illustrations sent to Andy Warhol, 1954–55. 1998.3.3926.1–.2, T3316.1–.8, T3319.1–.3, T3314.1–.2, T3307.1–.2, T3308a–c, 1998.3.3878, 1998.3.3909.1–.3, T3306, T3317.1–.3b

228
Postcard from Andy Warhol to Julia Warhola, posted June 24, 1956, Higashiyama, Japan. Printed ink on coated paper, 3 9/16 × 5 5/8 in. (9 × 14.3 cm). 1998.3.3978

Letter from Lance Loud to Andy Warhol, ca. 1967. Pen on paper, 11 × 8 1/2 in. (27.9 × 21.6 cm). T3350a–d

229
Decorated envelope from Peter Beard to Andy Warhol & Co., 1984. Ballpoint pen, felt-tip marker, on paper and coated paper, envelope: 4 × 9 1/4 in. (10.2 × 23.5 cm). TC522.48.1

Decorated postcard from Peter Beard to Andy Warhol, posted April 6, 1983, Venice. Ballpoint pen, felt-tip marker, printed ink, and stamped ink on paper, 4 1/4 × 8 5/8 in. (10.8 × 21.9 cm). TC526.16.1

Decorated envelope from Peter Beard to Andy Warhol, posted July 7, 1976, London. Printed ink and pen on paper, envelope: 4 1/4 × 8 5/8 in. (10.8 × 21.9 cm). TC147.3.1

T is for TOOTH FAIRY

231
Dental model, ca. 1982. Aluminum, plaster, and printed ink and ballpoint pen on paper, 1 5/8 × 1 3/4 × 1 3/4 in. (4.1 × 4.4 × 4.4 cm). TC526.30.8

232
Jasper Johns, *The Critic Smiles*, 1959. Sculpmetal, 1 5/8 × 7 3/4 × 1 1/2 in. (4.1 x 19.7 x 3.8 cm). Collection of the artist

233
Andy Warhol, *Screen Test: Jane Holzer (Toothbrush) [ST147]*, 1964. 16mm, black-and-white film, silent, 4 mins. 24 secs. 1997.4.113.147

234
Harry Shunk and János Kender, *Andy Warhol in Hotel, Paris*, May 8–9, 1965. Gelatin silver print, 9 3/8 × 7 1/4 in. (23.8 × 18.4 cm). 2001.2.2210

235
Andy Warhol, *Dental Molds*, 1982–83. Two Polacolor ER Polaroids, each: (top) 3 3/8 × 4 1/4 in. (8.6 × 10.8 cm), (bottom) 4 1/4 × 3 3/8 in. (10.8 × 8.6 cm). 2001.2.1508–.1509

Andy Warhol, *Photostat (Advertisement Collage)*, ca. 1961. Positive photo print on sensitized paper, 24 1/2 × 18 in. (62.2 × 45.7 cm). 1998.3.4532

236–37
Andy Warhol's collection of dental molds and models, ca. 1982–85. TC526.30.1–.12.12

238
Andy Warhol, *Saint Apollonia*, 1984. Four screen prints on Essex Offset Kid Finish paper, each: 30 × 22 in. (76.2 × 55.9 cm). 1998.1.2482.1–.4

239
Dental models from Columbia Dentoform Corp., ca. 1982. Aluminum, plaster, and printed ink and ballpoint pen on paper, envelope: 4 7/8 × 3 in. (12.4 × 7.6 cm), loose teeth, each approx.: 7/8 × 3/8 in. (2.2 × 1 cm). TC526.30.1–.5

Andy Warhol, *Lips and "Home Rum" Cigarette*, drawing in sketchbook, 1950s. Ballpoint pen on Manila paper, 16 15/16 × 13 3/4 in. (43 × 34.9 cm). 1998.1.1787.28

U is for UNDERGROUND

241
John Wilcock, *Other Scenes*, December 1968. 12 1/4 × 9 1/4 in. (31.1 × 23.5 cm). 1998.3.6589

245
Oracle, April 1967. 16 × 12 1/2 in. (40.6 × 31.8 cm). TC472.98

Rat, May 9–15, 1969. 16 1/2 × 11 1/2 in. (41.9 × 29.2 cm). TC-10.69

246
Eight of Andy Warhol's many artists' books and publications, 1963–68. 1994.8.1, 1998.3.4705, 1998.3.7754a–b, 1998.3.7761, 1998.3.8299a–b, T562, TCFilm.2.5.1–.2, TCFilm.2.9a–h

247
Five of Andy Warhol's many underground publications related to sexuality, 1969–70. TC-10.61, TC1.100, TC-10.62, TC1.124, TC10.509

248
Andy Warhol's collection of *Fuck You: A Magazine of the Arts*, 1962–65. 1998.3.10343–.10350, 1998.3.10355.1a–b, 1998.3.10359a–bbb

249
Steve Lawrence, *Newspaper*, April 1969. 22 3/4 × 16 7/8 in. (57.8 × 42.9 cm). 1998.3.9006.2

Al Hansen, *Incomplete Requiem for W. C. Fields*, 1966. Printed ink on paper, 8 7/16 × 5 1/2 in. (21.4 × 14 cm). 1998.3.4659

Babel I, 1951. Letterpress ink on paper, 8 1/2 × 5 1/2 in. (21.6 × 14 cm). 1998.3.8298.1

Steve Lawrence, *Ark*, 1968. Printed ink and ballpoint pen on newsprint, 22 3/4 × 16 3/4 in. (57.8 × 42.5 cm), 1998.3.9006.1

Andy Warhol, *"Unsalted Butter,"* 1968, artwork created for *Ark* magazine. 22 3/4 × 16 3/4 in. (57.8 × 42.5 cm). 1998.3.9006.1

250
Andy Warhol:
Screen Test: Allen Ginsberg [ST115], 1966.
1997.4.113.115
Screen Test: Bibbe Hansen [ST128], 1965.
1997.4.113.128
Screen Test: Edwin Denby [ST75], 1964.
1997.4.113.75
Screen Test: Ron Padgett [ST251], 1964.
1997.4.113.251
Screen Test: Ted Berrigan [ST22], 1964.
1997.4.113.22
Screen Test: Ed Sanders [ST294], 1964.
1997.4.113.294
All: 16mm, black-and-white film, silent,
4 mins. 30 secs.

251
Andy Warhol, *Gerard Malanga and Edwin Denby*,
1963. Two Type 47 Polaroids, each: 4 1/4 × 3 1/4 in.
(10.8 × 8.3 cm). 1998.3.14438.3, 1998.3.4956

C: A Journal of Poetry 1, no. 4 (September 1963),
with photograph by Andy Warhol on cover.
Screen print and mimeograph on paper,
14 × 8 7/8 in. (35.6 × 22.5cm). T3655

V is for VIVA

253
Photographer unknown, *Viva with Andy
Warhol's Art*, ca. 1968. Chromogenic color print,
3 1/2 × 3 1/2 in. (8.9 × 8.9 cm). 1998.3.15006

255
Photographer unknown, *Andy Warhol, Penelope
Tree, Lita Hornick, Viva, Fred Hughes, and
Ultra Violet*, 1968. Chromogenic color print,
3 1/2 × 3 1/2 in. (8.9 × 8.9 cm). 1998.3.14790

256
Hickey & Robertson, Houston, *Andy Warhol
and Viva in Houston*, 1968. Gelatin silver print,
8 × 10 in. (20.3 × 25.4 cm). 1998.3.14798

257
Andy Warhol:
Viva, ca. 1981. 1998.1.3070
Viva and Brigid Berlin, ca. 1981. 1998.1.3071
Viva and Brigid, ca. 1981. 2001.2.111
Three gelatin silver prints, each: (top) 10 × 8 in.
(25.4 × 20.3 cm), (bottom) 8 × 10 in.
(20.3 × 25.4 cm)

258
Village Voice, February 22, 1968. 17 1/2 × 12 1/2 in.
(44.5 × 31.8 cm). TC-15.59

Andy Warhol, *San Diego Surf*, 1968. 16mm film,
color, sound, 85 mins. 1997.4.153

Andy Warhol, *Lonesome Cowboys*, 1967–68.
16mm film, color, sound, 109 mins. 1997.4.75

259
Photographer unknown, slide (Viva), 1968.
Color transparency with printed ink on
cardboard mount, slide: 2 × 2 in. (5.1 × 5.1 cm).
2000.2.2973.9

260
Postcards sent from Viva to Andy Warhol
in the hospital, 1968. TC4.253–.254, TC4.258,
TC4.261–.263, TC4.349–.350

261
Photographer unknown:
Viva in Black Dress, 1968. 1998.3.15014
Viva Holding a Cigarette, 1968. 1998.3.15020
Viva on Airport Tarmac, ca. 1968. 1998.3.15013
Three chromogenic color prints, each:
3 1/2 × 3 1/2 in. (8.9 × 8.9 cm)

Envelope with note from Viva to Andy Warhol,
1968. Felt-tip marker and ballpoint pen on
paper and cardstock, envelope: 2 3/8 × 3 5/8 in.
(6 × 9.2 cm), each card: 2 1/8 × 3 1/4 in.
(5.4 × 8.3 cm). T3523.1–.2

W is for WIRETAPPING

262
TV Guide, March 5, 1966. Printed ink on coated
paper, 7 1/2 × 5 in. (19.1 × 12.7 cm). Gift of Janice
Hulme, 1995.9

265
Andy Warhol, *Ten Portraits of Jews of the
Twentieth Century: Louis Brandeis*, 1980. Acrylic
and silkscreen ink on linen, 40 × 40 in.
(101.6 × 101.6 cm). 1998.1.471

266
"Snooping" by Walter Goodman, *New York Times
Book Review* (review of *Privacy and Freedom* by
Alan F. Westin), September 17, 1967. 13 × 11 in.
(33 × 27.9 cm). TC25.74

267
Photographer unknown, *Robert F. Kennedy*,
ca. 1968. Gelatin silver print, 6 3/16 × 4 7/8 in.
(15.7 × 12.4 cm). T581

The Nation, July 14, 1962. 10 3/4 × 8 1/2 in.
(27.3 × 21.6 cm). TC32.93

268
Photographer unknown:
Bernard Spindel and Emanuel Cellar
("Electronics expert Bernard Spindel [left]
gives Emanuel Cellar of the House Judiciary
Committee, a firsthand lesson in the powers
of wire-tapping, May, 1955, Washington, D.C."),
1955. 1998.3.10667.5
Mort Davis ("For eavesdropping through
a wall, door, etc., a microphone and hearing
aid do the trick. The mike picks up sound,
magnifying the reception by hearing-aid"),
ca. 1955. 1998.3.10667.6
Mort Davis ("One of the tiniest tapping gadgets
is demonstrated by Mort Davis of the New
York Mirror, equipped with hearing aid and
small pack-hearing antenna aimed at phone"),
ca. 1955. 1998.3.10667.7
Three gelatin silver prints, grease pencil, ink,
and pressure-sensitive tape, each: 7 × 9 1/8 in.
(17.8 × 23.2 cm)

269
Photographer unknown:
Wire-Tapped Telephone ("1277289—A simple
induction coil [left] obtainable in any electronics
shop, can pick up a two-way conversation on a
telephone wire by placing it over the wire. The
impulse goes through the electronic device that
leads to recorder or earphones"), ca. 1955.
1998.3.10667.8
Mort Davis ("1277290—For eavesdropping on
conversants in the same room as the pick-up
microphone (which is shown being secreted
behind a picture frame) which may be attached
to a recorder in the adjoining room or another
part of the building"), ca. 1955. 1998.3.10667.9
Mort Davis ("1277288—A phone is about to be
placed back on the induction platform, which
picks up both ends of a conversation and
records it on another machine. This gimmick
permits a person 'in the know' to make a
permanent record of the talk without the other's
knowledge"), ca. 1955. 1998.3.10667.10
Tape Recorder ("Tape recording device which
Chas. Binaggio, Kansas City Democratic leader,
installed in his desk in an apparent effort to
trap his enemies"), ca. 1955. 1998.3.10667.11
Four gelatin silver prints, grease pencil, and ink,
each: 9 1/8 × 7 in. (23.2 × 17.8 cm)

270
Andy Warhol, *Vote McGovern*, 1972. Screen print
on Arches 88 paper, 42 × 42 in. (106.7 × 106.7 cm).
1998.1.2399

271
Rick Meyerowitz, Richard Nixon and Spiro
Agnew hand puppets, 1970–71. Painted, molded
vinyl with synthetic fiber and felt clothing, each:
14 × 8 × 4 in. (35.6 × 20.3 × 10.2 cm).
1998.3.8705.1, 1998.3.8705.3

X is for X-RATED

273
Kiss newspaper, June 23, 1969, with "Andy Warhol Underground Column." 14 1/2 × 11 1/4 in. (36.8 × 28.6 cm). TC-10.50

274–75
Andy Warhol, *Time Capsule -10*, 1939–73; bulk 1969–70. Mixed archival material. TC-10

276
Photographer unknown, *Josephine Baker*, ca. 1938, reprinted from the collection of Gotham Book Mart & Gallery, New York. Gelatin silver print, 8 5/16 × 8 1/2 in. (21.1 × 21.6 cm). TC-10.12.2

277
Photographer unknown, *Josephine Baker*, ca. 1924–25, reprinted from the collection of Gotham Book Mart & Gallery, New York. Gelatin silver print, 9 7/16 × 6 11/16 in. (24 × 17 cm). TC-10.12.5

278
Six Polaroids of unidentified nude man found inside June 1969 issue of *Film* magazine from *Time Capsule -10*, n.d. Six Polacolor Type 108 Polaroids, 75 speed, each: 4 1/4 × 3 3/8 in. (10.8 × 8.6 cm). TC-10.22.2–.7

279
Magazines from *Time Capsule -10*, 1967–69. TC-10.31, TC-10.37–.39

Y is for YVES

280
Yves Tanguy exhibition announcement and catalogues, 1942–77. TC15.60, 2000.2.2985.1–.5, TC163.124.3

281
Andy Warhol, *Yves Saint Laurent*, 1972. Acrylic and silkscreen ink on linen, 10 × 10 in. (25.4 × 25.4 cm). 1998.1.643

282
Invitation to Yves Klein exhibition opening at Centre Georges Pompidou, March 1, 1983. Printed ink on paper and coated cardstock, 5 7/8 × 8 1/4 in. (14.9 × 21 cm). TC344.257.3

Invitation to wedding of Yves Klein and Rotraut Uecker, January 21, 1962. Printed ink and ballpoint pen on coated paper, folded: 8 1/2 × 5 3/4 in. (21.6 × 14.6 cm). 1998.3.4221

283
Photographer unknown, *Andy Warhol and Unidentified Piaget Polo Jockey and Horse,* 1984. Gelatin silver print, 8 × 10 in. (20.3 × 25.4 cm). 1998.3.4978

Piaget building paperweight, June 21, 1979. Brass, 4 7/8 × 3 1/8 × 2 3/4 in. (12.4 × 7.9 × 7 cm). TC227.67.3.2

Photographer unknown, *Yves Piaget, Cornelia Guest, Andy Warhol, and an Unidentified Woman at the Piaget Polo World Cup Palm Beach*, 1983. Black-and-white photograph, 3 1/2 × 5 in. (8.9 × 12.7 cm). TC361.134.3

Boehm porcelain invitation to the Piaget World Cup Ball, April 16, 1983. Ink on porcelain, satin, and printed ink on cardboard, box: 6 3/4 × 6 3/4 in. (17.1 × 17.1 cm), invitation, diameter: 5 3/8 in. (13.7 cm). TC346.149.2

284
Photographer unknown, *Yves Saint Laurent Posing Outdoors with Life-sized Lalanne Sheep Sculpture*, ca. 1978. Gelatin silver print, 14 × 11 in. (35.6 × 27.9 cm). 2000.2.3281

285
Note from Yves Saint Laurent to Andy Warhol, ca. 1972. Graphite on stationery, 7 3/4 × 7 7/8 in. (19.7 × 20 cm). TC93.100.2

Telegram from Yves Saint Laurent to Monsieur Andy Warhol, June 22, 1981. Typewritten ink on paper, 5 1/2 × 8 1/2 in. (14 × 21.6 cm). TC559.271.2

Invitation for first New York showing of Yves Saint Laurent's Haute Couture collection sent to Andy Warhol, November 5, 1974. Printed ink on paper, 5 × 6 7/8 in. (12.7 × 17.5 cm). TC98.204

Campbell's Onion Soup candle signed "for Andy—Yves Saint Laurent," 1970–75. Metal can, candle wax, and wick, 4 3/4 × 4 1/8 × 4 1/8 in. (12.1 × 10.5 × 10.5 cm). TC67.11a

Announcement for retrospective exhibition of Yves Saint Laurent at the Palace of Fine Arts, Beijing, May–July 1985. Printed ink on coated paper, closed: 7 3/4 × 5 15/16 in. (19.7 × 15.1 cm). TC421.102.2

Z is for ZOMBIE

286
Andy Warhol, *Self-Portrait in Santa Costume*, 1978. Polacolor Type 108 Polaroid, 4 1/4 × 3 3/8 in. (10.8 × 8.6 cm). 1998.1.2868

287
Tom Savini, *Andy Warhol as Zombie*, ca. 1984. Chromogenic color print, 11 × 8 in. (27.9 × 20.3 cm). Gift of Tom Savini, 1994.9.3

288
Photographer unknown, *Allen Midgette Impersonating Andy Warhol*, 1967. Gelatin silver print, 4 15/16 × 4 in. (12.5 × 10.2 cm). 1998.3.5422.11

Andy Warhol, *Self-Portrait*, 1963–64. Photobooth photograph, 5 7/8 × 1 5/8 in. (14.9 × 4.1 cm). TC21.73.196

289
Edward Wallowitch, *Andy Warhol with Girl Projected on Face*, 1957. Gelatin silver print, 10 × 7 in. (25.4 × 17.8 cm). 2001.2.2117

290
Photostat, "Noses Reshaped," 1961. Positive photo print on sensitized paper, 8 1/4 × 10 1/4 in. (21 × 26 cm). 1998.3.4524

Otto Fenn, *Andy Warhol with Altered Nose*, ca. 1952. Gelatin silver print, 10 × 8 in. (25.4 × 20.3 cm). 1998.3.4858

Photographer unknown, Andy Warhol passport photograph, 1956. Gelatin silver print, 2 3/4 × 2 1/2 in. (7 × 6.4 cm). 1998.3.5224

Andy Warhol, *Self-Portrait (Passport Photograph with Altered Nose)*, 1956. Graphite on gelatin silver print, 2 3/4 × 2 1/2 in. (7 × 6.4 cm). 1998.3.14803

291
Edward Wallowitch, *Andy Warhol Dressed as a Clown*, 1950s. Gelatin silver print mounted on board, 13 3/16 × 9 5/8 in. (33.5 × 24.4 cm). 1998.3.5193

292
Andy Warhol, *Self-Portrait in Drag*, 1981. Three Polacolor Polaroids, each: (top) 3 3/8 × 4 1/4 in. (8.6 × 10.8 cm), (bottom) 4 1/4 × 3 3/8 in. (10.8 × 8.6 cm). 1998.1.2904, 1998.1.2923, 1998.1.2929

293
Andy Warhol, *Self-Portrait*, 1986. Acrylic and silkscreen ink on linen, 80 × 76 in. (203.2 × 193 cm). 1998.1.816

294
Andy Warhol, *Self-Portrait*, ca. 1982. Polacolor print, 4 1/4 × 3 3/8 in. (10.8 × 8.6 cm). TC337.134.11

Tom Savini, *Tom Savini and Andy Warhol*, ca. 1984. Chromogenic color print, 11 × 14 in. (27.9 × 35.6 cm). Gift of Tom Savini, 1994.9.1

Photographer unknown, *Unidentified Man and Woman with the Andy Warhol Audioanimatronic Robot*, ca. 1982–83. Chromogenic color print, 4 × 5 5/8 in. (10.2 × 14.3 cm). 1998.3.2668.2

295
Tom Savini, *Andy Warhol*, ca. 1984. Chromogenic color print, 11 × 8 in. (27.9 × 20.3 cm). Gift of Tom Savini, 1994.9.2

Director's Afterword

A is for Archive: Warhol's World from A to Z is a publication that serves as many purposes as the archives of The Andy Warhol Museum themselves. Packed with wildly divergent images and information leading down many roads, this book can be read as a metaphor for Warhol's fascination with objects, celebrity, and the most minute of personal details. It can also serve as a high-level overview of the thousands and thousands of items that collectively constitute the scholarly and artistic puzzle Warhol left behind. On the most personal level, *A is for Archive* is a reflection of the spirit of my friend and colleague Matt Wrbican, one of the museum's original archivists, who dove into Warhol's boxes and piles, gleefully digging deeper and deeper until we feared he might lose us all. But his stories, passion, and downright staggering knowledge were always so compelling that it was unquestionably worth accompanying him on the ride.

Many people made *A is for Archive* possible, and they are acknowledged in the following pages. But I must call out two in advance. Our director of publications, Abby Franzen-Sheehan, conceived of this book out of her love for this museum and her love for Matt. I am grateful to Abby and her long service to this institution. And this book would not have been possible without the unending generosity of Lea Simonds. Lea served as the first chair on The Warhol's board. Since that time, she has never been far away in spirit, and her philanthropy is matched only by her generosity of heart and mind.

The Andy Warhol Museum is the definitive source for all things Warhol. We achieve that goal in a quirky way particular to this museum and to Warhol himself. I am proud that *A is for Archive* carries on that tradition.

Patrick Moore
Director
The Andy Warhol Museum

Acknowledgments

A book is not the product of a single person, despite formal attributions to the contrary. This volume has relied on the efforts of a large and varied team to achieve realization. I may be unable to list them all here; I am indebted to so many wonderful people. First, my parents, who sacrificed comforts so that I could be given educational advantages. To my college mentor, Professor Bruce Breland, from whom I learned about his firsthand experiences in the New York art scene of the 1950s and early 1960s, including, significantly, the real reason that Andy Warhol painted soup cans. Special thanks to Abigail Franzen-Sheehan, director of publications, and Patrick Moore, director of The Warhol, who together shepherded this book to reality. My beautiful partner, Sharon, who performs a first edit of nearly everything I write, among countless other invaluable efforts; without her, there's not very much of me. Lea Simonds, who has supported my work for the museum for many years. My amazing colleagues at the museum, including previous directors Tom Armstrong, who encouraged me to learn all that I could about the collection; Tom Sokolowski, who insisted that I share that knowledge with visitors by writing extensive label copy; and Eric Shiner, who in recognizing my work, rewarded me with an overdue promotion in my job title, taking me from the "assistant" of about twenty years to "chief" with the stroke of a pen. My former supervisor, archivist John W. Smith, who broadened my understanding of Warhol's life and significance. The people who have developed the Archive: The Andy Warhol Foundation (which donated Warhol's widely varied "papers" to the museum under the leadership of Arch Gillies); Sally King-Nero, executive editor of The Andy Warhol Catalogue Raisonné; Claudia Defendi, independent curator and former chief curator and curator of prints, The Andy Warhol Foundation for the Visual Arts; the late Callie Angell, authority on Warhol's films and author of volume one of a catalogue raisonné devoted to Warhol's *Screen Tests*. Frayda and Ronald Feldman, codirectors of Ronald Feldman Fine Arts; and curator Donna de Salvo, who I understand was the first to recognize the significance of Warhol's entire Archive and sought to keep it whole. Gretchen Berg, John Wallowitch, and Jay Reeg, who has kept the Archive high on his list of priorities for many years through his donations and Warhol knowledge. Several of Warhol's close associates at his studio, the Factory, who shared with me their memories and knowledge of Warhol's life and practices, beginning with Jay Shriver and Vincent Fremont and continuing with Brigid Berlin, John Giorno, Billy Name, Benjamin Liu, Glenn O'Brien, Paige Powell, and Susan Pile, as well as his family, including brothers Paul and John and their children, and his cousins. I must also recognize my doctors and nurses at the Allegheny Health Network (#LivingProof).

Matt Wrbican
Archivist
The Andy Warhol Museum

A is for Archive was made possible by the generosity of many individuals and institutions. Our heartfelt thanks go to Lea Simonds, Carnegie Museums life trustee and The Warhol emeritus board member, for her long-standing, enthusiastic advocacy for Matt Wrbican's work and whose generosity, through the Juliet Lea Hillman Simonds Foundation, made this project a reality. The Barron Family Foundation, Dr. Branden W. Joseph, Jay Reeg, and Jarka and Donald Warhola provided additional support.

The Andy Warhol Museum is indebted to Blake Gopnik and Neil Printz for so eloquently sharing their personal insights into the complexities of the Warhol Archive and Matt's contributions. Their research, writing, and observations help to shape a greater understanding of the deep reaches of the artist, the archivist, and the Archive.

For Matt's museum colleagues, this project has been a work of pure joy. The range and depth of Matt's knowledge of Warhol has informed this institution for almost three decades. To all of us, he is a brilliant archivist, a thoughtful scholar, and an enduring friend. This collection of his work was produced by the determination of talented staff. Erin Byrne has shouldered the mantle of archivist and striven to honor Matt's legacy in her role, devoting long hours to this project and providing critical review while simultaneously facilitating researchers' visits, supervising staff, and caring for the Archive collection. Brianna Treleven, special project cataloguer, worked exclusively on this project, tracking down missing information, cataloguing thousands of *Time Capsule* objects, and organizing large data for future research. Matt Gray, cataloguer, supplied countless new object records, essential primary source research, and support for many chapters. The beautifully staged imagery in this volume is the work of Rebecca Shock, digital collections assistant, with the guidance of Kristin Britanik, manager of rights and digital collections. Their artistry and careful attention to detail cannot be overstated. A work of this breadth and scope could never be achieved without the digital asset management support and procurement of third-party clearances completed by Britanik.

Additional advisory support was provided by Geralyn Huxley, curator of film and video, and Greg Pierce, associate curator of film and video. Patrick Moore, director; Rachel Baron-Horn, deputy director; Karen Lautanen, director of strategic initiatives; and Rick Armstrong, director of marketing and communications, have cultivated this project from its inception and helped it reach the finish line.

The comprehensive research provided by Signe Warner Watson improves the quality of many museum projects and was invaluable to this book. Thank you to Julie Albright, freelance editor, who read an early draft of the manuscript and shared her astute comments, and to Richard Stoner, photographer, for providing his skill when objects proved too large for our on-site cameras. We recognize the immense work completed over the years by previous Archive staff who laid the foundation for the research in these chapters.

At Yale University Press, the skillful editing and oversight of the manuscript through design, production, and publication was at the hands of Patricia Fidler, publisher; Kate Zanzucchi, managing editor; Sarah Henry, art book design and production manager; and Jane Friedman, freelance copyeditor. In addition, designer Daphne Geismar, proofreader Jessica Skwire Routhier, and indexer Krister Swartz must be thanked for embracing the nuance and depth of this project.

Lastly, we thank The Andy Warhol Foundation for the Visual Arts, Inc., for their institutional support for the museum and the legacy of Warhol's work.

Abigail Franzen-Sheehan
Editor
Director of Publications
The Andy Warhol Museum

Credits

Illustrations

22–23. Book: Hergé © Hergé/Moulinsart 2019

43–47, 50–53, 58–63, 65, 71, 75, 77–78, 113,
115–19, 121, 129–31, 141, 162, 166–67, 189, 197,
200–201, 220, 235, 238–39, 249, 251, 257, 265,
270, 281, 286, 288, 290, 292–94. Artworks: Andy
Warhol © The Andy Warhol Foundation for the
Visual Arts, Inc.

53, 216, 289, 291. Photo: Edward Wallowitch
© 2019 all rights reserved.

58–59, 61–64, 66, 70–71, 76. Artworks
© Association Marcel Duchamp / ADAGP, Paris /
Artists Rights Society (ARS), New York 2018

61. Photo © CNAC/MNAM/Dist. RMN-Grand
Palais / Art Resource, NY

64. Photo © The Metropolitan Museum of Art.
Image source: Art Resource, NY

66. Photo © Munson-Williams-Proctor Arts
Institute / Art Resource, NY

70. Photo © ADAGP Paris | The Vera and Arturo
Schwarz Collection of Dada and Surrealist Art in
the Israel Museum

72–73. Photo: Nat Finkelstein © Nat Finkelstein
Estate

81. Photo: David McCabe © David McCabe

84, 95. Photo: Stephen Shore © Stephen Shore,
Courtesy 303 Gallery, New York

85, 145, 150, 172, 203, 233, 250, 258. Film stills:
Andy Warhol © 2019 The Andy Warhol Museum,
Pittsburgh, PA, a museum of Carnegie Institute.
All rights reserved.

86–87. Drawings: Courtesy Michael Post

89, 234. Photo: Shunk-Kender © J. Paul Getty
Trust. Getty Research Institute, Los Angeles
(2014.R.20)

91. Photo: Melton-Pippin

94. Photo: Robert J. Levin © Robert J. Levin

94. Photo: Patrick McMullan/Getty Images
© Patrick McMullan

98. Photo: David Montgomery © David
Montgomery

106. Periodical: LA Free Press courtesy of
Stephen Finger

110. Photo: Gretchen Berg

120, 258. Periodical: Village Voice © Village
Voice, Courtesy Wright's Media, LLC

128. Artwork: Jason Arthur Sapan © Jason
Arthur Sapan

147. Photo: Michael (Felix) Katz © Michael
(Felix) Katz

173. Photos: William John Kennedy © William
John Kennedy, Courtesy Kiwi Arts Group, Inc.

190–94. Photo: Courtesy of ICA Philadelphia

202. Photo: Jack Mitchell © Jack Mitchell

224. Artwork: Michel Hosszú

232. Artwork © 2018 Jasper Johns / Licensed
by VAGA at Artists Rights Society (ARS), NY

271. Puppets: Rick Meyerowitz
© Rick Meyerowitz

287, 294–95. Photo: Tom Savini

290. Photo: Otto Fenn © 2018 D. Hallam
holder of the Otto Fenn Personal Papers.
All rights reserved

Note to the reader: All exhibitions featured in this book were at The Andy Warhol Museum.

Published with assistance from The Juliet Lea Hillman Simonds Foundation

The Andy Warhol Museum
One of the four Carnegie Museums of Pittsburgh

Yale

yalebooks.com/art

Designed by Daphne Geismar
Set in Akkurat type by Daphne Geismar
Printed in Singapore by Pristone Pte. Ltd.

Library of Congress Control Number: 2018961797
ISBN 978-0-300-23344-5

A catalogue record for this book is available from the British Library.

This paper meets the requirements of ANSI/NISO Z39.48-1992 (Permanence of Paper).

10 9 8 7 6 5 4 3 2 1

Cover illustration
Andy Warhol, *Time Capsule 79*, 1941–72, undated, bulk 1963–66. Mixed archival material, box: 10 × 14 × 18 in. (25.4 × 35.6 × 45.7 cm). TC79

Page 1
Andy Warhol, *"Unsalted Butter,"* 1968, artwork created for *Ark* magazine. 22 3/4 × 16 3/4 in. (57.8 × 42.5 cm). 1998.3.9006.1

Page 4
Selection of Andy Warhol's *Time Capsules* in the Archives Study Center, The Andy Warhol Museum, Pittsburgh

Page 316
Cookie tin used by Andy Warhol to store money, n.d. Coated ink on tin, 2 3/4 × 9 1/4 × 8 3/4 in. (7 × 23.5 × 22.2 cm). T940a–b

A few years after Warhol's death in 1987, one of the artist's mystifying secrets was finally revealed. Matt Wrbican and others were reviewing many boxes of materials from Warhol's studio that were going into storage. Within a shortbread cookie tin, Wrbican found a large envelope that contained another envelope. Hidden inside was a shocking discovery: a neat stack of 140 $100 bills ($14,000). Jay Shriver, Warhol's former studio assistant, remarked, "You found it! If Andy wanted any of us to buy something he needed, he always gave a $100 bill, and we all wondered where he kept the stash."[1] The money was returned to The Andy Warhol Foundation, but the Archive still has the tin.

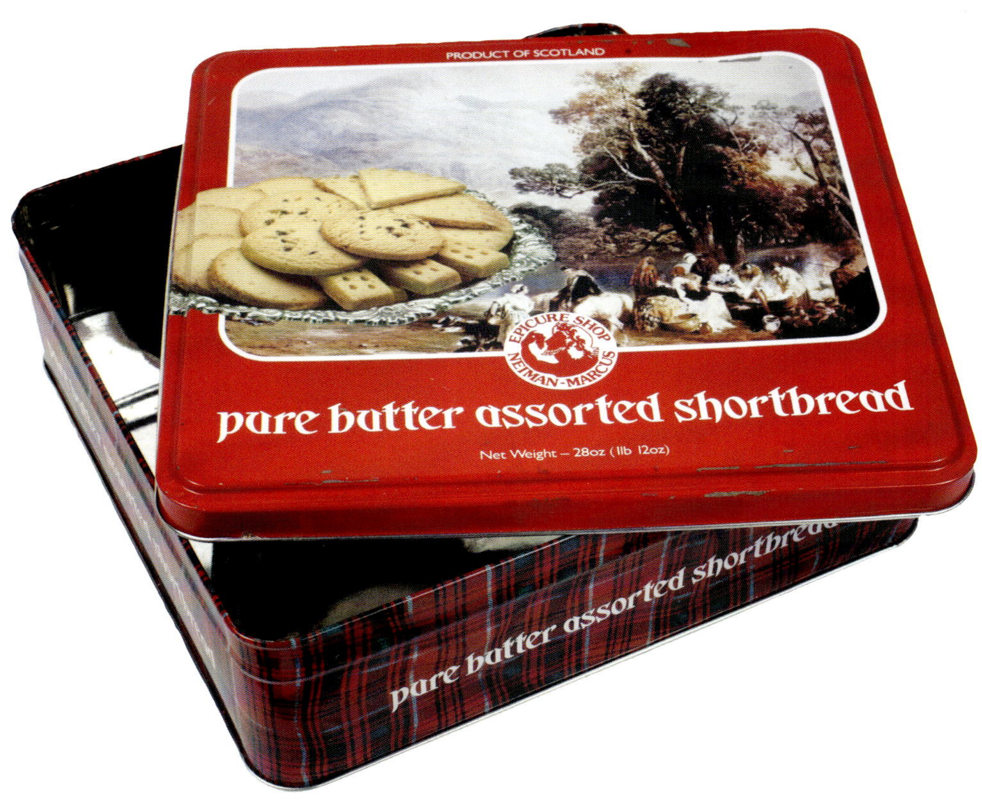

1. The author's experiences.